MUSIC AND MUSICAL LIFE
IN SOVIET RUSSIA

BORIS SCHWARZ

Music and Musical Life in Soviet Russia

Enlarged Edition, 1917–1981

INDIANA UNIVERSITY PRESS
BLOOMINGTON

Library of Congress Cataloging in Publication Data

Schwarz, Boris, 1906–
  Music and musical life in Soviet Russia.

  Bibliography: p.
  Includes index.
  1. Music—Russia—1917–   . I. Title.
ML300.5.S37   1983   780'.947   82-48267
ISBN 0-253-33956-1
1 2 3 4 5   87 86 85 84 83

*First edition published by Barrie & Jenkins under ISBN 0–393–02152–1 and by W. W.
Norton under ISBN 0–393–00699–9 (pbk.).*

TO THE MEMORY OF MY PARENTS

Contents

Preface to the Enlarged Edition

Twelve years have passed since the original volume of *Music and Musical Life in Soviet Russia* was completed. An updated edition was clearly in order. It proved more difficult than expected.

The 1970's were a decade of contradictory manifestations. Outwardly, the Soviet Union was as monolithic as ever. Musical life progressed and expanded, there was internal growth and international success, and there was a rapprochement between East and West on various levels—cultural exchanges, copyright agreement, and even a modest equalization of musical idiom. "Many new devices evolved by the world's compositional practices in the twentieth century have entered the arsenal of Soviet music", admitted Tikhon Khrennikov, the conservative "boss" of Soviet composers. "The musical cultures of East and West have rarely been so close together", observed critic Nigel Osborne after attending the 1981 International Moscow Festival.

Yet, beneath that controlled façade, there was much unrest among Soviet intellectuals and artists. The 1970's and early 1980's were characterized by dissent, dissatisfaction, and defection. For the first time in its history, the Soviet Union had to acknowledge the existence of a protest movement: tens of thousands of its citizens demanded the right to emigrate. The fact that a majority of the emigrants were Jews eager to escape internal oppression should not obscure the fact that many of the protesters (and some of the most prominent) were ethnic Russians, Baltics, Ukrainians, Volga Germans, and Baptists, among others, who demanded their civil rights as defined by the Helsinki Agreement. In the world of music, the pivotal events were the departure of Mstislav Rostropovich in 1974; the death of Dmitri Shostakovich in 1975; and the defection of his son, Maxim, in 1981. My conversation with Maxim Shostakovich after his arrival in New York seemed to form a natural conclusion to this volume.

The final two chapters of this book, newly written for the enlarged edition, focus on Soviet consent and dissent. The dedicated efforts of the Composers' Union to reach remote regions and outlying districts, to bring music to the rural population and the factory workers, to motivate creative young people, and to rejuvenate the ranks of composers and critics achieved manifold success. We witness the emergence of new composers in distant republics and the increase of public participation in musical events. Among the rising composers are Alfred Shnitke (acclaimed more in London than in Moscow), Giya Kancheli, Shirvani Chalayev, and other exotic names which will be new to the reader. We also observe the legacy of Shostakovich and the influence of the "New Folkloristic Wave".

Soviet virtuosos continue to win international acclaim and musical contests, unperturbed by the talent drain through emigration and defection. Often they are in direct competition with Soviet emigré artists in quest of new careers in the Western world, and some of them are spectacularly successful.

New York, July 1982   BORIS SCHWARZ

Preface

"Music and Revolution are deeply related . . . Every revolution is a grandiose symphony," proclaimed an early Bolshevik intellectual. But the relationship was not one of equality: music was made to serve and extol the revolution. Soviet music was to be "an art national in form and socialist in content," according to Stalin. To what extent was this edict accepted? The history of Soviet music is punctuated by conflicts between high-minded artists and low-minded bureaucrats, alternating between defiance or compliance by the musicians, concessions or repressions by the Government and the Party.

The regimentation of the arts is Stalin's responsibility. After the dictator's death in 1953, every move toward liberalization was hailed by Soviet officials as a return to true Leninism. Though Lenin disliked futurism and all other "isms", he advocated tolerance toward artists. But his tolerance had limits, "But of course we are communists. We must not allow the chaos to ferment as it chooses." Guidance or enforcement—these are the two alternatives open to Soviet leaders in dealing with the intelligentsia. A third alternative—complete freedom of musical expression—does not seem to be under consideration, though it prospers in Communist Poland.

Attempts to control music through censorship and autocratic rules have been made since antiquity. The Council of Trent regulated church music in the sixteenth century. Puritan England persecuted music and musicians. The French Revolution censored an opera because the word "liberty" was not used conspicuously. Imperial Vienna interfered with Beethoven's *Leonore*. The Tsarist regime forbade Rimsky-Korsakov's opera *Le Coq d'Or* because it pictured an autocrat as a fool. Shostakovich's *Lady Macbeth of Mtsensk* was branded as "chaos instead of music". The list could be prolonged ad infinitum. But music won out in every case because its spirit is free and unfettered, its meaning implicit, not explicit. "A Symphony to Man's pure and noble spirit," this is how Prokofiev described his own Fifth Symphony.

This book is not a history of Soviet Russian music; rather it is an attempt to picture the broad spectrum of musical life and culture during a half-century of Soviet rule—a period of immense suffering and proud accomplishments. Despite Revolution and War, social changes and physical deprivation, the Soviet leaders never lost sight of the country's cultural needs.

Traditionally, music histories concentrate on composers. They are the creative *élite* among musicians; their works form the musical heritage of a nation. This privileged position has been preserved, and even enlarged, in the Soviet Union where the composers speak on behalf of all Soviet music. At the same time, equal standing has been accorded to the musicologists. Used rather loosely, the term includes all those who write *about* music—historians, theorists, critics, commentators, authors of music books. Composers and musicologists form the exclusive membership of the "Union of Soviet Composers" which represents the musical "establishment". Not admitted, though highly admired and respected, are the great virtuoso performers who add so much to the international prestige of Soviet music.

No picture of the Soviet scene is complete without thorough consideration of the musical institutions—the opera and ballet theatres, the philharmonics, the libraries and museums of "musical culture", the State publishing establishments, the conservatories and research institutes, together with the entire system of music education which has many unique features.

And finally, there are the people themselves—receptive as listeners, creative as participants. Russian composers from Glinka to Shostakovich have been filled with an almost mystic belief in the creative powers of the people. This belief is the cornerstone of the Soviet artistic credo.

The book makes extensive use of quotations from original Russian sources. The translations are my own, unless otherwise indicated. Incorporated are also memoirs and observations of Western visitors to the Soviet Union, from H. G. Wells to John Reed and from Benjamin Britten to Aaron Copland. Most of my material was collected during my three prolonged visits to the Soviet Union, in 1930, 1960, and 1962, in particular my three-month stay in 1962, when under the sponsorship of the Soviet Academy of Sciences, I was enabled to study musical institutions at close range, and to make contact with leading Soviet musicians. I was received with much hospitality and friendship for which I am truly grateful. My professional observations are incorporated in this book. I have avoided political comments although, in the Soviet Union, art and politics are so intertwined and ideological viewpoints so dominant that a separation of the issues is virtually impossible.

My gratitude extends to several institutions and organizations that have supported my research in the field of Soviet music. They are:

The John Simon Guggenheim Memorial Foundation,

The American Council of Learned Societies, in conjunction with the Academy of Sciences of the USSR,

The American Philosophical Society.

The following libraries and institutions have facilitated my research:

Moscow—Institut Istorii Iskusstv; Tchaikovsky Conservatory; Glinka Museum; Lenin Library; Union of Soviet Composers.

Leningrad—Research Institute of Theatre and Music; State Public Library; Pushkin House; Rimsky-Korsakov Conservatory.

London—British Museum; Westminster Library; London University; Society for Cultural Relations with the U.S.S.R.

United States—Library of Congress; New York Public Library; Harvard University Library; Columbia University Library. Princeton University Library; Queens College of the City University of New York.

My warm personal thanks go to my publisher, Mr Leopold Ullstein, for his encouragement and support of my project from the outset; and to my editor, Mrs Bobby Ullstein, for her perceptive advice and assistance.

Part I

EXPERIMENTATION 1917-1921

1   *The Musical Scene before the October Revolution*

All cultural efforts of the Soviet State are guided by the following thoughts of Lenin,

> "Art belongs to the people. It must have its deepest roots in the broad masses of workers. It must be understood and loved by them. It must be rooted in, and grow with, their feelings, thoughts, and desires. It must arouse and develop the artist in them. Are we to give cake and sugar to a minority when the mass of workers and peasants still lack black bread? . . . So that art may come to the people, and the people to art, we must first of all raise the general level of education and culture."[1]

Long before Lenin, Russian musicians had identified themselves with the people. Glinka, revered as the "father" of Russian music, once said, "Music is created by the people; we—the artists—merely arrange it."[2] Balakirev and his group, known as the "Mighty Five", stressed the folk roots of Russian music. Mussorgsky wrote to the painter Repin in 1873, "It is the people I want to depict: when I sleep I see them, when I eat I think of them, when I drink—I can visualize them, integral, big, unpainted, and without any tinsel."[3] Even the most "Western" of nineteenth-century Russian composers, Tchaikovsky, never relinquished his ties with the native musical idiom. This tradition was carried into the twentieth century by composers like Arensky, Liadov, and Glazunov.

Politically, many Russian musicians opposed Tsarist autocracy and stood in the forefront of the liberal movement. They sympathized with the oppressed people and the rebellious youth. This was particularly evident during the revolutionary year 1905. The massacre of peaceful demonstrators in front of the Winter Palace in St. Petersburg on 9 January 1905—remembered as Blood Sunday—shook the intelligentsia to the core. A few weeks later, on 2 February, the Moscow paper *Nashi Dni* published an open letter signed by twenty-nine prominent Moscow musicians, among them Rachmaninov, Chaliapin, Taneyev, Grechaninov, and Glière. The letter read in part,

"Only free art is vital, only free creativity is joyful . . . When in the land there is neither freedom of thought and conscience nor freedom of word and print . . ., then the profession of 'free artist' becomes a bitter irony. We are not free artists but, like all Russian citizens, the disfranchised victims of today's abnormal social conditions. In our opinion, there is only one solution: Russia must at last embark on a road of basic reforms . . ."[4]

No sooner had the issue of the paper reached St. Petersburg than Rimsky-Korsakov endorsed the letter: "With all my heart I sympathize with the statement of the Moscow composers and musicians . . . and I ask you to attach to it the signature of a Petersburg musician."[5]

Rimsky-Korsakov was deeply troubled by the political crisis; to a friend he confided that the recent events had turned him into a "blood-red". At the Petersburg Conservatory, he was considered the spokesman for the liberal faction of the faculty. Soon he became embroiled in a protest action at the Conservatory where the students went on strike in support of educational and political reforms. The repressive measures taken against the students made Rimsky-Korsakov so angry that he demanded the resignation of the director, August Bernhard, and internal autonomy for the Conservatory. On 19 March 1905, the unexpected happened: Rimsky-Korsakov was brusquely dismissed from the faculty for having "protested publicly, with sharp words and distorted facts, against the actions of the directorate".[6] As a gesture of appeasement, Bernhard's resignation as director was accepted at the same time.

This shabby action brought an outcry of public indignation. Other faculty members, among them Glazunov and Liadov, resigned in sympathy. Suddenly, Rimsky-Korsakov had become the symbol of defiance for the Russian intelligentsia. A performance of his opera Kashchei the Immortal, which took place on 27 March, became the occasion for a public demonstration and fiery oratory. The watchful police interrupted the event by lowering the asbestos curtain and dispersing the audience. After that, the governor-general forbade further performances of Rimsky-Korsakov's music, and the composer was put under police surveillance.

By autumn, a compromise was reached: the conservatories were granted limited autonomy, including the right to elect their director. On 5 December 1905, Glazunov was elected to that post, and his first action was to ask Rimsky-Korsakov to rejoin the faculty. He agreed to return but did not abandon any of his liberal positions. However, he was perturbed by the reactionary atmosphere at the Conservatory: the liberal faction began to regret the concessions made to the students. At one point, Rimsky-Korsakov threatened to resign "forever", and he had to be placated by Glazunov.

The official harassment of Rimsky-Korsakov continued intermittently: a few days before his death in 1908, he was informed that the governor of Moscow refused to permit the première of his last opera, Le Coq d'Or, unless changes in the libretto were made. Indignant, Rimsky-Korsakov rejected any tampering with Pushkin's text. Le Coq d'Or, that supreme satire on the stupidity of autocrats, was given a posthumous première in 1909, with the censor's changes; the original text was not restored until after the Revolution.

At the Moscow Conservatory, the year 1905 was hardly less dramatic. Here, it was the autocratic directorship of Vassili Safonov that was resented by liberal faculty members and the students. The composer Sergei Taneyev led the opposition and attacked Safonov in the press. In September 1905, Taneyev resigned from the faculty and refused to return, even after Safonov left his post to become conductor of the New York Philharmonic Orchestra. Safonov's successor as director was the composer Mikhail Ippolitov-Ivanov who was to occupy this position until 1922.

Meanwhile, Taneyev played a leading role in the establishment of the "People's Conservatory", organized in the autumn of 1906; among the participating musicians were Glière, Kastalsky, Goldenweiser, Yavorsky and other prominent personalities. It was an experiment in democracy—to bring musical education to those who could not afford it. Within a few months, almost two thousand prospective students registered, including factory workers, postal and secretarial employees, railway clerks and young students. Other cities followed the Moscow example. However, this was not the first venture of its kind: as early as 1862, Balakirev had organized the "Free Music School" in St. Petersburg which survived until 1917; for a time, from 1878 to 1881, it was directed by Rimsky-Korsakov.

An enterprise of social significance was the series of "Historical Concerts" established in Moscow in 1907. The founder-conductor was the composer Sergei Vassilenko who felt that working people and students could not afford to attend the regular symphonic concerts. Assisted by the orchestra of the Bolshoi Theatre and prominent soloists, Vassilenko offered "historical" programmes at nominal admission prices and attracted throngs of the working intelligentsia.

Some of the musicians who had helped to organize the "People's Conservatory"—Taneyev, Kastalsky, and others—contributed their efforts towards bringing art music and folk music into closer contact. Under the sponsorship of the ethno-musicological committee of the

"Society for Natural Science, Anthropology, and Ethnography", professional musicians and folk performers appeared side by side in specially arranged concerts. Early in 1911, a folk chorus was organized by Mitrofan Pyatnitsky, and the work of this important ensemble was continued after the death of its founder in 1927. Today, the Pyatnitsky Folk Chorus, sponsored by the Soviet Government, is one of the glories of Soviet cultural life.

At the beginning of the twentieth century, Russian music stood at an important crossroad. The goals of the 1860's—the creation of a Russian national school of composition—were achieved, and the old slogans seemed outdated. Of the "Mighty Five", three members—Borodin, Mussorgsky, and Rimsky-Korsakov—enjoyed growing recognition abroad while Tchaikovsky had become an international celebrity.

The question was whether Russian music could hope to grow in isolation. There were two factions—one stressing traditional "Russianism", the other seeking to "Europeanize" the Russian musical idiom, to modernize its approach. Russian traditionalism was rooted in the conservatories and academic circles. Its outstanding representatives were Rimsky-Korsakov in St. Petersburg and Taneyev in Moscow; its younger adherents included Arensky, Liadov, Glazunov, Rachmaninov, and Glière. Many of these composers belonged to the "Belayev circle", named after the art patron Mitrofan Belayev in whose mansion in Petersburg the musical élite assembled every Friday. A man of great wealth, Belayev had established, in 1885, the "Russian Symphony Concerts" as well as a publishing house in Leipzig where the works of Russian composers were printed in exemplary editions. Belayev's chief advisor was Rimsky-Korsakov though his advice was not always followed. For example, Belayev sponsored the early career of Alexander Scriabin whom Rimsky-Korsakov disliked personally and musically— "the somewhat warped, posing, and self-opinionated Scriabin".[7]

As early as 1899, Rimsky-Korsakov complained of "signs of decadence wafted from Western Europe".[8] He ridiculed the "horizontal nonsense" of Max Reger and the "vertical nonsense" of Richard Strauss.[9] In a letter to his colleague Ossovsky, Rimsky-Korsakov expresses his irritation "against the Western 'progressive' tendencies in music", "against the myopic views of those who do not notice that the true progress in music is right here in Russia and exclusively here".[10] Yet Rimsky-Korsakov's reaction to Debussy's *Pelléas et Mélisande* which he heard in Paris in 1907, is amusing: "I'll have nothing more to do with this music lest I should unhappily develop a liking for it."[11]

Compared to the traditionalists, the musical modernists were a small but active group. In 1901, they organized the "Evenings of Contemporary Music" in St. Petersburg as an offshoot of the art circle *Mir Iskusstva* (The World of Art). A similar series of concerts was established in Moscow in 1909. The art journal *Mir Iskusstva* was founded in 1898 by Sergei Diaghilev and Alexander Benois; their circle represented the most advanced trends in Western and Russian art and proclaimed the slogan of *l'art pour l'art*. The same spirit pervaded the "Evenings of Contemporary Music" under the guidance of Vyacheslav Karatygin, a versatile musician and perceptive critic. His writings, republished in 1965 after almost forty years of deliberate neglect, furnish illuminating comments on musical modernism of the day. The "Evenings of Contemporary Music" sponsored the first public appearances of controversial young composers like Stravinsky, Prokofiev, and Miaskovsky. Prominent foreign composers were invited for personal appearances, among them Debussy, Reger, and Arnold Schoenberg. At these concerts, works by Ravel, Richard Strauss, and Florent Schmitt were introduced to Russian audiences.

But Soviet historians persist in describing the "Evenings of Contemporary Music" as decadent and representative of the "reactionary bourgeois ideology of the imperialist era".[12] This era is described by the official *History of Soviet Russian Music* in the following words,

"The activization of modernism and all other reactionary (*sic!*) tendencies increased sharply after the Revolution of 1905 and threatened Russian artistic culture—including music—with disintegration and decline. The Great October Revolution of 1917 saved Russian musical culture and opened unusual perspectives of fruitful development."[13]

To what extent the 1917 Revolution "saved" Russian music will be discussed in the pages of this book. In truth, the Leninist Revolution encouraged experimentation in the arts, including music. During the first fifteen years, modernism was fully explored through the activities of the "Association for Contemporary Music" (ACM) which flourished in Petrograd and Moscow during the 1920's. Soviet historians persist in drawing parallels between the pre-revolutionary "Evenings of Contemporary Music" and the post-revolutionary ACM and find them equally nefarious. Such misjudgments reflect the parochial, isolationist attitude that became so rampant during Stalin's time and still infests Soviet musicography. In fact, Prokofiev warned as early as 1934 against growing artistic isolation, "The danger of becoming provincial is unfortunately a very real one for modern Soviet composers."[14]

If parallels are in order, one could reflect on the fact that Tsarist censorship was comparatively tolerant towards free artistic expression as long as there was no political danger—in contrast to the heavy-handed ideological interference of the Stalin regime. In 1905, Stasov could protest publicly and forcefully against the shabby treatment of Rimsky-Korsakov. In 1936, no one dared to speak up against the humiliation of Shostakovich, nor did anyone defend Prokofiev and Miaskovsky against boorish accusations in 1948.

During the decade prior to the 1917 Revolution, the international prestige of Russian music rose to an unprecedented peak. This was due, ironically, to the initiative of Diaghilev whose "decadent" views on art were scorned by stalwart traditionalists. In 1907, Diaghilev organized a festival of Russian Music in Paris. Given at the Grand Opera during the month of May, the five programmes offered a panoramic view of the evolution of Russian music, from Glinka's *Ruslan and Ludmilla* Overture to Scriabin's Second Symphony, both conducted by Arthur Nikisch. The élite of Russian artists participated, including Rimsky-Korsakov and Glazunov who conducted their own works. The success was immense, the deficit amounted to 100,000 francs. Undaunted, Diaghilev organized an even bigger festival for the following year, with the focus on Russian opera. Mussorgsky's *Boris Godunov* and Chaliapin's interpretation of the title role created a sensation. The year 1909 brought the début of Diaghilev's ballet company, with such stars as Pavlova, Karsavina, Nijinsky, and Fokine. Diaghilev had an uncanny intuition for discovering new talent: he commissioned Igor Stravinsky, a former student of Rimsky-Korsakov, to write a ballet score for the 1910 Paris season. *The Firebird*, choreographed by Fokine and danced by Karsavina, was a great success, followed by *Petrushka* in 1912 and that *scandale célèbre*, *Le Sacre du Printemps*, in 1913. The following year, Diaghilev mounted a choreographic version of Rimsky-Korsakov's last opera, *Le Coq d'Or*. His novel stage ideas had their repercussions in Russia: for a new Petersburg production of *Boris Godunov* in 1911, the Parisian designs of 1908 (by Benois and Golovin) were used, to the distress of traditionalists.

Meanwhile, death claimed many of the great figures in Russian music. Rimsky-Korsakov died in 1908, Balakirev in 1910, Cui in 1918 —the last three members of the "Mighty Five". Liadov died in 1914, Taneyev in 1915, both highly regarded as composers and teachers. Perhaps the most tragic loss was the premature death in 1915, at the age of forty-three, of Alexander Scriabin who was undoubtedly the most original Russian composer of his generation. After years abroad, he had returned to Moscow in 1911 and exerted a strong influence on his

contemporaries. His personality overshadowed such minor experimentators as Vladimir Rebikov and Nikolai Roslavetz.

A strong new talent emerged with Sergei Prokofiev. In 1912 and 1913, while still a student at the Petersburg Conservatory, he performed his first two piano concertos at the summer concerts in Pavlovsk. "Half the audience hissed and the other half applauded," reminisced the composer.[15] For his graduation in 1914, Prokofiev chose to play the First Concerto since "the Second would have sounded too outlandish within the Conservatory walls". He was awarded a first prize—for his piano playing. Glazunov, who had voted against him, announced the result in a "flat, toneless mumble".[16]

The February Revolution of 1917, which brought about the abdication of the Tsar and the establishment of a Provisional Government, does not seem to have affected musical life too deeply. Prominent musicians described the events with a certain placidity, for example the conductor Nikolai Malko,

"In February of 1917 the first Russian Revolution took place. When life had more or less settled down the theatre continued as before. I had conducted the last pre-revolution performance at the Imperial Theatre . . . and after a short interval, performances were resumed. The only new thing in the theatre was the talkativeness which was a characteristic of the entire country at that time. I personally was given many non-musical duties to perform. I was the chairman of five different committees and, for a time, the chairman of the temporary board of the theatre as well as the chairman for the general meetings of the soloists . . . In the autumn, on 14 September, there was the official opening of the State Theatre in Petersburg. I conducted this opening: Borodin's Prince Igor . . . To begin with, at the insistence of the audience, we had to play the Marseillaise nine times . . ."[17]

The author John Reed confirms that "of course all the theatres were going every night. Karsavina appeared in a new ballet at the Maryinsky . . . Chaliapin was singing . . ."[18]

Prokofiev writes in his *Autobiography* with his usual laconicism, "The February Revolution found me in Petrograd. I and those I associated with welcomed it with open arms. I was in the streets of Petrograd while the fighting was going on, hiding behind house corners when the shooting came too close . . ."[19] The excitement of the day is reflected in one of his *Visions fugitives* (No. 19); it captures, so he says, "the feeling of the crowd rather than the inner essence of the Revolution". The summer of 1917 was spent in the country, and Prokofiev worked quietly on the *Classical Symphony*—decidedly an "escapist" piece of music. In the autumn, he left for the Caucasus where he stayed during the crucial early months of the October Revolution.

Prokofiev's political indifference was not unique. From the Bolshevik point of view, far too many artists were politically neutral and uninvolved during the historic year 1917. Blaming "the political apathy of the bourgeois intellectual circles" the historian Nestyev asserts that,

> "In these groups the very possibility of a relationship between art and politics was considered unthinkable. At meetings of writers and artists in the spring and summer of 1917, many outstanding representatives of the arts stubbornly asserted art's independence from the influences of the Revolution . . . Even the democratically-minded Miaskovsky . . . considered it a sign of banality for a composer to respond creatively to immediate events."[20]

In contrast, a sense of political involvement is conveyed in the reminiscences of Boris Asafiev, the versatile composer and writer, who was to become the foremost Soviet musicologist. In 1917, Asafiev—as yet mainly known as a fiery critic—was drawn into the circle around Maxim Gorky, who had recently returned to Russia. Gorky had founded a new journal, *Novaya Zhizn* (New Life), and persuaded Asafiev to collaborate. The editorial sessions were animated and often heated, "dialogues resembling duels". Here Asafiev met the poet Mayakovsky who was to become the symbol of revolutionary poetry, and the writer-politician Anatol Lunacharsky, soon to be appointed commissar of education in the new Bolshevik government. Lunacharsky seems to have had considerable influence on Asafiev's evolving political convictions. "I began to understand the political situation"— recalls Asafiev—"and since at the core of all disputes appeared more and more often the name Lenin, I began—by listening and questioning —to understand the trend of events."[21] This trend was indeed inexorable. The days of the Provisional Government were numbered. On 25 October (7 November)*, the Bolsheviks, a militant minority led by Lenin and Trotsky, seized power in Petrograd.

* The dates in brackets are according to the Gregorian (New Style, N.S.) calendar which replaced the Julian (Old Style, O.S.) calendar in Russia on 1 (14) February 1918.

A salvo from the cruiser *Aurora*, anchored in the river Neva, signalled the beginning of the "Third Revolution" proclaimed by Lenin. The roar of the guns could be heard at the Narodny Dom (People's House), across the river from the Winter Palace, where an opera performance of Verdi's *Don Carlo* was in progress. Chaliapin, on stage in the role of Philip II, calmed the frightened audience, and the performance was finished. On his way home, the artist had to dodge some stray bullets. It was Wednesday evening, 25 October (7 November).

The following day, the citizens of Petrograd awoke to realize that, during the night, the Provisional Government had capitulated and that the Bolsheviks had seized power. John Reed, the famous eye witness, described the scene,

> "Superficially, all was quiet . . . In Petrograd, the street-cars were running, the stores and restaurants open, theatres going, an exhibition of paintings advertised . . . All the complex routine of common life—humdrum even in war-time—proceeded as usual. Nothing is so astounding as the vitality of the social organism—how it persists, feeding itself, clothing itself, amusing itself, in the face of the worst calamities . . ."[1]

On that evening, 26 October (8 November), the Petrograd State Symphony gave a regularly scheduled concert. At the Maryinsky Opera (the former Tsarist court theatre), says conductor Malko, "I cannot remember even one performance being cancelled on any of the nights."[2] Nothing seems so reassuring to an unnerved population as the continuance of theatrical and musical events. This proved to be as true in revolutionary Petrograd of 1917 as in besieged Leningrad of 1941-3.

The man entrusted by Lenin to insure artistic continuity and ideological reforms was Anatol Lunacharsky. He became People's Commissar of Public Education on 26 October (8 November) 1917. From then until 1929, Lunacharsky, an "intellectual among Bolsheviks, Bolshevik among the intelligentsia", as he described himself,[3] guided the arts in the emerging Soviet state with imagination and flexibility.

In ideological matters, he could be firm, but he was not dogmatic. Lunacharsky's task was threefold—to educate a vast, untutored mass audience; to win the confidence of the arts intelligentsia faced with new social responsibilities; and to convince the political leaders that the support of the arts was an integral part of mass education. At times, Lunacharsky found himself at odds with Lenin himself, so in the affair of the PROLETKULT or the question of priorities. As Lunacharsky recalled, "Vladimir Ilyich's (Lenin's) attitude towards the Bolshoi Theatre was rather nervous . . . He insisted that its budget be cut and said, 'It is awkward to spend big money on such a luxurious theatre . . . when we lack simple schools in the villages.' "[4]

To Lenin, the Bolshoi represented "a piece of pure landlord culture", and he objected to the "pompous court style" of the opera. In a conversation with Klara Zetkin, a German fellow Communist, Lenin made clear his priority—education first, art second; he said, in 1920, "While in Moscow perhaps 10,000 people will come to the theatre, there are millions trying to learn how to write their name, how to count . . . We do not have enough schools . . ."[5]

Yet, Lunacharsky succeeded in reconciling the heterogeneous demands of artists, audiences, and politicians. He preferred to rule by persuasion rather than by decree, confronting the dissenters, arguing his case convincingly. Whether he met with the artists of the opera, the pedagogues of the Conservatory, or with a workers' audience, Lunacharsky always found the right words, the right approach. As Malko recalls, "Lunacharsky came to a meeting of singer-soloists of the Maryinsky Theatre and made a one-hour speech which dispelled the atmosphere of distrust and fright that nearly all of the intellectuals felt towards the Bolsheviks."[6]

On this point, Malko's recollections, after so many years, seem somewhat rose-coloured. There was considerable friction and pressure before the artists yielded to party directives. The democratization of the stages had led to a more active participation of the performers in guiding the affairs of their theatres. The "art workers" formed tight collectives and often resisted excessive pressures from Bolshevik bureaucrats. The official take-over of the theatres by the new government came in the first weeks of the Revolution, on 22 November 1917 "in order to satisfy the great cultural needs of the working population".[7] At the Bolshoi Theatre in Moscow , the change proceeded without too much friction, thanks to the conciliatory efforts of the famous tenor, Sobinov, who took charge as temporary director. However, at the Maryinsky Theatre in Petrograd there was open defiance of new government regulations, and some performances were disrupted. At a meeting of the artists' ensemble, a motion was passed "to send Lunacharsky an invitation to appear at the Maryinsky Theatre and to explain his policies to the soloists".[8] The invitation was signed by the leading singers Yershov and Andreyev, as well as by Malko. So strong was the resentment of some members (including the chief conductor, Siloti) that there were resignations "in protest against any negotiations whatsoever with the Bolsheviks".[9]

Lunacharsky accepted the invitation and appeared before the assembled soloists on 3 January 1918. He spoke in a conciliatory way and was well received. (This may have been the meeting Malko mentioned in his Memoirs.) Nevertheless, a week later, on 10 January, the chorus decided to go on strike. Having failed with persuasion, Lunacharsky chose force: he announced that any member, whether chorister or soloist, engaging in "sabotage" would be summarily dismissed. The ensemble yielded.

As a rule, Lunacharsky preferred to win the voluntary co-operation of the arts intelligentsia. On 1 December 1917 an appeal was published in *Pravda*, calling on all artists to fulfill their civic duty, "We ask all comrades—painters, musicians, and artists—who wish to work towards the rapprochement of the broad popular masses with art in all its aspects, as well as the comrade-members of the Union of Proletarian Artists and Writers, to report to the office of the Commissar of Public Enlightenment in the Winter Palace."[10] Among those who followed Lunacharsky's appeal were several musicians—the composer Shcherbachev, the critic Karatygin, and the composer-writer Asafiev.

Once the People's Commissariat of Public Education (abbreviated NARKOMPROS) was formally established, Lunacharsky began to build a vast, somewhat bureaucratic organization. There were subdivisions for the theatres (TEO), the fine arts (IZO), and music (MUZO). Administrative assignments were given to artists: Marc Chagall became arts commissar in Vitebsk, though only for a brief time, Vassili Kandinsky had the same duty in Moscow. The theatre division was headed by Vsevolod Meyerhold who in turn appointed the writer Ilya Ehrenburg to run the children's theatre. The poet Alexander Blok—despite his confessed coolness to Marxism—was put in charge of a theatre in Petrograd. "I like much about Lenin, but not Marxism", he told Lunacharsky.[11] In the field of music, Lunacharsky's chief assistant became Arthur Lourié, a young composer with strong modernistic leanings, whose aggressive policies alienated many musicians. But the ultimate control over the arts remained firmly in the hands of Lunacharsky. Thus, the theatre division (TEO) was denied jurisdiction over the great traditional stages—the Moscow Art Theatre, the Bolshoi, the Maryinsky. Explaining his position, Lunacharsky wrote that "the representatives of TEO, fanatics of their work—which is good and laudable—do not have the premises for correctly evaluating the importance of preserving the tradition of an already established culture."[12] Despite howls of protest from the leftist PROLETKULT and the futurist wing, Lunacharsky did not yield and maintained a close watch on the cultural heritage.

In dealing with the arts community, Lunacharsky was often caught between the traditionalists and the modernists. By appointing prominent futurists to policy-making positions in his own Commissariat of Public Education, Lunacharsky seemed to encourage the futurist movement. For a time, futurism in art and poetry seemed destined to become the official art of revolutionary Russia. On 1 May 1918—the first May Day of Red Russia—Moscow was "decorated with futurist and suprematist canvasses", as Ehrenburg recalls: "the futurists, the cubists, the suprematists—not the academic painters—were the ones who gathered in Red Square."[13] The poet Mayakovsky thundered against established art and signed a decree abolishing "those store-rooms and warehouses of human genius, such as palaces, galleries, salons, libraries, and theatres".[14] To build a new, proletarian, culture on the ruins of the old was the battle cry of the extremists. At this point, Lunacharsky stepped in. He had a firm mandate from Lenin to stem the tide of "artistic nihilism". He was instructed to "prevent by all means the collapse of the basic pillars of our culture, for the proletariat will never forgive us."[15] Lenin believed that "to preserve the heritage does not mean to be limited by it." Another of his guiding principles was, "By no means does Marxism reject the very valuable achievements of the bourgeois era; on the contrary, it absorbed and reworked all that was valuable in the more than two thousand years of evolution of human thought and culture . . ."[16]

Though Lenin and Lunacharsky did not see eye to eye in matters of art—Lenin called himself a "barbarian"[17] while Lunacharsky's taste was highly sophisticated—Lunacharsky was certainly in full agreement as to the preservation of the cultural heritage. His was one of the most sensitive assignments in the new regime, and he felt the weight of his responsibility, "It is particularly terrible in these days of violent struggle, of destructive warfare, to be Commissar of Public Education. Only the hope of the victory of Socialism, the source of a new and superior culture, brings me comfort."[18]

One of Lunacharsky's first statements was a lengthy "position paper" entitled "On Popular Education". Though designed as an interim pronouncement, it contained many ideas and plans that were incorporated into the evolving educational structure. Significant is Lunacharsky's distinction between "instruction" and "education": "One must emphasize the difference . . . *Instruction* is the transmission of ready knowledge by the teacher to his pupil. *Education* is a creative process. The personality of the individual is being 'educated' throughout life, is being formed, grows richer in content, stronger and more perfect. The toiling masses . . . are thirsting for elementary and advanced instruction. But they are also thirsting for education . . ."[19]

Lunacharsky was responsible for both instruction and education, and he wasted no time to try out new approaches. Under his guidance, NARKOMPROS proceeded "to give to all those who desire it the opportunity of acquiring musical culture, of learning to understand music in all its manifestations and to become musically literate."[20] A network of music schools was organized, for adults and children, for laymen and for future professionals. Many of these schools were placed near factories. Lenin himself helped establish the art studio at the Putilov* factory; it later became a "regional" music school and celebrated its fortieth anniversary in 1959.

Those early years were full of emotional appeals and challenges. They ring in the words of Asafiev, the active scholar-musician, "We need lecturers and musical propagandists; most importantly, we need prophets preaching the sacred significance of music as the art most cherished and closest to the human soul, and also as the art most powerful to solve the great problems of humanity."[21] These utopian words were backed up by strong practical action. Famous singers and instrumentalists formed mobile artistic "brigades" to carry music to the masses, into the factories and villages, for audiences of workers and peasants, soldiers and sailors. The conductor Malko reminisces about "the unforgettable examples of touching and tender reactions towards the new, unexplored, joyous experiences . . . Artists and musicians felt the electrified state of mind of the new audiences and treasured it."[22] Other artists remember the "romanticism of the early revolutionary years" when every performance would turn into a "festive event".

Occasionally, Lunacharsky would mark such "festive events" with a speech to the audience in an effort to create a special mood of receptivity. When Glinka's *Ruslan and Ludmilla* was reintroduced into the repertoire, he said, "To you, workers, will be shown one of the greatest creations, one of the most cherished diamonds in the wondrous crown of Russian art. On a valuable tray you are presented with a goblet of beautiful sparkling wine—drink it and enjoy it."[23] Or giving his speech a political twist, as he did when Mozart's *Requiem* was performed at the opening of a People's Concert Cycle on 1 May 1918 "We recognize the immense values created by the old culture and we make them available, not to a small group of parasites, but to the entire working population."[24]

* The famous armaments factory in Petrograd.

To involve the "entire population" was the gigantic plan. There was "a flood of concerts—big, small, chamber, symphonic, historic", wrote a tired critic; "never, it seems, did the pulse of our musical life beat so strongly and so unevenly." Next to important initiatives, there was also "so much casual and so much unnecessary music". In Petrograd alone, MUZO-NARKOMPROS sponsored 106 concerts in as many days (September to mid-December, 1918). To reach the broadest possible cross-section of listeners, these concerts were given, not only in established halls, but in workers' clubs, factories, and suburban centres. The Tsar's Winter Palace was renamed "Palace of the Arts" and opened to the public. No effort was spared to prepare and inform the new listeners —by lectures, pamphlets, programme notes, and introductory remarks. Chaliapin remembers singing "in a huge military riding school for nearly 15,000 sailors, soldiers, engineers, stokers, and some women. Most of the men were grimy and unwashed . . ." But, to illustrate the harshness of everyday life, he adds, "Little by little life became more and more difficult . . . I was glad to sing for the reward of a bag of flour, a ham, some sugar . . . Money had become of little value . . ."[25]

The harsh truth is that hunger, as much as idealism, drove the musicians to display their art under near-impossible conditions, on improvised stages, on decrepit instruments, in unheated halls, wearing overcoats and gloves. The musical mass circuit became known, somewhat contemptuously, as "khaltura"—hackwork—and one can readily understand, in view of the physical discomfort and uncritical audiences, that the quality of the performances tended to be careless. Yet, some of the finest musicians participated, out of necessity. The composer Alexander Grechaninov reminisces in his *Memoirs*,

"In the early years of the Bolshevik Revolution, lecture recitals for workers' children were given in various districts of Moscow . . . During intermission we were given herring and (horrible) black bread to sustain our physical strength. In lieu of a honorarium we received flour, cereals, and sometimes, as special premium, a little sugar and cocoa . . . My health had been undermined by undernourishment and cold to such an extent that I could hardly drag my feet. My hands suffered from frostbite, and I could not touch the piano . . . I had a chance to barter the silk ribbons from my laurel wreaths for flour, vegetables, apples, and other farm products . . . (Thus) the concerts were 'productive' . . . The poet Ivanov was given, in place of a laurel wreath, two logs of birchwood which he carried home as a treasured possession, to be stored in the apartment for fear that they might be stolen in the courtyard . . ."[26]

Already in July 1918 Lenin had put the entire country on a military footing to resist the armed intervention of the Great Powers and the attacks of the counter-revolutionary forces. Temporarily, three-fourths of Russia's territory was occupied by hostile troops. The country was a vast military camp. Music was used to raise the morale, to entertain the fighting men. Artists and ensembles were sent to the front lines; in the spring of 1919, more than one thousand artists performed at the front. At the same time, expenses for cultural projects had to be curtailed; in March 1919 Lenin said, "We are entering a difficult, hungry half-year."

The country had just gone through the terrible winter of 1918–19. Moscow was "buried in snow, cold, and rather hunger-stricken . . . The means of city transportation are almost immobilized; ever so seldom, a streetcar would rumble by. On the avenues one meets strange figures of shivering people, wrapped in strange pieces of clothing . . . Electric power functions only sporadically, the streets are dark, but every day, at a set time, the curtains rise in large and small theatres, before a crowded new audience—mainly workers and Red Army men . . ."[27] Soviet historians take justifiable pride in the fact that, during that severe winter, Lenin supplied the theatres with the necessary fuel although some factories had to be closed down. Even so, a few theatres had to suspend performances. As for the "new audiences", we have some revealing comments from Constantin Stanislavsky, the great director of the Moscow Art Theatre, who worked hard "to educate them up to the discipline of our theatre". His experiences were similar to those on other serious stages; so we read, "For some time after the February 1917 Revolution the public in the theatres was mixed; it was poor and rich, intelligent and non-intelligent . . . They were interesting performances and they taught us a great deal; they forced us to feel an altogether new atmosphere in the auditorium. We began to understand that these people came to the theatre, not in order to be amused, but in order to learn . . ."[28]

Things became more difficult, however, after the Bolshevik Revolution of October 1917, "The doors of our theatre opened exclusively for the poor people and closed for a time to the intelligentsia. Our performances were free to all who received their tickets from factories and institutions where we sent them. We met face to face . . . with spectators altogether new to us, many of whom, perhaps the majority, knew nothing not only of *our* theatre, but of any theatre . . ." The problem became not one of understanding, but of elementary behaviour, "We were forced . . . to teach this new spectator how to sit quietly, how not to talk, how to come into the theatre at the proper time, not to smoke, not to eat nuts in public, not to bring food into the theatre and eat it there, to dress in his best so as to fit more into the atmosphere of beauty ... At first this was very hard to do ..."

But with patience and firmness, Stanislavsky succeeded, and the rewards were rich. He speaks with great warmth of the "new audiences", "They were spectators in the best sense of the word; they came to our theatre not through accident but with trembling and the expectation of something important, something they had never experienced before. They treated the actors with peculiarly touching admiration ..."29

Conditions at the great musical stages—the Bolshoi, the Maryinsky —were comparable. So we hear from the singer Andreyev, "We used to call the subscription public the 'guillotine'. There were times one wondered whether or not there was an audience in the hall ... Now, though the listeners sit in rags, the enthusiasm has no bounds ..."30

Eventually, the restrictive admissions policy of the revolutionary government described by Stanislavsky was changed, "After about a year-and-a-half of the Revolution, material circumstances brought about a change in the theatrical policy of the government, and our doors (of the Moscow Art Theatre) opened again to the richer portion of the public ..."31

The control exercised by the Bolshevik government over all cultural institutions was absolute. One of the first steps was to nationalize the theatres. On 12 July 1918 the conservatories of Moscow and Petrograd were declared state institutions of higher learning; the decree was signed by Ulyanov (Lenin) and Lunacharsky. There soon followed the nationalization of the famed chapel choirs of Moscow and Petrograd, of all private music schools, publishing houses, and printing establishments, instrument factories, libraries, archives, and concert institutions. After seizing all physical means of artistic expression, the government turned to the music itself and declared the works of deceased composers to be state property. In the meantime, MUZO-NARKOMPROS worked towards establishing full supervision over all aspects of musical activities; by 1919, its decrees filled a 74-page volume. Artists were required to obtain MUZO's permission for concert trips. Programmes, announcements, placards, even tickets were subject to advance approval. The musical repertoire was regulated by a special commission, the GLAVREPERTKOM*. Concerts without "artistic value" were refused a licence. Model concert programmes were worked out by MUZO and distributed to organizations and individuals. Detailed reports on all musical activities had to be filed by all involved with music—composers,

* Abbreviation for "Glavnaya repertuarnaya kommissia", the "main repertoire committee".

performers, critics, historians, teachers, librarians, conductors, and theatre directors. In view of this avalanche of bureaucracy, it seems almost paradoxical to learn that Lunacharsky—in whose name many of these decrees were issued—did not believe in stringent surveillance. He confided to Ehrenburg that Communism should lead to multi-formity, not conformity; artists could not be cut according to a single pattern. Censorship was needed "in periods of transition", but Luna-charsky denied that "state control is inherent in the Communist system".[32]

On this point, Lenin was more realistic. He, too, said that "every artist takes it as his right to create freely, according to his ideal, whether it is good or not. There you have the ferment, the experimenting, the chaotic." Yet Lenin set limits, "But of course we are Communists. We must not drop our hands into our laps and allow the chaos to ferment as it chooses. We must try consciously to guide this development and mould and determine the results."[33]

Many Russian artists could not agree with such a type of "guidance" and chose emigration. Composers, performers, and pedagogues left in great numbers, either because they felt no sympathy with the Bolshevik Revolution, or because they saw no future for their pro-fession in a country torn by civil strife and bent on proletarian domina-tion. The list of musicians who requested, and received, exit visas and decided to remain abroad is formidable; equally large is the number who left illegally. That Russian music could survive such a drain of talent testifies to the immense reservoir of innate musical gifts to be found in Russia. Strangely enough, the Soviet government did not seem unduly concerned about the exodus of artists. Lunacharsky was personally helpful in obtaining exit visas for some prominent musi-cians, as we know from the memoirs of Chaliapin, Grechaninov, and Prokofiev. One can feel a slight note of regret in Lunacharsky's comment when he said to young Prokofiev in 1918, "You are a revolu-tionary in music, we are revolutionaries in life. We ought to work together. But if you want to go to America I shall not stand in your way."[34] Lunacharsky's trust proved justified: fifteen years later, Prokofiev resettled in Moscow.

Many others, however, remained permanently abroad. In discussing the artist-emigrés, Soviet historians make a careful distinction between those who left without political rancour, and those who became public antagonists of the Soviet regime. Certain noted emigrés have been "forgiven" posthumously, their works and achievements have been reintegrated into Russian-Soviet music; among them Rachmaninov, Medtner, Grechaninov, Glazunov, and Chaliapin. A historic "recon-ciliation" was Igor Stravinsky's visit to Russia in 1962, after an absence of some fifty years during which many bitter comments had been exchanged on both sides. The list of emigré-musicians is long, and the following enumeration is highly selective: the composers Rachmaninov, Grechaninov, Liapunov, N. and A. Tcherepnin, Lopatnikov, Schillinger, Medtner; the conductors Siloti, Kussevitsky, Malko, and Dobrowen; the pianists Borovsky, Orlov, Barer, and Horowitz; the violinists Heifetz, Achron, and Milstein; the cellists Piatigorsky, Graudan, Garbuzova; the theorists and critics Yasser, de Schloezer, Sabaneyev, Slonimsky. The violin teacher Leopold Auer who had been active at the Petersburg Conservatory since 1868 (!), departed with some of his best students in 1917. One of them, Miron Poliakin, returned to Russia in 1926 and continued to teach in the Auer tradition until his death in 1941. Even Lunacharsky's trusted assistant, the composer Arthur Lourié, emigrated to Paris in 1921 and ultimately settled in the United States. For Lourié and for the writer-historian Leonid Sabaneyev, the Soviets reserve some of their most vitriolic criticism: both are treated as "traitors" to the cause. For a time, in the mid-1920's, so many Russian composers worked abroad that professional critics distinguished between a "Russian school on Soviet territory" and a "Russian school in Western Europe". But—with few exceptions —the Russian composers "in exile" did not survive the permanent estrangement from their homeland. The future of Russian music remained on Russian soil.

But the leaders of Russian music "on Soviet territory" were by no means unanimous as to what that future should be. Lunacharsky favoured an evolutionary process, in the sense of Lenin's words, "Crushing capitalism will not feed us. We must take all culture that capitalism left us, and use it to construct Socialism. We must take all science and technique, all knowledge and art. Without this we cannot build the life of Communist society."[35] However, there were revolutionaries who had no use for the old bourgeois culture, who believed in a new "proletarian culture" that would arise from the masses.

Some of these extremist views were promulgated by an organization known as PROLETKULT (an abbreviation for "proletarian culture"). Its leaders stressed their ideological independence and competed with the official NARKOMPROS in the field of cultural mass education. Believing in the artistic "self-activity" of the labouring masses, PROLETKULT organized studio workshops in hundreds of towns and villages which were staffed by professional artists and cultural experts. At the first congress of PROLETKULT in October, 1920, more than three hundred organizations were represented. In the field of music, PROLETKULT attracted many good musicians who welcomed the opportunity of bringing music to the masses without much theorizing. Among them was Alexander Kastalsky, a noted folklorist and choral conductor. Choral studios were organized, each with sixty to seventy members, as well as model workshops for folk instruments. While the "orthodox" PROLETKULTISTS called for an end of the domination by "instructor-intellectuals", the musical leaders of the Moscow PROLETKULT dismissed any narrow interpretation of "proletarian" music. The Moscow musicians rejected the accusation that they were "saddling the proletariat with bourgeois culture: all genuine art has its eternal moments."

Despite some extremist theories, PROLETKULT played a useful role in the early years of the Revolution. However, Lenin was opposed to the principles of PROLETKULT; in fact, his opposition dated back to pre-revolutionary days when, in 1910, he wrote that, "In truth, all the phraseology about 'proletarian culture' merely conceals a struggle against Marxism." Lenin reasserted his opposition on 2 October 1920, when he said in a speech,

> "Proletarian culture is not something that has sprung from no-where, it is not an invention of those who call themselves experts in proletarian culture. That is all nonsense. Proletarian culture must be the result of the natural development of the stores of knowledge which mankind has accumulated under the yoke of capitalist society, landlord society, and bureaucratic society . . . One can become a Communist only when one enriches one's mind with the knowledge of all the wealth created by man-kind . . ."[36]

The end of PROLETKULT came rather unexpectedly, at the height of its success, late in 1920. At the PROLETKULT congress in October 1920 Lunacharsky was delegated by Lenin to present the government's views and to insist on Party discipline. However, Lunacharsky's speech at the congress did not satisfy Lenin who noted rather angrily, "Judging by *Izvestia* of 8 October, Comrade Lunacharsky said the *very opposite* of what he and I had agreed upon yesterday." Although Lunacharsky defended himself by saying that his speech was "wrongly reported", Lenin insisted on a draft resolution containing the following passage,

> ". . . The All-Russian Congress of Proletarian Culture most emphatically rejects as theoretically wrong and practically harmful all attempts to invent a special culture, all attempts to isolate itself in an exclusive organization . . . On the contrary, the Congress imposes upon all organizations of the PROLETKULT the absolute duty to regard themselves as being entirely auxiliary organs in the system of institutions of the People's Commissariat of Education,

and performing their duties under the general guidance of the Soviet government . . . as part of the duties of the proletarian dictatorship."[37]

This resolution spelled the end of any "autonomous" ambitions. By December 1920 PROLETKULT ceased to function independently though it was not abolished formally until 1923.

The PROLETKULT affair was only one aspect of the continuing struggle with dissident intellectuals, both on the right and the left of the Bolsheviks. With some bitterness, Lenin stated in a speech on 8 June 1918 addressing the All-Russian Congress of Teachers, that "the main mass of intelligentsia of old Russia are direct adversaries of the Soviet regime." It was Lunacharsky's thorny assignment to win over the intelligentsia by flattery or force. A good example was his method of dealing with such old institutions as the conservatories of Moscow and Petrograd. The faculties were self-governing bodies and viewed all interference with suspicion. They were headed by men who stood for old-time liberalism—Glazunov in Petrograd and Ippolitov-Ivanov in Moscow, but the type of liberalism fashionable in 1905 seemed strangely dated in 1917. Many of the pedagogues were antagonistic towards the Bolshevik regime and the "toiling masses" it represented. Lunacharsky tried to win their co-operation by persuasion. He welcomed the pedagogues "to the bright and honourable work of educating the people— the masters of the country" and envisioned "the co-operation of the pedagogues with the social forces". It was reassuring to hear that no educational measures would be adopted "without the attentive deliberation of the pedagogues", but this was coupled with the warning that "a decision cannot by any means be reached exclusively through the co-operation of specialists".[38] In other words, political as well as pedagogical considerations would play a part in making educational reforms.

In Tsarist times, the two oldest conservatories in the country—in St. Petersburg (founded in 1862) and in Moscow (founded in 1866)—were under the jurisdiction of the Russian Musical Society as were the conservatories in Kiev, Odessa, and Saratov. The conservatories were chafing under the domination of the Society and favoured autonomy. After the February 1917 Revolution, the five conservatories submitted a plan for autonomy to the Provisional Government, but no action was taken.

When the Bolsheviks assumed power, the deliberations about the future of the conservatories were resumed, with Lunacharsky and his assistant Lourié participating. It soon became apparent that no "autonomy" was possible outside the governmental structure. The decree of

12 July 1918 concerning the nationalization of the conservatories was but the last step in a protracted procedure. A final farewell was given to the defunct Russian Musical Society when Glazunov, at a meeting on 29 July 1918 recommended "to express thanks to the Directorate of the RMS for the more than fifty years of trusteeship of the Petrograd Conservatory".[39] A gracious but futile gesture.

De facto, the Conservatory had come under government control several months earlier when Lunacharsky authorized a budget allotment of 225,000 roubles to meet the urgent financial needs of the institution—a move gratefully acknowledged by the Conservatory. However, it was made clear that the subsidy was granted, not to the Russian Musical Society (which was still nominally in charge) but directly to the Petrograd Conservatory. An accompanying letter, dated 22 April 1918 contained some pointed observations, ". . . The People's Commissariat of Public Education, being the organization directly responsible for the financing of the Conservatory, reserves the right to enter into direct negotiations with the Conservatory concerning the necessary measures towards its democratization and towards a broader service to fulfill the musical needs of the working population . . ."[40]

This was more than the Conservatory had bargained for. Under the paternal rule of the Russian Musical Society, the faculty had enjoyed a certain degree of academic freedom. Now, the spectre of bureaucratic interference loomed threateningly. The first reaction of the faculty was one of concern and resentment, and Glazunov was delegated to seek clarification and reassurance. As a beginning, he replied with a statement addressed to Lunacharsky in which he rejected all hints of a lack of "democracy" at the Conservatory,

> "With regard to the 'democratization of the Conservatory', I must point out that—if the term is to be understood in the sense of an effort to raise the people's level of musical education and artistic taste—the Conservatory does not deserve any reproach . . . Students are admitted prevailingly from the poorer classes of the population, unconditionally and without consideration of national origin. The sole criterion for admission was, and is, exclusively the degree of talent and a certain degree of preparation (though there have been cases where exceptionally gifted individuals have been admitted 'in the raw'). The only wish one could express in the interest of a broader service of the Conservatory towards the musical needs of the working population is a lowering of the tuition an increase in scholarships, and an improvement in the material status of the faculty."[41]

Glazunov was justified in pointing with pride to the liberal past of the Conservatory—a liberalism that had often aroused the suspicion of the Tsarist authorities. But Lunacharsky's "democratization" aimed more deeply: the Conservatory seemed too remote from the needs and aspirations of the newly emerging proletarian society. Among the goals were the political activization of the students, the establishment of a new relationship between teachers and students, a re-examination of the curriculum in view of the new social needs. Above all, the government aimed at admitting a greater percentage of students from the, hitherto, underprivileged classes: workers and peasants. Glazunov was concerned about lowered admission standards, and the alarming drop in applications for admission to the Conservatory. In August 1918 there were only eighty applications by prospective students.

Glazunov's concern seemed justified. Lenin had just ordered that all admission tests to institutions of higher learning be abolished so as to eradicate "all privileges of the moneyed classes". However, Lunacharsky issued a special dispensation, dated 23 September 1918 which enabled the conservatories to continue with entrance tests. Since tuition was abolished and the conservatories were entrusted entirely "to the people", there was an obligation—so Lunacharsky argued—to select the most gifted applicants, justifying some sort of aptitude test.[42]

Undoubtedly, these selective procedures delayed the "proletarization of the student body" which proceeded far more slowly at the conservatories than at other institutions of higher learning—a fact much criticized by Party ideologists. In October 1918 a student council was elected; its members participated in the meetings of the faculty directorate and were entitled to vote. However, their influence on substantial decisions was negligible, and they concerned themselves mainly with student activities. One tangible achievement was that they were no longer called "pupils" but "students"—a term used in Russia for those attending an institution of higher learning.

This elevation of the conservatories to the status of a vuz (abbreviation for "Vyshye uchebnoye zavedenie"—institution of higher learning) brought about certain changes in the curriculum, particularly in the preparatory divisions. Lunacharsky set up two committees to study the problems involved. He also suggested new areas of study, including an Opera Studio which was realized in 1923.* The ensemble classes were revitalized, and the orchestra department received particular attention. Regular participation was made obligatory, with three to four rehearsals each week. The concert activities of faculty and students were expanded to include performances outside the conservatory, as part of the general educational campaign. Eventually, the post of "director"

* See pp. 103–4.

was abolished, and the administrative duties were assumed by the deans of the four "faculties"—theory, voice, piano, and orchestral instruments. In Petrograd, Glazunov remained as "rector" while Ossovsky became "pro-rector". The status of the teaching faculty was improved: all instructors having served more than five years received the title "professor" regardless of their previous standing or qualification.

The years of the Civil War—up to 1920—played havoc with organized instruction. The conservatory buildings had to remain unheated, group activities were suspended temporarily, and individual lessons were given at the homes of the professors. Faculty salaries remained unpaid for months. The academic year 1920–21 brought more normal conditions though the conservatories were plagued throughout the 1920's by problems of re-organization and curricular revisions. The teaching faculties remained stubbornly independent; thus, for instance, disregarding a decree about the separation of church and state (involving the closing of all churches attached to educational institutions), the "reactionary" professors of the Petrograd Conservatory not only kept their church open but succeeded in introducing a course in church chant into the curriculum. This incident, amusing in retrospect, is treated with the utmost seriousness in a recent Soviet book.[43]

The recalcitrance was not limited to artists and pedagogues but developed also among the rank-and-file musicians who resented the leadership of Lourié, the composer who was Lunacharsky's chief assistant. Lourié's active espousal of modern music aroused much opposition. He, in turn, accused the musicians of a "petit-bourgeois ideology", of being interested mainly in "making a rouble", and of being incapable of understanding the historic trend of events. The musicians, newly organized in a strong union, the VSERABIS ("Vserossiiski soyuz rabotnikov iskusstv"—All-Russian Union of workers in the arts)*, retaliated by complaining about the bureaucracy and inefficiency of MUZO, the music division of NARKOMPROS headed by Lourié. The split between the artists and the official NARKOMPROS became so dangerous that Lunacharsky convened a conference which began on 29 October 1920. The result was an important document, published as "Basic Policies in the Realm of the Arts" (Ob osnovakh politiki v oblasti iskusstva). In essence, these guidelines have remained valid until today, for they established the principle that the arts were subject to the supervision of the State and the Party. The document sought to end the factionalism in the arts and to channel energies towards a common goal. Here are some of the most salient passages,

* Thus, VSERABIS was not a "musicians' union", but a union of people working in all fields of the arts.

"The new proletarian and socialist art can be built only on the basis of all the achievements of the past . . . It must be cleansed mercilessly of all admixtures of bourgeois decay and depravity . . . The heritage of old culture must be absorbed by the proletariat not through student-like imitation but in an authoritative, conscious, sharply critical manner . . ."[44]

It was further stated that intense Communist propaganda among the "workers in the arts" should insure a "high ideo-revolutionary quality of artistic production". The proletarization of the teaching institutions was to be achieved through the establishment of workers' faculties, the so-called RABFAK. (These were special classes for workers and peasants lacking a secondary education, designed to prepare them for entry into institutions of higher learning.) The artistic self-expression of amateurs in all fields was to be encouraged; in music, choral singing and massed activities were to be stressed which would lead to an interpenetration of art and folk customs.

This document contains some of the creative ideas of PROLETKULT (so recently chastised by the Government), combined with the more orthodox approach favoured by Lenin. As for Lourié, his fight with the musicians brought him a Pyrrhic victory and he emerged with his prestige badly shattered. He left Russia the following year, in 1921, never to return.

Considering the "harsh and terrible realities of the situation in Russia", to quote H. G. Wells, the survival of the arts during the first years of the Revolution was a near-miracle. Wells visited Russia in September 1920 and was a sympathetic observer. He explained the survival of the theatres in the following words,

"For a time the stablest thing in Russian culture was the theatre. There stood the theatres, and nobody wanted to loot them or to destroy them; the artists were accustomed to meet and work in them . . . the tradition of official subsidies held good. So quite amazingly the Russian dramatic and operatic life kept on through the extremest storms of violence, and keeps on to this day (1920). In Petrograd we found there were more than forty shows going on every night; in Moscow we found very much the same state of affairs. We heard Chaliapin, greatest of actors and singers, in the *Barber of Seville* and in *Khovanshchina*; the admirable orchestra was variously attired, but the conductor still held out valiantly in swallow tails and white tie . . ."[45]

Wells lacked the time to penetrate beneath the surface. In truth, the physical condition of the theatres was catastrophic. Costumes, scenery, and other properties were falling apart. In the winter, the buildings remained virtually unheated, the temperature often hovering below freezing point. Musicians played in overcoats, singers shivered on the stage. No less lamentable was the appearance of the audience which struggled to attend a performance. Wells speaks movingly of the "underclad town population in this dismantled and ruinous city (Petrograd), appallingly under-fed", clinging in clusters to the outside of old tramcars for any kind of transportation. Moscow, though "far less grim", experienced similar hardships during the long winter months.

The subsidies required by the theatres and opera houses were very considerable, particularly since tickets were distributed free of charge through factories, trade unions, and schools as well as to soldiers and sailors. We have seen that Lenin himself doubted the educational importance of a theatre like the Bolshoi as long as there was a crying need for elementary schooling, both for children and adults. Particularly the opera had many detractors because of its "aristocratic" connotations. To counteract the polemics directed against the operatic genre by ideological extremists, the musicologist Asafiev developed certain novel ideas about the "democratic nature" of the opera. He maintained that, far from being an aristocratic fancy of "seventeenthcentury Florentine aesthetes", the opera actually grew out of folk roots and had absorbed song-like elements.

In a series of articles published in 1918–20, Asafiev refuted the idea that opera was "alien" to the working classes, and he elaborated on this subject in one of his best essays, entitled "Opera in the Worker-Peasant Theatre". He predicted that the classical Russian opera, with its affinity to folk images and national musical idioms, would serve as a firm basis for the development of a Soviet lyric theatre. Indeed, opera as a genre became as popular with the mass audiences as it had been with the bourgeois public in pre-revolutionary days. It became the ideal medium by which to introduce the untutored listener to "serious" music.

An interesting development within the Russian opera was the collaboration of famous stage directors drawn from the great dramatic theatres—directors who had revitalized the Russian stage by realistic techniques or futuristic fancy. Among them were Stanislavsky, Nemirovich-Danchenko, Fedor Komissarjevsky, Meyerhold, and Taïrov. At first, some of them were reluctant to apply their talent and energies to the "fossilized" opera. Komissarjevsky, asked for his opinion, suggested facetiously that the Bolshoi Theatre be blown up by a bomb. Stanislavsky, more seriously, recommended that the opera house be closed for two or three years so that an entirely new approach could be developed.

Such delays, however, were unacceptable to the newly-appointed commissar of the Moscow theatres, the capable Elena Malinovskaya. She decided to work towards an immediate rapprochment between the Bolshoi Opera and the Moscow Art Theatre in order to raise the "scenic culture" of the opera productions. In December 1918 the ensembles of the two houses met at a social gathering and performed for each other. "It was a triumphant rout," reminisced Stanislavsky, "the whole evening was joyful, touching, and memorable."[46] Almost immediately, work began in the studios of Stanislavsky and Nemirovich-Danchenko; the aim was to develop "actor-singers". Stanislavsky speaks of the "mutual" influence, combining the century-old tradition of the Bolshoi with the realistic acting techniques developed by the Moscow Art Theatre. Stanislavsky worked with a selected group of young singers whom he trained according to his "system" of acting. An "exceptional amount of attention was paid to diction in the opera", and the singers were exposed to "a whole series of exercises and classes for the development of feeling for the word and speech".[47]

Neither Stanislavsky nor Nemirovich-Danchenko undertook the staging of any productions for the Bolshoi Theatre. Both artists preferred to work independently in their own opera studios where they could control every aspect of a production. In 1941, the opera studios of Stanislavsky, who had died in 1938, and Nemirovich-Danchenko were combined into one opera theatre bearing the name of these two pioneers of the theatre. At present, the Stanislavsky-Nemirovich-Danchenko Theatre serves as Moscow's second lyric scene. It has preserved its own style—intimate, realistic as to theatrical details and acting—which contrasts with the more pompous and traditional style of the Bolshoi.

Petrograd, too, acquired another opera theatre. Next to the traditional Maryinsky, a smaller opera house was established in 1918, mainly through the initiative of Lunacharsky. It was housed in the former Mikhailovsky Theatre and became known under the abbreviated name, "Malyi" or "Malegot". At first, the performances were mere transplantations of productions taken from the Maryinsky repertoire. Soon however, the Malyi Opera became artistically independent; it acquired its own ensemble of singers and instrumentalists and staged its own productions. Being a smaller house, it stressed a more intimate repertoire of the *opéra comique* and *Singspiel* variety, as well as operettas. At the same time, the Malyi developed an interest in experimental work, both in terms of composers and stage directors.

The custodians of tradition were the two old theatres, the Bolshoi in Moscow and the Maryinsky in Petrograd. Their conservative policy was attacked violently by left-wing critics; one of them demanded the removal from the repertoire of the works of Tchaikovsky and Rimsky-Korsakov because they propagated ideas inimical to the proletariat. As late as 1929, a Western observer, Herbert Graf, remarked that "Tsarism has survived" in the Soviet opera houses, referring facetiously to the repertoire of classic Russian opera built on subjects of the Tsarist era. But Lunacharsky was a stout defender of a cautious approach, and he answered the critics, "Only naive people can discuss seriously that our great opera houses must change their repertoire. No revolutionary repertoire exists, and we cannot afford new productions. It means that, at present, we can only preserve and replenish carefully and slowly the repertoire of the academic theatres . . ."[48]

The "revolutionary" repertoire was, in fact, slow in developing. Nothing could be more conventional than the repertoire of the Bolshoi and the Maryinsky during the early revolutionary years. Next to the standard fare of Russian operas—by Tchaikovsky, Rimsky-Korsakov, Glinka, Borodin, Mussorgsky, Serov, and Dargomyzhsky—were equally standardized selections by Verdi (*Traviata, Aida, Rigoletto*) Bizet (*Carmen, Pearl Fishers*), Wagner (*Lohengrin, Rheingold, Walküre*), Gounod (*Faust*), Rossini (*Barber of Seville*), and Saint-Saens (*Samson and Delilah*). This familiar repertoire was regenerated, however, through the infusion of new directorial talent drawn from the legitimate theatres. Whether "realistic" or "futuristic", the new concepts breathed new life into stagnant productions. Increased attention was given to the scenic demands of opera and to the acting abilities of singers. The controversial director Meyerhold was entrusted with several new productions for the staid Maryinsky Opera: Stravinsky's *Rossignol* (May 1918), Gluck's *Orphée et Eurydice* (May 1919). He also restaged Auber's *La Muette de Portici* as a revolutionary drama, renamed *Fenella*. A new departure was to assign directorial duties to eminent singers who also participated in a leading role; it enabled the singer-director to shape an entire work according to his own concept. Thus Chaliapin was in charge of Boito's *Mefistofele*, Massenet's *Don Quixote*, and Rossini's *Barber*; Yershov directed Rimsky-Korsakov's *Kashchei*, Kurzner did the same for *Le Coq d'Or*.

Opera, however, was only part of the over-all musical scene. Orchestral performances played an important part, and here Petrograd led the way. In 1917, shortly after the February Revolution, the Court Orchestra was transformed into the State Symphony, and in May of that year, Sergei Kussevitsky was appointed principal conductor. After the October Revolution, he remained in charge though he continued to live in Moscow. Kussevitsky shared his conducting duties with several staff members of the Maryinsky Opera—Emil Cooper, Nikolai Malko, Albert Coates, and Grigori Fitelberg. Occasionally, Glazunov appeared as guest conductor. In May 1920 Kussevitsky was succeeded by Cooper. The Petrograd State Symphony played a decisive role within the governmental programme of mass education. During the difficult winter 1918–19, the orchestra gave ninety-six concerts, not counting children's concerts and other activities. On 19 October 1920 the name of the orchestra was changed to State Philharmonic Orchestra; now it is known as the Leningrad Philharmonic, and has the honour of being the oldest "philharmonic" orchestra in the Soviet Union.

In 1921, the concept of the "Philharmonic" was expanded and the orchestra became only one aspect of its responsibility. In addition, the "Philharmonic" sponsored chamber music concerts and music appreciation lectures; it also assumed the responsibility for a music library and a musico-historical museum and branched into the field of publication with explanatory booklets and printed programme annotations. This broad concept of a "philharmonic" organization has become the standard for the Soviet Union—the assumption of virtually complete responsibility for the musical life of a city or a larger territory. At present, there are some 130 "Philharmonics" spread over the entire Soviet Union. When the Petrograd Philharmonic was established, it was given a magnificent building for its headquarters; it dated back to the 1830's and had the imposing "Hall of Columns" which could seat some 2,500 listeners. Following the Petrograd pattern, the Moscow Philharmonic was established in 1925, the Ukrainian Philharmonic soon thereafter. At times, cities took the initiative: for example, Nizhni-Novgorod (now known as Gorky) organized some forty orchestral concerts during the season 1919–20 though there had been no permanent orchestra in that city before the Revolution.

In Moscow, the need for symphony concerts was filled mainly by the orchestra of the Bolshoi Theatre, with the assistance of other theatre orchestras. Various cycles of symphony concerts were given in 1918–19, under conductors like Orlov, Golovanov, and Vassilenko. The latter, long a champion of music for the masses, carried his concerts into workers' clubs, factories, and outlying districts.

Most interesting was the fate of the so-called Kussevitsky concerts which had been a hallmark of Moscow's musical scene since 1909. Kussevitsky had assembled his own orchestra whose members, by contract, were not permitted to play elsewhere. During the 1914–17 war, the ensemble was decimated by conscription. After the Revolution, the Kussevitsky orchestra was reorganized on a co-operative basis and the concerts continued under government sponsorship since private enterprise was no longer permissible. Kussevitsky remained as conductor though no longer as chief sponsor. He divided his time between activities in Moscow and Petrograd which led to a certain neglect of the Petrograd State Symphony. Kussevitsky's opposition to the Bolshevik regime was a matter of public record; in the early days of the Revolution, he had denounced it in an open letter as "the harshest, most despotic and violent regime that has ever reigned over us".[49] Nevertheless, the government treated him with consideration, and Lunacharsky tried hard to win his full co-operation within the framework of Russia's new cultural goals. Kussevitsky agreed to act as special consultant in musical matters and conducted the usual round of free concerts for workers, soldiers, and children. He even tried his hand at conducting opera at the Bolshoi—Tchaikovsky's *Pique Dame*—and cleansed the score of all spurious interpolations. His concert programmes continued to be challenging and instructive. In October 1919 he presented a cycle of Beethoven symphonies. In the spring of 1920, he commemorated the fifth anniversary of Scriabin's death with a series of five concerts devoted to his works. This anniversary was also observed in Petrograd by a concert cycle conducted by Cooper.

In May 1920 Kussevitsky and his wife left Russia, ostensibly for a year to give concerts abroad, but it was clear that he did not intend to return.

One of Kussevitsky's most notable achievements, the publishing firm *Edition Russe de Musique*, was nationalized by the Bolshevik government in 1918, as were all other private publishing enterprises. The *Edition Russe* had been established in 1909 by S. and N. Kussevitsky— the initial "N" stood for Madame Natalia Kussevitsky whose wealth provided the capital for his cultural enterprises. Kussevitsky's publishing house was dedicated to the sponsoring of young Russian composers; the first to receive a contract was Scriabin.* In 1915, Kussevitsky acquired the publishing house of A. Gutheil in Moscow, and the enlarged catalogue included such names as Rachmaninov, Medtner, Grechaninov, Stravinsky, and Prokofiev. The *Edition Russe* continued after Kussevitsky had settled in Paris, and the firm proved very helpful to Russian composers residing abroad. Kussevitsky's interest in Russian music remained undiminished. During his long tenure at the head of the Boston Orchestra, from 1924 to 1949, he encouraged Russian and Soviet composers, particularly Stravinsky and Prokofiev, and he never missed an opportunity to introduce new music from Soviet Russia. During the Second World War, he played a leading role in the American-Soviet Friendship Committee.

---

* Kussevitsky and Scriabin quarrelled in 1911, and the feud grew in bitterness until the composer's unexpected death in 1915.

Orchestral activities in Moscow and Petrograd were matched by a continuation of the choral traditions. In Moscow, the former Synodal Choir was reorganized in 1918 as the People's Choral Academy under its former director, Alexander Kastalsky, who stressed folk traditions. In Petrograd, the Court Chapel Choir, dating back to 1479, was transferred to State supervision; a continuity of work was insured by retaining the old conductor, Mikhail Klimov, who remained in charge until 1937. Needless to say, the repertoire became almost entirely secular, and there was a strong infusion of "political" texts and music. A break with tradition occurred in 1920 when twenty women's voices were added. Girls were admitted to the choir school beginning in 1923. The choir boys continued to double the soprano and alto parts but also functioned as an independent boys' choir.*

The Petrograd Choir gave some fifty to sixty concerts each year, not only in its own auditorium but also in club halls, for workers, students, and the Army. When the Petrograd Philharmonic Organization was expanded in 1921, the Choir became one of its constituent members, but in the following year it regained its independence. However, it continued to collaborate with the Philharmonic Orchestra in major performances. At present it is known as the Academic Glinka Choir.

A significant development of the early revolutionary years was the government-sponsored activity of small chamber ensembles. They added a new dimension to the drive for musical mass education. These ensembles were highly mobile and adaptable to small stages and improvised settings. In Tsarist days, chamber music was the domain of the élite. To make chamber music attractive to an untutored audience was a new and difficult task. Undeterred, Lunacharsky and his musical staff evolved an approach to "explain" chamber music to a new public. A type of lecture-recital was designed, and programmes were conceived with an educational purpose. So-called "concert-monographs" were devoted to the works of a single composer—Schumann, Schubert, Tchaikovsky, César Franck. The unsophisticated audiences expected full-blooded, strongly projected, and brilliant performances. This "externalization" of performing style proved very effective.

Encouraged and sponsored by NARKOMPROS and other government agencies, Russian musicians organized several excellent chamber ensembles. The first was the so-called Lunacharsky Quintet, named after the commissar who initiated its formation in late 1917. A few months later it was reduced to a quartet, retaining the same first violinist, Lukashevsky. In 1919 it was renamed the Glazunov Quartet and acquired much fame at home and abroad.

* By 1925, the choir had a membership of 30 men, 28 women, 40 boys, and 30 girls.

In Moscow, the Lenin Quartet, formed in 1919, was led by Lev Zeitlin, known as Kussevitsky's concertmaster; for a time, the cellist was the youthful Gregor Piatigorsky. Another ensemble (led by the violinist Mogilevsky) called itself the Moscow Quartet but changed its name to Stradivari Quartet when the government put four "Strads" at its disposal. The instruments came from a collection of rare musical instruments established by the government in 1921. Its holdings consisted mainly of valuable Italian string instruments expropriated from private collections.

Other string quartets formed in Moscow during the early 1920's were the Beethoven Quartet, still active today; the Komitas Quartet, also still in existence; the Moscow Art Theatre (MKHAT) Quartet; and the Glière Quartet. In Kharkov, the Vuillaume Quartet was formed in 1920 while Kiev acquired a permanent quartet in 1919.

The turbulence of the early revolutionary years engulfed the serious Russian composers; many of them fell almost silent, particularly the older generation. There was no immediate demand for complex sonatas or symphonies. The need of the day was served by the mass song, the "massovaya pesnia". New songs were written, old revolutionary songs were revived; at times, new words were adapted to old tunes. The "masses" were listeners, performers, and often creators—as Asafiev said, "The composer: his name—the people." A revolutionary folklore arose, captured and written down by professional musicians. Words and music reflected the martial spirit of the Civil War, the hatred against the "interventionists", the belief in a better future under Communism. Recognizing the political usefulness of these songs, the government subsidized the writing and publishing of "revolutionary" music. Within the State Publishing House, a "department of propaganda" was organized, to be known under the abbreviated name AGITOTDEL. It enlisted the help of professional musicians who were specialists in the song and chorus genres. The results were often dreary and became known disparagingly as "agit"-music. Musical opportunism flourished among hack musicians, but even serious composers were not averse to switching to "revolutionary thematics" as a means for survival. Later, Lunacharsky himself belittled that "homebred simplification with revolutionary pretences", which—in truth—merely paraphrased the "most trivial" aspects of older music.

The songs of the day, despite their ephemeral quality, represent, however, an integral part of the musical and social scene of the early revolutionary years. Serious or satirical, patriotic or inflammatory, many of these songs had an artless spontaneity that captured the imagination of the people. In later years, many noted composers have tried to write "mass songs", but the effort to be "folkish" is often painfully in evidence. Occasionally, one encounters some of these early songs in an opera, a ballet, or a descriptive symphony where they are used by composers for added "realism". The famous "Sailors' Dance" in Glière's ballet *The Red Poppy*, for example, is an adaptation of the revolutionary song *Yablochko* (The Little Apple). A certain type of folk ditty, the *Chastushka*, was very popular in those years; the contemporary Soviet composer Rodion Shchedrin has used the *Chastushka* genre in his opera, *Not Love Alone*, and in the orchestral concerto *Naughty Ditties*, both composed in the 1960's.

Among the older serious composers, the figure of Alexander Glazunov stands out. He guided the Petrograd Conservatory through the difficult years of readjustment and transition. Obviously he enjoyed the respect and affection of Lunacharsky; in fact, a personal directive of Lunacharsky (dated 9 March 1918), protected Glazunov from having his apartment on Kazanskaya Street requisitioned by the government. Yet, Glazunov was worn out, as Wells remarked, "He used to be a big, florid man, but now he is pallid and very much fallen away, so that his clothes hang loosely on him." Wells visited Glazunov in Petrograd in 1920 and found him rather depressed, "He told me that he still composed, but that his stock of music paper was almost exhausted. 'Then there will be no more.' I said there would be much more, and that soon. He doubted it . . ."[50] In fact, Glazunov's creative work came almost to a standstill during those years: his only major composition, written in 1920–21, was the String Quartet No. 6, Op. 106, dedicated to the newly named Glazunov Quartet. It showed traces of creative decline, described by Soviet critics tactfully as "a certain academization of style".

How hard living conditions were, even for artists of fame like Glazunov, can be gleaned from the reminiscences of a fellow composer and friend, Maximilian Steinberg.

"Glazunov, who all his life was used to living in a large flat with all conveniences, was now housed in one smallish room heated by a small stove; here he worked, composed, slept. In the next room was his mother, almost eighty years old. In the other rooms the temperature was freezing; some time later other people moved in. Under such circumstances, creative work was difficult . . . In this crowded room Glazunov received some of the most famous foreign musicians . . . I remember the conductor Hermann Abendroth. Entering the room, I saw Abendroth in a fur coat listening to the Second Piano Concerto of Glazunov, played by

the composer, also in a fur coat . . . In the same setting I met the
famous pianist Artur Schnabel . . ."51

The meetings recalled by Steinberg must in fact have taken place
around 1923, when conditions had actually improved compared with
the earlier revolutionary years.

While Glazunov represented a strictly conservative point of view,
the somewhat younger Nikolai Miaskovsky belonged to the progressive wing of Russian composers. Born in 1891, Miaskovsky's formative
years fell into the Tsarist era, yet he is usually considered a "Soviet"
composer since his creative life extended from about 1918 to 1950. In
his youth, around 1908, he belonged to the musical avant-garde, a
distinction he shared with his friend, Prokofiev. But Miaskovsky did
not become a professional musician until 1911 when he graduated from
the Petersburg Conservatory. During the First World War, he served
on the Austrian front. The outbreak of the Revolution found him in
Reval. Miaskovsky joined the Red Army, was transferred to Petrograd
in December 1917, and to Moscow the following year. Demobilized in
1921, Miaskovsky was appointed to the Moscow Conservatory where
he taught until his death in 1950. Although he described himself as
politically inexperienced, he had a sincere desire to co-operate with the
new regime. During the years 1919–23 he was active in the musical
affairs of Moscow: he helped organize the Composers' Collective, the
music division of the NARKOMPROS, and the Moscow Philharmonic.

The recognition of Miaskovsky as a major composer came rather late,
in the 1920's. A memorable date was 18 August 1920 when Nikolai
Malko conducted the Moscow première of Miaskovsky's Fifth Symphony. This work ranks high in the affection of Russian listeners
because of its serenity, its warmth, its closeness to Russian tradition.
Miaskovsky, by nature introspective and brooding, composed the
optimistic Fifth Symphony during the early months of 1918, and it
is tempting to assume that the work acquired its affirmative quality
under the impact of the Revolution. However, the composer informs
us that many of the themes were jotted down during the war, at the
front. Another aspect of the war is mirrored in Miaskovsky's Fourth
Symphony in E-minor, composed in 1917–18, which is filled with
tragic tension. For the next thirty years, Miaskovsky was to be one of
the most revered personalities of Moscow's musical scene. His influence
on the young generation of composers was very strong; his judgment
was generous but incorruptible. He was called "the musical conscience
of Moscow". His last years were embittered by the purge of 1948 which
engulfed him as well as his best friend—Prokofiev—and his best pupil—
Khachaturian. He died in 1950, a few months before the première of

his last—the Twenty-Seventh—Symphony, a work of "rehabilitation".

Comparable in importance, though in a different sphere, was Boris Asafiev who was destined to become the father of Soviet musicology. But this was only one aspect of this versatile mind: he was also active as a composer, a theorist, a critic, and an author. Born in 1884, Asafiev completed two courses of study: the philological faculty of the Petersburg University in 1908, and the course in composition at the Petersburg Conservatory in 1910. Asafiev began his activity as a critic in 1914; he wrote under the pen name Igor Glebov and published many of his books under that name.

The revolutionary year 1917 found Asafiev in Petrograd, writing mainly for the journal *Muzykalnyi Sovremennik* (Musical Contemporary). Early that year, he broke with the editor, Andrei Rimsky-Korsakov (a son of the composer), ostensibly because Rimsky had refused to print Asafiev's enthusiastic evaluation of the triumvirate Stravinsky-Miaskovsky-Prokofiev. One must admire Asafiev's acumen in sensing the great potential of these "avant-gardists".

When the October Revolution came, Asafiev was among the intellectuals who supported the Bolshevik regime with confidence. He worked tirelessly on behalf of the musical enlightenment of the masses, as journalist, author, lecturer, composer, and performer. For the journal *Zhizn Iskusstva* (Art Life), the official publication of NARKOMPROS, he wrote regular contributions—more than fifty articles in the years 1918-19 alone. They probed deeply into the topics of the day, dealing mainly with the relationship between art and the new audiences. Whether he explored methods of music appreciation for the masses, the thorny question of opera repertoire, or the organization of mobile opera units to reach the worker-peasant audience, Asafiev was always lucid and displayed a combination of practicality and idealism. His programme annotations for opera and concerts, published as leaflets and distributed to the public, set a style of musical commentary for the layman that became exemplary. A basic contribution to musical understanding was his *Dictionary of Musico-Technical Terms*, published in 1919 by the Petrograd Commissariat of Education, a slim volume of 102 pages which is a model of simplicity and thoroughness. Somehow, Asafiev also found time to serve the people as a composer: he conceived the ballet *Carmagnole*, based on materials of the French Revolution.

Valuable though the work of musical popularization was, Asafiev was fully aware of the need for research in depth. In 1919, he joined the staff of the Institute of Arts History in Petrograd, and became dean of the music division of that institute in 1921. Asafiev reached the pinnacle of his fame in 1943 when he was elected to full membership in the Academy of Sciences—the only musician ever so honoured.

The remarkable musical accomplishments during the first three revolutionary years become all the more impressive if viewed against the desperate economic and political situation. Wells observed in 1920 that the theatres enjoyed an exceptional status, but as "for the rest of the arts, for literature generally, there was overwhelming catastrophe . . . No one was left to buy books or pictures . . . The mortality among the intellectually distinguished men of Russia has been terribly high . . . through sheer mortification of great gifts become futile . . . The writing of new books, except some poetry . . . have ceased in Russia."

To keep writers alive, the government embarked on a "grandiose Russian encyclopedia of the literature of the world . . . In starving Russia hundreds of people are working on translations . . ."[52]

This was the intellectual climate as Wells saw it in September 1920. Yet he was immensely impressed when he met Lenin in person. "In him I realized that communism could after all, in spite of Marx, be enormously creative . . . He at least had a vision of a world changed over and built afresh."[53] Lenin stressed education. He said to Wells, "Come back and see what we have done in Russia in ten years time." Fate did not grant him that decade: four years later, Lenin was dead.

Part II

CONSOLIDATION 1921-1932

3   *New Economic Policy and the Five Year Plan*

"We are paupers. There is no paper. The workers are hungry and cold and have no clothing or shoes. The machines are worn out. The buildings are collapsing."[1] Lenin wrote these lines, almost in exasperation, in February 1921. The situation was bleak indeed. "Never in all history has there been so great a debacle before," observed Wells.[2] The war-torn country was exhausted and in desperate need of a breathing spell.

The year 1921 brought the end of the Civil War and of foreign military intervention. It also brought the historic reorientation of Party policy known as NEP, the "New Economic Policy". No one but Lenin, with his immense prestige, could have convinced the Russian Communist Party—assembled for its Tenth Congress in March 1921—that the new policy was a necessity for survival. In fact, such was Lenin's unequalled parliamentary skill that most delegates seemed unaware of the fundamental changes in economic policy, and the new measures were passed with a minimum of debate. "We have sinned . . . in going too far in nationalizing trade and industry, in closing down local commerce," declared Lenin.[3] Consequently NEP made certain economic concessions such as restoration of the wage system, free trade in grain, private ownership of some smaller businesses and factories, and the encouragement of foreign capital investments. Soon, small private shops reopened in Russian cities, and within two years they accounted for three-fourths of all retail sales. However, the "reversal" to capitalist techniques touched only the surface, because the State retained control over foreign trade, banking, large-scale industry, and education. Nevertheless, the new policy was bitterly resented by many dedicated Communists, old and young. "It's right, but it makes me sick," confided the poet Gerasimov to Ilya Ehrenburg.[4] A by-product of NEP was petty profiteering, and a new word, *rvach* ("grabber"), was coined; it is the title of one of Ehrenburg's books. In connection with NEP, the derogatory term "Nepmanstvo" came into use which could be translated as "the art of chiselling". Yet according to the American historian Ulam the "New Economic Policy" had achieved its purpose, "The economic and social wounds were healing. At the end of the NEP in 1927–28, the average Russian was probably better off than at

any time since the beginning of the World War, and he was not again
to enjoy the same standard of living until after Stalin's death."[5]

In cultural affairs, Lenin had won a significant victory in October 1920
by bringing the "leftist" advocates of PROLETKULT under control. He
kept a watchful eye on the modernists and distrusted even his close
associates. "Lunacharsky should be flogged for his futurism," he fumed
when he found out that his commissar had voted for printing 5,000
copies of Mayakovsky's poem *150 Million*. Such "double-dyed folly
and pretentiousness" should be printed in no more than 1,500 copies
"for libraries and cranks."[6]

Lenin made no secret of his conservative tastes, as we can see from
his conversation with Klara Zetkin,

> ". . . We must preserve the beautiful, take it as model, use it as
> starting point, even if it is 'old'. Why must we turn away from
> the truly beautiful . . . just because it is 'old'? Why must we bow
> low in front of the new, as if it were God, only because it is 'new'?
> Nonsense, utter nonsense! There is much hypocrisy and, of course,
> subconscious respect for artistic fashion dominating the West. We
> are good revolutionaries, but somehow we feel obliged to prove
> that we are on a par with 'contemporary culture'. But I have the
> courage to declare myself a 'barbarian'. I am unable to count the
> works of expressionism, futurism, cubism, and similar 'isms'
> among the highest manifestations of creative genius. I do not
> understand them. I do not derive any pleasure from them."[7]

When an "artist-realist" was slighted by Lunacharsky, Lenin coun-
tered, "Cannot dependable anti-futurists be found?" Such sayings—
taken out of context—are used over and over again in the continuing
battle of the Soviet government against modernist trends in the arts.
These Party bureaucrats forget too easily the patience and perception
with which Lenin faced all questions of creativity and enlightenment.
In defending the poet Demyan Bednyi against one-sided criticism, he
wrote to *Pravda* in 1913, "Don't dwell on human weakness, my friends.
Talent is a rare thing. It must be regularly and carefully supported."[8]

And in October 1921, Lenin urged a patient approach,

> "Cultural problems cannot be solved as quickly as political and
> military problems . . . It is possible to achieve a political victory
> during an acute crisis within a few weeks. It is possible to obtain
> victory in war within a few months. But it is impossible to achieve
> a cultural victory in such a short time; by the very nature of the

case a longer period is required, and we must adapt ourselves to this longer period, calculate our work accordingly, and display a maximum of perseverance, persistence, and system."[9]

The improvement in economic conditions brought about by NEP, the gradual return to "normalcy", was soon reflected on the musical scene. There was a lessening of the revolutionary militancy, a relaxation of ideological tensions, a greater permissiveness in matters of musical taste and style. Some of the new developments, however, were unforeseen: the number of music centres was reduced, the operational budgets were tightened, and the government proved less willing to subsidize unprofitable ventures. Concerts—especially those with serious programmes—became more difficult to arrange, orchestra musicians made monetary demands, and performers were reluctant to donate their services. Even prestigious organizations like the Philharmonics felt the strain. There was also a re-grouping of listeners: the "free" public dispersed, the audiences for serious concerts thinned out. The urban masses showed a preference for a lighter type of music which they could hear in clubs and meeting halls. This trend was exploited by individual entrepreneurs, operating privately, as was permitted under NEP rules. They sought to attract a paying public with presentations of doubtful musical value. After one such event in 1922, in the Philharmonic Hall of Petrograd, advertised lavishly as an "Evening of Beauty", the journal *Zhizn Iskusstva* (Art Life) published an indignant editorial entitled "Enough", "NEP in economics, despite its trends and drawbacks, is still a useful force. This cannot be said of NEP in art. Here this 'Nepomania' has so far produced nothing of value. On the contrary, it has succeeded in besmirching art."[10]

On the positive side, there was the resumption of Western contacts, interrupted since 1914. Foreign artists were invited to perform in Russia; often they brought a new repertoire and so provided a new stimulus. Soviet music began to be played at international music festivals, and many new scores were published in Vienna by the Universal Edition, under a special arrangement with the Soviet State Publishing House. Western music journals devoted increasing space to the music of new Russia. Even the *Christian Science Monitor* of Boston, disregarding the atheism of the Soviets, began to publish regular music reports sent directly from Moscow by the critic Victor Belayev. A high point was the "Russland-Heft" of *Anbruch* (March 1925) containing a complete survey of musical conditions in Russia by Russian and Western contributors. The discussion of Soviet Russia by genuine and half-baked experts became fashionable.

Among guest artist who visited the Soviet capitals, orchestral conductors predominated. Most of them belonged to the Austro-German school. Even in Tsarist days, Russia had imported many foreign conductors. Now, after years of isolation and weakened orchestral discipline, the foreign visitors revived vanishing traditions, renewed the repertoire, and brought new excitement to the Russian musical scene. Among the guests were Bruno Walter, Otto Klemperer, Pierre Monteux, Hermann Scherchen, and William Steinberg. Permanent conducting posts were given to Oscar Fried and Fritz Stiedry. Russia's novelty-starved audiences heard Bruckner and Mahler, Honegger and Krenek. Living composers were invited to conduct their own works, among them Darius Milhaud, Paul Hindemith, Franz Schreker, and Alfredo Casella. Among the foreign pianists, Artur Schnabel, Edwin Fischer, and Wilhelm Backhaus cultivated the classical repertoire, while Egon Petri and Eduard Erdmann explored modernism. The violinist Joseph Szigeti became a Russian favourite and visited the Soviet Union eleven times between 1924 and 1929. His intense, angular style—so different from the polished Russian tradition of violin playing—captured the interest of professionals and laymen alike, particularly because of his devotion to an unusual, mostly modern, repertoire. In his memoirs, Szigeti speaks warmly about Lunacharsky, "the intensely cultured, polyglot, widely read Commissioner of Education". He described the conditions of travel and concert giving as difficult, yet the experience was "bracing and tingling".[11]

Undoubtedly, these artistic visits produced mutual benefits. The peculiar responsiveness of Russian audiences, the eagerness of Russian orchestras, the musical curiosity of young Russian professionals—all this struck a responsive chord among the foreign visitors who returned home, deeply impressed. Musical discoveries were made, too: in 1926, Bruno Walter became acquainted with the twenty-year-old Dmitri Shostakovich. Upon hearing the young composer play the score of his First Symphony on the piano, Walter was so impressed that he promised to introduce the new work to Berlin. The Berlin première took place in 1927 and established Shostakovich's international reputation.

Walter, though critical of political conditions in Soviet Russia, spoke warmly of his first visit to Moscow and Leningrad in 1926, "To play music in Moscow . . . was more than a joy. The orchestra and the public were . . . enthusiastic and full of vital energy . . . and the excellent musicians' devotion to their work at rehearsals and performances was exemplary . . . The Leningrad Philharmonic Orchestra, the members of the opera, and the audiences made me joyfully aware of that spirit of enthusiasm which imparts to Russia's musical life its pulsating force."[12] The German edition of Walter's Memoirs contains a strange and sadly amusing reference to programme censorship: it seems that a performance of Mahler's Fourth Symphony was declined by the directors of the Bolshoi Theatre because "in new Russia one ought not to sing of heavens and angels, of Saint Peter and other saints".[13] This passage is omitted in the American edition.

West European composers found contact with the new Russian audiences particularly rewarding. So said Franz Schreker after having conducted his opera *Der Ferne Klang* in Leningrad in 1925, "It was indeed a time of great and unforgettable experiences and impressions, and something very special . . . The confrontations with a strange and alien world in the midst of fermenting evolution—this, for a sensitive person, amounts to an inner regeneration, a kind of new humanization. For the creative artist in particular it is air to breathe, a rejuvenating potion, staff of life."[14]

Alban Berg—who attended the Leningrad première of *Wozzeck* in 1927—was impressed by the "excellent" musical preparation, the *belcanto* singing, the modernistic stage sets—"it was a theatrically strong performance", he concluded, and the success was "stormy".[15]

Darius Milhaud expressed himself less ecstatically, but he was in essential agreement, "The players were docile and very understanding, and what an extraordinary audience! What love of music!" Milhaud spoke warmly of the achievements of the opera houses, of Meyerhold's theatrical daring, of the unlimited rehearsal time for every artistic enterprise. Comparing Moscow and Leningrad, he said, "In Moscow, academic influences were much more in evidence; the youthful musicians were more argumentative and inclined to hair-splitting . . . Generally speaking, the atmosphere seemed to us more formal and intellectual than in Leningrad."[16]

Accompanying Milhaud was the pianist Jean Wiéner, a specialist in Franco-American jazz. His subtle syncopations were much admired by young Russian pianists who, despite their technical adroitness, found his style difficult to imitate. Milhaud, like Walter, was much impressed by the talent of Shostakovich; in addition, he praised the somewhat older composer Vladimir Deshevov whose fame, however, did not outlive the 1920's.

But the spirit of musical adventure was not limited to the visits of foreign artists. Stimulated by the influx of musical ideas, encouraged by the tolerant view of the Soviet government, Russian musicians—composers, conductors, musicologists, and performers—joined forces to explore modern music, both foreign and Russian. An important event was the Leningrad première of the *Gurre-Lieder* by Arnold Schoenberg in 1927, conducted by Nikolai Malko. Prior to the First World War, Schoenberg had enjoyed a certain vogue among Russian intellectuals, and he had visited St. Petersburg in 1912 to conduct his own *Pelleas und Melisande*. But to the younger generation of Russians, he was virtually unknown though he had a few fervent advocates, among them the composer-critic Roslavetz. The *Gurre-Lieder*, a work dating back to the first decade of the twentieth century, evoked interest but no enthusiasm: the Leningrad critics treated it as a "museum piece" rather than a work of burning actuality.[17]

An interesting experiment in musical "collectivism" was the founding of an orchestra without conductor, known under its abbreviated name PERSIMFANS (PERVyi SIMfonicheskii ANSambl—meaning "First Symphonic Ensemble"). It functioned in Moscow from 1922 to 1932 and achieved international fame. The guiding spirit was Lev Zeitlin, violin professor at the Moscow Conservatory and former concert-master of the Kussevitsky Orchestra. PERSIMFANS performed not only the standard classical repertoire but also complex modern scores. The ensemble took immense pride in its accomplishments; from 1926 to 1929, it published its own musical journal. Occasionally, guest conductors were invited, for example, Otto Klemperer, but at one point the guest would be asked to sit in the audience to listen to the orchestra play on its own. The results were achieved through incessant rehearsals and mutual consultations until a point was reached when every player was familiar with the entire score. The composer Milhaud found the experiment "fully successful", but he remarked dryly that "a conductor would have obtained the same results, no doubt a little faster".

Another composer, Prokofiev, played with the PERSIMFANS in January 1927: it was his first visit to his homeland since his departure in 1918. On the programme of the two concerts were Prokofiev's Piano Concerto No. 3 and his orchestral suites from *Chout* (Buffoon) and *The Love for Three Oranges* as well as a novelty, his "American" Overture Op. 42. Prokofiev—always extremely critical when it came to performances of his own music—gives the following description of the events,

> ". . . I went to a rehearsal of the orchestra (Persimfans). As we approached the hall I heard the March from the *Three Oranges* being played. 'They are taking it a little too slow,' I said, thinking they were rehearsing it. But it turned out that the orchestra was playing the March in my honour. The conductorless orchestra coped splendidly with difficult programmes and accompanied soloists as competently as any conducted orchestra. Their main difficulty lay in changing tempo, for here the whole ensemble had to feel the music in exactly the same way. On the other hand,

difficult passages were easily overcome, for each individual musician felt himself a soloist and played with perfect precision."[18]

How these results were achieved is described by a French guest, the pianist Henri Gil-Marchex,

"The performers group themselves in a large circle, so as to be able to see each other easily, which necessitates some turning their backs to the audience. The utmost concentration and attention is demanded of each player, all of whom are fully conscious of their responsibility in that magic circle . . . Each member of the orchestra has his own important part to play, and glances, raising of the brow, and slight motions of the shoulders . . . are done by each instrumentalist, but so discreetly that the listener . . . seldom notices it. The rhythm of the interpreted work is completely felt by all, and the silence experienced by vigilance acquires for that very reason an unusual emotional importance. For the purpose of determining the rendering, a small group of performers meet and agree upon the nuances and other questions of interpretation, and at the rehearsals, one of them goes to the hall to get an idea of the effect produced. With such an orchestra, the technique of execution reaches its maximum . . ."[19]

Despite these acclaims, PERSIMFANS died as a noble experiment in collectivism. Interpretation by committee? At its best, it was impersonal, at its worst, imprecise. Every orchestra musician, deep down in his heart, feels that the conductor is expendable.* (Oscar Levant put it succinctly, "One hundred men and a louse.") Much depends on the repertoire played. Eighteenth-century music did not need a conductor aside from a strong "concertmaster" or leader of the first violins, with some assistance from the continuo-playing harpsichordist. The growth of the orchestra in the nineteenth century, in conjunction with the expressive demands of Romantic music, made a "director" necessary although the violin bow remained the tool of the conductor for many years—especially in Paris where François Habeneck conducted his famous Beethoven performances from a violin part. Judging by Richard Wagner's ecstatic comments, Habeneck and the Paris Conservatoire Orchestra took as much time—almost an entire winter—to learn Beethoven's Ninth Symphony in 1839 as the PERSIMFANS would in the 1920's. But we also know that Habeneck failed in his grudging attempts to conduct the music of Berlioz. As for the complex music of the twentieth century, it is virtually unplayable without a conductor.

*At a chance meeting in Baku in 1930, Professor Zeitlin told me, "We are not opposed to conductors—only to *bad* conductors."

The ever-increasing contacts between Soviet Russia and the West led to foreign concert tours of Russian performers. These were planned with the co-operation of Soviet authorities, often on an exchange basis. Very quickly, the Western world realized that Russian virtuosi were as brilliant as ever. The pianists Vladimir Horowitz, Alexander Borovsky, Simon Barer, and Nikolai Orlov, the violinists Nathan Milstein and Miron Poliakin, the 'cellists Gregor Piatigorsky and Raya Garbuzova, and many others were acclaimed in Europe and America. Most of them decided to settle abroad. Yet the Russian tradition of great instrumental performance remained unaffected. Still today, there emerges from the conservatories of Moscow and Leningrad a seemingly unending stream of dazzling virtuosi.

The rapprochement between Russia's musical life and the Western mainstream proceeded side by side with a more flexible arts policy within the country. High Party officials spoke out in favour of artistic tolerance, particularly in the field of literature. Lunacharsky did not believe that artists should be made to conform. Bukharin advocated "free and anarchic competition" in literature. Trotsky in 1924 dismissed "proletarian culture" in favour of a culture "above classes" and recommended a policy of "complete freedom of self-determination in the field of art",[20] though with certain revolutionary safeguards. These heated discussions culminated in a resolution of the Party's Central Committee, published on 1 July 1925, under the title "On the Policy of the Party in the Field of Belles-lettres".[21] It was a rambling, repetitious, and somewhat ambiguous document which lent itself to various interpretations. Some historians hail it as the Magna Carta of Soviet writers, others dispute its alleged liberalism. A few points deserve to be brought out. While supporting the proletarian writer in principle, the Resolution urged a patient approach towards the "fellow-traveller" ("poputchik")* and recommended free competition among various literary groups. "Communist criticism must drive out the tone of literary command," it warned at one point. And again, ". . . The Party cannot grant a monopoly to any of these groups, not even to the most proletarian in its ideology; this would be above all ruinous to proletarian literature." Clearly, the Party did not wish to permit any group—not even the proletarians—to speak on its behalf. This is an important point to remember, for a rebirth of proletarian artistic militancy, around 1930, led to the dissolution of all artistic organizations, proletarian or non-aligned, in 1932.

The Resolution of 1925—with all its ambiguity—was quoted in

---

* The term "poputchik", first used by Trotsky in 1923, meant all writers "who, without being Communists, vaguely sympathized with the Revolution and were certainly hostile to its enemies".

1965, after the fall of Khrushchev, when the new Soviet leaders endeavoured to rebuild the cultural front in a more liberal spirit.

In the mid-1920's, the Party's main concern was obviously with literature. But similar flexible guidelines were applied in the field of music. An intense, often acrimonious, debate between opposing musical groups and ideologies filled most of the 1920's. Throughout much of the decade, the adherents of Western-oriented modernism battled with the proponents of "proletarian" music. A third group—not formally organized but entrenched in academic positions—consisted of the Russian traditionalists; as guardians of the Russian classical heritage, they re-emerged as a potent force around 1932, after the other factions had been silenced.

The pages of Soviet music histories are filled with deprecations of the 1920's. All shortcomings of Soviet music—real or imaginary—are blamed on the activities of the two warring factions—the modern-oriented Association for Contemporary Music (ACM) or the leftist Russian Association of Proletarian Musicians (RAPM). Disparaging adjectives were formed out of the initials of the two groups: thus, an "asmovsky" position signifies decadent-modernist formalism, while "rapmovsky" stands for a simplistic musical primitivism. Throughout the Stalin era, and for years after, these two groups were considered a detriment to Soviet music, responsible for its failure to achieve early ideological significance, its slow and halting progress towards Socialist Realism. The ruinous influence of the feuding factions on immature young composers is also critically noted. Only in the last few years have there been some sobering voices calling for an end to such "anti-historism", and urging an objective evaluation of the 1920's which, in fact, was an important evolutionary decade. A simple comparison will illustrate this point: while the quasi-official *History of Soviet Russian Music* (1956) presents a narrow-minded view of the 1920's, the new *History of Music of the Soviet Peoples* (1966) takes a far more objective and reasoned position.

Certainly there was nothing sinister about the Association for Contemporary Music which was established in Moscow in 1923 by distinguished men like Miaskovsky, Belayev, Sabaneyev, and Paul Lamm. It followed by one year the founding the International Society for Contemporary Music (ISCM) which had its seat in London, with Edward J. Dent as first president. A proposal to organize the Russian ACM as an affiliate branch of the ISCM was quickly abandoned, and the Russian group remained autonomous. Nevertheless, there was collaboration between the Russian and the International Societies: modern Soviet composers were represented at the prestigious ISCM music festivals; in return, many modern West European scores were heard at the concerts sponsored by the Moscow ACM. Who were the Soviet composers selected by the ISCM to represent their country? Prokofiev in 1923 (Salzburg Festival) and 1924 (Prague), Samuel Feinberg in 1925 (Venice), Miaskovsky in 1926 (Zurich), Mossolov in 1927 (Frankfurt) and 1930 (Liège), and Knipper in 1931 (Oxford).* Considering the fact that Prokofiev—residing in the West at that time—was only nominally a "Soviet" composer, the representation seems somewhat meagre. But neither was the choice easy: by the mid-1920's, no young Soviet composer had as yet emerged to challenge the international competition. After 1926 came the meteoric rise of Shostakovich, but for some reason he was ignored by the ISCM selection committee.

This scant international list should not delude us into believing that there was a dearth of Soviet composers. The programmes of the Moscow ACM are studded with Russian names, but few have made a lasting impact. During the first season of 1924–25, six chamber music concerts were given. The following season in 1925–26, the chamber events were increased to eight; in addition, four symphonic concerts took place. In arranging the programme, care was taken to establish a balance between Soviet and Western composers though, quite naturally, the native composers prevailed. The selection of Russian works was eclectic, without emphasis on any particular school.

The first orchestral concert was devoted entirely to two symphonies of Miaskovsky—No. 4, composed in 1918, and No. 7, his most recent work. In the second orchestral concert, the post-romantic Symphony No. 3 by Alexander Goedicke was contrasted with music by Anatol Alexandrov, then considered one of the best young composers. The third orchestral concert brought works by the "avant-gardists" Lev Knipper and Vladimir Kriukov, At that time, Knipper was strongly influenced by German modernism while Kriukov was a disciple of Scriabin. A genuine sensation was the première of Prokofiev's Third Piano Concerto, played by the pianist-composer Samuel Feinberg at the last symphony concert of the series, on 22 March 1925.† All the orchestral concerts were conducted by the Armenian-born Konstantin Saradzhev; the orchestra was that of the "Theatre of the Revolution" where the concerts took place before large and appreciative audiences.

The chamber music concerts showed a significant representation of

---

* This list does not include composers like Igor Stravinsky, Nikolai Lopatnikov, and others who, though Russian-born, had left the Soviet Union permanently.

† In a two-piano version, the Third Concerto had been heard in Moscow on 24 October 1923; the 1925 performance was the first with orchestra. The world première of the Concerto took place in Chicago on 16 December 1921, with Frederick Stock as conductor and the composer as soloist.

contemporary West European composers with works mostly new to Moscow: string quartets by Hindemith (No. 1) and Bartok (Nos. 2 and 3), piano pieces by Satie, Ravel, Szymanowski, Honegger, and Poulenc, songs by Milhaud and Poulenc, and the Four Sonatas Opus 11 by Hindemith. Soviet composers represented by chamber works included Vassili Shirinsky, Nikolai Roslavetz, Georgi Catoire, Vissarion Shebalin, Alexander Dzegelenok, Sergei Vassilenko, Samuel Feinberg, and Leonid Polovinkin. Though largely—and, perhaps, unjustly—forgotten today, these composers were important in the 1920's and beyond; their works were published in Moscow and Vienna, and with one or two exceptions, they were on the whole a progressive group.

The ideas of the Moscow ACM were disseminated through the journal *Sovremennaya Muzyka* (Contemporary Music). During the five-year span of its existence (1924–29), the journal appeared usually every month, at times at greater intervals. It covered national and international music news and was edited by three progressive-minded critics—Sabaneyev, Belayev, and Derzhanovsky. Many of the articles were planned as commentaries on compositions performed at the Moscow ACM concerts and the level of writing and scholarship was extremely high. The Moscow ACM also sponsored two concerts of Soviet chamber music in Vienna.

In Leningrad, the cause of modern music took a somewhat more circuitous path. Here, the guiding spirit was the versatile Boris Asafiev. As director of an historical institute, he was not immediately involved in contemporary music; yet his interest in the contemporary scene was so strong that he was able to organize a study group, in the spring of 1922, with the purpose of exploring the latest musical developments. Under the pen name Igor Glebov, Asafiev contributed articles on modern music to a newly established Moscow journal, *K Novym Beregam* (To New Shores; published in 1923) as well as to *Sovremennaya Muzyka*. Early in 1924, Asafiev asked the Moscow ACM for the loan of foreign scores recently performed in Moscow. During May 1924 he organized three programmes of contemporary music in Leningrad's Philharmonic Hall; a similar series took place in December of that year. The concerts were co-sponsored by the Institute of Arts History, whose music division was headed by Asafiev, and the Leningrad Philharmonic. Coinciding with the concerts, several brochures entitled *Novaya Muzyka* (New Music) were published under the imprint of the Leningrad Philharmonic. Finally, on 1 January 1926 the Leningrad Association for Contemporary Music was officially formed. Very soon, however, a split developed, and Asafiev withdrew to re-establish his own group under the name "Circle for New Music"

(Kruzhok novoi muzyki). Led by Asafiev and the composer Vladimir Shcherbachev, the *Kruzhok* represented the more radical adherents of contemporary music by stressing the newest and most advanced trends.

Realizing that the internal feud was detrimental to the common cause, the two factions reunited in February 1927 under the banner of the ACM. A new series of brochures was launched under the editorship of Asafiev (alias Glebov) and his former student, Semyon Ginzburg.[22] Six issues were published in 1927–28, dealing with the music of Alban Berg, Ernst Krenek, Paul Hindemith as well as Soviet composers. The brochures were timely because they coincided with such Leningrad premières as *Wozzeck* by Berg, *Der Sprung über den Schatten* by Krenek. In 1924, Asafiev began work on his *Book on Stravinsky*, not published until 1929. Another brief monograph on Stravinsky, written by Yulian Vainkop, appeared in 1927. The intense activity of Asafiev and his circle on behalf of contemporary music brought about an artistic climate in Leningrad that made the city a centre of musical modernism, receptive to all kind of experiments. Thus, Georgi Rimsky-Korsakov, a grandson of the composer, founded a "Society for Quarter-Tone Music" in 1923 which gave concerts in 1925.* Nor was he the first: Ivan Vishnegradsky (born 1893), who emigrated to Paris around 1920, composed quarter-tone music—for string quartet—as early as 1918, while Lourié is said to have experimented with quarter-tones in 1910. In the mid-1920's, Russian interest in the quarter-tone system became so intense that Lunacharsky took personal note of it: he called it "one of the most important phenomena in the formal development of our music . . . for which one has already created special instruments".[23] Here, the "Termenvox" must be mentioned as the first electronic musical instrument; it was constructed by the acoustics engineer Lev Termen—known abroad as Leon Theremin—in 1920 and demonstrated to Lenin in 1921. The inventor brought the instrument to Western Europe and America where his demonstrations created a sensation in 1927. Theremin returned to Russia in 1938 and still worked as an engineer in Moscow in the 1960's.

The modernistic climate of Leningrad stimulated some over-zealous radicals into rejecting "old" music as out of step with the revolutionary developments. The following, rather amusing, statement could be dismissed as farcical, were it not for the fact that it was published under the auspices of the Leningrad Association for Contemporary Music in a brochure called *October and New Music* to commemorate the Tenth Anniversary of the Revolution in 1927,

* G. Rimsky-Korsakov's essay "The Basis of the Quarter-tone Musical System" was published in the yearbook *De Musica* in 1925.

"What is closer to the proletariat, the pessimism of Tchaikosvky and the false heroics of Beethoven, a century out of date, or the precise rhythms and excitement of Deshevov's *Rails*?* During the playing of Beethoven, the workers were utterly bored, and patiently, with polite endurance, waited for the music to end. But contemporary Soviet compositions aroused contagious emotions among the audience. Proletarian masses, for whom machine oil is mother's milk, have a right to demand music consonant with our era, not the music of the bourgeois salon which belongs to the time of Stephenson's early locomotive."[24]

On the whole, the Leningrad ACM was somewhat more adventurous than the Moscow ACM; in fact, the Muscovites were accused by the Leningrad group as fostering local patriotism, as being more interested in their local composers than in modern foreign music. This may well have been the case. For example, the composer Shebalin—in 1927 still a student at the Moscow Conservatory—wrote, "In fact, the Association for Contemporary Music mirrors the essence of contemporary *Russian* music; it has contact with 'Europeanism' on a formal plane, but not in substance."[25] In later years, when the ACM was under attack, Shebalin said apologetically that, to him and his Moscow colleagues, the ACM was merely "a circle for the purpose of becoming acquainted with new music, a 'non-programmatic' society of music lovers."[26]

This sounds rather innocuous and non-committal, but actually there were greater issues at stake. Some were practical, some were ideological. The practical usefulness is obvious: the ACM provided a "window" to the West and represented a vital link with the mainstream of modern European music. This exposure to advanced Western ideas was as stimulating to a mature composer like Shaporin as it was to a budding genius like Shostakovich. The ACM also helped propagandize Soviet music in Western countries. Under the heading "Modern Russian Music in Foreign Countries", the *Anbruch* of Vienna wrote in 1931, "In the last three years, the Russian State Publishing House brought out more than four hundred works of all categories. Lately, there were some two hundred performances in foreign countries, among them sixty-one of compositions by Miaskovsky, thirty-eight by Shostakovich, fourteen by Goedicke, ten by Ippolitov-Ivanov, six by Vassilenko, five each by Knipper and Krein . . ."[27] Particularly the First Symphony of Shostakovich and *The Iron Foundry* by Mossolov were performed with sensational success all over the world.

Ideologically, members of the ACM often engaged in polemics and challenged some of the views on music held by the "proletarian" wing

* A three-minute piano piece imitative of railway noises.

of musicians. The composer Roslavetz sneered at his proletarian critics when he declared, "Of course I am not a 'proletarian' composer in the sense that I do not write commonplace music 'for the masses'. On the contrary, I am so much 'bourgeois' that I consider the proletariat the rightful heir of all previous culture, worthy of the best in music."[28] As editor of the journal *Muzykalnaya Kultura* (Music Culture), Roslavetz attacked the concept of "representational" music. Using his slogan, "Music is music, not ideology," he wrote with sarcasm, "If we cross out the title 'Hymn of Thanksgiving' in Beethoven's Quartet Op. 132 and substitute 'Festive Victory Celebration of the Red Army' or 'Opening of the Streetcar Line in Baku'—does this in any way change the content of the quartet?"[29]

In a similar vein, the critic Sabaneyev wrote, "Music is not ideology to be attached to it in some way; music is organized sound. Music does not express ideas nor represent 'logical' structures: it exists in its own world of musical sound, musical ideas, and purely musical logic . . ."[30]*

The opponents in the proletarian camp vowed to "unmask the bourgeois character of Roslavetz and his ilk, to isolate him ideologically from the Soviet musical scene and thus to protect society from the destructive influence of such 'theorists'." Roslavetz was described as "the rotten product of bourgeois society" and the exponent of "petit-bourgeois reaction hiding behind leftist phraseology."[31]

Roslavetz suffered professional ostracism and eventual oblivion after 1930. Sabaneyev emigrated in 1926 and has remained the *bête noire* of Soviet musicology.

The strongest opponents of the Association for Contemporary Music were centred in groups of proletarian musicians. They were *not* identical with the leftist PROLETKULT that had been curbed by Lenin in 1920. A new group was formed in 1923 under the name of "Association of Proletarian Musicians"; later, the prefix "Russian" was added and the abbreviated name became RAPM. Originally, its members were a group of composers working within the propaganda division of the State Publishing House (AGITOTDEL).† Among them were gifted men like Kastalsky and Vassilev-Buglai, but also many hack musicians who busied themselves in turning out vocal music on revolutionary texts. This eminently practical activity was soon enriched by an excursion into the ideological field. RAPM published its first platform in 1924; later revisions appeared in 1926 and 1929. The original document was, in the words of the eminent Soviet musicologist Keldysh, "a crude

---

* It is interesting to note that Stravinsky expressed similar ideas in his *Poetics of Music* (1942).

† See p 33.

vulgarization of Marxist-Leninist teachings on culture."[32] While paying lip service to the "classical heritage", the RAPM ideologists narrowed that field by declaring almost all great composers of the past as "alien" to proletarian ideology. A similarly negative attitude was displayed towards many living composers.

A reflection of this attitude can be seen in a brash attempt of Moscow Conservatory students—members of the youth organization KOMSOMOL—to take issue with the views of Commissar Lunacharsky. In an open letter, published in 1926 in the RAPM journal *Muzyka i Oktyabr* (Music and October) the youthful rebels reproached Lunacharsky for listing, within the category of "our composers", such names as Miaskovsky, Shebalin, and Anatol Alexandrov; these composers, in the opinion of the students, represented a trend "technically skilful in form, but in content expressing the ideology of decadent bourgeoisie".[33]

Lunacharsky's "Answer to the Komsomols of the Conservatory" is a thoughtful and, for its time, significant document. Patiently, he advises his youthful critics to re-examine their scornful attitude towards the great masters,

"I cannot call Miaskovsky, Alexandrov, Shebalin, and Krein 'our composers' in the sense that they are composer–Communists or ideological fellow-travellers. I call them *our* because they are composers living and working in the USSR. The environment in which they live is undoubtedly reflected in their creative work . . . This group of composers has remained faithful to the homeland, they work in the spirit of the classics, yet they express certain experiences—perhaps not of our entire country, but certainly of a part of the intelligentsia."[34]

Significantly, Lunacharsky rejects any thought of a battle between "outlived formalism" and "revolutionary realism": these terms, he maintains, are not applicable to music. What are "class tendencies" in music? An imperialist march can just as well serve the revolutionaries, while the *Marseillaise*, with a changed text, could become a monarchist hymn. He adds, "This proves to what extent music is less explicit than literature."

Lunacharsky's statement—admirable in its simplicity and restraint—reflected the Party's patient approach to dissenters as embodied in the Party resolution of 1925. However, his stand on formalism and realism in music was swept aside in the 1930's, and music was made to conform.

Undaunted by criticism coming from the Party as well as influential non-political musicians, the Association of Proletarian Musicians (RAPM) continued to proclaim its simplistic approach to music. The ultimate goal was the "extension of the hegemony of the proletariat to the music field". It reflected the demands made by the comrades in the literary field, the Association of Proletarian Writers. The criticism levelled at the writers can also be applied to the musicians, "Their youth, their ignorance, and their enthusiasm for the Communist cause led them into gross over-simplification of all problems, and crude verbal excesses in their criticism of all who disagreed with them."[35]

There is no doubt that the proletarian musicians were stimulated by their literary confrères. In fact, the hard-hitting, earthy poetry of Demyan Bednyi was held up as a model to emulate, for he was "the only one whose poetry will be understood by every worker, peasant, and Red Army man". The musico-proletarian propaganda was disseminated by several journals under supervision of RAPM: first *Muzykalnaya Nov* (Musical News), 1923–24; then *Muzyka i Oktyabr* (Music and October), 1926; finally *Proletarskyi Muzykant* (The Proletarian Musician), 1929–32, and *Za Proletarskuyu Muzyku* (For Proletarian Music), 1930–32.

However, the proletarian musicians were divided among themselves. A splinter group left RAPM in 1925 to form its own organization under the abbreviated name ORKIMD.* As composers active in the "propaganda" wing of music (the so-called "agit-music"), they were dissatisfied with the "sectarianism of RAPM, unable to attract to its ranks a great many musicians active in the revolutionary realm". ORKIMD's views were expressed in the journal *Muzyka i Revolutzia* (Music and Revolution, 1926–29). But their aim—to participate in the "cultural revolution"—was not fulfilled; the group was too eclectic, the stress was too much on the production of functional music, easy to understand and simple to perform. For a time, the ORKIMD composers were popular in amateur circles, for they provided a topical repertoire of ready accessibility. The group was dissolved in 1929 without having played any significant role.

The year 1925 saw the formation of yet another "proletarian" group, to be known as PROKOLL (Production Collective of Student Composers). Attached to the Moscow Conservatory, this creative association consisted of serious and gifted young musicians who wanted to avoid both the complex modernism of the ACM and the simplistic utilitarianism of RAPM, to bridge the gap between "agitational" and "artistic" music. PROKOLL aimed at reflecting Soviet reality, at creating music that was meaningful to the Soviet listener. These young musicians believed that "revolutionary musical creation can only be achieved by those who grew up with the Revolution and are active participants in its development". Best known among the leaders of PROKOLL were the composers

* "Obyedinenie Revolutzionnykh Kompozitorov i Muzykalnykh Deyateley" (Association of revolutionary composers and musical workers).

Alexander Davidenko and Boris Shekhter, both of whom had won prizes for compositions in memory of Lenin. Others included Dmitri Kabalevksy, Victor Belyi, and Marian Koval. The group liked to work as a "collective" (hence its name). To reach the mass listener in a direct manner, it was decided to stress vocal music, particularly songs and choruses; larger forms, like opera and oratorio, as well as instrumental music, were to follow. To celebrate the Tenth Anniversary of the Revolution, eight of the young composers wrote a work for chorus, solo voices, and orchestra, often described as the "first Soviet oratorio". Its title was *The Path of October* (Put' Oktyabrya). Revolutionary poetry selected from the works of Gorky, Mayakovsky, and Alexander Blok was used as text. The aim was to transform the staid genre of the oratorio into a timely, meaningful, heroic-popular art form. The result was a stylistic hybrid of uneven quality. Some of the effects introduced —like stomping of feet or spoken recitations—were realistic but some-what crude. Still remembered are a few striking episodes, such as the two choruses by Davidenko—*The Street is in Turmoil* and *The Tenth Verst*. They reflect the groping intensity of the early revolutionary years, often described as revolutionary romanticism. The gifted Davidenko died young, in 1934, at the age of thirty-five.

In 1929, PROKOLL lost some of its founding members—among them Davidenko, Belyi, Shekhter, and Koval—who decided to join the more powerful RAPM (Russian Association of Proletarian Musicians). This move reflected important changes on the Soviet scene. In the politico-economic field, the lenient "New Economic Policy" was termi-nated, to be replaced by the hard-driving Five-Year Plan. In the cultural field, Lunacharsky—the symbol of an enlightened arts policy—was removed from the ministry of education. At the same time, the Party's Central Committee adopted a more militant policy towards literature, embodied in a resolution of December 1928. Gone was the flexibility of 1925; now it was decided that preference was to be given to Communist writers and to a type of literature serving the political aims of the Party. New authors belonging to the worker and peasant classes were to be encouraged. Significantly, these new directives were issued, not to the Writers' Union, but to the State Publishing Houses that controlled the choice of literature to be published. The implemen-tation of these directives lent a specific imprint to the literary output of those years, often called the "Five-Year-Plan literature".

The renewed awareness of "partyness" in literature found its reflec-tion in the field of music. While the Russian Association of Proletarian Writers (RAPP) moved into a favoured position, its musical counter-part, the RAPM, assumed new power and militancy. Many uncommitted authors and musicians joined the ranks of proletarian organizations following *Pravda*'s call for a "consolidation of Communist forces in proletarian literature" on 4 December 1929. It was this urge towards consolidation that impelled the young PROKOLL composers to join forces with RAPM, the musical organization most likely to gain the Party's open support.

The predictable happened: within the brief span of three years, between 1929 and 1932, RAPM acquired a monopolistic position of power on the musical scene. Prior to 1929, it had been an organization militant in spirit but weak in creativity. The influx of talented composers in 1929 raised the level of the group and gave it added importance. Yet, many influential musicians preferred to remain outside the organizational orbit of RAPM. They resented the bureaucratic mediocrity of the leadership, the intolerance towards the classical heritage, the simplistic views on the role of music in society, the contemptuous attitude towards dissenting fellow musicians. Although RAPM's professional standards were considered low, there was interference in the conservatory curriculum. Said Professor Shebalin in comic anger, ". . . My pupils who studied with Shekhter [one of the prominent proletarian musicians] bring me three-four bars of some clumsy melody. Then the discussion starts whether these three-four clumsy bars reflect the experience of the proletariat at the time of the Kronstadt uprising.* This is simply an idiotic exercise in semantics."

Nevertheless, the proletarian steamroller moved forward relentlessly. The new journal, *Proletarskyi Muzykant*, published the third—revised— platform of RAPM. Everyone was to be re-educated in the Marxist image —composers, critics, musicologists, listeners. The RAPM policy was violently anti-modern, anti-Western, anti-jazz, often anti-classical. RAPM fought the alleged bourgeois tendencies tolerated during the years of NEP. One such vitriolic attack was entitled "Against Nepmanski Music". A welcome target was the Association for Contemporary Music whose fortunes were declining in the midst of growing animosity towards modernism and Westernism. There was an attempt, in 1928, to re-organize the ACM; the name was changed to "All-Russian Society . . .", former members of ACM had to re-register, and the new by-laws contained the timely sentence "to bring contemporary music within the reach of the proletarian masses".[36] But the hostile tide could not be stemmed: the ACM's journal *Sovremennaya Muzyka* ceased publication in March 1929, followed in 1930 by the demise of the excellent monthly *Muzykalnoye Obrazovanie* which had represented the independent musical intelligentsia and the conservatory circles.

* In March 1921 the sailors at the Kronstadt Naval Base, who had played a conspicuous part in the Communist seizure of power in November 1917, mutinied against the Government and were suppressed by military action.

Only the brash voice of *Proletarskyi Muzykant* was left, pretending to speak for all the musicians. In the meantime, many important members had abandoned the ACM, among them Miaskovsky, and the organization simply ceased to function even prior to its dissolution in 1931.

In the midst of clashing ideologies and bitter feuds, it is remarkable that Russian musicians representing different views—traditionalist, modernist, proletarian—continued to meet at various conferences in an effort to explore areas of common interest and to chart a course for the future of Soviet music. One such meeting took place in June 1929 in Leningrad—the All-Russian Musical Conference convened by a government agency, the GLAVISKUSSTVO. The papers and resolutions of this conference were published in 1930 under the title *Nash Muzykalnyi Front* (Our Musical Front), many of them highly critical of musical conditions in the Soviet Union. Another All-Russian Conference was convened in Moscow in October 1930 to discuss the musical education of children.

In the meantime, RAPM continued to build its strength on a national scale. In the spring of 1931, two conventions were held—one Russian, the other all-Union. In attendance were more than one hundred delegates from many parts of the Soviet Union, including the Ukraine, Georgia, and Armenia. Perhaps this show of strength hastened the downfall of RAPM, for its policies towards the cultures of national minorities deviated from the guidelines established by the Party. The proletarian theorists of RAPM deprecated the musical heritage of the national minorities, neglected the wealth of native folklore, and belittled the composers writing in a "national" idiom.

In mid-1931, the dissension among musicians produced a new development. A number of composers—equally disenchanted with the dogmatism of RAPM and the modernism of the (defunct) ACM—issued a call for a "new creative association" though they declared themselves willing to co-operate with the proletarian group. Among the signers were Miaskovsky, Shebalin, Shirinsky, Kriukov, and Kabalevsky, representing a broad spectrum of the musical scene. The declaration was published in two journals: *Proletarskyi Muzykant* (1931 No. 7) and *Sovetskoye Iskusstvo* (8 August 1931). It called for "the implementation of Marxist-Leninist methodology in theoretical and practical work" and for contact with the "proletarian mass society". Creatively, the new group proposed to cultivate not only the mass genres, i.e. songs and light music, but also the large forms of opera and symphony. This was a marked departure from RAPM's dogmatic insistence on mass song as basis of all music making. Although many of the composers who signed the declaration were politically inactive, they displayed an increased awareness of the social responsibilities of the artist, "Every

Soviet artist and musician faces the task to reflect, through his work, the mighty process of Socialist construction, the changes taking place in the minds of millions of workers, the broad development of truly Socialist forms of labour, and the relentless struggle with the class enemy of the proletariat."[37] Only "through collective forms of work of the composers themselves, and with the active help of the musical and literary community" could these tasks be completed successfully.

Despite these conciliatory gestures towards the proletarian ideology, RAPM did not make any move to compromise with the composers. On the contrary, the official course remained inflexible, dogmatic, and dictatorial. The disenchantment of a majority of creative musicians with the policies of RAPM was shared by Party officials, though for different reasons. RAPM had become increasingly independent, and was often disinclined to recognize the guidelines issued by the Party: the proletarian theorists of RAPM, considering themselves the makers of musical laws, over-estimated their power. Similar signs of independence were noticeable in other proletarian organizations, particularly among the writers.

With one stroke, the Party's Central Committee ended all incipient insubordination and internal squabbles: on 23 April 1932 it dissolved *all* proletarian organizations in literature and the arts (including, of course, RAPM). The far-reaching resolution, entitled "On the Reconstruction of Literary and Artistic Organizations", marked the end of the "proletarian phase" in Soviet arts.

The Soviet composer of the 1920's was confronted by complex problems. He faced a public of the most heterogeneous character, ranging from the remnants of a sophisticated intelligentsia to a barely educated proletariat, while a stabilizing middle class was still lacking. Whatever approach the composer chose, he was certain to be assailed by one of the many feuding professional groups. Some found the traditional style alien to the revolutionary times, others considered the modern style too complex and meaningless for the masses. The artificial folksiness of the mass songs pleased no one, not even the masses who preferred their own urban ditties—the *chastushki*. Some composers switched to "Socialist topics", but this placated only the Party functionaries.

Thus, much Soviet music composed during the 1920's is strangely barren and synthetic—music manufactured by composers who aimed at a certain effect, at a certain type of audience, and who tried to satisfy the demands of the day. Often, a momentary success was achieved, but it proved illusory because the music was conditioned by a set of circumstances that could not be duplicated. The appeal of Soviet music became localized, aimed at audiences receptive to declamatory exhortations; few works evoked any response beyond the boundaries of Russia. Many important Russian composers settled abroad, forming an émigré school. Those who remained behind, struggled to find a new identity, a new focus in the face of social conditions that many of the composers found alien and bewildering.

Yet, though Soviet music of the 1920's failed to achieve greatness, it was by no means inconsequential. During that decade, a firm base was established that assured future growth. Everything was tried—music that was epigonal or futuristic, proletarian or esoteric, programmatic or absolute. This period of unchained experimentation was followed, in the 1930's, by a period of controlled restraints. Out of these conflicts arose a genuine Soviet style that reflected the travail and turbulence of the era.

To understand Soviet music of the 1920's, one must analyze the forces that shaped the composers—socio-political and musical. We have noted the essential political pressures. Let us look more closely at the musical influences.

The great Russian tradition was in the hands of the older masters—Glazunov, Ippolitov-Ivanov, Glière, Vassilenko, Kastalsky. In January 1922, surveying the remains of musical culture, Asafiev coined the often-repeated phrase, "There is Glazunov, hence there is Russian music."[1] In truth, however, the academicism of Glazunov and his generation had run its course and was no longer the guiding light of Russia's musical youth.

During the early 1920's, the influence of Scriabin was dominant. His memory was still fresh—he had died in 1915. His music, full of exaltation and passion, struck a responsive chord among some young revolutionaries. Statistics show that, during the 1922–23 season in Moscow, Scriabin ranked only behind Beethoven and Tchaikovsky as the most often performed composer. Lunacharsky who considered Scriabin to be "the culmination in music bearing the imprint of the premonition of our Revolution" wrote that, "Scriabin, despite his individualism, passed from the representation of passion to the representation of the Revolution, or to its prophecy. He was its musical prophet, and therein lies his social significance . . . The music of Scriabin is the supreme expression of the musical romanticism of the Revolution."[2]

Today these thoughts seem contrived. There is a streak of mysticism and decadence in Scriabin's music that, to us, appears more representative of the effete preciousness of pre-revolutionary days than of the harsh realities of post-October. Whatever influence Scriabin exerted on Russian music, it evaporated rather soon. As early as 1923, signs of a shift in attitude became apparent when the modernist journal *K Novym Beregam* (To New Shores) printed an article on Prokofiev. The author Zhilayev (a well-known pedagogue) compared the "healthy, somewhat rude masculinity" of Prokofiev to Scriabin's over-refinement and remarked, "In Russia, the dominating influence—until recently exerted by Scriabin—now seems to shift towards Prokofiev."[3] A few years later, young Shostakovich delivered this harsh verdict, "This is why we consider Scriabin as our bitter musical enemy. Why? . . . Because Scriabin's music tends towards unhealthy eroticism. Also to mysticism, passivity, and a flight from the reality of life."[4] Shostakovich said "we", speaking not only for himself but for his entire generation.

Prokofiev's affirmation of life, his abhorrence of sentimentality, his biting humour, his steely strength—all these traits endeared him to the young generation of musicians. When he paid a brief visit to Soviet Russia in 1927, after an absence of almost ten years, he was surrounded by admirers. Prokofiev and, to a lesser degree, Stravinsky exemplified to the young Soviet composers the possibilities of a creative fusion between Russian elements and advanced Western techniques. In addition, there were fresh influences from the West—Hindemith's neobaroque contrapuntal skills, Krenek's use of jazz elements in *Johnny spielt auf*, Bartok's folkloristic techniques, the high humour of France's "Les Six", the twelve-tone system of Schoenberg. New slogans came from Germany, such as *Gebrauchsmusik* (functional music) and *Neue Sachlichkeit* (new objectivity). Constructivist music imitative of technology—Honegger's *Pacific 231*, Milhaud's *Agricultural Machines*—stirred the imagination of Soviet youth. All these heterogeneous influences, rushing in after the near-isolation of the years 1914 to 1921, had to be absorbed by Soviet composers before they could bear fruit.

Impatient with the slow process of absorption, Soviet musicians tried imitation instead—and failed. The 1920's are filled with names of Russian composers, now dimly remembered, who copied external devices, modernistic tricks, sociological gimmicks. But the chaos of experimentation was not fruitless; it represented the growing pains of Soviet music and eventually led to a certain clarification, to the emergence of significant talents formed in a period of controversy. The 1920's were the formative years of Shostakovich, Kabalevsky, Khachaturian, Knipper, Koval, Shebalin; they shaped the—more mature—talents of Shaporin and Miaskovsky. Their strength was forged by conflict, while the next generation of composers was weakened by conformity.

A gap of some fifteen years separates the last great pre-revolutionary Russian opera—Rimsky's *Le Coq d'Or*—from the first Soviet opera of the mid-1920's. The turbulent years of war and revolution were not propitious for opera, the most complex of all musical genres. Yet, the interest in opera as a theatrical experience increased, stimulated primarily by the imagination of stage directors. Taïrov, Stanislavsky, Nemirovich-Danchenko, Meyerhold were fascinated by the problem of fusing action and music, of regenerating the static approach to the lyric masterpieces.

As for the composers, they seemed to view the opera as temporarily unapproachable. To be sure, there was much discussion of the need for "contemporary" opera, based on topics of actuality—war, revolution, social progress. But such goals could not be achieved in haste. To cast recent events into a valid artistic mould, to distill reality into a universal human experience is a process that requires time, reflection, and absorption. Attempts to exploit patriotism and revolutionary fervour on the stage were made, but they failed. Stanislavsky, in reminiscing about theatre life during the First World War, reflected on this point,

"In Moscow . . . theatres worked as never before. They tried to fit their repertoire to the moment and produced a series of quickly baked patriotic plays. And art showed that it had nothing in common with tendencies, politics, and the topics of the day.

When during the Russo-Japanese War somebody advised Chekhov to write a play about the war, the great writer was insulted.

'Listen,' he said, 'it is necessary that twenty years should pass. It is impossible to speak of it now. It is necessary that the soul should be in repose. Only then can an author be unprejudiced.'

The newly baked patriotic plays failed, one after the other, and there was nothing remarkable about that . . ."[5]

For lack of modern topical Soviet operas, the repertoire in Moscow and Petrograd clung to the established Russian composers, from Glinka to Rimsky-Korsakov. Verdi and Rossini, Bizet and Gounod continued to be given in traditional versions. Surprisingly, Wagner's operas were also often performed, particularly in Petrograd's Maryinsky Theatre which had a superb Wagnerian tenor in Ivan Yershov.

A revolutionary by-product was the rewriting of operatic libretti while leaving the music intact. Thus, *Tosca* became "The Battle for the Commune", *Les Huguenots* was transformed into "The Decembrists", *A Life for the Tsar* emerged as "Hammer and Sickle". New texts were also provided for *Rienzi* and *Don Giovanni*. More creative was a new version of *Carmen* under the name "Carmencita and the Soldier" (1924) staged by Nemirovich-Danchenko; it proved very popular.

In the second half of the 1920's, the conventional opera repertoire was enlivened by a vigorous infusion of West-European operas and ballets. Perhaps Western-oriented would be a more accurate description since Stravinsky and Prokofiev were among the composers represented. This trend was sparked off by the activities of the ACM whose leaders occupied important positions in the cultural world. For a few years, the Leningrad Maryinsky Theatre was almost in competition with Berlin, the citadel of modernism during the 1920's. A Soviet historian[6] gives the following comparative dates of premières:

Composer	Opera	Berlin Première	Leningrad Première (all at Maryinsky)
Franz Schreker	Der Ferne Klang	1925	1925
Alban Berg	Wozzeck	1925	1927
Stravinsky	Pulcinella	1925	1926
Stravinsky	Le Renard	1925	1927
Prokofiev	Love for Three Oranges	1926	1926

This is all the more impressive since the Leningrad ensemble had virtually no prior experience with the contemporary idiom. Judging by the exuberant comments of the composers Schreker and Berg, the performances were excellent. A friendly rivalry developed between the proud old Maryinsky Theatre and the newly established Malyi Opera Theatre. Unhampered by tradition, the Malyi turned to modernism and experimentation, both in terms of re-staging older works in a new spirit and in presenting new operas. After an unsuccessful *Mona Lisa* by Max von Schillings (a post-romantic work dating back to 1915) in 1926, two operas by Ernst Krenek followed in quick succession—*Der Sprung über den Schatten* in 1927 and *Johnny spielt auf* in 1928. Both were advertised as "satires on bourgeois decadence" depicting the "bankruptcy of the old civilisation". *Johnny*, in particular, was a big success, even in provincial theatres. Less successful was *Columbus* (1929) by Erwin Dressel, a nineteen-year-old composer. However, there was increasing agitation against the modernist policy, and several projects had to be cancelled, including *Le Pauvre Matelôt* by Milhaud and *Neues vom Tage* by Hindemith. The opposition branded the Malyi Theatre as the "herald of formalist art". While Leningrad was the leader in exploring the modern repertoire, other cities were not inactive. In Moscow the Nemirovich-Danchenko Theatre tried unusual works, with varying success: *La Vida Breve* by Manuel de Falla was well received, *Tyll Ulenspiegel* by Mark Lothar was a fiasco. In Kharkov, Max Brandt's *Maschinist Hopkins* reached the stage but was not given elsewhere.

Clearly, such a repertoire could appeal only to a sophisticated public. Not only did a large segment of the Soviet audiences reject modern Western operas, so alien in subject and idiom, but many performing artists were unwilling to study the new roles. The strongest support came from a handful of musicologists and music critics who laboured incessantly to acquaint the Soviet public with the new composers and their novel musical ideas. Most active were Victor Belayev in Moscow and Asafiev in Leningrad. Belayev detected in Krenek's works certain affinities to the idea of "proletarian mass opera". Asafiev stressed the importance of contact with advanced Western music. In an article "We and the Musical West", published in 1927 for the Tenth Anniversary of the October Revolution, he wrote, "Acquaintance with the best examples of Western music will help the development of Soviet music, will liberate it from the amateurishness and speculation about 'revolutionism', will lead towards the exploration of new forms and new means of musical expression. To show the masses the musical art of the West will provide criteria for the evaluation of Soviet musical creativity." After mentioning *Wozzeck* and *Der Sprung über den Schatten*, Asafiev continued, "As to quality of artistic accomplishment, can one compare these works with the Soviet operas that have appeared in the last years? Under no circumstances. Does it not follow that Soviet musicians ought to learn, ought to acquire the necessary techniques, not from the era of the 'Mighty Five', but from contemporary musical art?"[7]

Such thoughts became blasphemous in the 1930's. In 1927, it was still possible to believe that Soviet composers could explore Western methods without embracing Western ideologies. Asafiev felt justified to speak bluntly since the disappointing quality of contemporary Soviet opera was a matter of general concern.

The responsibility of creating a new genre of "revolutionary" opera did not rest with the composers alone; an essential prerequisite was a suitable libretto. Traditionally, the Russians attached great importance to the literary quality of a libretto—because the texts of Pushkin, used widely by Russian composers, had set such high standards. Soviet criticism has continued that tradition: the analysis of an opera is never limited to musical matters but extends into dramaturgy, delineation of characters, historical accuracy—in short, the totality of the work. To these criteria must be added the ideological stance which has caused some spectacular failures in Soviet opera.

Two types of libretti can be identified during the Soviet era. One deals with the historic past and such subjects as social rebellions or national wars of liberation, either Russian or foreign. The other type is concerned with the twentieth century—true or fictionalized events of the Revolutions of 1905 and 1917, the Civil War, and—since 1945— the Second World War. The heroic defence of the fatherland is always stressed, from the invasions of the Teutonic Knights to the invasions of Napoleon and Hitler. The revolt of the Decembrists in 1825 has been treated several times. Popular rebels like Emelian Pugachev and Stenka Razin are frequent protagonists. The presentation of the folk heroes of various national minorities who fought the oppression and encroachment of Greater Russia proved to be sensitive topics. Among foreign rebellions, the subjects range from Spartacus in ancient Rome to the French Revolutions of 1789 and 1848, as well as the fight against Fascism. Far more contemporary and more gripping than these doubtful historical excursions are the musical realizations of recent events—those dealing with October 1917, the Civil War of 1919–21, and the sufferings inflicted by the Second World War.

The problems of the librettist were matched by those of the composer. To find a musical idiom commensurate with the dawn of a "new era" was a troublesome task, even for a master like Prokofiev. During the unsettled decade of the 1920's, many young composers felt that the conventions of the opera were outworn, that musical language and form needed radical change. Some advocated the abandonment of tonality following the lead of the Schoenberg school. Others repudiated the conventional devices, such as arias, ensembles, and ballet insertions, as remnants of the "feudal and bourgeois world". They felt that the Soviet hero should express his thoughts in bold recitatives. The disappointing result of such a "primitive sociological method", as one Soviet author described it,[8] was that some traitorous villain sang a melodious aria while the Soviet hero had to be content with a dry, inexpressive recitative.

Among the early—often immature—attempts at creating a "Soviet" opera, two works, both staged in 1925, achieved more than passing attention—*Orlinyi Bunt* (Eagles in Revolt) by Andrei Pashchenko and *Dekabristy* (The Decembrists) by Vassily Zolotarev.

Pashchenko's opera was given for the first time at Leningrad's Maryinsky Theatre on 7 November 1925, the Eighth Anniversary of the Revolution. The hero was the eighteenth-century cossack Emelian Pugachev who, in 1773–75, led the peasant uprising against Catherine II and was executed in 1775. Though the musical idiom was essentially traditional, the score found a strong defender in the unpredictable Asafiev. Despite undeniable weaknesses, *Orlinyi Bunt* remained in the repertoire for some ten years and was performed in twenty-four cities.

Zolotarev's *Dekabristy* (not to be confused with Shaporin's later opera of the same name*) was produced at Moscow's Bolshoi Theatre on 26 December 1925 in commemoration of the centennial anniversary of the historic revolt. Lunacharsky spoke kindly about the work, but the critics tore it apart: they found the music trite and filled with "martial barrack tunes and lyrico-sentimental bathos".[9] The composer was at his best when imitating Tchaikovsky, remarked Asafiev caustically.

In selecting works of Soviet composers for the repertoire, the theatres were caught between the needs of an untutored audience and the demands of the sophisticated critics. One young composer, Piotr Triodin, claimed openly that his opera "aimed at an unqualified mass public, a public that does not go to the theatre in order to dabble in aesthetics after a good dinner, but people who go to learn about life, about the things that live mass-oriented theatre can contribute . . ."[10] The critics promptly accused him of musical oversimplification and slavish imitation of the "Mighty Five". The exasperated director of the Bolshoi wrote complainingly in 1926, "The democratic circles receive our productions with enthusiasm, the music experts react with coldness, but certain personalities treat our work like dirt."[11] These "music experts" considered themselves guardians of public

* Two scenes from Shaporin's first version, under the name *Paulina Goebel*, were given in Leningrad on 27 December 1925.

taste; they wielded considerable power and were able to decide the success or failure of a production. When the first Soviet opera, *Za Krasnyi Petrograd* (For Red Petrograd) was staged in Leningrad in 1925, it was subjected to so much criticism by "modernist and left-wing PROLETKULT circles"[12] that the work was withdrawn after thirteen performances.* Yet *Red Petrograd* was the first opera to be based on a Soviet revolutionary topic. As such it was "immeasurably more fruitful than all the involvement in the works of Krenek", to quote a Soviet historian.[13] The opera, subtitled "The Year 1919", described the victorious defence of Petrograd against the assault of the White-Guardists under Yudenich. It was planned as a realistic spectacle accessible to the mass public, a lively revue-like chronicle of events still vivid in everyone's memory. Various episodes described the blockade of Petrograd, a meeting at the factory, the call to arms, the Red and the White Armies, treason and victory. Musically, the "positive heroes" were characterized in lyric song, their foes in satirical terms. To add realism the composers used authentic tunes of those days. In 1930, Gladkovsky—the more gifted of the two composers—rearranged the opera as an oratorio under the new name *Front i Tyll* (War Front and Home Front), but the new version failed to make any impact.

The search for topical actuality led to theatrical experiments that were barely related to opera. In 1927, Leningrad's Malyi Theatre staged Mayakovsky's poem *Dvatzat piatoye* (The Twenty-Fifth) with a score by Shtrassenburg. The poem was divided into forty-eight episodes, describing events of the Revolution and the Civil War. Solo recitations alternated with choral speaking, choral singing was accompanied by pantomime. A narrator provided introductions to the various scenes. The music was assigned a secondary, merely supporting, role. The staging was elaborate, employing theatrical and cinematic effects "in the manner of heightened expressionism, in poster-like monumental forms".[14]

For lack of suitable operas, the Tenth Anniversary of the October Revolution was celebrated in 1927 with so-called "synthetic" spectacles. For example, the Moscow Bolshoi Theatre staged the *Geroicheskoye Deistvie* (Heroic Act) with music by Nebolsin. The five scenes were entitled Slavery, Battle, Victory, Liberty, and Epilogue. The naiveté of the concept can be gathered from the following description,

> "Capitalism—abominable, immense, bloated, hideous, filled with sucked blood—holds enslaved humanity in its gigantic, blood-stained, sharp-nailed paws. The toilers break their chains. Upward creep the victorious red banners. A colossal hammer is lowered

* Two composers were responsible for the score—A. Gladkovsky and E. Prussak.

from above . . . A few powerful strokes, and the head of evil is split open, the claws relax, evil is thrown into the abyss. One hears a stupendous victory hymn to humanity . . . a group of leaders on top of conquered evil . . ."[15]

Such cosmic allegories were characteristic of the "revolutionary romanticism" in Russian literature of the 1920's. However, the music critics took a dim view of this bombast, and one remarked dryly, "There is nothing heroic about a dull orchestral texture woven out of a monotonous repetition of altered chords."[16]

A comparable experiment took place at Leningrad's Maryinsky Theatre. The production was called *Shturm Perekopa* (Storm of the Perekop) and was designed as a chronicle of the famous Civil War battle. The score was by the noted composer Yuri Shaporin, but even he could not raise the significance of the music beyond a mainly illustrative function.

In the midst of so much mediocrity, the staging of Prokofiev's opera *The Love for Three Oranges* (based on a comedy of the eighteenth-century author Carlo Gozzi) came as a refreshing experience, a fluffy bit of "gay nihilism". The Leningrad performance of 1926 was fanciful and brilliant, almost over-produced, while the Moscow staging of 1927 was criticized as heavy-handed and pompous. A planned revival of the *Three Oranges*, to be directed by the "futurist" Meyerhold, was cancelled because the poet Mayakovsky—who was to have written additional "political" interpolations—ended his life in 1930.

Within the history of "non-Russian" Soviet opera, Reinhold Glière's *Shakh-Senem* had considerable impact. The story is placed in nineteenth-century Azerbaijan. In preparation, Glière made a thorough study of Azerbaijan folklore and folk music, and shaped his musical idiom accordingly. The score attempts a synthesis between native folk traditions and Russian compositorial techniques. First performed in Baku in 1927—though in Russian—the work was considered a milestone in the musical evolution of Azerbaijan, at a time when "minority" republics were struggling for cultural recognition. A second version, this time in the language of Azerbaijan, was given in Baku in 1934 and shown in Moscow in 1938, as part of the Festival of Azerbaijan Art.

The ideological cleavage between the adherents of musical modernism and those agitating for a "proletarian" stance was reflected in the repertoire of the musical theatres. In fact, this factionalism is blamed, by many official Soviet histories, for the slowness in the development of a truly Soviet opera. A prime example of the "nefarious" influence of Western modernism on Soviet composers are three operas that appeared in quick succession in 1930. They were—*Nos* (The Nose) by

Dmitri Shostakovich, *Severnyi Veter* (North Wind) by Lev Knipper, and *Lyod i Stal* (Ice and Steel) by Vladimir Deshevov. Each composer had distinguished himself with works related to revolutionary topics, and there was no reason to doubt their loyalty to Marxist ideals. Their preference for a modern musical idiom was certainly not intended as an ideological protest. Furthermore, two of these operas dealt with revolutionary subjects: *North Wind* treated the execution of the twenty-six commissars in Baku during the Civil War, *Ice and Steel* was based on the Kronstadt rebellion of 1921.

Both Knipper and Deshevov were criticized for not measuring up to their heroic topics. Knipper's concept was that of a drama with supporting music, and as such it was staged by Nemirovich-Danchenko in his Moscow studio theatre in March 1930. Obviously, composer and director wished to avoid any stereotyped operatic procedures. Much of the music moved in rather artificial recitatives; at climactic moments, the score became altogether silent. As one critic remarked sarcastically, "They 'sing' a telephone conversation, but they 'speak' an impassioned appeal to the masses."[17] Whatever success *North Wind* had was achieved "in spite of the score".[18]

While Knipper derived some of his modernistic ideas from his studies in Berlin, Deshevov was entirely Russian-trained. In 1926, Milhaud singled him out as the major talent among younger Soviet composers. Deshevov was determined to break with operatic traditions, both Russian and Western. One commentator pointed out certain affinities with the "realism" of Mussorgsky and the "naturalism" of Alban Berg. Actually, Deshevov was far simpler: he leaned towards illustrative music, the rhythmic noises of technology, the symbols of the "machine age". This was the fashion of the 1920's, but it could not sustain an evening's interest. The music was described as "cinematographically fragmented", and even a sympathetic critic like Ivan Sollertinsky felt that a potentially monumental topic had been denigrated by both composer and librettist. "The topic of Kronstadt is a topic of tragedy . . . The spectacle *Ice and Steel* can be called monumental only by a misunderstanding. Four short little scenes, of which the first three have a genre-like, slightly grotesque character, while the fourth is melodramatic with a battle apotheosis—all this is dramaturgically grey . . ."[19]

While the failures of Knipper and Deshevov need not detain us—neither achieved major status as a composer—the case of Shostakovich is far more significant. *The Nose* is a satirical masterpiece by a youthful composer—twenty-two years at the time—who eventually became the symbol of Soviet greatness in music. The opera was conceived in 1928 and given its première at the Leningrad Malyi Theatre on 17 January

1930. The score mirrors the grotesque-satirical mood pervading the 1920's. Strangely enough, the composer denies any intentional flippancy by saying, "The music does not have deliberately the character of parody . . . [it] is not comical."[20] Yet, from the orchestral "sneeze" that opens the opera, the score is full of biting humour and tongue-in-cheek caricature. Shostakovich learned from many contemporaries—from Prokofiev and Krenek, Hindemith and Stravinsky. But he also drew on Russian models—on Dargomyzhsky and Mussorgsky—to solve the problem of fusing speech and music, the characteristically Russian speech-song. The critic Belayev wrote at the time that Shostakovich came close to the solution of the problem that beset so many Russian composers, and he called *The Nose* "the musical equivalent of a great literary work".[21]

In explaining the choice of the libretto, Shostakovich writes almost apologetically that he was "forced to turn to the classics" because Soviet writers showed no interest in collaborating on an opera. Revealing his hesitant approach towards "the classics", the composer says that "in our time an opera based on a classical subject would be pertinent, provided it has a satirical character". Gogol's *The Nose* was a social satire on the era of Tsar Nicholas I. But Shostakovich's musical satire was too acid and over-drawn; besides, it proved too difficult to perform in provincial theatres. Despite a success in sophisticated Leningrad, *The Nose* was not performed on other stages; not even a performance in Moscow is listed. Belayev explained that, "The chamber music style in which it is written and the extremely difficult mode of musical declamation . . . manifest the development of a new style in our music for which we have not, as yet, the performers."

Soon, the spectre of formalism obliterated *The Nose* which, until today, is described as "the acme of 'ultra-left' trends".[22] It is one of the works not yet unfrozen by "the thaw". A few recent stagings—in Florence and in Santa Fe—did not lead to any rush of revivals. The Suite from the opera (consisting of seven numbers of which three are sung by soloists) was actually played before the première of the staged version—in Moscow in 1928 and in Leningrad the following year. One excerpt, the amusing and original "Percussion Interlude", is heard more frequently.

As a riposte to the inroads of modernism, the Association of Proletarian Musicians (RAPM) actively supported two operatic projects of its members, but neither was produced. One, entitled *The Year 1905*, was the joint effort of Davidenko and Shekhter, two of the most active RAPM composers. The work received a third prize in a competition and was to be produced by Stanislavsky; however, Davidenko died suddenly in 1934, and the project was abandoned. Davidenko left another opera, *The Year 1919*, of which only the first act was completed. RAPM attempted to describe the fragment as a step towards the realization of proletarian opera. However, by that time, RAPM's hegemony in music was broken, and Soviet critics reacted sharply by saying that Davidenko's unfinished work merely revealed "the full fallacy of RAPM's aesthetic position."[23]

The mediocre successes of Soviet operas should not obscure the fact, however, that opera as a *genre* was in a state of efflorescence in the Soviet Union. The novel theatrical techniques applied by Soviet stage directors in the production of repertoire works aroused the admiration of many Western visitors. Among them was the Austrian opera director Herbert Graf who, as a young man in his twenties, studied Soviet production methods. In 1929, he published a report in *Anbruch* that was full of high praise.[24]

Graf wasted little time on the traditional theatres—Moscow's Bolshoi, Leningrad's Maryinsky—and focused his attention on the work of the foremost directors and their own studios—Stanislavsky, Nemirovich-Danchenko, Meyerhold, Taïrov. Stanislavsky's "artistic realism" with its fidelity of milieu and the naturalistic treatment of the scene struck Graf as somewhat old-fashioned; yet, it was an "indescribable impression" to see *La Bohème* or *Eugene Onegin* performed as true *dramas*, without regard to operatic conventions. Taïrov's "unchained theatre" was another world: here was "abstraction of the human expression . . . grotesquely stylized gestures . . . opposition to realism". Taïrov treated the original work merely as raw material and reshaped it in an autocratic way—a "completely anarchic treatment of the work"—yet impressive in a highly personal manner.

Graf observed the synthesis of tradition and innovation achieved by Nemirovich-Danchenko: he overcame the clichés of operatic acting and reached beyond realism towards "modern concentrated expression". Yet he was not averse to treating a work freely, as for example in his colourful production of *Carmencita and the Soldier*. In Graf's opinion, probably the most gifted, certainly the most revolutionary, among the stage directors was Meyerhold. A confirmed Communist and one of the early adherents of PROLETKULT, he worked most successfully with the writer Mayakovsky—the production of the satirical play *The Bedbug* by Mayakovsky, with incidental music by young Shostakovich, was the sensation of 1929. Meyerhold's art was the achievement of a new realism in a wholly contemporary evolution; such slogans as constructivism and bio-mechanics give an imperfect description of his highly personal style.

Graf saw other, less spectacular, productions—at the Leningrad Malyi Theatre and at the Leningrad Opera Studio which stressed an intensely musical, rather than theatrical, approach. In general, Graf ascribed the success of Soviet opera productions to the slow, methodical preparation and a strict limitation in the number of new productions; usually, no more than four new productions are given each season, and the repertoire is limited to few works with frequent repeats. As an example, he cites forty-two performances within eighteen months of Krenek's *Sprung über den Schatten* and thirty-five performances within six weeks of *Johnny spielt auf* (also by Krenek). This led to "technically masterful" performances. One might compare these accomplishments with the impoverishment of the lyric stage during the next decade— due to the application of the "Socialist Realism" principle and to Stalinist terror. Meyerhold's theatre was closed in 1938 and he disappeared in the purge of 1939. Taïrov continued to work but was forced into a conventional style. The productions of the ageing Nemirovich-Danchenko eventually became a bulwark of traditional realism. Stanislavsky was spared the reorientation: he died in 1938.

The search for revolutionary topics also pervaded the Soviet ballet. No sooner was the October Revolution a *fait accompli* than Asafiev arranged the staging of his ballet *Carmagnole*, set at the time of the French Revolution of 1789. During the winter 1917–18, the work was given at various workers' clubs, with piano accompaniment. Though score and scenario are lost, it is generally assumed that Asafiev used much of the material for his later ballet, *Flame of Paris* (1932).

The classical Russian ballet had to be revitalized by new concepts and techniques if it were to serve contemporary topics. This was realized very early by choreographers and composers. The first attempts at innovation aimed at presenting spectacles rather than ballets. An example is *The Red Hurricane*, with a scenario by Lopukhov and a score by Deshevov, which was given at Leningrad's Maryinsky Theatre in 1924, first planned for the Fifth Anniversary of the Revolution. It was called a "synthecized theatrical performance in two processes, with prologue and epilogue", and it contained dancing, singing, declamation, acrobatics, and cabaret-like entertainment. Soviet historians describe the production as an "absurd mixture of decadent symbolism and primitivism combined with naive vulgar-philosophical attempts".[25] Nevertheless, Lopukhov soon was named one of the chief choreographers of the Maryinsky and was responsible for several Stravinsky premières (*Pulcinella* in 1926 and *Renard* in 1927). Earlier, in 1921, he had staged *The Firebird*. To the horror of traditionalists, Lopukhov attempted an updated version of *The Nutcracker* by Tchaikovsky in 1929, and his name is also connected with the spectacular fiascos of Shostakovich's ballets *Bolt* in 1931 and *The Limpid Stream* in 1935.

Moscow was more tradition-minded. At the Bolshoi Theatre, the greatest success of the 1927 season—the Tenth Anniversary of the Revolution—was the new ballet by Glière, *The Red Poppy*. Within two years, it was given two hundred performances, and it has retained its popularity. A separate number, the "Russian Sailors' Dance", has achieved world fame. The story, set in revolution-torn China of the 1920's, had topical appeal. It called for unity of proletarians across the borders, and the epilogue envisaged a free Chinese people. The—essentially traditional—score is colourful in its contrast of East and West, juxtaposing socio-political and lyrico-personal situations. Graf, who saw the production in 1929, found the music "sweetish" and objected to the use of conventional ballet techniques for the expression of new ideas. Nevertheless, Glière's *The Red Poppy* became a milestone in the evolution of Soviet ballet.

In 1930–31, within a span of twelve months, Leningrad saw three new ballets that aroused opposition by their "misguided" modernism. *Footbolisty* (The Football Players), with a score by Victor Oransky, was a naive attempt to compare the good world of the Soviets with the bad world of the capitalist West. Musically, the positive heroes were characterized by fragments of revolutionary songs, while the bad boys were condemned to jazz music. Unfortunately, the jazz seems to have had much more popular appeal. The score, now totally forgotten, also contained some organized noises and "soulless" machine rhythms, typical of the 1920's.

More significant were the failures of two other ballets, both with music by Shostakovich—*Zolotoi Vek* (The Golden Age) and *Bolt*, for they revealed the official hostility towards artistic experimentation. These ballet scores show Shostakovich in the same satirical, exuberant mood as displayed in his recent opera *The Nose*. This highly-strung young man—so tense, serious, and unsmiling—could write music of such humour, such casual wittiness that an audience would roar with laughter. It was his intent to write "good amusing music" and he fully succeeded. Shostakovich shows himself a master of orchestral effects and sly parody, whether achieved by instrumental cuteness, satirical allusion, or the high spirits of the unexpected. His orchestration is extravagant, and the use of unusual instruments makes the score sound like orchestral high jinks. However, the Soviet bureaucrats were not receptive to this kind of humour, especially when it concerned their football players, " . . . Formalist music—skimpy melodic content, exaggerated emphasis on effects of rhythm, timbre, harmony, the extravagance of orchestration, the unjustified grotesqueness—all this caused the complete failure of *The Golden Age*."

The scenario, too, is torn apart, and the flimsy story of a Soviet football team visiting an imaginary Western exposition is subjected to heavy-handed political analysis. "The image of the Soviet people in this ballet is inert and false. The representatives of the capitalist world are given much more play," is the complaint of an official Soviet historian.[26] One brief musical number from *The Golden Age*—the caustic, astringent "Polka"—has become a world-wide success. It occurs in Act III as music to a choreographic skit on the League of Nations, entitled "Once Upon a Time in Geneva". While the ballet failed to achieve success as a spectacle, a four-movement Orchestral Suite drawn from the score enjoyed considerable popularity in Soviet concert halls. Paradoxically, what was considered offensive as musical illustration of a weak plot became suddenly "witty and brilliant" as a work of absolute music. It proves that music *per se* cannot be ideologically right or wrong—it must be judged on its own, purely musical terms.

While *The Golden Age* offered international entanglements, *Bolt* was concerned with Soviet productivity—the "first industrial ballet" as it was called. The world of the *petit-bourgeois* was juxtaposed to that of the Marxist workers, the true builders of socialism. Urban folklore was used in grotesque distortion, but—to the chagrin of the critics—the positive aspects were allegedly neglected. Not even such scenes as the "Dance of Enthusiasm" or the "Work Pantomime", showing hammers striking an anvil, could assuage critical opinion. The fiasco was shared by composer, choreographer, and librettist. An abject admission of failure was written by Shostakovich a few years later, though under mental stress, "*The Golden Age* and *Bolt* were gross failures from the dramatic point of view. The depiction of Socialist reality in ballet is an extremely serious matter, it cannot be approached superficially . . . Insufficient thought had been given to the problem of a realist ballet performance, constructed around a Soviet theme."[27] It is, perhaps, not by accident that Shostakovich speaks of failure from a *dramatic* point of view while not actually admitting any musical shortcomings.

Among the Russian classicists, the symphony, in its pure abstract form, was not particularly favoured. Only Tchaikovsky and Borodin made significant contributions in this genre, and Glazunov followed their example. In general, however, Russian composers showed a preference for orchestral music with picturesque titles, tone poems with an implied or realistic programme, and colourful phantasies of national character. "Orientalism" was much in vogue.

On the whole, these traditions were continued during the Soviet era, but there are subtle differences. Strangely enough, the "absolute" form of the symphony received greater attention. Not only did Miaskovsky, Shostakovich, and Prokofiev make significant contributions, but the symphonic genre retained its attraction for every Soviet composer, old and young. With pride, Soviet historians point out that, while in Western Europe the post-Mahler era was one of symphonic disintegration, Soviet Russia preserved the symphonic heritage. Asafiev wrote in 1944, "Soviet symphonism is our pride, for only in our great land did symphonic music not lose itself . . . did not squander itself . . . in eccentric experiments . . . The West lives only in the memory of great symphonists and performs the past monuments of glorious symphonies."[28]

One can disagree with such a low estimate of Western symphonic achievement. Yet, it must be admitted that the Mahlerian concept of the symphony as a universe, as a "mirror of life"—to quote Asafiev— has remained strongest among Soviet composers.

Side by side with the "absolute" concept of the symphony, Soviet composers were using the large-scale form for ideological or topical purposes. Beginning in the 1920's, we witness new approaches and ideas—the *actualization* of the symphonic genre begins to take shape. Some of these works were not symphonic in the real sense of the term because their form was dictated, not by musical laws, but by external considerations, such as a topic, a text, or some ideological programme. In fact, such topical works were commissioned by the propaganda division (AGITOTDEL) of Lunacharsky's Commissariat of Public Education, and many compositions of the 1920's owe their existence to the initiative of that office.* In such works—usually in one movement—the symphony orchestra was often amplified by the human voice, either as narrator, vocal soloists, or chorus. There was a heavy stress on symbolism in the choice of texts—the ideological meaning had to be perfectly clear—and the scores contained significant quotes of revolutionary tunes. The "textual" practice became so widespread that a wordless symphony became almost suspect as to ideological purity. "Add a verse—that's 'content'; no verse, that's 'formalism'," grumbled Shostakovich.

Among Western composers of the twentieth century, descriptive music was considered rather old-fashioned, though "hidden" or implied programmes were admitted. On this subject, a comment by Gustav Mahler, expressed in a letter to Max Kalbeck around 1902, is of interest, "*Beginning with Beethoven*, there is no modern music without

* See p. 84.

an inner programme. But no music is worth anything if the listener has to be told what experience it embodies or what he—the listener—should experience. Therefore again: perish any programme . . . A remnant of mystery always remains—even for the creator!"[29]

In Soviet Russia, on the other hand, programme music in its concrete form was encouraged officially, and the encouragement became the more urgent, the more Socialist Realism was enforced. In the 1920's, many Soviet composers turned to programme music of their own volition because a programme made instrumental music more accessible and, hence, more enjoyable to the new mass audiences. This purpose was served not only by symphonies but also by shorter descriptive pieces, overtures, and suites. The latter were usually drawn from scores composed for ballets or films, and this custom has continued until today. It has enriched the Soviet repertoire by many colourful and effective works. Prokofiev, in particular, made it a practice to extract suites from every score he composed for stage or screen; Shostakovich, Khachaturian, and many other Soviet composers followed his example.

Another Russian tradition, the "orientalism" so dear to the "Mighty Five", was more systematically exploited in the Soviet era. In keeping with the official policy of developing a "multi-national" culture, Soviet composers concentrated on music based on various folk sources—Caucasian, Uzbek, Turkmenian, Burat-Mongolian, and similar exotic material. Eventually, this led to the systematic development of national, indigenous potentials—the creation of music schools, the collection and notation of folklore, the preservation of oral musical traditions. The groundwork for this development was done in the 1920's.

The emergence of Nikolai Miaskovsky as the foremost Soviet symphonist was an important feature of the 1920's. It was his strong, positive Fifth Symphony that brought him decisive, somewhat belated, recognition . . . not so much at the time of its première in 1920, but in 1924 when the conductor Emil Cooper gave two repeat performances in Leningrad and Moscow. A few months later, Miaskovsky's Sixth Symphony, a far more complex work, was given its première. In quick succession followed the symphonies No. 7 to No. 12. But they were not written with ease; each testifies to the inner struggle of the composer to find a musical idiom less subjective, more universally valid and meaningful.

Miaskovsky's Sixth Symphony is an important human document. Composed in 1922–23, it was his personal, almost anguished reaction to the revolutionary era which he saw as a period of suffering, tragedy, and pain. It was, he admits, "a weak-willed, neurasthenic, and sacrificial

concept".[30] In the Finale, he used two songs of the French Revolution
—the *Carmagnole* and *Ça ira*—but their vigour is over-shadowed by
the *Dies irae* and an old Russian chant, *O rasstavanii dushy s telom* (The
parting of body and soul). The work is essentially a tragic experience.

In his Eighth Symphony, composed in 1924–25, Miaskovsky followed
"a genuine impulse towards those objective moods that I was seeking".
He used folk-related themes, mostly of Russian origin, while an exotic
Bashkir melody forms a lovely contrast in the Adagio movement. Yet,
Miaskovsky's inclination towards complex textures overwhelmed the
natural flow of the material, and the "objective mood" he was seeking
yielded to a subjective treatment not free from a streak of pessimism.

While programme music did not play an important part in Miaskovsky creative work, he provided occasionally some clues as to the source
of his inspiration. The first impulse for the Eighth Symphony, for
example, came from the hero of Russian folklore, Stenka Razin. In his
Tenth Symphony, written in 1927, the composer wanted to give "a
picture of the inner turmoil of Eugene in Pushkin's *The Bronze Horse-
man*". Since the protagonist was mad, it is not surprising—says one
Soviet historian—that the Tenth Symphony "borders on a nightmare
. . . an individualistic concept of pessimism realized through expressionistic images".[31] To convey this inner tumult, Miaskovsky—using
an "immense" orchestra—adopted a strongly modernistic idiom, with
dissonant counterpoint, and wildly leaping melodic lines—all this com-
pressed into a one-movement form. Problems arose during the rehearsals in March 1928, which were compounded by the fact that the work
was to be performed by the conductorless orchestra, PERSIMFANS. The
composer was not happy, "Nothing goes smoothly, the symphony
does not please." Nor was the première entirely to his liking; there
were "misunderstandings" and he felt that the work did not make the
desired impression.

Perhaps chastized by this experience, Miaskovsky turned in his next
orchestral compositions to a simplified and accessible musical idiom.
He conceived the idea of several "village concertos" for smaller orchestra. Three such works appeared as Opus 32: a Serenade, a String Sinfonietta, and a Lyric Concertino, all written between December 1928
and January 1929. A feeling of estrangement between composer and
public may have led Miaskovsky to compose these works, so charming
in their simplicity. He also tried his hand at writing mass songs, though
the popular choral medium was alien to him. This need to communicate in more direct musical terms coloured his creative work during
the next few years.

These were the years—the early 1930's—when Miaskovsky abandoned the Association for Contemporary Music of which he had been

a founding member, when he signed a declaration calling for a new grouping of creative musicians. Non-political in the past, Miaskovsky did some reading of Marx and became more acutely aware of social and political trends.

No such problems beset the younger generation, those born around 1906, among them Shostakovich and Kabalevsky. They were not luke-warm towards the Revolution—they were unquestioningly dedicated to its goals and ideals, for they belonged to the first generation edu-cated under the Soviet system. This unconcerned, unproblematic nonchalance is the immediate asset of the First Symphony of Shostako-vich which, in 1926, catapulted the nineteen-year-old conservatory student into world fame. Shostakovich had studied at the Leningrad Conservatory since 1919, first piano, then composition. The Symphony was his graduation piece, though he continued at the Conservatory as a post-graduate student. The work bears the opus number 10, for he had started to compose seriously at the age of fifteen, in 1921. His teacher Maximilian Steinberg was proud of the fact that the symphony was written "at the Conservatory"—meaning, under his supervision—and he was distressed when Shostakovich, in 1936, declared that "he was hindered in composing" while he was a student. Whatever the case, Shostakovich's First Symphony is touched by genius. It speaks the language of youth with the skill of age; it reveals, in a composer not yet twenty, a fully formed personality, able to balance inspiration and technique.

Six months after the success of his First Symphony, Shostakovich startled Leningrad with his newest work, the Piano Sonata Opus 12, which he named *October*.* On 2 December 1926 he performed the work himself at a concert of the Association for Contemporary Music. It proved to be a rather wild, expressionistic piece, full of aggressive dissonance and angular linearity, showing the young composer on the road towards a far more modern musical idiom. Undoubtedly he was influenced by the Western avant-garde, particularly Hindemith, Krenek, and Toch whose works were just then becoming known in Soviet musical circles. Was it imitation, was it inner necessity? His former teacher Steinberg saw mainly the outside influences,

"On leaving the Conservatory, Shostakovich came under the influence of people who believed in the musical principles of the

* The subtitle *October* does not appear in the printed version of the Sonata, perhaps to avoid confusion with the Second Symphony, sub-titled *To October*. However, the turbulent mood of the Piano Sonata suggests the spirit of rev-olutionary October.

'extremist' West. This was in 1925... One of his first compositions
was the Piano Sonata, written in contemporary idiom, which he called *October Symphony*.* Already there was the unhealthy trend to 'adapt' the formalist idiom for the expression of revolutionary ideas."[32]

Shostakovich's "Storm and Stress" period—as we may call it—lasted
until about 1936, for almost ten years. It led to the official censure in
1936 when *Pravda* published the now historic denunciation, "Chaos
instead of Music".

Shostakovich's "new style" permeated his Second and Third Symphonies which failed to match the success of his First. Soviet historians
brand these two works as youthful formalistic aberrations; the composer
himself expressed his dissatisfaction in later years. Yet, flawed though
the Symphonies Nos. 2 and 3 may be, they cannot be simply dismissed
as a creative error, for—in truth—they are symbols of a confused and
turbulent time. Both were written in the late 1920's, at the height of the
musical feud between "modernists" and "proletarians". Shostakovich's
symphonies absorbed elements of both—but instead of achieving a
fusion, these elements seem to co-exist in these strangely hybrid works.

The Second Symphony (1927) is entitled *To October: A Symphonic
Dedication*, the Third (1929) is called *The First of May*. Both are cast in a
one-movement form, introducing a chorus at the end. The texts are
contemporary revolutionary poems that help clarify the message of the
symphonies. (For this reason, any performance omitting the chorus, as
was done in Philadelphia in 1932 or in London in 1962 is meaningless.)
While the setting of the words is straightforward and direct, the purely
instrumental parts of the symphonies are extremely complex, dissonant,
and at times intentionally cerebral. However, this idiom was found
timely when these symphonies were first heard, in 1927 (No. 2) and
1930 (No. 3). For once, the modernist as well as the proletarian critics
agreed that the idea of the Revolution was presented with dynamic and
explosive sweep. The theatrical, declamatory style was found justifiable; the aural harshness seemed to disturb no one. Asafiev referred to
the Third (*May*) Symphony as "the birth of the symphony out of the
dynamism of revolutionary oratory".

But as Soviet musical aesthetics changed in the 1930's, so did the
evaluation of Shostakovich's "revolutionary" symphonies: they were
discarded for almost thirty years as symbols of "formalism". As late as
1956, we can read in the semi-official *History of Soviet Russian Music*
that, at the time, Shostakovich was "imprisoned by bourgeois-
modernistic influences, with a strange admixture of 'rapmovski'†

---

* See footnote on page 79.
† Influenced by the proletarian RAPM (see p. 49).

schematicism". As for the Second (*October*) Symphony, "its extremely complex character . . . the anti-melodism, the intentional harshness of sound transform the music into cacophony which is deprived of all artistic value."[33]

Ten years later, in 1966, Keldysh—the dean of Soviet musicologists—wrote in an equally semi-official History, "At times (especially in the Second Symphony) one is reminded of the most involved examples of modern linearism, at times of the brain-twisting contrapuntal edifices of the old Flemish School."[34] Keldysh felt that this "intentional cerebralism" negated the avowed purpose of the music—a hymn to "The Great October and its inspirer, Lenin".

But younger Soviet historians, for example, Orlov, try to re-evaluate the controversial symphonies of Shostakovich in the light of their turbulent times and customs—the choral declamations accompanied by rhythm orchestras, the musico-theatrical, poster-like spectacles on revolutionary topics, the intrusion of cinematic techniques by the use of quick-changing "frames". All these elements needed time to fuse into a new style. In the meantime, says Orlov, "the Second and Third Symphonies of Shostakovich are, in many respects, significant for that stage in the evolution of Soviet symphonism without which its further development would have been impossible".[35]

Lest one believes that all criticism is an outgrowth of Stalinist evil, it is useful to remember that Western critical opinion was, at best, divided as to the musical value of Shostakovich's two "ideological" symphonies. The American critic Lawrence Gilman called the *May Day* Symphony "brainless and trivial music"[36] when it was first played in New York's Carnegie Hall in January 1933, again without the "propagandistic" final chorus. Gerald Abraham, an authority on Russo-Soviet music, wrote in 1943, on the same symphony, "One cannot help feeling that the composer is playing a part . . . He tries to be Marxian, but fantastic Gogolian humour keeps breaking in. A stranger hotch-potch of commonplace, bad taste and misdirected cleverness has never been called a symphony."[37]

Others were kinder, but they were in a minority. Calvocoressi, for example, another Russian specialist, found the music of the Third Symphony remarkable for its freshness and brightness, for its abundance of ideas and the power of its drive. To him, the programme of the symphony was obvious, and its special purpose was never out of sight. To less sympathetic critics, the same work was "not primarily an aesthetic experience but an utterance of political and economic faith".[38] Leopold Stokowski, who conducted the Philadelphia and New York premières of the Third, took it as a work "written to a Bolshevik programme" and as such "completely radical" though not necessarily from the musical point of view. He heard in it passages "suggesting the march of the Soviet armies", even possibly the "hum of industry".[39] Russian commentators recognized in it certain melodic idioms reminiscent of youth and "pioneer" songs of that time.

Actually, aside from their ideological bond, the Second and the Third Symphonies of Shostakovich are quite dissimilar. Musically, the Second is more radical, more daring, obviously influenced by some Western techniques, such as Milhaud's "horizontal" or linear counterpoint. At one point there are thirteen autonomous voices moving in canon, without regard to any perceptible tonality. Shostakovich uses polyrhythm, polytonality, he conjures organized chaos, industrial music until a factory whistle (in F-sharp) sets the stage for the final chorus. The basses begin with the sombre words,

> "We marched, we asked for work and bread,
> Our hearts were gripped by pain and grief,
> The factory chimneys were stretched to the sky,
> Like hands too weak to clench a fist."

The first full-throated climax is reached with the outcry,

> "Lenin! Our destiny is FIGHT"

Here, the Russian word "bor'ba" (fight) is set in a sharply accentuated rhythm. At the end, the chorus is identified with the masses: men and women declaim, rather than sing, the final words "October, The Commune, Lenin."

There is, essentially, a sombre mood about the Second Symphony. Perhaps the composer thought of it as leading from Chaos to Light, from Suffering to Victory. The musical texture is dense, involved, with few points of repose. There is obviously a deliberate break with convention, a complete negation of the traditional technique of thematic development. Shostakovich never repeats a theme, neither in its original form nor transformed; he even avoids repeating a motive or melodic fragment. Every measure has to be new, freshly invented. It is a youthful *tour de force*.

Contrasting in mood, the *May Day* Symphony (No. 3) is a work of exuberant gaiety, a hymn to joy, to spring, to solidarity among workers. There is far less dissonance than in its predecessor, the *October*, and the writing is largely diatonic. Although the over-all design is in one movement, one can discern four or five subdivisions or sections, thematically unrelated to each other. The symphony has been called a "symphonic divertimento"; again there is virtually no thematic development and the composer prefers to work with an abundance of episodic material. The gay mood is punctuated by a lot of percussion;

in fact, the single unifying element seems to be a persistent rhythm—a longer note followed by two short notes—that has remained one of Shostakovich's favourite rhythmic devices.

Preceding the final choral section are instrumental recitatives set against a continuous drum roll: one can think of orators exhorting the masses. The choral part is brief and full-throated; the dynamics range from forte to fortissimo and the emotional pitch is ever-rising. A climax is reached with the words,

> "Hoisting the flags in the sun
> A march resounds in our ears
> Every First of May
> A step closer to Socialism."

A strong orchestral coda, led by a triumphant trumpet, concludes the work on a note of victory. In shaping the choral finale, with its introductory instrumental recitatives and brisk ending, Shostakovich seems to recall Beethoven's Ninth Symphony. He reached for the unreachable, but he was too young to realize it.

Was Shostakovich, as Gerald Abraham suggests, really "playing a part"? Perhaps, but if so, certainly subconsciously. For there is an aura of incorruptible sincerity about Shostakovich which does not admit any sham. He believed in what he was doing: "There can be no music without an ideology . . ." He said this in 1931, to a woman reporter from *The New York Times* who visited him in Leningrad. She described him as "a pale young man, withthe tremulous lips and hands and the manners of a bashful schoolboy".[40] But behind that bashful look—which he never lost—was a disciplined mind, a roaming imagination, and a self-critical honesty that would not permit shabbiness, musical or otherwise.

Many other symphonies were written in the 1920's though none could match the depth of Miaskovsky or the ingenuity of Shostakovich.

In Leningrad, Vladimir Shcherbachev—appointed professor of composition at the Conservatory in 1923—occupied a position similar in importance to that of Miaskovsky in Moscow. But while Miaskovsky was circumspect and methodical, Shcherbachev was impulsive and improvisational. Miaskovsky was rooted essentially in Russian classicism, while Shcherbachev was more Western-oriented, towards Scriabin, Mahler, and Richard Strauss. The Second Symphony of Shcherbachev, composed in the years 1922–26, is a monumental work in five parts, using texts by the great poet, Alexander Blok, which are set for solo voices and chorus. The poems, selected by the composer,

are predominantly dark and pessimistic in mood; at times, as in the
Finale, the chorus sings wordlessly, adding a sinister colour to the
orchestra. The entire work resembles more an oratorio than a symphony. It is one of those grandiose failures, mentioned admiringly in
histories as a milestone, yet unperformed and only dimly remembered.
Shcherbachev's next Symphony (No. 3) was begun in 1926, allegedly
under the impact of Shostakovich's First Symphony; it is a purely
instrumental work of a more positive, optimistic character. Despite an
admiring analysis by Asafiev, however, the Third Symphony—following its première in 1931—did not establish itself permanently in the
symphonic repertoire though, in the opinion of some historians, the
neglect is unjust.

Too much grandiosity also impaired the effectiveness of Yuri
Shaporin's Symphony for orchestra with chorus, composed in the years
1926-32 and first performed in 1933. The epic concept was to portray
the grandeur of Russia, past and present, a kind of immense historic
fresco. The result, however, was—to quote Gerald Abraham's witticism—"Borodin inflated to the dimensions of Mahler".[41] Nor did the
Soviet critics appreciate Shaporin's efforts to sound "contemporaneous"
by introducing revolutionary tunes and even a brass band playing the
well-known *Budyonny March*; the work was found "static" and
unconvincing, ideologically as well as musically.

The process of transformation of the "Russian" symphony into the
"Soviet" symphony has intrigued various historians, among them
Asafiev who wrote that it was "as yet very difficult to establish with
any kind of exactitude the development of content and form leading
from the past Russian 'intelligentsia' symphony to the Soviet symphony,
i.e. the emergence of an unmistakeably new quality in music".[42]
Unquestionably, the transformation began in the 1920's when the
"old" and the "new" genres existed side by side. A few symphonic
works—by Miaskovsky, Shcherbachev, Shaporin—straddle the line;
while rooted in the past, they courageously face the present, however
strange and unsettling it may be.

We have mentioned the "actualization" of the symphonic genre, a
process actively encouraged by Lunacharsky's initiative. Among the
works commissioned by his Commissariat were the *Agricultural Symphony* by Alexander Kastalsky (1923), the *Symphonic Monument 1905-
1917* by Mikhail Gnessin (1925), the *Mourning Ode to Lenin* by Alexander Krein (1926), and the *October* Symphony by Shostakovich (1927).
The "concreteness" of revolutionary content was enhanced by the use
of such melodies as the *International*, the *Varshavianka*, and the *Workers'
Funeral March* ("Vy zhertvoyu pali"). When, some thirty years later,
Shostakovich turned to "programme" symphonies such as the Eleventh

and the Twelfth Symphonies, he used similar techniques and even some of the same tunes, though with far greater discretion and skill.

At times, the exploitation of the "Soviet topicality" seems rather crude, as in the *Symphonic Dithyrambus* by Krein (1932), subtitled "The USSR—the Shock Brigade of the World Proletariat". Set for narrator, bass choir, collective declamation, and orchestra, it represents an ideological and musical hodge-podge during which the narrator reads excerpts from Stalin's speech "On the Tasks of Economists". When the musico-political trend became too obvious, it was rebuffed; such was the case of the *Hymn to Labour* (1927) by Ippolitov-Ivanov who was criticized for adapting the "good old times" to modern use.

That such music was not limited to the circle of "proletarian" musicians is proved by the activities of the ACM, the modernistic association. In honour of the Tenth Anniversary of the October Revolution, on 4 December 1927, the ACM sponsored a concert with the following programme (all premières): Second (*October*) Symphony by Shostakovich, Suite from the ballet *Steel* by Alexander Mossolov, *Prologue* by Lev Polovinkin, and the cantata *October* by Nikolai Roslavetz. A few days earlier, at a concert of PERSIMFANS, the symphonic rhapsody *October* by Joseph Schillinger was played.★ All these works were written in a modernist idiom—at times neo-classical, at times constructivist, yet all were dedicated to the celebration of the Revolution. As yet no artistic group had a monopoly on *October*!

Among the last-named composers, two demand our attention: Mossolov and Roslavetz. In the late 1920's, Alexander Mossolov was considered a young composer of tremendous promise who had won quick international acclaim. His early fame was based on a brief orchestral piece, *The Iron Foundry* (actually "Zavod", meaning Factory). It was a "symphonic episode" from a projected ballet, *Steel*, that was not staged. The piece is a picturization of industrial noises, musically rather primitive, yet very effective in its motoric rhythm and churning drive. The prototype of such "mechanistic" pieces was probably Honegger's *Pacific 231*, a huge international success in 1924. In Soviet Russia, the fad of such constructivist music became very popular in the late 1920's, but none was as highly acclaimed as Mossolov's *Iron Foundry*, called "a mighty hymn to machine work" by one Soviet critic,[43] a symbol of the enthusiasm of Socialist industrialization. Today, the same work is assailed as a "grossly formalistic perversion of a contemporary topic" and is vilified at every turn by Soviet historians.[44]

★ Schillinger emigrated to the United States in 1929 and settled as a successful teacher of composition in New York where he died in 1943. *The Schillinger Method of Musical Composition* (published posthumously in 1946) describes his system of mathematically controlled composition.

But *The Iron Foundry* was played around the world, hammering the bourgeois audiences into masochistic submission with its pitiless "Bolshevik barbarism". This piece, a symbol of the technological *Zeitgeist*, was even staged in 1932 at the Hollywood Bowl. Established as an international celebrity, Mossolov was accepted as musical representative of the new Russia, and two of his works were performed at the International Festivals of the ISCM—his String Quartet in 1927 at Frankfurt-am-Main and *The Iron Foundry* in 1930 at Liège; the score of the latter was also printed in Vienna. Mossolov's career was cut short in 1936 when he was expelled from the Composers' Union, allegedly for drunken brawls. He continued to compose and was eventually reinstated, but never regained a significant role.

While Mossolov is still remembered and listed in Soviet histories, the name of Nikolai Roslavetz has been completely expunged. If his name happens to be mentioned, it is either with venom or ridicule for having aspired to be a "Russian Schoenberg". Roslavetz was a dedicated Communist with leftist convictions, close to the original PROLETKULT. He vented his radical ideas in various essays in the mid-twenties, and his opinions earned him the enmity of virtually everybody except a small group of extreme modernists. Roslavetz considered classical Russian music as an "outgrowth of a feudal culture" which deserved to be swept aside by the Revolution. "Russian musical culture—still unsteady, still without strong roots—was completely routed by October," he wrote in 1924.[45]

As a composer, Roslavetz was a rebel as early as 1912 when he completed his courses at the Moscow Conservatory. His Violin Sonata of 1913 is the first atonal work by a Russian composer, and his String Quartet No. 3 of 1920 employs a "tone row" technique. Following his own theories—independent of both Scriabin and Schoenberg—Roslavetz worked towards the dissolution of tonality and the substitution of other principles. However, his works—among them a Violin Concerto in 1925—found only limited response. Eventually, he seemed to relent in his doctrinaire approach: the cantata *October* (1927) used a "somewhat too sentimental idiom and orchestral means reminiscent of Strauss and Wagner".[46] In the 1930's, Roslavetz wrote lighter theatre music; he then accepted an invitation to Tashkent where he switched to folk music in Uzbek style and composed the first national Uzbek opera.

All music dictionaries published in the West speculate that Roslavetz was banished from Moscow and that he disappeared without trace in the wake of the political purges of the 1930's. Perhaps he moved to Tashkent to escape political reprisals. But according to private information his death occurred in Moscow on 23 August 1944. Be this as it may, he is a forgotten man as far as Soviet music history is concerned, and no effort has been made to rehabilitate him in his own land. Abroad, there is growing interest in Roslavetz—and other avant-garde composers of the 1920's—and he is now recognized as one of the important pioneers in the evolution of non-tonal serial music.[47]

Musical research in Russia was well established over a century before the word *muzykoznanie* (musicology) was coined. The first collection of Russian folk music was published in 1790, edited by Ivan Prach with the assistance of Nikolai Lvov; it served Beethoven as source for Russian themes. In the earlier nineteenth century, Russia had noted authors on music who established a European reputation— Vladimir Odoyevsky, Alexander Ulybyshev (also spelled Oulibicheff), and Wilhelm von Lenz. A chair for music history and aesthetics was established at the St. Petersburg Conservatory in 1865; the first professor was Alexander Famintzyn. In 1866, Nikolai Kashkin was appointed to teach music history at the newly established Moscow Conservatory. The noted experts on Russian church music and the old notation—Dmitri Razumovsky and Stepan Smolensky—taught there as well. In the second half of the nineteenth century, Vladimir Stasov, Alexander Serov, and Herman Laroche built their reputations as keen critics and essayists. Nikolai Findeisen founded the *Russian Musical Gazette* in 1894, a publication that served as forum for serious musical debate until 1918. In the early twentieth century, several associations based in St. Petersburg and Moscow were dedicated to the cultivation of musical knowledge.

Yet, musicology as an independent musical discipline lacked formal recognition; there was no uniform method or approach. A decisive change occurred in 1921 when the Soviet Government established two research centres—the Russian Institute of Arts History* in Petrograd and the State Institute for Musical Science** in Moscow. The remarkable efflorescence of Soviet musicology can be traced in a large measure to the work of these institutes which have survived many vicissitudes and are still active creatively today.

Lunacharsky was primarily responsible for the establishment of the institutes. His close adviser was Asafiev, the dynamic composer-historian-critic. As a historian, Asafiev was primarily interested in the

---

* "Russkii (from 1924 Gosudarstvennyi) Institut Istorii Iskusstv (abbreviated RIII, later GIII).

** "Gosudarstvennyi Institut Muzykalnoy Nauki" (abbreviated GIMN).

exploration of Russia's musical past. In his essay *Nash Dolg* (Our Duty), written in 1918, published in 1920, he issued a call to collect everything pertaining to the life and work of Russian musicians, "It is the duty of every person active in Russian music, to explore all possibilities to search, collect, classify, and find ways and means to publish even raw materials touching upon the past of our music."[1]

With such an appeal, backed by Asafiev's personal work and a devoted circle of disciples, it is not surprising that Soviet Russia has provided—and is continuing to provide—the most exhaustive series of publications concerning Russian music: complete works editions, letters, diaries, and archival materials. But Asafiev's appeal would have been a cry in the wilderness, had it not been for officials like Lunacharsky and his successors who supported the musicological projects by government-sponsored publications and the provision of a staff of experts.

The Petrograd Institute (RIII) had its beginnings in pre-revolutionary years. In 1912, Count Zubov opened his private arts library to the public, and courses were offered there beginning in 1913. In 1916, it was recognized as an institution of higher learning. After the Revolution, Zubov's institute was nationalized and reorganized. Four divisions were established—fine arts, theatre, linguistics, and music. The academic work of the music department opened formally on 19 February 1920 with a lecture on Russian secular music by Sergei Liapunov. A committee headed by Alexander Glazunov, then director of the Conservatory, was charged to recommend a curriculum and a faculty. Selected as subjects for research and instruction were the history of music—general and Russian—, acoustics and tone psychology, musical aesthetics, and musical theory. The faculty consisted of experts in every field, some of whom also taught at the Conservatory. Sergei Bulich, a distinguished philologist and historian, was named dean; among the faculty members were Asafiev, Karatygin, Liapunov, Maximilian Steinberg, Antoni Preobrazhensky, and Alexander Ossovsky.

After Bulich's death in 1921, Asafiev was elected dean of the music division, to be known under the abbreviated name RITM,* later changed to OTIM.** He attracted a number of post-graduate students and younger associates. Among them were several future leaders of Soviet musicology—Roman Gruber, Semyon Ginzburg, Alexei Finagin, Ivan Sollertinsky, Yuri Tyulin, Mikhail Druskin, Arnold Alshvang, and Anatol Butzkoi. Asafiev gave new impetus to the work of his group;

* "Razryad istorii i teorii muzyki" (Division of History and Theory of Music).

** "Otdel teorii i istorii muzyki" (Department of Theory and History of Music).

the research acquired cohesion of thought and method, bearing the indelible imprint of the leader's personality. He directed the group's research towards Russian music of the late eighteenth and early nineteenth centuries—the pre-Glinka period hitherto little explored. The discoveries made in the course of these studies threw a new light on Russia's musical past and paved the way for a fresh approach to the history of Russian music.

Not content with the past, Asafiev also organized a study group concerned with modern music, reflecting the wide range of his musical interests. As a result, two concert series of "New Music" were given in 1924 and 1925; explanatory brochures were published at the same time. These activities led, as we have seen, to the establishment of the Leningrad Association for Contemporary Music.

Asafiev preached the gospel of "living" musicology, of research related to contemporary life. He discouraged any retreat into an "ivory tower" by making his young musicology students aware of their social responsibilities. Research was important, but no less important was the popularization of music, the task of musical education in the schools. Asafiev shaped Soviet musicology in his own, wide-range image, and he established a tradition that balanced the study of the past with an awareness of the present. This—until today—is the profile of Soviet musicology, moulded through trial and error by one dynamic personality—Asafiev.

During the first years of the Petrograd Institute, the Soviet government did not interfere in the curriculum. Gradually, there was pressure to include sociological studies. This led, in 1924, to the establishment of a special commission for sociological research in the arts. Gruber offered the first lecture series, "Dialectical Materialism and Contemporary Musicology", while Semyon Ginzburg lectured on "Sociological Influences in Musicology".

As to publications, the Petrograd Arts Institute fared less well. During the early 1920's, economic conditions were extremely strained, and the printing presses were unable to fulfil the excessive demands made upon them. In 1923, the Institute established its own printing outlet, *Academia*, but musicology—being one of the youngest disciplines—was not among the favoured subjects. For years, much valuable research had to remain unpublished; for example, *Music and Musical Life in Old Russia* (Muzyka i muzykalnyi byt staroi Rossii) was ready for print in 1923 but was not published until 1927. Though a slim volume—a sequel was planned but did not appear—it contained the collective research on pre-Glinka music done in 1921–22 and proved of far-reaching importance.

The publication, in 1924, of Preobrazhensky's book *Liturgical Music in Russia* (Kultovaya Muzyka v Rossii) was all the more valuable because it dealt with a subject that was increasingly neglected in view of the atheist policies of the regime. Preobrazhensky died in 1929; one of his students, Maxim Brazhnikov, active in Leningrad, is today the lone expert in the field of old church chant.

Another faculty member of the Institute, Karatygin—who died in 1925—was honoured by a volume devoted to his life and his activities as a critic and protagonist of modern music. It appeared in 1927 but was unavailable for decades because Karatygin's fight on behalf of the musical avant-garde of his time was out of step with official policy during the Stalin regime.

Among the earliest volumes to appear under the Institute's imprint were, quite significantly, two translations of German musicological publications, done by students of Asafiev under his editorship; they were the *Tabellen zur Musikgeschichte* by Arnold Schering and the *Geschichte der Oper* by Hermann Kretzschmar. Asafiev also contributed much material to the prestigious *Musik-Lexikon* by Hugo Riemann. Maintaining his interest in Western musicology, Asafiev translated and expanded the *History of Music* by the Swiss scholar Karl Nef (1930). Leningrad's musicologists received a signal tribute from the German journal, *Melos*, which devoted an entire issue (1926 No. 6) to the research work done at OTIM, the Institute's music division. In fact, international journals began to pay increasing attention to the musicological research done in Leningrad and Moscow.[2]

No report on Asafiev's achievements at the Leningrad Institute would be complete without mentioning the yearbook *De Musica* of which three issues appeared in 1925, 1926, and 1927.* A fourth issue was published in 1928 under a changed name, *Muzykoznanie*, but the format and direction remained the same. By then, the music division had over thirty staff members, and twenty-three authors made scholarly contributions to the volumes. The contents are wide-ranging— from old church chant and ancient Hebrew psalmody to Scriabin's colour theories and quarter-tone music. Several important articles dealt with the sociological aspects of music. Lunacharsky personally reviewed the first issue, expressing delight at the progress of the Institute but also criticizing certain sociological deductions made in an essay by Gruber. Clearly Lunacharsky favoured a musico-sociological

---

* A similar collection of essays, under the same name *De Musica*, edited by Asafiev (Glebov), had appeared in 1923 under the imprint of the Petrograd Philharmonic. The contributors belonged to the same circle of Asafiev disciples —Gruber, Ginzburg, Finagin, and Boris Zotov. Asafiev himself contributed two essays.

study in depth and hoped for the development of a "Marxist musicology". On the whole, he found Asafiev's progress towards that goal encouraging.[3]

While the Petrograd Institute had the advantage of an established educational framework—the pre-revolutionary Zubov Institute—the Moscow Institute had to be built from the ground up. Such pre-revolutionary institutions as had existed in Moscow—for example, the Society for Natural Science, Anthropology, and Ethnography or the Musico-Theoretical Library*—had ceased to function.

After the October Revolution, Moscow's musical intelligentsia gathered around the Music Division (MUZO) of Lunacharsky's Commissariat of Education. On 1 November 1921 the State Institute for Musical Science (GIMN) was officially established in Moscow although meetings had already begun in September of that year. It soon became the focal point of musical research. However, GIMN's independence lasted only a few years. In 1923, the Moscow Academy for Arts Sciences (GAKHN) formed a music division. In order to avoid duplication with work done at GIMN, the latter was incorporated into the Arts Academy, though with some internal autonomy. The division of responsibilities was not always clear; it would seem that, for a time, the "Music Sector" of GAKHN and the "incorporated" GIMN continued to function side by side. GAKHN, as the parent organization, assumed the responsibility for broader cultural areas of music history and theory, while GIMN concentrated on musico-technical matters such as musical acoustics, tone psychology, pedagogy, and ethno-musicology.

In contrast to the Petrograd Institute where, under the guidance of Asafiev, a veritable "school of musicology" arose, very little—if any—teaching was done at the Moscow Institute. From the very beginning, the stress in Moscow was on research and publication. There was less flamboyance than in Leningrad, and more theoretical introspection. The first dean of GIMN was Nikolai Garbuzov, a distinguished theorist and specialist in acoustics. On the staff were noted music historians and critics—Mikhail Ivanov-Boretzky, Konstantin Kuznetsov, and the controversial Leonid Sabaneyev, as well as the eminent theorist Boleslav Yavorsky, author of the theory of "Modal Rhythm" (Ladovoi Ritm).

The Moscow Arts Institute issued a bulletin, *Iskusstvo* (Art), which occasionally printed shorter essays on music. In 1923 it contained contributions by Yavorsky and Sabaneyev, in 1925 by Lunacharsky and Kuznetzov, in 1927 by Victor Belayev and Ivanov-Boretzky. That

---

* The valuable library was eventually incorporated into the library of the Moscow Conservatory.

GAKHN was receptive to modern trends is proven by the fact that it assumed the sponsorship for the Moscow Association for Contemporary Music founded in 1923. In fact, Belayev's essay of 1927 dealt with "New Trends in Contemporary Western Music".

But the most valuable contribution published by the Moscow Institute was a series of four volumes under the general heading *History of Russian Music in Research and Materials* (Istoria Russkoi Muzyki v issledovaniakh i materialakh). The first volume (1924) was a collection of articles by various authors on topics ranging from Old Russian Church Music to Prokofiev, from the relationship of Tolstoy with Tchaikovsky to the Moscow visit of Richard Wagner in 1863. The contents seem less esoteric than the comparable Leningrad anthology *De Musica*: less emphasis was placed on sociology and aesthetics, more on tangible and useful information. The second volume (1925) was devoted entirely to the life and work of Sergei Taneyev, the revered Moscow composer and theorist who had died ten years ealier, in 1915. Volume 3 in the series (1926) was written entirely by Kuznetsov and is entitled *Glinka and his Contemporaries*. In a number of essays, the author examines Glinka' relationship with Western musicians (Field, Mendelssohn, Berlioz) and Russian colleagues (Odoyevsky, Wielhorsky, etc.). The fourth (and last) volume aroused international attention: published in 1927—the Beethoven Memorial Year—it was called *The Russian Book on Beethoven* (Russkaya Kniga o Bethovene). It reflects Russia's unique attitude towards Beethoven which is admiring and possessive. Already in the nineteenth century, Russian musicians were absorbed by Beethoven studies. After the Revolution, a new element was added—the identification of Beethoven's personality and music with revolutionary ideals. This idolization of Beethoven as a revolutionary hero became a Soviet obsession, stimulated by Lunacharsky, Asafiev and many other authors. Yet, *The Russian Book on Beethoven* was not a propagandistic book in the ideological sense; on the contrary, it was deliberately historical which makes it all the more valuable.

The year 1927 also saw the important Russian publication of the so-called "Moscow Sketchbook" of Beethoven. It contains pencilled sketches for the String Quartets Op. 130 and Op. 132 (commissioned by Prince Galitzin). The facsimile was published in the journal *Muzykalnoye Obrazovanie* (1927 Nos. 1–2), with annotations by Ivanov-Boretzky. At the Beethoven Centenary Celebration held in Vienna in 1927, Ivanov-Boretzky gave a lecture on the "Moscow Sketchbook" and published several articles on this subject in Western music journals. At present, the "Moscow Sketchbook" is kept at the Glinka Museum in Moscow, together with another Beethoven sketchbook named after its previous owner, Wielhorsky.[4]

A characteristic of the multifaceted intellectual life of the 1920's was the profusion of printing presses sponsored by various educational institutions or related organizations. We have already mentioned the Leningrad Arts Institute with its *Academia* imprint. Modern music was served in Leningrad by the *Triton* imprint sponsored mainly by the Association for Contemporary Music. The Leningrad Philharmonic, too, printed its own materials. Somehow, Asafiev, usually under his pen name Ivor Glebov, was involved in all these enterprises. In Moscow, the Arts Academy, the Conservatory, even the conductorless orchestra PERSIMFANS had their own publications, not only books but also pamphlets and journals. All this led to a colourful, though fragmented intellectual picture, but most of the new journalistic ventures were short-lived. All the printing had the earmarks of austerity—soft covers, brittle paper, bindings that fell apart after one reading. But the intellectual message came across—blazing, aggressive, controversial, refreshingly different from the stale conformity that was to engulf Soviet cultural life after 1932.

Towering above all smaller enterprises was the State Publishing House and its Music Sector (often referred to under its abbreviated name MUZGIZ). Working slowly but methodically (and undoubtedly with greater financial resources), the State Publishing House brought out some sumptuous publications. Among them was the monumental *Essays on the History of Music in Russia from the Oldest Times until the End of the Eighteenth Century* (Ocherki ob istorii muzyki v Rossii s drevneishykh vremen do kontza XVIII veka) by Nikolai Findeisen. Born in 1868, Findeisen was the Nestor of Russian musicology, and the publication of his *magnum opus* occurred in the year of his death, 1928. The two volumes, lavishly illustrated, were the sum-total of forty years of assiduous work, and they are considered a most valuable contribution to the study of Russian music history.

Also in 1928 began the monumental enterprise of the Complete Works Edition of Mussorgsky, under the editorial supervision of Paul (Pavel) Lamm assisted by Asafiev and other experts. After the publication of six volumes the edition was abandoned in 1939 and remained incomplete. The 1920's were a period of international agitation for the restoration of Mussorgsky's original versions, particularly of *Boris Godunov*. In Soviet Russia, the fight was carried mainly by Asafiev and Victor Belayev. The fiftieth anniversary of Mussorgsky's death, in 1931, saw the publication of several volumes of his letters, documents, and scholarly studies; among the editors were Andrei Rimsky-Korsakov, a son of the composer, and Yuri Keldysh. Strangely enough, the initial enthusiasm for "restoring" Mussorgsky died down, the implied criticism of the editorial work of Nikolai Rimsky-Korsakov, done after Mussorgsky's early death, became muted, and at present the Rimsky-Korsakov editions of *Boris Godunov* and other works are in general use in the Soviet Union.

Among other publications of the 1920's, the three-volume *General History of Music* (Vseobshchaya Istoria Muzyki, 1922–27) by Yevgeni Braudo should be mentioned; it was followed, in 1928 by his shorter *History of Music* in one volume. Braudo, who belonged to the Asafiev circle, approached history as a Marxist, but his interpretation was criticized for alleged sociological over-simplifications or, to use the Soviet expression, "vulgar sociology".

Asafiev (alias Glebov) kept up his incredible productivity with three books published within two years: the *Book on Stravinsky* (1929), *Russian Music from the Beginning of the Nineteenth Century*, and *Musical Form as a Process* (both 1930). Each has its particular points of excellence, though some of his views were soon to be challenged.

Least controversial was his book *Russian Music*—an elegantly written history, arranged not chronologically but by genres, i.e. Opera, Folksong, Instrumental Music, and so on. Asafiev avoids dry academicism and offers many fresh viewpoints. It is a survey, not a textbook, and appears rather summary at times. But he could afford this condensed approach since he had published many scholarly studies on the subjects touched upon in the book. Incidentally, it is the only major work by Asafiev translated into English.

Asafiev's *Book on Stravinsky*, written over a period of years during the 1920's, reflects his intense involvement in the music of his time. While he is not uncritical of Stravinsky, he analyzes his development and achievements in a perceptive and sympathetic way. At the same time, Asafiev speaks with such unrestrained enthusiasm about certain aspects of modern music, that the book became unacceptable in terms of Stalinist aesthetics; it was never reprinted. In later years, Asafiev retracted some of his earlier views.

His theoretical treatise, *Musical Form as a Process*, came also under attack and remained a controversial issue for decades. It was even excluded from the posthumous edition of his *Selected Works* (1952–57), and a reprint of this important book had to wait until 1963. In the meantime, a companion volume, *Intonation*, was published in 1947 and found full acceptance; in fact, Asafiev's concept of "intonation" and its germinal role in music became a mainstay of Soviet theoretical thought.*

In contrast to the institutes—newly founded in 1921—the conservatories had a long history of traditions, customs, and time-honoured

* See also p. 125.

methods which resisted any rapid changes. Although Lunacharsky had expressed the need for reforms as early as 1918, at the time of the nationalization, no one among the administrators expected quick action. There was, in addition to bureaucratic slowness, a strong tradition of academic self-rule, and the faculty had considerable power. The retention of the respected directors, Glazunov in Petrograd and Ippolitov-Ivanov in Moscow, seemed to ensure continuity.

Rather than impose reforms from above, the Soviet Government—through Lunacharsky—enlisted the co-operation of "progressive" educators. For it had become obvious that neither the old-style curriculum of the conservatories nor the hurriedly established new music schools could fill the growing needs of the country for performers and teachers, as well as for all-round musicians specifically trained for the task of musical mass education. In this new field, too much professionalism could be ineffectual while, on the other hand, too much amateurism could be disastrous.

An important reform plan, adopted in October 1922, for the Moscow and Petrograd Conservatories had been worked out by faculty committees of both institutions, in collaboration with Lunacharsky's Department of Education. Three levels of instruction were to be established within the conservatory—preparatory, intermediate (also called "technicum"), and "higher learning" (vuz in Russian). Certain principles were enunciated: the task of the conservatories was not to create "narrow specialists" but broadly educated musician-artists capable of responding to the demands of contemporary life and adaptable to practical work. The level of achievement of the Soviet conservatories had to be on a par with the "contemporary development of the musical art of the world, the contemporary stand of European science on music, and the contemporary musico-pedagogical systems and methods".[5] These three important points reflected the desire of the Soviet cultural leaders to be thoroughly up-to-date in matters of methodology, research, and musical style. Such an "international" orientation was characteristic of the 1920's; it was to be abandoned in the 1930's.

An important issue was the proletarization of the student body. The Soviet Government was eager to increase the percentage of students from worker and peasant families. Obviously this process could not be hurried if admission standards were to be maintained, for the applicants from the previously underprivileged classes often lacked the necessary preparation. After an intensive recruiting campaign, a new group of applicants presented themselves in the autumn of 1922; they were selected by KOMSOMOL (the Communist youth group) and similar Party organizations. The examiners of the conservatories, unimpressed, failed almost all of them for reasons of "weak specialized preparation".

Amid general uproar, the Party forced a re-examination, and the proletarian students were admitted, though many were placed in remedial courses. Even after this forced entry, the statistics—from the Party's point of view—were dismal: at the Leningrad Conservatory, out of a total of 1,756 students only thirty-three students had a working-class background.[6]

Another source book furnishes statistical figures somewhat more favourable to the proletariat. Here, the social backgrounds of the Leningrad Conservatory students during 1922–23 are given as follows,[7]

workers	33
peasants	333
bourgeois	1114
gentry	65
functionary	44
clergy	7
honour citizens	125
merchants	3
intellectuals	27
Total	1751*

A re-examination of all registered students took place during the academic year 1922–23. While the report of the Moscow Conservatory speaks only of a placement test in order to redistribute the students according to the three "levels", the Leningrad Conservatory admits that the examination was not only musical but also political. This led to the elimination of a number of students who were "professionally inadequate and particularly reactionary".[8] Those among the faculty who protested were branded as "anti-social", and their protests were disregarded.

At about the same time, the Communist Party cell among students became more active, trying to attract and influence the non-aligned, non-political student. Led by young KOMSOMOL members, the student organization increased its influence, not only in matters affecting student activities, but also in matters of admission, academic standards, curriculum, and faculty. There were clashes between over-zealous students and so-called reactionary professors, not only at the conservatories but in many other institutions of higher learning. Lenin was aware of these "errors" and warned that "in relations with those professors, strangers not belonging to our class, one must pursue a more cautious line".[9]

* The total figure in the source book is given as 1307. Either the addition is wrong or some of the individual figures are incorrect.

The internal squabbles were particularly abhorrent to Glazunov who continued to enjoy the confidence of all the factions. An old-time liberal who had sided with the students in 1905, he suddenly found himself caught between resentful professors and rebellious, often arrogant, students. While Glazunov remained as director until 1928, Ippolitov-Ivanov resigned his directorship of the Moscow Conservatory in 1922.

1925 was an important milestone in the history of the conservatories. In a major revision of the entire music curriculum, the teaching of musicology was transferred from the institutes to the conservatories. From now on, the institutes were to concentrate on research and publications while the conservatories were entrusted with the added responsibility of training musical scholars and theorists.

After long consultations between the faculties and Lunacharsky, the "Statement concerning the Moscow and Leningrad Conservatories" was officially released on 5 December 1925.[10] Already earlier, Lunacharsky had stressed that the educational goal was not only to produce an artist-musician but a citizen, who would not isolate himself from society but share its life. In the new curriculum worked out in conjunction with the "Statement", stress was laid on the socio-political education of the students and their ideological preparation. In terms of the music curriculum, the conservatories were now reorganized into three "faculties": (1) composition and musicology, (2) performance, (3) pedagogy. Musicology included the history and sociology of music, theory, acoustics, and pedagogical methodology. The performing faculty was subdivided into keyboard instruments, orchestral instruments, vocal art, and conducting. The pedagogical faculty included general music education, theory, and musical performance. The length of instruction was set at three years for brass instruments and double bass, four years for woodwinds, harp, singers, and general music education, and five years for all other subjects. No one older than twenty-five could enter the performing faculty. Every student applicant had to undergo a rigorous examination, except the graduates of a so-called RABFAK.* This was a concession to speed the "proletarization" of the student body.

At the same time, the conservatories acquired a post-graduate department—the so-called *aspirantura*, a three-year course leading to the degree of "candidate". The entire re-organization brought the two conservatories—the oldest in the country—closer to the ideal of a "music university" envisaged by their founders, Anton and Nikolai Rubinstein. From now on, the conservatories were to be concerned only with the higher level of musical education.

* See page 26.

To strengthen the scholarly aspect of the curriculum, the Leningrad Conservatory appointed Asafiev to head the new musicology division, though he remained at the Institute. At the Moscow Conservatory, Ivanov-Boretzky was already installed as chief historian. Asafiev was assisted by a group of young pedagogues, mainly his former disciples at the Institute. They brought fresh ideas and a readiness for innovations. Already in 1923, the composer Vladimir Shcherbachev had joined the Leningrad faculty, and with him, modernism had entered the traditional halls of the Conservatory.

The changes in the faculty brought about changes in approach and philosophy. As the ranks of the older members thinned out, younger men entered, with less concern for traditions and with plans to modernize the Conservatory, musically as well as politically. Eventually, a split developed between the old-line "Rimsky-Korsakov group" and the younger faction. Rightly or wrongly, Glazunov considered Asafiev to be the chief trouble-maker. In 1928 he wrote from Paris, "It is very hard for me to part with the faculty members of the performing division with whom I've never had any friction, but the prospect of being in the hands of the composers' faction headed by Asafiev is not to my liking."[11]

A year later, Glazunov, still in Paris, admitted that his "authority as a musician" had decreased. He continued to enjoy the affection and respect of many musicians and government leaders, particularly Lunacharsky, but his musical influence was on the decline. This was not necessarily due to any intrigue, but rather because the ageing master was out of touch with the musical trends of his time. Even Scriabin's late style was alien to him; he once admitted that he could not follow him beyond the Fourth Sonata of 1903. All the more was he unable to comprehend such students of the Leningrad Conservatory as Prokofiev and Shostakovich. He tried to be fair but he could not hide his musical dislike. Technically on leave of absence, Glazunov left the Conservatory in 1928, visited the United States in 1929, and then settled in Paris where he died in 1936, at the age of seventy.

Glazunov's departure did not leave an irreplaceable void. Since the reorganization of 1925, his position had really been that of a figurehead. Each of the faculties enjoyed considerable autonomy. Within the "dual" faculty of composition and musicology, the balance was somewhat delicate: it was headed by a conservative dean, Maximilian Steinberg, yet each department had a progressive director, Shcherbachev in composition, and Asafiev in musicology.

Much controversy was created by the establishment of the special "instructorial-pedagogical" faculty. Its practical purpose was to fill the need for teachers and musical leaders in all fields, from pre-school music to adult appreciation, including guidance work with clubs and amateur groups. Obviously, these eminently practical aims did not require the ultimate artistic finish, but the —often mediocre—level of this particular faculty provoked criticism of the artist teachers who feared a general lowering of standards. Lunacharsky tried to mediate by pointing out, in 1925, that there was a two-fold responsibility—to educate the "most talented creators and virtuosi", as well as to raise the "general level of mass education in the arts". The eminent composer-educator, Ippolitov-Ivanov, former director of the Moscow Conservatory, came to the defence of the new faculty,

> "Our country needs composers, needs artist performers in all specialties and with various qualifications, from the virtuoso to the modest ensemble player and orchestral musician; but at the same time, the country—so backward in musical culture—urgently needs large cadres of pedagogues, musical appreciationists, leaders of music circles in clubs, of musical activities in schools and preschools. This justifies the great attention paid by our professional schools to the instructorial-pedagogical faculties and divisions— new units created after the October Revolution."[12]

The controversies raging within the musical life of Moscow and Leningrad during the mid-1920's—particularly the issue of "modernism" versus "proletarianism"—reached disturbingly into the life of the conservatories. They not only created dissensions among faculty members and among students, but they pitted students against certain teachers. A prime example was the case of the Moscow Conservatory KOMSOMOLS which had to be mediated by Lunacharsky. The militancy of the students had increased with the shift in their social background: by 1925, for example, of the 836 students at the Leningrad Conservatory 172 had a "workers" background and 128 were of peasant origin. The Communist student organization had 300 militant members. This was an enormous increase compared to the status of 1922–23.[13]*

The mood of the students was rebellious, the respect for tradition and professorial authority was weakened. Not only politically but also musically, the students were in search of new solutions and fresh approaches. They were encouraged by Asafiev and other progressive members of the faculty. The old-style pedagogy, jealously guarded by conservative teachers, seemed dry and dogmatic, estranged from the

* See page 97. The lower total number of students can be attributed to the elimination of the preparatory department.

living pulse of music. Modern Western ideas entered through the books of Ernst Kurth, Guido Adler, and Egon Wellesz. The performers were stirred by the "anatomic-physiological" approach of Rudolf Breithaupt (for pianists) and Dr. Friedrich Steinhausen (for string players).

Asafiev himself scorned the canonization of Rimsky-Korsakov's teaching when he spoke sarcastically of the "Petersburgian-bureaucratic chauvinistic academicism which perverted a good harmony book into a 'symbol of faith' ".[14] Soviet authors wrote new textbooks to bring the theory and practice of music closer together, attempting to teach the elements of music on the basis of examples drawn from the works of the great masters. Thus, Tyulin wrote a textbook of harmonic analysis based on the Bach chorales, while *solfeggio* was taught on the basis of Russian and foreign folk songs.

A divisive factor, within faculty and students, was the attitude towards musical modernism. It would be wrong to assume that the conservative faction of professors were *a priori* opposed to all modern trends. On the contrary, when the Leningrad Association for Contemporary Music was formed in 1926, the entire musicological and compositorial faculty joined, including traditionalists like Steinberg, Leonid Nikolayev, and Ossovsky. They considered the ACM as a forum for *all* kinds of new music, while Asafiev and his circle saw contemporaneousness expressed mainly through an ultra-advanced idiom.

At the same time, the Proletarian Musicians (RAPM) were increasingly active and interfered in all phases of musical instruction, trying to shape the academic standards according to their simplistic outlook. Particularly among Moscow conservatory students there was a "leftist" trend towards "collective" work while deprecating the individual talent. An outgrowth of this trend, as we have seen, was the organization PROKOLL (Production Collective).* As usual, Lunacharsky was a moderating influence, trying to placate the young rebels. In a speech in 1925, on "The Foundations of an Artistic Education", he said, "It is highly incorrect—and, from the viewpoint of Communism, almost heretical—to say that we are entering a period of mass life in the sense that we all shall act in masses, that the collective itself, as a complex of individuals, will replace the master himself."[15]

The dissensions within the conservatories reached such proportions that they became the subject of public criticism late in 1928, both in Moscow and Leningrad. With the growth of "proletarian" power in music, pressures and attacks increased; they were directed as much against traditionalism as against modernism. Posing as the strong arm of the Party in musico-ideological matters, the proletarian RAPM

* See p 56.

became a real threat to the existence of the conservatories: between 1930 and 1932 there were serious attempts to dismember the conservatories, to transform them into practical workshops attached to opera theatres, philharmonic orchestras, and so on.

After the All-Russian Musical Conference of 1929, RAPM acquired a virtual musical monopoly, and its simplistic approach, its contempt for tradition and for "abstract formalism" infected government circles. An official journal like *Artistic Education* made the rash demand that young composers stop writing "in the spirit of Rachmaninov and Scriabin" and that performers stop playing "Bach, Beethoven, and Liszt" . . . as being "alien to the proletariat".[16] By then, Lunacharsky had been displaced as head of NARKOMPROS, while Glazunov's absence weakened the traditionalists. Early in 1930, an old Party member, Mashirov, was named director of the Leningrad Conservatory—an incredible appointment considering the fact that Mashirov was not even a musician. A Party boss was also named as head of the Moscow Conservatory, one Pshibyshevsky, who antagonized everybody (except RAPM) by pushing the "leftist" policies. The emphasis at the conservatories shifted from the education of accomplished professionals to the training of leaders and organizers of non-professional musical activities. Under the pretence of the "activization of teaching methods", academic standards tumbled. Students were taught and evaluated collectively on the basis of their record in group work, the so-called "laboratory brigade" approach, while individual examinations were abolished. The performing students were given the task of learning a repertoire that could be readily understood by an untutored audience. Similar directives were issued to the composition classes. The normal learning processes were further disrupted by the ukase that students had to work no less than two hundred hours as labourers during which time their stipends were suspended since they were paid for their work like their fellow workers.[17]

By 1930 and 1931—so Professor Steinberg confided in his diary—there was "real bedlam, threatening the annihilation of professional art and the reduction of everything to complete dilettantism". And Professor Shcherbachev wrote, "The students walk around from class to class and don't know what to do with themselves". The mood of the faculty members was desperate, yet those who dared to protest were dismissed or forced to resign. Teachers could no longer afford to be non-political "fellow-travellers"; as was expressed at the Leningrad Conservatory in 1930, on behalf of the faculty, "All the best forces among the teaching staff cannot fail but go with the Party at the present time . . . Let the Party deal with us as it sees fit . . ."[18]

By this time, the role of the faculty as a self-governing body had come to an end. In line with a Party decision, all institutions of higher learning abandoned academic self-rule in favour of a system of "one-man management" ("yedinonachalie"), and that "one man" was a Bolshevik, regardless of other qualifications. Perhaps this decision was a reaction against the over-permissiveness advocated by an over-zealous faction of the faculty which had led to an erosion of educational discipline.

Obviously, the "leftist" ideologists of the proletarian RAPM had gone too far and pushed too hard. In 1931, NARKOMPROS (though no longer under Lunacharsky's guidance) condemned the "vulgarization" of Marxist concepts concerning the social role of music as well as the general decline in regard for historic tradition and technical mastery. The Conservatories of Moscow and Leningrad were required to report, by 1932, on the progress of reforms made within the institutions. The near-chaotic conditions were brought under control by a decree dated 19 September 1932, "On the Educational Programmes and the Regime in the Higher Schools and Technicums".[19] The innovations of the last few years were annulled, examinations were re-established, academic standards were raised. The crisis of "leftism" had passed, soon to be replaced by Stalinist Party conformity.

The recurrent dissensions and arguments within the conservatories were not necessarily signs of a decline but rather "growing pains", a search for innovation without abandoning tradition. Some of the crises were actually imposed from above, by Party bureaucrats and proletarian dogmatists. But one need only leaf through the pages of the journal *Muzykalnoye Obrazovanie* (Music Education), published under the auspices of the Moscow Conservatory from 1925 to 1930, to realize the high intellectual and musical standards that governed that institution.

An aspect stressed both in Moscow and Leningrad was the activization of students through practical work in the field. Individual performers, chamber groups, and orchestras were sent out to perform in clubs, factories, and outlying districts—to gain experience and to share their talents. The opera studios became increasingly active. Student composers presented their works. Student teachers taught in special schools. Student musicologists wrote programme annotations and delivered introductory lectures. Student folklorists went on expeditions to collect new materials. All this involved the students actively in the social life of their community—making them "citizens" as well as "artists".

Some of the most noteworthy work was accomplished in the Opera Studio of the Leningrad Conservatory. Although Lunacharsky had mentioned the need for such an enterprise as early as 1918, the project did not take shape until 1922 when the students were given the use of the "Large Hall" for opera purposes. They laboured to transform the hall into a suitable theatre; they pumped the basement dry, installed stage and pit, restored curtains and costumes. The first season in 1923 lasted only a month (11 June to 13 July) and offered eleven performances of three full-length operas—Gluck's *Orfeo*, Gounod's *Faust*, and Rimsky-Korsakov's *The Snow Maiden*, in addition to single scenes from Russian operas. The orchestra and chorus were "borrowed", but the following season these duties were assumed by the students. In 1928–29, the Opera Studio gave sixty performances for some 80,000 listeners, not only in their own hall but also in clubs, factories, and cultural centres. International recognition came to the Opera Studio of the Leningrad Conservatory in August 1928 when it offered guest performances at the Salzburg Mozarteum. The repertoire consisted of two Russian operas—*The Stone Guest* by Dargomyzhsky and *Immortal Kashchei* by Rimsky-Korsakov, Mozart's *Bastien et Bastienne*, and an opera by Bernhard Paumgartner, *Die Höhle von Salamanca*.* The Western press comments were very favourable, and there was particular praise for the fusion of acting and singing—a trait characteristic of the Soviet opera style of that time. The Studio proved an invaluable training centre for young singers, conductors, and stage directors. Within a decade, one-third of the ensemble of the Leningrad Maryinsky Theatre and fully one-half of the Malyi Opera Theatre consisted of graduates of the Opera Studio. In order to insure a continuity of work, outstanding student-performers remained at the Studio for a period up to two years after graduation from the Conservatory; these artist-members were called "studiitzy" (a coined word meaning approximately "studioists") to distinguish them from the regular "studenty" (students).

In Moscow, the need for such a studio was, perhaps, less acute since the opera studios of both Stanislavsky and Nemirovich-Danchenko were active. Full opera performances were, however, presented by the opera class. In April 1926 Rimsky-Korsakov's *The Tsar's Bride* was given, with an eighty-piece orchestra and a fifty-five-voice chorus. A year later followed Mozart's *Cosi fan tutte*, and then, in December 1927, Mussorgsky's *Khovanshchina*. In the next few years, only excerpts were given until, in 1933, an Opera Studio was organized as a branch of the Moscow Conservatory.

The student orchestras of the conservatories, though very proficient, did not achieve an independent artistic life. Closest came, perhaps, the

* The première of this work had been given earlier that year in Leningrad (23 April 1928). Paumgartner was the director of the Mozarteum and visited the USSR as conductor of the Mozarteum as recently as 1965.

senior orchestra of the Leningrad Conservatory which gave its initial concert under the name Young Philharmonic Orchestra in May 1928 under the baton of Glazunov. Despite the enthusiasm of the participating students, this independent effort did not develop significantly.

An outgrowth of student ensemble playing was the so-called Beethoven String Quartet of the Moscow Conservatory; the four gifted string players, recent graduates of the Conservatory, gave their first public concert at the end of the 1923–24 academic year and stayed together for over forty years. Until the recent death of the second violinist, the ensemble remained unchanged—Tzyganov and V. Shirinsky, violinists; Borissovsky, viola; and S. Shirinsky, cello. Virtually all the string quartets of Shostakovich were written for the Beethoven Quartet.

In 1927 began the remarkable triumphs of Soviet-trained virtuosi at international competitions. The first Chopin Competition in Warsaw in 1927 was won by Lev Oborin, a recent graduate of the Moscow Conservatory. An honorary mention was awarded to Dmitri Shostakovich, composer-pianist and at that time still a post-graduate student at the Leningrad Conservatory. In the field of virtuoso performance, the traditional training of young Russian players has proved highly beneficial and successful. The fact that each virtuoso is expected, in turn, to devote part of his time to teaching insures the continuance of tradition. This same adherence to tradition is less successful when applied in the creative field; it rather inhibits the young composer. That was one of the complaints of Shostakovich after his graduation. Ultimately, creativity cannot be taught, only skills.

Part III

REGIMENTATION 1932-53

1932 was a crucial year in Soviet history. The first Five-Year Plan was nearly completed, and the partial collectivization of the land had been accomplished, though at the price of incredible hardship. The second Five-Year Plan, inaugurated in 1932, was to stress industrialization and productivity. Masses of people were moved to provide the necessary labour force in far-away regions. There was much idealism among young people assigned to these tasks, but there was also much unrest and discontent aggravated by the famine of 1931–33. The atmosphere was one of crisis.

Returning from Paris in the early summer of 1932, Ehrenburg described the mood at home and the new generation born on the eve of the First World War.

> "Those were extraordinary days; for the second time our country was shaken up by a tornado; but if the first one—during the Civil War years—had seemed elemental . . ., this time collectivization and the laying of the foundations of heavy industry . . . were determined by an exact plan . . . subordinated . . . to the iron laws of necessity".[1] . . . "To them [the new generation], the Tsar, the factory owners, the policemen were abstract notions . . . Observing them closely, I detected many contradictions. The process of democratization of culture is slow and complicated. During the first twenty-five years, culture was broadened at the expense of depth; at the outset, universal literacy led to an intellectual semi-literacy, to over-simplification."[2]

One of the most effective means to mould the minds of this eager generation was through literature—a literature purposeful and controlled. One of Lenin's earliest tenets was the "partyness" of literature; he and his successors considered the printed word of paramount importance while the other arts were subordinate. It was primarily this concern with literature—torn by internal dissent—that brought about the Party Resolution of 23 April 1932, entitled ' 'On the Reconstruction of Literary and Artistic Organizations".[3]

This Resolution has been called historic. It signified the end of an era of flexibility, and inaugurated one of regimentation. It transformed Soviet arts from multiformity to conformity and, ultimately, to uniformity. On the surface, the tone of the Resolution was conciliatory. There were no denunciations of the past; on the contrary, it was stated that "literature and the arts have, in the past few years, exhibited a considerable growth" which was due to the "success of Socialist construction". However, it was found that "the framework of existing proletarian literary-artistic organizations had become too narrow" and that there was danger of sectarianism leading to the alienation of many artists who were otherwise sympathetic to the Socialist cause. Therefore, the Party's Central Committee resolved to "liquidate the Association of Proletarian Writers" and similar artistic organizations. In place of these dissolved groups, single unions were to be established, each containing a Communist faction. Membership was to be open to all artists "upholding the platform of the Soviet regime and striving to participate in Socialist construction". Despite the voluntary aspect of membership, the political climate was such that no artist could afford not to join.

The Resolution of 1932 achieved several purposes: it displaced the rebellious proletarian "leaders" who had outlived their usefulness, it widened the organized circle of artists under the banner of "Socialist construction", and it insured Party control of the new organizations by the built-in "Communist factions". To many artists, who were repelled by the proletarian arrogance of the previous leaders, the Resolution seemed a liberalizing step, and it was received with widespread approval. Little did they realise that they exchanged the dictatorship of a small clique for the control of a super-power—the Soviet government and the bureaucratic machinery of the Party.

At the First All-Union Congress of Soviet Writers, held in 1934, Gorky's presence lent prestige to the keynote address of Andrei Zhdanov, the Party's representative—the same Zhdanov who acquired such notoriety in the cultural purges of the late 1940's. Zhdanov defined the aims of Socialist Realism, "to depict reality in its revolutionary development", and he called for "works attuned to the epoch". A year earlier, in 1933, Gorky had published an essay, *On Socialist Realism*, which is still considered valid as a basic definition of this new concept. Gorky's words are those of an artist, while Zhdanov spoke as a political realist.[4] Stalin, too, made a contribution to the definition of that elusive term: he mentioned "cultures, national in form and Socialist in substance".

The Writers' Congress—coming as it did two short years after the Resolution and the establishment of the Writers' Union—was a festive occasion. For two weeks, Moscow was the meeting place of Soviet writers from all over the country and prominent guests from the West. "The Congress has remained in my memory as a great and marvellous festival," wrote Ehrenburg. "The crowded hall was like a theatre: ovations greeted favourite authors, felicitous speeches elicited applause." Among the speakers were Pasternak, Isaac Babel, Fadeyev, Malraux and Aragon from France, Ernst Toller from Germany. Yet, the outlook was clouded: "the smoke of the Fascist book-burning reached us from Germany . . . Fascist riots in Paris, the crushing of the Schutzbund . . . We were conscious of the looming menace of war," recalls Ehrenburg.[5]

Compared to literature, music was in a more unsettled position. The composers lacked a dominant personality comparable to Maxim Gorky, and there was no one to pull the feuding factions together. Glazunov— once a tower of strength in the early years of the Revolution—was in Paris, old and ill. Miaskovsky was politically too naive. Prokofiev had recently returned to Moscow after fifteen years abroad, and for a time was a stranger in his own land. Asafiev was temporarily compromised by his activity in the modernist faction. Worst of all, the music-loving Lunacharsky had been removed from his post as cultural commissar in 1929. His successor was a Party functionary, Andrei Bubnov, who had no connection with music.

On the eve of the Resolution of 1932, Soviet composers were in a state of tension, disunity, and frustration. Critics pointed out the creative failure in the field of the topical Soviet opera—a genre considered most important. The attempts to switch to "Soviet thematics" were clumsy and artificial. The traditionalist composers felt neglected and ignored, the Association for Contemporary Music had quietly disintegrated, while the Association of Proletarian Musicians (RAPM) dominated the musical scene almost unopposed. Early in 1932, rumours were rife that some official action was impending. An important meeting was held at the People's Commissariat of Education on 23 April at seven o'clock. Here is an eye witness report,

'There is an atmosphere of excitement—all the composers and musical workers of Moscow and Leningrad are gathered here. All ages and all wings of creative musical craft of Soviet culture are represented, from Ippolitov-Ivanov to the leaders of RAPM . . . Those assembled are grouped according to trends and tendencies. There is restrained talk. The serious faces reflect one question: what is going to happen? It is apparent that something unusual is in the air. Possibly a decisive battle . . . Comrade Bubnov opens the discussion dealing with problems of construction in Soviet musical culture; he points out some deficiencies in this field. He asks for a frank discussion, to the bitter end . . . Those present take the floor one after another, and attack the RAPM with extraordinary vehemence. Its theoretical, creative, and tactical attitudes are under fire. Many speeches reveal rancour: theoretical contentions give way to echoes of recent feuds. Feelings run high . . . It is clear that RAPM's rule, which limits the sphere of creative work, causes unhealthy conditions for the development of Soviet music . . . On 24 April, the Moscow papers publish the decree of the Central Committee, announcing the dissolution of all Proletarian arts associations . . ."[6]

Clearly, this was not an overnight decision, but a well-prepared political coup. The public debate did not influence the decision, yet it was useful as a barometer of public sentiment: the Proletarian Musicians were doomed.

The ban of RAPM and the plans for a new creative organization produced a surge of unity among composers. Most elated were the academicians and traditionalists who for years had felt constricted by extremist factions. One composer is reported to have quipped, "Now I can write music in three-four time"—alluding to RAPM's insistence on march rhythms as most appropriate for a proletarian society. Approval came from older, highly respected masters like Ippolitov-Ivanov, Vassilenko, Glière, Miaskovsky. In Leningrad, such contrasting figures as Shaporin, Asafiev, and Shostakovich spoke up in favour. In fact, support for the new Resolution came from all quarters. Musicians who had belonged to the—now discredited—proletarian RAPM or the modernist ACM hurriedly abandoned their lost causes to join the Party-decreed union. By this time, the *volte-face* had become a technique indispensable for survival.

The new association of composers and musicologists, established in accordance with the 1932 Resolution, was named *Soyuz Sovetskikh Kompozitorov* (Union of Soviet Composers)*. The first to be organized were city groups in Moscow and Leningrad, followed quickly by state-wide unions in the Ukraine, in Byelorussia, Georgia, and Armenia. By 1940, there were composers' unions in most of the republics and in many urban centres. At first, the nation-wide organization seems to have been rather loose until, in 1939, the Organizational Committee (ORGKOMITET) of the Composers' Union of the USSR was established by government decree. Compared with progress in the field of literature, the organization of composers proceeded rather

* In 1957, the name was changed to *Soyuz Kompozitorov SSSR* (Union of Composers of the USSR). See pp. 399–400, 472.

slowly; while the Soviet writers were able to mount their first national congress in 1934, the Soviet composers did not hold a nation-wide conference until 1948, sixteen years after the establishment of the Union. Numerically, the Composers' Union was always small: its prestige and influence is not based on numbers but on quality. Only the creative musical *élite* is admitted: those who write music—composers, and those who write *about* music—musicologists. Among the latter are included, rather broadly, critics, theorists, historians, lecturers, and authors on various musical subjects. Uniting composers and critics in a single organization was not accidental; the aim was to promote an atmosphere of creative stimulation. The practical results, however, were not quite so idyllic; the composers did not care to be criticized, creatively or otherwise, while the critics did not dare to criticize whenever the works of a well-known composer were involved. Lesser composers felt neglected and resentful while their prominent colleagues were boosted by the press. The smouldering animosity burst into the open during the cultural purge of 1948 when the "kowtowing critics" received their share of public castigation.

The position of the newly established Composers' Union was strengthened when it acquired its own journal, *Sovetskaya Muzyka* (Soviet Music). It began to appear in 1933 as a bi-monthly, with an initial printing of 3,000 copies, each containing some 150 pages (of course without any advertising). The following year, *Sovetskaya Muzyka* became a monthly, and today it has a circulation of 18,000. During the war years, the regular publication was interrupted and replaced by several yearbooks. While the Composers' Union is primarily responsible for the journal's contents (it is run by an editorial committee), the Ministry of Culture appears as co-sponsor on the masthead which adds to its official status.

At the time *Sovetskaya Muzyka* was established, there was a desperate need for a publication reflecting the broad spectrum of the musical scene. During the cultural crisis of 1930, most music journals had ceased publication; the only one to survive until 1932 was *Proletarskyi Muzykant* (Proletarian Musician), the wildly partisan mouthpiece of the proletarian wing.

The editorial policy of *Sovetskaya Muzyka* was based on the assumption that the Resolution of 1932 had eliminated all intra-musical factionalism. Discussion was permitted, but not dissent; the cultural policy dictated by the Party's Central Committee could not be questioned. Within this framework, however, there was still room for lively discussion of musical subjects in the fields of theory, history aesthetics, and performance. There were important debates on the problems of genres—the opera, the symphony—there were analyses of new compositions, book reviews, critical columns on new operas, ballets, concerts, interviews with foreign visitors, translated excerpts from foreign publications. The monthly issues of *Sovetskaya Muzyka* were a lively mirror of musical life in the entire Soviet Union; the reports from abroad (often rather partisan) became the only contact with the outside world available to a Soviet musician. Aside from the repetitive political harangues, *Sovetskaya Muzyka* is still an excellent musical journal; because it attempts to cover so much, it cannot allot sufficient space to lesser events. To fill this gap, and to provide a more popular survey of the musical scene, a new bi-weekly journal, *Muzykalnaya Zhizn* (Musical Life) was established in 1957. Special mention must be made of the musical supplements carried in both journals. Occasionally, good short pieces are published, but for the most part the music printed consists of political mass songs or patriotic marches which are embarrassingly mediocre.

The first editorial of *Sovetskaya Muzyka*, in January 1933, stated as the main task the development of a Marxist-Leninist musicology; it also promised to fight the ideology of the modernists as well as the leftist interpretation of Marxism. While the organizations representing these views (mainly the modern ACM and the proletarian RAPM) were dissolved, the editorial rightly assumed that former members of these groups had not renounced all dangerous thoughts. Conformity or silence became the formula for survival. Asafiev, until recently the guiding spirit of the modernist wing, defined the process glibly as "the growth of political consciousness of the Soviet composer searching persistently for creative solutions".[7]

The new "creative solution" was to be Socialist Realism. Musicians began to discuss this concept a year prior to the historic Writers' Congress in 1934. The first issue of *Sovetskaya Muzyka* printed an article by the critic Gorodinsky entitled "On the Problem of Socialist Realism in Music". Indeed it was a problem to translate this—essentially literary—concept into musical terms. The Composers' Union contributed the following guidelines which make up in belligerence what they lack in clarity,

> "The main attention of the Soviet composer must be directed towards the victorious progressive principles of reality, towards all that is heroic, bright, and beautiful. This distinguishes the spiritual world of Soviet man and must be embodied in musical images full of beauty and strength. Socialist Realism demands an implacable struggle against folk-negating modernistic directions that are typical of the decay of contemporary bourgeois art, against subservience and servility towards modern bourgeois culture."[8]

The negative "modernistic directions" soon gained the label of Formalism. The term was used so loosely that Prokofiev once quipped, "Formalism is music that people don't understand at first hearing."[9] Though poorly defined, Socialist Realism and Formalism became the two opposing concepts which have bedevilled Soviet musical aesthetics from the early 1930's to the present day.

The Resolution of 1932 came at a time when Soviet music was in a state of crisis. A vicious campaign by the proletarian RAPM had discredited musical modernism by equating it with "bourgeois decadence". It forced the withdrawal of several modern productions that were in the planning stage, among them Prokofiev's ballet *Pas d'acier*. The mood of the country was not geared to stylized experiment. On the contrary, there was a general retreat into rose-coloured "realism".

As a result, advanced composers turned conventional, and conventional composers became commonplace. Young composers endeavoured to be inoffensive, and conservatism became a cherished virtue, while musical nationalism experienced a revival. But music merely reflected a general trend in changing Soviet attitudes during the 1930's. Realizing that the plan for world revolution had failed— at least temporarily—Soviet leaders became avowed nationalists. Patriotism was no longer limited to pride in the "conquests of the Revolution" but was extended to include Russia's historic past. In fact, the entire concept and teaching of history was reversed. The views of Mikhail Pokrovsky, until his death in 1932 the leading Soviet historian, were discarded as a vulgarization of Marxism and a distortion of Russian history. The glory of Russia was restored, the tsars re-evaluated, including Peter the Great and Ivan the Terrible. In literature, the new attitude produced a large number of historical novels and plays. In music, this mood was reflected in epic works like the symphonic cantata *On the Field of Kulikovo* (1939) by Yuri Shaporin, commemorating the battle with the Mongols in 1380, or the oratorio *Alexander Nevsky* by Prokofiev, depicting the defeat of the Teutonic Knights in 1242. The latter was originally a film directed by Sergei Eisenstein (1938) for which Prokofiev had written a stirring score.

The decade of the 1930's also witnessed the emergence of what has been called a "new respectability" in Soviet life. On the home front, there was a revival of almost Victorian standards of morality, restoration of school discipline, and abandonment of many "progressive" innovations. The Constitution of the USSR was adopted with great pomp in December 1936. In foreign policy, the Soviet Union restored diplomatic relations with the United States, entered the League of Nations, and concluded an alliance with France. Even the atheism campaign seemed to slacken: the famed poet, Demyan Bednyi, wrote a new libretto for an old opera pasticcio, *Bogatyri* (with music by Borodin and others). Performed in Moscow in October 1936, it had to be withdrawn because Bednyi had belittled Russia's conversion to Christianity in the tenth century!

Under these conditions, it is not surprising that Soviet music moved to a plateau of safe conservatism. Topical symphonies, descriptive tone poems, and folklore genres dominated the field, with the use of traditional materials in the time-honoured tradition of the "Mighty Five" school. Prokofiev, recently returned from abroad, foresaw the implications of this trend and warned the composers against incipient provincialism. His prophetic words created deep resentment, and years later they were repeated accusingly.

In the midst of this flight into "provincialism", the position of Prokofiev is of particular interest. After his permanent return to Moscow in 1933, he faced a difficult problem of musical readjustment. True, he had received an enthusiastic welcome in 1927 when he visited the Soviet Union for an extensive tour of concerts, all devoted to his own works. The reception was noticeably cooler when he returned in 1929 and again in 1932 because the works he now presented were more problematic. It was difficult—and perhaps painful—for him to realize that many of the compositions he had written abroad, between 1918 and 1932, failed to impress his Soviet compatriots.* They warmly responded to the brilliant Third Piano Concerto, the charming *Classical Symphony*, the humorous Suite from the *Three Oranges*, but they were cold and critical towards such works as the Second Symphony, the Fifth Piano Concerto, the Overture Op. 42, or the Quintet Op. 39, all written in his more astringent style. Prokofiev was frankly puzzled by this lack of understanding and response to what he considered some of his best music. "I do not want Soviet audiences to judge me only by the March from the *Three Oranges* and the Gavotte from the *Classical Symphony*," he wrote in 1933.[10] But eventually he realized that he had to make certain concessions.

Prokofiev's mastery was such that he could write "accessible" music without lowering its quality. He had done it in his opera *The Love for Three Oranges*, a commission from Chicago, where he took into account the "American taste". He was ready to do the same for Soviet

* It was generally assumed that Prokofiev remained a Soviet citizen throughout the years abroad. However, Nestyev's first American biography of Prokofiev (1946, never published in Russian) states, "One of the first steps Prokofiev took upon reaching his homeland in 1927 was to take Soviet citizenship."[11] It proves that Prokofiev must have obtained some non-Soviet travel document prior to 1927. This sentence was suppressed in Nestyev's later Russian biography of Prokofiev (1957).

audiences as he wrote in 1934, "In the Soviet Union music is addressed to millions of people who formerly had little or no contact with music. It is this new mass audience that the modern Soviet composer must strive to reach." At the time he seriously believed that these new millions needed a special approach—a type of "light-serious music, primarily melodious, written in clear, yet original terms."[12] Among the music in this category Prokofiev named the symphonic suite *Egyptian Nights* and the score to *Lieutenant Kije*. But by 1937 he changed his position and became convinced that the new audiences needed no concessions, "The masses want great music . . . they understand far more than some composers think . . . I consider it a mistake to strive for simplification . . ."[13]

Despite all rationalizations, some of Prokofiev's newer works were received with indifference, others even remained unpublished and unperformed. For example, the Fifth Piano Concerto, introduced by the composer in December 1932 left the Moscow audience completely cold; even his old friend Miaskovsky found two of the movements "not very pleasing". The Moscow première of the Symphonic Song Op. 57 in 1934 was a failure; Miaskovsky recalled that "there were literally three claps of applause in the hall". One critic called the work "a sad tale of the decline of the fading culture of individualism"; it was not published. A painful disappointment was the jubilee Cantata Op. 74 for the Twentieth Anniversary of the October Revolution, set to words by Marx, Lenin, and Stalin: it remained unperformed* and unpublished. His first Soviet opera, *Semyon Kotko* (1940), produced a controversy and was removed from the repertoire. In his efforts to find a musical idiom accessible to broad audiences, he approached a new genre, the mass song, yet the results were not memorable.

But outweighing these failures were a number of masterpieces that added new lustre to Prokofiev's fame. Suffice it to mention *Lieutenant Kije* (1934), the ballet *Romeo and Juliet* (1935–36), the children's tale *Peter and the Wolf* (1936), the Second Violin Concerto (1935), the score to *Alexander Nevsky* (1939). Generally speaking, there is greater warmth and more spontaneous expressiveness in Prokofiev's musical idiom of the 1930's. It was undoubtedly the effect of his confrontation with the "new" Soviet audiences; the problem of reaching the people was constantly in his mind, as he expressed it in 1937, "Music in our country has become the heritage of vast masses of people. Their artistic taste and demands are growing with amazing speed. And this is something the Soviet composer must take into account in each new work."[14]

It was this desire to compose music in his homeland, for the Russian

---

* Delayed by thirty years, the première took place in 1966. See pp. 465–6.

people, that explains in part his decision, in 1933, to settle in Moscow. It was a decision dictated by nostalgia rather than politics, for Prokofiev was essentially non-political. At the time, he was in the midst of a creative crisis: his career in the West was stagnant, and his style was no longer considered trend-setting in modern music. He confided to a French critic, Serge Moreux, in 1933, "The air of foreign lands does not inspire me because I am Russian, and there is nothing more harmful to me than to live in exile . . . I must again immerse myself in the atmosphere of my homeland . . . I must hear Russian speech and talk with the people dear to me. This will give me what I lack here, for their songs are my songs . . . I'm afraid of falling into academicism. Yes, my friend, I am going home."[15]

It was Russia that beckoned him, not the Soviet regime nor Marxism. The last twenty years of his life, spent "at home", were not cloudless: there were failures, brutal disappointments and unjustified criticism. But there were also warm response, sincere admiration, and that intangible flow of inspiration filtered through people and landscape, language and tradition. Here, his music acquired a quality of lyric expansiveness, of deepened humanism that created a new bond of communication with his audiences.

Prokofiev's return to Russia was a milestone in the development of Soviet music. It was more meaningful than the return of Gorky, for Prokofiev was at the peak of his creative power while Gorky was in his decline. Prokofiev was refreshingly frank and outspoken, as yet unafraid of political pressures, willing to learn but equally willing to criticize. He had always been cool to a certain stale Russian traditionalism whose personification he saw in Glazunov. He once reproached his old friend Miaskovsky for occasional "Glazunovisms". His critique of "academicism" came at an awkward time when Soviet music was turning academic, retrospective, when the entire cultural policy of the Soviets was redirected towards conservatism. This led to some clashes with his confrères who did not hesitate to criticize his occasional "relapse" into a style too "modern" or "formalistic", as the term went. On such occasions he was treated like a recidivist.

Shortly after his return to Moscow, Prokofiev agreed to teach a few post-graduate composition students at the Conservatory although he had no previous pedagogical experience. He began by attending some of Miaskovsky's and Shebalin's classes where he met two star students —Khachaturian and Khrennikov. "Prokofiev's remarks were friendly, specific, and to the point," recalled Khachaturian;[16] others remembered him as somewhat aloof and haughty. However, teaching did not appeal to Prokofiev: he was so immersed in his own creative plans that he was reluctant to spend time for anything not directly connected with composing. He even declined to give a recital of his own works, remarking that the preparation "would cost him half a piano sonata". Prokofiev's connection with the Moscow Conservatory was short-lived, but he continued to take an interest in the development of young talent, and he was always ready to contribute creative criticism.

At the time, the Composers' Union inaugurated a new type of "collective" work. New compositions, often half-finished, were played in closed sessions to fellow composers and musicologist-critics. These auditions were designed to guide young composers although experienced masters also participated in such try-outs, mainly to check the reaction of professional listeners. The mutual criticism was often sharp and controversial, and particularly a young composer would not dare disregard the judgment of such an illustrious forum. The system—which has survived until today—was designed to be helpful, but in practice it amounted to a control of creativity, well-meaning but nevertheless decisive. The insistence on conformity was particularly hard on young talents who were eager to explore new paths. The directorate of the Composers' Union was expected to offer guidance and to be vigilant, and during the cultural purge of 1948, the entire directorate was held responsible for creative failures of composers . . . failure meaning, in this case, the deviation from the principles of Socialist Realism and the preoccupation with Formalism.

The year 1934 brought two events—totally unrelated at first; yet, what grew out of these events became later strangely intertwined. One was the rise of an opera, the other the violent death of a politician. On 22 January a new opera by Shostakovich, *Lady Macbeth of Mtsensk*, had a triumphant première in Leningrad; it was hailed as a great achievement of Soviet culture. On 1 December the leader of the Communist Party in Leningrad, Sergei Kirov, was assassinated in his office. He was succeeded by Andrei Zhdanov, the Party's spokesman at the Writers' Congress in 1934.

The impact of these two events did not become fully apparent until two years later: in 1936, a virulent attack on Shostakovich and musical modernism forced the withdrawal of *Lady Macbeth* and a general re-orientation of Soviet music; that same year brought an intensification of political terror, culminating in the great purge that cut deeply into every stratum of Soviet life. So intimidated was the musical community that hardly anyone dared to speak up in defence of Shostakovich who, at thirty, had reached the pinnacle of musical fame.

Shostakovich's music of the early 1930's cannot be categorized as

belonging outright to one or the other of the opposing musical
philosophies. The modernists pointed with pride to his satirical opera
The Nose, the ballets *Bolt* and *The Golden Age*. The proletarian wing
claimed him on the strength of his symphonies *October* and *May Day*
as well as the collective farm ballet *The Limpid Stream*. The tradition-
ists took comfort in his euphonious Cello Sonata. Shostakovich
belonged to all, and to none. He proved his independent spirit by
taking Leskov's classical short story, *Lady Macbeth of Mtsensk*, re-
shaping it into a psychological drama with socio-critical overtones, and
providing it with a score of modern *verismo*, in turn glowing, crude,
satirical, and impassioned.

Soviet critics, while deploring some of the more lurid aspects of the
opera, considered it nevertheless "the result of the general success of
Socialist construction, of the correct policy of the Party"[17] as stated in
the "historic decree" of 23 April 1932. Such an opera "could have been
written only by a Soviet composer brought up in the best traditions of
Soviet culture". Shostakovich was credited with having "torn off the
masks and exposed the false and lying methods of the composers of
bourgeois society . . ."[18] The conductor of the première, Samosud,
summarized the general feeling in these words, "I declare *Lady
Macbeth* a work of genius, and I am convinced that posterity will confirm this estimate. One cannot help feeling proud that, in a Soviet
musical theatre, an opera has been created that overshadows all that
can possibly be accomplished in the operatic art of the capitalist world.
Here, too, our culture has indeed not only overtaken, but surpassed,
the most advanced capitalist countries."[19]

American critics were not slow in taking up this challenge: they
blamed every shortcoming of the opera on Communism. In his article,
"Socialism at the Metropolitan", the critic-composer Virgil Thomson
described this reaction, "The New York critics hedged. In fact, the
degree of approval expressed by them was in pretty close proportion
to the political leftness of the respective newspaper for which they
work . . ." Thomson—who liked the opera—added, "For educated
people to protest at this late date about the rough-and-ready tone of
Socialist art is really just a shade more than stupid."[20] But, in fact, how
"Socialist" is this art? Neither the Soviets nor Virgil Thomson present
a convincing case. Closer to the truth is Gerald Abraham who wrote,
"So little was Socialist Realism understood at first that *Lady Macbeth*
was accepted as an embodiment of it."[21]

Be this as it may, some of the capitalist critics were outraged at the
lurid happenings on the stage and in the pit. William Henderson wrote
in *The New York Sun*, "Shostakovich is without doubt the foremost
composer of pornographic music in the history of the opera." He

called *Lady Macbeth* a "bed-chamber opera" and said that "passages which in their faithful portrayal of what is going on become obscene. If this is musical art, then it is time for sackcloth and ashes".[22] Henderson must have been thinking of the suggestive trombone slides that accompanied the seduction scene—an effect described by an American journal as "pornophony". It shocked and delighted the New York audience, though it was dropped in Leningrad, and Olin Downes of *The New York Times* wrote, "Its cheapest and most obvious features . . . won the most frenzied applause . . ." Downes, incidentally, was quite critical of Shostakovich's score which he found "flimsily put together, full of reminiscences and obvious and shallow tricks, with almost no originality or creative quality, attached to a libretto of Communistic hue, lurid, overdrawn, naive, sensational . . ." (Why "Communistic" is a mystery.) Yet, Downes concedes the "immense success" of the work and ascribes it to the "composer's feeling for the theatre". "The music, whatever its inner lacks, seldom fails to emphasize the doings on the stage." But "pages of this music are puerile in immaturity and naïveté" and he accuses Shostakovich of "effrontery and lack of self-criticism".[23]

Obviously, the New York reviews were carefully read in Moscow. When Howard Taubman, representing *The New York Times*, met with members of the Soviet Composers' Union in Moscow in September 1935,* he was told that *Lady Macbeth* was a significant work of "powerful realism and satirical pungency"; the occasional "overripe naturalism" was allegedly "misunderstood" by American critics as vulgarity.[24]

The conductor Artur Rodzinski, who regarded *Lady Macbeth* as "a sensational masterpiece and one of the most important contributions to contemporary music brought out in the past twenty-five years",[25] was primarily responsible for the American performances of *Lady Macbeth* and conducted the première in Cleveland on 31 January 1935 and a performance in New York on 5 February.**

The Swiss musicologist R.-Aloys Mooser (who in his youth had studied Russian music in St. Petersburg) heard *Lady Macbeth* during the "First Leningrad Music Festival" in June 1934. The music, Mooser wrote, is "of prodigious intensity and brutal realism . . . The dramatic scenes are treated with incredible vigour. They are impassioned and exciting, and they move at an extraordinary pace without ever being lengthy. And the musical idiom is so powerful and evocative, the accents are so spontaneous and so truthful that the impression is

---

* The three members, whom Taubman interviewed, were the composers Veprik and Kabalevsky, and the musicologist Shneerson. They pointed out that after the Resolution of 1932, "democratic tendencies" prevailed in music.

** A narrator was used before each act to tell the story. These were semi-staged concert performances.

infinitely perturbing." Mooser admits that some effects are deafening—as are so many Soviet compositions. But there is, in this opera, "such a sense of action and movement, such intense and vibrant vitality, something so frenetic and hallucinatory, that the spectator, even the coldest and most sceptic, emerges breathless, shaken, moved almost against his will by the violence and insight of the composer's language."[26]

The opera aroused a great deal of international interest. Stockholm, Prague, London, Ljubljana, Zurich, Copenhagen are among the cities that performed the work in 1935–36. In Russia, the success was extraordinary: by 1936 there had been eighty-three performances in Leningrad and ninety-seven in Moscow. The piano score, with Russian and English texts, was published by MUZGIZ in 1935. Everything pointed to a lasting success.

The crushing blow came on 28 January 1936, when *Pravda* published a slashing attack on Shostakovich's opera under the title "Sumbur vmesto muzyki" (Chaos Instead of Music).[27] It was followed a week later (6 February) by a second article, this time directed against a recent ballet of Shostakovich on a Soviet topic, *The Limpid Stream*. Both articles were unsigned which gave them the standing of official policy pronouncements, and it was revealed in 1948 that they were written on instructions from the Party's Central Committee. Whether Stalin personally was involved in giving these instructions, whether Zhdanov was the actual author of the articles, cannot be ascertained though these facts were widely rumoured.

While Lenin was reluctant to be drawn into artistic controversies—he referred such matters usually to Lunacharsky—Stalin knew no such modesty. Opera particularly attracted Stalin's personal interest. His taste for pompous spectacles influenced the performance style of the Bolshoi Theatre, especially in classical Russian works. On direct instructions from Stalin, Glinka's masterpiece *A Life for the Tsar* was re-staged in 1939, with a revised libretto and under the name *Ivan Susanin*—the first revival, twenty-two years after the Revolution.* The finale was transformed into an apotheosis of patriotism, cutting the music to fit the new concept: masses of people, horses on the stage, warriors and priests in resplendent armour and robes, the gleaming white walls of the Kremlin topped by the golden cupolas of the churches.

* Actually, Glinka's original name for his opera was *Ivan Susanin;* the change to *A Life for the Tsar* was made at the behest of Tsar Nicholas I prior to the première in 1836. The revised libretto stresses Susanin's love for his homeland while minimizing his monarchic allegiance. An earlier attempt to provide Glinka's score with a completely new libretto (under the title *Hammer and Sickle*, 1924) was a complete failure.

Stalin also had his own ideas on contemporary Soviet opera. He listed its desirable basic attributes—a libretto with a Socialist topic, a realistic musical language with stress on a national idiom, and a positive hero typifying the new Socialist era. These criteria were submitted to a group of opera specialists at a meeting on 17 January 1936.

That same evening, Stalin—accompanied by Molotov and commissar of education Bubnov—attended a performance of an opera by a young composer, Ivan Dzerzhinsky, *The Quiet Don*, based on Mikhail Sholokhov's famous novel. Stalin was highly pleased, and his comments were given wide publicity. A few days later, Stalin saw *Lady Macbeth of Mtsensk* by Shostakovich and found it repugnant. Indeed, nothing could be further from Stalin's idyllic concept of contemporary Soviet opera than Shostakovich's explosive psychological drama, based on a story of murder, greed, and lust—though Leskov's heroine Katerina Izmailova was re-shaped into a more sympathetic character.

Pravda's attack on Shostakovich was two-pronged, the opera libretto was criticized for its crudity and vulgarity, the ballet for ideological "falsehood". More important, however, was the critique of the music, for it transcended the specific case of Shostakovich by condemning modernism in general.

> "From the first moment, the listener is shocked by a deliberately dissonant, confused stream of sound. Fragments of melody, embryonic phrases appear—only to disappear again in the din, the grinding, and the screaming . . . This music is built on the basis of rejecting opera . . . which carries into the theatre and the music the most negative features of 'Meyerholdism'* infinitely multiplied. Here we have 'leftist' confusion instead of natural, human music . . . The danger of this trend to Soviet music is clear. Leftist distortion in opera stems from the same source as the leftist distortion in painting, poetry, teaching, and science. Petty-bourgeois innovations lead to a break with real art, real science, and real literature . . . All this is coarse, primitive, and vulgar. The music quacks, grunts, and growls, and suffocates itself, in order to express the amatory scenes as naturalistically as possible. And 'love' is smeared all over the opera in the most vulgar manner. The merchant's double bed occupies the central position on the stage. On it all 'problems' are solved . . ."

With this abusive outburst, *Lady Macbeth* was expelled from the Socialist orbit. As an ideological parting shot, *Pravda* added, "*Lady*

---

* The theatre director Vsevolod Meyerhold, with whom Shostakovich had worked on several occasions, was still active in 1936, though under attack. He was arrested in 1939 and died in 1942.

Macbeth enjoys great success with audiences abroad. Is it not because the opera is absolutely unpolitical and confusing that they praise it? Is it not explained by the fact that it tickles the perverted tastes of the bourgeoisie with its fidgety, screaming, neurotic music . . .?"

Ostensibly, the *Pravda* article was directed against Shostakovich alone, but it contained sufficient warnings against his admirers and potential imitators. While the Resolution of 1932 was supposed to have silenced all factionalism, the modernists among musicians and critics had not simply vanished—they just kept still. In fact, Shostakovich was the lone survivor of what, in the 1920's, had been a vigorous avant-garde school of music. Roslavetz and Mossolov were silenced, Miaskovsky and Shcherbachev had become middle-of-the-road composers, Knipper and Deshevov had turned to realist music. Only Prokofiev could be mentioned in the class of "advanced" Soviet composers at that time—and he understood the veiled threat, as he admitted later, in the tense year 1948.*

The *Pravda* articles were interpreted by the entire musical community as a timely warning. Immediately, meetings were called at all chapters of the Composers' Union, discussions were initiated, statements were issued, and in general the future of Soviet music was charted. The transcripts of the discussions in Leningrad and Moscow, published in the journal *Sovetskaya Muzyka*,[28] make sad reading. Few voices were raised in sympathy or defence of Shostakovich, everybody had to think of his own career, involvement, and safety. These were far from normal times in the Soviet Union—the purges were on—and this might excuse, or at least explain, the detached attitude of colleagues and friends towards Shostakovich. His works were removed from programmes; conductors and soloists made quick readjustments. Yet, one sentence in *Pravda*'s diatribe permitted some lenience; after enumerating the composer's "errors", it said, "All this is not due to a lack of talent, or to a lack of ability to depict simple and strong emotions." Not Shostakovich's talent, but his "formalistic" tendency was condemned. Hence, the composer Knipper was on safe ground when he said during the discussion, "One must not remove Shostakovich from the rolls of Soviet music. One must not drive nails into his coffin. One must help him to straighten himself out." In the same vein, Asafiev and Dzerzhinsky warned against dismissing him from the front ranks of Soviet composers. Rather touching were the words of Professor Steinberg, Shostakovich's former composition teacher at the Conservatory,

> "The drama of Shostakovich is my own personal drama, and I cannot remain indifferent to what my pupil experiences in his

* See pp. 232-3.

creative work . . . The most extreme expression of Shostakovich's 'new' tendency were the *Aphorisms* Op. 13 (1927). When he showed them to me, I told him that I understood nothing in them, and that they were quite alien to me. After that he stopped coming to me . . ."[29]*

Everybody expected some utterance from Asafiev, known as the spiritual leader of the Soviet modernists of the 1920's, the author of a book on Stravinsky and of various essays on modern music. Asafiev did not participate in the debate; he was given the privilege of answering in writing, and his answer—entitled "Exciting Questions" (Volnuyushchie voprosy)—was printed in the same issue of *Sovetskaya Muzyka* as the transcript of the discussion; hence it became part of the record. Asafiev's apologia is cleverly written. He admits past errors of judgment from which he was rescued by two circumstances—his intense study of the music of Mussorgsky** and his involvement with, and final rejection of, Alban Berg's *Wozzeck*.*** His final sentence is rather limp, "The problem of the improvement of the idiom and creative method of Shostakovich as well as of a number of other composers—this, in sum, is the problem of the evolution of Soviet music, stated brilliantly in the timely articles of *Pravda*."[30]

Of course this is a shrewd over-simplification. Yet, Asafiev's position must not be viewed as a clear-cut capitulation. For some time he had shown signs of disenchantment with modernism and "Westernism". In 1929, he warned against the "rootlessness" of Stravinsky's later music. In 1930, he wrote an essay, "The Crisis of Western Musicology". His famous appeal, "Composers, hurry up!"—published as early as 1924—revealed his inner dichotomy: a passionate interest in musical newness, and an equally passionate belief in music as a reflection of the people. Nevertheless, he was branded by the proletarian journal, *Music and October*, as the "most consistent formalist". During the years 1929-32, he felt increasingly attacked and misunderstood, particularly by the proletarian musical faction, and he withdrew in discouragement. On 15 April 1930 he wrote to his old friend, the composer Miaskovsky, "I cannot work. Nothing succeeds. My job *was* to infect myself with music and to write in such a way as to infect others . . . I have no other

---

* See pp. 79–80.

** Asafiev was co-editor, with Paul Lamm, of the Academic Edition of Mussorgsky.

*** In 1927, Asafiev had written a number of articles on *Wozzeck* in conjunction with the Leningrad première of the work. He was also co-editor of a booklet entitled *Alban Berg's Wozzeck*.

concept of musicology or criticism. Now, alas, one cannot write this way. So I've turned sour." In his "total revulsion" against musicology, he turned to his first love, composition, where his style was wholly traditional. His ballets *The Flame of Paris* (1932) and *The Fountain of Bakhchisarai* (1934) were immensely successful.

Thus, at the time of the musical controversy around Shostakovich and formalism, in 1936, Asafiev's position was that of a successful ballet composer, entirely acceptable to the Socialist Realist ideology. Hence, his article was not so much a defence as voluntary self-criticism. His was the problem of many Russian intellectuals—an attempt to justify their inner re-orientation in the face of irresistible pressures. *Wozzeck* revealed to Asafiev "the senselessness of human suffering in the grip of inhuman capitalist culture"; he became aware of the "helplessness of West European *petit-bourgeois* musical intelligentsia in the face of growing fascism". After *Wozzeck*—so Asafiev explained—all dabbling in contemporaneousness—in view of Soviet reality, in view of the masses creating a new world—became nonsensical.

Still to be explained was Asafiev's earlier praise of *Lady Macbeth*. Here he stated simply that he was blinded by the brilliant talent of Shostakovich: the mirage of the "quality of talent" obscured the quality of the utterance. He admitted certain reservations about the style of Shostakovich—a trend towards cynicism, crude naturalism, taunting gibes, which were in jarring contrast to his "Mozartian" youthfulness. But the negative aspects, so evident in *The Nose*, were about to be overcome in *Lady Macbeth*. "We must not fail to preserve the exceptional talent of Shostakovich," warned Asafiev. Here he paraphrased Lenin's remarkable defence of the poet Demyan Bednyi, "You will be guilty of a sin, a great sin . . . if you fail to attract, to *help* a talented co-worker . . ."*

All in all, Asafiev's essay was a dialectic masterpiece. Without undue submissiveness, he extricated himself from a vulnerable position; it was a dignified retreat. It also encouraged others to take similar steps; if the "master" could explain away his entire past in fifteen hundred well-chosen words, there was no need to feel any compunction about offering retractions and apologies when their work, their careers, possibly their liberty was at stake. In the light of Soviet music history, however, Asafiev's statement was more than one man's apologia: it meant the end of an era.

While Asafiev's "position paper" saved him from becoming involved in the acrimonious debate raging around Shostakovich and modernism, three younger critics—described as a "group of militant formalists" in

*See p. 42.

Leningrad—had to bear the brunt of verbal attacks by vengeful colleagues. They were Mikhail Druskin, Alexander Rabinovich, and Ivan Sollertinsky. All three were among the most brilliant disciples of Asafiev, and their unwillingness to recant immediately only increased the anger of their accusers. Eventually, they yielded to pressure and made the expected admissions of "error".

At the time, Sollertinsky was the most important member of the group. He began his career as a lecturer and art critic in 1924, and entered the directorate of the Leningrad Philharmonic in 1929. About that time he formed a close friendship with Shostakovich. They both shared an admiration for the music of Mahler, and Sollertinsky may have influenced Shostakovich in the direction of modernism. In 1934, Sollertinsky wrote a perceptive study of Arnold Schoenberg—perhaps the last sympathetic account in Russian of that great modernist who became anathema to the Soviets.

In 1936, Sollertinsky was branded as the "bard" of formalism. At first, he had a defeatist reaction and wanted to abandon temporarily the field of music in order to re-think his position. He explained it later as his "unwillingness to lie, since I could not yet envisage the path of my reorientation". On second thoughts, however, he decided to recant. In a lengthy statement, he admitted that this decision was prompted by the position taken by Asafiev. "Yesterday, at last, I heard the exhaustive, clear statement of Asafiev. I personally, like all musicologists who studied at Leningrad, consider myself his student. His silence confused me immensely. In particular, I was puzzled by the ambiguous evaluations in his book on Stravinsky. Asafiev's clear, unmistakable clarification of his position was for me an incentive to speak out definitely and with conviction against myself and my former errors."[31]

In his apologia, Sollertinsky was understandably more concerned with his own defence than with that of Shostakovich. He pointed out that he did not care for Shostakovich's *The Nose* nor the dry calculations of Ernst Krenek. But he admitted that he succumbed to the emotionalism of Berg's *Wozzeck*. He also admitted that he "overlooked" the fact that the "animalic eroticism" in *Wozzeck* (Maria and the Major) was "transferred" by Shostakovich to *Lady Macbeth* (Katerina and Sergei). Sollertinsky ended his statement with a flattery so obvious as to be facetious—he promised to study the language and folklore of Georgia—which happened to be Stalin's native land.

Despite the general animosity displayed towards him, Sollertinsky's career seemed hardly affected. He continued his duties at the Philharmonic. In addition, he was invited to join the Leningrad Conservatory and the Institute of Theatre and Music. Sollertinsky was a brilliant lecturer, and his printed *oeuvre* is rather small, though important. His rich background in philology and theatre arts enabled him to discuss music in a large context, encompassing the inter-relationship of the arts. Sollertinsky died in Novosibirsk in 1944, at the age of forty-one. Shostakovich dedicated his Piano Trio Op. 67 to the memory of his friend.

The career of Alexander Rabinovich was also cut short by premature death at the age of forty-three, in 1943. His particular interests included the music of Mahler, Richard Strauss, and Stravinsky, which exposed him to attacks during the critical year 1936. His defensive statement did not satisfy the editors of the journal *Sovetskaya Muzyka* who branded his ideas as nonsensical. This applied particularly to Rabinovich's thesis that there were two types of formalism—"conservative" and "innovational", of which the latter was allegedly "more dangerous". Among the few published works of Rabinovich, the most important is a slim volume, *Russian Opera prior to Glinka*, considered a pioneering work in its field; it was published posthumously in 1948.

Mikhail Druskin, the youngest of the "formalist trio", was trained as a pianist and showed a predilection for the modern repertoire. In 1928, at the age of twenty-three, he published a remarkable first book, *New Piano Music*, for which his teacher Asafiev wrote a preface. Some of Druskin's statements must have startled the tradition-minded: thus, he described Schoenberg's Opus 25 as a "sample of highest mastery, placing this work on a level with the best polyphonic achievements of J. S. Bach." He also gave enthusiastic endorsement to the piano music of Hindemith and Stravinsky, calling the latter's *Piano Rag Music* "the turning point in piano literature" and "the gospel of modern rhythm".[32] Druskin's booklet on *Petrushka*, published in 1935—at a time when Stravinsky was already under attack by the Soviets—is still laudatory though more reserved. For the witch-hunters of 1936, Druskin was a welcome target but he defended himself with skill. Today, Druskin is a major figure in Soviet musicology, a professor of music history at the Leningrad Conservatory, and an authority on Western music as well as the Russian revolutionary song. He has lost none of his interest in modern music; in 1962, he was reported to be at work on a biography of Anton Webern.

During the debates at the Composers' Union, the names of a few other musicians were drawn in—the composers Mossolov, Popov, and Litinsky. But the over-riding issue of the 1936 controversy was, not the fate of any individual composers, but the issue of musical modernism and its status within Soviet music. True, there is never any direct censure of modernism: it is always referred to as "formalism", for modernism and formalism are *not* synonymous in Soviet usage. Soviet critics often stress the "progressive" nature of the Socialist-Realist type of "modern" music, as contrasted to the decadence of Western-style dabbling in modernism. Formalism—officially defined as the "separation of form from content"—is a term to be used with care, as one can read in an authoritative Soviet encyclopedia, "Formalism must not be confused with individualized original creativity, genuine innovations in terms of form as well as content, which constitute an indispensable trait of valuable realist art."[33]

The Resolution of 1932 considered formalism a dead issue, for its entire weight is directed against proletarian factionalism. Indeed, the anti-modernist campaign of RAPM in the years 1929–32 had routed the advanced musical forces. But the issue of formalism smouldered below the surface. In 1934, the journal *Sovetskaya Muzyka* published an article "Against Formalism in Music" in which the allegedly formalistic works by Litinsky were taken as a pretext to caatigate all unnecessary complexity in music. The author was the critic Ostretsov who, paradoxically, found himself on the defensive in 1936 because he had praised *Lady Macbeth*.

Pravda's anti-Shostakovich article of 1936, "Chaos Instead of Music", had far-reaching implications: it was meant as a warning not only to music, but also to literature and the other arts. Yet, to *Pravda*'s pained surprise, other publications did not immediately join the campaign. Three weeks later there was some prodding in *Pravda*, "It is with surprise that we note that the *Literary Journal* treated the editorials in *Pravda* as an affair apart from literature, and even uninteresting. The paper has not carried a word of comment . . . In the same blissful state of ignorance are also the other newspapers. *Izvestia* is silent. The usually energetic *Komsomolskaya Pravda* is in the same position. Is it possible that these papers have nothing to say?"[34]

Eventually, the arts were blanketed with conformity. In the visual arts, we witness a dreary revival of academicism with a stress on representational realism. In the theatre, the experimentalism of Meyerhold and Alexander Taïrov came under attack and their theatres were soon to be closed. In literature, sycophantism became an art practised by opportunist writers. Alexei Tolstoy, an author of stature, is reported by the painter Annenkov as saying, "I am simply a cynic . . . I am an ordinary mortal who wants to live . . . I don't give a damn; I'll write whatever is wanted. If he (Stalin) wants Ivan the Terrible and Rasputin rehabilitated and turned into learned Marxists, I don't care."[35]

But it was music that captured the international headlines. Shostakovich became a test-case—the "first clear demonstration of what Communist totalitarianism in art meant".[36]

What was the effect of the 1936 censure on the creative development of Shostakovich? This question has been discussed repeatedly by Soviet and by Western authors. Generally speaking, the Soviets maintain that Shostakovich benefited by the public criticism, while Western critics feel that his talent suffered permanent damage and was stunted at a sensitive point of its natural evolution. Recently, both sides have withdrawn from their extreme positions. Since the Soviet rehabilitation of *Lady Macbeth* in 1963, Shostakovich's opera has been declared an undisputed masterpiece, and much of the original criticism of *Pravda* has become obsolete. In the Western camp, an article in the British music journal *Tempo* (1966) found that Shostakovich's musical idiom underwent a salutary clarification after the 1936 castigation. These findings were based on an analytical comparison between his Fourth Symphony of 1935–36 and his Fifth Symphony of 1937. Both are pivotal works; the Fourth, withdrawn by the composer prior to its première in 1936 and the Fifth, a "creative reply to just criticism". In the opinion of the British critic of *Tempo*, this work of "repentence" is "more convincingly and profoundly original than the one whose 'excesses' it was meant to atone for" (namely the Fourth).[37]

To what extent did Shostakovich have to "repent"? It is wrong to picture him as a misunderstood rebel oppressed by an inimical regime. Even at the height of his involvement with modernism—around 1927–31—he never thought of challenging Marxist-Leninist aesthetics. He made this clear in an interview granted to *The New York Times* in December 1931,

> "There can be no music without ideology . . . We, as revolutionaries, have a different conception of music. Lenin himself said that 'music is a means of unifying broad masses of people'. It is not a leader of masses, perhaps, but certainly an organizing force! For music has the power of stirring specific emotions . . . Even the symphonic form, which appears more than any other divorced from literary elements, can be said to have a bearing on politics . . . Music is no longer an end in itself, but a vital weapon in the struggle. Because of this, Soviet music will probably develop along different lines from any the world has ever known."[38]

It is important to remember that Shostakovich never posed as an "ivory tower" artist nor as a misunderstood futurist. He had a vital need to communicate with his audiences and with his performers, and nothing seemed to frighten him more than a possible alienation from his surroundings. This might explain his apparent submissiveness to official criticism. He said in 1931, "I consider that every artist who isolates himself from the world is doomed. I find it incredible that an artist should want to shut himself away from the people who, in the end, form his audience. I think an artist should serve the greatest possible number of people. I always try to make myself understood as widely as possible, and, if I don't succeed, I consider it my own fault."[39]

As early as 1931, Shostakovich considered some of his older works a bit "old-fashioned", meaning in the Russian sense too sharply revolutionary. "A children's disease of the Left Wing" he described some of his earlier theories. From this point of view, he called his *October* Symphony (No. 2, 1927) "not entirely successful". Undoubtedly, Asafiev was right in saying that *Lady Macbeth*, composed in 1930–32, showed Shostakovich on a musical path leading away from his earlier modern eccentricities. The whole *Pravda* attack on Shostakovich appears in retrospect a stupid, misinformed, ill-timed blunder. Yet, one can also admit another point of view, as for example that of the editor of *Tempo*, ". . . It is possible to understand, if not condone, the moral indignation and censure once aroused by the blatant heartlessness and sardonic 'objectivity' of the music (to *Lady Macbeth*), and to feel that a deeper emotional involvement was desirable . . . though it is also true that the Fourth Symphony almost bursts at the seams with feeling . . ." The pattern of Shostakovich's career, remarks the same editor, is that of the "daring young man, who is suddenly checked by doubts, and sobers up" though his doubts were "forced on him by extra-musical criticism".[40]

Obviously, the evolution from "sardonicism" to "emotional involvement" took place within Shostakovich as a matter of course, without outside prodding, during the three-four years that separate *Lady Macbeth* from the Fourth Symphony, for he worked on the Fourth during 1935 and 1936, before and after the *Pravda* attack. The decision to withdraw the Fourth Symphony from the planned performance was not a spontaneous act. The symphony was put into rehearsal by the Leningrad Philharmonic under the German conductor Fritz Stiedry, a man well disposed towards Shostakovich. Several rehearsals were held before the composer, apparently discouraged by the reaction of the orchestra and various listeners, decided to cancel the première. He must have felt instictively that the Fourth Symphony was not the kind of work expected of him at that critical juncture of his career. What was expected and needed, was not a work of turbulence and involvement, but a work of clarity and affirmation. Thus, the score of the Fourth Symphony was put aside for twenty-five years.* Unbowed, Shostakovich concentrated on a new symphony, the Fifth, which was first

---

* One could draw a parallel between the twenty-five year delay of Shostakovich's Fourth Symphony and the delay in publication of the second part of the novel *Virgin Soil Upturned* by Sholokhov; the first part of the novel was brought

played on 21 November 1937 to triumphal acclaim. It re-established Shostakovich at the top of his generation—the success was a full vindication—and it brought him world-wide praise, though with some intermingled reservations. The next few years added lustre to Shostakovich's fame; the First String Quartet, the Sixth Symphony, various film scores, and particularly the Piano Quintet Op. 57 (1940) which brought him a Stalin Prize. He had reclaimed his position, and he kept it until 1948, when the next storm broke.

Turning from musical controversies to the positive aspects of Soviet musical life, one must mention the *Dekadas* of national art introduced in 1936. These were ten-day festivals, each dedicated to the arts of one of the Soviet republics, opera and ballet, art and folk music, orchestras, composers, and performers. Co-ordinated with the performing arts were exhibits of painting and sculpture. The main *Dekadas* took place in Moscow though other capital cities planned similar events. From 1936 to 1941, ten Festivals were presented, showing the arts of the Ukraine, Kazakhstan, Georgia, Uzbekistan, Azerbaijan, Kirghizia, Armenia, Byelorussia, Buriat-Mongolia, and Tadzhikistan. After a ten-year interruption due to war and post-war conditions, the *Dekadas* were resumed in 1951 on a broader scale, including literature as well as the performing and visual arts.

Needless to say, the *Dekadas* served political as well as artistic purposes. They demonstrated the success of the Communist policy towards the nationalities with its stress on cultural autonomy—the development of national cultures within a Socialist society.

Artistically, the *Dekadas* were immensely valuable, both for the visitors and the Muscovites. To be evaluated by a sophisticated metropolitan public was a challenge for the visiting ensembles, while the Moscow hierarchy welcomed the opportunity to gain first-hand information about the cultural climate in the provinces. In developing national cultures, there were unavoidable frictions between local factions: the so-called local bourgeois nationalists resisted the Russian influence and preferred the preservation of what the Russians called condescendingly "national archaism". Some regions had old musical traditions worthy of preservations, as for example the Ukraine, Georgia, Azerbaijan, and Armenia. But there were also regions where, before the Soviet era, no written musical documentation had existed,

---

out in 1932, the second was actually ready in 1936 but not published for twenty-five years. The première of Shostakovich's Fourth took place on 30 December 1961.

where the reliance was on oral traditions. Schooled composers were brought to these regions to teach musical notation and theory, and there were frequent controversies as to how much to preserve, how much to modernize. In the process, some of the old traditions undoubtedly became lost or distorted; often a compromise had to be reached. The Russian composers and scholars made genuine efforts to preserve the folklore, the national traditions of singing and playing folk instruments. As soon as native musicians were ready to assume the cultural leadership, they took over. A certain degree of Russification was unavoidable, particularly since all conservatories in the Soviet Union had to follow a unified curriculum. Among Russian composers who worked and taught systematically in remote sections of the Soviet Union were Glière, Vassilenko, Vlassov, Feré, Roslavetz, and Ippolitov-Ivanov.

In addition to these national *Dekadas,* there were also "all-Union" festivals of Soviet music, extended to two-month surveys of musical accomplishments. The first such festival, in celebration of the Twentieth Anniversary of the Revolution, was held in 1937 in Moscow, Leningrad, Kiev, and Tbilisi. The second, in 1938, was expanded to thirty cities, with some 600 concerts which stressed exchanges of performers between the republics. The third and fourth festivals, in 1939 and 1940, were done on a truly national scale, with concerts in every urban centre of the Soviet Union.

While the *Dekadas* and festivals stressed mainly professional performers, the musical Olympiads were dedicated to amateur musicians. The first such Olympiad assembled in Leningrad on 13 June 1927, when 5,000 amateur musicians met at the Communist Youth Stadium. There was a chorus of 2,000, many bands and folk instrument ensembles. To create musical outlets for laymen was a prime concern during the early revolutionary years, and Leningrad in particular had many organizations devoted to group singing, folk instrument ensembles, and similar activities. Each succeeding year saw an Olympiad with an ever growing number of participants (up to 100,000) and increasingly sophisticated musical programmes, including pieces by Glière, Shostakovich, Knipper, and Dzerzhinsky. After the Tenth Olympiad in 1936, a temporary halt was called. The next Olympiad, planned for 1941, was cancelled because of the outbreak of the Second World War.

Other cities followed the Leningrad example. Moscow had an all-Union Olympiad of national theatres in 1930, and one for amateur artists in 1932. The first all-Ukrainian Olympiad took place in Kharkov in 1931, and critical observers from abroad were impressed by the spontaneity and elemental strength of massed performances by non-professionals. The unifying force of such musical gatherings had already been recognized during the French Revolution when virtually the entire population of Paris would assemble on the *Champs de Mars* to join in revolutionary festivities.

The establishment of diplomatic relations between the United States and the Soviet Union in 1933 led to a thaw in artistic relations. Actually, the musical contacts had never been completely severed; such journals as *Modern Music* published regular reports on Soviet music written by its Moscow correspondent, the critic Victor Belayev and others. In 1935, *The New York Times* sent a special correspondent, Howard Taubman, to the Soviet capital, and his sympathetic survey of the musical scene was published in three major articles, during August and September of that year. But the Soviet people knew little about what was happening in American music. That lacuna was filled in July 1934, when *Sovetskaya Muzyka* published a major article, "Music in the United States", by the American composer Henry Cowell. Understandably, the activities of left-wing organizations were stressed in reports from America, as in Elie Siegmeister's article on New York's "Composers Collective".[41] The Moscow critic Shneerson began to publish regular summaries on music in America, usually based on material from American journals. In such reports, the seamy side of American musical life was emphasized to create a contrast with the paradisiac state of the arts in the Soviet Union. But good or bad, there was intense interest in Western musical events, and the journal *Sovetskaya Muzyka* gave considerable space to reports from abroad.

The 1930's brought new successes to Soviet performers: they won virtually every international musical contest. The Wieniawski and Chopin competitions in Warsaw, the Pianistic Concours in Vienna, the Ysaye Prize in Brussels—everywhere, Soviet instrumentalists were among the finalists. The prize-winning pianists were Lev Oborin, Yakov Flière, Emil Gilels, and Yakov Zak, while David Oistrakh dominated the violin field. New conductors emerged through national contests, particularly in 1938—Yevgeni Mravinsky, Melik-Pashayev, Rakhlin, Ivanov, all of whom were to reach top positions. Even string quartets competed for prizes, and in 1938 the Armenian Komitas Quartet shared the first prize with the Quartet of the Bolshoi Theatre.

Soviet artists are taught early to be competitive, to be able to perform under stress. Those who are sent abroad to participate in competitions are trained like teams for Olympic events, exposed to trial performances, and prepared both technically and psychologically. The results are astounding, and there is hardly a musical contest in which young Soviet musicians are not among the top winners.

While Soviet virtuosi were popular abroad, Soviet music was less readily accepted. Prokofiev, of course, was famous before he acquired the label of "Soviet" composers, and his popularity was undiminished. The works he composed after his return to Moscow in 1933—notably the Suites from *Lieutenant Kije* and *Romeo and Juliet*, the Violin Concerto No. 2, *Peter and the Wolf*—were warmly received and widely played. He continued to make concert tours in Western Europe and the United States, the last in 1938, and his personal appearances stimulated interest in his music.

Miaskovsky, considered a leading personality among Soviet composers during the 1920's, lost some of his appeal in the West and was more rarely performed. The Symphony of Yuri Shaporin, played in London in 1935, was found to be dull and disappointing. According to Gerald Abraham ". . . There was a curious sense of disillusionment at the discovery that Revolutionary Russia could produce such far from revolutionary music."[42]

Among the young composers Shostakovich was the recognized leader. Though he was often criticized for the occasional flippancy and banality of his musical ideas, each of his new works was received with interest. The controversy surrounding *Lady Macbeth* gave him a halo of martyrdom in the West, but the opera—despite the momentary flurry of interest—did not become a repertoire piece. When the Fifth Symphony reached Philadelphia in 1939 and London in 1940, it was well received though without the exaggerated huzzas accorded it in Moscow. Other young newcomers who aroused international interest were Dmitri Kabalevsky and Aram Khachaturian.

But it became clear, during the 1930's, that the platitudinous music of Socialist Realism was not really exportable. The West was simply not interested in symphonies and cantatas glorifying Lenin, Stalin, and Kirov, the Red Army and the Kolkhoz. What Prokofiev had predicted in 1934 became a reality—Soviet music became "provincial". The harder Soviet officialdom clamoured for music "Socialist in content, national in form", the more Soviet music became estranged and isolated from the musical mainstream of the West.

In one field, however, Soviet music gained quick and uncontested international recognition—music for the cinema. The new medium of sound film attracted Russia's best composers who were drawn into this field by extraordinarily talented film directors. Most prominent was the collaboration between Prokofiev and Sergei Eisenstein. Prokofiev's colourful imagination, controlled by a disciplined mind, responded to the challenge of the new medium, to the split-second needs of musical illumination of the moving picture. Eisenstein reminisced, "Prokofiev works like a clock . . . His exactness in time is a by-product of creative exactness . . . His music is amazingly plastic. It is never content to remain an illustration, but everywhere . . . it wonderfully reveals the inner movement of the phenomenon."[43]

In 1940, after having completed *Alexander Nevsky*, Prokofiev wrote, "The cinema is a young and very modern art that offers new and fascinating possibilities to the composer. These possibilities must be fully utilized. Composers ought to make a study of them, instead of merely writing the music and then leaving it to the mercy of the film people. Even the most skilled sound technician cannot possibly handle the music as well as the composer himself . . . Eisenstein's respect for music was so great that at times he was prepared to cut or add to his sequences so as not to upset the balance of a musical episode."[44]

This unique collaboration produced such film classics as *Alexander Nevsky* (1938) and *Ivan the Terrible* (in two parts, 1942–45). Earlier, Prokofiev had written the score to *Lieutenant Kije* (1933), directed by Feinzimmer.

Every Soviet composer, major and minor, has done some work for films though few were so fortunate as to have an Eisenstein at their side. Shostakovich said in 1939, "Cinema music is often regarded as a mere illustration, supplementary to the screen. In my opinion, it should be treated as an integral part of an artistic whole."[45]

Shostakovich's contact with the film world started early, when, as a seventeen-year-old, he earned a meagre living playing the piano in a cinema. His first film score was actually an accompaniment to the silent film *The New Babylon* (1928–29), to be played by an orchestra in place of the customary pianist. The following year, he wrote his first sound film, *Alone*. By 1963, the number of his film scores had reached thirty-two, the last being *Hamlet*. Shostakovich provided each film score with an opus number and has arranged ten orchestral Suites, each based on one of his films. At times it almost seems as if Shostakovich sought "refuge" in writing film music, particularly after the public castigation suffered in 1948; at that time he was warned not to "retire" completely into the film medium. For films, Shostakovich used an idiom less complex and less inclined towards "formalism" in the Soviet sense because of the subject matter involved. One Soviet biographer wrote in 1959,

"The ideological conceptions underlying such films were the exact opposite of those displayed in *The Nose* and *Lady Macbeth* . . . Shostakovich's work . . . in the cinema gave him a more correct outlook on life, it enabled him to obtain a more profound understanding of the traits of the Soviet character . . . It did much to change his style . . . Under the inspiration of this new work he turned to the so-called mass-genres . . . Shostakovich enjoyed writing songs for his cinema productions. In the early 1930's Soviet youth throughout the country took up the refrain of his 'Song of the Young Workers' from the film *The Passer-by,* and made it the most popular song of the day."[46]

This contradicts Gerald Abraham's contention that Shostakovich "cannot write even a moderately good tune". In fact, Soviet composers have a knack of writing functional music, and they put this gift to good use in their film scores. Among those active in film work during the 1930's were Kabalevsky, Shebalin, Dunayevsky, Khachaturian, Khrennikov, Dzerzhinsky, Sviridov . . . composers of every hue and conviction. It is safe to say that in no other film-producing country have so many composers of note lent their talents to the film industry. In turn, the peculiar and specific requirements of film music—its adaptability to quick-changing moods, illustrative needs, and concrete realism—have occasionally influenced the "absolute" music of Soviet composers. In the 1920's the term "cinemafication" of music was coined. A British critic compared the Twelfth (*Lenin*) Symphony of Shostakovich to a "sound track". Shchedrin's Second Symphony of 1963 was likened to music composed for cinematic "frames" because of its rapid changes of moods. Indeed, in listening to some colourful— and not over-profound—Soviet scores, one can easily imagine the sound track of a non-existing moving picture. Certainly, the demands of Socialist Realist aesthetics—concreteness, closeness to life—came nearest to implementation in Soviet film music.

Despite the internal tensions and the threatening international situation, the 1930's brought constant expansion to the musical life of the Soviet Union. In 1936, Moscow acquired a third symphony orchestra, the USSR State Symphony, which was to function next to the Philhar-monic and the Radio Orchestra. The activities of the radio network played an increasingly important role that was emphasized by two gigantic festivals, in 1936 and 1937. The Soviets, always aware of com-memorative dates, made the year 1939 into a Mussorgsky anniversary and dedicated 1940 to Tchaikovsky, in both cases celebrating the centenaries of the composers' births. This meant not only musical festivities but also the publication of documentary materials, letters, scholarly editions, all prepared with painstaking care. The Shostakovich revision of *Boris Godunov* was planned for the Mussorgsky anniversary though it was not performed until 1959 and did not succeed in dis-placing the entrenched bowdlerization of Rimsky-Korsakov. Inci-dentally, it was in 1940, during the Tchaikovsky year, that the Moscow

Conservatory was re-named in honour of Tchaikovsky—just as in 1944 the Leningrad Conservatory was re-named in honour of Rimsky-Korsakov, born in 1844.

Visits by foreign artists contributed to the richness of Soviet musical life of the 1930's. Several conductors, displaced by Hitler's persecution, received permanent appointments—permanent until the growing xenophobia in Russia made their activity undesirable. Fritz Stiedry was conductor of the Leningrad Philharmonic from 1933 to 1937. Georg Sebastian was in charge of the All-Union Radio Orchestra in Moscow from 1931 to 1937. Oscar Fried—who had been the first foreign conductor to visit Russia after the First World War in 1921—settled permanently in the Soviet Union in 1934, acquired Soviet citizenship, and died in Moscow in 1941. Eugene Szenkar led the Moscow Philharmonic from 1934 to 1937. Heinz Unger conducted the Leningrad Radio Orchestra from 1934 to 1936. There was a rumour in 1933 that Arnold Schoenberg might settle in the Soviet Union, though eventually he emigrated to the United States.*

Other artists came for short visits: the pianists Egon Petri, Casadesus, Artur Rubinstein, the violinists Szigeti and Thibaud, the singers Marian Anderson, Ninon Vallin, and Paul Robeson, the cellist Maurice Maréchal, the conductors Ansermet, Kleiber, Klemperer, and Coates. Received with particular enthusiasm were some native Russian virtuosi who had settled abroad before the 1917 Revolution—the violinist Efrem Zimbalist and the incomparable Jascha Heifetz. These two—both former students of the unforgotten Leopold Auer—had carried the glory of Russian violin playing throughout the world. Now, in 1934, they celebrated a unique homecoming.

The late 1930's were harsh years for the Soviet people. The Great Purge swept through the country in 1936–38. No one felt safe. "People who had never belonged to any opposition, who were loyal followers of Stalin or honest non-party specialists were arrested. These years came to be known as 'Yezhovshchina',," wrote Ehrenburg in his Memoirs.[47] People held Nikolai Yezhov, the head of the dreaded Secret Police 1936–38, responsible for the "senseless violence committed against the Communists, against the Soviet intelligentsia". Stalin continued to be revered by millions as a "sort of mythical demi-god". If we are to believe Ehrenburg, he—and many others like him—Meyerhold, Pasternak—were convinced that Stalin knew nothing about the terror. "One night . . . I met Boris Pasternak . . .; he waved his arms about as

* See p. 427.

he stood between the snowdrifts, 'If only someone would tell Stalin'."
This was in 1938. Ehrenburg, who survived ("how, I shall never
know") told some of the story, "The life we led in those days was quite
exceptional . . . There was no one in the circle of my acquaintance who
could be sure about the morrow; many of them kept a small suitcase
. . . permanently in readiness . . . I once met Prokofiev at the Club—he
played some of his compositions. He was unhappy, even grim, and
said to me, 'Today one must work. Work is the only thing, the only
salvation'."[48]

As happens so often in times of extreme stress, the mood of the
populace turned towards light entertainment—operettas, popular songs,
humorous films were in demand. Dunayevsky and Blanter, composers of light music, rose to renewed fame. After all, "life is easier,
life is gayer" was the slogan of Stalin's regime. The harsh every-day
reality was seen through rose-coloured glasses. ". . . Life of the Soviet
people was often presented as a continuous holiday, and the labour of
the people as an easy and gay occupation," writes a Soviet historian in
retrospect. All this sailed under the flag of Socialist Realism. "One must
admit," writes the same historian, "that the adaptation of the new
method (i.e. Socialist Realism) was complex and controversial. At
times, a one-sided inclination towards official parade-like, festively
pompous forms was noticeable, often connected with the cult of
personality of I. V. Stalin."[49]

Somehow, musical creativity continued despite the oppressive mood.
New operas and ballets were staged, such as Khrennikov's *Into the
Storm* (1939), Dzerzhinsky's *Virgin Soil Upturned* (1937), Prokofiev's
Semyon Kotko (1940) and his long awaited ballet *Romeo and Juliet* (1940).
During the All-Soviet Music Festival of 1939 (November–December),
two historic cantatas aroused fervent patriotic feelings—Shaporin's *On
the Field of Kulikovo* and Prokofiev's *Alexander Nevsky*. Significant new
instrumental works were heard—three symphonies by Miaskovsky
(Nos. 19, 20, and 21, 1939–40), the Sixth Symphony of Shostakovich
(1939), the Violin Concerto of Khachaturian (1940).

In the meantime, the international situation—deteriorating since
Hitler's ascent to power in 1933—moved inexorably towards a crisis.
The German annexation of Austria, the defeat, with German help, of
the Spanish Loyalists, the Munich Pact of 1938 and the subsequent
dismemberment of Czechoslovakia—all this pointed towards an unavoidable conflict. Anglo-French negotiations with the Soviet Union
were dilatory and inconclusive. Memel was annexed by Hitler in
March 1939, and a threat to Poland followed immediately. A last-
minute "deal" with Hitler was almost certainly at the back of Stalin's
mind in April and May of 1939, in the opinion of Werth and other

historians. Yet, when the Soviet-German Non-Aggression Pact was signed on 23 August 1939, the Soviet population was totally unprepared.

This is not the place to discuss the "morality" of the Soviet-German pact, "the pact that was also a duel", as Walter Duranty has said. The Soviet Union gained a breathing spell of twenty-two months, as far as the military confrontation with Germany was concerned. Otherwise, the Soviets were embroiled almost immediately in war-like situations: the occupation of Eastern Poland in September 1939, the bloody Finnish War in 1939-40, the annexation of the Baltic States in the summer of 1940, and the simultaneous move into Rumanian Bessarabia and Northern Bukovina. Although these were "victories", they were won not without sacrifice—40,000 Russians died in the brief Finnish War alone. The home front became tense when industrial labour was put on a virtual war basis. Preparedness was the watchword, and it gained "spontaneous" support from workers and state employees.

In 1940, Ehrenburg returned to Moscow having witnessed the defeats in Spain and France. He was appalled by the lack of concern he found at home, "I went back to Moscow on 29 July. I was convinced that the Germans would soon attack us; the terrible scenes of the exodus from Barcelona and from Paris were still before my eyes. But in Moscow the general mood seemed calm. The press said that friendly relations between the Soviet Union and Germany had grown stronger."[50]

Another year passed while Yugoslavia and Greece fell to the Germans. By 1941—so Ehrenburg surmises—Stalin had become concerned. Yet, when the blow came on 22 June 1941 the Soviet Union was relatively unprepared. It was Molotov, not Stalin, who told the people over the radio that their country had been invaded by the Germans. In a "faltering, slightly stuttering voice", Molotov spoke of a "treacherous attack". Ehrenburg recalls, "We sat for a long time by the radio. Hitler made a speech. Churchill's speech was relayed. But Moscow was broadcasting gay lighthearted songs which in no way corresponded to the mood of the people. No speeches, no articles had been prepared; they were playing songs . . ."[51]

The war for survival had begun.

In the field of opera, Soviet composers made a determined effort to achieve in the 1930's what they had failed to achieve in the 1920's—the creation of a contemporary Soviet opera genre reflecting Soviet reality and aspirations. In this context, the two operas by Shostakovich must be disregarded: they were atypical works, at variance with Soviet aesthetics, and "unsuited" for the Soviet public of the day. As Nestyev commented as late as 1957,

> "Naturally during the years when Socialist culture was advancing, when more and more workers and peasants were beginning to enjoy the treasures of mankind's cultural heritage, it was quite impossible to accept the modernistic distortions which appeared now and then in music, poetry, painting, and architecture. These distortions could only seem offensive and incomprehensible anachronisms in the pure and beautiful world which the Soviet people were creating."[1]

This laboured explanation illuminates the mentality of those who felt responsible for protecting that "pure and beautiful world". *Lady Macbeth* was simply the wrong opera at the wrong time; the whole subject was too "depraved" for the tender sensitivities of Stalin and his cultural satraps. They decreed that the ideal Soviet opera should be positive in outlook, Socialist in content, and national in musical idiom. Since the operas of Shostakovich possessed none of these attributes, the official rejection was almost hysterical. The irony of it is that the crassness and brutality in *Lady Macbeth* were called "Communistic" by some Western critics, while the Soviets rejected it as "bourgeois". When the opera reappeared twenty-five years later as *Katerina Izmailova*, it finally received a fair evaluation in depth—a sign of the growing maturity of Soviet society and its aesthetic standards.

In shaping *Lady Macbeth*, Shostakovich had very definite ideas, both literary and musical. Despite his innate reluctance to discuss himself and his work, he wrote a lengthy commentary on his opera and on his artistic intentions. He had tried—so he said—to make "the musical language of the opera very simple and expressive . . . all my vocal parts are built on broad cantilena". (This is what impressed *Pravda* as "neurotic screaming".) Shostakovich explained that the music of each act was conceived as an integral whole, without being separated into individual numbers; and that the orchestral *entr'actes* were meant to form essential bridges between scenes. Hence, the orchestra, in *Lady Macbeth*, "plays perhaps an even more important part than the soloists and the chorus". As for the libretto, the composer admitted that Katerina "commits several acts that are not compatible with ethics and morality", but he saw some justifications though he did not quite trust his verbal powers as he says, "It would take a lengthy explanation for me to describe how I justify these acts—this is better accomplished by the musical material which, I consider, plays the leading and decisive part in an operatic work."[2] At the time, Shostakovich is reported to have planned a trilogy portraying Russian womanhood, and *Katerina Izmailova* was to be the first of the intended cycle. Needless to say, the plan was dropped after the fate of *Katerina*.

To understand the initial acceptance and subsequent rejection of *Lady Macbeth* within a span of a few years, one must visualize the profound changes in Soviet attitudes towards the arts that took place in the early 1930's. The Resolution of 1932 paved the way for stricter Party guidance of all creative work. In literature, the guidelines were spelled out at the Writers' Congress of 1934. In music, the formulation of certain principles was somewhat slower, the application of Socialist Realism more tortuous. The genre of opera was recognized as being most urgently in need of reform, and by January 1936 the Stalin-sponsored principles had been transmitted to, and adopted by, an assembly of operatic experts. In view of the newly evolving policy, the condemnation of *Lady Macbeth* was unavoidable.

By a quirk of fate, the fall of *Lady Macbeth* coincided with the acclaim given to a new opera—*The Quiet Don* by Ivan Dzerzhinsky. Here was a work that seemed to fill all the requirements of the "new" Soviet opera: it was simple, wholesome, socialist, and patriotic. On 21 January 1936—a week before the attack on Shostakovich—*Pravda* reported that Stalin was favourably impressed by *The Quiet Don*. Obviously, it represented a type of opera to be patronized officially.

Prior to its unexpected success, *The Quiet Don* had had a checkered history. In 1932, the young composer—while still a student at the Leningrad Conservatory—entered the work in an opera contest sponsored by the Bolshoi Theatre and the journal *Komsomolskaya Pravda*. When the results were announced in 1934, *The Quiet Don* did not even receive an honourable mention, and the evaluation of the jury was near-disastrous,

"The libretto is ragged and consists of fragments from Sholokhov's novel, tied together without observing the elementary rules of scenes and dramaturgy. In many instances the saving grace is the nearness of the material to the contemporary listener. The music reveals the unquestioned talent of the composer; the gift for song are traits of his originality. Unfortunately, the technical skill of the author is on a very low level. The creative means are monotonous, there are many empty spots. The orchestration is primitive. All this lends the entire work a stamp of monotony. Nevertheless, certain fragments convey an impression of talent."[3]

This, then, was the newly discovered masterpiece. But young Dzerzhinsky found an unexpected champion in Shostakovich who recognized a certain potential, "In spite of the sketchiness and unfinished state of the material, I felt the great gifts of the author . . . I realized immediately that what I had heard would make a good piece . . . One had to help Dzerzhinsky . . . who was as inexperienced as he was talented . . ."[4] Shostakovich referred Dzerzhinsky to the conductor Samosud who offered his rich theatrical experience in putting *The Quiet Don* into final shape for a production at Leningrad's Malyi Theatre. It is safe to say that the version shown on 22 October 1935 was a substantial improvement of the one rejected by the jury of the 1932–34 contest.

The libretto, written by the composer's brother, was based on "motives" from Sholokhov's—as yet unfinished—novel. The author of the libretto had to invent his own ending which, as it turned out, was different from the one Sholokhov eventually wrote. Nevertheless, the libretto was serviceable and effective; the Soviet listener could identify himself with the people and the events. The score had the same directness: it was simple, uncomplicated, melodious, it used the musical idioms of mass songs and revolutionary folklore, though without actual quotations. Certain songs from the opera, like the final chorus "From border to border" swept the country. The effect, particularly on an unsophisticated public, was irresistible. But even the critical listeners were captivated by the freshness and unpretentiousness of the spectacle.

Shostakovich, usually so reserved and sparing with praise, wrote even before the première that *The Quiet Don* was an "outstanding work, destined perhaps to play a significant role in the evolution of Soviet opera." These turned out to be prophetic words. Asafiev, writing in retrospect in 1944, pointed to "certain imperfections of technique" but found them outweighed by "the freshness of folk lyricism and the realism of the characters . . . People with living intonations, behaving in a natural way, appear once again on the stage. The melodies have been revived with song elements, and lyricism once again expresses healthy emotions."[5] Rather pointedly, Asafiev remarked that the public preferred this type of wholesome experience to the "grotesque artificiality" of Shostakovich's *The Nose* or the "cynical sensuality" of *Lady Macbeth* —a gratuitous jog at two works he himself had admired at one time.

But the decisive factor in catapulting *The Quiet Don* into fame was the personal approval of Stalin. His comments were designed not merely to encourage a young composer but to stimulate the development of Soviet opera. The first press release was entitled "Conversation of Comrades Stalin and Molotov with the authors of the operatic production *The Quiet Don*,"

> ". . . During the conversation, comrades Stalin and Molotov gave positive appraisals of the work of the theatre (the visiting Leningrad Malyi Theatre) in the field of the creation of Soviet opera, and remarked on the ideological and political value of the production of *The Quiet Don*. At the conclusion of the talk, comrades Stalin and Molotov expressed the need of remedying certain shortcomings of the production and also expressed their best wishes for further success in the work on Soviet opera."[6]

This statement received some elaboration when Dzerzhinsky and the conductor Samosud reported in their own words what had been said during the conversation. The twenty-six-year-old composer was obviously overwhelmed by the occasion, and his comments sound stereotyped, "Comrade Stalin said that the time was ripe for the creation of a classical Soviet opera. He pointed out that such an opera should be emotionally inspiring, and that melodic inflections of folk music should be widely used. The music ought to make use of all the latest devices of musical techniques, but its idiom should be close to the masses, clear and accessible."[7]

Samosud's comment was more pertinent. He had been the musical director of the Leningrad Malyi Theatre—an outpost of modern opera—since its inception in 1918, and he was vitally concerned with the future course of Soviet opera. Samosud asked Stalin whether the policy of the Malyi Theatre—the struggle on behalf of Soviet opera —was justified. Stalin answered in the affirmative: while operatic classicism was needed, it was time to have "our own Soviet classicism". When Samosud said that his theatre was often "whipped" for its advanced stand on Soviet opera, Stalin asked, "who whips you?" and added jokingly, "probably the oldsters". While pleased with much of the performance, Stalin remarked that Dzerzhinsky still had to learn to marshal all the musical resources needed to give full musical expression

to the ideas and passions motivating the Soviet heroes. Stalin and
Molotov also made a few comments about the staging which must
"help, not confuse" the understanding of the spectator. Samosud concluded that the "creation of a Soviet opera" was not the task of the
Malyi Theatre alone, but was of concern to all people active in Soviet
music. That same year, Samosud's career advanced significantly: he was
appointed to the highest post in the country—the conductorship of the
Bolshoi Theatre in Moscow. In 1943 he joined the Stanislavsky-
Nemirovich-Danchenko opera theatre in Moscow—a smaller but more
adventurous establishment. During the 1940's, he formed a close
artistic friendship with Prokofiev, helping in the various revisions of the
opera *War and Peace,* and conducted the première presentation of the
first eight scenes of *War and Peace* in Leningrad. Samosud died, highly
honoured, in 1964.

As for Dzerzhinsky's *The Quiet Don,* it became—with the blessing of
the Party and the public—the prototype of a new Soviet genre—the
"song opera". Intuitively, Dzerzhinsky had anticipated the official
criteria which were actually quite simplistic. During the next few years,
a number of operas appeared, attempting to emulate the new principles
but none proved durable. Dzerzhinsky himself was unable to repeat his
first success.* His next opera, *Virgin Soil Upturned,* again based on
Sholokhov, was given at the Bolshoi Theatre—under Samosud—on
23 October 1937. His limited compositorial technique proved to be a
hindrance though he avoided the issue by saying that "it would be
wrong to employ complex musical forms to express uncomplicated
emotions and thoughts". In fact, he turned his artlessness into a virtue
by remarking, "In general, I have a negative attitude towards musical
ensembles in opera. When five people start to sing simultaneously—one
smiling, the other frowning, and each speaking his own words—one
cannot make any sense out of it."[8]

Dzerzhinsky's utterance points out the pitfalls of the new operatic
trend—the deliberate simplification of the musical idiom, the primitive
professional approach, the neglect of established traditions. Discussing
this impoverishment of Soviet opera during the later 1930's Asafiev
criticized the "primitivists",

> "The healthy trend . . . proved incapable of accomplishing the task
> set before it and finally resulted in over-simplification . . . The
> importance of recitative was reduced . . . either to a sort of 'metric
> speech' . . . or to a dry, primitive, and naturalistic presentation of

* Between 1940 and 1960, he produced no fewer than eight operas without a
single success. After *The Fate of Man* in 1960 he was criticized for professional
deficiencies bordering on wilful negligence.

prose speech, set to intervals. Rhythm became monotonous. The constant use of the marching step of the mass song, the inevitable scheme . . . of the rousing finale, turned into a cliché of the choral mass song expression of heroic emotions . . . The art of ensemble writing . . . was completely lost. Melody was supplanted by strophic and fragmentary modern street ditties ('chastushki') . . . This may have been necessary to provide a realistic atmosphere, but it also caused the degeneration of the aria as an expression of depth and passion of feeling."[9]

Among the "song operas" of the 1930's, one work stood out above the general mediocrity—*Into the Storm* by Tikhon Khrennikov. It was proclaimed the best of its type after the première in 1939. Less than a year later, in June 1940, the opera *Semyon Kotko* by Prokofiev was staged. The musical community took sides and played one work against the other. The temper of the times was unfavourable to Prokofiev's more complex musical conception. *Semyon Kotko* was adjudged "formalistic" and disappeared from the repertoire for almost twenty years. A concert performance was given in 1957 in Moscow, four years after the composer's death, and the piano score was not published until 1960. Since then, however, the work has been fully rehabilitated.

The unfair treatment meted out to Prokofiev's opera should not obscure our judgment of Khrennikov's *Into the Storm*. It has a youthful freshness, an engaging charm, and far more technical skill than that displayed by most of his *confrères* in the field. Khrennikov—born in 1913—wrote a symphony and a piano concerto while still a student at the Moscow Conservatory. But his true inclination was—and has remained—the theatre. During the 1930's he wrote incidental music for the progressive Vakhtangov Theatre, and his score to Shakespeare's *Much Ado about Nothing* was highly praised. His first opera, *Into the Storm*, has the insouciance of youth and adheres to the principles of the "song opera"—simplicity, directness, folkishness, "real" people mirrored in their environment. All this was heightened by the composer's gift for idiomatic melodic invention and his innate sense of dramatic effectiveness. In a second, slightly revised version, *Into the Storm* has remained successfully in the Soviet repertoire.

Incidentally, the libretto calls for an appearance of Lenin on the stage —the first (though not the last) time in operatic history. The action takes place in the year 1920, and the peasant Frol Bayev, seeking "the truth", meets Lenin in the Kremlin. The brief conversation is not set to music; even the orchestra remains temporarily silent. The device of avoiding music at this culminating point has been hailed as the only right solution. However, since then, Lenin has been heard to raise his voice in song—in the opera *October* by Muradeli (1964)—though this fact alone was not sufficient to lift that work above mediocrity.

Prokofiev, too, was interested in furthering the cause of a truly Soviet opera. As early as 1933, shortly after his permanent return to Moscow, he said, "I very much want to write an opera on a Soviet topic, but it is not so simple to find a suitable libretto: while much space is given in our plays and libretti to a satirical, caricature-like picturization of the negative hero, little is said about the positive and heroic type, or—if at all—it is done too schematically . . ."[10] Prokofiev wanted a subject "heroic and constructive . . . for these are the traits characteristic of the present era in the Soviet Union". Unable to find the material he wanted, he turned for advice to Alexei Tolstoy who suggested a story by Valentin Katayev, published in 1937, under the title *I, the Son of the Working People*. The action is set in a Ukrainian village at the time of the Civil War. The hero is Semyon Kotko, a young peasant and partisan.

Katayev agreed to work on the dramatization, but his concept of a folk opera, with songs and dances, did not please Prokofiev who is reported to have said, "I don't need rhymes and arias." Instead, Prokofiev insisted on prose dialogue which he set to music in a kind of melodic recitative. Yet he was not unmindful of the folk idiom, and he familiarized himself with texts and tunes of Ukrainian folklore which he remembered fondly from his childhood spent in the village of Sontsovka. But it was not in Prokofiev's nature to compromise. He deliberately challenged the—then fashionable—rousing marches and "song and dance" routines. Prior to the première of *Semyon Kotko* he wrote a lengthy essay, setting forth his ideas on the subject. It was not published until 1956 though it was meant for a printed symposium in connection with the production of the opera. Thus, the critics who—at the time—passed a negative judgment, were ignorant of the composer's own ideas, of his motivation in writing as he did. Today, in retrospect, one can see how cautiously Prokofiev had approached his project, though all his caution could not prevent a failure. Here are some of his thoughts,[11]

> "To write an opera on a Soviet theme is by no means a simple task. One deals here with new people . . ., a new way of life, and hence many of the forms applicable to classical opera might prove unsuitable . . . I had long wanted to write a Soviet opera . . . I did not want a commonplace . . . plot or, on the contrary, a plot that pointed too obvious a moral. I wanted live human beings with human passions . . . arising naturally from the new conditions . . ."

Prokofiev felt that certain types of arias had a retarding effect on the stage action. "When a person goes to the opera, he wants not only to *hear* but to *see*. Hence the action must be dynamic . . . In composing my opera I have tried not to let the action on the stage lapse for a single moment . . ." In his desire to "activate" the happenings on the stage, Prokofiev decided to avoid recitatives "as the least interesting element in opera". Here is how he dealt with this problem. "At the more emotional moments, I have tried to make the recitative melodious, producing a sort of recitative melody. In the more 'matter-of-fact' parts, I have used rhythmic speech . . . something in the nature of a chant . . . I have endeavoured to make the transition from singing to speaking sound natural . . . the listener is not even aware of the transition . . ."

Prokofiev felt, though others disagreed, that he did not neglect the melodic aspects, but sought originality, "Although it would obviously have been more advantageous from the standpoint of immediate success to have filled the opera with melodies of familiar design, I preferred to use new material . . . of new design. New life, new subject matter demand new forms of expression, and the listener must not complain if he has to exert a little effort to grasp these forms . . ."

Alas, the "little effort" for which the composer pleaded was not forthcoming, neither from the public nor from the professionals. In bitter debates, fought in the Composers' Union and on the pages of *Sovetskaya Muzyka*, Prokofiev's *Semyon Kotko* was torn apart, compared unflatteringly with the song style of Khrennikov's *Into the Storm*, and ultimately discarded. There were many petty minds who were resentful of Prokofiev. Had he not said that Soviet composers were "provincial"? Had he not said that "formalism" was something people did not understand at first hearing? The acrimonious debate was not soon forgotten; those who defended *Semyon Kotko* were regarded with suspicion years later when mere sympathy with modernism became a sin.

One must admire the resilience of Prokofiev who, during the next decade, wrote three more operas. Of these, only the comic opera *La Duenna* had a measure of success. The monumental *War and Peace* was never fully staged during the composer's lifetime while his last opera, *The Story of a Real Man*, was rejected in harsh terms during the crisis year 1948.

Midway between Prokofiev's "expressionistic idiom" (a term used pejoratively by Asafiev in 1944) and Khrennikov's simplified song style are the works of several other composers which do not veer towards either extreme. Here we find Kabalevsky and his first opera, *Colas Breugnon*. Given in Leningrad in 1938, it was never produced elsewhere in the Soviet Union. Perhaps it was the remoteness of the libretto that failed to interest a wide audience: the chronicle of a Burgundian master craftsman in the sixteenth century is not exactly close to Soviet reality. The original book by Romain Rolland, written in 1913 and published in 1918, was popular among Russian intellectuals.* Rolland called his book "*sans politique, sans métaphysique, un livre à la 'bonne françoise'* . . .", though it contains some social criticism. This point is stressed in the opera where the librettist enlarged upon the social conflict between the master craftsman and the feudal patron-duke. Rolland liked Kabalevsky's music but was not so sure about the shift in emphasis. He wrote to the composer, "The libretto did not preserve much of the specific French and Burgundian character of my *Colas Breugnon*. I no longer recognize my basic protagonist whom the librettist has transposed—if I may use the expression—into a different tonality."[12]

Kabalevsky's score is sparkling, transparent, full of Gallic gaiety, probably as French as a Russian can get. He made a study of French folklore, but there are no direct quotations, except for two brief motives. The composer said, "I believe that in writing a work on an 'historic' subject one must not attempt a photographic reproduction of the era, nor should one stylize the work—the result will be cold, dry and alien to the contemporary listener. One should strive to convey the colour and character of the period . . ."[13]

In the West, only the Overture to *Colas Breugnon* is known, a sparkling, effective curtain raiser, brilliantly orchestrated and of engaging melodiousness. Essentially, Kabalevsky's musical language is conservative, and it has changed little over the years. But it exudes such good humour and is built with so much skill that the listener is carried away despite some critical reservations. Kabalevsky's versatility—he is an excellent pianist and conductor as well as a convincing and scholarly writer—and, above all, his integrity have earned him the highest regard at home and abroad.

Other operas composed and produced during the 1930's had short-lived careers. Many of the failures can be attributed to over-simplification, operatic "primitivism", and plain lack of technique. Tunefulness and folkishness were not sufficient to ensure success, as many young composers discovered to their disappointment. Often, the librettists were equally at fault. Among the unsuccessful operas of that decade were *The Kamarinsky Peasant* (1933), *Nameday* (1935), and *Mother* (1939) all by Valery Zhelobinsky**; also *Mutiny* (1938) by Leon

* It went through some 120 printings in a Russian translation before Kabalevsky chose it as a libretto.

** Zhelobinsky died at the age of thirty-three in 1946. See Prokofiev's comment on p. 234.

Khodzha-Einatov, *Battleship Potemkin* (1939) by Oles Chishko, and *The Perekop* (1939) by Yuli Meitus. All dealt with topics related to social rebellion, past or present, and followed in general the trend of the "song opera".

Western critics who visited Moscow and Leningrad during the 1930's, found the achievements of the Soviet ballet highly disappointing. Kurt London's impression in 1936 was that, "Russian ballet, as it is to-day, makes an out-of-date and reactionary impression and is an anachronistic relic of *l'art pour l'art* pageantry . . . Quite generally it must be unfortunately established that the choreography and dancing style of the Soviet ballet is a good hundred years behind the times . . . Soviet ballet . . . has become an art fit only for the museum. Even in those scenes in which toe-dancing is not used, movements are still conventional."[14]

He found the entire effect "external, based on hollow form" and could not discover "a trace of Socialist Realism". Nor did London care particularly for the musical side; the accompaniments, mostly by Soviet contemporary composers, rivalled the standards of the dancing.

Only the musical aspects need interest us here. The success of the ballets by Boris Asafiev are puzzling to any Western observer, and London is right in saying that Asafiev "cherished a misguided ambition to compose". Yet, the Soviet audiences remain loyally devoted to such excruciatingly boring spectacles as *The Flame of Paris* or *The Fountain of Bakhchisarai*.

According to Soviet historians, *The Flame of Paris* is the "first of the Soviet heroic mass ballet representations". The events depicted are those of the French Revolution, culminating in the taking of the Tuileries in 1792. "The Revolution is enacted on tiptoe. Nothing more ridiculous . . . than pretty little dances with red flags," commented London. Asafiev's music is compiled rather than composed. He used the music of the period—not only popular songs and dances of the Revolution, but also art music by composers like Gossec, Grétry, and Méhul. The court of Louis XVI was depicted by using the music of Lully and Gluck. "These passages were chosen by Asafiev for their gloomy, tragic character in order to show the doom of the old world," explained a Soviet commentator rather naively.[15] It is true that Asafiev calculated every effect, anticipated every mood. He approached the ballet, as he said, "not only as a dramatist and composer, but as musical scholar, historian, theorist, even as an author, resorting to the methods of the modern historical novel."

For his next ballet, *The Fountain of Bakhchisarai*, he abandoned the principle of collecting "authentic" material and wrote what he considered an "original" score—which, unfortunately, lacks any originality. Since the libretto was based on Pushkin, Asafiev chose an early nineteenth-century musical idiom. This led to several strange anachronisms, such as a waltz in a harem. The story is a lyrico-psychological drama, and it gave Galina Ulanova one of her most famous roles—the pure and fragile Maria. It also provided an opportunity for stunning stage effects which were to become the hallmark of Bolshoi ballet productions. "There's more applause when the curtain goes up on the scenery than there is when it comes down on the dancers," was a wisecrack among Russians.[16]

But what Asafiev lacked in musical originality, he made up in thoroughness and musical scholarship. In each of his ballet scores—and there were ten in the brief span from 1935 to 1941—he adjusted his musical language to the given topic, lending it "concreteness" in matters of historical details, national colour, and popular customs. His participation in the production was not limited to the music alone; he worked closely with the choreographer, the librettist, the stage director. He chose the topics, turning often to literary classics by Pushkin, Lermontov, Gogol, Ostrovsky, Gorky, Kuprin, and even Balzac. He used many national colours—French and Italian, Tartar and Caucasian, Polish and Ukrainian, Gypsy and Persian—not to mention genuine Russian. In his archives, Asafiev kept innumerable notations on customs, songs and dances, folk tunes, harmonizations, and many other details needed for a "concrete" realization of a given subject. With his theatrical experience and his superior intellect, he created almost single-handedly a new "science" of ballet writing.

Following the example of Asafiev, other composers—musically more original—made use of his innovations. Highly acclaimed was *Laurencia* with a score by Alexander Krein, staged in Leningrad in 1939. The scenario, based on Lope de Vega's *Fuente Ovejuna*, had already attracted Glière in the 1920's.* The Spanish Civil War revived interest in the topic, and Krein created a heroic ballet stressing the revolutionary struggle. The score is full of Spanish colour and—aside from a few quotations—the material is the composer's own. Krein, born in 1883, belonged to the older generation, and his rich experience as a composer is evident in the solid craftsmanship of the score.

* Faubion Bowers (in his book *Broadway, U.S.S.R.*) retells the story amusingly, "A village maiden, after having been raped, leads the villagers in a happy revolution, and they burn (typically for the Bolshoi) the castle full of wicked soldiers. Against the gaiety of a Spanish setting . . . the brutality of the soldiers is enacted. A rock is painfully crushed in the face of the hapless hero. But all this is wiped away in the joyous triumph of the villagers over evil authority."

Quite successful was the first Georgian ballet, *The Heart of the Mountain*, with a score by Andrei Balanchivadze (brother of the choreographer George Balanchine). The story is based on an incident from eighteenth-century Georgian history—the peasant revolt against Prince Eristhavi. The score uses folk melodies and native dance rhythms in a well-integrated manner. The première was given, almost simultaneously, in 1938 in Leningrad and Tbilisi.

A clever production was the satirical comedy-ballet *Tale about the pope and his workman Balda* (after Pushkin) with a score by young Mikhail Chulaki (born in 1908). Incorporating a wide assortment of folk material, the composer paid special attention to the orchestral sound. It acquired a "folk" timbre through rich display of wind instruments, imitations of balalaikas and actual use of the "bayan", an accordion widely used in Russian folk music. Chulaki's ballet was first staged in Leningrad in 1939.

Yet the creeping conventionality afflicting Soviet music during the 1930's was reflected in all the ballets mentioned so far. In stark contrast are the three ballets of Shostakovich composed between 1927 and 1935: they are refreshingly unconventional, pert, and almost insolent. All three—*The Golden Age, Bolt*, and *The Limpid Stream*—have disappeared from the ballet repertoire, but some of the music survived in orchestral suites arranged by the composer. *The Golden Age* was a persiflage, an irreverent romp, "actually a typical revue disguised as ballet", as one Soviet biographer remarked. *Bolt* tried to deal with the topic of industrial productivity—and failed.★

The Limpid Stream, produced in 1935, was a different story altogether. The scenario attempted to portray the life on a collective farm in the Kuban Cossack region, but the attempt misfired—neither the Kolkhoz nor the Kuban were adequately pictured, according to Soviet critics. The collective farmers resembled "peasants painted on pre-revolutionary candy boxes", and the whole spectacle was "concocted by opportunists". As for the music, it was found to be "without character, it jingles, it is meaningless. The composer apparently has only contempt for national songs . . ."[17] Indeed, Shostakovich seems to have taken his task somewhat lightly: he had transferred fragments of his earlier ballet *Bolt* into *The Limpid Stream* and—horror upon horror!—his previously industrial music now had to serve agricultural purposes. All this strained Soviet patience to breaking point and led to a public condemnation of *The Limpid Stream* a week after the attack on *Lady Macbeth*. The critical article "Ballet Falsehood", published in *Pravda* on 6 February 1936, rivals in vehemence the castigation of the opera and sealed the

★ See pp. 74-5.

temporary misfortune of Shostakovich. It ended his career as a ballet composer.

The truly great achievement of the Soviet ballet during the 1930's—and perhaps one of its greatest altogether—was Prokofiev's *Romeo and Juliet*. The music was composed in 1935–36, but the ballet was not staged until 1940 at the Leningrad Kirov (former Maryinsky) Theatre. The delay reflects the bewilderment of the ballet experts who considered the completed score unsuitable for dancing. There was also some wrangling about the scenario which was to have a "happy ending", with both lovers alive and reunited; only strong protests from literary authorities succeeded in restoring the original ending. The vicissitudes of the production were well expressed by Galina Ulanova, who danced Juliet, when she proposed a humorous toast in rhyme after the première,

> "Never was a tale of greater woe,
> Than Prokofiev's music to Romeo."*

She herself had to overcome many reservations before she grew into the role which was to become her greatest achievement.

The suggestion to write *Romeo and Juliet* came from the Kirov Theatre as early as 1934. In the spring of 1935, Prokofiev worked on the scenario with Sergei Radlov, a staff member of the Kirov Theatre. Radlov knew Prokofiev's style, for he had directed the Russian première of the opera *The Love for Three Oranges* in Leningrad in 1926. As director of his own theatre studio, Radlov was also familiar with problems of Shakespearean production; he had staged *Othello* and *Romeo*. Prokofiev completed the piano score by September 1935; the following month, he played some excerpts in piano transcription at a concert in Moscow. The critic of *Izvestia* commented warmly on the new "realistic language" of the composer. Impatient with the delays at the Kirov Theatre, Prokofiev arranged several orchestral suites from the ballet score. Suite No. 1 was performed in Moscow on 24 November 1936 under Georg Sebastian; Suite No. 2 received its première on 15 April 1937 in Leningrad under the composer's baton. The scores of both suites were published in 1938 as Opus 64 *bis* and 64 *ter*. In addition, Prokofiev arranged a piano suite of ten excerpts from the ballet which he performed in Moscow in 1937; it was published the following year

---

* In Russian, 'Nyet povesti pechalneye na svete/Chem muzyka Prokofieva v balete", translated literally, "There is no sadder tale in the world/Than Prokofiev's music for ballet".

as Opus 75. Thus, the music for *Romeo and Juliet* was played and acclaimed several years before the ballet was actually staged.

The world première of *Romeo and Juliet* was in fact given outside the Soviet Union, at the provincial theatre of Brno in Czechoslovakia, in December 1938. For a work commissioned by a Soviet theatre to be given a première abroad was a surprising, almost embarrassing development. In the meantime, there had been changes at the Kirov Theatre; a new choreographer was appointed in 1938, Leonid Lavrovsky, who had a fine reputation as a dancer and, later, ballet master. In the autumn of 1938, he came to Moscow to confer with Prokofiev. He described the first meeting as immensely impressive, yet he had to tell the composer that changes and additions would have to be made. Reluctant though Prokofiev was to make any concessions, he was anxious to have the work staged after so much delay. A decision to produce the ballet at the Kirov Theatre was not made until 1939, and it took another year, until 11 January 1940, before the curtain finally rose.

From the reminiscences of Lavrovsky and Ulanova[18] we know that choreographer and dancers had to struggle with Prokofiev for every change and adjustment. Lavrovsky wanted some additional music, but Prokofiev stubbornly refused, saying "I've written exactly as much music as is necessary, and I shan't add a single note . . . You must manage with what you've got." Exasperated, Lavrovsky looked through some older music of Prokofiev, chose the Scherzo of the Second Piano Sonata, dating back to 1912, and inserted it in the first scene without telling the composer. Prokofiev was furious and refused to orchestrate the piece. "We'll do it on two pianos," replied Lavrovsky. Prokofiev stormed out of the rehearsal but eventually relented. Other frictions occurred when the dancers found the orchestration too delicate. Compared to the "full, powerful 'dansante' orchestra", as Lavrovsky called it, Prokofiev's orchestration was at times so intimate as to be nearly inaudible to the preoccupied dancers. Unbelieving, Prokofiev climbed on the stage: "I can hear everything," he declared. The principal dancers. Ulanova and Sergeyev, kept complaining, "We can't hear the music." Prokofiev shouted furiously, "I know what you want. You want drums, not music." Ultimately, though still angry, he agreed to "add something".

Problems arose when action and music were not fully co-ordinated at various places. The scenario had been changed, sometimes without sufficient adjustment to the flow of the music. "While stormy passions raged on the stage, the orchestra would be playing music that was delicate and refined," recalled Lavrovsky. Prokofiev was inclined to blame Lavrovsky; "the staging was often at odds with the music" and he complained at rehearsals that the dancers often moved "against the music". The dancers, on the other hand, were struggling with a musical style that was novel and alien to them. "At first," says Ulanova, "the music seemed to us incomprehensible and almost impossible to dance to . . . But the more we listened to it, the more we worked . . . the more clearly emerged the images that music created . . ." Yet it took some time. Ulanova was frank: when asked during a rehearsal what she thought of the music, she said, "Ask Lavrovsky, he has instructed me to like it." The "intricate harmonies, the angularity of the rhythms" seemed to inhibit the dancers. "The rehearsals were in full swing," Ulanova recalls, "but we were still badly hampered by the unusual orchestration and the chamber quality of the music. The frequent changes of rhythm, too, gave us a great deal of trouble. To tell the truth, we were not accustomed to such music, in fact we were a little afraid of it . . ."

The dancers were not only afraid of the music but also of Prokofiev, who appeared stern, unapproachable, and haughty—"disapproving heartily of everything he saw and especially of us, the dancers." Lavrovsky had to mediate, and it is entirely to his credit that the production took shape; miraculously, his friendship with Prokofiev survived. Nor were the dancers alone in their bafflement: the orchestra musicians held a meeting two weeks before the première "at which it was decided that, to avoid a scandal, the performance should be cancelled". Despite all opposition, the première took place, and it was a triumphal success.

The professional problems encountered by Prokofiev in shaping *Romeo and Juliet* are all the more surprising in view of his rich experience in the field of ballet. He had worked with Diaghilev, Massine, Balanchine, Lifar, and his ballets of the Parisian period were not all pursued by "bad luck", as Ulanova surmised. *The Buffoon* (Chout, 1921), *Pas d'Acier* (1927), *The Prodigal Son* (1929), and *On the Dniepr* (Sur le Borysthène, 1932) had been notable achievements, though perhaps not in terms of Soviet aesthetics. There was a deliberate tendency among Soviet critics to belittle Prokofiev's compositions written abroad during the 1920's, and this attitude is still noticeable in Nestyev's biography published in 1957,

"*Romeo and Juliet* presents a striking contrast to the ballets Prokofiev composed in Paris. When he wrote *The Prodigal Son* and, especially, *Sur le Borysthène*, he had no vital material to fire his imagination, nothing to stimulate his talents for portraiture, dramaturgy, and poetry . . . *Sur le Borysthène* amounted to providing a musical accompaniment for an entire ballet which had neither plot nor characters."[19]

Fortunately, such supercilious evaluations have become rare in Soviet musicography; today, Prokofiev is recognized as the modern classic, and Nestyev himself has revised many of his former opinions.

Lavrovsky, the choreographer, was to work again with Prokofiev towards the end of the composer's career: he was the co-author of the scenario for *The Stone Flower* and directed the posthumous production. What Prokofiev's ballet music meant to the choreographer is expressed in the following recollections of Lavrovsky, "Prokofiev carried on where Tchaikovsky left off. He developed and elaborated the principles of symphonism in ballet music. He was one of the first Soviet composers to bring to the ballet stage genuine human emotions and full-blooded characters. The boldness of his musical treatment, the clear-cut characterizations, the diversity and intricacy of his rhythms, the unorthodoxy of his harmonies . . . serve to create the dramatic development of the performance."[20]

Prokofiev's *Romeo and Juliet* is too well known today to require elaboration, analysis, or praise. However, not all Western observers are carried away by the Soviet interpretation of this work. In the late 1950's, the critic-author Faubion Bowers saw a performance with Ulanova at the Bolshoi Theatre and wrote,

> "Predictably, *Romeo and Juliet* is gargantuan . . . The actual effect it gives is that of a pageant on an extravaganza scale. The choreographers . . . have taken the highlights of the Shakespeare play . . . and chained them together in dance form . . . Prokofiev has scored his music for an enormous orchestra, and if this is not enough . . . he places an additional orchestra of a dozen mandolines and four cornets onstage . . ."[21]

The "enormous" orchestra described here is completely at odds with the composer's original, more intimate concept. Certainly, considerable padding and coarsening of instrumental texture must have been done without Prokofiev's knowledge or approval.*

Undoubtedly, many a Western spectator will find the Soviet ballet version of *Romeo and Juliet* artificial and disturbing, as indeed did some Soviet critics. But to the Soviet dance world, the concept of this ballet opened new perspectives in terms of danced drama, of psychological search in a—basically extrovert—medium. *Romeo and Juliet* was seen as the beginning of a new ballet era, revealing uncharted vistas.

To the concert-goer, the orchestral suites drawn by the composer from the ballet score have become a familiar treat. The music is strong without being daring, colourful without being extravagant, and it

* See p. 241.

reflects an emotional involvement that was often hidden in earlier works—a new facet of Prokofiev's immense talent that endeared him to millions while baffling some of his old admirers. Actually, it was not new, but merely a shift in emphasis, a stress on the gentler, lyrical side of his creative personality. This process of mellowing was to come to full fruition in Prokofiev's great works of the 1940's.

In February 1935, the Composers' Union held a three-day conference on the topic of Soviet Symphonism. Composers, critics, and theorists from Moscow and Leningrad engaged in a "creative discussion" of Soviet symphonic music, its successes and failures, its achievements and prospects.[22] There was a notable polarization of opinions, with composers and critics on opposite sides. The critics read lengthy prepared statements which were answered during the debate by the composers. The critics freely dispensed advice, praise and blame, but the composers struck in rebuttal.

One critic derided "the rotting musical culture of the West" (including Schoenberg, Webern, Milhaud, Honegger, Stravinsky), but Shostakovich thought differently, "We Soviet composers do not know enough about Western compositions . . . We should have a seminar at the Composers' Union to become acquainted with the musical culture of the West; there is much that is interesting and instructive . . ." Critics tended to overpraise Soviet symphonic art, but young composers, among them Shostakovich and Kabalevsky, urged restraint. One of them, Victor Belyi, who had been in the forefront of young "proletarian" musicians, acknowledged the bitter truth ". . . Soviet symphonism does not as yet exist. Let's be modest and admit that we do not as yet have musical works in extended form that reflect the stylistic, ideo-emotional segments of our life—and notably reflect it in *beautiful* form . . . We must admit that we have, in our symphonic music, so far only a few tendencies towards the realization of a new musical language, musical thought, timid hints of a future style . . ."

Had such an evaluation come from a critic, it might have seemed an impertinence. Coming, as it did, from a composer who had contributed towards creating a "Soviet" style, it was an admission of collective failure. Exaggerated though it may be, such self-criticism was refreshing in view of the fulsome praise heaped on works, mediocre in musical substance, but rich in ideological appeal. Already in 1934, Kabalevsky had pointed to the discrepancy between Soviet titles of musical compositions and their non-Soviet content. He maintained that Soviet composers had not yet found "expressive means corresponding to the topics selected, and that even the topics were not always thought out thoroughly". Kabalevsky's criticism was obviously aimed at the shift to Soviet thematics that became so widespread around 1930. In lieu of "content", the composers simply attached a catchy title or a programme to their music. This, Kabalevsky felt, was a "remnant of the RAPM times . . . the distrust of purely instrumental music which allegedly was incapable of fully reflecting our Soviet reality". And in a final blow at "concrete musical images", Kabalevsky said, "It does not mean at all that Soviet music must 'depict' and 'portray' concrete facts and occurrences—things of which, perhaps, music is not even capable.* We must keep in mind the concrete ideo-emotional basis of creativity."[23]

Kabalevsky expressed what was on the mind of many serious composers. Shostakovich said it bluntly and rather ironically, "There was a time when the problem of content was simple: put in some verses, there's content; no verses—formalism. Now there is serious talk that the question is not one of text, but of music . . . There is no shortcut to content in music."[24]

Coming from Shostakovich, this statement is not without piquancy: had he not used that "simple" expedient of putting "verses" into his *October* and *May Day* symphonies? But he must have realized the drawbacks of this method, for he did not write a symphony between 1929 and 1935, and when he returned to the symphonic form with his Fourth Symphony, it was non-textual and non-programmatic.

Not all young composers were as self-critical as Shostakovich or Belyi. There was Gavril Popov, the composer of a much-discussed Symphony (1932) who spoke up confidently about new creative methods, "Soviet symphonism is a new category of musical work which ought to permeate the creative practice of the composer . . . Soviet symphonism must spread its influence into the forgotten, backward segments of instrumental and vocal music . . . in terms of genuine emotional exposure and intensification of socio-political ideas embedded in the literary part of vocal compositions."[25]

This sounded somewhat fuzzy and bombastic. What was this new category "Soviet symphonism"? The word was not new: Asafiev had coined the Russian term in the 1920's to describe large-scale musical works not necessarily in symphonic form or belonging to the symphonic genre. Subsequently, a thoughtful critic—Sollertinsky—was quick to point out that such works had existed long before the term was coined—Mahler's *Lied von der Erde*, for example, as well as other compositions of the nineteenth and even eighteenth centuries.

But now, in the mid-1930's, the term Soviet Symphonism acquired

* One is reminded of Lunacharsky's statement in 1925 to the KOMSOMOL that realism in literature and realism in music could not be equated. See p. 55.

a slogan-like significance, it became a rallying point and revealed the crisis condition of the Soviet symphony. The critic-composer Bogdanov-Berezovsky tried to provide a more specific answer, "Symphony as a genre is nothing but a sonata for orchestra . . . Symphonism, on the other hand, is the definition of a creative method, a definite procedure for the development of musical material . . . Symphonism as a principle, as a means of musical representation and of concrete reality in the highest philosophical categories, is becoming the leading and dominant method of the Soviet composer, independent of the genres and forms he uses."[26]

Through all this grandiloquence, one perceives the aim to pre-empt the term Soviet Symphonism for large-scale works (not necessarily instrumental nor even "symphonic") representative of the Soviet concept of Socialist Realism. Vague as this aim may be, it was pursued with vigour by a number of Soviet composers during the 1930's.

However, the composers were far from unanimous as to how this aim could best be achieved. They seemed to agree on one point: the traditional non-topical, "absolute" symphony was outdated. The pressure on composers for a "symphonism" with ideological meaning became well-nigh irresistible. Unresolved, however, was the problem of how best to instil meaning into the symphonic genre, and it led to many experiments. Some composers used the purely instrumental approach, usually with titles or programmatic indications, others combined vocal and instrumental textures. The critic Ostretsov remarked in 1935,

"The process of the topical enrichment of Soviet symphonism is proceeding with seven-mile boots . . . Soviet composers are interested in the profound and complex processes taking place in the customs and personal lives of those who participate in the building of a new society and culture . . . the general tenor of our life and construction—collectivization, industrialization, struggle for peace, the defence of our country. All this makes us ponder anew the problems of Soviet lyricism, heroism, epos . . ."[27]

In keeping with the new thematicism, some works were dedicated to the image of a national hero, particularly Lenin, others to national institutions, like the Red Army. A few described historic revolutionary events, while others painted aspects of Soviet life and labour. Many composers turned to works with "national" colouration, incorporating the folklore of an ethnic or national unit within the Soviet Union, occasionally also beyond her borders. The orchestral repertoire was enriched by suites drawn from films, ballets, or from incidental music to plays; usually, the content of such suites was easily identifiable since the music had originally served illustrative purposes.

Within this variety of approaches, an important—though short-lived
—development was the so-called Song Symphonism. It was a hybrid
genre combining voices and instruments in large-scale compositional
cycles. The songs inserted into the instrumental framework were of the
"mass" type—accessible, easily retained, with the customary ideological
slant. There was little effort to integrate the instrumental and vocal
elements, and it led to what some critics called a "deformation" of a
noble genre. But there were also learned defenders of the song symphony. The musicologist Ryzhkin, for example, observed a fusion of
two arts—music and literature—and of two textures—vocal and
instrumental. He referred to the multiplicity of genres traceable in the
song symphony—cantata, suite, oratorio, symphonic poem. By way of
the mass song, the choral element contributed the ingredient of accessibility, while the orchestral element added philosophic depth and scope.[28]

These fanciful theories, however, came too late to save the "song
symphonism"—it disappeared around 1936 from the symphonic genre.
There remained, within Soviet music, a predilection for large-scale
works set for voices and instruments—works that fit neither the definition of oratorio nor that of symphony, but are truly a synthesis of both.
Georgi Sviridov became the master of this genre, though Shostakovich,
Prokofiev, Kabalevsky and many others cultivated it.

The typical song symphony of the 1930's was a rather primitive
affair, deliberately artless in form and thematic invention. Its most successful and characteristic representative was Lev Knipper, a composer
once counted among the modernists. Knipper's Third Symphony
(1932–33) was dedicated to the Far Eastern Red Army; it was scored
for symphony orchestra and military band, vocal soloists, a non-
professional chorus, and accordion. His Fourth Symphony (1933–
34) was entitled *Poem about the Fighting Komsomol* (Poema o boitze-
komsomoltze) and required somewhat smaller forces—a symphony
orchestra, and a chorus of professional and non-professional male
voices. Both symphonies had texts by the popular poet, Victor Gusev.
The Fourth Symphony contains the song *Meadowland* (Poliushko),
a happy melodic inspiration in Russian folk style. There is an incongruous lack of coherence between the rather complex orchestral
sections and the folkish vocal parts. Knipper defended this use of dual,
heterogenous material, "The song is invented so as to be sung independently of the symphony. This is the path an author should follow in
creating large-scale works for the masses." His hope was fulfilled: the
song *Meadowland* became famous on its own (most people believe it to
be an authentic folksong which it is not) while the Fourth Symphony
fell into total oblivion.*

* A second version in 1964 failed to revive interest in the work.

Knipper himself abandoned the song symphony temporarily in his Fifth Symphony, subtitled *Lyric Poem* (1935). When he returned to the genre with his Sixth Symphony (1936), the critics tore it apart. His Seventh Symphony, a martial opus glorifying the Soviet armed forces, was considered rather old-fashioned in its pictorial methods when it was first heard in 1939. None of his twenty symphonies—the last in 1973—entered the permanent repertoire.

But in 1935, at the symphonism conference, Knipper's symphonic methods were discussed with great intensity. The critic Ostretsov placed Knipper's *Far Eastern* Symphony (No. 3) "among the outstanding compositions of the day". To which Shostakovich replied heatedly, "I categorically disagree. In my opinion, the method chosen by Knipper in his symphonies cannot serve as the starting point for the development of the Soviet symphony . . . I find neither purity nor simplicity . . ."[29] At the precise time of this debate—as if to prove what he thought a symphony should be—Shostakovich began work on his own Fourth Symphony, that sprawling, ill-starred work, far removed from either song symphonism or Soviet thematicism—the work that he decided to withdraw rather than expose to the critical fanaticism rampant in 1936.

Shostakovich, incidentally, was not alone in his disapproval of Knipper's symphonic method; even earlier, in 1934, Kabalevsky had found that the songs "had no inner connection with the symphony. The crucial point is not the *song* . . . but *songfulness*; and Knipper errs because his material is not imbued with songfulness."[30]

How to balance the vocal and instrumental elements in a song symphony was a problem solved differently by every composer. In some works, the vocal element was so prevalent that all semblance of a symphonic concept was lost. Such was the case in the three *Vocal Symphonies* (1931–35) by Klimenti Korchmarev, set for vocal soloists, chorus, and orchestra. The same is true of the cycle *The West* (1932) by Alexei Zhivotov which uses revolutionary poetry by Western writers in a setting for tenor, chorus, and orchestra. Worthy of mention is also *The Crusade of Hunger* (1931) by Victor Belyi, for chorus and orchestra.

Composers steeped in the symphonic tradition were better able to cope with the manifold problems of vocal and instrumental integration. From this point of view, the Fourth Symphony (1932–35) of Vladimir Shcherbachev achieved more idiomatic fusion of all forces involved. As early as 1925, in his Second Symphony, Shcherbachev had used texts by Alexander Blok. After a purely orchestral Third Symphony (1931), Shcherbachev returned to the mixed genre in his Fourth which was intended as an immense canvas of Russian revolutionary history—a "musico-historical novel", as one critic called it. The subtitle *Izhorsk* refers to the history of a factory and its workers who played an important role in the 1905 Revolution. Of the seven movements originally planned, only four were completed; as it stands, the work has a cycle of movements roughly corresponding to the symphonic scheme though the slow movement is at the beginning—as so often in the Soviet symphony. Despite his experience as a composer, Shcherbachev was not able to resolve the conflict between the programmatic content and the purely musical development of thematic material. His ultimate failure was the failure of the genre itself.

The application of "song symphonism" techniques to an essentially tragic theme can be observed in two works dedicated to Lenin—the dramatic symphony *Lenin* by Vissarion Shebalin (1931) and the Third Symphony, subtitled *Requiem** (1933), by Kabalevsky. Shebalin conceived his work as a monumental trilogy for symphony orchestra, narrator, four vocal soloists, and chorus, based on the poem *Vladimir Ilyich Lenin* by Mayakovsky. Although only the first third of the plan was executed, the work is complete in itself. There are three movements. The first, for orchestra alone, is a massive fugue, rather free in form, with an assertive main subject. Additional brass players reinforce the powerful orchestral climaxes. This movement is self-contained, without "quotations" of any kind, and is often performed separately. The second movement—a somewhat operatic concept—brings the narration to the day of Lenin's death. Here, the solo singers and the chorus carry the main part while the orchestra is merely an accompanying and illustrating factor. The finale uses an impressive accumulation of forces, somewhat in oratorio style, with polyphonic choral sections and strong orchestral support. The fugal theme from the first movement—at least its initial phrase—reappears both in the second and third movements, and serves as a musically unifying link.

Despite the imposing musical plan and Mayakovsky's moving text, the *Lenin* Symphony by Shebalin was not an unqualified success: it lacked thematic distinction. Critics felt that its melodic inspiration was more suitable for "water-colour landscapes and melancholy nocturnes" than for the "heroic epoch of the Revolution". Though the symphony has not survived as a viable work, it is—in retrospect—a notable "period piece". "This work," a young Soviet historian comments, "combining the elements of instrumental-polyphonic and operatic forms, the oratorio, and musico-literary superimpositions, is perhaps the most striking and artistically the most significant example of that hybrid genre known . . . under the slogan 'song symphony'."[31]

Compared to Shebalin's mature skill, Kabalevsky's *Requiem* Symphony was a simplified concept: two movements only, the first orchestral,

* Not to be confused with his *Requiem* of 1963.

the second combining chorus and orchestra, with a text by Nikolai Aseyev, a disciple of Mayakovsky. Kabalevsky's eclectic idiom was not, however, able to sustain interest in a large-scale work that over-emphasized the mournful aspects of life. In fact, none of the funereal pieces dedicated to Lenin have survived in the repertoire. The Soviet nation—or rather, its leaders—decided to change the character of memorialization from one of mourning to one of "ever-living": the tragedy of his death was obliterated by the immortality of his life's message.

Next to the song symphony, the most widely used method of expressing Soviet thematicism was to stress national and folkloristic aspects. This could be accomplished without using vocal forces. Within a purely instrumental genre, folk melodies could be included side by side with original thematic material, as long as the entire work was impregnated with the idiom of a particular region. Such a method was used extensively by Russian composers of the late nineteenth century, particularly the school of the "Mighty Five", and Soviet composers merely revived the time-honoured precepts of Balakirev, Rimsky-Korsakov, and the others. Unfortunately, this revival failed to revitalize the out-dated methods of the past century; instead, there was much imitative, epigonal writing, a sort of flight into the past that brought Soviet music almost into disrepute. This "search for new simplicity" was being misunderstood abroad as a kind of primitivity. "Democratic music need not be primitive," was the explanation given by a representative group of Soviet musicians to *The New York Times* in 1935. "Our style must reflect the life around us . . . Song is the main element of music . . . Our style demands that the heart of song exist in our music." The democratization of the musical idiom was to come through folklore that is not merely "arranged" but used creatively, reflecting the "social awareness".*

The creative use of this method was indeed a touchstone of the originality and skill of the composer. For the older generation the theories of Balakirev were still valid. Consider the case of the veteran composer Ippolitov-Ivanov. In 1894 he wrote the successful *Caucasian Sketches*. In the 1930's, as a septuagenarian, he composed the *Turkish Fragments* (on Azerbaijan themes), *On the Steppes of Turkmenistan*, and *Uzbek Pictures*. Though forty years separate the early work from the later ones, the technique is essentially the same. There is nothing particularly "Soviet" about Ippolitov-Ivanov's last compositions; it is simply that the exoticism of the nineteenth century had come back into fashion, disguised as cultural encouragement of the ethnic minorities.

* See p. 121.

Somewhat more modern are the orchestral suites of Sergei Vassilenko who had been a student of Ippolitov-Ivanov. Vassilenko's *Turkmenian Pictures* (1931) and particularly his suite *Soviet East* (Sovetskii Vostok, 1932) were popular in their time. The latter consists of seven movements, each built on folk melodies of a different nationality or region —Pamir, Armenia, Uzbekistan, Kazakhstan, Tadzhikistan, Azerbaijan, and Daghestan. The colourful orchestration uses a rich assortment of percussion instruments in an attempt to recreate certain native timbres.

In the evolution of the topical Soviet symphony, Maximilian Steinberg's *Turk-Sib* (actually his Fourth Symphony) is considered significant by Soviet historians. The work was written to celebrate the opening of the Turkestan–Siberian railway, built in the years 1926–30. The composer's aim, revealed in a preface to the score, was to convey the idea of the "mighty struggle with the forces of nature", the crossing of deserts and mountains, the evolution of the "new man" who conquered all obstacles. Each of the four movements is headed by a motto from the poetry of Semyon Kirsanov and Demyan Bednyi, lending the work a quasi-programmatic character. Though there is occasional tone-painting, the basic form of the symphony is preserved. The thematic material—some derived from authentic Kazakh songs—has a folkloristic flavour. Despite the grand design, however, the total effect is one of epigonism.

Composers of the younger generation also tried their hand at orchestral exoticism, but the results were not memorable. Among such works were the *Mari* Suite (1931) by Nikolai Rakov, *Turkmenia* (1932) by Boris Shekhter, and *Vanch* (1932) by Lev Knipper. As usual, the technique employed was to use local folk material within a framework of musical forms belonging to European art music. But the two elements never quite fused, and the results were potpourri-like rhapsodies where authentic-sounding themes were subjected to alien development techniques. Nonetheless, such rhapsody-like compositions have remained in favour with Soviet musicians until today.

One must distinguish, however, between the efforts of Western-trained composers to capture the idiom of far-away regions, and the emergence of native-born composers attempting to preserve age-old folklore while adapting some Western-type technical devices to their specific needs. To what extent the conservatory-taught methods of harmonization, rhythm, and pitch can be used is a question as yet unresolved. Some of the native material is not adaptable to our chromatic twelve-note system or to our limited variety of meter, nor can the Western musician fully reproduce the quasi-improvisational style of performance. The solution may come from the emerging national schools of composers, encouraged by the Composers' Union.

"Native" composers, having followed a normal conservatory curriculum, are able to use these techniques judiciously and creatively without violating the genuine folk idiom. Composers like Kara Karayev of Azerbaijan, Fikret Amirov of Georgia, Edward Mirzoyan of Armenia, to name but a few, have acquired national reputations while preserving their native heritage. Aram Khachaturian's music, often based on Caucasian folk material, might sound too "Westernized" for some tastes, as does the idiom of the Ukrainian Konstantin Dankevich. But the younger generation is more concerned to preserve the authenticity of folk material.

Despite the widespread preoccupation with topical symphonism, the grand old design of the genuine symphony refused to die. Too much of the precious heritage of Russian music was symphonic. Even the young generation, while seeking new solutions, felt the challenge of the great traditional form. Kabalevsky, Khachaturian, Khrennikov all wrote "absolute" symphonies early in their careers though their talents pointed in a different direction.

The great tradition of Russian symphonic art was kept alive primarily by Nikolai Miaskovsky. During the 1930's, he composed nine symphonies, Nos. 11 (1931–32) to 19 (1939). Two of them could be called "topical" symphonies though there is no explicit programme: the Twelfth, nicknamed the *Kolkhoz*, and the Sixteenth, known as the *Aviation* Symphony. Miaskovsky dedicated the *Kolkhoz* to the Fifteenth Anniversary of the October Revolution, and it was first performed on 1 June 1932. The three movements had a suggestive programme later withdrawn by the composer: he had planned to picture the Russian village "*before* and *during* the struggle for a new life, and finally the *new* village". There is something calculated in the whole scheme—a self-conscious adjustment to the times, a rationalization of the problems involved. We must assume that Miaskovsky was sincere though he does not seem entirely at ease with himself, as he says in his Autobiography,

> "The Twelfth Symphony did not quite come off as I had wished; in some way it had become schematic although, in keeping with its content, I broke some rules of formal schemes; but mainly I did not succeed in finding the idiom and form for the Finale which conveys my intentions externally but remains not quite convincing internally."

Even though not wholly successful, the Twelfth Symphony has remained a milestone in Miaskovsky's creative evolution—a symbol of his increased awareness of social changes. Like so many of his fellow-artists, he felt compelled to be more responsive to the cultural appeals of the Party: the non-political intellectual of the 1920's was *passé*—the so-called "fellow traveller" had to yield to the committed artist.

In the Thirteenth Symphony, a one-movement work, Miaskovsky went so far as to experiment with a "linear-constructivist attempt at destroying tonality", but it remained an isolated departure. To meet the repeated criticism that his musical idiom was too "subjective", he searched for a more "objective" style and discusses it in his *Autobiography*,

> "My Fifteenth Symphony (1933–34) . . . is highly regarded by many for its optimism and lyric excitement. Yet, this is not quite the idiom I am seeking. I do not know what this idiom should be, and I have no recipe how to find it. Neither the trend towards the folk-song, nor the idiom of our urban tunes in their pure form seem to me to be the only factors for the creation of a musical language of Socialist Realism in instrumental music—basically so different from vocal music."[32]

Miaskovsky's Sixteenth Symphony (composed 1935–36) came closer to the ideal envisaged by the composer, and it was greeted with exuberant praise by Soviet critics who named it the "Soviet Eroica". A superficial resemblance to Beethoven's Third Symphony explains this honorary title: Miaskovsky's penultimate movement was a funeral march, followed by an "optimistic" finale. The march was composed under the impact of the tragedy that befell the giant airplane "Maxim Gorky", while the finale contains one of Miaskovsky's own mass songs, "There fly the airplanes" (Letyat samolyoty); hence the Sixteenth Symphony is called the *Aviation* Symphony. Miaskovsky's obvious aim was to capture the mood of the Soviet people, the concern, sorrow, and pride felt by his compatriots, and he succeeded in writing a work that was meaningful in its contemporaneousness. Prokofiev, usually a detached and impartial critic, wrote about the Sixteenth Symphony with great warmth,

> "The beauty of the material, the mastery of its presentation, and the over-all harmonious construction—all this is genuinely great art . . . There is no sweetish naivety, no sneaking into the graves of dead composers to obtain stale material."[33]

Only the self-critical composer was not fully satisfied, "Neither do I consider my last, the Sixteenth Symphony, as a fully successful solution of the problems of form or idiom, though the tendency of its content is closer to contemporaneousness than in my other works."[*][34]

* This quote is from the *Autobiography* written in 1936, hence the reference to the Sixteenth Symphony as the "last". In fact, Miaskovsky wrote twenty-seven symphonies; the last was completed in 1950, the year of his death.

In his continued search for an "objective" musical idiom, Miaskovsky produced several lighter-weight works which were rather non-symphonic in form and content. The Eighteenth Symphony, dedicated "To the Twentieth Anniversary of the October Revolution", has a Russian folk flavour; in fact, the composer felt that some of the themes were, so to speak, "songs without words". The style is unpretentious, bright, clear-cut, and incisive—one could call it "Homage to Balakirev" —yet the simplicity is artificial and seems untypical for Miaskovsky.

The popularity of this Eighteenth Symphony was increased by a skilful transcription for band by Petrov, a military band conductor. Miaskovsky heard the band version and liked it so much that he decided to write his next symphony (the Nineteenth) for the Red Army Band. It was conceived as a sort of engaging Divertimento, in an idiom accessible to players and listeners. Characteristically, Miaskovsky avoided the obvious style of a band piece: there is none of the martial posture, heroism, and monumentality expected of a military band. In fact, some of the lyrical themes might sound just as well on string instruments. On the whole, the wind instruments are treated idiomatically and with refinement. Miaskovsky's Band Symphony requires instrumental finesse and was a salutary influence on the further development of band playing in the Soviet Union.

This series of light-weight compositions was broken by the Twenty-first Symphony, one of Miaskovsky's most mature works. It is conceived in an artful one-movement form, used by him only once before, in his Tenth Symphony. In the Twenty-first Symphony, a sonata-allegro is framed by a slow introduction and a—thematically related—slow coda. It is a compact work, only about sixteen minutes in length, and its original title, *Symphony-Fantasy*, fits it to perfection. The mood of the outer sections is lyric and intensely pensive, in contrast to the impetuous central Allegro part.

Originally, the Twenty-first Symphony was commissioned by the Chicago Symphony Orchestra whose conductor Frederick Stock had been a tireless champion of Miaskovsky's music for many years. Stock visited Moscow in 1938 and asked Miaskovsky to write a symphonic work for the Golden Jubilee of the Chicago Orchestra that was to occur in 1940. Miaskovsky accepted willingly.* The dedication (in French!), written by Miaskovsky on the autograph score, read, "Composed for the fiftieth anniversary of the Chicago Symphony Orchestra and dedicated to its illustrious conductor, Dr. Frederick Stock." It is note-worthy that the symphony was dedicated, not to the orchestra, but to

* Among other composers who wrote special works for Chicago on this occasion were Casella, Milhaud, Walton, and Roy Harris.

its conductor. This was done deliberately, as can be gathered from a letter of the composer addressed to Shneerson,* dated 20 July 1940, ". . . I am sending you the score of the *Symphony-Fantasy* for Chicago. The dedication is somewhat artificial, but I realize that if I am under obligation to this orchestra, it is only thanks to Stock . . . I enclose a letter confirming that this symphony can be used by Stock *without compensation* . . ."35 The last sentence is not quite clear: did Miaskovsky wish to offer the symphony as a gift to the orchestra, in recognition of past artistic ties, or had he received compensation at the time he accepted the commission?

Soviet historians avoid any mention of the connection between Chicago and the Twenty-first Symphony, as if it had been an embarrassing incident. Details of the story did not become known until 1959 when Shneerson published a brief article, "Meetings with Miaskovsky", in a two-volume collection of materials on the composer. Miaskovsky and Stock met in an atmosphere of warmth. The composer "was glad to make the acquaintance of the outstanding conductor, a sincere friend of Soviet music . . . Stock told Miaskovsky how beloved his music was by the Chicago audiences, especially the Sixth Symphony which is played every year.** He took Miaskovsky's word to write a symphonic work for the forthcoming fiftieth jubilee of the Chicago Orchestra. Miaskovsky kept this promise . . ."36

The Chicago première of the Twenty-first Symphony took place on 26 December 1940 under the baton of Stock. The Chicago programme booklet indicates that this was a "world" première. However, all Soviet sources list the first performance of the Twenty-first Symphony as having taken place six weeks earlier, on 16 November 1940, in Moscow under Alexander Gauk. The matter takes on an air of mystery in view of the composer's statement in a letter to Shneerson that the première performance was given in Chicago.37

By now, the question of priority between Chicago and Moscow seems rather academic. The Twenty-first Symphony was warmly received in both cities, and in the Soviet Union the work was awarded the Stalin Prize of 1941. In retrospect, the discernment of the judges was fully justified: the Twenty-first Symphony is recognized as one of

* At the time, Shneerson was secretary of the Foreign Commission of the Composers' Union. He handled the foreign contacts of Soviet composers, including the mailing of orchestral materials for performances abroad.

** The popularity of Miaskovsky in Chicago can be gauged by the following statistics: between 1925 and 1941, his Fifth Symphony was performed twice, the Sixth eleven times, the Seventh five times, the Fifteenth twice, the Twenty-first three times. One performance each was given of the Symphones Nos. 8, 10, 12, and 13.

the finest achievements of Miaskovsky. Yet, it is also sad to contemplate how the entire symphonic output of Miaskovsky has somewhat faded out of the repertoire, not only in the West but—more importantly—in the Soviet Union.

This makes Miaskovsky's creative efforts during the 1930's all the more significant. For there can be no doubt that he was searching for a clarification of his musical idiom—away from a "subjective" style (that is, music as self-expression) to an "objective" style—the communion with a vast audience. This quest, it must be admitted, was not always successful, and what was hailed by some Soviet critics as music "expressing the world outlook of Soviet man" turned out to be a rather shallow optimism and simplification. But even in his errors of judgment, Miaskovsky remained the consummate master, the conscientious, self-critical artist.

Prokofiev's position, during the 1930's, was altogether different. After the disastrous reception given to his *Symphonic Song* Op. 57 when it was performed in Moscow in 1934, he simply withdrew from the symphonic genre for the next ten years. Nevertheless, Prokofiev contributed to the orchestral repertoire; as already mentioned, the suites *Lieutenant Kije* and *Romeo and Juliet* became highly successful. His Second Violin Concerto—originally planned as a sonata—was completed in 1935 and first performed that same year in Madrid by the French violinist Robert Soetens, with the conductor Fernàndez Arbos. The work, lyrical and expressive, does not have the "bite" of the First Violin Concerto and stresses a more songful approach to the violin; it has become a favourite repertoire piece of many virtuosi, including Heifetz who first popularized it in America. The idiom of the Second Violin Concerto pleased the Soviet critics who felt that Prokofiev had realized "the utter futility of formalist experiments".[38] This critical smugness was premature, for Prokofiev went his own way in the Cello Concerto Op. 58 which was heard in Moscow in 1938. It was not well received, to the composer's consternation who thought it to be "very much like the Second Violin Concerto".[39] Nevertheless, he made certain changes; many years later he reshaped it completely into the monumental Sinfonia Concertante Op. 125. An attempt of Prokofiev to follow the "national" trend with the *Russian Overture* Op. 72 (1936) merely proved the artificiality of such a deliberate adjustment.

While the symphonic genre was in a state of flux and experiment, while composers attempted unsuccessfully to revive "symphonism" with an infusion of Soviet "topics" and "songs", one composer stood on the sidelines—Shostakovich. He did not avoid the issue—he had gathered his experience with "ideological" symphonies in the late 1920's, and he spoke during the discussion on the symphony in 1935 against the intrusion of articifial "meaning", of so-called topicality.

Shostakovich's creative solution to the symphonic ills was his Fourth Symphony on which he worked in 1935-36. His withdrawal of the Fourth Symphony, and his immediate decision to write a new and entirely different symphony was an act of supreme self-discipline and creative maturity. It was a self-imposed purgatory out of which he emerged victorious, though not unscathed.

What can one say about the Fourth Symphony—that long-banished child of Shostakovich's creative youth—banished not so much by narrow-minded Soviet aesthetics as by its creator himself. For it is clear that Shostakovich, who withdrew the work in 1936, could have had it performed at any time after 1953—the year of the beginning of the "thaw"—without waiting another nine years. As late as 1956, in his autobiography, he speaks of the Fourth in the same vein as of his Second and Third Symphonies—as failures. He says "Also a failure was my Fourth Symphony, not played as yet. It is—as far as form is concerned —a very imperfect, long-winded work that suffers—I'd say—from 'grandiosomania'. However, the score contains some parts I like."[40]

Today, after thirty years, the listener is stunned and bewildered by Shostakovich's Fourth. For sixty minutes, one listens tensely for something momentous to happen, yet that culmination somehow never comes. The Symphony resembles a volcanic eruption, the eruption of an unbridled imagination, spewing forth music almost at random, without apparent logic or design, producing flashes without consistent illumination, driving forward without audible aim. This, at least, is the impression one gains from the sprawling first movement where one musical idea follows the other without visible connection or development. It is as if the young composer, barely thirty, set out to remake with one sweep the exalted world of the symphony, the stratosphere inhabited by Beethoven and Mahler. Another first movement comes to one's mind in which a composer in his early thirties swept aside tradition but harnessed his onrushing imagination—the first movement of Beethoven's "Eroica".

But the Fourth by Shostakovich is a different story: it is a titanic failure, yet one which leaves the listener strangely moved. After the first movement, which resists all formal analysis, comes the *Ländler*-like centre movement—a short pacifier with bitter-sweet Mahlerian accents. And then the massive Finale which is built, if not with convincing logic, at least with an over-all plan: five large sections, each more or less self-contained. One recognizes, of course, Bruckner and Mahler in the mock-funereal Largo opening section. Never before or after has Shostakovich been closer to Mahler than in his Fourth Symphony; yet the Mahlerian influence has been over-stressed by both Soviet and Western critics who needed something tangible by which to evaluate this strange hybrid of a symphony. On the whole, the Fourth is purest Shostakovich—there is not one element (save one—massiveness, which *is* Mahlerian) that one could not trace back to the earlier three symphonies, to his operas, to his ballets, to all of his music from 1926 to 1935. There are the obsessive ostinato rhythms, the power-drunk percussion, the tongue-in-cheek humour, the biting satire, the down-to-earth stomping, the widely arched melodies so afraid of sentiment, the quirks of orchestration. Finally he reaches the extended coda of the finale, the long pedal point on C, resolved to speak leisurely and to let his thoughts float. The quiet ending is strangely sad, yet one must hesitate to call the entire work "pessimistic" as has been done.

To say that the Fourth Symphony lacks "form" is a mis-statement: it does not lack it (for Shostakovich knew the textbook rules) but it deliberately rejects form in favour of a free-flowing stream of music. After the Fourth, Shostakovich seems to have lost confidence in this approach and abandoned it in favour of clearer organization of his musical materials. The change did not come easy; even much later in life he admitted that he had never succeeded in writing—to his own satisfaction—a good symphonic sonata-allegro movement. Be this as it may, he came to the conclusion—after the completion of the Fourth—that a symphony without firm architecture was not viable.

In reaching to the conclusion that the Fourth was a *cul-de-sac*, did the composer act out of creative conviction or did he yield to outside pressure? The question is often asked, and usually answered peremptorily, in favour of the pressure theory. The composer himself made the answer easy by calling his next—the Fifth—Symphony "an artist's creative answer to justified criticism".

It should be understood that the composer's "admission"* did not refer to the Fourth Symphony (a work not known to the general public since it was withdrawn before the première). It referred, in a general sense, to the *Pravda* articles of January–February 1936 in which Shostakovich was criticized for a penchant for "formalism", meaning extreme modernism.

Shostakovich's answer, then, was the Fifth Symphony of 1937. It is often overlooked that it *could have been* the Fourth Symphony, had he

* The wording of the "admission" is all the more poignant if one realizes that Shostakovich never spoke up in his own defence; his voice was not heard during the debate which dragged his work into the mud. Whether he really used the words "justified criticism" is open to question though the quote is repeated in many Western reports. Soviet historians refer to it as "My creative answer" or "My creative answer to criticism"; the elimination of the word "justified" makes Shostakovich's utterance sound far less submissive and does not imply any admission of "guilt".

so desired. The Fourth Symphony was begun on 13 September 1935 and completed on 20 May 1936. In the four months that elapsed between the first article in *Pravda* and the completion of the Fourth Symphony, Shostakovich could have reshaped the Fourth Symphony to make it more acceptable in terms of the official criticism. Shaken though he was by the criticism, he followed his artistic conscience and left the Fourth intact. The new (Fifth) Symphony was not begun until 18 April 1937; the date of completion was 20 July, that of the première 21 November—all of it incredibly swift.

Compared to the primordial chaos of the Fourth Symphony, the Fifth is a well-ordered organic work along fairly traditional formal lines. The exception is the essentially slow tempo (Largo) of the first movement. Otherwise, the composer merely continued where he left off in 1926 with his First Symphony—at least so far as form is concerned. In texture, however, the massiveness of the Fifth is far removed from the chamber-music-like transparency of the First.

What about the musical idiom of the Fifth? A possible concession is the Finale which is rousing and obvious; yet much of this obviousness can be mitigated by adhering to the composer's moderate tempo markings (as expressed in the precise metronome figures) instead of vulgarizing it by the head-long rush so popular with some conductors. The final pages—the obsessive reiteration of the D-major tonality—are overextended, but the procedure itself is not new: Mahler, for example, used it effectively at the end of his First Symphony of 1888. In the mid-1930's, Shostakovich's admiration for Mahler was in full bloom, and the influence is evident.

But after registering this reservation, one must recognize the grandeur of the first movement with its jagged opening theme (though the second subject, beautiful in its mood, is somewhat sweeter than usual with Shostakovich). One is amused by the boisterous Scherzo and moved by the intense Adagio—the movement found most problematic by 1937 standards of Soviet aesthetics. All in all, the Fifth Symphony possesses the *"gesellschaftbildende Kraft"*,* an expression coined by Paul Bekker to describe the power of Mahler.[41] It is the power given only to the great symphonists—the power to weld an audience together, to uplift and to move masses of disparate people in one single emotion-controlled wave, sweeping aside all intellectual reservations. This was the effect the Fifth of Shostakovich produced at the very beginning, and it has withstood the test of time. In the Soviet Union, a dozen articles appeared, praising the work in exaggerated terms, and favourable opinions were elicited from non-musicians like the writer Alexei Tolstoy and the aviator-hero Gromov. It was as if the Soviet intellectual

* Community-moulding power.

community wished to atone for the maltreatment given to one of its genius members. The chorus of praise drowned the few voices of reservation. Only much later, in 1948, when Shostakovich was once again under attack, did one writer—the fellow-composer Koval—refer to the "uncritical overpraise" of the Fifth Symphony.[42]

Nor did the Soviet public wish to hear about adverse opinions from abroad. When the Symphony was first played in the West—on 14 June 1938 in Paris under Désormière—the favourable review in the Communist *Humanité* was widely reprinted, while the summary dismissal of the new work by several important French critics remained unmentioned. Even prior to the Paris performance, Artur Rodzinski—who had introduced *Lady Macbeth* to America—conducted a broadcast performance of Shostakovich's Fifth on 9 April 1938 over the N.B.C. network. The Fifth Symphony has remained the most widely played of Shostakovich's fifteen symphonies.

The Sixth Symphony was composed two years later and first performed in Leningrad under Mravinsky (who had also conducted the première of the Fifth) on 5 November 1939. This new symphony received a more sobre and more critical appraisal than its predecessor. Given during the annual Festival of Soviet music, the Sixth of Shostakovich was overshadowed, in public interest, by such colourful works as the cantatas *Alexander Nevsky* by Prokofiev and *On the Field of Kulikovo* by Shaporin—both arousing patriotic fervour because of their texts. Some critics found a retrogression in Shostakovich's development. The form was subjected to criticism: a three-movement cycle in which the first—an extended Largo—was more than twice as long as the two following movements, an airy Scherzo and a gallop-like Finale. The inner contrast between the philosophical subjective beginning and the extrovert, flippant ending seemed too sharp. But there was also some public disappointment which had nothing to do with the actual quality of the new symphony: hopes had been aroused—on the basis of the composer's statement in the autumn of 1938—that his new symphony would deal with the subject of Lenin, using poetry and folk materials.[43] Instead, without any explanation, the Sixth Symphony was presented, bearing not the remotest relationship to the announced topic. This somehow impeded an objective evaluation of the Sixth, at least within the Soviet orbit.

Abroad, the Sixth was received with studied indifference. By now it had become customary to assume that Shostakovich, in composing, had to follow the dictates of the Party—a nonsensical prejudice, to be sure, but one particularly widespread in America. Thus, the composer-critic Virgil Thomson wrote after the première given by the Philadelphia Orchestra under Stokowski,

"Shostakovich's Sixth . . . is clear, obvious, effective, old-fashioned
. . . Its allegiance seems to be divided between a romanticized, and
hence attenuated, neo-classicism and a full-blooded Muscovite
orientalism à la Borodin . . . It is a pleasant piece and not without
a certain concentration at moments. If it were signed by an
American composer, . . . it would be classifiable as good saleable
academicism."[44]

How easy it is to dismiss as mere "academicism" music that is clean
and clear at first hearing. Just as easy as it is—according to Prokofiev—
to stamp as "formalism" anything *not* accessible at first hearing. What
most critics overlooked was that, in his Sixth Symphony, Shostakovich
was true to himself. Whether introvert or extrovert, neo-classic or neo-
banal, the Sixth has its roots in ballets like *The Golden Age* and *Bolt*, in
the Piano Concerto, in *The Nose*—all music pre-dating *Lady Macbeth*.
In Shostakovich's musical make-up, Bach and Offenbach had always
been friendly neighbours, and so they are again in the Sixth Symphony.

If one looks back on the symphonies of the 1930's and on the contribution of Shostakovich—the silenced turbulent Fourth, the triumphant
Fifth, the underrated Sixth—there is one fact standing out with
brilliant clarity: this young composer, barely thirty, preserved and
reaffirmed almost single-handed the grandeur of the symphonic genre,
the Mahlerian vision of the world within a score. During that decade,
he absorbed more abuse than anyone of his confrères, and he proved
more resilient, more true to himself than the best of them. While
Shostakovich is thought of as having made "concessions" to the regime,
he was actually less accommodating than, say, Prokofiev or Miaskovsky; at least his work list is not studded with cantatas to the glory of
Stalin and Kirov. It was Shostakovich who lifted the symphonic genre
out of its ideological doldrums, freed it from the hollow verbiage and
the pseudo-programmatic doubletalk. The impact of his Fifth Symphony was such that everything else paled in comparison. Soviet
aesthetic thought turned away from such palliatives as the "song
symphony" and recognized anew the dignity and grandeur of the
symphony as a supreme expression of the musical mind.

To the vast masses of Soviet people, Hitler's attack on 22 June 1941 must have come as a complete surprise. But among better informed citizens—those in government circles, Party officials, the intelligentsia —a mood of ominous foreboding had prevailed for some time. Ehrenburg felt in the summer of 1940 that "the Germans would soon attack us". Konstantin Simonov described the mood of those days in his novel, *The Living and the Dead,* "It seemed that everybody was expecting the war for a long time and yet, at the last moment, it came like a bolt from the blue; it was apparently impossible to prepare oneself in advance for such an enormous misfortune."[1]

The next few months were a nightmare. The reverses on the battle-fields were staggering, the losses beyond belief. By the end of 1941, Kiev was captured, Leningrad was encircled, and the Germans were at the gates of Moscow. On the Soviet side, there was heroism, confusion, even occasional treachery—but in the end, heroism prevailed. "The moral fibre of the people" was—as Alexei Tolstoy wrote in 1942—the determining factor in this cruel war. But there were moments when even the moral fibre gave way. One such day of panic was 16 October 1941 when it was thought in Moscow that the Germans had broken through the defences of the city. That day was "certainly not a tale of the 'unanimous heroism of the people of Moscow' as recorded in the official *History,*" writes Alexander Werth.[2] The panic was hastened by the government's decision, taken a few days earlier, to evacuate all important scientific and cultural institutions.* The Bolshoi Opera and Ballet were sent to Kuibyshev, the U.S.S.R. State Symphony to Frunze, the Moscow Conservatory to Saratov. Leningrad's institutions had also been transferred: the Kirov Theatre to Perm, the Philharmonic to Novosibirsk, the Conservatory to Tashkent, the Malyi Opera to Orenburg. The headquarters of the Composers' Union was established in Sverdlovsk. Many individual musicians were evacuated from Moscow, first to the Caucasus, then—as the front moved dangerously closer—further inland. Among them were Prokofiev, Miaskovsky,

---

* The panic abated when it was announced, the following day, that the Kremlin leadership, including Stalin, had remained in Moscow.

Shaporin, Alexander Krein, Paul Lamm, Samuel Feinberg, the veteran pianist Goldenweiser. Eventually, Prokofiev found himself in Alma-Ata, Miaskovsky in Tbilisi and later in Frunze. Despite the tensions and dislocations, the composers not only continued to be creative, but were stimulated by their new surroundings; for example, Caucasian folk material forms the thematic basis for Prokofiev's Second String Quartet and Miaskovsky's Twenty-third Symphony, both composed in 1941. The stimulation also worked in reverse: the provincial cities, as hosts, derived lasting cultural benefits from the presence of renowned institutions and great artists settled in their midst.

Despite these evacuations, there was no wholesale abandonment of the beleaguered population. Moscow and Leningrad retained a nucleus of artistic institutions—the radio orchestras, the Stanislavsky-Nemirovich-Danchenko Opera Theatre, the Bolshoi Affiliate. Individual artists continued to perform in the cities and at the front, undeterred by danger, cold, and hunger. Just as during the blitz in London, music and musical performances proved their regenerative strength in Moscow and Leningrad—a lifeline, as it were, for the beleaguered, famished populace. In blockaded Leningrad "listeners came to us at the Philharmonic in any weather, despite the most dreadful frost. They even came from the front—and the front was only six kilometres from the centre of town,"[3]—reminisced the conductor Eliasberg. One isolated statistical fact will illustrate what music meant to the population under stress: on a single Sunday, 1 February 1942, sixteen thousand Muscovites attended sixteen different concerts. That summer, Werth was in Moscow, "I noted in my Moscow diary... the extraordinary emotional atmosphere ... even at any routine Tchaikovsky concert—as though all Russian civilization were now in deadly danger. I remember the countless tears produced on one of the worst days in July 1942 by the famous love theme in Tchaikovsky's Romeo and Juliet Overture. Irrational no doubt, but true!"[4]

Indeed, Russian civilization was in deadly danger. Shostakovich, who saw the destruction wrought by the Germans in Klin, wrote, "The Nazi barbarians seek to destroy the whole of Slavonic culture ... Never will the Russian people forgive or forget this ..."[5] Klin is a village near Moscow where Tchaikovsky spent the last years of his life; his house is preserved as a national shrine. The German army occupied Klin on 22 November 1941 but had to retreat three weeks later. In this brief space of time, a great deal of damage was done in the village itself, and in the Tchaikovsky House, though the Soviet authorities had evacuated many valuable manuscripts and memorabilia, "The Germans tore the woodwork from the walls and used it for heating purposes and threw books, music, and scores into the stove."[6]

Serious though the situation was around Moscow, it cannot be compared to the agony of Leningrad. This city of three million people was cut off, encircled, and condemned to death by starvation. The blockade lasted from September 1941 to February 1943; but even after the blockade was broken, the Germans were entrenched only two miles from the Kirov Works. During the eighteen months of the blockade, 632,000 people died of hunger and privation, according to official figures. Unofficially, the estimate is closer to one million deaths, or one-third of the population. According to Harrison Salisbury, "This was the greatest and longest siege ever endured by a modern city, a time of trial, suffering and heroism that reached peaks of tragedy and bravery almost beyond our power to comprehend . . ."[7] In addition to hunger and cold, the city was subjected to shelling and air raids. The winter of 1941-42, when the official food rations—if they could be obtained—were reduced to under 500 calories a day for many adults, was particularly cruel. People died everywhere, on the street, at work, in offices and factories. Water pipes burst, and people had to drink the infested water of the Neva or of the canals. Electric power was cut to a minimum and there were no lights in houses and offices.

Under such desperate conditions, one would assume that nothing but physical survival would matter. Yet theatres struggled to function, musicians continued to play, composers managed to write music. Cold and starvation decimated their ranks. Actors appeared in overcoats and felt boots, musicians played in wool gloves with cut-out finger tips. The Radio Orchestra was forced to remain inactive for about three months, from January to March 1942: too many players were ill or dead, starving and unable to move. But in March of that year, an orchestra was reassembled and gave its first concert on 5 April. The conductor Eliasberg recalled that "The temperature in the hall (the Pushkin Theatre) was 7° to 8° centigrade below zero. People cried from excitement and joy . . . The hall was filled to overflowing . . . On 1 May, under heavy shelling, we played the Sixth Symphony of Tchaikovsky."[8] Subsequently, this orchestra moved to the Philharmonic Hall. Three months later, on 9 August 1942, it gave the première of Shostakovich's famed Leningrad Symphony.

The war-time diary of the composer Bogdanov-Berezovsky mentions the early genesis of that symphony. On 17 September 1941, we find the following entry,

"Tonight we went to Shostakovich. Twice he played for us two movements of his new symphony (the Seventh). He told us of the over-all plan. The impression we all had was tremendous. Miraculous is the process of synchronization, of instantaneous creative reaction to the surrounding experiences, clad in a complex and large form with no hint of 'belittling of the genre' . . . While he played there was an air raid. The composer suggested that we continue the music; only his family went to the shelter . . ."⁹

Shortly after this fragmentary audition, Shostakovich published a brief memorable essay on the subject of his new symphonic project, "Never in my life have I dedicated my compositions to anyone. But this symphony—if I succeed in its realization—I shall dedicate to Leningrad. For all that I wrote into it, all that I expressed in it, is tied up with that beloved native city of mine, is connected with the historic days of its defence against fascist oppressors."¹⁰

By the time these lines were published, on 9 October 1941, Shostakovich was no longer in Leningrad; reluctantly, in late September 1941, he agreed to be evacuated to Moscow. From there he was sent to Kuibyshev where he completed the symphony in December 1941. On 5 March 1942 the first performance took place in Kuibyshev, played by the evacuated orchestra of the Bolshoi Theatre conducted by Samosud. On 29 March, it was heard in Moscow, also under Samosud.

In the meantime, life in Leningrad was slowly grinding to a halt. Here are some more entries from Bogdanov-Berezovsky's diary.

5 November 1941	"We all met in Asafiev's room at the Pushkin Theatre where he lives. There we listened to the entries of the song competitions for the Twenty-fourth Anniversary of the Revolution . . ."
28 November	"Four days without warm food, only some bread rations . . ."
25 December	"The end of the financial year—and the funds of the Union are exhausted. We are cut off from the central Muzfond, we don't even know to what place they have been evacuated . . ."
6 January 1942	"The pulse of creative life in the Composers' Union weakens from day to day. It weakens but does not die. Many are no longer able to come in from outlying districts . . . The streetcars have stopped altogether . . ."
29 January	"The city is paralyzed. Since the 25th there is no water, since the 26th no bread as it cannot be baked for lack of water. The telephones do not work, the radio is mute . . . The only creative activity in the Union consists of excursions of composers to give free concerts for front units, hospitals, Navy ships anchored in the Neva . . ."

6 February	"Our ranks are thinning . . . Evacuations, deaths . . ."
25 February	"The radio functions again . . ."
23 March	"Received 25,000 rubles for the Union's account for 1942 . . ."
11 April	"At home the stove is warm, the first time this winter . . . Tomorrow to Eliasberg's Symphony Concert . . ."
15 April	"Streetcars are running again, and the city is in a holiday mood . . ."[11]

The summer brought some improvement; at least one did not have to fight darkness and cold. In July, Bogdanov-Berezovsky—who was head of the Leningrad Composers' Union—was flown to Moscow where he presented the creative work of the Leningrad composers, written during the siege. He returned on 6 August, laden with food and medical supplies for his colleagues. He arrived just in time for the last rehearsal of Shostakovich's Seventh Symphony, dedicated "To the City of Leningrad".

Even before Leningrad could hear "its" symphony, the work had reached the United States. The microfilmed score had been flown to America by military plane via Iran, North Africa, and South America. On 19 July 1942 Arturo Toscanini conducted the National Broadcasting Symphony Orchestra in a radio première heard by millions. During the season 1942–43, sixty-two performances of the symphony were given in the United States alone, by every conductor of stature— Kussevitsky, Stokowski, Ormandy, Rodzinski, Mitropoulos, Monteux, and many others. The symphony was played around the world, in Great Britain, Australia, Latin America . . . These were no longer concerts, but tributes to the indomitable spirit of a great people fighting for its survival. And that spirit was expressed by one of its sons, in terms of the one universal language—music. It was music "written with the heart's blood", as the American poet, Carl Sandburg, expressed it.

No première, however glittering, could have had the significance of the first performance in Leningrad on 9 August 1942 while the city was still under siege. Bogdanov-Berezovsky wrote in his diary,

"Exciting sight of the hall, festive as of old, in its pristine white, the gold and the dark red, with its faultless architectural proportions . . . The hall is fancifully lit by the large crystal candelabras . . . In the audience, all—or nearly all—the representatives of the musical life of besieged Leningrad—composers, opera artists, pedagogues . . . many soldiers and officers who came with their automatic weapons directly from the front line. The orchestra was reinforced by army musicians temporarily on leave for this occasion: the score demands eight horns, six trumpets, six trombones, an enormous battery of percussion.

With excitement we hear the first sounds of the unison theme in the strings . . . Quite new for me were the last two movements written by Shostakovich after his departure from Leningrad . . . One cannot speak of an impression made by the symphony. It was, not an impression, but a staggering experience. This was felt not only by the listeners but also by the performers who read the music sheets as if they were reading a living chronicle about themselves . . ."[12]

Obviously, this particular symphony could not be discussed objectively, dispassionately, in terms of its musical qualities. An entire people adopted the work as the symbol of its struggle, as a commentator wrote at the time, "The Seventh Symphony of Shostakovich is significant beyond the bounds of a merely musical event. It has become a cultural entity of our people, a fact of political and social significance, and an impulse to struggle and victory."[13]

The war period can be divided into two phases: the first, from 1941 to 1943, comprises the initial shock, the disastrous reverses on the battlefields; the second, from 1943 to 1945, covers the halt of the enemy, the counter attack, and the ultimate victory. The initial mood of grief and anger turned gradually to determination and a will to win. All this is reflected in the music of the time. A symphony like the Seventh ("Leningrad") by Shostakovich, written early in the war, in the midst of an inconclusive battle, mirrors an atmosphere different from, say, the Fifth Symphony of Prokofiev, which was composed when victory was already in sight. To encompass the magnitude of the events, one needs a certain distance—and the greater the event, the more time is needed to absorb all its significance. Whatever the ultimate evaluation of Soviet music of the war years will be, one fact is clear: it cannot be judged in a detached, "objective" manner. To do that is to misinterpret ist function, and its motivation.

The music of those days was meant to console and uplift, to encourage and exhort; nothing else mattered. Composers did not think of eternal values, not even of tomorrow—only of today, of the moment, of the immediate impact on the listener. Gone were all controversies, all the quarrels about epigonism and realism and formalism; forgotten was all aestheticizing. Only the survival of body and soul mattered, and the essential element of music was its morale-building force. In detached retrospect one finds occasional shallowness, posturing, hollow heroics; but under fire it all seemed real and very vital.

Wedded to the music was the word, for the spontaneous reaction to the war must not be sought in symphonies—which represent a sublimated experience—but in the songs, whether improvised by unknown folk artists or composed by professional composers. In the first days of the war, literally hundreds of songs were sung and written down by poets and musicians, amateurs and professionals. They vowed defence of the fatherland and death to the enemy; but there were also songs of quiet resolve and stoic suffering—all deeply imbued with that unique Russian love for the *rodina*, the homeland, its rivers, meadows, trees, villages, its countryside. And then there was the pride in past history, the memories of repulsed invasions by the Tartars, Mongols, Teutonic Knights, Napoleonic armies. In the grimmest days of the war, during November 1941, the "Holy Russia" speeches of Stalin stressed the mood of indignation and uplifted the sagging spirits of the entire nation.

Of all the war songs, one achieved the distinction of being called the "emblem of the Great War"—the song *Sacred War* (Sviashchennaya Voyna) with words by Lebedev-Kumach and music by Alexander Alexandrov. Composed in 1941, this song—in stately three-four time —captured the minds and hearts of millions. It also served as a marching song, despite the unsuitable metre and the absence of any martial "dotted" rhythms. The song is rather hymn-like and shows a certain resemblance to old-time revolutionary Russian songs. Alexandrov was a professional musician, the organizer, in 1928, of the Red Army Choir and Dance Ensemble. He had the army rank of major-general but was also active as a professor at the Moscow Conservatory. He died in 1946, in Berlin, after having witnessed the victory.

Other successful writers of war songs were Zakharov, Novikov, Mokrousov, Fradkin, Belyi, Blanter, Soloviev-Sedoi (better known lately as the composer of "Moscow Nights"). Some of these songs were written at the front, under the impact of death and destruction, imbued with courage and determination. One such story is told by Kabalevsky,

> "Early in 1942 I found myself on the South-Western front, near Kharkov, still occupied by the Germans. My loyal comrade on this trip was the poet Evgeni Dolmatovsky. In one of the Ukrainian settlements, just liberated from the Germans, we met a group of partisans . . . I listened with tremendous interest to what they had to say . . . Not surprisingly, Dolmatovsky and I had the idea of writing a song cycle about the partisans. That evening, in a tent . . . at a table dimly lit by a smoky kerosene lamp, we began our work. Dolmatovsky penned the first four lines and gave them to me . . . While he was writing the remaining lines, I composed the music. In a half-hour, we had the entire song ready to be sung

accompanied by a soldier on an accordion who improvised a few chords. In a few days, the song was already sung by a front ensemble . . . Further songs followed. The work went well. To see the real images of the partisans, to feel the atmosphere of this settlement just liberated, inspired and helped us—pictures of joy and sorrow intermingled in a most curious manner."[14]

Such was the genesis of Kabalevsky's *The People's Avengers* for chorus and orchestra. Innumerable songs were similarly conceived in the heat of the battle. True, some songs turned out to be synthetic or sentimentalized, cheapened . . . but a great many were filled with sincerity and served as an outlet for the pent-up emotions of an entire people.

A song could be born in an outburst of spontaneous creativity, but the writing of a symphony or an opera, a cantata or an oratorio was a laborious and involved undertaking. The impulse may be spontaneous, yet the realization is slow and cumbersome. All the more surprising is the fact that more than thirty symphonies were composed in the Soviet Union during the war years, though not each of them was necessarily a "war" symphony. But there are few, very few great works among them—they often lack composure because they were written under pressure, without the benefit of that period of gestation so important for any work of art.

Even more complex than the symphony is the genre of opera: before a note of music is written, the libretto must provide a suitable dramatic framework. Current events cannot be transferred to the stage like a newsreel; they need artistic distillation and reflection. For this reason, several operas built on current war stories turned out to be well-intentioned failures; written in 1941–43, they were hastily conceived and insufficiently matured. Of all the war operas, only the titles have remained—like memorial plaques commemorating sincere but futile efforts: *At the Gates of Moscow* (Pod Moskvoi), also called *Under Fire*, by Kabalevsky, *Stronger than Death* (Silneye Smerti) by Voloshinov, *The Blood of the People* (Krov naroda), *Nadezhda Svetlova* by Dzerzhinsky, and a few others. The opera *Emelyan Pugachev* by Koval was, in essence, a transference to the stage of his earlier oratorio of the same name. Years later, in 1950, Kabalevsky succeeded in sublimating his war experience in a strong opera, *The Family Taras*.

Only one opera of the early 1940's stands out as a masterpiece—*War and Peace* by Prokofiev. Most of the score was composed in the years 1941–43. For some time, the composer had thought of Tolstoy's epic novel as a possible operatic subject; the outbreak of the war provided a renewed impulse to proceed with the immense project. "The pages describing the struggle of the Russian people against the Napoleonic hordes in 1812," wrote Prokofiev, "and the expulsion of Napoleon's army from Russian soil had somehow a particular poignancy at this time."[15] *War and Peace* was not given until 1955 in a near-definitive version, two years after the composer's death.*

The related genre of cantata and oratorio fared somewhat better than the opera. The most impressive work was Shaporin's *Saga of the Battle for the Russian Soil* (Skazanie o bitve za russkuyu zemlyu), composed in 1943–44 and first performed in Moscow in April 1944. In contrast to his previous historic oratorio, *On the Field of Kulikovo*, Shaporin's *Saga* deals with a contemporary topic, "the life of the people in their struggle for the homeland". But it must be said that Shaporin's musical idiom showed no change, whether he dealt with the fourteenth or the twentieth century: he did not attempt any contemporary characterizations, and his score was mildly criticized for being somewhat too "archaic" and stylized. The texts were provided by four writers. The first part of the *Saga* consists of seven sections describing the first months of the 1941 War in terms of episodes. The second half, in five sections, moves on a more abstract plane. Essentially, Shaporin leans towards lyricism rather than drama, and the work ends, not in an apotheosis of sound, but with a chorus of lyric patriotism.

The poem-cantata *Kirov is with us* (Kirov s nami) by Miaskovsky, completed in early 1943, belongs to the vocal-choral genre. The text, by Nikolai Tikhonov, was written in besieged Leningrad. Kabalevsky contributed several choral works, including the cantata *Great Homeland* (Rodina velikaya) based on poems by seven writers. Koval's *The People's Holy War* (Narodnaya sviashchennaya voina) belongs to the same category; it is effective in a poster-like manner and lacks depth and introspection.

The Soviet ballet, on the other hand, did not even attempt to deal with contemporary problems like war and patriotism. The best new works of the period are removed from reality—like Prokofiev's *Cinderella* (Zolushka) which is an escape into the realm of fairy tale. Khachaturian's *Gayane* (one of his best-known and most successful works) paints in vivid colours village life in Soviet Armenia; it is based on materials from an earlier ballet, *Happiness* (1939). Asafiev created no fewer than seven ballet scores during the war years, several of them written in blockaded Leningrad (he did not leave for Moscow until 1943). One of the ballets, *Militza*, portrays the freedom fight of the

* See p. 238.

Yugoslav people against fascism; others deal with subjects drawn from
Pushkin.

Far more contemporaneous were the films made during the war
years: they conveyed an immediacy which was often absent in more
complex genres. The courage of the partisans, the suffering and
quiet heroism of the Russian people, the cruelty of the invaders—these
are the favourite topics. Music forms an indispensable, integral part of
these films, and the best Soviet composers were called upon to provide
the scores—Shostakovich, Khachaturian, Khrennikov, Dunayevsky,
Soloviev-Sedoi, Popov, Shaporin. Time and again, the contrast between the peaceful Russian countryside and the brutal invasion is
explored musically—just as it was by Tchaikovsky in the *Overture 1812*.
In keeping close to the folk idiom, these film scores have an immediate
melodic and rhythmic appeal, and it is not surprising that some of the
songs used in films became immensely popular as mass and marching
songs. A new genre of film emerged in the form of variety programmes
called *Kine-Sbornik* (Cinema Journal) or *Film-Kontsert* (Film Concert);
they were used primarily for entertainment at the front.

At the same time, the genre of historic Russian films was continued.
Eisenstein and Prokofiev (whose collaboration had produced the immensely successful *Alexander Nevsky*) worked together to create *Ivan
the Terrible* in the years 1942–45. Shaporin composed the musical scores
to several films glorifying Russia's military past; the protagonists were
famous generals of the eighteenth and nineteenth centuries—Suvorov
and Kutuzov. All this was in keeping with the new approach to
Russia's historic grandeur.

After the defeat of the Germans at Stalingrad in January 1943, the
general mood in the Soviet Union became more confident, though
much fighting and suffering was still ahead. Day-to-day life was hard,
women and children worked at man-sized jobs, food was in short
supply, and the houses were barely warm enough to keep the water
pipes from freezing and bursting.

Nevertheless, the musical scene in Moscow became more varied;
concerts and theatres were full—as Ehrenburg observed, "People felt
the need both to relax and to get warm." Early in 1943, two new musical ensembles were formed: the State Chorus of Russian Folksong
(under Sveshnikov) and the Choral Ensemble of the Russian Republic
(under Stepanov). The State Symphony Orchestra of the U.S.S.R.
resumed its activity. In August 1943 the Bolshoi Theatre returned from
Kuibyshev, in September the Moscow Conservatory came back from
Saratov. (A "rump" conservatory had continued to function in

Moscow.) Leningrad had to wait longer: not until the autumn of 1944 were the two opera theatres (Kirov and Malyi) and the Conservatory repatriated. Despite the difficult times, new performers emerged—the pianist Sviatoslav Richter, the cellist Mstislav Rostropovich, the conductor Kyrill Kondrashin.

Regardless of war-time disruptions, Moscow welcomed the visits of various arts ensembles from other Soviet republics. During 1943, for instance, the following events took place: in April, choral concerts by ensembles from Latvia and Estonia; during the summer, Kirghiz artists were heard; in August, the Byelorussian Opera—evacuated to Gorky—staged a series of performances. Even in the grimmest period of the war—during November 1942—the city of Sverdlovsk succeeded in arranging a ten-day festival honouring the arts of the Ural region.

In true Russian tradition, commemorative dates were observed with concerts and oratory. The fiftieth anniversary of Tchaikovsky's death, in November 1943, was the occasion for a six-day festival of his major works, held in Moscow and near-by Klin. Rachmaninov's death in 1943 was mourned with commemorative concerts of his works, though the composer had lived abroad since 1917. Glinka's 140th, Rimsky-Korsakov's 100th anniversary (both of which occurred in 1944) were observed with musical ceremonies. All this, it should be remembered, took place while a grim war was in progress and while enemy troops still occupied vast stretches of Russian land. The observance of these commemorative occasions acquired greater scope through the participation of Soviet scholars. Complete Works editions of the great Russian composers were prepared, new documentary material was published, scholarly conferences were held, research papers were read and printed. Soviet musicologists were extremely active all through the war. Pure research faded into the background because of the dislocation of archives and the enforced closure of some libraries, but other—more timely—activities were stressed. Musicologists joined performance groups who visited front lines, factories, and villages; they contributed explanatory talks and used the radio to communicate with the music-hungry population. The art of "cultural popularization"—a tradition of the early revolutionary years—was revived and was considered an important civic assignment. During the war, lecturing activity acquired added significance, not only in Leningrad and Moscow, but also in the cities of the interior. For example, three prominent Leningrad musicologists—Sollertinsky, Druskin, and Vainkop—were evacuated to Novosibirsk with the Leningrad Philharmonic. They gave hundreds of illustrative lectures and contributed to the musical development of the entire region and near-by cities like Tomsk and Sverdlovsk.

Among those who remained in besieged Leningrad were the two

eminent music scholars, Asafiev and Ossovsky. In 1943, both were honoured by the Academy of Sciences in Moscow: Asafiev was elected to full membership in the Academy—the first "academician" with a musico-scholarly background—while Ossovsky became a corresponding member. Their reports on their creative work during the war have been published—work accomplished under incredibly harsh conditions. Even under normal circumstances, Asafiev's creative output in the years 1941-45 would have been impressive; under the conditions prevailing in Leningrad his achievement seems superhuman. His waning physical strength was supported by an indomitable will and an ever-active mind. In his reminiscences, he writes that he spent much time in bed—simply to reduce the need for food and heat. Lying in bed, he would work mentally—either composing or working on a literary project. Then, during the few daylight hours—and they were brief in Leningrad's winter climate—he would write down hurriedly what he had conceived in his mind. One photograph shows him playing the piano in a fur hat and overcoat, his legs in felt boots. Asafiev also participated actively in the continuing work of the Composers' Union— judging contests, holding auditions, and similar tasks. Apart from composing several ballets and a number of other works, he also wrote books, brochures, and essays, dealing mainly with Russian music, past and present. His catalogue lists some fifty compositions and almost one hundred literary items, written in the years 1941-45.

Asafiev's innate patriotism became more fervent during the war. His vivid style lent itself to proclamatory appeals: he—the avant-gardist of the 1920's—now called for a "united popular front of artists" and exhorted the composers to listen intently to the events surrounding them in order to rise to their greatness. This was not mere patriotic oratory. Even while preaching modernism, Asafiev had always been an impassioned protagonist of Russian music. The fusion of "modernism" and "Russianism" that he saw in the early Stravinsky, explains his enthusiasm, and later disappointment, in that composer. Just as Asafiev had appealed to the composers of the 1920's to create works worthy of the great Revolution, so he now stressed the need for a supreme patriotic upsurge in the arts to match the people's war effort. Asafiev's opinions, often strongly subjective and at times flowery, have nevertheless the strength of conviction and sincerity.

Asafiev remained in Leningrad until early 1943; in February of that year, he was evacuated to Moscow in a greatly weakened physical condition. He recovered and led an active life as head of the musicology section of the Moscow Conservatory and of the Institute of Arts History—a branch of the Academy of Sciences. He died in 1949 at the age of sixty-four, and no musician took his seat in the Academy.

The career of Alexander Ossovsky (1871-1957), though less versatile, was nevertheless rich in accomplishment. He played a leading role in Leningrad's Institute of Theatre and Music. Under the impact of the war, he re-examined the relationship between the musical cultures of the Slavic, Germanic, and Romance nations. His interest was caught by the music of the Russian allies—by the "undervalued" music of Britain and the "little known" music of the United States. Ossovsky prepared an essay, "The Musical Cultures of England and the United States" which he used as a lecture topic. Others followed suit, as we shall see. When Rimsky-Korsakov's 100th anniversary was commemorated in 1944, Ossovsky was invited to Moscow to deliver the official address at the Bolshoi Theatre—an address which honoured his old teacher.

Ossovsky's war reminiscences are brief, but he concludes them with a significant observation, "Summing up, there is a remarkable psychological observation I have made concerning myself and some of the other musicologists who had remained in Leningrad: never in peacetime did our scholarly work proceed with so much enthusiasm, with so much concentration and such fruitful results; never did this work give us so much inner satisfaction as in those war years, in the midst of the difficulties and dangers of the blockade."[16]

Indeed, the musicologists carried on, in besieged cities and evacuation centres. Conferences were held regardless of dangers: the Twenty-fifth Anniversary of the Revolution in 1942, for example, was observed at the Leningrad Institute with festive lectures on Soviet music and musical theatre; the lecturers were Bogdanov-Berezovsky and Ossovsky. The same year, the twenty-fifth jubilee of the Red Army was the occasion for a scholarly meeting at the Moscow Conservatory, dealing with the role of music under war-time conditions.

Shortly after the outbreak of the war, the journal *Sovetskaya Muzyka* interrupted its regular publication schedule. In place of monthly issues, the Composers' Union published six volumes of collected articles. Beginning in 1946, *Sovetskaya Muzyka* re-established its regular publication as a journal. The war-time volumes were edited by the composer Kabalevsky; the contents were often geared to commemorative dates—Rimsky-Korsakov, Rachmaninov, Anton Rubinstein—and the stress was on Russian music, although the music of the Allied nations received more than usual attention. Articles on musical subjects also appeared in the journal *Literatura i Iskusstvo* (1942-44), a war-time merger of two publications, *Sovetskoye Iskusstvo* and *Literaturnaya Gazeta* (Soviet Art and Literary Gazette).

Scholars continued to work on their favourite subjects: Roman Gruber's first volume of his imposing *History of Musical Culture* appeared in Leningrad in 1941, Rabinovich investigated the pre-Glinka

Opera, Sollertinsky worked on the subject of Symphonic Dramaturgy, Druskin on Western Piano Music of the seventeenth and eighteenth centuries, Vainkop on Rimsky-Korsakov. During the winter 1943–44, a cycle of radio lectures illustrated by performances was offered by Yuri Keldysh. The subject was, once again, Russian Music. War-time patriotism led to a re-evaluation of the achievements of the Russian "classics". A certain chauvinism, already noticeably on the rise during the 1930's, became more pronounced. The indigenous sources of Russian music were stressed while foreign influences were minimized or simply ignored. These issues became magnified and distorted during the Zhdanov purge of 1948.

As a by-product of the war-time alliance between the Soviet Union and the Western powers, more attention was paid by the Russians to the music of Britain and America. Ossovsky's lectures on this topic have already been mentioned. The voks* bulletin carried a report on a concert of English music given in Moscow; among the composers were Cyril Scott, Lennox Berkeley, William Alwyn, Eric Coates—not a very representative list, to be sure, but at least an attempt to create good will. The concert was introduced by Igor Boelza, then professor at the Kiev Conservatory, who spoke on "The Musical Culture of Contemporary England". voks also published an essay, "New Material on the Cultural Relations between Russia and Great Britain and America", which resembled a historic survey. On 3 July 1945 the U.S.S.R. State Symphony Orchestra played a programme of American music; represented were Gershwin, Samuel Barber, Roy Harris, Wallingford Riegger, and Elie Siegmeister. Several books and brochures on music of the West appeared in 1945, among them Alshvang's *French Musical Impressionism*, Shneerson's *Contemporary British Music* and *Contemporary American Music*, and Boelza's above-mentioned lecture.

Direct contacts between Soviet and Western musicians were encouraged and given publicity. voks printed a letter by the British composer Alan Bush addressed to Sergei Prokofiev, in reply to a letter from Prokofiev who had sent him some Soviet musical materials. Bush wrote on 1 August 1941, "We have been singing the popular Soviet songs in Hyde Park and elsewhere to interested and sympathetic audiences . . . The B.B.C. made its first broadcast of the Soviet National Song last Sunday . . ." Bush did much on behalf of Soviet music. So did Gerald Abraham with his excellent essays on Soviet composers

* voks—abbreviated for "Vsesoyuznoye Obshchestvo Kulturnoi Svyazi s Zagranitsoi" (USSR Society for Cultural Relations with Foreign Countries). Founded in 1925, voks became quite active during the war and published bulletins in English (for example, four issues in 1942).

which appeared in 1943. Calvocoressi's *A Survey of Russian Music*, including the Soviet era, was published as a Penguin Book in 1944. The sympathies for the valiant struggle of the Soviet people were carried into the field of music and led at times to almost uncritical acclaim, as in the case of Shostakovich's "Leningrad" Symphony.

In the United States there was a similar sympathetic climate. The Music Committee of "The National Council of American-Soviet Friendship", organized in 1943, was active under the chairmanship of Sergei Kussevitsky; he was supported by prominent musicians—Aaron Copland, Roy Harris, Fritz Reiner, Dimitri Mitropoulos, Lily Pons, André Kostelanetz, and Benny Goodman. After the war, in 1946, the American-Soviet Music Society was set up as an independent organization; among their officers and members were Leonard Bernstein, Marc Blitzstein, Morton Gould, Daniel Saidenberg, Elie Siegmeister. There was a national Advisory Board of thirty-five members, and an "American-Soviet Music Review" was published, but it did not flourish beyond the first issue in autumn 1946. The political circumstances of the late 1940's—The Cold War, McCarthyism—made the Society cease its activities within a few years. The tragic post-war estrangement between the Soviet Union and its former allies was reflected almost immediately in the field of music.

Symphonies of War and Peace is the title of a book by the Soviet musicologist Boris Yarustovsky.[17] Written two decades after the end of the Second World War, it surveys and compares a number of symphonic works, both Soviet and foreign, which were composed under the impact of the war. Included among the Western composers are Honegger (Symphony No. 2, 1941, and No. 3, 1945–46), Stravinsky and his Symphony in Three Movements, Bartok and his Concerto for Orchestra, and several works by Bohuslav Martinu—the Double Concerto, the Third Symphony, and "Lidice". Treated more briefly are Milhaud, Britten (the Symphony-Requiem), Dallapiccola, Petrassi, Auric, the Sixth Symphony of Vaughan Williams, and the Fifth Symphony (1943) of Roy Harris, with a rather grandiloquent dedication to "our great Ally, the Union of Soviet Socialist Republics . . ."

Among Soviet works, Yarustovsky singles out the Symphonies Nos. 5 and 6 by Prokofiev, the Seventh and Eighth by Shostakovich, the Twenty-second and Twenty-fourth by Miaskovsky, and the Second Symphony by Khachaturian. Briefly mentioned are also symphonies by Khrennikov and Muradeli.

The author points out a strange phenomenon: in Soviet music, the strongest impact of the war was felt in two wholly unrelated genres—

the song and the symphony; in other words, in the simplest and the most complex of forms. The essential difference between East and West —in the opinion of Yarustovsky—is the fact that the "Western" war symphonies were composed at a safe distance from the battlefield, while the Soviet composer—though not precisely "in battle"—was engulfed by the war, surrounded by it on all sides, physically and psychologically. Thus, the war experience of the Western composer was one of intellectual absorption rather than physical exposure, while the Soviet composer was in daily contact with soldiers and survivors, with the horror and the despair. The Soviet composer shared the agony of his people as well as the supreme joy of victory. There is, perhaps, less polished perfection in the scores of the Russians, but far more immediacy of personal involvement which—so Yarustovsky believes—transmits itself more forcefully to the listener. This, of course, is a rather personal reaction by a Soviet citizen whose own emotional response colours his objectivity and scholarship. But it is safe to assume that his view is shared by virtually every musician and music lover in the Soviet Union. Disagree as one may, one must accept it as a fact: the Russians are fiercely proud of their music and very sensitive about any—even the slightest— foreign criticism.

In order of chronology, the two "war" symphonies of Shostakovich were the first; the Seventh was completed in December 1941—barely six months after Hitler's invasion—the Eighth was composed in 1943 and performed that same year, on 4 November. For Shostakovich, the symphonic idiom was a natural means of expression while other composers struggled to translate their patriotic feelings into the formal terms of the symphony.

Western critical opinion is almost unanimous in considering the Seventh Symphony a second-rate work. Its thin musical substance is out of proportion with its inordinate length. To the Seventh Symphony one can apply a rather *méchant* witticism of Ernest Newman: the position of a Shostakovich symphony on the musical map of the future will be located "between so many degrees longitude and so many degrees platitude". The length of the Seventh is not conditioned by the development of thematic material nor by an over-abundance of new ideas. It is due to excessive repetition which appears to be intentional, a part of the over-all design of the composer. There is nothing accidental or slipshod about the construction of the work; Shostakovich is a master craftsman, always in control though working at a furious speed. "I never composed as quickly as now," he said in October 1941 while working on the Seventh. Perhaps he wanted to be as simple, as direct as possible so that no artifice would stand between him and his com-patriots. Shostakovich's sayings and writings during that time betray an almost naive desire to be unmistakably clear about his reasons for writing this symphony, his impulse, his emotions, his intent, about the underlying programme and the implied meaning. There appears a need to communicate in words as well as in music—a loquaciousness which, in fact, is unlike Shostakovich. Usually, he is inclined to understate or to remain silent when it comes to his own music; in the case of the Seventh, he overstates and overtalks. This might prove that he was under tremendous strain. Perhaps he did not intend to write *the* im-mortal masterpiece, but to write "from the heart to the heart", to communicate without fussiness with all and everyone who felt as he did. So many of his utterances sound just that way. For example, on 1 September 1941, he said on the Leningrad radio, "Soviet musicians, my dear and numerous brothers-in-arms, my friends! Remember that our art is threatened by an immense danger. Let us defend our music, let us work honestly and unselfishly . . . An hour ago I finished the score of the second movement of a new, large-scale symphonic work . . . If I succeed in completing the third and fourth movements of this work, it will be my seventh symphony."[18]

It was—one must remember—a work conceived in the heat of battle, and neither the sincerity of his words nor of his music can be doubted. The following description of his new symphony must have been written by the composer shortly after he completed it; the state-ment (in an inadequate English translation) was published by VOKS early in 1942. The prose is artless, at times naive, but somehow moving,

"My Seventh Symphony I began in besieged Leningrad. Every day of the heroic defence of this great town was a new link in the sub-lime symphony of the fight carried on by our people. I hearkened to the life and saw the struggle of the Russian people and tried to inculcate the pictures of their heroic deeds in my music.

The first part, a symphonic allegro, was inspired by the month of August in Leningrad. The war burst into our peaceful life . . . Our people—workers, thinkers, creators—became warriors. Ordinary men and women became heroes . . . The first part of the symphony has something tragic, it includes a requiem. It is full of grief for those who died the death of heroes on the field of battle.

However, we are unconquerable in our great national war, because ours is a righteous cause. We know that Hitler will be defeated and that our enemy will find his grave in Russian earth. Therefore, the general spirit of the first part is bright, cheerful, and life-asserting.

I composed the second and third parts—a scherzo and an adagio
—at a time when the dark clouds gathered over our country,
when ... every step of the retreating Red Army evoked a smarting
and painful echo in our hearts. But the Soviet people knew that
they were invincible ... The scherzo and adagio express the confidence in the near triumph of freedom, justice, and happiness.

The fourth part is to a certain extent a continuation of the first.
It is the Finale of the symphony; it too is composed in the form of
a symphonic allegro. And if the first part may be conditionally
given the name of 'war', the fourth part ought to be called
'victory'. The fourth part begins with the idea of the struggle for
life and death. The joint struggle of life and darkness grows into
radiant exultation. We are carrying on the offensive. The fatherland is victorious.

My dream is to hear in the near future the production of
this symphony in Leningrad, in my own native city which
inspired me to create it. I dedicate my dearest work of art to
the heroic defenders of Leningrad, to the Red Army and to our
victory."[19]

This statement must have been written in Kuibyshev, during the
darkest hours of Russian withdrawal. The unshakeable belief in ultimate victory is indeed inspiring. It is clear that each of the movements
represents a programmatic idea, and in fact the composer intended to
give a title to each; the first was to be "War", the second "Reminiscence" (of pleasant happenings), the third "Native Expanse", the
fourth "Victory".

While the first movement has that long episode built on an ostinato
theme—picturing the invasion by the enemy—(a theme that has an
obsessive quality through sheer repetition and build-up), the composer
does not consider this the main section. "I did not write so-called
battle music," he said, "I wanted to convey the meaning of dreadful
events. The central place in the first movement is taken by a requiem
for the heroes who died for us ..."[20]

The entire Seventh Symphony has a programmatic meaning which
must be taken into consideration. Shostakovich had very specific ideas
about programme music; he set them down almost ten years later in
an essay "On Real and Alleged Programme Music".[21]*

No criticism written "far from the battlefield" is really valid as far
as the "Leningrad" Symphony is concerned. The important question is
—what was the impact on the people *for whom* it was written, *at the time*
it was written? Did the work achieve the intent of the composer? It did,

*See pp. 338–39.

and fully so. Ehrenburg wrote after hearing it, "I came away from the concert deeply stirred: voices of the ancient choruses of Greek tragedy had suddenly resounded. Music has one great advantage: without saying anything it can express everything."[22] Even a foreign observer— emotionally less involved—had to admit, as Werth did, "The impact of the first movement depicting the German invasion—which was now continuing—was truly overwhelming."[23]

There is no need to analyse the work any further. It stands rock-like, imperfect though it may be, like a monument to agony and faith. And the same faith that inspired the composer must permeate the listener . . . a condition not so easily fulfilled.

Decidedly, the New York critics did not belong to that category of listeners. Virgil Thomson of *The New York Herald Tribune* and Olin Downes of *The New York Times* riddled the Seventh Symphony. Thomson, who had written sympathetically about the opera *Lady Macbeth*, found the symphony "thin of substance, unoriginal, and shallow"; he accused the composer of intentionally lowering his quality, "willing to write down to a real or fictitious psychology of mass consumption in a way that may eventually disqualify him for consideration as a serious composers."[24] These harsh words did not prevent the Seventh Symphony from being a huge commercial success in the United States. For a year or two, it was played everywhere; then it disappeared completely from the orchestral repertoire.

Its companion piece, the Eighth Symphony—also a war-time work —arrived on the scene two years later. Serious critics value it higher than the Seventh although its success in Russia was not unanimous. Soon, the chorus of Soviet criticism increased, and the Eighth was pushed into temporary oblivion, to the distress of the composer who wrote in 1956 (!), "I regret very much that the Eighth Symphony has remained unperformed for many years. In this work there was an attempt to express the emotional experience of the people, to reflect the terrible tragedy of the war. Composed in the summer of 1943, the Eighth Symphony is an echo of that difficult time, and quite in the order of things, in my opinion . . ."[25]

In the meantime, the cries of "formalism" raised around the Eighth Symphony have died down, and Soviet critics have evaluated it more objectively. For a time, the Eighth was condemned as a depressive, self-pitying confession of subjective emotions, of tortured expressionism; now one has recognized its validity as a document of deeply-felt humanism. A British critic, Andrew Porter, has expressed it perceptively: "(Shostakovich's Eighth Symphony) must be set beside Goya and *Guernica* . . . a shattering experience . . ." "The Seventh Symphony was heroic. The Eighth is not heroic, but rather a direct and dreadful presentation of what all good men must hate (war)."[26]

A young Russian historian, Orlov, calls the Seventh a "heroic chronicle", the Eighth a "philosophical tragedy".[27] For although both symphonies deal essentially with the same topic, there is an important difference: the Seventh is a description of war, the Eighth is a contemplation of war and its horrors. The Seventh is a spontaneous reaction—comparable to an eyewitness account or a documentary; the Eighth represents the matured thoughts, more bitter, more resigned, and more strongly yearning for peace . . . for true peace, not a noisy victory celebration.

The lack of an "apotheosis" in the Eighth, the alternation of savagery and contemplation, the quiet, inconclusive ending seem to be the reflection of utmost strain on the sensitive psyche of Shostakovich. The war was in its third year, the cruelties multiplied each day, and no end to the bloodshed was in sight. There can be no doubt that the composer was deeply affected: the spirited mood of the Seventh became dispirited, punctuated by anger in the Eighth.

The Seventh was provided by the composer with copious commentary; about the Eighth he remained laconically silent. He wanted to paint horror as well as hope; omitted from the range of his images was triumph. It was a lack sadly noted by critics and public.

The Eighth has a curious, somewhat lopsided form. The first movement is an immense, tripartite structure (Adagio—Allegro—Adagio): the slow sections are suggesting a bitter contemplation, the fast part a battle or invasion. There follow two scherzo-like movements, though drained of any "jest": both—according to Soviet interpretations—are distorted pictures of the "enemy", aggressive, savage. Particularly the second scherzo is a motoric movement, driving forward relentlessly in a toccata-like fashion and topped by screams of despair. This leads without break into a sombre Largo—a set of variations on a theme in the bass, that is, a Passacaglia. (Shostakovich is fond of this Baroque technique; it reappears in several of his compositions of the 1940's, notably the First Violin Concerto.) After the pitiless frenzy of the preceding movement, the Passacaglia appears deliberately static, almost frozen in time and space. "It is as if the music wished to say, 'here, there *was* life'," said one Soviet commentator.[28] The grave Passacaglia theme is repeated twelve times in the bass instruments; the variations built above it feature the strings, the clarinets, a haunting solo horn, the flutes . . . all clad in a mood of desolation and loneliness. Suddenly, almost imperceptibly, the music modulates into a more cheerful key—C-major—and the final movement begins. There is a pastoral mood about this Finale, although the centre section builds into a rather incongruous climax, with a mighty theme played against snarling drums. But the excitement subsides, and the movement trails off in a coda of peaceful dreams.

There were critical voices both in Russia and abroad calling the Finale an anti-climax. Even a well-disposed listener feels a certain imbalance in the over-all structure and "dramaturgy"—to borrow a favourite Russian expression—of the Eighth Symphony. Perhaps it is the fault of the strange sequence of tempo indications, the two successive fast movements (the second and third), the two successive slow movements (fourth and fifth), the tying-together—without interruption—of the three last movements. But most likely it is the lack of a completely satisfying final movement—a miscalculation of mood and weightiness. By itself, the movement has many charming moments; but coming as it does at the end of four tension-filled movements, it disperses the tension rather than resolves it. It leaves the listener limp and drained as the music trails off into nothingness. Yet Shostakovich's Eighth contains some of his greatest pages, some of his most sincere utterances.

Five years after the première of the Eighth Symphony, Shostakovich was in deep trouble with the Soviet cultural bureaucracy led by Zhdanov. The Eighth became a prime target of his opponents: its dissonant language, defeatist mood, lack of affirmation, its brooding subjectivism was unacceptable to the ideologists of 1948. Less than a decade later, in 1957, the Eighth was "rehabilitated" in the course of the cultural "thaw", and the Composers' Union—through its First Secretary Khrennikov—retracted its former "dogmatic position".[29]

Unlike Shostakovich, Prokofiev was not by nature a "symphonist". Not that he could not handle large forms: his numerous concertos and sonatas—altogether some twenty—are proof that form was no impediment. But his imagination was sparked by the element of virtuosity, and he was at his best when a solo instrument—be it piano, violin, or violoncello—could display its brilliance and idiomatic qualities. The genre of symphony demands a different approach—the grand gesture, the massive eloquence.

The fact that Prokofiev's final catalogue contains seven symphonies should not deceive us. The first, the so-called "Classical Symphony", was a happy spoof, a youthful, though masterly, romp. The second, made of "iron and steel", pleased neither the Parisians nor, in fact, the composer when it was played in 1925; later plans to revise and re-orchestrate the work came to nought. The Symphonies Nos. 3 and 4 were based on materials originally written for other media: the Third was derived from the opera *The Flaming Angel*, the Fourth from the ballet *The Prodigal Son*. Fourteen years separate the Fourth from the Fifth Symphony—a long span (1930–44) during which Prokofiev displayed a wealth of creative activity . . . ballet, opera, concerto, vocal music, film scores, even orchestral music, but nothing in the symphonic genre. Then came the Fifth Symphony in 1944, the Sixth in 1947 (though sketched in part in 1944–45), and the Seventh in 1952. Thus, the Fifth Symphony belongs directly to the war period, while the Sixth represents, as it were, a delayed reaction to the war.

However, neither the Fifth nor the Sixth form Prokofiev's complete portrayal of the war. As early as July 1941, he sketched an orchestral suite, *The Year 1941*, in three programmatic movements, entitled "Night", "In the Battle", and "For the Brotherhood of People". The music was later used for the film *The Ukraine in 1941*. Prokofiev also wrote a cantata, *The Ballad of an Unknown Boy*, based on verses by Antokolsky: a boy avenges the killing of his parents by the Nazis. Composed in 1942, the cantata received only a single performance in 1944 and was criticized even by friendly colleagues like Miaskovsky and Shostakovich. "*The Boy*, I'm sorry to say, has been trampled to death", remarked Prokofiev regretfully.[30] War-like echoes can be heard in his *Ode to the End of the War* (1945) and in his last opera, *The Story of a Real Man* (1947–48), which is based on a war topic.

Except for the two symphonies, Prokofiev's war-inspired works—like so many of his *pièces d'occasion*—are dutiful and unconvincing. Despite his immense technical skill, his ability to organize at will his musical materials, Prokofiev failed to transmute the innermost meaning of politico-patriotic events into music of commensurate greatness. It almost seems that his approach was too "objective", that his subjective emotions were not fully involved. There was, perhaps, too much intellectualization, too much mistrust of the initial impulse. "In striving for greater clarity and comprehensibility, Prokofiev sometimes lapsed into over-simplification or abstraction," wrote Nestyev.[31] These are, of course, diametrically opposed extremes; but whichever way Prokofiev "lapsed", neither critics nor listeners responded favourably to his war-connected works.

This relative failure does not reflect upon the stature of Prokofiev. The romantic notion—so prevalent in Soviet aesthetics—that an artist, to be great, must mirror the problems and turmoil of his time, is not always applicable. The inspiration of many great masters often flows from inner sources that are seemingly detached from outer events. Prokofiev produced—next to deliberately "topical" works—a number

of lyrical masterpieces, all written during the war years: the serene
Flute Sonata in D, the Eighth Piano Sonata, the ballet music to *Cinderella*. Prokofiev was not given to paroxyms of joy or sorrow; he was
controlled and collected—it was intellect over impulse.

Was the Fifth Symphony an exception, was it written in a spontaneous response to the war? The composer does not give any such indication, "The Fifth Symphony was intended as a hymn to free and happy
Man, to his mighty powers, his pure and noble spirit. I cannot say that
I deliberately chose this theme. It was born in me and clamoured for
expression. The music has matured in me, it filled my soul . . ."[32]

The Fifth Symphony was composed during the war, but it is not
necessarily a "war" symphony. 1944 was the fourth year of the war,
and the Soviet people had become psychologically adjusted to the
struggle; the feeling of outrage had been replaced by confident determination, and victory was in sight.

There is such nobility, confidence, and serene humour in Prokofiev's
Fifth that the thought of war seems remote. It is his next symphony,
the Sixth, not completed until 1947, that truly reflects the tension,
turbulence, and sorrow of the war years; and the composer—usually
reticent about discussing the "meaning" of his music—admitted that
much to his biographer, Nestyev, "Now (in 1947) we are rejoicing in
our great victory, but each of us has wounds which cannot be healed.
One has lost those dear to him, another has lost his health. This must
not be forgotten."[33]

Even later, in 1950, Prokofiev returned to the topic of war in his
oratorio, *On Guard for Peace*, and he described it in the following
words, "It tells of the grim days of the Second World War, of the tears
of mothers and orphans, of towns swept by fire, of the terrible trials
that fell to the lot of our people; of Stalingrad and the victory over the
enemy . . . I have sought to express my ideas about peace and war, and
my firm belief that there will be no more wars . . ."[34]

All this goes to prove that Prokofiev was far from indifferent to the
tragedy of war. But it is useless to search for it in the Fifth Symphony
although Yarustovsky—in his book on "war symphonies"—succeeds
in assembling a list of war-related idiosyncrasies. They all apply more
to the Sixth Symphony (begun before the Fifth was entirely completed), but not to the Fifth which simply does not lend itself to a
martial interpretation.

Nestyev's analysis is more convincing. He views the Fifth as a kind of
synthesis of Prokofiev's creative evolution of the 1930's. He senses
affinities with the operas *War and Peace* and *Semyon Kotko*, with *Romeo
and Juliet* and *Alexander Nevsky*, with *Ivan the Terrible* and *The Duenna*.
Without wishing to "disparage" the composer, Nestyev feels that the

development of musical material in the Fifth Symphony is less symphonic than theatrical in the "shifting of various moods and scenes".[34]
True, Prokofiev does not engage in any heavy-handed, drawn-out
elaboration: his development is concentrated, succinct. (Did not
Debussy refer to "development" contemptuously as the "necessary dismemberment"?) Be this as it may, the first movement of Prokofiev's
Fifth moves with a sturdy grace towards the culmination in the coda
where the initial theme reappears on a pedal point—one of the great
moments in symphonic literature. The two quick movements of the
Fifth—the Scherzo and the Finale—are in pure Prokofiev style: jaunty,
humorous, full of spirit and vitality. They form a delightful contrast to
the stately, unhurried unfolding of the first movement and the noble
lyricism of the third, the Adagio.

In characterizing Prokofiev's "new" symphonic style, Soviet authors
conjure the epic Russian tradition—Borodin, Rimsky-Korsakov,
Glazunov, the *bogatyri* . . . Poor Prokofiev must be turning in his grave:
there was nothing he abhorred more than the good old Russian
academicism, and Glazunov was sheer anathema to him.

At the première in Moscow, on 13 January 1945, Prokofiev conducted his own work, and it was a festive occasion. In June of the same
year, the Fifth Symphony was heard in Leningrad, in the autumn in
Paris, in November in Boston. Some American critics were mystified
by the accessibility of the musical idiom and suspected that the composer appealed "too openly to the masses".[36] But Olin Downes, the
New York Times critic, gave Prokofiev a rare accolade which contrasted
with the cool critical response to the recent Shostakovich symphonies:
"The (Prokofiev) Symphony is certainly one of the most interesting,
and probably the best, that has come from Russia in the last quarter-
century. It is unquestionably the richest and most mature symphonic
score that the composer has produced. There are new spiritual horizons
in the serenity of the opening movement and wonderful developments
that come later . . ."[37]

This highly favourable review escaped the attention of Nestyev who,
instead, reprints another American opinion which he considers laudatory. However, due to faulty translation or a bit of over-eager editing,
the Russian version of the American review is subtly misleading and
transforms various reservations into a hymn of praise. The words in
square brackets are omitted in the Russian translation but appear in the
American original,

> "The eagerly awaited Fifth Symphony of Prokofiev burst [more]
> like [a bon-bon than] a bombshell upon the musical horizon of
> New York . . . It is difficult, without understating, to describe

[*original*: This is not written to disparage] a work so beautifully orchestrated, so cleverly linked together, so packed with wit and invention . . ."[38]

It is amazing what a little manipulation can do to a review!

While the Fifth Symphony was received with enthusiasm by Soviet critics and the public, the Sixth aroused bewilderment, even among musicians. Miaskovsky, friendly but incorruptible, had to admit, "I began to understand the Prokofiev Sixth only on the third hearing, and then I was won over: profound, but somewhat gloomy, and harshly orchestrated."[39]

Prokofiev's Sixth Symphony is as forbidding and uncompromising as the Fifth is ingratiating and lucid. The public was disappointed, for after the Fifth it had expected more of the same. One could draw a parallel with the Symphonies Nos. 7 and 8 by Shostakovich; here, too, enthusiasm for the Seventh, disappointment with the Eighth. In the case of Prokofiev's Sixth Symphony, the times were not propitious: in 1947 there was growing official impatience with the revival of "formalism" in the arts, and Prokofiev's harsh-sounding new symphony further irritated the cultural hatchet men. Four months later, the blow fell, and Prokofiev—together with Shostakovich, Miaskovsky, Khachaturian, and others—received the public castigation of the Party.

Prokofiev's Sixth Symphony—like Shostakovich's Eighth—has long since been rehabilitated, re-analyzed, and declared a masterpiece. But it is not a work that one longs to hear repeatedly, and it has not established itself in the orchestral repertoire, certainly not to the extent of the Fifth. The orchestral sound is—as Miaskovsky rightly remarked—harsh and metallic; the sonorities of the low brass instruments are often snarling, and those of the high woodwinds shrill. Prokofiev uses this type of sound when he wishes to describe animosity or desolation—in *Alexander Nevsky*, in the *Ode to the End of War*, and in the Sixth Symphony (particularly the first two movements). Pictured here are the reminiscences of the horrors of war, the cruelty of the enemy, the devastation of the land. The clangorous sound is increased by the use of percussion and piano. The lyrical moments provide only occasional respite. The centre movement, the Largo, is framed by austere progressions, but it has a songful middle theme, rather Russian-sounding, which brightens the tonal picture. The Finale (there are only three movements) is a rollicking Rondo, quite playful and somewhat out of character with the ascetic first two movements. It is definitely entertaining, and becomes quite involved when, at the culmination, Prokofiev superimposes both first and second themes. Shortly before the end, there is a return to the austerity of the first movement, followed by a brief, rapid, and none too convincing coda.

With inimitable laconicism, Prokofiev has left a few lines concerning his Sixth Symphony. In discussing his creative work of the years 1945–46, he wrote on 1 February 1947, "The first movement is of an agitated character, at times lyrical, at times austere; the second movement—Andante*—is brighter and more songful; the Finale—rapid and in a major key, resembles in character my Fifth Symphony, were it not for the austere echoes of the first movement. Now I'm busy orchestrating the symphony—two movements are already orchestrated, and I am beginning the scoring of the third movement."[40]

As we have seen, Prokofiev jotted down themes for the Sixth Symphony as early as 1944, while he was at work on the Fifth. In outline and sketches, the Sixth was already finished in the summer of 1945. It is surprising that two essentially so dissimilar works as the Fifth and Sixth Symphonies could have been conceived at almost the same time. However, other composers (Brahms, for example) used to produce works in pairs that were sharply contrasting in character. Yarustovsky surmises that some themes that Prokofiev thought unsuitable for the Fifth were put over for the Sixth, and that both works complement each other. Be this as it may, there is no doubt that the Sixth Symphony is among the most complex compositions written by Prokofiev during his Soviet period. Thus Nestyev writes, in 1957, "It seems as though the two Prokofievs, the old and the new, were engaged in a struggle with each other, revealing in the course of this struggle both powerful, genuine lyricism and sudden outbursts of unrestrained expressionism utterly incomprehensible to the listener."[41]

Here, Nestyev speaks of the Soviet listener, no doubt. Abroad, it was well received, and a French critic even found the instrumentation "transparent" and was pleasantly surprised by its "melodic elements".[42] The Sixth Symphony was introduced to America by the New York Philharmonic under Leopold Stokowski on 24 November 1949, two years after the Moscow première. The journal *Musical America*, which had characterized the Fifth as a "bon-bon", found the Sixth more to its liking: "Perhaps because the work is a kind of autobiographical confession, it is loose in structure and repetitious, and the gorgeous effects of scoring seem to tempt the composer to excess. Nevertheless, there is no resisting the passion, sincerity, and drive of large sections of the work."[43]

Nikolai Miaskovsky, the foremost Soviet composer in the field of the symphony, was sixty years old at the outbreak of the Second World

* Changed by the composer to "Largo".

War. He was one of the few composers who had experienced war as a soldier. Educated at a military school, Miaskovsky spent most of the First World War in the front line; in fact, some of his earliest symphonies—the Fourth and the Fifth—were written in 1917–18.

Three of Miaskovsky's symphonies were composed during the Second World War, in addition to four string quartets, the cello concerto, the cantata *Kirov Is With Us*, and marches for military band. Much of it was written under difficult conditions, during the evacuation from Moscow, and his ability to concentrate on creative work is wholly admirable.

The three "war" symphonies are No. 22, composed in September 1941; No. 23, on Caucasian folk themes, completed in December 1941; and No. 24, written after his return to Moscow during the summer of 1943. The "Caucasian" symphony was based on folk material collected by the composer during his stay in Nalchik, the capital of the Kabardino-Balkar Autonomous Republic, in the autumn of 1941. His friend Prokofiev was there, too, and both musicians were fascinated by the original Kabardian folk tunes, some of which Prokofiev used for his Second String Quartet. Miaskovsky's Twenty-third Symphony is more of a genre piece—rather a symphonic suite—and its inner connection with the war experience is slight.

On the other hand both the Twenty-second and the Twenty-fourth Symphonies have strong reflections of grief and defiance. The composer himself described some of the themes and episodes in a letter, characterizing a part of the second movement of the Twenty-second as the "evil image of the enemy" and the main theme of the same movement as an expression of "deepest sorrow and even despair". In fact, Miaskovsky planned to call the Twenty-second Symphony a "Symphony-Ballad about the Great Patriotic War", and each movement had originally a programmatic subtitle: the first—images of "peaceful life, overshadowed occasionally by threats", the second— "Harkening to the Horrors of War", the third "And the Enemy trembled . . ." To this, Miaskovsky added in a letter, "Perhaps it is not superfluous to give each movement some epigraph, but if the sensitive listener will understand without it, it might be better to omit titles, because most of the time they result in even greater vagueness."[44]

Shortly after the first performance in Tbilisi, on 12 January 1942, Miaskovsky wrote to a friend, the critic Derzhanovsky,

"The Symphonic Ballad does not have concrete images like the Seventh Symphony of Shostakovich, and my subtitle 'About the Patriotic War of 1941' is meant as my personal reaction: dark forebodings penetrate the beautiful, serene life, then everything is submerged in sinister gloom and suffering; the emerging forces of resistance raise the hope for liberation, and the sharp conflicts bursting forth in the development of the Finale lead to liberation —the hymn of victory. Said in this manner it seems crude; in music it is, of course, much smoother . . ."[45]

Later, the composer discarded all references to a programmatic meaning and kept only the title *Symphony-Ballad*, but the "narrative trend"—a term used by Miaskovsky—left a certain imprint on the Twenty-second Symphony. Its three movements, played without interruption, are of modest proportions, and the work is not counted among his best.

The Twenty-fourth Symphony was written in the same year—1943 —as Shostakovich's Eighth. By that time, the spontaneous reaction to the war had given way to meditation, and both works have certain traits in common: the sombre colours, the tragic images, and a trend towards contemplation. Miaskovsky is, perhaps, more heroic in places, but it is the traditional heroism—fanfare-like themes, brass instruments . . . The work is full of good and noble intentions, but it does not rise above an essentially conventional concept, and was received as an appropriate tribute to its times, rather than a significant illumination.

There were other symphonies composed and performed in the Soviet Union during the Second World War—symphonies that were timely but not timeless enough to survive. (Beethoven knew the difference when he excluded, from his numbered symphonies, his so-called *Battle Symphony*, "Wellington's Victory".) Nevertheless, the Soviet "war" symphonies played a certain role in the evolution of Soviet music: they showed the composer's active involvement in the national struggle for survival, they helped release the emotional surge of the people, and they contributed to the maturing of the symphonic idiom, to a widening of its scope and expressive power. In the words of a young Soviet historian,

"In order to re-establish the equilibrium of inner strength and to free oneself from the wrath of horrible reality, time was needed. The composer-symphonists, engulfed by the staggering course of events, failed to realize at first that the specific task of the symphony does not lie in the rendering of temporary day-by-day evil; its sphere is the enduring element in the life of man and society. The exclusive limitation within the confines of the current experiences must not become the rule. It does not matter whether the composer chooses the form of documentary publicism, the philosophical-symbolical poem, or the agitated jottings in his personal diary. The works, created under the first , the strongest impression, confirm this thought."[46]

Among symphonies composed during the war years, we may mention those by Khachaturian, Gavril Popov, Vano Muradeli, Khrennikov, and Balanchivadze. They were played, discussed, praised, and laid aside, with the exception of the Symphony No. 2 by Khachaturian because of the strong personal imprint of his musical idiom.

In 1945, the Soviet armies entered Germany; by April, they had reached Berlin, on 2 May the German capital surrendered. The feeling of elation inside Russia was indescribable. Although there was still Japan . . . But here the Soviet involvement was brief: on 8 August the war on Japan was declared, on 2 September the capitulation was signed. The Great Patriotic War was ended, but peace did not begin, neither for the Soviet people nor for the world at large. The post-war years of readjustment were to be a painful experience, particularly for the Soviet intelligentsia. Even before the end of the war, heralding the approaching change in the Party line, Ehrenburg was silenced in April 1945. . . . Ehrenburg whose voice had been a clarion call of resistance against rhe Nazi onslaught, against Fascism everywhere.

> "The end of the war was to be followed by years of disappointment and frustration for the Russian people. The war-time hopes of a Big Three Peace gave way to the reality of the Cold War and the 'Iron Curtain'. The happy illusion of 1944 that the Soviet regime would become more liberal, and life freer and easier after the war, soon went up in smoke . . . The NKVD (Secret Police), which had shown a certain discretion during the war, came into its own again, and a new terror developed which did not come to an end until 1953, after Stalin's death."[1]

This is the conclusion of Alexander Werth's monumental book, *Russia at War*.

It had been a costly victory, and the Soviet leaders were determined that its fruits were not to be dissipated. To cope with the reconstruction of the devastated land, the forty-eight hour week was retained, work discipline was tightened, and a new five-year plan was imposed. To counteract the relaxation of Party vigilance, the Central Committee launched an ideological campaign in all fields of the arts and sciences. The arts became the domain of Andrei Zhdanov, and the period of cultural purges—the years 1946–48—became known as *Zhdanovshchina*.

The term itself is significant, for it proves to what extent the cultural policy of the late 1940's was identified with his personality. But one must guard against over-simplification. In the arts, the ideological post-war battles were, in many ways, the continuation and enforcement of policies established in the 1930's. The Resolution of 1932 had re-directed the Party's cultural policy, the Writers' Congress of 1934 had provided guidelines for literature, the *Pravda* articles of 1936 had censored Shostakovich and—indirectly—the state of music. The total enforcement of these decisions was held in suspense during the war. Once the war was ended, old regulations were reactivated and additional guidelines decreed. But ultimately, the cultural policy of the 1940's must be seen in the larger context of the general course set for the Soviet Union by Stalin and the Party hierarchy after the victorious conclusion of the war. Immense national pride, strong anti-Western feelings fanned by vicious propaganda, and renewed stress on ideological discipline were some of the characteristics. Stalin himself set the tone—in his toast to the Russian people on 24 May 1945, and particularly in his speech of 9 February 1946. In this speech he extolled the Soviet world concept and restated the implacable Bolshevik enmity towards the capitalist system. This placed the Soviet Union in total ideological opposition to its war allies—whose role in winning the war was belittled in official pronouncements.

Stalin's speech of February 1946—which actually ranged over a wide area—indicated that a new course for stricter control of cultural activities was in the making. Zhdanov did not set the policy, but he must have had an important voice in shaping it, and he was in full charge of executing it. And so the *Zhdanovshchina* began in August 1946.

This was not, as we have seen, Zhdanov's first excursion into the field of the arts. At the First Writers' Congress in 1934, standing side by side with Maxim Gorky, he delivered the Party's ideological dictum, forging Socialist Realism into an ideo-political weapon. When he was put in charge of the ideological front, in 1946, he was determined to make a clean sweep. Cultured and well-educated, cold and ruthless, Zhdanov had the fanaticism of conviction. He did not shrink from anything that could help him achieve his aims which he believed to be in the best interest of his Party and his country. He resorted to abuse, insinuations, threats, even flattery if need be. He knew the intelligentsia; he was aware of the secret divisions, the hidden jealousies, the artistic foibles. He exploited the resentments of the young and the unrecognized against the "establishment". Whatever he did, he always posed as the protector of true Russo-Socialist art. After calling together a group of intellectuals or artists, he would set the tone with a keynote address and then merely preside over day-long sessions of mutual vilification, disguised under the euphemism of "creative debates". So demoralized was the intelligentsia, so fresh were the memories of the

1938 purges, that hardly anyone dared to disagree. Once Zhdanov's accusing statement was heard, the artists fell into line: everybody echoed the charges, defended his own position, and apologized profusely if that position was vulnerable. Those criticized by name recanted publicly; to remain silent was an admission of guilt. Zhdanov obviously enjoyed his dual role as prosecutor and judge; he manipulated the meetings with shrewdness, always maintaining a certain intellectual level. The real drama was acted out by writers, musicians, and artists, each trembling for his own career and safety. Pasternak, Prokofiev, Shostakovich and others were vilified and condemned by their fellow artists. To read the minutes of those "debates" in the Writers' Union or Composers' Union is a saddening experience, for they prove how decent men can be perverted by fear and ambition.

Zhdanov can be considered the architect of four ideological resolutions enacted by the Central Committee of the Communist Party. The first, dated 14 August 1946, was entitled "Resolution on the Journals *Zvezda* and *Leningrad*" and dealt with literature. The second, published two weeks later, on 26 August, was called "On the Repertoire of the Dramatic Theatres and Measures for its Improvement", followed on 4 September by the resolution "On the film *Bolshaya Zhizn*". Finally, after a considerable interval during which "voluntary" compliance was tried, the blow fell on music: on 10 February 1948 the resolution "On the Opera *Velikaya Druzhba* by V. Muradeli" was made public.

Zhdanov—having brought about the complete subjugation of Soviet intellectual life—died unexpectedly later in the year, on 31 August 1948. But the policies he had initiated continued for at least another five years, until Stalin's death, and some of his principles have remained valid until today. It is remarkable that, in all the dethroning of great leaders—from Stalin down—the name of Zhdanov has remained inviolate. Any errors committed during the cultural purges—and some of them were formally admitted—were charged to the "subjective views" of Stalin and his advisers, Molotov, Malenkov, and Beria.

How the purges affected the intellectual community is best expressed by Ehrenburg in his Post-War Memoirs, "I had believed that, after the Soviet people's victory, the 1930's could not repeat themselves, yet everything reminded me of the way things had gone in those days: writers, film directors, and composers were called together, 'abettors' were singled out, and every day new names swelled the list of those censured. Accusations were levelled against Pasternak and Shostakovich, Eisenstein and Pudovkin . . ."[2]

The three Resolutions of 1946, concerning literature, theatre, and film, also have a bearing on music because they foreshadowed the course of events. The guidelines of the Party were made clear; it became the responsibility of the intellectuals to carry them out. In the Resolution of 14 August 1946—dealing with the two literary journals *Zvezda* and *Leningrad*—the core of the accusations is contained in the following sentences,

> "Works which cultivated a non-Soviet spirit of servility before the contemporary bourgeois culture of the West have appeared in the journal. Contributions saturated with gloom, pessimism, and disillusionment with life have been published . . . The editors . . . have forgotten the thesis of Leninism that our journals—whether scientific or literary—cannot be non-political . . . They are a mighty instrument of the Soviet state . . . Any preaching of 'art for art's sake' . . . is harmful to the interests of the Soviet people and the Soviet state . . ."[3]

The repercussions in the Writers' Union were far-reaching: the militant Alexander Fadeyev took over as first secretary—a writer who believed in Stalin and who committed suicide in 1956 during the de-Stalinization campaign of Khrushchev. In his first speech, Fadeyev attacked Pasternak as a representative of "that individualism which is profoundly alien to the spirit of our society". (This was—one should remember—a decade before the furore broke over *Doctor Zhivago*.)

To reinforce the impact of the Party's resolution, Zhdanov's personal attacks against writers were vitriolic. He called Zoshchenko a "scum of literature" and he vilified Akhmatova—"not exactly a nun, not exactly a harlot, but rather nun and harlot, with whom harlotry is mixed with prayer."[4]

The resolution on theatre affairs (26 August 1946) dealt less with personalities than with issues: too few plays on contemporary Soviet topics, too many plays "idealizing the lives of tsars, khans, and great lords", too many foreign plays by "foreign bourgeois dramatists" who only serve "the propaganda of reactionary bourgeois ideology and morals".[5]

The resolution on film (4 September 1946) provides a curious illustration of Soviet attitudes. "Socialist Realism" for instance is fine as long as it does not portray Soviet life too realistically. The film *Bolshaya Zhizn* gave a "false and perverted picture of Soviet people" as it showed "backwardness, vulgarity, and ignorance"; even its title, *The Great Life*, "sounds like ridicule of Soviet society". The tender sensibilities of the critics were obviously offended by the portrayal of Soviet workers as being at times semi-literate, vulgar, and not averse to vodka and sex. Even more important was the condemnation

of such Soviet films as the second part of Eisenstein's *Ivan the Terrible**
and Pudovkin's *Admiral Nakhimov*, a hero of the Crimean War. The
reason for this criticism was Stalin's new approach to history, a glorification of Russia's past regardless of accuracy. The official condemnation read: "Eisenstein exhibited ignorance of historical facts by portraying the progressive army of *Oprichniki*** as a band of degenerates,
similar to the American Ku Klux Klan, and Ivan the Terrible, a man
of strong will and character, as weak and spineless, something like
Hamlet."[7]

Eisenstein's spirit was broken; after making an abject confession—
"The sense of historical truth betrayed me"—he died less than two
years later, in 1948, without having returned to work. The censured part
of *Ivan the Terrible* was released in 1958, during Khrushchev's regime,
and is now widely recognized as a cinematic masterpiece. Both parts of
the film have impressive musical scores by Prokofiev which escaped
criticism.

The three resolutions of 1946 had a twofold purpose: to correct alleged
shortcomings in certain artistic fields, and to warn all potential dissidents that the Party would enforce its ideological aims. Obviously, no
fellow-travellers, like those of the 1920's, would be tolerated. Total
commitment to Leninism—in Stalin's interpretation—was expected.
And the Soviet intellectuals understood the message. They gathered in
hurriedly called conferences, they discussed the issues of the resolutions
within their unions. Invariably, such meetings ended in unanimous
expressions of fervent approval and undying loyalty to the Party, often
accompanied by a direct letter to Stalin. Such letters usually began
with "Our dear Yosif Vissarionovich" and ended with flowery
exclamations, "Long live our great leader and teacher, the greatest
scholar of our epoch, J. V. Stalin."

At the time, the Composers' Union was ruled by the ORGKOMITET
(Organizational Committee), set up in Moscow in 1939 to co-ordinate
the activities of the local chapters (there were twenty-eight in 1945).
The ORGKOMITET was directed by a small group of recognized composers—Glière, Khachaturian, Shostakovich, Shaporin, Kabalevsky,
and Belyi—and lacked any representation of young members; on the
whole, the committee did not function very effectively. The composer

* In Ehrenburg's words, "Eisenstein, at Stalin's demand, was working on a
film on *Ivan the Terrible*. The second part of the film aroused Stalin's wrath; after
seeing it through, he said briefly, 'Scrap it'."[6]

** The *Oprichniki* were Tsar Ivan's henchmen guilty of hideous atrocities in
the decade 1565–1575.

Knipper—who had no axe to grind—described the activity of the ORGKOMITET, "Occasionally, they met, often without a quorum. It is customary to be either politely silent, or to raise objections, but very tactfully . . . All must be nice and quiet."[8]

However, the events on the ideological front aroused the ORGKO-MITET from its usual lethargy. Khachaturian, the vice-chairman, issued a call for a plenary meeting. Delegates representing all local chapters convened in Moscow for a seven-day session, from 2 to 8 October 1946. Khachaturian delivered the key address, and more than fifty speakers participated in the discussion.[9]

There were numerous basic complaints. Many out-of-town speakers were unhappy about the Moscow-based ORGKOMITET, about the lack of leadership and guidance, about the isolation of the Moscow "establishment" from the rank-and-file of Soviet composers. Even the delegates from Leningrad confirmed that they had hardly any contact with the Moscow directorate. Khachaturian, under pressure, had to admit certain shortcomings in organizational work.

Ultimately, the plenum adopted eleven recommendations addressed to the ORGKOMITET, consisting mostly of weak generalities—the need for more creative guidance, more ideological-educational work, more criticism and self-criticism, closer ties between Soviet composers and Soviet reality. Barely mentioned was the struggle against formalism and Western modernistic influences—actually the basic issues. Besides, neither the plenum nor the ORGKOMITET had any power to enforce compliance with its recommendations—and persuasion alone proved insufficient. As Shebalin, director of the Moscow Conservatory, observed, in retrospect,

> "I must admit that, although we had many discussions on the Party's resolutions on literary and art questions, we have so far failed to change some of our composers' direction. Not all our students and professors have realized the necessity of reorganizing their work in the light of their Party's decisions; and, as the director of the Conservatory, I must admit that we have not done enough in that direction."[10]

Throughout the discussion at the 1946 plenary session of the composers, there seemed to be a certain feeling of uneasiness about the state of Soviet music. A noted Soviet musicologist summarized the musical scene of the immediate post-war years:

> "The ties of music with life weakened noticeably. The communal 'temperature' of musical art was lowered, its social edge was dulled. Great works dedicated to contemporary topics became relatively

rare, and their ideological-artistic level was by no means always high enough ... The ideas and images of our socialist 'today' found hardly any reflection in our musical theatre. The development of programme music was slowed down. Little was written in terms of appealing songs, popular instrumental pieces designed for wide circles of players and listeners. Some of the symphonies, quartets, and sonatas found no response among the large audiences. Many listeners said that the music of Soviet composers often failed to satisfy the aesthetic needs of our people, and that many of the works, in content and form, were alien to the masses and to the traditions of realist art."[11]

The reason—the author found—was not only a certain "creative emotional depression" after the tensions of the war. Many of the composers simply failed to grasp the new "socio-historical" period of the Soviet land. During the war, many musicians worked closely with the fighting army; after the war, no similar ties were established with the Soviet masses. Shostakovich called it the "demobilization mood—the war is ended, we can rest".[12]

In fact, the artistic reaction of Soviet composers to the victorious conclusion of the war was surprisingly tepid. Prokofiev was the first to respond. On 12 November 1945, Moscow heard his symphonic *Ode to the End of the War* (Op. 105), but it proved to be a far from accessible work. The composer chose an odd instrumentation for band and percussion, four pianos, eight harps, and—as the only string instruments—an enlarged double bass section. He aimed at achieving a certain severity of timbre, but succeeded only in producing a thick, thunderous sonority without the mitigating warmth of the strings. Besides, the instrumental demands of the *Ode* were too complex for most of the country's orchestras, and so the work was laid aside and remained unpublished. Another musical contribution to the end of the war was an overture, *Victory* (Op. 85) by the veteran composer Glière; but the Moscow audience, at the première on 30 October 1945, found it rather shallow and superficial.

Perhaps the most exuberant tribute to the victory mood was the Ninth Symphony of Shostakovich, first performed in Leningrad under Mravinsky's baton on 3 November 1945. It was a "joyous sigh of relief", as if a burden had been lifted from all humanity. No sharper contrast can be imagined between this merry, light-hearted scherzo-symphony ("Probably the least symphonic music ever written," commented a British critic[13]) and the preceding "war" symphonies Nos. 7 and 8, alternating between obsession and depression. Yet, Shostakovich's Ninth Symphony was not the "victory symphony" that had been expected by the Soviet public. Rumours had been circulating that the composer planned a significant work to crown a trilogy begun by the two war symphonies. In 1944, Shostakovich had hinted in a conversation that he thought of a Ninth Symphony with chorus and soloists although he was afraid of "immodest analogies". Twice he started on a new symphony, with "powerful, victorious music in the major mode",[14] only to abandon the project. In the summer of 1945, he made a renewed attempt, and the result was the joyous, irreverent present Ninth. A critic described the first reaction after an informal reading,

> "We were prepared to listen to a new monumental fresco, something that we had a right to expect from the author of the Seventh and Eighth Symphonies, especially at a time when the Soviet people were still full of the recent victory over fascism. But we heard something quite different, something that at first astounded us by its unexpectedness."[15]

Shostakovich must have taken a boyish delight in deflating the pompous expectations of his compatriots. How they would have welcomed a choral-instrumental victory monument that would have out-Mahlered Beethoven. Instead, here was that nose-thumping opus which immediately aroused the "sharply negative attitude" of many leading musicians.

Quite a different reaction to the end of the war can be felt in the Symphony No. 25 by Miaskovsky, composed in 1945–46. The veteran symphonist conveyed the mood of peace by music of a relaxed, idyllic nature. His biographer Livanova wrote, "It is beautiful and transparent, but not sufficiently democratic and bright."[16] We may guess that a "democratic" symphony is one with mass appeal—not necessarily a hallmark of quality.

It is remarkable, though, that so many Soviet composers of that period tried to reach the mass audience by means of the—rather esoteric—symphonic genre. Between September 1945 and January 1946, the Moscow Philharmonic alone gave premières of twenty-four symphonies. These were mainly works completed during, or immediately after, the war. Most of them were undistinguished and disappeared quickly.

The prevalence of instrumental music at the expense of vocal genres becomes even more pronounced if one considers the many concertos and chamber music works written shortly after the war. Among them were—to mention only the best-known composers—the cello concertos of Miaskovsky and Khachaturian, the string quartets No. 3 by Shostakovich, No. 2 by Kabalevsky, Nos. 10, 11, and 12 by Miaskovsky, the Second Violin Sonata and the Ninth Piano Sonata by Prokofiev.

In the eyes of Soviet officialdom, this trend towards "abstract" instrumental music was objectionable, for it did not fulfill "the aesthetic needs of the people".

As the Thirtieth Anniversary of the October Revolution approached —to be observed in October 1947— the role of music in the celebrations was expected to be important. Strangely enough, the composers were in no rush to be represented by new works specifically written for this occasion. Shostakovich, for example, made only a minor effort: he prepared a "mass cantata", the *Poem about the Homeland* (Op. 74) for vocal soloists, chorus, and orchestra. Actually, it was little more than a medley of tunes, mainly by other composers like Dunayevsky, Alexandrov, and others, reset by Shostakovich. His biographer Rabinovich calls it "a rather short piece, extremely simple in structure and very modest in the artistic devices employed; it does not make any claims to greatness".[17] A fellow composer, Khrennikov, put it more bluntly, "Just a small job . . . for the occasion since he has had no time to do anything else." What angered Khrennikov, however, was the cliquishness in the Composers' Union, the hero worship among critics, "There were some who immediately proclaimed Shostakovich's orchestral fantasia to be a work of genius. It seems to be that even Shostakovich himself was taken aback by this fulsome praise; he did not consider this work important . . ."[18] It should be mentioned that Shostakovich's cantata was not performed at the occasion for which it was written.

Prokofiev showed more foresight. For the Thirtieth Anniversary celebration, he had prepared two compositions: the *Festive Poem* (Op. 113) for symphony orchestra, and the cantata *Flourish, Mighty Land* (Op. 114) for chorus and orchestra. Neither ranks high in his work.

Prokofiev's major contribution was to be his latest symphony, the Sixth, whose roots, as we have seen, reach back into the war year 1944. The première was timed for the festive month of October 1947, and the Leningrad Philharmonic played the work on two successive evenings, the 11th and the 12th. It is curious to note that this work—which was soon to be subjected to much official and unofficial criticism— aroused at first a favourable reaction. The critic Shneerson confided privately to Alexander Werth, "I heard the work in Leningrad. It is wonderful; better than the usual Prokofiev. It is philosophic, has the depth of Shostakovich. You'll see". He wrote in his programme notes:

> "It is one of the most beautiful, most exalted of his works, imbued with the creative spirit of Soviet humanism . . . It is a great landmark not only in the art of Prokofiev, but in the whole history of Soviet symphonism . . . This great work shows once again how immeasurably superior Soviet music is to the music of the capitalist

West, where symphonism has long ceased to be an art of lofty ideas and high emotionalism and is now in a state of profound decadence and degeneration . . ."[19]

Prokofiev's Sixth Symphony reached Moscow on 25 December 1947. A brief notice in *Pravda* merely said that the audience had been "very appreciative". The same programme contained a recent work by Khachaturian, the *Symphony-Poem*, now known as Symphony No. 3, which uses a symphony orchestra reinforced by organ and fifteen trumpets. Werth called it a "noisy, bombastic *tour de force* . . . crude and eccentric". The current evaluation is more lenient; Orlov suggests that Khachaturian's piece belongs to the genre of "music for street and square",[20] comparable to Beethoven's *Battle of Vittoria* or Tchaikovsky's *1812 Overture*. With this "jubilee" piece, the hapless Khachaturian— never a modernist—got himself into a formalist mess.

It was the opera *The Great Friendship* by Vano Muradeli, however, that was designed to be the major musical work of the Thirtieth Anniversary celebration. Born in Georgia in 1908, Muradeli was—like Khachaturian—the prime example of a successful "minority" composer. After early studies in Tbilisi, he had completed his musical education at the Moscow Conservatory under the guidance of Miaskovsky. He was the recipient of many official honours, the latest in 1947.

The opera *The Great Friendship* was conceived as a tribute to Stalin's native Georgia. Not only were the composer and librettist born in Georgia, but the story dealt with a noted Georgian, the Communist commissar Ordzhonikidze, who had played a major role in the Sovietization of Georgia. Appropriately, the première of the opera was given in the city of Stalino (now Donetsk) on 28 September 1947. Thanks to the active sponsorship of the Party's Arts Commission, *The Great Friendship* was staged almost simultaneously in twelve additional cities. Four of the premières were set for the actual anniversary date, 7 November. Of these, the most important was the performance at the Moscow Bolshoi Theatre where over 600,000 roubles had been spent on the lavish production.* It was a success story that was as extraordinary as it was short-lived. Within two months, the opera was denounced, the composer was publicly humiliated, and the Soviet musical world was thrown into panic. Muradeli's opera entered the annals of Soviet music as a *cause célèbre*.

What had happened? Zhdanov saw a closed performance of *The Great Friendship* which was attended by "a rather well qualified audience

* The Moscow première took place on 7 November 1947. Werth's date for the première as "sometime about the New Year" is obviously erroneous.

of about 500 people".[21] (How "well" qualified? The musicologist Livanova complained that she could not get a ticket while "all kinds of people from the Food and Fish Ministries were there".) Zhdanov disliked the opera intensely, both on grounds of the music and the libretto. Whether the closed performance was a preview or the actual première—possibly limited to an invited public of Party officials—is unclear. Slonimsky claims that *The Great Friendship* was given in Moscow only once, on 7 November,[22] but this would not necessarily exclude a private showing. At any rate, the opera was not immediately withdrawn, for there were three more premières later in November, and two in December—the last in Alma-Ata on 14 December.

It is not known whether Stalin was present at the Moscow première, but it is safe to assume that, on some occasion, he had seen the work. Muradeli's opera was especially designed to flatter Stalin's concept of opera. What was not known until recently, however, is the fact that there was some antagonism between Stalin and Ordzhonikidze, the hero of the opera. During the "unmasking" of Stalin at the Twentieth Party Congress, Khrushchev intimated that Ordzhonikidze was driven to suicide by Stalin; at any rate, the commissar had died in obscure circumstances during the 1937 purges. It may well be that Stalin did not like the idea of having "The Extraordinary Commissar", as the opera was called originally, glorified on the stage. The alleged "historical inaccuracies" of the libretto—one of the major criticisms of the opera—may have been simply facts displeasing to Stalin. There must have been reasons other than musical or artistic to justify the immense scandal raised around Muradeli's mediocre opera.

Whether or not Stalin was directly involved in this sordid affair, is unknown; his name was not mentioned at the time. Zhdanov carried the action, nominally on behalf of the Party's Central Committee. He met with Leontiev, the director of the Bolshoi Theatre, in the presence of Muradeli. It was an "ugly row",[23] which may have caused Leontiev's sudden death of a heart attack. Next, Zhdanov summoned the Moscow composers to a meeting which lasted three days, in January 1948. This was an informal airing of opinions, and the musicians who attended were encouraged to speak their mind. Zhdanov's closing words sounded ominous, "The Central Committee will take into consideration what has been said here, and draw the necessary conclusions. The creative workers must also take account of the results of the discussion."[24]

The "necessary conclusions" came on 10 February 1948 when the Central Committee published its Resolution, "On the Opera *Velikaya Druzhba* by Muradeli."[25] It is a spiteful document, full of unjustified attacks against composers—including Miaskovsky, Prokofiev, Shostakovich, and Khachaturian—who had achieved world renown. Ten years later, in 1958, the Central Committee withdrew some of its baseless accusations, but by then irreparable damage had been done to Soviet music, and to its reputation abroad. The domestic aftermath of the Resolution was predictable. The Composers' Union—mainly the resident members of Moscow—convened immediately for a week of daily meetings, from 17 to 26 February. The Resolution was debated and endorsed, and the customary letter of adulation to Stalin was duly dispatched. Similar meetings were held in all local chapters throughout the land. The old leadership of the ORGKOMITET was deposed. Thirty-four-year-old Tikhon Khrennikov, best known for his "song opera" *Into the Storm* (1939) emerged as the new spokesman. He represented the "hard" line advocated by Zhdanov.

The "new order" in Soviet music was given the final stamp of approval by the "First All-Union Congress of Composers", held in Moscow from 19 to 25 April 1948. It was a national convention attended by delegates from all the Soviet republics. A new directorate of fifty-one members was elected by secret ballot. On 25 and 26 April, this directorate held meetings and elected the following officers: Asafiev, chairman; Khrennikov, general secretary; Koval, Zakharov, Chulaki, and Shtogarenko, secretaries. It must be said that the new presidium was no more representative of the multi-national character of the Composers' Union than was the old ORGKOMITET. Shtogarenko, a Ukrainian composer, was the only non-Russian, just as Khachaturian had been the only non-Russian in the ORGKOMITET. Inefficient though the old ORGKOMITET may have been, it was a group of distinguished personalities. The new slate of officers was mainly an assemblage of Party-line stalwarts—with one exception: Asafiev. But his chairmanship was an honourary post, and his name was used as window-dressing. He was a sick man, too ill to attend the Congress in person; the statement read in his name was a severely "edited" document. Less than a year later, Asafiev died, on 27 January 1949. The position of chairman was not filled, and Khrennikov—as first secretary—remained in full charge of the Composers' Union. In 1968, he could look back on twenty years in this sensitive post which he retained through Stalinism, Khrushchevism, and the present collective regime.

It is difficult to summarize the Zhdanov era; there is always the danger of over-simplification. A well-informed expert like Edward Crankshaw, for example, asserts that

> "This point about the apparent total acceptance of the Zhdanov Edict is worth remembering. From 1946 to 1953 there was hardly a surface flicker in all the arts (only Prokofiev and Shostakovich

among the musicians put up a sharp resistance to the Zhdanov line: they were supposed to produce the sort of music that the moronic blondes of the New Soviet Society could sing in unison in the fields) to show that the artists were unhappy in their work."[26]

Crankshaw's information about the "sharp resistance" of Prokofiev and Shostakovich is not borne out by available facts. All of Shostakovich's public statements were meek and apologetic; he looked and acted like a broken man. Prokofiev, in poor health, made a written statement which was a dignified apologia. As for the "moronic blondes of the New Soviet Society" in the fields, they probably sang the same songs as the, equally dumb, blondes of Tsarist times, namely the old Russian folksongs, so melodious and idiomatic that they needed no enrichment by any composer. Much as one would have liked to see the composers resist Zhdanov, there was no resistance but rather an effort to compromise, at least temporarily.

Ilya Ehrenburg, one of the writers silenced for a time, is responsible for a rather flippant remark on the music situation, "Early in 1948 Prokofiev and Shostakovich told me that Zhdanov had also invited the composers to meet him and told them that the most important element in music was a melody that could be hummed."[27]

We know what Zhdanov told the composers, for there is a complete transcript of the meeting. The issues were much more complex. For those who cannot study the 176 pages of verbatim reports, however, Alexander Werth, who was in Moscow at the time, has provided a skilful and most readable condensation, under the title *Musical Uproar in Moscow.*[28]

Of all the documentary evidence, the transcript of Zhdanov's informal meeting with the composers is, perhaps, the most interesting. It took place in January 1948, several weeks before the Resolution was published. The debate quickly revealed the dissensions and antagonisms within the Composers' Union. The older generation hated virtually all modern music, Soviet or otherwise. Said Professor Goldenweiser, the highly respected old piano pedagogue, "In recent years I have often expressed my disapproval of the road chosen by most Soviet composers, with the 'stars' at their head . . . When I hear the clatter of false chords in some of our new symphonies and sonatas, I am horrified to feel that they are akin to the decadent ideology of the West—or even of Fascism —and not to the healthy nature of Russian, Soviet humanity . . ."[29]

The younger composers chafed under the domination of the "establishment" which controlled commissions, prizes, and critics. Khrennikov spoke for this faction, "The big four—or five*—. . . found themselves in a sort of privileged position: they were immune against criticism . . . They became musical top bureaucrats. Kowtowing critics described everything they wrote as a work of genius . . . Young composers followed blindly in their footsteps . . ." Dzerzhinsky had the same complaint, "The critics are . . . nothing but flunkeys in the service of the big composers . . ."

Another dissatisfied faction consisted of the composers of "light" music who resented the fact that so much official attention was given to "serious" music. Among them were highly successful men like Zakharov and Dunayevsky. Zakharov was particularly vicious, "Our symphonists have put up an iron curtain . . . between the people and themselves . . . They have done it, not accidentally, but quite consciously. Because to them the song is something 'plebeian'. To make use of a song in their work is degrading—so they think." He denied that Muradeli's opera was a major issue, "It is, in fact, one of the most intelligible works. But let us look at our symphonic music . . . These composers are alien and completely incomprehensible to our Soviet people . . . In order to lead the people, one must speak to the people in a language they can understand . . ."

Shostakovich's Eighth Symphony aroused Zakharov's particular ire, "There are still discussions around the question whether the Eighth is good or bad. Such a discussion is nonsense. From the point of view of the people, the Eighth is not a musical work at all; it is a 'composition' which has nothing to do with art whatsoever."

Zakharov's diatribe did not remain unanswered. Knipper, a highly respected composer of the middle generation, rebuffed him, saying

> "It is not true that we have no gifted composers. It is not true that they do not wish to serve the people. It is not true that nothing is done in this direction . . . We are asked to democratize music, and to write more simply and intelligibly . . . Democratic musical language is not such a simple matter. In these last thirty years our literary language has changed greatly . . . New conceptions require new words. Musical language . . . develops. We cannot speak today in the language of Borodin or Tchaikovsky . . ."

Shebalin called Zakharov's approach "absurdly narrow" and rejected the contention that "all our composers write nothing but cacophony". Another composer, Victor Belyi, tried to explain that "our

* Presumably Prokofiev, Shostakovich, Khachaturian, Kabalevsky, and possibly, Miaskovsky.

whole middle generation studied during those years when Western modernism was in great vogue". Disappointing were the statements of Kabalevsky, Khachaturian, and Shostakovich who sounded too apologetic. Muradeli—apparently in a state of shock because of the sudden notoriety—positively grovelled in the dust, blaming teachers, colleagues, and circumstances for his alleged shortcomings. The veteran composer Miaskovsky attended the meeting but did not speak. Prokofiev's presence was not recorded, and his "rude" behaviour at the meeting (sitting on a piano stool with his back turned to Zhdanov) is pure rumour.

There was near-unanimity on only one point: the ineffectiveness of the Union's leadership and the shortcomings of the ORGKOMITET. Shebalin compared the ORGKOMITET "to the Boyars' Duma in *Boris Godunov* . . . the sort of machine that will do nothing until there is some strong outside interference . . . It needs thorough democratization."

That was all Zhdanov needed to hear. If the distinguished director of the Moscow Conservatory felt the need for "strong outside interference", something ought to be done. Actually, the entire debate played into Zhdanov's hands and confirmed his belief that the composers could, or would, not act on their own. Had not the venerable Shaporin said that the plenary meeting of 1946 "came to no conclusions on musical aesthetics"? Clearly, they needed help . . . the same kind of "help" that he had given the writers, the theatre directors, and the film makers.

In his opening speech, Zhdanov spent comparatively little time on Muradeli's opera, ostensibly the main issue. He found a lack of melody and harmony, insufficient musical characterization, and an inclination towards cacophony. He criticized, among other aspects, the historical inaccuracy of the libretto. But then came the important parallel with Shostakovich's *Lady Macbeth*: both operas had many faults in common. Zhdanov quoted lengthy passages from the 1936 article of *Pravda*, "*Chaos instead of Music*", and he added, "It is clear that the tendency that was then condemned is now alive, and not only alive, but setting the tone to Soviet music." This clarified the issue: a fight to the finish against formalism, naturalism, modernism, Westernism.

In his final summary, Zhdanov elaborated on the issue of the whole direction of Soviet music. He found it lagging behind the achievements of literature and the other arts. He declared the formalist school to be "radically wrong . . . It is anti-People and prefers to cater for the individualistic experience of a clique of aesthetes." He contrasted the "false, ugly, idealistic music of the formalists" with the "beautiful, natural, human intonations", the "healthy and progressive things in Soviet music". He warned against "decadent Western influences", against "bourgeois cultural decay". He challenged the composers, "Music that is unintelligible to the people is unwanted by the people. Let the composers not blame the people, let them blame themselves."[30]

When, a few weeks later, the actual Resolution was made public, it contained whole sentences taken from Zhdanov's speeches, repeated *verbatim*. It only shows to what extent the whole ideological drive was masterminded by Zhdanov. A few curious divergences deserve to be mentioned, however.

Zhdanov, in his speech, had been guilty of a minor historical inaccuracy when he said, "You realize how keenly interested we all were in this new opera [Muradeli's *Great Friendship*], after an interval of more than ten years, in the course of which no new Soviet operas were produced."

This was simply not true: among Soviet operas produced between 1937 and 1947 were Khrennikov's *Into the Storm*, Prokofiev's *Semyon Kotko*, Kabalevsky's *Under Fire*, Koval's *Emelyan Pugachev*, and several operas by Dzerzhinsky. In addition, one could name operas not being narrowly "Soviet" because of the libretto, like Prokofiev's *Duenna* or *War and Peace*. Zhdanov's slip was not repeated in the Resolution; the key sentence was changed to "no Soviet operas comparable to Russian classical opera have been produced in recent years".

Another important change occurred in the list of composers accused of "formalism". Officially named are "comrades Shostakovich, Prokofiev, Khachaturian, Shebalin, Popov, Miaskovsky, and others." (Muradeli's name was already contained in the title of the Resolution.) These composers were found guilty of "formalistic distortions and antidemocratic tendencies which are alien to the Soviet people and its artistic taste". Originally, Zhdanov had also included Kabalevsky, and during the discussion, the name of Shaporin was added. These two were not mentioned in the formal Resolution and thus they escaped direct censure. Actually, neither of the two had any modernistic leanings, and their sole "guilt" was their membership in the discredited ORGKOMITET.

For the seven composers mentioned by name in the Resolution, the censure had many disagreable side-effects: loss of jobs, cancellation of performances, delays in production plans. Even before the Resolution was published, rumours were flying that the "big" composers were in trouble, and their names began to disappear from the programmes. Shebalin told Zhdanov in January 1948,

"A certain feeling of panic has been aroused . . . in the theatres, all Soviet operas are being scrapped, and it is already said that certain names, which might be considered 'seditious', are to be removed from the MUZGIZ (State publishers) catalogue. This morning . . . a certain professor from the Conservatory phoned me and asked, 'May we, at a closed performance in the Small Hall, perform Soviet works?' "[31]

When Zhdanov interjected that "panic was a poor counsellor", Shebalin replied, "That is why I thought it necessary to mention it. There are some servile idiots (if you'll excuse my saying so) who might cause a lot of trouble."

Nevertheless, there were—as one Soviet biographer wrote in 1959—"many morbid manifestations in Soviet life . . . For example, the Central Committee of the Communist Party had to take measures to put a stop to the tendency of some concert organizations to curtail the performances of Shostakovich's works."[32] In fact, as we shall see, the Central Committee took an unprecedented step in 1958—it corrected some of the "unjust and unjustifiably sharp criticism" levelled against the individual composers in 1948.

But the criticism of formalism was not withdrawn, and the definition of 1948 remained on the books: it is "the cult of atonality, dissonance, and disharmony", the rejection of melody, and the involvement with the "confused, neuro-pathological combinations that transform music into cacophony, into a chaotic conglomeration of sounds". This music reflects the "decay of bourgeois culture" and represents a "total negation of musical art".

The formalistic trend, according to the Resolution, has led Soviet composers to favour "complex forms of instrumental textless symphonic music" while disdaining opera and choral music. In this context, the term "textless" symphonic music means absolute, non-programmatic music in juxtaposition to "programme" music, i.e. orchestral music provided with some underlying idea or story. This type of music, advocated in the nineteenth century by Western composers like Liszt and Berlioz, found many adherents among Russian composers, from Glinka to Glazunov, as well as Soviet composers. While the popularity of "programme" music declined sharply in the West during the twentieth century, Soviet theorists and composers continued to cling to the "pictorialization" of music as a means of making it more accessible. Zhdanov considered the neglect of programme music as a break with the classical heritage, saying that "The neglect of programme music is also a retreat from progressive traditions. As you know, Russian classical music was, as a rule, programme music."[33]

Taking his cue from Zhdanov, the critic Gorodinsky made the sweeping statement that "all the six symphonies of Tchaikovsky are programme pieces." And he continued, "Programme, subject matter, clear dramatic significance—all these are in the Russian tradition. No proper programme music was written for the Thirtieth Anniversary [of the Revolution]; hence one reason for the failures."

Tchaikovsky's attitude towards programme music was ambivalent. There can be no doubt that his imagination was stirred by literary images—*Romeo and Juliet, Francesca da Rimini* are prime examples. But in the symphonies, the issue is not quite that clear, as we can see in a letter to Madame von Meck, concerning the Fourth Symphony,

> "You ask if the symphony has a definite programme, Ordinarily, when asked that question concerning a symphonic work, I answer, 'No, none whatever.' And in truth it is not an easy question . . . Our symphony has a programme definite enough to be expressed in words; to you alone I want to tell—and can tell—the meaning of the work as a whole and in part . . ."

Tchaikovsky's reluctance is obvious—"it is not an easy question".* But for Soviet aestheticians, the question of programme music has remained vitally important—at a time when Western theorists look upon it with condescension and even contempt. In Soviet musicology, the analysis of a musical composition is often based on extra-musical aspects, on images and thoughts, on putting tangible "meaning" into music. Zhdanov treated this tendency with some irony: he would have preferred straight programme music, with the "meaning" provided by the composer in unmistakable terms,

> "Things have come to the point where the content of a new musical composition has to be interpreted after its performance. A new profession has come into being—that of the critics, friends of the composers, who try on the basis of personal intuition to decipher *post factum* the content of musical works already performed, the hazy idea of which, it is said, is not quite clear even to their composers."[34]

But the issue did not die with Zhdanov. Programme music continued to be discussed, at conferences and on the pages of *Sovetskaya Muzyka*. In 1951, that journal published various contributions on programme music, including one by Shostakovich. He brought his ideas to fruition with two topical symphonies, the Eleventh (*The Year 1905*) in 1957 and the Twelfth (*Lenin*) in 1961. They represented a vindication of programme music by Russia's greatest living composer.

* Gerald Abraham goes so far as to say that Tchaikovsky "disliked genuine programme-music" (*Slavonic and Romantic Music*, p. 110). See p. 316.

An area criticized sharply by the Resolution of 1948 was musical education at the conservatories:

> "The fallacious, anti-national, formalistic tendency in Soviet music exerts a pernicious influence on the . . . education of young composers . . . especially in the Moscow Conservatory . . . where the formalistic tendency is predominant. Students are not inculcated in the respect for best traditions of Russian and Western classical music . . . The creative output of many students of our conservatories consists in blind imitation of the music of Shostakovich, Prokofiev, and others."[35]

At Zhdanov's pre-Resolution conference with the musicians, the directors of the Moscow and Leningrad Conservatories—Shebalin and Serebriakov—had been heard. Both had to admit that neither faculty nor students had paid much attention to the Central Committee's previous ideological resolutions, and that more could have been done to enforce compliance. Shebalin used the opportunity to complain to Zhdanov about poor physical conditions: there were not enough instruments to teach the students, the dormitories were over-crowded, the State Publishing House was short of paper and could not supply enough music, the progress of the *Complete Works* editions was "catastrophically" slow; even the roof of the Conservatory was leaking. Whereupon Zhdanov replied coolly, "A roof can be repaired, but there is a great big hole in the very foundation of Soviet music." Shebalin's courage got him nowhere; he was dismissed as director of the Moscow Conservatory.

Serebriakov—less distinguished a personality than Shebalin—was more cautious in his speech, and he kept his job. He blamed the creative failure of the students on the teachers "who have not reached a high political and ideological level". Some of what he said was repeated almost verbatim in the Resolution,

> "Our professors—men like Shostakovich, Shcherbachev, and Prokofiev—are men of great talent and therefore have a particularly strong influence on our students. In the final examinations we often see nothing but little Prokofievs or little Shostakoviches . . . And what they learn from their teachers is chiefly a certain complexity of musical language, which does not appeal to the people . . ."[36]

A brief but important section of the 1948 Resolution dealt with the "utterly intolerable state of Soviet musical criticism". All the critics—classified as "musicologists"—belonged to the Composers' Union.

Since the daily newspapers in the Soviet Union rarely carry reviews of musical events, the profession of a "music critic" is a kind of free-lance occupation. Only in exceptional cases, like the 1962 visits of Stravinsky or Menuhin, are summary articles printed in *Pravda* and *Izvestia*, usually written on special assignment by some noted musical personality not necessarily a "critic". The task of the so-called critics consists mainly of contributing to journals like *Sovetskaya Muzyka*, *Sovetskaya Kultura* and similar publications. Several critics were employed by VOKS, the semi-official organization for cultural relations with foreign countries. When—after the war—the Soviet cultural policy took a xenophobic turn, the staff members of VOKS became immediately suspect because of their foreign contacts and their sympathetic attitude towards Western music and musicians. Indiscriminately, the critics received their share of blame in the Resolution, "Musical criticism has ceased to express the opinion of Soviet society . . . and has become the mouthpiece of individual composers. Some music critics, instead of writing objective criticism, have begun, because of personal friendship, to fawn upon this or that musical leader, glorifying their works in every conceivable way."[37]

Actually, things were not as sinister as they were made to appear, and there was no plotting to subvert Soviet music. True, some critics formed friendly ties with certain composers; the results were biographies, analytical articles, work catalogues, and programme notes. Among the authors, Nestyev and Shlifstein were close to Prokofiev; Martynov and Rabinovich, later also Danilevich, were linked with Shostakovich; Ikonnikov wrote on Miaskovsky, Boelza on Shebalin, Shneerson on Khachaturian. In fact, we owe to their biographies and studies a great deal of inside information about the composers' workshop, their original plans and creative concepts. Under the given circumstances it was not always easy for the authors to remain impartial although, on the whole, a certain objectivity was observed.

As soon as the 1948 Resolution had censured the prominent composers, the censure was extended almost automatically to all those critics and biographers who had praised them. They became suspect and were described as "bootlicking" and "kowtowing" critics though no names were mentioned. The Resolution affected not only critics of contemporary music, but also music historians and authors of textbooks.

The shake-up in the Composers' Union, in the wake of the 1948 Resolution, propelled young Khrennikov into prominence. Obviously, he was Zhdanov's choice to provide new leadership in accord with the ideological principles of the Resolution. But Khrennikov seemed also favoured by many disaffected composers who were tired of the entrenched ORGKOMITET and the "domination" of the top composers. During the first years in office, Khrennikov brought about some organizational improvements and useful innovations, such as the nationwide surveys for young composers. But as the years went by, he and his directorate became in turn an "entrenched establishment", silencing all critics and stifling all opposition, particularly the timid rise of the so-called avant-garde. For five years after taking office, Khrennikov followed the "hard" Stalin-Zhdanov line. The greater flexibility of the Khrushchev era found him ready to yield to the "thaw", and he helped prepare the ground for the important Party Resolution of 1958 which exonerated some of the composers victimized during the Zhdanov era. That Khrennikov had been one of Zhdanov's most enthusiastic aides in 1948 was readily forgotten. In 1962, at the height of the "liberalization", there were rumours that Khrennikov might step down in favour of a younger, politically untarnished leader, and Rodion Shchedrin was often mentioned as a candidate. But Khrushchev's cultural "clamp-down" vindicated Khrennikov's arch-conservative position, and he remained in his post, even after Khrushchev's exit.

Khrennikov's long tenure in office reflects his ability to represent the Party line in cultural matters, and to make adjustments whenever required. In the process, he did not hesitate to make friends with men he had formerly attacked and insulted, like Shostakovich and Stravinsky. This may seem highly unprincipled to many, especially his Western critics. In fact, Western observers usually consider him little more than the iron-fisted "boss" of the Soviet composers. New Yorkers will remember his conduct in 1959 as leader of a delegation of composers whose every move and every word he controlled.* But "bossism" alone does not explain Khrennikov's success. He built a numerically weak and dispirited group of musical intellectuals, less than 1,500 all in all, into a voice powerful enough to be heard by the Party hierarchy. The Composers' Union profited immensely by his political acumen and his excellent relations with the Kremlin leaders. In 1962, during private conversations, Soviet musicians—though critical of Khrennikov's ideological rigidity—admitted freely that he was irreplaceable as effective leader of the Composers' Union.

Khrennikov changed with the times. This becomes clear if one reads his first important speech of 1948—a piece of demagogical rhetoric which leaves the reader incredulous. With Zhdanov's approval, Khrennikov took the Resolution of 1948—a spiteful and narrowminded document—and applied its generalized invectives to Soviet

* See p. 317.

and Western music of the twentieth century. Hardly anyone escaped his censure, and those who were left were not worth saving.

"This Resolution deals a decisive blow to the anti-democratic formalist movement which has spread in Soviet music. It administers a crushing blow to modernist art as a whole...",[38] Khrennikov said in 1948, and then proceeded to enumerate the musical "fiascoes" of the last three decades. He worked his way back from the most recent failures of Prokofiev and Shostakovich to the long-forgotten eccentricities of Mossolov and Deshevov. They all represented formalistic experimentation, abstract musical idiom, and "a break between listener and musical art". He also found "images and emotions alien to Soviet realistic art—expressionistic tenseness, neuroticism, escape into a region of abnormal, repulsive, and pathological phenomena".

Having wiped nine-tenths of Soviet music off the map, Khrennikov went on to demolish the foreigners. First came Stravinsky, to some extent still a "Russian", as well as Diaghilev and his circle. The *Sacre du Printemps* expressed Russian "Asianism" in "boisterous, chaotic, intentionally coarse, screaming sonorities". Not much better fared *Petrushka, Les Noces, Le Rossignol, Mavra*. Into the same "decadent" category belonged Prokofiev's *Chout* (The Buffoon). While Stravinsky is called "the apostle of reactionary forces in bourgeois music", other European composers are not neglected on Khrennikov's blacklist, as he says, "One can hardly name a single important composer of the West who is not infected with formalistic defects, subjectivism, and mysticism, and bereft of ideological principles." Thus, Hindemith, Krenek, Berg, Britten, Messiaen, Menotti, Max Brandt all favour "a conglomeration of wild harmonies, a reversion to primitive savage cultures . . . eroticism, sexual perversion, amorality, and the shamelessness of the contemporary bourgeois heroes of the twentieth century".

This ludicrous speech requires no comment; it only shows to what depth of degradation the Soviet musical intelligentsia had sunk under Zhdanov's prodding. Suffice it to say that within a dozen years, everyone of the insulted composers was performed in Soviet concerts, and that quite a few were welcomed personally by Khrennikov with a show of affection and friendship.

In this bizarre spectacle of 1948, the position of the academician-musicologist Asafiev was strangely ambiguous and puzzling. Zhdanov and Khrennikov had blasted everything and everybody cherished by Asafiev. He had been a lifelong friend of Miaskovsky and Prokofiev. In the 1920's, he had fought for Stravinsky, Krenek, Berg, and Hindemith. In the 1940's, he has praised the Soviet symphonists and their great achievements, foremost among them Shostakovich.

Yet, when the 1948 Resolution became a reality, when his friends and associates were humiliated and his former idols crushed, Asafiev did not protest. On the contrary, he gave support to the "new line" by accepting the chairmanship of the new directorate of the Composers' Union. He also wrote an important endorsement, "Thirty Years of Soviet Music and the Tasks of Soviet Composers",[39] which was read on his behalf at the All-Union Congress of the Composers in April 1948. This document is considered by many as tantamount to a betrayal of his former ideals, a dismal ending to a distinguished career.

But there were mitigating circumstances. We know now that the statement read on his behalf was not written by him alone—a fact suspected for some time. In a recent monograph on Asafiev, we read that "The statement was prepared collectively, with participation of other Soviet musicians. However, a sketch of the statement is preserved in manuscript, and it testifies to the fact that Asafiev played an important role in its preparation."[40]

Thus, Asafiev can be partially—though not totally—absolved of the responsibility for his April 1948 statement. But to what extent did he understand all the ramifications of his action? At the time, he was a very sick man, too feeble to attend the conference in person, and he died the following year. He was surrounded by colleagues counselling him to compromise, and he seems to have been on friendly terms with Khrennikov. As Werth says, "It may have been impressed upon Asafiev that State reasons demanded this address."[41]

Yet, those who believe that Asafiev simply yielded to persuasion or pressure had better examine other of his essays written at about the same time. He did call for a rejuvenation of Socialist fervour and ideals in music, so—for example—in his brief article "Music for the Millions", published on 20 December 1947, in *Sovetskoye Iskusstvo*. Coming as it did at the height of tension caused by Muradeli's ill-fated opera *The Great Friendship*, Asafiev's article was considered an encouragement to those who favoured drastic reforms and Party intervention. This was the interpretation of Khrennikov when he said at the January conference with Zhdanov, "The coming of the crisis was foreshadowed in a short article by Asafiev . . . in which he said that our symphonists 'had forgotten about the listener'. Though a sick man, almost bedridden, Asafiev is a highly sensitive judge, and he felt the growing alienation between our big symphonists and the people."[42]

What exactly did Asafiev say? Here are a few key sentences, couched in his usual, somewhat flowery, style,

> "There are composers who fight rigidly and sternly for sharp, individualist principles and tastes, for a personal 'sediment' in invention so as not to be repetitious, not to resemble anyone, and

to speak only in a personal idiom. Such composers ought to think hard about their future creative development. The country exudes all-unifying feelings and slogans—this is the gigantic triumph of Soviet democracy. The composers must strive towards a musical language that will reach multi-million hearts . . . This must be the aim of the ideas, and of the forms revealing these ideas. I do not mean cheap simplification for the 'non-understanding' and allegedly backward listener, but the grand simplicity that is always understood by people who sincerely crave for the excitement of native art . . ."[43]

These thoughts of Asafiev are not much different from his convictions expressed in the revolutionary fervour of the 1920's. He had always believed that truly great art could reach the masses. In pleading for the "grand simplicity", he certainly did not envisage the spiteful language of the 1948 Resolution, the crude speeches of Zhdanov and Khrennikov, the niggardly persecution of great composers who were also his friends.*

The fatal weakness of the 1948 Resolution was that it initiated a musical witch-hunt and stifled creativity. It also exposed the cultural policy of the Soviet Union to world-wide ridicule and contempt. The creative shackling of artists like Prokofiev and Shostakovich produced an international tremor comparable only to the Pasternak-Zhivago affair of 1958. The ultimate indictment of "Zhdanovism" is the fact that it did not produce great music: the masters vilified in 1948 still represent Soviet music at its greatest. In terms of international recognition, the music of "Socialist Realism" has failed, despite all the efforts of cultural exchanges.

That the monstrous machinery of the Party was mobilized to curb a few composers was another major miscalculation of Zhdanov. Why did this astute politician embark on such a heavy-handed policy? In 1936, he had disciplined Shostakovich—and modernism—with an article in *Pravda*; in 1948, he used a sledge-hammer approach against composers who, by nature, were not rebellious. As Werth said, "Zhdanov destroyed a great nucleus of musical culture—and he did it quite deliberately . . . Was it really necessary . . . would not another warning have been sufficient? But that was clearly no longer Zhdanov's objective . . . [he] wanted a clean sweep . . . He had added, perhaps, to

---

* Rostropovich, in defending Solzhenitsyn, remembered the year 1948, "How much nonsense was written about those giants of our music, Prokofiev and Shostakovich . . . Now, when one looks back at the newspapers of those years, one becomes unbearably ashamed . . ." ("Open letter to *Pravda*", 31 October 1970).

the whole process a certain ruthlessness which others might have avoided."[44]

Although Zhdanov died some six months after the Resolution was made public, his policies were carried out relentlessly by organizational bureaucrats. The new directorate of the Composers' Union, led by Khrennikov, displayed a show of furious activity, in contrast to the *laissez-faire* of the defunct ORGKOMITET. The immediate aim was to prove that Soviet music had been helped, not hindered, by the 1948 Resolution. Since the top composers had been censured, it was up to the secondary talents to produce great music on demand. Public opinion had to be convinced that, after the purge, "Soviet music is on the rise". This was, in fact, the title of a volume of collected essays published by the Composers' Union in 1950.[45] The essays were better than the music they discussed.

The new leaders of the Composers' Union understood only too well that Soviet music could not keep its level of accomplishment without the co-operation of the censured composers, and conciliatory overtures were made. On the other hand, the composers knew that they could not battle with the Party machine, and that their livelihood and their careers were at stake. Recantations were in order, and only Miaskovsky remained silent. As a further gesture of co-operation, the composers involved—each in his own way—strove to write more simply, to avoid harmonic and melodic complexities, to devote more time to vocal genres and Soviet topics. The Party reciprocated by awarding Stalin Prizes* to several of the composers it had so recently indicted. Among the recipients, within the next few years, were Shostakovich (for the oratorio *Song of the Forests*), Prokofiev (for the cantata *On Guard for Peace*), and Miaskovsky (for the Twenty-seventh Symphony, the Cello Sonata, and the Thirteenth Quartet). Incidentally, while the censured composers were willing to "co-operate" in music, they avoided any active participation in the affairs of the Composers' Union—a fact that, as Khrennikov said, created "great uneasiness".

The new directorate of the Composers' Union was determined to supervise the "creative reorientation" of its members. For this purpose, a plenary session was convened in Moscow to hear new works written

---

* Stalin Prizes (renamed Lenin Prizes in 1956) were divided into first, second, and third class. The first class consisted of 100,000 roubles, the second of 50,000 roubles, the third of 25,000 roubles. In Music, four categories were set up, (1) Large musico-scenic and vocal works, (2) Large instrumental works, (3) Works in small forms, (4) Concert and performance activities. Within each of these categories, prizes of first, second, and third class were awarded, and within each prize class, several recipients were eligible.

since the February 1948 Resolution. From 21 to 27 December 1948 almost one hundred new compositions were performed—from oratorios and symphonies to quartets and songs—and the results were discussed for two days. Khrennikov offered a summary in a major address, "Creative Activities of Composers and Musicologists since the February Resolution".[46]

He had words of encouragement and warning. Despite partial success, he found that the reorientation of the censured composers was proceeding rather slowly, and he spoke of "unliquidated formalistic elements". Shostakovich had submitted the film score to *Molodaya Gvardia*, Khachaturian a *Symphonic Dithyramb in Memory of Lenin* (originally a film score), Shebalin his Seventh String Quartet, Miaskovsky his Twenty-sixth Symphony; there were also choruses by Muradeli and Popov, and—last but not least—the most recent opera by Prokofiev, *The Story of a Real Man*. The only one to receive a fully positive evaluation was Muradeli. Otherwise—said Khrennikov—"not one so far gave us a work commensurate with his talent as to full artistic worth and expressive power". The film scores by Shostakovich and Khachaturian were found acceptable, but both composers were warned not to concentrate too much on film music as an easy escape—an advice both of them disregarded. The instrumental works of Miaskovsky and Shebalin were judged unimpressive, while Popov's contribution was minimal. The sharpest rebuff was reserved for Prokofiev's new opera, "Formalism still lives in the music of Soviet composers. This is demonstrated by the new opera of Prokofiev . . . In the modernistic, antimelodic music of his opera, in the treatment of the Soviet people, the composer remains on his old positions, condemned by the Party and by Soviet Society."[47]

Prokofiev's failure at the plenary session was a foregone conclusion since a closed preview of the opera, given at Leningrad's Kirov Theatre on 3 December 1948, had been denounced by *Sovetskaya Muzyka* in an editorial.[48]

Khrennikov found it necessary to extend his criticism to the artistic leaders of the Kirov Theatre for having prepared the Prokofiev work on their own responsibility. It was also held against Prokofiev that he had kept the opera to himself while the work was in progress, and had not sought "constructive criticism".

The composers censured in the 1948 Resolution were in a highly uncomfortable position. Whatever they wrote was immediately scrutinized and analyzed as to "realism" and "formalism". It mattered less to composers like Khachaturian and Muradeli whose modernism was a temporary affectation; they could—and did—discard it by simply returning to their natural, folk-related mode of expression. It was more difficult in the case of Shebalin and Miaskovsky who, through life-long efforts, had arrived at a musical idiom of a certain complexity that did not lend itself to instant simplification. It was almost impossible in the case of Prokofiev and Shostakovich who were wedded to the music of the twentieth century and to many of its modernistic aspects: to them, a radical change meant almost a denial of all previous creativity. Each of these composers approached the problem in his own way—and the results were not always happy.

Miaskovsky was the oldest of the censured composers and, perhaps, the one most deeply involved because three of his best students— Khachaturian, Shebalin, and Kabalevsky—were also under attack. It is reported that he was deeply embittered, but he made no formal reply. Nevertheless, he was not inattentive to the issue of "formalism" raised by Zhdanov and the Resolution. His last works, written in 1948–50 (he died of cancer on 9 August 1950) show his renewed desire for clarity and directness of musical expression. This, in fact, had been his goal for most of his creative life; his was a continuous search for communication with his fellow man. To facilitate the accessibility, he built his Twenty-sixth Symphony (1948) on "Old Russian Themes", but the work was found colourless and static when it was played at the plenary session on 28 December 1948. However, his next major work, the Second Cello Sonata, was acclaimed at the performance on 5 March 1949 by the cellist Rostropovich, for whom it was written. The ingratiating work received the Stalin Prize for 1949 (awarded in the spring of 1950). This already signified the rehabilitation of Miaskovsky, all the more since he had been invited to resume his teaching at the Moscow Conservatory, beginning in the autumn of 1948.

Miaskovsky's greatest success, however, came posthumously, with his last—the Twenty-seventh—Symphony. At its première on 5 December 1950, it was greeted as a consummate masterpiece. In his last symphony, Miaskovsky succeeded in fusing subjective and objective elements, in finding a musical language that was as much akin to the mysterious Russian "soul" as it was to the Soviet image of the "positive hero". The latter found expression in the final march-like theme with its somewhat forced optimism. In the other movements, Miaskovsky chose a traditional musical language, which strikes a Western listener as rather retrospective. The Soviet critics, however, saw in the Twenty-seventh Symphony the ultimate reorientation of the old master and his acceptance of the new aesthetic ideals.

The case of Vissarion Shebalin is similar to that of his teacher Mias-kovsky. Shebalin, too, had a life-long association with the Moscow

Conservatory, first as a student, then, beginning in 1928, as a teacher. In 1942 he was named director of the Conservatory, or—more precisely—of the branch that remained in Moscow while the major section was evacuated to Saratov. During the difficult war years, Shebalin served the institution with devotion and efficiency. In his encounter with Zhdanov, he acted with dignity and courage. His dismissal from the faculty in 1948, both as director and teacher, was as unjustified as it was stupid. He was reinstated as professor of composition in 1951 and died in 1963 after a prolonged illness.

As a composer, too, Shebalin had certain traits in common with Miaskovsky . . . the ties with Russian tradition, the search for his own idiom in the 1920's, the effort to adjust himself to Soviet topicality in the 1930's. After the 1948 Resolution, he continued to write chamber music—the string quartets No. 7 (1948) and No. 8 (1960), a piano trio (1949), and a viola sonata (1954). But his greatest success came in 1957 with the opera *The Taming of the Shrew*, after Shakespeare. It is one of the truly successful comic operas of the Soviet repertoire—elegant, sparkling, written with a master's touch.

Khachaturian took the events of 1948 rather philosophically and he indicated privately that the whole thing "shouldn't be taken too seriously".[49] But at the meetings he was quite nervous and he babbled some incoherent excuses. At the bottom of his heart, however, he knew that he was innocent of the formalist "heresy" though he had strayed occasionally from the true path. For this he blamed outside advice. One of his errors was, he felt, his preoccupation with "technicism" because he had been criticized for an alleged lack of technical skill. Another error was to follow the advice of "critics and musicologists" to free himself from the limitations of a narrow national style. He explained, "I was receptive to these instructions, I could not liberate myself in time from these pernicious creative principles. Lately I estranged myself increasingly from my own Armenian element; I wanted to become a cosmopolitan."[50] The naiveté of this apologia shows the inane level of the entire "discussion" at the Composers' Union.

Following the events of 1948, Khachaturian concentrated on writing music for motion pictures and completed four film scores in the years 1948–50. In 1950 he expanded his musical activities into two areas new for him—teaching (at the Gnessin Institute and at the Moscow Conservatory) and orchestral conducting. He showed a natural aptitude for the baton and has since then appeared in many foreign countries as interpreter of his own music.* In 1950, he visited Italy, and shortly

* One of his latest successes was an American concert tour in 1968 during which he conducted sixteen of the major American symphony orchestras in all-Khachaturian programmes.

thereafter began to work on his ballet score *Spartacus* which was to become a major success in the mid-1950's. After Stalin's death in 1953, Khachaturian became the first of the prominent musicians to speak out publicly for greater creative freedom.

In his Post-War Memoirs, Ehrenburg speaks of the painter Konchalovsky* and of his successful career, then continues, "How a painter or a writer is treated is bound to influence him; a man has to be fanatically hard-headed to remain impervious to kicks or plaudits, the pillory or prizes. I know from personal experience that sometimes one hardly realizes that one has given in at some point or surrendered something or another . . ."[51]

These words of experience apply, of course, to all artists and intellectuals. The stronger the creative personality, the greater the inclination to be "fanatically hard-headed". But even the strongest personalities among Soviet composers—Prokofiev and Shostakovich—bent and yielded under the impact of the 1948 Resolution with its avalanche-like public pressure.

Prokofiev's case was particularly complicated because he was a "modern" artist, fully committed to the twentieth century, and with few—if any—longings for the "good old times". His last five years—1948-53—are characterized by a struggle to reconcile his artistic convictions with the simplistic guidelines imposed by the Party. This explains the stylistic unevenness of this last period. Prokofiev had faced similar crises before, and in the past he had succeeded—despite a few outward concessions—in retaining his creative independence. The first of these crises came in the early 1930's, after his return to his homeland, when he realized that many of the works he had composed during the 1920's and early 1930's were beyond the comprehension of his countrymen. The inner readjustment to face his new audiences, to gauge their receptivity, was not an easy task. A second crisis occurred in 1936 when he felt that much of the criticism directed against Shostakovich was applicable to his own creative work. In a letter to Khrennikov read at the February 1948 plenary meeting of the composers, Prokofiev wrote:

> "When formalistic errors in Shostakovich's *Lady Macbeth* . . . were exposed by *Pravda*, I gave a great deal of thought to creative devices in my own music, and came to the conclusion that such a method of composition was faulty. As a result, I began a search

* In 1934, Konchalovsky painted a fine portrait of Prokofiev, reproduced in Nestyev's Russian biography of the composer.

for a clearer and more meaningful language. In several of my subsequent works, I strove to free myself from the elements of
formalism and . . . succeeded to a certain degree."[52]

It is a remarkable document, flexible yet confident, and full of implied
meaning. Prokofiev—to demonstrate his own reorientation of the
1930's—enumerates in this letter such model compositions as *Alexander
Nevsky*, *Romeo and Juliet*, the cantata *Zdravitsa*, the Fifth Symphony.
He admits occasional deviations into formalism, over-complexity, even
atonality, but he reaffirms his belief in tonal music and in melody.

In juxtaposition with this statement of 1948, it is useful to recall what
Prokofiev had said in 1937, "In the music written during this productive year, I have striven for clarity and melodiousness. But at the same
time I have not tried to get by with hackneyed melodies and harmonies.
This is what makes it so difficult to compose clear music: the clarity
must be new, not old."[53] This, in essence, was the difference between
Prokofiev and most of the other Soviet composers: their clarity was
old, not new.

In 1948, Prokofiev faced the same problem, but he was no longer the
same man. Beset by illness, unable to work at full speed, careworn by
personal and political adversities, Prokofiev had little of the old fighting
spirit left. Age, experience, and disappointments had mellowed him.
There was, as Khachaturian recalled, "a vast difference between the
Prokofiev we knew in the years immediately following his return from
abroad [i.e. the early 1930's] and the Prokofiev of the last ten years of
his life." At first, he was "curt, businesslike, a trifle haughty . . .", later
he "grew more friendly and considerate towards his associates . . ."[54]★
Kabalevsky made a similar observation during Prokofiev's first visit to
Moscow in 1927—"he seemed to treat all the other composers with
condescension".[55] Indeed, Prokofiev was very critical of many contemporary composers, not excluding Stravinsky, and the Moscow
group of composers—in their enforced isolation from the mainstream
of European music—seemed rather provincial to him. In a revealing
letter addressed to the composer Vladimir Dukelsky (alias Vernon
Duke), dated 29 September 1935, Prokofiev writes,
    "I plan to be in Paris in a month for the première of the Violin
    Concerto . . . Shostakovich is talented but somehow 'unprincipled'
    and—like certain friends of ours—bereft of melodic invention; he

★ My personal experience with Prokofiev, in 1932, was a very pleasant one.
At the time, I was preparing his Violin Concerto No. 1 for a concert performance, and I asked for an opportunity to play it for him. We met at Steinway's
in Berlin, he played the accompaniment at the piano, and—far from being
"haughty",—he was most considerate and encouraging.

is made too much of here. Kabalevsky and Zhelobinsky *sont des zéros-virgule-zéros*.* I am flattered that you find certain works of mine 'timeless'. It's possible that therein lies the reason why men who are *too much of our time* often fail to understand my language . . ."[56]

In Dukelsky's opinion, the last sentence hints at an "already existing ideological friction" between the composer and Soviet music authorities.

Another time, in the early 1940's, Prokofiev criticized Shostakovich's lack of musical daring which proves that he did not believe in writing "safe" music. After becoming acquainted with the Piano Quintet of Shostakovich—which received the Stalin Prize in 1940—Prokofiev said, "What astonishes me in this Piano Quintet is that so young a composer, at the height of his powers, should be so very much on his guard, and so carefully calculate every note. He never takes a single risk. One looks in vain for an impetus, a venture."[57]

Around 1950, Prokofiev lost some of his oldest and closest friends—Miaskovsky, Asafiev, Paul Lamm. A new circle had formed around him, mostly young performers who looked to him as the venerated older master—Oistrakh, Richter, Rostropovich, Samosud. All the more painful to him, therefore, were the vicious and rather personal attacks of Khrennikov who, to him, must have seemed an upstart.

Nevertheless, in his letter to Khrennikov—his official reply to the accusations—Prokofiev was careful not to show any signs of irritation. He drew attention to the new opera he was writing, *The Story of a Real Man*, "I intend to introduce trios, duets, and contrapuntally developed choruses for which I use some extremely interesting folk songs of the North. Lucid melodies and, as far as possible, a simple harmonic idiom—these are elements that I shall strive to achieve in this opera."[58] Though Prokofiev knew by December 1948 that his opera was doomed, he still pleaded for understanding at late as 28 December, "In depicting my heroes, I was concerned, first of all, with revealing the inner world of the Soviet man, love of his country, Soviet patriotism . . .".[59] Obviously, Prokofiev was convinced that—in terms of libretto and music—the new opera fulfilled the requirements of Soviet ideology.

The rejection of Prokofiev's last opera was dictated by the harsh mood of the times, not by rational evaluation. The music, far from being "modernistic and anti-melodious", is appealing and often ingratiating, rather simple but skilful, and it avoids pseudo-heroics. The four

* Original in French, meaning "are zeros-comma-zeros". Zhelobinsky was at the time a promising young composer.

acts are organized into short scenes or numbers connected by orchestral interludes. The version presented at the Bolshoi Theatre in 1960—seven years after the composer's death—condensed the opera into three acts and made dramaturgical changes, which are a definite improvement. Even so, Prokofiev's *The Story of a Real Man* did not enter the permanent repertoire of the Bolshoi. Perhaps it is the fault of the libretto; based on a strong story by Boris Polevoi about the heroism and the suffering of a Soviet flyer in the Second World War,* it is not the kind of material one longs to see on the opera stage.

With admirable resilience, Prokofiev turned to other projects. Among the important works of his last years are the oratorio *On Guard for Peace* Op. 124 (1950), the ballet *The Stone Flower* (1948–50), the Cello Sonata (1949), the Symphony-Concerto for cello (1950–52),** the suite *Winter Bonfire* (1949), and the Seventh Symphony (1951–52). It is an impressive list though it leaves the objective listener with mixed feelings. Simplicity seems to have been foremost on Prokofiev's mind —perhaps that "grand simplicity" Asafiev spoke about in his essay *Music for the Millions.* But there is a fine dividing line between simplicity and simplism, and at times one wonders whether Prokofiev did not yield too much to the simplistic mentality of Party hacks. At one time he had said that clarity must be "new"; now he provided clarity that was old. *The Stone Flower,* a score widely admired in the Soviet Union, struck a Western critic as "music of such retroversion that—more than once—one was tempted to doubt Prokofiev's authorship".[60]

Another example is the Seventh Symphony—Prokofiev's last completed work—to which East and West respond in different ways. Soviet critics hail it as a consummate masterpiece. Olin Downes, a sincere admirer of Prokofiev's genius, called the Seventh "a retrogression and not a step forward".[61] No sooner had the opinion of Downes become known in Moscow than Shostakovich, Nestyev, and others began to belabour the American critic.[62]

A very touching episode is reported by Kabalevsky in connection with the first "audition" of the Seventh Symphony at the Composers' Union, in a piano arrangement. Prokofiev could not attend. Kabalevsky recalls,

"We found him ill in bed. He questioned us anxiously about the

---

* Polevoi's *Story* . . . sold six million copies in bookform (Werth, *Russia under Khrushchev,* p. 235).

** The often used title *Sinfonia Concertante* is an inexact translation of the Russian "simfonia-kontsert". This work (Op. 125) should not be confused with the Concertino Op. 132 for cello and orchestra, a posthumous work completed by Rostropovich and Kabalevsky.

audition and brightened up at once when he heard that it had been successful. Again and again he asked us about it, as if he feared we had only been trying to pacify him, 'Isn't the music rather too simple?' he asked, but he was not doubting the correctness of his search for a new simplicity; he merely wanted to be reassured that his creative quests had been understood and appreciated."[63]

How right is Kabalevsky in assuming that Prokofiev "was not doubting the correctness of his search for a new simplicity"? Doubts seem to have been on his mind, perhaps justified doubts. The Seventh Symphony, despite its lack of tension and conflict, remains a work of autumnal glow, a gentle farewell to life's struggle.

Some of this serenity can also be found in the Cello Sonata Op. 119, unaffected, lyrical, relaxed, even sweetish in its melodiousness. One almost longs for a strong contrast, a bit of the barbarism that spiced some of his earlier works. Yet the ties with his youth are not entirely broken: there is, in the first movement of the Sonata, an almost literal quotation from the score of *Alexander Nevsky*—the melody sung by the mezzo-soprano in the "Field of the Dead". But again, the Cello Sonata is another deliberately non-controversial work, presented to general applause at the Composers' Union in December 1949 and testifying to the "reorientation" of the great master.

Like the Cello Sonata, the Symphony-Concerto for Cello owed much to the faithful collaboration of young Rostropovich who not only edited the solo part but also assisted Prokofiev in the scoring. It is a monumental work, symphonic in its concept, as its title indicates, yet fully exploiting—even straining—the technical and lyrical potentials of the solo instrument. Particularly intriguing is the fact that the new Symphony-Concerto is based on Prokofiev's Cello Concerto of 1933–38, a work not well received at its première. Nor was the reception accorded the new Symphony-Concerto overly enthusiastic, but Prokofiev continued to revise the score until he was fully satisfied. The reason for the initial coolness is well described by Nestyev,

"In the Symphony-Concerto, just as in the Sixth Symphony and the last piano sonatas, the old and the new in Prokofiev stand side by side. The old manifests itself chiefly in the harshness of timbre and harmony and in the deliberately disjointed character of certain passages . . . But these particular passages, which displeased some members of the audience at the première . . . must not be construed as the predominant stylistic elements of the work. On the contrary, it is the broad and idiomatic singing themes . . . that are the most prominent features of this composition . . ."[64]

To Western ears, it was refreshing to recognize some of the "old" Prokofiev, the bite, the sweep, the unusual orchestral timbres, and the disregard for conventional virtuosity. The stylistic dichotomy is not disturbing because the entire work is put together with such a sure hand. Unquestionably, the Symphony-Concerto is the high point of Prokofiev's last creative years.

The last years also produced such dutiful "Socialist Realism" as the oratorio *On Guard for Peace* or the Festive Poem *The Volga Meets the Don*. There are instances in Prokofiev's last years when he listened, perhaps more than necessary, to the advice of Stalinist intellectuals. One of them was Alexander Fadeyev, the writer who had become leader of the Writers' Union in the wake of Zhdanov's cultural purge in 1946. It was Fadeyev who helped Prokofiev plan *On Guard for Peace* though the text was written by Samuil Marshak, an expert in children's literature. Despite the distinguished collaboration and the varied means employed (narrator, solo alto, boys' chorus, mixed chorus, and orchestra), the oratorio did not fuse into a convincing artistic entity. As for the Volga-Don Canal piece, it was *Gebrauchsmusik* for radio use; its sole distinction was that it was "the only symphonic work dedicated to this historic event".

There are also non-musical indications that Prokofiev, in his very last years, was more amenable to Party-sponsored ideas. Again, outside influences seem to have been at work. Take. for example, one of his last essays, "Music and Life", published in 1951.[65] To anyone familiar with Prokofiev's prose style, it must seem like a ghost-written—or at least heavily edited—piece. His usual style is laconic, unadorned, artless, and devoid of empty phraseology. This essay, on the other hand, is verbose, pretentious, self-advertising, and full of such hollow phrases as the composer being "duty bound to serve Man, the people". As a point of departure, the essay uses an incident in Salt Lake City (Utah) where an anonymous telephone call tried to prevent a performance of Prokofiev's Fifth Symphony. It was a typical crank call, and the performance took place as scheduled. But the incident is used in the essay to juxtapose the peace-loving Soviet society with those who scheme "new sanguinary wars", presumably the bloodthirsty Mormons of Utah. The whole essay is vacuous and pompous; it reflects the mentality of the circle surrounding Prokofiev, but hardly his own. As in the case of Asafiev, a great name is used for propaganda purposes by unprincipled "collaborators".

Prokofiev in all his mature glory reveals himself in the opera *War and Peace*. He worked on it intermittently from 1941 to 1952 and—as Kabalevsky recalls—"considered the opera the best thing he had written". Shortly before he died he said, "I am prepared to accept the failure of anything else I have written, but if you only knew how I would like *War and Peace* to be produced!"[66] That joy was denied to him. Sections were performed during his life—but the complete version was not given until 1955. Even so, the opera was dragged into the debate during the 1948 purge when Serebriakov, the director of the Leningrad Conservatory, remarked, "I venture to suggest that Prokofiev's *War and Peace* is not an opera that can appeal to the people. It gives nothing to either head or heart. Yet I am a trained musician. Admirers of the opera tell me that, to appreciate it, I ought to hear it five times. For whom, then, has it been composed? For a narrow circle of connoisseurs? Or for the people?"[67]

This "judgment" was rendered before the complete version of the opera was known. The history of *War and Peace* is a history of its revisions. The first version, composed in 1941-43, was given two concert readings in Moscow in October 1944 and June 1945, by different ensembles. This version consisted of eleven scenes, to which Prokofiev, upon the advice of the conductor Samosud, added two more scenes. This made a division into two evenings advisable. Part I (eight scenes) was staged in Leningrad at the Malyi Opera on 12 June 1946, with Samosud conducting. Part II was heard at a closed preview in 1947. Dissatisfied with the division, Prokofiev began the task of condensing the score to make a performance on a single evening possible. Many of his cuts were found too drastic when *War and Peace* was staged in Leningrad on 1 April 1955, two years after the composer's death. There began a gradual restoration of the cut-out sections which ultimately led to the complete staging—thirteen scenes and a choral epigraph—at the Moscow Bolshoi Theatre on 15 December 1959, combining Parts I and II into one, rather long, operatic evening. Even before that, Moscow audiences saw a somewhat shorter version at the Stanislavsky-Nemirovich-Danchenko Theatre (in November 1957). At present, both houses have Prokofiev's *War and Peace* in their repertoire, each in its own version.

The—virtually uncut—Bolshoi production is a stirring experience, both musically and theatrically. Prokofiev's score shows some stylistic inconsistencies caused by the many years of revision during which his approach underwent certain changes. In the first version, the vocal line consisted almost entirely of a continuous song-speech (like an extended recitative) since Prokofiev considered the traditional operatic "numbers", such as aria, ensemble, etc., as obsolete. Being his own librettist— a task he shared with the writer Mira Mendelson, his second wife— Prokofiev took whole sections of Tolstoy's prose and set the unaltered text to music. Although he had used such a method in some of his previous operas, it proved unsatisfactory in the case of *War and Peace* and led to extensive revisions. Prokofiev then reverted to a more traditional approach, inserting arias, choruses, and ensembles. Some problems remained unresolved since Tolstoy's speech patterns did not always lend themselves to a smooth vocal line.

In making the revisions and additions, Prokofiev relied heavily on the vast operatic experience of the conductor Samosud, though the final decisions were of course his own. Nevertheless, there is at least one hint that the composer made adjustments in order to make the opera more acceptable to the Party experts. His last essay, published in 1953, weeks before his death, contains this sentence, "I have been working a great deal latterly on a new version of the opera *War and Peace* in the light of the tasks with which we Soviet composers were confronted by the decision of the Central Committee of the Communist Party of 10 February 1948. Much in the opera has been revised and altered, much rewritten completely, in particular Kutuzov's aria at the council of war in Fili."[68]

Actually, Prokofiev had become aware of certain shortcomings in *War and Peace* prior to the 1948 Resolution. Extensive revisions were made during a year's interval between the concert performance on 7 June 1945 in Moscow under Samosud (the "first version") and the staged performance on 12 June 1946 in Leningrad (the "second version").

Prokofiev's third return to the opera was not only for the purpose of condensing it into one evening's length but also for "inner" revisions. This is how Kabalevsky described it,

"Realizing that one of the main shortcomings of the opera was the dearth of melodious arias and the general lack of broad melody, Prokofiev rewrote a good part of it. Among the parts substantially revised at the third editing of the opera were the duet of Natasha and Sonya, Andrei's arioso in the first scene (almost entirely written anew), Kutuzov's aria in the Fili scene, the grand choral finale. Much of the other music was condensed at the same time."[69]

Thus, in the end, Prokofiev felt the need to abandon some of his earlier ideas on opera, to return to a more traditional approach. Did he decide on a compromise because he was "confronted" with the 1948 Resolution and its demands for more "melody", or was it his own decision, made after he had heard his "first" version and felt dissatisfied? Let us assume that the decision was made on artistic grounds, that Prokofiev's innate spirit of innovation yielded to the great classic tradition of opera. True, the compromise left flaws, but they are minor compared to the sweep and grandeur of the concept.

No Western opera house can hope to match the stunning production of *War and Peace* staged by the Bolshoi Theatre in 1959. Yet it is regrettable that the operatic establishments of Europe and America have so far been unwilling to risk the presentation of Prokofiev's monumental masterpiece.* Admittedly, it is an involved and costly enterprise—but it is also a cultural obligation which the opera entrepreneurs should no longer eschew.

The delay in the production of *War and Peace* worried Prokofiev more than he wished to admit. Similar delays were encountered by Prokofiev's last ballet, *The Stone Flower*. For four years, the score gathered dust at the Bolshoi. Finally, on 1 March 1953, the rehearsals began. Prokofiev was at work on a revision in Act 4 when death overtook him five days later, on 5 March. It took another year before the ballet was ready for the première.

The genesis of *The Stone Flower* goes back to 1948. The choreographer Lavrovsky—who had been so successful with *Romeo and Juliet*—was eager to create another ballet with Prokofiev. After much search for a suitable story, a Russian subject was selected—a fairy tale from the Ural mountains by Bazhov. For Prokofiev, this was to be his first ballet with a "Russian" setting, and the prospect of using some genuine folk material spurred his interest. The music was written—in piano score—between September 1948 and March 1949—at a time when illness kept him from working more than one hour a day.

In June 1949 the score was played for the officials of the Bolshoi Theatre, and it was received with great praise. Everything seemed set for a speedy production, yet nothing happened. Undoubtedly, the delay was due to the tense politico-cultural situation, the aftermath of the 1948 Resolution. While Prokofiev became increasingly impatient, there was—unbeknown to the composer—backstage bickering about his score. According to Lavrovsky,

"The music was sharply criticized at a number of auditions. It was said to have little in common with the artistic imagery of Bazhov's tales, that it was gloomy, heavy, and difficult to dance to. A great many hasty, inconsiderate, and indeed tactless, judgments were passed. Prokofiev chafed at the delay in the production and felt hurt. At this time his health took a turn for the worse . . . Unforfortunately I could do nothing to bolster his spirits, in fact I was

* Among the few foreign performances were the production in Florence in May 1953, and the television version (in an English translation by Joseph Machlis) by the Opera Theatre of the NBC in New York in 1957. The latter had merits but was cut too drastically.

compelled to conceal much from him for fear of affecting his health . . ."[70]

Once again—as during the preparation of *Romeo and Juliet* in the 1930's—Prokofiev was faced with demands to make alterations in the score—"to make the dramatic parts louder, which means to coarsen the texture of the score", as he put it. Despite his misgivings, says Kabalevsky,

> "He agreed to a few changes which he considered more or less reasonable. Unfortunately, having obtained the composer's consent 'in principle', the theatre took the liberty of revising the score on their own after his death. A comparison of both scores—the author's and the one 'edited' by the theatre—will show how much more subtle and colourful is Prokofiev's music."[71]

This observation by a fellow composer shows that Prokofiev's ballet scores—and not only *The Stone Flower*—have been tampered with by unauthorized editors of the Bolshoi staff, particularly in matters of thickening the orchestration.* But apparently Prokofiev was more willing to co-operate than in his young years—one remembers the clashes with choreographer and dancers during the rehearsals of *Romeo*. This time, things went more smoothly, and Lavrovsky remarks with some satisfaction, ". . . Rehearsals began. Prokofiev livened up at once. More than two years had passed since he had written the music. We had altered and revised much of the material in the light of some of the criticism. Prokofiev rewrote a good deal, for example, the duet of Katerina and Danila in the fourth act . . ." It was this duet that occupied Prokofiev to the end. As Lavrovsky recalls, "Prokofiev was sitting over the orchestral score of the duet. He seemed quite well, was absorbed in his work . . . I spent the rest of the day staging the duet, and that evening I called up Prokofiev to tell him about it . . . Mira Alexandrovna (Mrs. Prokofiev) answered the phone and in a barely recognizable voice told me that Sergei Sergeyevich was dead."[72]

Eleven months later, on 12 February 1954, the long delayed première of *The Stone Flower* took place at the Moscow Bolshoi Theatre. The experienced Yuri Faier conducted, the title role of Katerina was danced by Galina Ulanova. While the beauty of Prokofiev's score was recognized, the production itself was not an unqualified success. Nestyev reports that, "Because of its sumptuous and overly ornate conception, the simplicity and wisdom of Bazhov's folk material were all but obscured. What is more, the choreographer Lavrovsky failed to achieve an organic synthesis of classical ballet and Russian folk dance . . ."[73]

---

* See p. 156.

In retrospect, it would seem that Prokofiev was more deeply affected by the damning 1948 Resolution than any of the other censured composers. Three of his stage works—ready for production—were delayed for years. The Sixth Symphony disappeared from the repertoire, the première of his Ninth Piano Sonata was cancelled and did not take place until 1951. On the other hand, there was no prolonged vendetta on the part of Party officials. Prokofiev continued to receive commissions, he was awarded a Stalin Prize—"second class"—in 1951 for the oratorio *On Guard for Peace* and the suite *Winter Bonfire*, and he was granted a special government pension in 1952 because of his precarious health.

But the effects of the 1948 Resolution went deeper than some day-by-day adversities—they are reflected in Prokofiev's music of the last five years. The official drive against "formalism" (i.e. modernism), the simplistic stress on tunefulness and accessibility elevated musical insipidness to a status symbol. Prokofiev had loathed all such trends throughout his life; now he had barely the strength or spirit to fight back. The problems worked in his mind; he became doubtful, he listened to the advice of friends and colleagues while in his youth he had recognized no judgment but his own. Madame Mendelson-Prokofiev describes one such instance in connection with the—already completed—oratorio *On Guard for Peace*, "[Prokofiev] . . . simplified the harmony and modulation of the oratorio at the request of [the conductor] Samosud . . . and the choirmaster Ptitsa after an audition in the Radio Committee."[74]

Simplicity and lyricism became the guiding features of Prokofiev's late style, while his satirical streak and motoric drive weakened. Yet to what extent was this an enforced development? There was always a strong bent towards lyricism in Prokofiev which, in his younger years, was often submerged by other facets of his personality. In some of his early works, lyricism and roguishness co-exist side by side, as for example in the First Violin Concerto which dates back to 1916–17. It disconcerted the critics by its "Mendelssohnism" when played in Paris in 1923. According to Prokofiev's self-analysis, there are five traits in his creative personality: classical, innovatory, "toccata" (i.e. rapid, precise motion), lyrical, and scherzo-humourous. At various periods of his life, different facets became prominent. Environment played its part —his migrations from Russia to America, to Western Europe and back to Soviet Russia shaped his tastes in music and influenced his relationship to his audiences. With age came mellowness, compassion, a sense for tradition, and a feeling for simple beauty. The "classical" and the "lyrical" facets of his personality became dominant, while "innovation" and "motion" faded into the background. As for the "scherzo", it lost its earlier bite and became good-humoured.

Seen in this light, it is conceivable that Prokofiev's creative evolution —in its broad aspects—might have been the same regardless of outside pressures. True, there are a number of compositions of his Soviet period that were clearly designed to appease the Party bureaucrats. But his truly great works were conceived from within, and only those works matter in the final analysis.

Ultimately Prokofiev did not bend under criticism, no matter how harshly some of his works were attacked by Soviet culture "experts". Self-criticism was his ultimate criterion, and self-confidence his most effective weapon. That self-confidence was wellnigh unshakeable. Yet, there is an unforgettable line in his Autobiography. After the near-failure of his Second Symphony in Paris in 1925, he wrote, "This was perhaps the only time it occurred to me that I might be destined to be a second-rate composer."[75] Only a genius or a fool could have written such a line. And Prokofiev was no fool.

The case of Shostakovich was altogether different. For him, public castigation was not a new experience: he had endured the attack of 1936 when he had stood alone. Now, in 1948, he shared the burden with the most distinguished composers of his time. Also, Shostakovich was conditioned to accept the infallibility of a Party dictum: he was a product of the Communist educational system, and he had lived in Soviet Russia all his life. Prokofiev had been educated under the Tsarist regime, he had left Russia as soon as the Revolution broke out, and he had lived fifteen years in the West; he was a cosmopolitan in the best sense of the word. Prokofiev returned to Moscow, not because he loved Stalin, but because he loved Russia. No doubt, both Prokofiev and Shostakovich were patriotic citizens, but over and above that Shostakovich was part of the political system to an extent that Prokofiev never could be.

The difference in background and "status" also explains, to a degree, the difference in the apologias of Prokofiev and Shostakovich. Prokofiev, in his letter to the Union, pleaded guilty "with an explanation". Shostakovich just pleaded guilty, pure and simple. There was dignity in Prokofiev's words, humility in what Shostakovich had to say—as if to indicate that "he should have known better". A literary historian, Struve, commenting on the recantations during the "trials" of that period, said that, "An important aspect of the Zhdanov inquisition is to be seen in the sinner's 'confessions' and 'recantations' which remind one of Galileo's trial. These recantations are perhaps the saddest feature of this newest phase of mind control: in character and in scope they far exceed anything that happened during the 1929–32 period . . ."[76]

Shostakovich answered his accusers several times. At the informal

January 1948 meeting—in presence of Zhdanov—he calmly admitted the need for criticism, "The composer must not be offended when he is criticized; he should be offended when there is no criticism." With equanimity, he rejected the abuse of songwriter Zakharov, interpreting the criticism as general rather than directed against him personally, "Comrade Zakharov was not very thoughtful in what he said about Soviet symphonies. It seems to me that he was not right, because there are, in our symphonic music, many great achievements, though there are also faults and failures . . ."[77]

However, once the February Resolution was published, singling him out by name, Shostakovich answered more specifically. After the "creative failure" of *Lady Macbeth* (going back to 1936!), he had thought that he had, to a certain extent, eradicated the "pernicious elements" of his musical style. But the "reconstruction", Shostakovich admitted, was not complete, "Certain negative characteristics pertaining to my musical thought prevented me from making the turn . . . I again deviated in the direction of formalism, and began to speak a language incomprehensible to the people . . . I know that the Party is right . . . I am deeply grateful . . . for all the criticism contained in the Resolution."[78] The directives of the Party testified to a "stern but paternal solicitude for us, the Soviet artists".

In fact, Shostakovich was not alone in being "grateful". Prokofiev, too, expressed "gratitude to our Party for the clear directives set forth in the Resolution",[79] and so did the other composers involved. It was part of the accepted formula.

For the next few years, Shostakovich planned his creative output in such a manner as to avoid political controversy. He wrote works that were ideologically unassailable—scores for patriotic films such as *Meeting at the River Elbe* and *The Fall of Berlin*, the oratorio *Song of the Forests*, choruses on words by revolutionary poets, and so on. On the other hand, he composed several important works in a more complex idiom and laid them aside without having them performed at the time; he obviously decided to postpone the premières until the artistic climate would be more relaxed and receptive. Among the latter works are the Violin Concerto No. 1, composed in 1947-48 and first performed in 1955, the String Quartet No. 4, composed in 1949 and first played in 1953, and the vocal cycle "From Jewish Folk Poetry", written in 1948 and first heard in 1955. There can be no doubt that all three works would have been considered "controversial" during the Zhdanov era. The delay proved a wise move, for they were highly acclaimed when first played after Stalin's death.

It is now realized by Soviet historians that Shostakovich—especially during the critical Zhdanov years—used two musical idioms: one more simplified and "realistic" to satisfy the terms of the 1948 Resolution, the other more complex and abstract to satisfy the connoisseurs and—his own artistic conscience. His biographer Rabinovich describes it in the following paragraph but draws the wrong conclusions,

> "There seems to be good grounds for the widespread opinion that the musical language used by Shostakovich in his cinema work, his mass cantatas, and in the two song cycles to Dolmatovsky's texts [Op. 86 and Op. 98] differs essentially from the artistic devices used in other works, even in the later Tenth and Eleventh Symphonies and the Violin Concerto. This is true of other composers as well . . . [the author cites Prokofiev and Khachaturian]. As far as Shostakovich is concerned, the difference is not only in genre conventionalities, nor is it due to the fact that different groups of works are addressed to different sections of the public. To understand the real nature of this phenomenon, we must recall the stylistic evolution of Shostakovich in the course of more than two decades. The basis of these intricate processes was the urge to get rid of the influence of modernism and at the same time get closer to, and be understood by, the people."[80]

This is a specious argument. It is highly doubtful that Shostakovich, in writing simply, wanted "to get rid" of the influence of modernism; what he wanted to get rid of was the constant quibbling of Party scribes. True, Shostakovich wanted to be "understood" by the people. But—like all genuine artists—he wanted to be understood through his *best* efforts, not by "writing down" to the people.

The fallacy of Soviet aesthetics—in the narrow interpretation of Stalin and Zhdanov—is not so much that "art must be understandable by the people", but that *all* art must be understood by *all* the people. That is an impossibility unless art is brought down to the lowest common denominator. The ultimate goal is to raise the people's receptivity to great art, and significant progress has been made in the Soviet Union to bring art closer to the people. But that goal cannot, and should not, be made the yardstick for the creative efforts of an entire nation.

As for Shostakovich, his musical language was never wholly estranged from his public, even when he spoke the so-called modern idiom. He was eager for contact with his audiences, and happy when he felt he had achieved it. But he also wanted to be true to himself—and this inner struggle weighed heavily on him. His apologetic statements in 1948 were, as Werth observed, "words of a great artist, utterly bewildered by what was happening . . . words of a man—still just over forty—who feels himself crushed and beaten ..."[81] He, a national idol since the "Leningrad" Symphony, saw his entire creative output subjected to vicious criticism by a fellow composer, Koval, on the pages of *Sovetskaya Muzyka*, while third-raters like Zakharov insulted him to the ill-concealed glee of other nonentities. The accumulation of sorrow that Shostakovich experienced during that time came out with elemental, explosive force in his Tenth Symphony, written in 1953—the great work that heralded the liberalization of the human spirit.

In the meantime, a sense of duty—so pronounced in Shostakovich—induced him to agree to be a member of the peace delegation that was sent by the Soviet Union to the Peace Congress in New York in 1949. This was another unhappy experience, though of a different nature.

The "Cultural and Scientific Conference for World Peace", as it was officially named, was held on 25 to 27 March 1949 in New York under the auspices of the National Council of Arts, Sciences, and Professions. American visas were granted to seven Soviet delegates, including the writer Fadeyev, the film director Gerasimov, and Shostakovich. A week before the Congress was to convene, a message of greeting and welcome was cabled to Shostakovich, then in Moscow; it was signed by leading musicians in America—Kussevitsky, Walter, Mitropoulos, Horowitz, Barber, Copland, Bernstein, Piston, Morton Gould, Tibbett, Spalding, Efrem Kurtz, Erica Morini, and others. The Soviet delegates arrived at La Guardia Airport on 24 March and were officially greeted by Norman Mailer and Aaron Copland.

On 28 March *The New York Times*, reporting on the front page Shostakovich's speech at the Congress, commented that it "rivals in bitterness" that of Soviet Foreign Minister Vishinsky. Shostakovich spoke briefly in Russian, thanking the conference for inviting him. Then, his 5,200-word speech was read in English by an interpreter while he watched intently the reaction of the public. Though Shostakovich's speech, in general, avoided politics, it aroused surprise by its ferocious attack on the West. He criticized the "small clique of war mongers" and accused the United States by implication of "trampling upon international obligations". Speaking of his own creative work, Shostakovich found it necessary, once again, to recant his "bourgeois formalism". He conceded that—particularly in some of his post-war works—he had lost contact with the people and failed. He repeated the old formula that musical culture was brought to *all* the people of the Soviet Union. Shostakovich said that "Prokofiev is in danger of relapse into formalism" if he failed to heed the Party directives. He also found it necessary to attack Stravinsky who "betrayed his native land and severed himself from his people by joining the camp of reactionary modern musicians". Such was the partisanship of the audience present that Shostakovich received a standing ovation after the speech had been read.

The final session of the Conference took place at the immense Madison Square Gardens. It was attended by 18,000 people, while 2,000 demonstrators opposed to the Conference assembled outside. At this session, Shostakovich received his greatest ovation. A scroll was presented to him, signed by forty-two prominent musicians: "Music is an international language and your visit will serve to symbolize the bond which music can create among all people. We welcome your visit also in the hope that this kind of cultural exchange can aid understanding among our peoples and thereby make possible an enduring peace." Shostakovich ended the session at 11.40 p.m. by playing on the piano the second movement (Scherzo) of his Fifth Symphony, and he received a tremendous ovation.

In the meantime, however, nation-wide resistance to the Conference had grown throughout the United States, and pressure was building up in Washington to cancel the further itinerary through the United States, planned for the Soviet delegation. Yale University refused the use of a hall for a concert and lecture by Shostakovich. In Newark, a programme at the Mosque Theatre was held without him.

The Soviet press reacted with bitterness. Though calling the Conference a tremendous success, the "terrorism" in the United States was denounced; it was said that the U.S. Government and the "Black Hundreds" repressed all who advocated peace.[82]

On 4 April, the Soviet delegation—barred from travelling to other cities—left New York by plane for Stockholm.

However, this was not the end of the affair. Upon his return, Shostakovich wrote a report for the literary journal *Novyi Mir*, summarizing his impressions of America. *The New York Times* lost no time in informing its readers of the content of the Shostakovich article. The headline read, "Shostakovich holds U.S. fears his music"; further quotes added, "The rulers of Washington also fear our literature, our music, our speeches on peace—fear them because truth in any form hinders them from organizing diversions against peace."[83]

Shostakovich repeated some of his views in the satirical journal *Krokodil*. The Russian visitor expressed shock that the audiences sat sprawled in hats and coats (in Soviet theatres, as in West European theatres, the public leaves them in the cloak room). Shostakovich was also dismayed by abridged editions of literary classics; he mentioned Tolstoy's *Anna Karenina* in a 32-page paperback with a "pornographic" cover. The skyscrapers were "depressing", and there was "disorder" at La Guardia Airport.[84]

Thus ended the saga of Shostakovich's first American visit. What really went on in his mind we do not know. The speech that was read for him was hardly his own. There were enough professional writers in his entourage to give it the necessary ideological slant; just as in the case of Asafiev's and Prokofiev's utterances, the editors had the final say. As for his impressions of America, they were uncharacteristic; he had seen nothing but New York in a turmoil of police and hostile demonstrators; he had spoken to no one without the help of interpreters. But even if Shostakovich had found something likeable about America, he would not have dared to express it; even under Khrushchev, almost fifteen years later, the writer Nekrasov faced expulsion from the Writers' Union for publishing his favourable impressions of the United States. In 1949, Shostakovich was caught in the web of xenophobia manufactured by Stalin. But it should be admitted that the political climate created by McCarthyism in America must have struck the Soviet visitors as highly inhospitable.

In sending Shostakovich to New York in 1949, the Kremlin leaders made a purely political choice. He was no Stalinist like Fadeyev or Gerasimov; in fact, he had just been "convicted" of being "anti-national". The normal choice to represent Soviet music would have been Khrennikov who occupied a position within the Composers' Union analogous to that of Fadeyev in the Writers' Union. But Khrennikov was internationally unknown, and his recent vitriolic speech, directed against all modern musicians, would have provoked repercussions in New York. Hence, Shostakovich was pressed into service; to clear his ideological record, he had to insert into his speech another recantation. By now, one surmises, it no longer mattered to him.

While the 1948 censure of prominent composers aroused a storm of international indignation, a parallel action against the "musicological" wing in the Composers' Union was barely noticed. Yet, the purge of critics, historians, theorists, and authors was every bit as harsh and harmful as that of the composers. In fact, more personalities were singled out by name, and many more lost their jobs. The shackling of the musicologists did more permanent damage to Soviet music than the action against the composers. The books (especially textbooks) written under the ideological knout contained so much bias and distortion of facts that the Soviet student was likely to emerge with a distorted view of history. Sadly enough, the authors of such books and articles—some of them outright "hate literature"—were often well-informed writers who today are embarrassed by having produced such trash. Yet, their actions must be understood as acts of self-preservation in the face of overwhelming pressure.

In February 1949—almost exactly one year after the 1948 Resolution —the action against the musicologists began. A three-day meeting of the Moscow musicologists—on 18, 21, and 22 February—provided a forum for a full debate of the issues. A few weeks later, on 5 and 6 March, the Leningrad musicologists convened for the same purpose. In both instances, the pattern was identical. The chairman made a general statement deploring the "intolerable" situation and castigating a number of individuals. During the ensuing discussion, those accused had an opportunity to recant, while those who had escaped censure delivered self-righteous speeches. Finally, the entire assembly voted censure of those accused by the chairman, sometimes adding or omitting a name. The entire procedure seemed like a well-rehearsed drama in three acts, with some lines left to improvisation.

Actually, there were only two issues. One was the campaign against "servility towards the West", aiming at historians and critics. The other concerned the critics in the so-called formalist camp, particularly those considered excessively friendly towards the composers censured in the 1948 Resolution. Within these two issues, virtually every Soviet musicologist of stature was caught in some "wrong-doing" in the eyes of the Party prosecutor. Guilty were even those who had taken no position at all, for this was construed as proof of political aloofness, of sabotage by silence.

With Zhdanov and Asafiev no longer alive, Khrennikov was in full command. His major statement was entitled "About the Intolerable Lag of Musical Criticism and Musicology". The term "intolerable" was borrowed from the 1948 Resolution, and so were lengthy quotations from Zhdanov's speeches. Khrennikov's opening remarks can be paraphrased as follows,

"The principal task of high-principled criticism is to help the Soviet composer along the path towards Socialist Realism, in the spirit of Bolshevik partyness. This task remains unfulfilled; not only do critics not help, but they hinder this development. Still in circulation are certain historical and theoretical 'works' that belittle the mighty Russian musical culture, deny its indigenous national path, and imply its full dependence on Western models. Still among us are critics who until recently were heralds of formalism in Soviet music and who now are taking up a position of taciturnity, even with thoughts of eventual revanchism. Still among us are some cosmopolite critics who are not willing to surrender, who still peddle their 'theoretical systems' providing a so-called 'scientific' basis for the formalistic mockery of music."[1]

These introductory remarks were followed by itemized accusations against individual critics and musicologists. Khrennikov's blacklist was, on the whole, accepted *in toto* by the assembly when it voted formal censure of the accused. They were grouped into three categories. Most damning was the first, described as "anti-patriotic, harmful activity, bent on undermining the ideological basis of Soviet music". Named in this group were Lev Mazel, Daniel Zhitomirsky, Igor Boelza, Alexei Ogolevetz, Semyon Shlifstein, Yulian Vainkop, Grigori Shneerson, Israel Nestyev, and Ivan Martynov. Added in Leningrad was the name of Semyon Ginzburg.

A second group was blamed for "cosmopolite errors", "grovelling before Western music", and disregard for Russian music. Here, the guilty were Grigori Kogan, Mikhail Pekelis, Roman Gruber, and Tamara Livanova. The Leningrad section added Mikhail Druskin, Anatol Butzkoi, Alexander Dolzhansky, Yuli Kremlev, and Bogdanov-Berezovsky.

Finally, for holding themselves "aloof" from the work of the Composers' Union and thus denying their help to the composers, the assembly censured Yosif Ryzhkin, Viktor Zukkerman, Vladimir Protopopov, Viktor Berkov, Boris Levik, and Vera Vasina-Grossman; in Leningrad, this list was enriched by eight names, including Elena Orlova and Maxim Brazhnikov. In his summing up, Khrennikov also berated Boris Shteinpress, Alexander Shaverdyan and Yuri Keldysh, but all three escaped official censure.

This monumental list requires some comment. Though most of the names are virtually unknown abroad, they represent the cream of Russian musical thought. Most of them were faculty members of the conservatories and institutes of Moscow and Leningrad; others were biographers, critics, lexicographers, lecturers—each and everyone an authority in his field. There are some thirty-five names—five times as many as the composers censured in 1948.

Whether, in view of the anti-Jewish campaign which began in late 1948, any Anti-Semitism played a part in the purge of musicologists is difficult to determine. Roughly half of the accused were of Jewish origin. But the percentage of Jewish writers and critics had always been, and still is, high. Some of the most fiercely attacked writers were non-Jewish, as for example Ogolevetz and Boelza. On the whole, the issues seem to have been more important than the national or religious origin of the accused.

In examining the "issues" at stake, one is struck by the vindictiveness and flimsiness of most of the accusations. Often it was merely a sort of "guilt by association"—a positive opinion about a composer now out of favour. Prime targets were Shostakovich and his critical supporters. Martynov—who had written a monograph on Shostakovich in 1946—was charged with an attempt to revise and reverse the judgment on *Lady Macbeth*, the opera so thoroughly condemned in 1936. Those who had spoken or written in favour of Shostakovich's Eighth and Ninth Symphonies were called to account for their opinions. For instance, Mazel's praise of the Ninth, his perceptive analogy of its jolly character with Charlie Chaplin and Walt Disney's film *Bambi* was scornfully ridiculed by Khrennikov. "This"—he thundered—"is supposed to be a positive criterion for Soviet music according to Mazel!" The antagonism towards Shostakovich bordered on vindictiveness.*

The advocates of Prokofiev were treated with slightly more leniency. The brunt of the attack was directed against Nestyev for what Khrennikov called an "anti-patriotic fact": Nestyev's monograph on Prokofiev was printed in America prior to its publication at home. There is indeed some mystery as to how the publisher Alfred Knopf obtained the English translation (done in Moscow by Rose Prokofieva—no relation to the composer) which was published in 1946.[2] That version,

---

* Koval's series of viciously critical articles on Shostakovich in *Sovetskaya Muzyka* have been already mentioned.

in fact, never appeared in Russian. Not until 1957 was Nestyev's mono-graph on Prokofiev published in Moscow,[3] and it bore only a super-ficial resemblance to the earlier "American" version.

With particular venom, Khrennikov turned against those critics who had concentrated on modern foreign music because it presupposed "formalism" and "servility towards the West". The adherents of Stravinsky—Ogolevetz, Druskin, Vainkop for example—became the prime targets. Was not Stravinsky "the apostle of reactionary forces in bourgeois music"? Yet, it must be remembered that Stravinsky had lashed out sharply against "Bolshevik" music and Soviet policies in his *Poetics of Music* (published in 1942), and no love was lost between him and the musical establishment in Moscow. Characteristically, the name of Asafiev was never mentioned in this phase of the debate though Asafiev had been the main champion of Stravinsky, and other Western modernists, during the 1920's.

The harshest treatment was reserved for Alexei Ogolevetz, a re-spected theorist who envisaged an expansion of the tonal system from the traditional twelve tones to seventeen and twenty-two tones. He had the temerity of quoting examples from Stravinsky, of calling Stasov a "dilettante", of deprecating Asafiev. He stated that "The path of the growing complexity of harmony corresponds to the gradual enrichment of the content of musical art." Khrennikov called Ogolevetz a "rootless cosmopolite", a "fake musicologist" who tried to gloss over the "seriousness of his crimes". Ogolevetz' "stillborn" books had cost "the Government hundreds of thousands of roubles to print". Khren-nikov's extensive "exposé" of Ogolevetz' theories were based primarily on his book *Introduction to Contemporary Musical Thought*, published in 1946. Another work by Ogolevetz, *Fundamentals of Harmonic Language* —an enormous tome of 972 pages—had appeared in 1941 with a resumé of the contents in French.

Soviet authors who had written on contemporary American and English music in the spirit of wartime *rapprochement*, were now con-demned as "anti-patriotic". But this post-war hysteria was not limited to Moscow. In Washington, during the McCarthy era, American musicians who had participated in the activities of the American-Soviet Music Society were eyed with great suspicion.

The result of the persecution of music critics was that Soviet musi-cologists shunned any commitment to discuss the contemporary musical scene. Journals began to complain about the refusal of critics "too busy" to write for publication. But was it any safer to write about the musical past? Not if one looks at the fate of the historians.

Here, the prime example is Mikhail Pekelis and his two-volume *History of Russian Music*, published in 1940 and adopted as a textbook for conservatories. It was a co-operative endeavour; next to Pekelis (the chief editor), the authors were Livanova, Popova, Groman, Zhitomirsky and Keldysh.

Khrennikov criticized Pekelis' principle of tracing "influences" of Western music upon Russian composers. This "pernicious" book, he said, was teaching young Russian musicians in the spirit of "grovelling" before the West while scorning their own musical culture. Curiously enough, one of Pekelis' co-authors, Keldysh, became sharply critical of Pekelis' approach as early as 1947 when he—Keldysh—published the first two volumes of his own *History of Russian Music*.* Having disavowed Pekelis' historical approach even prior to the 1948 Resolution, Keldysh strengthened his own status as a historian and disarmed any possible criticism of "opportunism". It was the beginning of Keldysh's rise to eminence in Soviet musicology.

During the 1949 debate, however, Keldysh was still somewhat on the defensive. In discussing the Pekelis *History*, he admitted that "we as authors approached Russian music with West European concepts of genre, style, and form". Therefore, "in explaining one or the other Russian composer we always considered it necessary to apply European models which were established as something universal, obligatory, and immutable. This, in essence, is the cosmopolitan approach, the kow-towing before the Western culture, so justly and sharply condemned in Party documents."[4] This speech saved Keldysh from further embarrassment; in the meantime, his own *History* was replacing the Pekelis *History* as the approved textbook.

While Keldysh apologized profusely for having collaborated on Pekelis' *History*, Pekelis himself was far less remorseful. He spoke vaguely of the "harmfulness of historic comparative methods, individualism, and a-political attitudes". In the opinion of *Sovetskaya Muzyka*, Pekelis' reply "revealed a complete lack of understanding for the events of the day".[5] Eventually, Pekelis was rehabilitated.**

Another eminent historian, Roman Gruber, was humiliated before the assembly. Two volumes of his *General History of Musical Culture* had appeared in 1941 and covered the history of music until the end of the sixteenth century. During the 1920's, Gruber was one of Asafiev's brightest disciples; later, he outgrew his "radicalism" and became one of Russia's most erudite historians. Khrennikov's absurd charge was that Gruber, "having upheld blindly the concepts of Western bourgeois scholars, ignored completely the contributions made by Slavonic

* The preface containing the criticism was dated November 1947; the volumes appeared in 1948.
** See pp. 394–5

cultures and the cultures of the peoples of the Caucasus and Central Asia."*

Gruber seemed unruffled by the criticism, and his reply indicated that "he did not understand the difference between a conservatory class and the tribunal of an assembly", to quote *Sovetskaya Muzyka*; his "pedantic summary" consisted of vague generalities; his "wordy, unclear and uncritical statement proved once again the gulf between Gruber and reality, and the extreme backwardness of his ideological position".[6] Gruber was the prototype of a scholar immersed in his studies and oblivious to the world around him; there was indeed a "gulf" between him and reality. The first volume of his completely revised *Music History* appeared in 1960, but the project remained unfinished. He died in 1962 while occupying the position of chief music historian at the Moscow Conservatory.

A very special case was Tamara Livanova. Born in 1909, she studied at the Moscow Conservatory under the historian Mikhail Ivanov-Boretzky. Her dissertation of 1936, *Essays and Materials concerning the History of Musical Culture in Russia in the Seventeenth and Eighteenth Centuries* (Ocherki i materialy po istorii muzykalnoi kultury v Rossii XVII–XVIII vekov) established her prominence among young Soviet musicologists. When the dissertation appeared in book form in 1938, it received a harsh review in *Sovetskaya Muzyka*; the critic, Ivan Martynov, objected to the alleged belittling of the Russian past and called the work "a falsification of history".[7] Livanova's career, however, was not affected; she remained in her teaching post at the Moscow Conservatory and, in 1940, published a two-volume *History of Western European Music until 1789* that was accepted as a textbook.**

All went well until 1949 when Khrennikov took up the attack. He accused Livanova of being an adherent of Alexander Veselovsky—a famous literary historian who had died in 1906—whose "comparativist school" was condemned by Zhdanov in 1947.*** This condemnation had created panic in literary circles. Struve reports that there was a "mass recantation of literary scholars accused of 'Veselovskyism' in the big auditorium of the University of Leningrad in April 1948"; they "mounted the rostrum in turn and abjured their 'comparativist' sins . . . promising to 'reform'."[8]

---

* Two further volumes followed in 1953 and 1959, but the work never reached beyond the seventeenth century. The last volume contained a chapter on West Slavic Music (Polish and Czech).

** In the same year 1940, Livanova's husband, Valentin Ferman, published a *History of nineteenth century European music from 1789 to Wagner*, also adopted as a textbook. Ferman died in March 1948.

*** Veselovsky's name was cleared in 1956.

Livanova admitted her guilt, "I committed a very grave error by following the line based on the views of Veselovsky. The juxtaposition with Western cultures and the stress on all sorts of borrowings lowered the significance of Russian music. Now, re-reading my book, I have a feeling of sharp shame for what I have written."[9]

Otherwise, Livanova's defence did not satisfy the assembly; "giving a great deal of attention to the errors of others, she spoke disproportionately little about her own".[10] In fact, Khrennikov reproached Livanova for not having repudiated her erroneous views and termed her recent interest in Soviet music as "opportunism". Livanova, however, was undeterred by this insinuation. She published a monograph on Miaskovsky in 1952 which was criticized by many, among others by Shostakovich. Far more significant is her two-volume publication *Russian Musical Culture of the Eighteenth Century in its Relationship with Literature, Theatre, and Social Life*. There is an immense amount of basic material in the 1,000 pages and two separate music supplements. The first volume was published in 1952, the second in 1953. Livanova proved that it is possible to write valuable historiography despite political oppression and thought control.

In a lengthy Introduction of thirty-eight pages Livanova refers to her former "erroneous point of view" but explains that she had merely followed Asafiev's trend of thought. (Veselovsky is no longer mentioned.) Asafiev, too—says Livanova—had assumed at one time that Russian music of the eighteenth century was based on "the theoretical principles of the academic Bologna school, the traditions of the Venetian concerto style, and the musical practice of that first 'Italian' period of Russian music",[11] but she hastens to add that Asafiev had later revised this view.

Not only was "dependence on the West" a forbidden subject, but even within Russian music, every comparative evaluation of composers produced sensitive reactions. Nothing was permitted to be said that would reflect adversely on Russian composers, even minor ones. Only the most spineless flattery of everything Russian and Soviet was acceptable, at the expense of everything foreign. In this spirit, the composer Koval —a member of the new directorate of the Composers' Union— declared, "The Musicologists must become politically educated people. Many of them have long been in need of such an education, not to mention the young cadres . . . We must eliminate from our ranks those musicologists who retard and hinder the development of the new, realistic, Socialist musical art . . ."[12]

It is not surprising that Soviet critics and musicologists yielded to this type of public pressure. They were forced to denounce what they once praised, to turn on former idols and friends. They had no choice but to heed the Party line, to produce hackwork in praise of Soviet realism and propaganda literature against Western music and musicians. But music was only a part, and a small part at that, of the over-all intellectual scene. In literature, the same happened on a much larger scale. Ehrenburg tells us that the files of *Literaturnaya Gazeta* for the years 1951–52 read "like records of legal proceedings, though today it is difficult to understand of what the crimes consisted".[13] One by one, literary personalities were taken to task—for a poem, an opera libretto, for being critical of a book that had found approval in *Pravda*. To counterbalance this destructive criticism, Party-line publications were extolled as "unrivalled flowerings of creative work". (Ehrenburg himself admits that he "sugar-coated" Soviet life and Soviet people in his new book *The Ninth Wave* which he calls "a bad novel"). What is true of *Literaturnaya Gazeta* is also true of *Sovetskaya Muzyka*. The pages bulge with new names being pushed forward as the great composers of the future—names of obvious nonentities who disappeared as fast as they appeared. Yet, critics had to be found to praise them . . . and they were found.

A year later, in March 1950, the musicologists and critics were subjected to yet another indoctrinating session. This time, the sponsor was, not the Composers' Union, but the Council of Ministers and its Committee on Arts Affairs; in fact, Khrennikov and his Union showed little interest in the proceedings, a fact that was noted with displeasure in the final report.[14]

The meeting in March 1950, was named "All-Union Scientific Session on Musicology" and was designed to be constructive rather than punitive. The musicologists attended in large numbers; but since the Party line was unchanged and inviolable, they vented their aggressiveness on each other.

It was, as the name indicated, a national rather than a local session. 262 delegates, including sixty-two from outside Moscow, represented all the institutions of higher learning concerned with music: the conservatories, the institutes of Moscow and Leningrad, arts committees of various Soviet republics, and the Composers' Union.

The purpose of the assembly was the critical evaluation of projected new textbooks dealing with Russian and Soviet Russian music as well as with the musical cultures of the Soviet peoples. At the same time, some musico-theoretical books were to be evaluated and approved as textbooks. All of the projects and plans under discussion were required to reflect the principles of the 1948 Resolution on Music.

At the March 1950 session, the key address was delivered by Alexander Ossovsky, at seventy-nine the oldest active musicologist and a corresponding member of the Academy of Sciences. He asserted, "The task of the musicologists is to advance that which exalts Russian music and ensures its foremost role in the development of the world's musical culture—its grand ideas and the high perfection of its artistic and musical embodiment."[15]

A more detailed set of aims for Soviet musicology was provided in *Sovetskaya Muzyka* by its correspondent, Blok:

> To rebuild musicology on the basis of Marxist-Leninist methodology;
>
> To incorporate the ideas formulated by Zhdanov and the 1948 Resolution;
>
> To obliterate all formalist and cosmopolitan tendencies as well as all traces of bourgeois ideology;
>
> To overcome the idea of a "single" cultural current, and to examine the musico-historical process in the light of Lenin's teachings of two cultures;
>
> To show the evolution of musical culture through the process of two competing tendencies—realistic versus anti-realistic (or anti-people);
>
> To reveal the interrelationship between Russian musical culture culture and that of the fraternal peoples of the Soviet Union;
>
> To emphasize the world-wide significance of Russian and Soviet musical cultures.[16]

This list is mainly a reiteration of prior goals, some going back as far as the 1920's, as for example the application of Marxist-Leninist methodology to the history of music. But this summary demonstrates anew the narrow and predetermined scope allotted to Soviet musical research.

It is noteworthy that almost all the projects presented to the March 1950 session originated with musicologists who were censured only a year earlier, some of them for the serious offense of "anti-patriotism", and that the lively discussion was dominated by previous "dissenters". There were no "untainted" musicologists left, but since the offenders were busily engaged in "re-orientation", all seemed well on the surface. Yet, the correspondent of *Sovetskaya Muzyka* predicted that the ringing ideological promises contained in the "projects" would become diluted by the time the manuscript went to print.

Some of the historical "adjustments" are amusing to the Western historian. Secondary composers previously classified as "epigones"—men like Ippolitov-Ivanov, Goedicke, Glière—were suddenly elevated to a master's status because they had preserved the classic tradition against the onslaught of modernistic, anti-realist, and anti-people trends. A projected course on Polyphony was sent back for further study to include more material about Russian polyphony and its use in non-polyphonic genres like opera and symphony. The extent to which everything Russian|was emphasized is ludicrous to any but a Russian mind.

Yet, despite this ideological rigidity, the Musicological Conference of 1950 was an important step in the evolution of Soviet musical research. Several large-scale projects were initiated—the *History of Soviet Russian Music* (five volumes completed in 1963), the *History of Music of the Soviet Peoples* (vol. 1, 1966), a *History of Russian Music* (three volumes, 1957–60). Recognizing the shortage of materials dealing with music of the Soviet peoples other than Russian, the assembly recommended the writing and publication of shorter studies, each devoted to a different national musical culture of the Soviet Union. These were to be accompanied by collections of musical examples ("readers") and phonograph records. A special request went to Professor Semyon Ginzburg—so harshly attacked the previous year—to speed the completion of his brief textbook on Soviet music. The assembly also examined outlines for history courses and theory textbooks.

Out of the holocaust of the 1948–49 purges, Soviet musicology began to emerge with confidence in the future. The debates were lively, the criticism sharp and outspoken. Most important, the scholars censured only a year earlier demonstrated that they were not cowed, and that they were determined fully to participate in the future expansion of musical research.

While the musicologists were engaged on long-range projects, the composers were fortunate in that music did not have to be published before it was performed. There was a steady stream of new compositions, and the annual surveys of recent works, sponsored by the Composers' Union, tried to convey the impression that the 1948 Resolution had given new impetus to Soviet music and that great progress was being made.

The truth of the matter was, however, that the bustle of activity merely disguised the lack of quality. Mediocre talents with half-baked technical skills were pushed forward, only to collapse at the first real challenge. Older composers expressed concern, as for example Kabalevsky—always well disposed towards youth—who wrote in 1952, "It must be said in all honesty that the Composers' Union attaches far too little importance to technical mastery. Indeed, until recently these matters were removed from the order of the day under the false pretence that the battle with formalism must be won first; then only could

one worry about the problems of artistic mastery . . . Genuine realism
is unthinkable without accomplished mastery . . ."[17]

But the lack of technical skill was not the only problem. Music became dull, bland, conventional, inoffensive. The new tendency was to
avoid depicting conflict, even if it involved bending historical truth
or sugar-coating contemporary life, glossing over any negative aspects
of Soviet existence. This theory of *non-conflict* infested literature, theatre,
film, and music; eventually, it was denounced by the Party. In the meantime, however, it produced anaemic art, glossy but quite unreal.
Looking back on those years, the critic Danilevich wrote in 1962,

> "There were people in the arts who treated the method of Socialist
> Realism as a diagram based on the principle—this is permitted,
> this is not. Anything that did not fit into the narrow frame of the
> diagram was termed 'anti-realistic'. The trend towards vulgariza-
> tion led unfailingly to parochial narrowness, to a denial of the
> variety of forms and styles in art."[18]

And Danilevich adds, "Where there is no creative originality, initiative,
genuine innovatory spirit, there is no true art."

All this is hindsight. In 1948, Danilevich was among those who
advocated "partyness" of criticsm. Yet the originator of "partyness",
Lenin, knew that one could not approach the arts with a sledgeham-
mer, when he wrote in 1905,

> "There is no question that literature is least of all subject to
> mechanical adjustment or levelling, to the rule of the majority
> over the minority. There is no question, either, that in this field
> greater scope must undoubtedly be allowed for personal initiative,
> individual inclination, thought and fantasy, form and content . . .
> Far be it from us to advocate any kind of standardized system, or a
> solution by means of a few decrees . . ."[19]

We have already discussed the creative work of the formost composers
subjected to censure in 1948—Miaskovsky, Prokofiev, Shostakovich,
Shebalin, Khachaturian—and we have seen to what extent they were
forced into a precarious compromise. Not all composers were equally
affected. Kabalevsky, for example, wrote his charming "youth concertos"* which seem totally unconstrained and unself-conscious,
bubbling with vitality and joy.

Other composers, particularly the young generation born around

* Violin Concerto, Cello Concerto (both 1949); 3rd Piano Concerto (1952).

1920, were even less concerned with the demands of musical "accessibility". Their formative years fell into the period of the emerging Socialist Realism. Isolated, as they were, from Western models, they turned quite naturally to a homegrown idiom—not only traditionally "Russian" but also indigenous to their specific national origin. There was a surge of composers belonging to minority groups who felt encouraged to speak a simpler musical language, without fear of being considered "backward" by their sophisticated Moscow colleagues. They all had a common denominator—the traditional academic Russian schooling in music theory since all Soviet conservatories, whether in Moscow or Alma Ata, follow a standard curriculum. The extent of "Russification" varied, however, from one individual composer to another. Although familiar with Western techniques, they all attempted to draw from native lore, to preserve certain indigenous traditions, and to effect a musical compromise between the Russian tradition and their own national heritage. Among the new names coming to the fore around 1950 were Andrei Eshpai of the Mari Autonomous Republic, Otar Taktakishvili and Sulkhan Tzintzadze of Georgia, Alexander Arutiunyan and Arno Babadzhanyan of Armenia, Sultan Gadzhibekov and Fikret Amirov of Azerbaijan. Already known at that time were the somewhat older Kara Karayev, also of Azerbaijan, and the Armenian Edward Mirzoyan.

But new talent did not come only from the "peripheral" sections of of the country. There was Eduard Balsis of Lithuania, Moissei Vainberg, originally from Warsaw but living in Moscow, and the Russians Herman Galynin, Boris Tchaikovsky, and Georgi Sviridov. All these young composers lacked neither talent nor technical skill. Yet around 1950 there was a blandness, a conventionality about their work that reflected the post-Zhdanov freeze.

Zhdanov had made an appeal to the composers to cultivate realistic-vocal music in place of abstract-instrumental genres. Composers and librettists heeded the call: new works were written, older works were revised and brought up to date, usually by strengthening the ideological content while simplifying the musical idiom. After 1948, "second versions" became a common procedure, and the libretti were as much subject to scrutiny as were the scores. Among revised operas were *The Family Taras* by Kabalevsky (1947 and 1950), *The Young Guard* by Meitus (1947 and 1950), and *Bogdan Khmelnitzky* by Dankevich (1951 and 1953).

Oratorios and cantatas, based on crudely political texts and often containing a hymnic flattery of Stalin became the favourite outlet for Socialist Realism. According to the critic Georgi Khubov, speaking in 1953,

"Some one hundred cantatas and oratorios were written in the last five years. Of course it is not bad that we have so many cantatas and oratorios, but it is bad that too many are bad: they are composed with indifference, without mastery or inspiration, and they are cut according to a stereotyped pattern. Is it necessary to enumerate the many typical cantatas in which we heard the noisy 'introductory' declamation at the beginning, the traditional 'optimistic lullaby' in the middle, and the festive 'concluding' declaration at the end? This is the standard type . . ."[20]

The problem of Soviet opera was far more involved—the difficulty of selecting a suitable contemporary libretto, the complexity of production, of finding a theatre willing to undertake the staging of a new work, possibly by a—not as yet established—composer. Even a well-known composer like Shebalin complained in 1948, "I composed an opera before the war, right down to the last bar of the piano score. It met with complete disregard at the theatres, the Composers' Union, and everywhere else . . . Now I can't be bothered with the thing any more. Many others have had the same experience . . ."[21] The veteran Shaporin also stressed this point in 1948, "Opera is of course the most democratic musical form. And we are faced with the problem of creating a Soviet style of opera. In the last thirty years, 300 operas have been written . . . Yet the number of operas that have established themselves is very small indeed. Many operas never got as far as the stage. The fault lies here with the theatres . . ."

Khachaturian (who, despite his melodic gifts, never attempted to write an opera) made some constructive suggestions in 1948:

"There ought to be an experimental opera theatre, and closer contact between opera composers and the theatres; it is not good for an opera composer simply to turn up at the theatre and put his manuscript on the director's table. A composer must also have some assurance that, if he writes a good opera, it will be produced. You can't decide, sitting at the piano, whether an opera is good or bad. Theatres are extremely slow in deciding on new productions. Hence our preference for symphonic music . . ."[23]

At the same meeting in 1948, the question of libretto was brought up, too. "Where is a young composer to find a libretto", asked Shebalin, "when established composers find it hard enough to get one; where is a student to get one?" He went on to suggest that the Composers' Union organize the production of libretti; otherwise the creation of operas will be "sabotaged from the start".

By a long-standing tradition, the Russian public is used to opera libretti of literary quality. Pushkin's writings, for example, provided libretti for *Boris Godunov, Eugene Onegin, Pique Dame, Ruslan and Ludmilla, Le Coq d'Or, Tsar Saltan, Russalka, Mazeppa, The Stone Guest* . . . Gogol, Lermontov, Ostrovsky, Turgeniev, Leskov, Tolstoy —all were used for operatic purposes.

Hence, it is quite natural that Soviet composers would turn to Soviet literature in their search for opera topics, and the following list provides an illustration of this point:

Author	Original title	Composer	Opera title
Sholokhov	Quiet Don	Dzerzhinsky	Unchanged
„	Virgin Soil Upturned	„	Unchanged
„	The Fate of Man	„	Unchanged
Maxim Gorky	The Mother	Khrennikov	Unchanged
„	Foma Gordeyev	Kasyanov	Unchanged
Gorbatov	The Unvanquished	Kabalevsky	Family Taras
Ivanov	Armoured Train 14–69	„	Nikita Vershinin
Polevoy	Story of a Real Man	Prokofiev	Unchanged
Fadeyev	Young Guard	Meitus	Unchanged
Katayev	I am the Son of the Working People	Prokofiev	Semyon Kotko
Virta	Loneliness	Khrennikov	Into the Storm
Kirshon	City of Winds	Knipper	North Wind
Fedin	First Joys	Chernov	Kyrill Izvekov
Azhayev	Far from Moscow	Dzerzhinsky	Unchanged
Alexei Tolstoy	The Way through Hell	Spadavecchia	Unchanged
Maltzev	From All One's Heart	Zhukovsky	Unchanged
Korneichuk	Bogdan Khmelnitzky	Dankevich	Unchanged
Antonov	Short Stories	Shchedrin	Not Love Alone

In no other country did contemporary literature provide its native composers with so much material. Yet very few of these works entered the permanent repertoire. In some cases the librettist did not succeed in building a dramaturgically sound book; in others the composer used an outdated musical idiom to depict the contemporary scene. But at least a concerted effort was made to lift the operatic genre out of its retrospective doldrums and into twentieth-century life, linking it to the destiny of the country. Events from the Revolutions of 1905 and 1917, the Civil War of 1918–21, the Second World War, were used as subjects, as well as Soviet communal life on the land, and the collectivization and industrialization of the country.

Russian history provided two of the finest operatic examples, Prokofiev's *War and Peace* and Shaporin's *The Decembrists*. Rebels against the feudal order became operatic heroes (*Stepan Razin* by Kasyanov*

---

* Recently also a cantata by Shostakovich, on a text by Yevtushenko.

and *Emelyan Pugachov* by Koval). Even Kabalevsky's *Colas Breugnon* acquired antifeudal overtones. Foreign rebellions were not neglected: *The Gadfly* by Spadavecchia is set in Italy in 1834–48, while Kyril Molchanov's *Del Corno Street* has an anti-Fascist plot.

Although "classic" literature was avoided by those who sought to be up-to-date, Soviet composers occasionally delved into the literary past and were singularly successful, as can be seen from this list:

Author	Original title	Composer	Opera title
Gogol	The Nose	Shostakovich	Unchanged
Leskov	Lady Macbeth of Mtsensk	Shostakovich	Katerina Izmailova
Sheridan	The Duenna	Prokofiev	Betrothal in a Monastery
Tolstoy	War and Peace	Prokofiev	Unchanged
Shakespeare	Taming of the Shrew	Shebalin	Unchanged
Gozzi	The Love for Three Oranges	Prokofiev	Unchanged
Dostoyevsky	The Gambler	Prokofiev	Unchanged
Bryusov	The Flaming Angel	Prokofiev	Unchanged

Admittedly Prokofiev's three last-named operas belong to his "foreign" period, and only *The Love for Three Oranges* was given in Russia—in Leningrad in 1926, but *The Gambler* was actually completed in a first version in 1916. In general the "typical" Soviet composer prefers a Russian or Soviet subject. It gives him the opportunity to incorporate folk material, whether it be old revolutionary songs, as in Khrennikov's *The Mother*, or urban ditties ("chastushki") as in Shchedrin's *Not Love Alone*. Such a procedure increases—to use a Soviet term—the "concreteness" of the musical realization. In the absence of actual folk material, composers tend to write music in the folk idiom, and the dividing line between "real" and "invented" folk music is often blurred.

But the conventional Soviet formula for opera does not always work. The year 1951 saw two spectacular failures, approaching in magnitude the débâcle of Muradeli's *The Great Friendship* in 1948. They were *From All One's Heart* by Herman Zhukovsky and *Bogdan Khmelnitzky* by Konstantin Dankevich.

A composer of minor talent, Zhukovsky, born in 1913, had written an opera that seemed a perfect model of Socialist Realism: the libretto portrayed life on a collective farm, the score was folkish and inoffensive. On the basis of an incomplete piano reduction, Zhukovsky's work was recommended for performance by the Composers' Union and the Arts Committee. *From All One's Heart* opened in Saratov on 17 December 1950 and reached the Bolshoi Theatre in Moscow on 16 January 1951. The opera received advance publicity and favourable reviews in *Sovetskaya Muzyka* and *Sovetskoye Iskusstvo* (Soviet Art) by reputable critics.[24] On 15 March 1951, the Stalin Prizes for 1950 were announced, and Zhukovsky's opera was awarded a Third Prize of 25,000 roubles.

Suddenly, on 19 April, *Pravda* published a blistering criticism of the opera: libretto, music, and production were found equally objectionable. *Sovetskaya Muzyka* reprinted the article in its May issue. On 11 May, the Stalin Prize committee recommended to the Council of Ministers that the Prize be revoked; two days later the revocation was published in both *Pravda* and *Izvestia*. The chairman of the Arts Committee and the director of the Bolshoi Theatre were relieved of their duties; but Khrennikov remained unscathed although the secretariat of the Composers' Union had actively promoted Zhukovsky's opera.

The entire affair is incredibly stupid on two counts: first, a work as weak as *From All One's Heart* should not have been staged; second, once staged, it should not have been recommended for the Stalin Prize. The repeal of the Prize exposed the Committee to mistrust and ridicule. Reading the indictment of the opera in *Pravda*, one wonders how a responsible group of professional judges could have failed to see the creative impotence of the entire production. But in the post-Zhdanov years there was a general desire to satisfy the Party bureaucrats, a blind urge towards ideological conformity that dulled all critical faculties of those appointed to be critical.

According to *Pravda* of 19 April 1951 the libretto shows kolkhoz life in a "false light, and many episodes are over-simplified and vulgarized". Instead of describing the patriotic work of the Soviet peasantry, a family drama is the main subject. The samples of the libretto text given in *Pravda* border on the burlesque, as for example, "A rare stroke of luck. We need this seed variety very much. It is obvious from the shoots that the grafting has taken." Or the aria of Vanya, "And thus I dream of realizing my plan—of bringing electricity to the fields, of putting machines into motion. It will be easier for us to work, and life will be easier."

Reading such lines, one is not surprised that Zhukovsky's musical inspiration faltered. But one is also reminded of the prophetic warning of Prokofiev in 1940, discussing the pitfalls of writing a Soviet opera, "For example, an aria sung by the chairman of a village Soviet could, with the slightest awkwardness on the part of the composer, be extremely puzzling to the listener. The recitative of a commissar making a telephone call may also be misunderstood".[25]

Zhukovsky's awkwardness was not "slight", it was colossal. *Pravda* found his score "weak and colourless". The dances lacked national profile, the melody was without individual shadings, the recitatives were lifeless and awkward. Only the choruses, in Ukrainian style, were satisfactory ,but they seemed "inserted", not integrated. The orchestral sound was out of touch with the stage action; the sweetish musical style "serves to emphasize the ideological falsity of the libretto . . ."

Finally, *Pravda* tore the production to pieces. Instead of showing a "modern" kolkhoz with "mighty machinery", one sees "a sorry rickety wattle fence . . . in the middle an abandoned log . . . in the distance a greyish landscape. In this setting are crowds of opera peasants who do not quite know what they are supposed to do on the stage."

Obviously, Communist pride was hurt because a kolkhoz was made to look like a dilapidated pre-revolutionary village. It may be recalled that in 1936, Shostakovich's ballet *The Limpid Stream*, was found similarly guilty of "faulty portrayal" of kolkhoz life. The sugar-coating of Soviet life was obligatory in the 1930's as it was in the 1950's.

No second version of the opera *From All One's Heart* was attempted; it was beyond repair. As for the composer Zhukovsky, his career was finished before it had begun. "There is no substitute for talent", Aldous Huxley once observed. Yet, in 1956, Zhukovsky was elected to the directorate of the Composers' Union, and in 1958 he was formally vindicated. The 1958 Resolution admitted that the judgment of Zhukovsky's work had contained "blatant exaggerations" though the criticism of music and libretto was basically "correct". In other words, *From All One's Heart* was bad, but not sufficiently bad to justify such a major uproar.

While Zhukovsky's opera failed on the grounds of plain ineptitude, the motivation for the censure of the Ukrainian opera *Bogdan Khmelnitzky* by Konstantin Dankevich was more complex. It was undoubtedly related to a Party drive—almost a purge—directed against Ukrainian intellectuals who exhibited too much nationalism for the Kremlin's liking. One of the authors of the libretto was the Ukrainian dramatist Alexander Korncichuk, a leading member of the Writers' Union since the Zhdanov shake-up of 1946.

Bogdan Khmelnitzky was given its première in Kiev on 29 January 1951, in Ukrainian. However, *Pravda* did not review it until 20 July of that year, when the opera was given as part of a ten-day festival of Ukrainian arts. The verdict was, "Serious ideological defects have made the opera an unworthy work. The librettist and the composer have failed to create a unified and organic musico-dramatic work." Yet, *Pravda* did not consider the opera beyond redemption; a revision was urged to bring the action "into complete accord with historical truth".

The libretto of the opera dealt with the Ukrainian hetman, Bogdan Khmelnitzky, who fought for his country's independence in the seventeenth century. Struggling against Polish oppression, the hetman accepted the help of the Russian tsar but became his virtual vassal in 1654. In Soviet histories, this is described as the "reunification" of the Ukraine and Russia, though Ukrainian patriots hold a different view of this "brotherly" event.

It was *Pravda*'s contention that the Ukrainians fought, not against the Polish people, but against the Polish gentry and that this issue was not made visually clear in the opera. The audience, therefore, did not fully understand the reasons motivating the "Ukrainian desire to join with the Russians". Nor was there "genuine joy in the victory" because the War of Liberation lacked realistic portrayal. All this was considered "an utterly unjustified departure from the historical truth". As for the score, *Pravda* praised certain parts but found it, on the whole, too "static". There was an over-all lack of "musical dramaturgy", and the protagonist, Bogdan Khmelnitzky, appeared phlegmatic and rhetorical.

The Ukrainian authors saw the handwriting on the wall. Korneichuk and the co-librettist, Wanda Vassilevska, sent a four-line statement to *Pravda* saying, "We consider the criticism entirely correct . . ." Dankevich was more effusive in his apologies. In his letter to *Pravda*, he thanked "from the bottom of his heart" for the "strict but just criticism of the serious defects" in his opera. He promised a thorough revision, indeed a "second version". Aligning himself with the librettists, he accepted his full share for the "ideological faults". The criticism, Dankevich wrote, will "help me to raise the ideological level of my work". He promised to devote "all the efforts of my spirit" to merit "the finest thing in the life of a Soviet artist—the trust and concern of our great Soviet people and our great Party of Lenin and Stalin".

When, in 1953, the second version proved satisfactory, Dankevich rose to prominence in the Composers' Union; he was elected to the directorate in 1956 and visited the United States as a member of a delegation of composers that included, among others, Shostakovich, Khrennikov, and Kabalevsky.

Next to the Italians, the Russians are probably the world's most opera-loving and most opera-conscious people. Long before there was a "Russian" opera, there was opera in Russia. The Soviet rulers have continued the century-old tradition; a number of new theatres for opera and ballet have been built in cities which had no theatre before.* The subsidies are generous. Artists, composers, directors—all are well provided for. But a vital new repertoire is rather slow in emerging.

* See p. 474.

Lenin once planned to cut the subsidy for the Bolshoi Theatre which he sneeringly called a "landowner's culture". In order to make it a "people's" culture, a relevant new repertoire was needed; hence the frantic search for a formula to produce the meaningful "Soviet" opera in addition to the classical Russian repertoire that was the people's cherished heritage. Discussion around the opera raged in the 1930's, in 1948, again in the 1950's and 1960's. Books were written studying the "dramaturgy" of the opera, looking at the genre as musical theatre. Yet, some of the dullest opera performances can be seen and heard in Moscow and Leningrad, with hardly a new idea since Stanislavsky staged his last opera.

As for the new Soviet opera—most of which deal with contemporary subjects—the problem seems to be that Soviet composers have not yet found the appropriate musical idiom. They deal with twentieth-century topics in a nineteenth-century language. They are trapped in an idiom made up of different ingredients—part *verismo* à la Puccini, part Russianism à la Borodin, a bit of exoticism, when needed, à la Rimsky, and a new self-conscious Sovietism with flag-waving rhetorical declamations, while the new Socialist hero triumphs over the evil enemy, either a fascist or a capitalist. This does not apply, of course, to the best contemporary works, but all too often Soviet opera retreats into a bland, conventional, predictable sameness.

The Soviet public is comparatively unsophisticated. To the Russian listener, opera must have an emotional meaning; rationalization is insufficient. The Soviet listener does not go to the opera to aestheticize: to him, opera is a living theatrical experience—as it should be. The West may smile at the "realism" of melodic line in an opera by Kabalevsky or Khrennikov—but *Taras* or *Frol Skobeyev* cannot sing a twelve-tone row; their idiom must be related to the straightforward, folk-connected story line. The chorus—whether partisans or peasants—cannot break out into atonal sophistry; it would make no sense. Even the genius of Prokofiev struggled—not always successfully—with the problem of "musical idiom". Ultimately, it does not matter whether Covent Garden or the Metropolitan Opera approve or disapprove of Soviet opera—as long as it has a meaning for the people for whom it was written.

Perhaps a regeneration of Soviet opera will come through a revival of theatrical experimentation. Fifty years ago, the great theatre directors, Stanislavsky and Nemirovich-Danchenko, Meyerhold and Taïrov, revitalized Russian opera by developing singing actors, by applying their theatrical experience to the stagnant operatic stage. Just as there are now new choreographers active in Moscow and Leningrad, breathing fresh air into the convention-ridden Soviet ballet, so there may be—soon—new ideas about operatic staging, about the scope and aim of the opera in general. This, in turn, might stimulate young composers to new thoughts and new departures . . . if they can overcome the limitations of Socialist Realism.

The genre of opera was not the only musical problem of the post-Zhdanov years, though it seems to be the one most intensely discussed. In February 1953 the critic Georgi Khubov made a thoughtful survey of musical conditions in a report entitled "Music and Contemporaneousness".[26] He found much to criticize. He recommended reorganization of the Composers' Union and urged an end to the interminable meetings, and the bureaucratic methods. He pleaded, "Lets' finish with the pernicious theory of 'non-conflict'." Khubov objected to the many mediocre orchestral suites that seemed ready to displace the genre of the symphony. He pointed out that at the Sixth Plenum of the Union only two symphonies were played: Prokofiev's Seventh and Knipper's Thirteenth. Khubov also criticized—as we have seen—the flood of stereotyped cantatas and oratorios.

Khubov's statement was reprinted in *Sovetskaya Muzyka* in three consecutive issues—March, April, and May of 1953. Little did Khubov think—when he delivered his report in February—that within a few weeks the great Stalin would die, leaving a legacy of artistic parochialism that well-nigh paralyzed Soviet arts. Khubov's report reads like an eulogy on an unlamented past. Soon, many of the old problems would fade away, only to be replaced by new ones. Yet, Stalinism and Zhdanovism—particularly that half-decade 1948 to 1953—were to be remembered as a nightmare for years to come.

Part IV

LIBERALIZATION 1953-64

Stalin died in the evening of 5 March 1953. He had suffered a stroke on the night of 1 to 2 March, but the news was not released until 4 March. The population had barely any forewarning of his approaching end. There was consternation, bewilderment, and grief. "I saw many people in tears in the street,' reminisced Ehrenburg, "we had long lost sight of the fact that Stalin was mortal. He had become an all-powerful and remote deity . . ." At his funeral, there was a wild rush to have a last glance at the revered leader, and several persons were trampled to death. On 9 March, eulogies were delivered by Malenkov, Beria, and Molotov who were to form a short-lived triumvirate. They exhorted the country not to yield to despair and disorder. "On the next day, Moscow resumed its normal life . . . Stalin had died, but life went on . . . though it would never be the same . . ." reflected Ehrenburg.[1]

On the same 5 March—by a strange coincidence—the Soviet people lost another great figure: the composer Sergei Prokofiev. So stunned was Moscow by the death of its political leader that the death of the composer remained unreported to the outside world for several days. Not until 9 March did *The New York Times* carry Prokofiev's obituary. The dispatch from Moscow contained an erroneous date which has since been perpetuated in many Western dictionaries: it reported that Prokofiev had died on "Wednesday" (i.e. 4 March) while the actual death occurred on Thursday, 5 March. As for relative values—*Sovetskaya Muzyka*, the official music journal, carried the obituary of Stalin on page 1, the one of Prokofiev on page 117 of the April 1953 issue.

Stalin's death occurred at a tense moment in the internal life of the Soviet Union. The Nineteenth Party Congress—which met in Moscow in October 1952 (there had been no Party congress since 1939!)— revealed smouldering discontent within the highest Party circles. Stalin's deteriorating health made the question of possible succession more acute. Malenkov emerged as the top contender. Shortly afterwards, in January 1953, the "Jewish Doctors' Plot" threatened to unleash a new wave of terror, directed not only against "Cosmopolitanism and Zionism" but against anyone being suspect as a sympathizer or anyone harbouring critical thoughts about the government's newest policy twist. In the words of a German historian,

> "A strange atmosphere of uneasiness and uncertainty made itself felt, such as had not been experienced since the great *chistka** . . . The increasing fear of espionage and its accompanying call for watchfulness, and the renewed ideological attacks on Soviet scientists and artists . . . were all part of the almost pathological nervousness with which the Soviet Union reacted to Eisenhower's inauguration as president. At times, there were unmistakable signs of collective hysteria."[2]

The passing of such a symbol as Stalin—virtually deified during his lifetime—made a re-examination of Stalinist ideology almost inevitable. But no one expected the changes to come quite as fast as they did.

Within a month of Stalin's death, on 4 April, the affair of the "Doctors' Plot" was revoked. On 10 July, Beria, for years head of the security police, was arrested; on 23 December, he was executed with a number of co-defendants, mostly Georgians like himself and Stalin.

To the Soviet population, Beria symbolized ruthless terror and extermination. With his arrest, an oppressive weight seemed to be lifted from the minds of Soviet artists and intellectuals. Literature led the way, music soon followed. A new spirit of intellectual inquisitiveness, of critical self-evaluation made itself felt, reflected in the pages of the literary journals *Novyi Mir* and *Znamya*, in contributions by Alexander Tvardovsky, Konstantin Paustovsky, and Ilya Ehrenburg, among others. The appearance of Ehrenburg's short novel *Otepel* (The Thaw), first published in the May 1954 issue of *Znamya*, became the literary sensation of the year, a topic for endless discussions in Russia and abroad, alternately praised and criticized. The work's title became symbolic for the "thaw" in literature and the arts of the immediate post-Stalin years—a *détente* that, in spite of some wavering, lasted for almost ten years, until December 1962. The zigzag course of Soviet cultural policy was caused by the tug of war between the adherents of a Stalinist "hard line" and the advocates of a liberalized approach, always under the watchful—indeed fretful—eye of Party officials. Every period of comparative permissiveness was followed by tough demands for ideological restraints.

There was only one constant—virtually unchallenged until today—the concept of Socialist Realism, though it was subject to flexible interpretation. A broad-minded approach to Socialist Realism was advocated in an authoritative article in *Pravda*, published on 27 November 1953, and it gave much encouragement to liberal-minded forces,

* "cleaning", purge.

"One of the worst disasters for art is standardization, however high the standard may be. To pattern all art on one model is to obliterate individuality . . . and rob the artist of creative experimentation.

Socialist Realism offers boundless vistas for the creative artist and the greatest freedom for the expression of his personality, for the development of diverse art genres, trends, and styles. Hence the importance of encouraging new departures in art, of studying the artist's individual style, and . . . of recognizing the artist's right to be independent, to strike out boldly on new paths."[3]

While Soviet literature tested cautiously the limits of the new "tolerance", music proceeded on its own course. In 1953—during the summer following Stalin's death—Shostakovich composed his Tenth Symphony, breaking an eight-year silence as a symphonic composer. It was a work of inner liberation, a human document that astounded listeners and critics at the première on 17 December 1953. Its role in Soviet music is comparable to Ehrenburg's *The Thaw* in literature, and it caused almost as much discussion. But ultimately, Shostakovich's Tenth Symphony was accepted on its own terms.

Almost simultaneously, the composer Khachaturian turned to words instead of notes in order to claim greater freedom for music. In the November 1953 issue of *Sovetskaya Muzyka*, his article "On Creative Boldness and Imagination" called for the abolition of excessive bureaucratic "tutelage" of composers. The literary critic Struve[4] compared Khachaturian's statement to an essay by Ehrenburg—also published in the autumn of 1953—entitled *On the Work of a Writer*. Here, Ehrenburg abandoned Zhdanov's anti-Western line and spoke objectively about the literary production of the West. There were many parallel developments in literature and music as far as "liberalization" was concerned, though music—being less explicit and less vulnerable—was treated more leniently.

For a time, the liberalizing trend in the arts received encouragement in certain Party circles. The Kremlin leadership must have realized that Zhdanov's methods had brought stagnation to the artistic and intellectual life of the country. An end to that sterile period was indicated when Georgi Alexandrov, one of Zhdanov's former antagonists, was appointed minister of culture.* Though Alexandrov served for only a brief time, 1954-55, he permitted a certain loosening of controls

* In 1947, Zhdanov attacked Alexandrov's *History of Western European Philosophy*. However, Alexandrov was no political novice: from 1939-47 he had been propaganda chief of the Party's Central Committee, and he had signed the *Pravda* article of 14 April 1945 directed against Ehrenburg.

in all fields of the arts—theatre, music, film, and radio. The sciences, too, pursued a more liberal policy; international contacts were resumed, and Soviet scientists began to participate in international congresses. But liberalization was not to proceed smoothly. All too soon, the Party realized that the arts (and especially literature) were moving too fast, and the reins were tightened. A reaffirmation of Party discipline was evident at the Second Writers' Congress in December 1954—the first meeting after a hiatus of twenty years!—though there was some open discussion. Ehrenburg was called to task for *The Thaw*, but he was not afraid to answer his critics.

Yet, while the key address of the poet Alexei Surkov (a high official of the Writers' Union) reiterated the "partyness" of literature, it also quoted Lenin's flexible thought, ". . . Literature is least of all subject to mechanical adjustment . . ."* Nevertheless the intelligentsia seemed intimidated and chastened after the Writers' Congress. "For a time a hush descended over the artistic scene," says Edward Crankshaw who visited the Soviet Union in 1955.[5] But there was no "reversion to Stalinism", as so many Western observers feared; in fact, Crankshaw found "an atmosphere of hope and purpose". This cautious pause lasted until February 1956 when the Twentieth Party Congress heard Khrushchev's momentous speech, unmasking Stalin. A new era had begun.

Khachaturian's article[6] did not merely express his personal feelings. Within the Composers' Union there were creative forces chafing under the petty restrictions of the "system", and he emerged as their spokesman. It may well be that he was not the sole author of the article and that he had expert help in formulating some of its bolder passages. But the fact that the article appeared over his signature and that he expressed dissatisfaction with certain existing conditions was in itself a significant step. At the time, his reputation—both national and international—among living Soviet composers was second only to that of Shostakovich.

There is considerable verbal "padding" in Khachaturian's article. He had to be careful, he had to reassure everyone concerned that he did not intend to overthrow the established principles. Yet it is not by accident that he speaks only of "the great teachings of Marx and Lenin" without mentioning Stalin.

First of all, Khachaturian criticizes the "drab, outworn musical verbiage" in many recent Soviet compositions: "How often have we witnessed such opportunism, particularly in the last few years. How often have we listened to 'monumental' works . . . that amounted to

* Quoted in full on p. 259.

nothing but empty prattle by the composer, bolstered up by a contemporary theme announced in descriptive titles." Time and again he mentions "deliberate or unwitting opportunism". He praises his great colleagues, Shostakovich and the late Prokofiev. Then comes one of the key paragraphs, "About Confidence and Creative Responsibilities",

> "We must, once and for all, reject the worthless interference in musical composition as it is practised by musical establishments. Problems of composition cannot be solved by official bureaucratic methods . . . The sensible planning and careful guidance of the country's musical life must not be usurped by interference in the actual process of creativity or interpretation, by imposing on composers the tastes of musical institute officials—who take no part in creative work but imagine themselves as standing 'above' it."

Khachaturian argues against the "tutelage" system that "relieves" the composers of responsibility, "Tutelage must go. Let the composer and librettist work conscientiously . . . *on their own responsibility.*" And he criticizes his own Composers' Union, "Let there be the sharpest, most impartial criticism . . . But do not let such criticism assume the character of 'directives'. Our musical institutions must stop their petty surveillance of composers . . . The Composers' Union must not assume the mantle of infallible 'arbiter' . . ."

Apparently, Khachaturian was not prepared for the heated national and international response to his article. A few months later, he published a lengthy sequel, entitled "The Truth about Soviet Music and Soviet Composers" which appeared in the April 1954 issue of *Sovetskaya Muzyka*. He denied any intent of artistic "rebellion" or a renunciation of "the fundamental principles of Socialist Realism".

> ". . . All my sharply-worded criticism levelled at certain mediocre composers of the 'opportunist variety' (unfortunately, some members of the species are still extant), all my barbs levelled at the 'musical bureaucrats' (this type, one hopes, will soon be extinct) are evidence not of any 'change of course' in Soviet art policy . . . but quite the reverse. While urging the need to combat errors and shortcomings in both the creative and organizational aspects of our musical life, I most emphatically uphold the great principles of Socialist art . . ."[7]

To bolster his arguments, Khachaturian quotes an extensive passage from the *Pravda* article of 27 November 1953 on the rights of the artist to be bold.

Another musician who took the *Pravda* article very seriously was Shostakovich. He elaborates on it in an article entitled "The Joy of Seeking New Ways", published in *Sovetskaya Muzyka*'s January 1954 issue. Referring to *Pravda*, he says,

> "These wise words cannot, of course, remain unheeded in the Composers' Union . . . In our controversies, the most important argument must be the high ideological and artistic quality of the work, not the author's affiliation with any creative trend.
>
> In my opinion, the Union should not 'protect' our composers against exploring the new, against independent movements along an unbeaten track in art. This is not the bold creative search for new paths but 'safe' sliding into superficiality, dullness, and clichés, that must be fought.
>
> Attempts to smooth out the rough edges are, in my opinion, a peculiar expression of the wrong-headed 'no-conflict' theory. The sooner we reject these levelling-out tendencies, the better it will be for the development of Soviet art."[8]

These fighting words acquire added significance if one considers that they coincided with the appearance of the Tenth Symphony in which Shostakovich asserted "the artist's right to be independent".

While the articles of Khachaturian and Shostakovich can be said to represent the "liberal" point of view—a demand to let the artist create according to his own conscience, without outside interference—other voices were heard fearing a "relapse" into formalism. Among them was Dzerzhinsky, embittered by his lack of success since his first opera, *The Quiet Don*, had brought him recognition—and an approving nod from Stalin—in 1935. Now, almost twenty years later, Dzerzhinsky calls for vigilance against the resurgence of the formalists. *Sovetskaya Muzyka*, as the official journal, printed Dzerzhinsky's article "Fight for Realistic Art" in the same issue that contained the contribution of Shostakovich. Said Dzerzhinsky,

> "After February 1948 the Secretariat of the Composers' Union at first actively campaigned for realism . . . We all expected the leaders of the Union to keep a vigilant eye on any development of cliquishness or a relapse into formalism in any disguise . . . The secretariat, however, being content with initial successes, soon lost the fighting spirit that prevailed in 1948-49 . . . Familiar notions of 'pure music', 'pure skill' apart from a work's concept and idea, and so on, became current. Saddest of all, there are among the upholders of these sentiments many young people . . . These

groups of young snobs look down on their 'backward' contemporaries who are trying to write simple and melodious music."[9]

Dzerzhinsky's annoyance with the "young snobs" is understandable for they must have regarded his music as hopelessly "backward". But he was also annoyed by the Union's position. Indeed, Khrennikov, who had assumed leadership in 1948 as a "Zhdanovist", found his power structure attacked in 1954 from two sides: the "liberal" wing, demanding less tutelage and artistic surveillance, and the "hard liners", calling for vigilance and continued discipline. The problem became even more acute after 1956 when de-Stalinization was carried out.

How deep-seated Dzerzhinsky's suspicions were, and he was certainly not alone, can be seen from the following paragraph in his article,

> "I would like to mention some of my anxieties as regards further development of Soviet music . . . Have formalist influences been fully overcome? Are our musicologists acting correctly in scarcely touching on this theme? These questions have to be answered in the negative . . . In my opinion, formalism has . . . taken up other forms . . . There is anxiety, for example, over Shostakovich's artistic development in the past six years, for a good many young composers are influenced by him."

Though these lines were written before the Tenth Symphony was heard in public, Dzerzhinsky's "concern" about Shostakovich was justified. After the death of Miaskovsky in 1950 and of Prokofiev in 1953, the moral leadership of Soviet music passed to Shostakovich—a heavy responsibility for a man not yet fifty. Perhaps because he stood between the generations, he was regarded with equal respect by the old and the young.

Dzerzhinsky's attitude towards Shostakovich was probably typical of many so-called conservatives; a belief in creative "guidance" to keep a composer from straying from the "correct" path:

> ". . . After the 1948 Resolution . . . healthy tendencies were again to be seen in Shostakovich's work . . . Then he seemed to be going back to his former positions; . . . there appeared the Twenty-four Preludes and Fugues, the Fifth String Quartet, and other works. I do not want to analyze every complexity and contradiction in these works. I only want to ask: what part have the Composers' Union and musical criticism played in Shostakovich's creative development? How have they helped him and other composers in their difficult struggle with the grave consequences of formalist delusions?"

Continuing in this vein, Dzerzhinsky deplored the absence of "really militant criticism" and asserted that "Shostakovich throughout his stormy creative life, has never really met with creative criticism", only "panegyrics" or "cautious silence". ". . . Our musicologists wait a decent span of time and then again begin with their 'Hurrah! Shostakovich has reformed! Formalism is done for! All's well!' The source of this non-objectivity is the critic's lingering sympathy for the negative sides of Shostakovich's work."

This puerile belief in collective righteousness—so typical of the Soviet approach to creative work—is both amusing and saddening. What kind of "creative help" did Shostakovich really need? What kind of collective pressure should be exerted on a mind like his? Yet, so steeped was Shostakovich in that peculiarly Soviet method of "group therapy" that he permitted himself to be subjected time and again to previews and auditions of works in progress. Whether he was influenced by the collective opinions is another matter.

Incidentally, the dissatisfaction with the critics was not limited to music. At the Writers' Congress in 1954, the literary critics were accused of cowardice. "Many critics," said Surkov, "take heart only the day *after* the Stalin Prize is awarded." Their activity was described as "being permanently late". A theatre play would not be reviewed "until several months after the première when the fog in the 'authoritarian' sky had lifted and the guiding star of official viewpoint had become visible". There were privileged famous authors who were above criticism, "untouchable" as it were.[10]

But there was nothing "untouchable" about Shostakovich in 1954. After the première of the Tenth Symphony in Leningrad on 17 December and in Moscow on 29 December 1953 the work was subject to intense critical debate, both favourable and unfavourable. A three-day discussion took place at the Composers' Union in the spring of 1954, on 29/30 March and on 5 April. Lengthy articles appeared in *Sovetskaya Muzyka*—by Khachaturian in the March issue, by Yarustovsky and Volkonsky in April, and a reprint of the entire discussion in June. More articles appeared in later issues and in other publications. The debate aroused by the Tenth Symphony seemed to transcend the significance of the work and centered on a vital principle: the right of an artist to express himself, individually rather than collectively, subjectively rather than objectively, without bureaucratic interference and tutelage.

Shostakovich won this battle—and more; in the summer of that year 1954, he was awarded the highest artistic honour of the Soviet Union—the title "People's Artist of the U.S.S.R.". The other two recipients were Khachaturian and the veteran composer Shaporin. This act signified the ultimate erasure of the grave injustices suffered by these artists in 1948. It also proved that the "liberal" stance of Shostakovich and Khachaturian during the post-Stalin era was found acceptable in the highest Party circles.

When Shostakovich was asked whether the Tenth Symphony had a "programme", he answered with a smile, "No, let them listen and guess for themselves."[11] In a very general sense, he said, "In this composition, I wanted to portray human emotions and passions." Prior to the debate in the Composers' Union, Shostakovich spoke with disarming simplicity and modesty about his latest work,

> "I worked on the Tenth Symphony during the summer of last year (1953) and finished it in the autumn. Like other works of mine, it was written quickly. That perhaps is not a virtue . . .
>
> "The Symphony consists of four movements. Appraising the first movement critically, I see that I did not succeed in doing what I have dreamed of for a long time: writing a real symphonic allegro. It did not come to me in this symphony, any more than it did in my previous symphonic works . . . In this first movement, there are more slow *tempi* and lyric moments than dramatic, heroic, and tragic . . .
>
> "The second movement, in my opinion, answers my purpose in the main, and occupies its intended place in the cycle. It is perhaps too short, however, especially since the other movements are rather long . . .
>
> "As for the third movement, I think that my purpose was more or less successful, though it is a bit too long; here and there, however, there are places that are a bit short. It would be very valuable to have the comrades' opinions on this.
>
> "The Finale has a somewhat lengthy introduction, although the last time I heard it, I thought it fulfilled its function and more or less balanced the whole movement.
>
> "Authors often like to say: I was trying, I was attempting, and so on. I have refrained, I think, from speaking in that way. I shall be very interested to learn what my hearers feel, to hear their opinions. I would say only one thing: in this composition I wanted to express human emotions and passions."[12]

Rarely has an author expressed himself with more self-effacement. He seems to look at his own work with complete detachment. One wonders, though, why—finding one movement "a bit too short", the other "a bit too long"—he did not do some retouching and revising before publication. But apparently it was not in Shostakovich's nature to brood over a piece already completed. As he said,

"As soon as a work is written, the creative spark dies; and when you see its defects, sometimes large and substantial, you begin to think that it wouldn't be a bad thing to avoid them in your next work; but as for the one just written, well, that's done with, thank goodness.

"I advise everyone, especially myself, not to hurry; it is better to compose slowly and to correct faults as you work."

But as a rule, he did not follow his own advice. He composed with incredible speed and apparent ease, as if consumed by an elemental creative urge, as if afraid that the "creative spark" might die before he could complete the work. It almost seems that he barely took time to sort out his thoughts, to separate the wheat from the chaff. Once finished, he was reluctant to look back. Perhaps he instinctively agreed with Robert Schumann, that "The first concept is always the best and most natural. The intellect can err, the sentiment—never."[13] This explains, to a certain degree, the unevenness of Shostakovich's creative output. He is capable of lofty heights and embarrassing triteness. But as time goes on, the flaws are forgotten, and the great moments remain.

Certainly, his Tenth Symphony contains some of Shostakovich's greatest moments. While it may have been written down quickly, it had matured slowly, perhaps subconsciously. There are affinities with the Violin Concerto No. 1 which, as we know, was nearly completed in 1948.

This slow process of gestation explains, perhaps, the essentially tragic character of the Tenth Symphony. The first three movements of the Tenth capture three moods of tragedy—pensive, fierce, wistful. But the tragedy of the Tenth is retrospective; it does not truly reflect the mood of the country in mid-1953. "In the late summer of 1953, after the arrest of Beria, everyone started singing, at first tentatively, then, in a rush, as a full dawn chorus" writes Crankshaw. The Tenth of Shostakovich does not fit into this picture, except for the fourth and final movement. It starts in an introvert mood but soon shifts into a somewhat forced, artificial gaiety, which brings a jarring note into an otherwise beautifully integrated work. Even the reappearance of the "author's theme"—the notes D–S–C–H which represent his initials*—does not succeed in lifting the movement to anything more than a pleasant afterthought. If Shostakovich bemoans his inability to write a "real symphonic allegro", it does not prevent him from writing great

* D, E flat, C, B (in German D, Es, C, H); Shostakovich used this "motto" theme frequently, in the First Sympany, the Fifth and Eighth Quartets, and the Concertos for violin and for violoncello.

first movements. Far more critical is his apparent inability to write a good Finale—one that would bring a large cyclic work to a satisfactory conclusion, both emotionally and intellectually. But there are critics who are less concerned with the quality of the Finale of the Tenth, as for instance David Lloyd-Jones.

"By the time Shostakovich came to write the Tenth, the (elegiac) quality had deepened into tragedy, and in the refinement of his language he had shed the Mahlerian bombast of the Finale of the earlier work [i.e. the Fifth]. It is true that instead he gives us a Finale which is perhaps even less satisfactory taken in its context, but nevertheless musically it is altogether on a different plane, and the work (the Tenth) remains the composer's deepest and most original utterance in this form."[14]

While this is a rather left-handed compliment for the Finale of the Tenth Symphony, another British musicologist, Robert Layton, is of the opinion that

". . . The Finale of the Tenth is the first in the symphonies to achieve real unity. It meets the traditional classical requirement for the Finale to be positive in outlook without compromising the integrity of the symphony as a whole. There is no need for the optimism encouraged by Soviet critical opinion to be synonymous with . . . emptiness . . . this [Finale] lacks neither depth nor pathos. There is a good deal of both behind the innocent, childlike façade presented by the main theme . . . This darker side emerges in the tragic outburst towards the end of the work . . ."[15]

The question is actually not so much whether the Finale of the Tenth is a *good* movement (which it is), but whether it is the *right* movement in its place. This is a very personal matter of judgment, and critics can debate this point endlessly, right up to the Finale of Beethoven's Ninth, which has as many admirers as it has detractors. The symphonic repertoire is not over-rich in great final movements. What composer, after all, can hope to match Mozart's Finale to the "Jupiter", or Beethoven's to the "Eroica", or the final Passacaglia of Brahms' Fourth?

The best that can be said about the Finale of the Tenth Symphony by Shostakovich is that it is finely wrought, in good taste, but somewhat lightweight and distracting in mood. To some listeners, this may come as a relief after the dark colours of the earlier movements, to others, the contrast may be disconcerting. But this is a minor flaw when the grand concept of the whole, the masterful integration of the musical material, and the deep humanity pervading the entire work is considered.

In America, the Tenth Symphony was received with immense satisfaction. After the New York première on 15 October 1954, given by
the Philharmonic under Mitropoulos, the critic Olin Downes called it
"powerful, outspoken, and at times grossly impolite". The latter
probably refers to the "swift, furious, battledrunk" scherzo movement
Downes rightly mentions Shostakovich's indebtedness to Mahler,
Prokofiev, and Tchaikovsky. "But these influences are no longer
quoted. They are assimilated and made part of an expression that is now
wholly personal, and eminently racial and ancestral in its nature.
Shostakovich, born of troubled times, has gone through much to reach
this symphony. It seems to us the sure token of his arrival at the master's
estate, and it should precede more scores of his growing power."[16]
Downes' acclaim of the Tenth Symphony helped establish this work
as a major contribution to the symphonic repertoire, and moreover
signified a musical "rehabilitation" of Shostakovich whose standing in
the West had sunk rather low at that time.

Because it was the first major work to be composed after Stalin's death,
the Tenth Symphony of Shostakovich was awaited with particular
anticipation. The Western world was eager to know whether the composer, after a creative stagnation of some five years (a stagnation which
in the Western view was politically enforced) was able to reassert his
leading position on the international musical scene. This question was
answered in the affirmative by the Tenth Symphony, and even more
emphatically by the Violin Concerto No. 1.
    In the Soviet Union, however, both works were received with
initial hesitation. The question in Moscow was not so much musical as
political, and this became quite obvious during the debate in the
Composers' Union dealing with the Tenth Symphony. There were
two opposing factions: one, unfavourable to Shostakovich, feared the
resurgence of the creative permissiveness that had prevailed before
the Resolution of 1948, and urged a rigid adherence to Zhdanov's
principles. The other faction, acclaiming Shostakovich—while not
openly attacking the Zhdanov guidelines—rejected excessive bureaucratic tutelage and asserted the right of the artist to be guided by his
own integrity. Shostakovich was a good "test case" because his loyalty
to Soviet ideals was unassailable, despite his previous clashes with
artistic officialdom.
    Almost all the composers of note, spoke in support of Shostakovich.
The conspicuous exception was Dzerzhinsky. An interesting point,
however, was the absence at the debate of some composers known
to oppose the Tenth Symphony, notably members of the directorate

of the Composers' Union. It may well be that the "internal" opposition to the new symphony was greater than the debate indicated. The opponents were led by two musicologist-critics, Yuli Kremlev and Victor Vanslov. The tenor of the opposition was that the Tenth Symphony was a "non-realistic" work, deeply pessimistic in approach, and not representative of Soviet life. These are, in fact, non-musical criteria, but they are applied time and again in Soviet criticism. Characteristically, Khrennikov expressed the opinion that Shostakovich's *Song of the Forests* "succeeded in a far more convincing manner, with far more impressive means, in representing the truth of our life than the Tenth Symphony".[17]

Thus, it was not the symphony's musical quality, but its prevailing mood that came under Soviet attack. Its defenders, too, used non-musical arguments. The young composer Volkonsky called the Tenth "an optimistic tragedy". Others praised it as the end of the "theory of non-conflict". Important critics—like Yarustovsky, Nestyev, Zhitomirsky, and Danilevich—spoke in favour of the new symphony, although with some reservations. In the course of the discussion it became clear that the Tenth Symphony of Shostakovich heralded a new, freer approach to musical creativity and that the "dogmatists" (those favouring a "hard line") were retreating, at least temporarily.

Editorially, the journal *Sovetskaya Muzyka* favoured the more flexible approach. This was already apparent in the printed transcript of the debate that was published under the heading "An Important Event in Soviet Music" (June 1954).[18] The editorial introduction tried to be impartial, rejecting both glorification and negation of the work. But it was clear that the editors were impatient with the speakers who took "hackneyed and worn-out clichés" as the basis for their criticism.

The discussion surrounding the Tenth Symphony of Shostakovich signalled a new stage in musical criticism. The three-day debate at the Composers' Union was only a beginning. The dispute continued a year later at the Eighth All-Union Plenum of the Union's directorate when "Soviet Symphonism" was discussed.[19] Some twenty papers of a specialized nature were read, all dealing with Shostakovich's new symphony. Not only professionals, but many laymen participated in the discussion. Never before had there been such a divergence of opinion about the same work, and never before had there been such acid sharpness, such fierce clashes in public forums. At last, the strait-jacket of silent conformity was loosened, and honest disagreements were once again vented in public debate.

Shortly after the momentous debate in the Composers' Union, the Moscow correspondent of *The New York Times*, Harrison Salisbury, had a lengthy personal interview with Shostakovich, which was given great prominence in its Sunday supplement on 8 August 1954. The article was published under the title "Visit with Dmitri Shostakovich" and a sub-heading, "Despite official criticism of his work, the noted composer insists that Soviet artists are allowed freedom of expression."[20] (As if to counterbalance the favourable impression created by Salisbury's article, *The New York Times* attached a "contrasting view on the subject" by Julie Whitney under the title "Music in a Cage".*)

Salisbury was greatly impressed by Shostakovich's obvious "honesty and sincerity" though he disagreed with some of his views. For example, Shostakovich put forward the thesis that "the artist in Russia has more 'freedom' than the artist in the West". He felt that the rôle of the artist in the Western world was haphazard and ill-defined, while the Soviet artist enjoyed a firm relationship with state and society, based on recognized principles. Salisbury argued that this "relationship" presented certain dangers, namely the artist's dependence on the State and his confinement to a "single outlet" which limited his "freedom".

Shostakovich admitted that "there is a 'line' which is established by the Party for the general guidance of artists—a line asking of art that it be appealing to people, that it have depth and perfection of form. But this does not make Soviet composers mere automatons. Great differences of opinion continue to exist and are strenuously expressed . . . The Western conception of an iron hand and of rigidity of doctrine is quite wrong . . . " Speaking of himself as a much-criticized composer, Shostakovich said, ". . . Who can say that my work suffered from this criticism? My works are played all over Russia. Just because one work is criticized, does not mean that orchestras stop playing the others. And I go on writing and the Government goes on supporting me, and generously, too."[21]

Almost by coincidence, very similar ideas were expressed by Khachaturian at about the same time. In the April 1954 issue of *Sovetskaya Muzyka*, Khachaturian described the plight of the artist in the West by quoting Artur Honegger, "The position of the composer in the West today is as hopeless as that of a shoe manufacturer trying to sell ladies' high button boots on the modern market." Speaking of the futility of trying to create under present conditions, Honegger compared the status of the modern composer to that of an uninvited guest who insists on taking a seat at a table where he is not wanted. In contrast, says Khachaturian, "the Soviet composer is an honoured member of society. He is surrounded by the care and solicitude of the people.

* Julie Whitney, a Soviet-born composer-pianist, is the wife of Thomas Whitney who spent the years 1944–53 as Associated Press correspondent in Moscow. They now live in the United States. In his book *Russia in My Life* (London, 1963), Mr. Whitney gives a vivid picture of those years.

He has no material worries and he knows that he is highly valued by society."[22]

Again as if by prearrangement, both Shostakovich and Khachaturian, referred to the—already mentioned—article in *Pravda* of 27 November 1953 as a proof that freedom of creativity is encouraged in the Soviet Union. "All my life I have written only what has appealed to my artistic imagination," wrote Khachaturian, "and I therefore find it hard to believe in the sincerity of lamentations over the alleged lack of creative freedom of the Soviet composer." Here, then, we have two leading Soviet composers, publicly castigated as recently as 1948 for having composed music according to their "artistic imagination", now singing the praises of creative freedom in Soviet Russia in 1953.

The "changing times" were evident in many other ways. Shostakovich had shown the way. His Tenth Symphony was neither the dawn of a new musical era, nor was it a reversion to formalism. It was the self-confession of an individualistic artist. He had demanded, and he had won, the right to express himself on his own terms, though the right was granted reluctantly. Many considered the Tenth as the tragedy of a "deeply lonely individual"—an interpretation that the composer himself resolutely rejected. Nevertheless, the mood proved contagious, many a younger composer imitated him, and the result was a wave of "pessimistic", pseudo-tragic Soviet music.

The fact that composers felt free enough to be pessimistic if they so chose was significant in itself. People began to discuss controversial matters without fear of reprisals. Musicians began to revaluate the state of music, the provincial taboos imposed by Zhdanov and his coterie, the long list of proscribed composers so venomously denounced by Khrennikov. Especially the younger composers—those who were too young to be involved in the 1948 purge—felt encouraged to speak up. Among them were Volkonsky and Shchedrin, then both in their early twenties. Volkonsky wrote a warmly appreciative article about Shostakovich's Tenth Symphony and welcomed a widening of the concept of Socialist Realism,

> "I believe that Socialist Realism is such a rich and fertile soil that the most varied flowers can grow in it. The Soviet man is many-sided, and so must be his art. The tendencies towards levelling all creative individuality are not yet eliminated; this leads unavoidably to the appearance of grey, monotonous, inexpressive works. Those are not needed. It is our task to create works of different stylistic directions, but—be it understood—in the framework of Realism."[23]

These optimistic words of Volkonsky—the most adventurous among the young composers—proved to be premature. He was soon to discover that his own brand of modernism was not permitted to "grow" in that "fertile soil" of Socialist Realism. But in 1954 he still had illusions.

The following year, Shchedrin published an essay in *Sovetskaya Muzyka* entitled "For Creative Courage".[24] He appealed to his generation for a more daring and creative search. Too many of the works of the young, he said, lacked the spirit of innovation and life. "Youth is eager to throw itself into the thick of battle and polemics," he exclaimed. After paying tribute to the great contemporary Soviet composers, Shchedrin then turned to twentieth-century Western Europe and confessed that young Soviet musicians knew little about the "latest vintage", namely Mahler, Debussy, Ravel, etc. (How pathetic it is to realize that these names, dating back to the early twentieth century, represented "the latest" for a Soviet composer in the year 1955!) Shchedrin expressed the opinion that works like Debussy's *Nocturnes* or Ravel's *Boléro* and *Daphnis et Chloé* "can stand side by side with great classics". He found it hard to understand that French musical Impressionism was characterized as "deeply decadent" in the latest edition of the *Great Soviet Encyclopaedia* (1952).*

Shchedrin called for separating the youthful Stravinsky, "the disciple of Rimsky-Korsakov", from the later Stravinsky, "the enemy of his homeland". Early works like *Firebird* and *Petrushka*, he felt, belonged to the history of Russian music. This opinion was supported by Shostakovich a few months later who said that *Petrushka* was not really an example of "anti-people"[25] music. Thus began a cautious, partial rehabilitation of Stravinsky.

All this seems ludicrous, weird, and yet it carries deep significance. Shchedrin is merely the prototype of the young Soviet composer, reared in isolation and misinformation by official ukase, who suddenly becomes aware of the musical world around him. Within the next few years, many young Soviet musicians went through the same process of revelatory experience. By 1962 one could see a conservatory class in Leningrad rediscovering Berg's *Wozzeck* after a gap of almost forty years, and the young people were enthralled by the experience.

Side by side with the young generation, the older composers continued their demands for freer creative scope. Once again, Khachaturian

---

* The lingering Soviet hostility towards French Impressionism is indeed a curious phenomenon. In 1956, both *Izvestia* and *Pravda* printed an attack on Igor Grabar, the eminent Russian art historian. Grabar was allegedly friendly towards Impressionism and had said that Repin—Russia's foremost painter—had not been an enemy of Impressionism. Untrue, cried *Izvestia*: Repin disliked Impressionism, and Grabar was guilty of historical falsification!

spoke up, and his article "Exciting Problems" was published in the same issue of *Sovetskaya Muzyka* as that of Shchedrin. Khachaturian reopened the question of the relationship between the composer and bureaucratic criticism,

> "As soon as one touches Soviet music, one finds comrades who try to regulate the natural and necessary competitiveness of creative trends, who interpret the term Socialist Realism as a style and exclusively as such. By assuming the difficult responsibility of defining the style characteristics of Socialist Realism in music, they reduce the whole matter to a simplified concept of folkishness, programmaticism, and a generalized demand for skill. As for the ideological content of music, it is often reduced to a superficial, fanfare-like declaratory pronouncement, to an official and—hence —cold pathos."[26]

Khachaturian objected to the hasty "labelling" of an unsuccessful composition. There are cases when a composer fails while searching for newness and individual expression, "And, then, certain over-zealous critics hasten to denounce the unsuccessful work as formalistic, ideologically harmful, etc. I categorically object to this. Moreover, I should prefer to excuse the composer's failure rather than praise an insipid mediocrity trying to make headway under cover of well-sounding titles and ready-made, worn-out formulas."

Yet he himself had not overcome those "worn-out" taboos, "Of course, the decadent, formalist trends are still very strong in the musical art of bourgeois countries . . . We have good reasons to be outraged at the crude formalistic perversion characteristic of modern bourgeois music, and we reject uncompromisingly the anti-popular, cosmopolitan principles of modernism."

This type of twaddle—the faded equation of "modernism" with "bourgeois decadence"—was repeated *ad nauseam*, not only by the so-called dogmatists, the "hard-liners", but also by those who advocated more liberalism in music. They wanted liberalism, but not too much of it, and only of the approved kind. As soon as anything like dodecaphony or similar formalistic "deviations" came up for discussion, even the most liberal threw up their hands in horror and repudiation. During the following years, we shall hear many self-righteous statements from Shostakovich, Kabalevsky and others of similar stature concerning the evils of dodecaphony.

The Tenth Symphony represented a musical peak in Shostakovich's life. Nothing comparable happened in the next few years; in fact, one can speak of a creative lull during the years 1954–55. While the Tenth was an ideological "victory" in musical terms, Shostakovich made no effort to widen and exploit this victory. The works he wrote in those two years—the *Festival Overture*, the Two-Piano Concertino, a few film scores and songs—contained no hint at musical "liberalization", at a widening of musical idiom.

Nevertheless, the year 1955 brought two Shostakovich premières that demanded the attention of friends and foes—delayed premières of works written earlier, during the *Zhdanovshchina*, but withheld by the composer. One was the song cycle *From Jewish Folk Poetry* (for three solo voices with piano), first given in January 1955, though composed in 1948.* The other was the Violin Concerto No. 1, composed in 1947–48 and first played by David Oistrakh in Leningrad on 29 October 1955, and in Moscow on 4 February 1956.

Shostakovich's Violin Concerto No. 1 occupies a pivotal position between his gay Ninth and the tragic Tenth Symphonies. For a time, the Concerto bore the opus number 99, placing it *after* the Tenth Symphony (Op. 93). However, the composer later indicated that he wanted the Concerto to be numbered Op. 77, in keeping with the time of its composition (1947–48), rather than of its publication (1956). Whether the Concerto underwent any changes during the seven-year span between composition and première is not known. As it stands, it is a perfectly logical bridge between the Ninth and the Tenth Symphonies; in fact, it has traits in common with each of them. One can trace the earthy exuberance of the Concerto's Finale to the Ninth Symphony, while the contemplative and tragic elements foreshadow the Tenth. In depth and seriousness, the Violin Concerto is closer to the Tenth Symphony; in fact, there are thematic relationships. This is all the more remarkable since the two works are separated by some five years—years of great inner strain and outside pressure. But the spiritual link between the two works appears unbroken, seemingly unaffected by the intervening years.

Both as to form and content, the Violin Concerto is one of Shostakovich's most original works. Cast in a four-movement cycle, it approaches his favourite symphonic form while it breaks with the concerto tradition. Unusual—for a concerto—is the number and the sequence of movements, opening with a moderately slow movement (Nocturne), continuing with a Scherzo, a stately Passacaglia, and ending with a Burlesca. Bridging the last two movements is a large-scale Cadenza, almost long enough to be counted as an individual movement.

---

* The composer had selected the texts from a collection of Jewish Folk Poems published in Moscow the previous year (1947).

While the solo part requires a virtuoso, it does not offer any technical display for its own sake. The entire concept is that of a "symphonic concerto"—a concept thought to be more German than Russian prior to this Concerto by Shostakovich and the Symphony-Concerto for Cello by Prokofiev.

The four movements of the Concerto represent exciting contrasts: the Nocturne is contemplative and ethereal, the Scherzo is sparkling, with a rough hewn-middle section suggesting a Jewish folk dance. Since the Concerto was composed at almost the same time as the cycle *From Jewish Folk Poetry*, it may well be that Shostakovich's imagination veered in that direction. There follows a Passacaglia, one of Shostakovich's favourite compositional devices, a movement of lapidary grandeur, while the final Burlesca has a devil-may-care abandonment. The Concerto does not aim at easy effectiveness; there are no memorable, ingratiating melodies nor virtuoso pyrotechnics designed for immediate audience response. Just as its first performer, David Oistrakh, admitted that he had to "live" with the work for some time until he penetrated its meaning, so the listener must exert some patience and intellectual effort to grasp its full message.

The musical community remained strangely silent after the première of the Violin Concerto. Finally, Oistrakh exchanged his bow for a pen and wrote an analytical article for *Sovetskaya Muzyka* which appeared in July 1956.[27] He noted that silence was also a sort of criticism and he blamed the leaders of the Composers' Union for the failure of the musicologist-critics to come forth with any significant comments on the new work. After the enormous attention given to the Tenth Symphony, the silence surrounding the Violin Concerto seems strange indeed. But lacking that nod of approval from the "leaders", no musicologist was willing to assume the responsibility for a favourable appraisal. This is where Oistrakh stepped in. He was fully committed to the Concerto, he had accepted its dedication, he had played the first performance, he was not a member of the Composers' Union and hence not subject to any internal pressures. However, by publishing his article in *Sovetskaya Muzyka* Oistrakh added weight to his opinion.

His comments served the immediate purpose of not letting an important work slip off into oblivion. Much of what he had to say is refreshingly direct and simple. Violinists might be comforted by his confession that the Concerto does not "fall easily into one's hands". In speaking of the Nocturne, Oistrakh mentions the tempo as Adagio while the printed score has Moderato. The Scherzo, in his words, has something "evil, demoniac, prickly". Oistrakh points towards the sparing use of the orchestral violins in the Scherzo so that the solo violin stands out vividly, "concertizing" with the woodwind instruments. Speaking of the Cadenza, Oistrakh recommends to build it slowly and cautiously so as not to run out of "breath"—good advice indeed in view of the length and technical demands of that section. The title of the Finale—*Burlesca*—is not to Oistrakh's liking; to him, it fails to convey the brightly-coloured mood of a folk festival, Russian in character. All in all, Oistrakh describes the Concerto as "innovational"—a very apt term.

Shortly after the Leningrad première of the Concerto on 29 October 1955, Oistrakh embarked for his first visit to the United States, and he brought the new work with him. Thus, the audiences of the New York Philharmonic Orchestra heard the Concerto before Moscow did—it was played at Carnegie Hall on 29 December 1955, with Mitropoulos conducting. The performance was then perpetuated on a phonograph recording*—an interpretation of rare perfection. But nothing could duplicate the excitement generated by the actual première at Carnegie Hall—the unique experience of discovering, at the same time, a great composition and a great performer. Those who were privileged to be present (and I was among them) will cherish that experience forever.**

Seen from the West, Shostakovich seemed to dominate the Soviet musical scene, almost dwarfing the other composers. But this impression can be misleading. True, the Tenth Symphony had become the rallying point of all liberal-minded musicians. But it did not result in any spectacular change of direction in Soviet music. Moscow was fairly bursting with musical activity, but most of the new music offered was not "new". Now that the right to greater creative freedom was won, composers seemed unsure how to use it. To clamour for innovation proved easier than to innovate. Besides, the concept of Socialist Realism had become ingrained, and there was nothing comparable to replace it. However, the more Soviet music became "tainted" by Socialist Realism, the less acceptable it became in the Western world.

Inside the Soviet Union, however, the vast productivity of Soviet composers was considered a healthy sign of continuing vitality. Composers who conformed to the rules of the establishment, continued to enjoy material support, performances, publications, and commissions. Once the "cultural exchanges" got under way, composers were sent abroad to represent Soviet culture—only to discover that Moscow was

* Columbia Records ML 5077.

** In response to the enthusiastic applause, Mitropoulos—in a symbolic gesture—lifted the score of the Concerto toward the audience as if to let the new work share in the ovation accorded the masterful performance.

not the world, and that the rhetoric of the Composers' Union was ineffective at a New York press conference. But this rude awakening did not come until 1959.

In the meantime, many premières were given in Moscow and Leningrad, old composers were acclaimed, new composers were discovered, and some events proved to be of more than local importance. Let us look more closely at some of the works produced in the years 1953–56, the first years of the "thaw".

Among the operas were the historic drama *The Decembrists* by Shaporin (1953), *Nikita Vershinin* (on a Soviet libretto) by Kabalevsky (1954), and the Shakespearean comedy, *The Taming of the Shrew*, by Shebalin (1957). Several works by Prokofiev were heard posthumously —the ballet *The Stone Flower* (1954) and the Leningrad version of the opera *War and Peace* (1955). Khachaturian's ballet *Spartacus* was completed in 1954 and first performed in 1956. Among younger composers, Georgi Sviridov gained belated prominence with his cantata-like *Poem to the Memory of Sergei Yesenin* (1955). (The "peasant-poet" Yesenin, who belonged to the Imagist group, had committed suicide in 1925; his works were not reprinted during the Stalin regime and were still unavailable in 1954.) The composer Moissei Vainberg also gained more recognition, particularly with chamber music. Several new names emerged among the very young composers—Andrei Eshpai, Rodion Shchedrin, and Andrei Volkonsky.

Shaporin's *The Decembrists* is an opera in the great Russian tradition. The composer spent a lifetime shaping this particular work. A first version, under the title *Paulina Goebel*, was given in 1925; a second version was ready in 1938 but did not satisfy the composer. At the time Gerald Abraham referred to the score as a "curiously satisfying synthesis of those seeming incompatibles, Mussorgsky and Tchaikovsky".[28] The final version took shape in 1947–53. Over the years, the libretto underwent so many changes that the various drafts filled seven filing boxes in the archives of the Bolshoi Theatre. Despite the efforts of several prominent writers (including Alexei Tolstoy), the libretto is undramatic and structurally deficient, and the opera remains static and oratorio-like. Shaporin's score, though full of nobility, is not strong enough to overcome these weaknesses. Although his musical idiom belongs essentially to the nineteenth century, one cannot dismiss the score as purely epigonic. Every page shows the thoughtful and skilled musician who consciously recreates the musical language of the 1820's, the age of Pushkin and Glinka. This is most noticeable in the choral settings and folk scenes which have an indefinable Russian character without resorting to any direct quotations of folk material.

Shaporin—who died in 1966 at the age of seventy-nine—was a

towering figure in Soviet music. Outwardly impassive, he impressed by a kind of moral integrity comparable to that of Miaskovsky. As a teacher, he had an open mind; thus, he went to the defence of his student Volkonsky though musically they were at opposite poles.

Another work by an older master—Shebalin—achieved a notable success: *The Taming of the Shrew*. It was not only a matter of recognizing its musical excellence but also of rehabilitating a composer who had suffered grave injustice during the 1948 purge. Shebalin's opera displays spirit, humour, and charm; it has stylized elegance without any attempt at "period" music. Shebalin succeeded in the genre of comic opera which in general is not congenial to the Russian temperament. The score is extremely skilful, and an important role is assigned to the orchestra.

Kabalevsky's opera *Nikita Vershinin* was not successful although it had a contemporary Soviet libretto of great potential. Soviet critics blamed a dramatically weak finale, but there were more basic deficiencies. Kabalevsky had planned a music drama with the people as protagonists, in the great tradition of Glinka and Mussorgsky, but his musical gifts were not commensurate with this plan. His talent tends more towards the smaller-scaled genres. Everything is planned with supreme intelligence, but the spark of genuine inspiration is too rarely present.

The two most successful ballets of those years were composed by non-Russians—*Spartacus* by the Armenian-born Khachaturian, and *Path of Thunder* by Kara Karayev, Azerbaijan's foremost composer. Both scenarios deal with rebellions. In *Spartacus* (whom Karl Marx once called the "true representative of the proletariat of antiquity"), we perceive ancient Rome through Armenian eyes: full-blooded rhythms, romantic lushness, and unabashed sentimentality. The ideological meaning—"struggle of the enslaved colonial people rising . . . against imperialist tyranny"—is drowned in lavishness. The Roman "Sword Dance" is a twin to the Armenian "Sabre Dance" from *Gayaneh*. In his music, Khachaturian deliberately avoided any stylization; he adhered, as he said, "to my individual style, my idiom, describing the events the way I understood and felt them".

As a ballet, *Spartacus* had a checkered history. The Leningrad version of 1956, choreographed by Leonid Yacobson, was a successful spectacle, though more mimic action than ballet. The Moscow production of 1957, for which the famous Igor Moiseyev was responsible, did not satisfy the critics who objected to its facile effects and the predominance of pantomime. When *Spartacus* was brought to New York in a modified Yacobson version, it suffered a critical debacle and was hurriedly removed from the repertoire, at least for the American tour. In 1968, *Spartacus* underwent a metamorphosis that made it into a virtually new work as to scenario, choreography, and even music. The new production is the work of Yuri Grigorovich, chief choreographer of Moscow's Bolshoi Theatre. The dance critic of *The New York Times*, Clive Barnes—sceptical at first—called it a "turning point" in Soviet ballet history. The transformation in scenario and choreography concern us less than the changes in music. Khachaturian was induced to revise the score which was "turned inside out", with music added, "newly orchestrated" from the composer's piano works. Barnes called it a "scissors-and-paste job—switching, cutting, changing, and rearranging". What resulted was "not the greatest ballet score ever written, but it is at least serviceable".[29] We must assume, however, that basically Khachaturian's musical style remained the same through all the changes.

Another ballet dealing with social revolt was Kara Karayev's *Path of Thunder* ("Tropoyu Groma"), first staged in 1958. Karayev had acquired a solid reputation with an earlier ballet score, *Seven Beauties* (1952), in which he used the songs and dances of his native Azerbaijan. *Path of Thunder* presented a different problem: the scenario was based on a novel by the South African writer Peter Abrahams and dealt with the racial tensions in that country. While preparing the score, Karayev made a study of African music which (as he said) was more time-consuming than the writing of the score itself. He used not only tribal music of South African natives but also themes from Northern Africa, from African urban centres, and even some Afro-American rhythms and tunes. Far from being an ethno-musicological endeavour, the material is developed in an almost symphonic manner. Karayev has a predilection for strong rhythms and ostinato basses. A student of Shostakovich, Karayev's musical "ancestors" include Prokofiev, to whose memory the score is dedicated, Khachaturian, Ravel, and an occasional dash of Gershwin. In writing for orchestra, Karayev favours a battery of percussion instruments, lending colour and excitement to the score. In the last few years, Karayev's musical style has become more sophisticated and experimental, and his creative evolution points towards bridging the gap between East and West.

In 1968, the name of Georgi Sviridov appeared in the news when he succeeded the ailing Shostakovich as head of the Composers' Union of the Soviet *Russian* Republic (RSFSR). As a composer, Sviridov is virtually unplayed in the West. There is a reason for this neglect: Sviridov is mainly known for his cantata-like compositions in which texts and music are so tightly interwoven that a translation seems well-nigh impossible. But even in the Soviet Union, Sviridov's rise to prominence has been very slow. Born in 1915, he studied composition at the Leningrad Conservatory under the guidance of Shostakovich and did not complete his formal education until 1941. Apart from a few modernistic flings—as with so many of the young composers under Shostakovich's influence—Sviridov is essentially a composer of conservative bent. In 1955, he moved to Moscow and achieved his first success on a nation-wide scale, the *Poem to the Memory of Sergei Yesenin* for soloists, chorus, and orchestra. This was followed, in 1959, by an even greater success, the *Pathetic Oratorio* on texts by Mayakovsky centred on the memory of Lenin. The two works are as different as the two poets. Yesenin's poems are sensitive, nostalgic, and imbued with that unique Russian love for their countryside. Mayakovsky's poetry is extrovert, assertive, and filled with "revolutionary romanticism". In each case, the moods of the texts are captured to perfection by Sviridov. His musical means are entirely traditional; yet one is willing to forget the basic conventionality of the musical idiom because words and music create an intense rapport between stage and audience. Without an understanding of the texts, however, the music sounds outdated: "steady, solid, unhurried (all euphemisms for 'boring'...); it does not venture beyond a primitive triadic scheme..." This is the evaluation of Robert Craft,[30] Stravinsky's amanuensis, who heard Sviridov's music on his trip to the Soviet Union in 1962. As a foreigner, Craft could not possibly grasp the fusion of words and music, the total interpenetration of the two media, which is Sviridov's essential accomplishment.

Another composer who deserves wider attention abroad is Moissei Vainberg. Born in 1919 in Warsaw, he received his musical education in Poland. When his country was overrun by the Germans in 1941, Vainberg sought refuge in the Soviet Union and eventually settled in Moscow. He is one of the few Soviet composers of Jewish origin who has achieved genuine equality among his colleagues: he is extremely well liked and receives many commissions and performances. In contrast to the older generation of Jewish-Russian composers who stressed their Jewishness (among them Engel, Achron, Krein, Veprik, Gnessin), the younger generation does not limit itself ethnically. Composers like Lev Knipper, Yulian Krein, Boris Kliusner, and Vainberg have acquired a Russian or international musical idiom. In Vainberg's music, there is neither avoidance of, nor stress on, Jewishness; some of his works contain elements of Jewish folklore, while others employ a musical idiom related to Shostakovich and Bartok.

After the 1948 decree, Vainberg enjoyed the doubtful privilege of being praised by Khrennikov for his "re-orientation"—enough to ruin anyone's career—when he reviewed the accomplishments of the year 1948,

"A shining proof of the fruitfulness of the realistic path is the Sinfonietta by Vainberg. As a composer, Vainberg was strongly influenced by modernistic music which badly mangled his undoubted talent. Turning to the sources of Jewish folk music, Vainberg created a bright, optimistic work dedicated to the theme of the shining, free working life of the Jewish people in the land of Socialism. In this work Vainberg has shown uncommon mastery and a wealth of creative imagination."[31]

Among Vainberg's best works is his Second Sinfonietta, composed in 1958 for Rudolf Barshai and the Moscow Chamber Orchestra. In addition, Vainberg has written eight symphonies, eleven string quartets, some twenty sonatas for various instruments, several concertos, and various chamber music works with piano, including an impressive piano quintet. Whether his style is strong and personal enough to win acceptance abroad is still untested since hardly any of his music has been heard in the West.

A young composer of peculiar charm is Andrei Eshpai, born in 1925 in the Mari Autonomous Soviet Republic (the "autonomy" was acquired in 1936). This small state is inhabited by some 600,000 people, half of them Mari (a Finnic people), the other half Russian with an admixture of Tartars. The son of a composer, young Andrei was brought to Moscow as a boy of ten, and there he received his entire musical education. Yet, true to the cherished theory of national heritage, he was expected to play the role of a "Mari" composer. By incorporating some folkloristic material, Eshpai gives his music an attractive "exotic" flavour, heightened by a Ravel-like treatment of harmony and texture. Eshpai's Piano Concerto of 1954, dedicated "To the Memory of Ravel", is refined and elegant, with a particularly lovely slow movement built on a folk-like theme. His Violin Concerto of 1956, which received a First Prize at the Sixth International Youth Festival in Moscow in 1957, is highly praised. Some affinity to his teacher Khachaturian is evident, though Eshpai is more refined in his treatment of folk and dance rhythms. During the 1960's, Eshpai's reputation as a composer developed significantly.

Among the youngest composers, two students of Shaporin deserve special mention—Rodion Shchedrin and Andrei Volkonsky.

Shchedrin, born in Moscow in 1932, completed his studies at the Conservatory in 1955. While still nominally a student, he played his own piano concerto in 1954. That year he was sent to Prague to represent the Soviet Union at the Fifth World Festival of Democratic Youth.

Shchedrin's music to *The Hump-Backed Horse* ("Konyok-Gorbunok") became known as an orchestral suite in 1955 before it was staged as ballet in 1960. The score uses an electronic instrument, the "clavioline" imported from France. But essentially, the music is old-fashioned; as the British critic Arthur Jacobs rightly remarks, "in basic idiom it would have been modern if composed in 1910 along with Stravinsky's *Firebird*".[32] Shchedrin's talent developed rapidly; he soon became the darling of the musical establishment, the "official" modernist, a "reliable" composer of realistic tendencies despite occasional modernistic experiments.

One of the hallmarks of Shchedrin's style is the use of the urban folk ditty, the "chastushka"—racy rhymes and impudent tunes which he incorporates into many of his scores. His music is full of youthful insouciance, bold orchestral effects (with obvious derivations from early Stravinsky scores), and a delightful sense of humour. Shchedrin is a new breed of Soviet composer—unafraid, open-minded, and without the pompousness that makes Socialist Realism so dull in the hands of older composers.

In contrast to Shchedrin's officially approved modernism, his fellow student Volkonsky became the *enfant terrible* of the establishment, whose open avant-gardism exasperated his elders. A descendant of the princely family of Volkonsky, he was born in "exile"—in Geneva in 1933, Andrei studied piano with the legendary Dinu Lipatti, and composition with Nadia Boulanger. He was far advanced musically when the Volkonsky family resettled in Moscow in 1947. From 1950–54 Volkonsky studied at the Moscow Conservatory under Shaporin but was expelled for infraction of some minor rules. One Soviet writer, criticizing the action of the Conservatory, said that, instead of trying to help the young artist, the authorities used an excuse to get rid of a "difficult" student. In 1956, Volkonsky began a second career as a harpsichordist and is considered a specialist in Renaissance and Baroque music.

Because of his Western upbringing, Volkonsky had a grasp of modern music that was infinitely broader than that of any of his Soviet colleagues. To him, the neo-classic idiom of Stravinsky was a perfectly normal mode of musical self-expression while "neo-classicism" remained virtually unacceptable to Soviet musicians for another decade. True, Shostakovich had occasionally used a kind of "neo-Bachism". But Volkonsky was not oriented towards Shostakovich—he openly leaned on Stravinsky. Hence, Volkonsky's Concerto for Orchestra (composed in 1953, performed the following year) was received with caution and distrust; there was linear counterpoint, occasional polytonality, and similar "deviations" from accepted rules.

Volkonsky's next major work, a Piano Quintet, caused a controversy on the pages of *Sovetskaya Muzyka*.[33] It proved that an open debate was possible and that a controversial work could be judged from various angles. Two years later in 1956, the Quintet appeared in print as Opus 5 (with a dedication to his former teacher, Shaporin). The work is talented but immature and not unified in style. The first movement has a traditional Russian flair, the second—a Burlesca—is dominated by a Stravinsky-like repetitive, "motoric" drive. The last two movements, Passacaglia and Fugue, tend to be cerebral and contrived. At the time the Quintet was written, the young composer still believed that a wide range of music could be accommodated under the concept of Socialist Realism.*

The more Volkonsky tried to expand the experimental range of his music, the more he was singled out for criticism—criticism that was usually coupled with recognition of his basic talent, unfortunately so "misguided". Thus, Kabalevsky wrote in 1958, at a time when "liberalization" was expanding,

> "For example, I highly value the bright talent of Volkonsky, evident in his Second String Quartet, especially the first movement. Yet, one cannot help but feel that Volkonsky gets involved in search for the 'unusual' expressive means, and he occasionally over-steps that line where chaos begins and where complexity . . . degenerates to a sheer piling-up of sounds. For example, the second movement of the String Quartet No. 2 . . . To write chaotically, non-organically, illogically is not that 'new' and not that difficult. It requires no specific mastery. True, to be a disciple of Schoenberg or Hindemith is much easier than to be a follower of Chopin or Mussorgsky . . ."[34]

The last sentence, so restrictive and provincial, is a reflection not on Volkonsky, but on Kabalevsky. Yet there were others who remained open-minded, among them Volkonsky's old teacher, Shaporin. Alexander Werth reports a conversation with Shaporin— "one of the Grand Old Men of Russian music"—in 1959,

> "Volkonsky—Shaporin said—was an exceptionally brilliant and original composer . . . 'polyphonic, lapidary, classical, and rather chromatic music'; I gathered, however, that Volkonsky was proving a little too 'original' to some orthodox tastes."[35]

Since then, Volkonsky has become the unofficial leader of Soviet avant-garde composers, a small but determined group. More about this later.

* See p. 285.

The Twentieth Party Congress, held in Moscow from 14 to 25 February 1956, signified a turning point in Soviet policy. Almost four years had elapsed since the Nineteenth Party Congress—still dominated by the ailing Stalin—had seen the emergence of Georgi Malenkov as the most powerful contender for the highest post. After Stalin's death in March 1953, the power structure was in a state of flux—the execution of Beria, the gradual rise of Khrushchev, the failure of Malenkov as premier and his replacement by Bulganin in February 1955—these top events were symptomatic of the bitter power struggle waged on every level of the Party and the Government.

The most dramatic development of the Twentieth Congress was the deliberate destruction of the Stalin legend. The decision to end the "cult of personality" must have been taken collectively by the Presidium, but it was left to Khrushchev to deliver the ultimate blow. In a seven-hour speech that began at midnight on 24 February, Khrushchev unmasked the rule of Stalin. The original intent was apparently to balance praise and blame, but ultimately the condemnation overshadowed everything else. The full text of the speech was not released in the Soviet Union, but was published in the West.[1]

By spring 1956, the essence of Khrushchev's speech was known in every Party organization within the Soviet Union. On 30 June of that year, the Central Committee of the Party released a lengthy statement commenting on the evils of the "cult of personality". Werth describes this statement as "something in the nature of a compromise between 'Stalinites' and ' anti-Stalinites' ": it warned that the abolition of the 'personality cult' was not to be interpreted as a basic change in Soviet society or Soviet aims.[2]

Nevertheless, the impact on the arts was strong and immediate. First to react to de-Stalinization was Soviet literature, with series of exposés, of accusatory writings in poetry and prose. New names attracted attention, among them Daniel Granin, Yevgeni Yevtushenko, and Vladimir Dudintsev. It was Dudintsev's novel *Not by Bread Alone*—first published in *Novyi Mir* in 1956, then in book form in 1957—that became the symbol of that momentous period. It was not a great novel, but—for that matter—neither was Ehrenburg's *Thaw*. Yet these books mirrored the mood and satisfied the needs of the moment, and therein lay their importance. Dudintsev's novel was read everywhere; it caused considerable unrest among university students and in intellectual circles. The students were disciplined, the author was publicly criticized and eventually recanted. This incipient rebellion among the intelligentsia was embarrassing for the Soviet leadership which was battered by the unrest in Poland and the revolt in Hungary. No additional internal dissatisfaction could be tolerated, and the dissidents were reined in with a firm hand. Dudintsev, however, was not cowed by the criticism (which included Khrushchev's personal condemnation); he spoke up in his own defence and proved that a semblance of open debate was possible under the new regime.

In the field of music, major readjustments were overdue. It had been planned to convene the Second All-Union Congress of Composers in May of 1956. Without explanation, the Congress was postponed until April 1957. Obviously, more time was needed in the aftermath of the Twentieth Party Congress to gauge the temper of the new political directorate, to explore the ideological trends, to evolve new guidelines for the arts. Such matters could not be left to an open debate; they had to be argued in high-level conferences between Party ideologists and arts leaders.

All during the year 1956, *Sovetskaya Muzyka* published a number of essays under the general heading of "Pre-Congress Discussions". These were position papers written by "conservatives" and "liberals", presenting divergent views, as if to probe the reaction of Party officials. There was obvious uncertainty among composers and critics as to the future course of music policy.

The uncertainty was dispelled, once the Second Composers' Congress began its sessions on 28 March 1957. Nine years earlier, in 1948, the First Composers' Congress had stood—it will be recalled—under the domination of Zhdanov who exercised his control through Khrennikov, the newly elected secretary of the Composers' Union. The Second Composers' Congress of 1957 had the political guidance of Dimitri Shepilov, a high-ranking Party official, assisted by the ubiquitous Khrennikov. Shepilov was well prepared for a "cultural" assignment: he was a corresponding member of the Academy of Sciences and had served as editor of *Pravda* from 1952 to 1956. His elevation to the post of foreign minister was short-lived: he succeeded Molotov in 1956 and was replaced by Gromyko in February 1957.

Nevertheless, the presence of Shepilov, Secretary of the Party's

Central Committee, at the Composers' Congress added official importance to event. His status was comparable to that of Zhdanov in 1948. But Shepilov commanded less respect and less fear than Zhdanov who had been the "engineer" of the cultural purges. Shepilov attended the Composers' Congress, not to make policy, but to communicate decisions taken by the Party's Central Committee.

The opening address was delivered by Khrennikov. Compared to his militant harangue of 1948 when he had lashed out against all domestic and foreign "modernists", his speech of 1957 was moderate. It was his task to salvage Socialist Realism from the wreckage of Stalinism. By doing so, Khrennikov dampened all hopes for a liberalization of artistic concepts. Giving the usual dull survey of Soviet music history, he said,

> "I dwell particularly on the 1930's because it is precisely this period when the concept of Socialist Realism ripened . . . that certain foreign critics have recently represented in a distorted light as the beginning of the decline of Soviet art. By automatically linking the development of our art since 1934 with the mistakes and flaws of the cult of personality, in considering Socialist Realism merely an offshoot of this cult, these 'theoreticians' wish to represent the weaknesses and shortcomings of our creative work as the genuine history of Soviet art; they try to discredit the very method of Socialist Realism and the principle of Party spirit; under cover of the slogan 'freedom of creation', they try to put Soviet artists in opposition to the Communist Party and to Party direction of the arts.
>
> "Such views, whether they be a link in the openly reactionary propaganda campaign or the result of confusion among ideologically unstable circles of the arts intelligentsia in certain of the People's Democracies, cannot of course make us change our stand in the fundamental questions of principle of Soviet aesthetics."[3]

Speaking of the "ideologically unstable circles", Khrennikov must have had the Poles in mind, for they were the first among the "people's democracies" to free the arts from outdated dogmas. Khrennikov seemed to imply that all the artistic unrest was caused by "foreign" critics and he serenely pretended that there was no internal opposition to the *status quo*. He went even further by declaring that, "The direct, consistent criticism of formalistic manifestations and the broad, positive programme for the development of music contained in the 1948 decree, had a beneficial influence on the further growth of our music."

This reveals a strange concept of "growth". As we have seen, the 1948 decree encouraged mediocrity, not growth, and paralyzed efforts at creative originality. Khrennikov had to admit "occasional serious errors in evaluating works", such as Zhukovsky's opera *From All One's Heart*, a "nefarious" example of the non-conflict theory. In this connection, Khrennikov provided some interesting statistics: since 1948, some 120 operas had been written, of which more than half had reached the stage or were in process of production.* Notwithstanding this large number, only six operas were performed at more than a single theatre —namely Kabalevsky's *Family Taras*, Meitus' *Young Guard*, Shaporin's *Decembrists*, Prokofiev's *War and Peace*, Dankevich's *Bogdan Khmelnitzky*, and Kreitner's *Tanya*. This is indeed a disappointing record, all the more since neither *War and Peace* nor *The Decembrists* were—strictly speaking—operas of the post-1948 era. For some reason, Khrennikov does not include *From All One's Heart* which was given at several theatres before it was officially disgraced.

Only towards the end of his speech did Khrennikov hint at a broader vista; but similar phrases had been used repeatedly since 1953 and did not constitute anything new.

Despite the rigidity of his approach, Khrennikov was re-elected as head of the Composers' Union. Yet, there had been considerable criticism of the Union machinery—bloated bureaucracy, red tape, factionalism, excessive tutelage. But the *status quo* won out. It soon became apparent that the principles enunciated by Zhdanov in 1948 were indestructible; only the methods of application tended to become less rigid.

The key address of the Composers' Congress was delivered by Shepilov on 3 April 1957; it was entitled "To Create for the Welfare and the Happiness of the People".[4] It was a flexible speech: he appeased the conservatives and gave hope to the liberals. Shepilov, too, declared that Socialist Realism was to be retained. But his formulations did not exclude an artistic expansion of the concept. "In the creation of works of art, the rules of arithmetic or apothecary's formulas are not applicable . . . The question is decided . . . primarily by the artist's ideological position and his talent . . . The method of Socialist Realism is the most progressive in the realm of music . . ."

Recalling Lenin's flexible attitude towards art and artists, Shepilov said, ". . . The Leninist style of guidance requires a high adherence to principle, and essential flexibility, and patient care when it deals with cultural workers who honestly and unselfishly fulfill their patriotic duty, and essential sensitivity; such a style precludes high-handed commands and petty tutelage."

At the same time Shepilov made it clear that the direction of the arts would remain the responsibility of the Party and the Government in

* Compare Shaporin's statistics, p. 261.

order to "create ever-improving material conditions for a flowering of the arts". Here is the key sentence, "The Party and State guidance of the arts on the basis of Leninist standards and principles is a life-giving element, an all-important prerequisite for the development of art in conformity with its great task—service to the people."

Shepilov clearly stated what kind of music was expected "Soviet music cannot reconcile itself either to shabby primitivism or to aestheticized formalism . . . We are for simplicity, for music accessible and near to the people, rich in thought and emotion, saturated with the lofty ideas of our day, music that inspires, that is beautiful by its melody and artistic perfection."

These guidelines are similar to those expressed by Zhdanov in 1948; in fact, much of what Shepilov said in his address confirmed the validity of the cultural decrees of 1946–48. Yet, in one key paragraph, Shepilov held out a promise of reconsideration where past judgments had been unjustifiably harsh,

> "It would be wrong to insist on the immutability of every case in everyone of its [the Party's] decisions. The evolution of Soviet musical art testifies that there is no need to consider individual composers as representing an anti-people tendency even if there are serious flaws in their work. In the work of some important masters of Soviet music there were errors or weaknesses of an ideological, creative nature. But this must not obscure their undoubtedly serious contribution to the development of Soviet musical culture."

There can be no doubt that the liberal elements in the Composers' Union were heartened by Shepilov's speech and by the promise of greater flexibility. There were others who disliked any idea of liberalization and who feared the return of modernist influences.

But the fact alone that there were *two* factions, with opposing views, was in itself a sign of progress towards freer expression. Among those who participated in the debate, Shostakovich stood out—he who had suffered so much from unfair intolerance. Shostakovich pleaded for no particular concessions, only for the opportunity of free discussions,

> "We could quickly overcome the many shortcomings of the recent phase if broad creative discussions would develop productively among our composers. Unfortunately, this has yet to occur. The development of discussions is impeded, most of all, by one of the survivals of the 'cult of personality' . . . the unacceptable method of debate . . ., discrediting and denigrating one party to the

debate. As soon as the position of one side is ideologically discredited, the debate dies. Yet, it is quite clear that the debate is between people who adhere strongly to the positions of Soviet ideology and strive towards the same goal, but who interpret the path to those goals differently."[5]

At this point, Shostakovich was interrupted by applause. He continued,

"Why resort to evil demagogy and impede the creative discussion so necessary to us . . . Unfortunately, the secretariat of the Composers' Union has done more to freeze discussion than to develop it."

Shostakovich also defended the journal *Sovetskaya Muzyka* against persistent attacks based solely on the journal's effort to spark creative discussions. Earlier, he had a word for the critics, "In recent years, musical criticism . . . has given us a great deal of pedantry and opportunism. However, I am not disposed to hold the critics entirely responsible . . . since their position has often been none too independent." Here, Shostakovich put his finger on a sensitive spot: the so-called "critics" were not always free to express their own opinions but were delegated to present official viewpoints.

"Criticism and Creativity" was the subject of another major address at the Second Composers' Congress, delivered by Georgi Khubov.[6] He defined criticism as a "science in the sphere of art", and in his speech leaned towards the liberal side. He spoke sharply against "dogmatism", against a simplistic interpretation of "folkishness", against a primitive understanding of "accessibility". He defended the use of dissonance which, all too often, is confused with cacophony. Tchaikovsky, he said, called dissonance "the greatest power in music . . . though it has to be used with skill, taste, and art". Khubov warned against the indiscriminate stress on "optimism" (a favourite Soviet art concept) by quoting Lenin, "Nothing is more vulgar than self-satisfied optimism." What was needed was imagination, not reglementation; here again a Lenin quote was handy, "Fantasy is a quality of the highest value."

At one point, Khubov took issue with the loose usage of the term "modernism" in Soviet criticism. As an example, he cited the definition in the *Great Soviet Encyclopaedia* which reads as follows,

"*Modernism* (from the French new, contemporary), a general concept of various decadent trends (impressionism, expressionism, constructivism) in bourgeois art and literature of the imperialist era. Modernism is characterized by the distortion of reality, the refusal to represent the typical, the confirmation of reactionary tendencies, anti-people, cosmopolitanism (see decadence, formalism)."*

By such a "mechanical levelling"—Khubov said—composers like Debussy and Ravel, Mahler and Strauss, Stravinsky and Hindemith, Berg and Honegger are all thrown together as representatives of "reactionary" modernism. While Khubov admitted that the roots of "formalist, cosmopolitan" modernism reach back into the early twentieth century and even further, modernism is a distinct style evolved later, after the First World War.

When Khubov tries to reconcile the irreconcilable, he resorts to verbal acrobatics. He rejects the cult of personality but praises the 1948 decree which, in fact, was a shameful manifestation of the "cult". He states that, despite the harm done by the "cult", Soviet music flourished, and then he proceeds to name compositions that were written in defiance of the "cult"—Shostakovich's Tenth Symphony and the Violin Concerto, Prokofiev's *War and Peace*, Khachaturian's Second Symphony and the Cello Concerto. As for Socialist Realism, Khubov glowingly reaffirms its validity—it is "as wide as life itself". But he detaches the concept from Stalinism—"the theory of Socialist Realism is based on Lenin's writings on proletarian culture", he maintains. After a lengthy quotation from these writings, Khubov concluded,

"The art of Socialist Realism is an organic, inalienable part of proletarian, socialist culture that we are building, and building successfully, despite some difficulties . . . Socialist Realism is a concept that has grown historically, that is concrete and exact . . ."

Thus, Khubov joined Shepilov and Khrennikov in proclaiming the continuance of Socialist Realism, freed from Stalinist stigma and newly rooted in Leninism. The return to the principles of Leninism was to become a *cantus firmus* of the next decade.

In the course of his speech, Khubov labelled much of Soviet historical writing as "factography" (a word he coined). More should be written about Soviet contemporary music though it was a difficult subject and "for a music critic, I should say, not without peril". A rather significant admission to be made by the chairman of the Composers' Union's committee on musical criticism!

The Second All-Union Composers' Congress ended on 5 April 1957 with a resolution that embodied many of the points brought out by

* It must be said that most musical definitions in the *Great Soviet Encyclopaedia* (2nd ed., 1952) are equally dogmatic, distorted, and at times downright stupid. The articles were written by carefully selected Party-line musicologists and reflect Stalinist and Zhdanovist aesthetics. A new edition has begun to appear in 1970.

Khrennikov, Shepilov, and Khubov. It was stated that the period between the First and the Second Congress (i.e. the years 1948 to 1957)
had been one of "new and major successes of Soviet music". It was
acknowledged that the Composers' Union had become a truly nation-
wide organization. Certain shortcomings, particularly in the running
of the secretariat and in the journal *Sovetskaya Muzyka*, were to be
eliminated. An important paragraph of the resolution reads,

> "The entire work of the Composers' Union should be directed to-
> wards helping composers carry out creative tasks, and contributing
> to their close solidarity on the basis of Socialist Realism. Further-
> more, there should be no room for any limitations, for any con-
> straint of the freedom of creative search. One must remember the
> need to combat both the preoccupation with formal aesthetic
> experiments and vulgar naturalism, dullness, and clichés . . . The
> method of Socialist Realism permits endless ways of resolving
> creative tasks that are common to all Soviet art . . ."[7]

The composers had every reason to be satisfied with the results of
the Second Congress. It was a constructive session, in contrast to the
First Congress in 1948 which had been punitive. Neither the conservatives nor the liberals could claim victory, but the fact alone that rigidity
was rejected was indicative of a liberalizing trend. And finally, the hope
was raised in Shepilov's speech that past injustices migh be rectified.

As it happened, Shepilov's appearance at the Composers' Congress in
April 1957 was virtually his political swan song. A few months later,
on 29 June, he was expelled from the Party's Central Committee for
having joined an anti-Khrushchev faction (often called the "anti-
Party group") which included Molotov, Malenkov, and Kaganovich.
Among the reasons given was "dogmatic adherence to out-dated
methods". Shepilov was transferred to Frunze in Kirghizia where
he became director of a scientific institute.
Shepilov's removal from power had immediate repercussions: it
boosted the hopes of the "hard-line" adherents of reversing the trend
towards greater flexibility. A few weeks after his downfall, in July
1957, he was bitterly attacked for having quoted Lenin out of context.
An editorial in *Kommunist*, entitled "For Leninist Adherence to Principle in Questions of Literature and the Arts", asserted that Shepilov
". . . bears a tremendous share of responsibility in the spread of unsound
tendencies among a part of the art intelligentsia . . . He retreated from
the line charted by the Twentieth Congress (1956) in questions of
literature and the arts, and took a liberal position that was at variance
with Leninist adherence to principle."[8]

The editorial denied that Lenin was "liberal" and continued, "Some critics and literary scholars began to represent Lenin as a sort of believer in non-resistance, as someone with a liberal attitude towards alien tendencies in literature and arts, as an exponent of 'non-interference' in the work of art institutions and the arts intelligentsia generally . . . Attempts have been made . . . to demand such anarchic freedom from public control . . ." Nothing of the kind was ever on Lenin's mind: he was for Party control of literature though he advised caution and "more breadth"; ". . . yet the facts show that Lenin did not advocate broad scope for every thought and all imagination."*

Almost simultaneously, Shepilov was attacked in the leading cultural journal, *Sovetskaya Kultura*, by a minor Soviet musicologist, Pavel Apostolov, known for his "hard-line" views. In an article, "For the Purity of Realism in Soviet Music", Apostolov opposed "revisionist" tendencies and feared a possible "dilution" of realism by modernism. He warned that "The Party's correct demands for tactful and flexible guidance in the arts have been used as a 'bogey' against proponents of consistent realism and as a weapon for silencing the slightest criticism of modernistic tendencies . . ."[9]

How quickly things seemed to have changed! Suddenly, the "hardliners" felt persecuted. As for modernism, Apostolov coined colourful new epithets: bourgeois music of the latest period is described as the "gangrened appendix of decadence". While "early modernism" (like Debussy, Ravel, Mahler, Strauss, even some early Stravinsky) is partially acceptable, the post-modernism of the mid-1920's and later years is decisively rejected.

Apostolov entered into polemics with various liberal-minded musicologists. One must assume that he was not merely speaking for himself but for a strong anti-revisionist faction, by no means limited to musicians. The fact that his views were published in *Sovetskaya Kultura* —a journal addressing itself to a cross-section of the intelligentsia— assured them of a much wider readership.

There can be no doubt that a great deal of rethinking took place among musical authors and critics. The traumatic experience of the Zhdanov years had finally worn off, and musicologists began to question anew the validity of certain principles, concepts, and value judgments that had gained currency during the past decade. Composers long under a cloud began to be rediscovered. Such re-orientations

---

* In fact, Lenin can be interpreted in many ways; he has made "rigid" as well as "flexible" statements, and there are enough quotes to support both positions. But essentially, a return to "Leninism" is not—as some Western idealists wish to believe—a return to "liberalism" but merely a more humane approach to the creative processes, contrasted with Stalin's dehumanized dogmatism.

were most apparent in essays and articles, while books could not keep pace with the fast-changing scene. Repeatedly, books were outdated by the time they appeared in print. It happened to the monumental *History of Soviet Russian Music*, a collective work sponsored by the Academy of Sciences; the first volume, dealing with the years 1917–34, was published in 1956 and reflected all the prejudice and dogmatism of the Zhdanov years. It was received with harsh criticism. The same happened to Keldysh's third and final volume of his *History of Russian Music*, published in 1954; here, the author's formulations on twentieth-century modernism no longer fitted the concepts of 1957. It also happened to Nestyev's imposing monograph *Prokofiev*—published in 1957 but reportedly completed by 1955—which denigrated the composer's foreign period and misjudged the "modern" elements of his style. Since then, Keldysh, Nestyev, and other authors have revised their opinions. Such revisions merely highlight the "elasticity" of individual views which must conform to the officially established policy on any given subject. Under these confining circumstances, it is remarkable how much excellent work has been accomplished by Soviet musicologists. Because subjective evaluations are not always possible (indeed at times "perilous", as Khubov said in his speech), Soviet research is at its best in the presentation of documentary material, the painstaking exploration of primary sources within the history of Russian music. Such "Factography"—used by Khubov in a pejorative sense—may well be the most valuable contribution of Soviet musicologists.

Shepilov's career was, after all, a minor interlude in the evolving history of Soviet arts. Even before his dismissal in June 1957, Nikita Khrushchev had taken personal charge of dealing with the intelligentsia. His manner was ebullient and earthy, he could be reasonable as well as rude. In May 1957, Khrushchev spoke to the assembled Moscow writers who were his guests at a garden party. Alternately cajoling and threatening, he left no doubt that the Party would remain firm and vigilant. There was stunned silence when he said that force could be used against recalcitrant writers.

Khrushchev's speeches on literature and the arts, delivered on various occasions during the spring and summer of 1957, were collected and published in August 1957, under the title *For Close Ties Between Literature and Art and the Life of the People* (Za tesnuyu svyaz literatury i iskusstva s zhiznyu naroda).[10] Though often rambling and wordy, Khrushchev's utterances provided the official cultural guidelines until his fall in October 1964. Hence, they merit close attention. The following quotes are taken from the published version, at times expurgated since his extemporaneous remarks were not always fit to print.

Khrushchev interpreted Lenin's position as rather rigid, "Lenin took an irreconcilable attitude towards those who deviated from fidelity to principle in questions of literature and the arts, and who slid back to liberal positions with regard to ideological mistakes."

And while he admitted that errors were made "in the last years of Stalin's life", these errors were in the process of being "consistently" rectified. "However, the Party vigorously opposes those who try to make use of these past errors to resist the guidance of literature and the arts by the Party and the State."

Nor did Khrushchev pose as a "liberal". He discredited all "chatter about an allegedly 'creative attitude' toward Party guidance" and called them "false positions". He continued,

> "Certain liberally inclined people may accuse me of issuing a call to battle. Yes, we have never denied that we have been and are urging a principled ideological battle. There is a sharp conflict today in the world between two ideologies, the Socialist and the bourgeois culture, and in this conflict there can be no neutrals. The development of literature and art is proceeding in conditions of ideological battle against the influences of bourgeois culture, which is alien to us, against obsolete concepts and views, and for the affirmation of our Communist ideology."

Khrushchev showed understanding for the emotional reaction "particularly among writers" to the criticism directed against Stalin. Some seemed to think that "practically all their past creative work was wrong". (It will be recalled that such an "emotional reaction" had driven Fadeyev to suicide in 1956.) In fact, Khrushchev found kind words for Stalin's "positive role", and he also defended the Stalin Prizes against denigration although some mistakes in selecting the recipients had been made.

After praising the intelligentsia for having "proven itself politically mature, steadfast, and loyal to the ideas of Marxism-Leninism", Khrushchev charted a course for the future that offered nothing new,

> "Our people need works of literature, painting, and music that reflect the grandeur of labour and that they can understand. The method of Socialist Realism ensures unlimited opportunities for the creation of such works. The Party relentlessly combats the infiltration into literature and art of influences of alien ideology; it combats hostile attacks on Socialist culture."

These "attacks", he said, originate not only from the West but also from within Soviet art circles: attempts are made by "some creative workers to push literature and the arts onto a wrong path . . . The main line of development is that literature and the arts must always be inseparably linked with the people's life, must truthfully portray the wealth and variety of our Socialist reality."

Khrushchev is equally opposed to those who "prettify" reality (he calls them "lakirovshchiki"—lacquerers) as he is to the discontented critics who stress only the negative aspects. But he deals more harshly with the critics and takes Dudintsev and others to task for "taking malicious delight" in harping on shortcomings. "We have opposed, and continue to oppose, . . . a one-sided, unfaithful, mendacious distortion of our reality in literature and art." To Khrushchev, the Party and the people are inseparable; one cannot serve the people without actively carrying out the Party's policy.

Khrushchev's ideas on the role of Soviet literature and arts were a rehash of hollow phraseology. The stress was on conformity, not creativity. There was nothing vacillating in his cultural policy as is so often assumed; it remained constant throughout his rule and was rudely reaffirmed in late 1962 and early 1963. The "zigzags" were usually caused by adventurous writers, artists, and composers who wanted to test the limits of the allegedly "unlimited opportunities" of Socialist Realism, only to be disciplined periodically by zealous officials or, if the breach was important enough, by Khrushchev himself.

From the "official" point of view, music was the least troublesome of the arts because it was ideologically less sensitive. A cacophonous score could be silenced simply by non-performance, and the public would not even be aware of its existence. Khrennikov and the musical establishment could be trusted to keep "discords" within the walls of the Composers' Union. Besides, the leading composers like Shostakovich, Kabalevsky, and Khachaturian—all in their fifties—were becoming more conservative as they grew older; in fact, they presented a united front against any experimentation in music, such as twelve-tone technique. This attitude made Khrennikov's watchful position very much simpler.

Nevertheless, the Khrushchev era—particularly the early years—brought a relaxation of tensions, a reconsideration of certain Stalinist taboos. The denigration of Western culture was stopped, and the cultural exchange programme—initiated in 1958—contributed to the re-establishment of ties with the West. Gradually, certain writers and composers of the 1920's and 1930's, Soviet as well as foreign, who had been blackballed during the *Zhdanovshchina*, began to reappear in print and in performances.

Khrushchev knew how to flatter the intelligentsia. On 8 February

1958, an important reception was given at the Great Kremlin Palace "in honour of the Soviet People's intelligentsia". Khrushchev addressed the gathering several times, since each group represented was honoured by a separate toast. At one point he said, "What does one wish our writers and workers of theatre, cinema, music, and fine arts? Greater daring in their quests, more attention to life and people! Address yourselves more persistently to our own times!"[11]

The task of toastmaster was distributed among various high officials. After Khrushchev had honoured the scientists and the writers, Bulganin toasted the cinema, Mikoyan the theatre. Each toast was acknowledged immediately by a prominent representative of the group addressed. Music was assigned to a comparatively minor official, Pospelov, who said the expected, "We are happy to see that in new Soviet music there are many works of great social content, imbued with the lofty and heroic ideas of proletarian revolution. Our musicians achieved great successes at international contests. Soviet music lives a full and active life . . ."[12]

Shostakovich answered on behalf of the musicians. He said that, throughout the history of music, there had never been such remarkable conditions for the development of a composer's talent, skill, and art, as now in the Soviet Union. He praised all the "material care that the Party and Government give to the Soviet composers. I want to talk about the constant, paternal, attentive, and thoughtful guidance of our music." Finally, Shostakovich toasted "the Communist Party and its Leninist Central Committee, the Soviet Government, and the Soviet People."

One can be certain that the choice of Shostakovich (instead of Khrennikov) as spokesman was not accidental: having been the most prominent victim of the "paternal" attention of the Party back in 1936 and 1948, his speech symbolized complete reconciliation between the Party and the once-formalist composers, paving the way for the retraction by the Party which was to come a few months later.

Sceptics might doubt the sincerity of Shostakovich's word, but one cannot doubt the sincerity of his deeds. In celebration of the Fortieth Anniversary of the October Revolution—observed in 1957—Shostakovich presented his Eleventh Symphony, subtitled *The Year 1905*. It is a large-scale programmatic work depicting the first revolution—a composition that is the embodiment of Socialist Realism. Despite the tendency among Western critics to sneer at this timely work of Shostakovich, the "1905" Symphony represents to the Soviet people the fulfilment of the dream of a great Socialist art.

The other major musical work, prepared and presented for the Fortieth Anniversary, was a new opera by Khrennikov, *The Mother*, based on Gorky's novel. By coincidence, it also dealt with the revolutionary events of 1905. The opera was staged at the Bolshoi Theatre in Moscow on 26 October 1957, followed within a few days by premières in Gorky and Leningrad. *The Mother* was praised as an outstanding example of Soviet opera in the realist idiom, and it has established itself in the repertoire. It is an effective though uneven work. There are lyrical sections of appealing "folkishness" while others (like the flag-waving finale) strike the Western listener as commonplace and stereotyped. With innate theatre sense, Khrennikov draws on urban revolutionary songs of the period (a technique known as "historical concreteness") and invents his own tunes in a similar idiom. There are certain intimate qualities in this work which are overwhelmed by the grandiose production at the Bolshoi.

Thus, unlike the musical débâcle at the Thirtieth Anniversary in 1947, the celebration of 1957 was considered worthy of the great occasion. Other events of importance included a new production of Prokofiev's *War and Peace* at Moscow's Stanislavsky-Nemirovich-Danchenko Theatre, and a tuneful operetta by Kabalevsky. Some provincial opera theatres staged new works among which *The Gadfly* by Antonio Spadavecchia (a Russian of Italian parentage) had particular success in Perm. All in all, it appeared that Soviet ideology had conquered the field of music and that Socialist Realism was indeed capable of inspiring impressive works. For their devotion to the cause, Soviet composers had clearly deserved some sort of signal recognition.

This recognition came on 28 May 1958 when the Party's Central Committee adopted a resolution entitled "On Rectifying Errors in the Evaluation of the Operas *Great Friendship*, *Bogdan Khmelnitzky*, and *From All One's Heart*."[13] It was a rare document—rare because the Central Committee admitted "blatant errors" in some of its past evaluations and made a gesture of reconciliation. The censure of these operas (respectively by Muradeli, Dankevich, and Zhukovsky) was termed "incorrect and one-sided". The resolution went on to admit other injustices, "Gifted composers, comrades Shostakovich, Prokofiev, Khachaturian, Shebalin, Popov, Miaskovsky, and others, whose works at times revealed the wrong tendencies, were indiscriminately denounced as the representatives of a formalist anti-people trend ..."

These errors were explained in a curious way, "Some incorrect evaluations in the decree [of 1948] reflected J. V. Stalin's subjective attitude to certain works of art ... As we know, a very adverse influence was exercised on Stalin in these matters by Molotov, Malenkov, and Beria ..."

Yet Zhdanov, the true villain of the 1948 purge, was omitted from this list of scapegoats. While the 1958 decree acknowledged the excesses of the past, it stopped far short of nullifying the decree of 1948. On the contrary, great care was taken to point out that the 1948 decisions "had played, on the whole, a positive role in the subsequent development of Soviet music". There was renewed emphasis on the "inviolability of the fundamental principles expressed in the Party decrees on ideological questions".

Since the Resolution of 28 May 1958 could not encompass all the details of the musical situation, the editor of *Pravda* was officially instructed to publish an article based on the present decree "presenting a profound and comprehensive analysis of the fundamental questions concerning the development of Soviet music". This editorial appeared on 8 June 1958—a rambling, tortuous, and pedestrian restatement of the 1948 principles which were deemed essentially "correct"; the errors, admitted with reluctance, consisted merely in the "unjustifiably severe" evaluations of Soviet music. At the same time, however, *Pravda* was still concerned about the "alien and unsound phenomena in music" and warned against "indiscriminate rehabilitation of all the works justly criticized". Such "revisionist attempts" were resolutely rebuffed.

Nevertheless, the decree of 1958 was received with immense satisfaction by the musical community. It rehabilitated the leading composers (two of whom—Prokofiev and Miaskovsky—had died in the meantime); it improved the international standing of Soviet music that had been severely impaired by the shameful events of 1948; and it opened an era of new cordiality between the Party and the composers. Paradoxically, among the first to hail the new decree was Khrennikov who had been Zhdanov's right-hand man and who had implemented the policy set in 1948. Yet nobody expressed surprise.

The official reaction of Shostakovich was somewhat curious. His statement reads as if he had never been personally involved, and it was prominently published in *Pravda,*

"I have been deeply moved by the manifestations of the Communist Party's care and attention for Soviet music and Soviet composers. The Central Committee's Resolution of 28 May 1958 made me happy, first and foremost because it stresses the high place Soviet music rightly takes in the promotion of Socialist culture. The resolution wipes out the unfair and sweeping appraisals of various Soviet composers, and opens up wonderful prospects for the further advance of Soviet music along the path of realism. The exceedingly high ideological, moral, and ethical standard of this resolution delights us Soviet musicians and all the legions of admirers of Soviet music."[14]

The year 1958 had begun auspiciously with the signing, on 27 January, of the cultural exchange agreement between the United States and the Soviet Union. *Pravda* commented that "the Soviet people support the broadest possible cultural and scientific exchange" (certainly a change of attitude!) but warned that the exchange should not be used for resurrecting the "cold war".[15] The first American conductor to lead Soviet orchestras in Moscow and Kiev—in June 1958—was Leopold Stokowski. His programme included the Eleventh Symphony of Shostakovich and the *Adagio for Strings* by the American composer Samuel Barber. This "beautiful meditation" had to be repeated at the concert (wrote *Izvestia* on 18 June) because of the enthusiasm of the audience.

Another important event of 1958 was the establishment of the "International Tchaikovsky Contest" in Moscow. Before a distinguished international jury, violinists competed in March of that year, followed by pianists in April. The violin prize was won by the Russian Valeri Klimov while the pianists' contest ended in the sensational victory of a young American from Texas, Van Cliburn. No political machinations were involved: Cliburn's first prize was as unexpected as it was merited. For once, the professional jury and the Soviet audiences were unanimous. Soviet commentators pointed with pride to the Russian-type schooling of Cliburn as a student of Rosina Lhevinne, herself a pianist born and trained in pre-revolutionary Russia. Yet, Cliburn's interpretations did not always conform to Russian traditions. Among the judges was Genrikh Neigaus (Neuhaus), the celebrated pedagogue who taught Gilels and Richter. Asked whether he really liked Cliburn's Chopin playing, he answered, "I don't particularly like his Chopin, but I like *him*", and he called Cliburn "a pianist of genius".[16] Van Cliburn became an idol in Russia, and he has contributed more to mutual understanding and goodwill than many a diplomat.

The Soviet Union heard the Philadelphia Orchestra under Eugene Ormandy, the Boston Symphony under Charles Munch, the New York Philharmonic under Leonard Bernstein, later also the Cleveland Orchestra under George Szell. The United States became acquainted with the art of David Oistrakh, Emil Gilels, Svyatoslav Richter, Leonid Kogan, Mstislav Rostropovich, and the Moscow State Orchestra under Konstantin Ivanov. Perhaps, more of the truly "new" music of each country should have been performed during these visits (nothing more stale could be envisaged, for example, than the programmes of the Moscow Orchestra given in New York). On both sides, anything approaching "experimental" was avoided. It must be said that the visiting Americans were more generous in presenting Russian and Soviet music in the Soviet Union; it never seemed to have occurred to the Russians to study and perform some American music on their visits to the United States.

At times, a well-intentioned remark could produce a minor crisis. Thus, Bernstein's highly successful visit was marred by an incident involving his admiration for Stravinsky, a composer still "under suspicion" in the Soviet Union at that time. His Moscow programme included the Piano Concerto (played by Seymour Lipkin) and *Le Sacre du Printemps*. He felt it necessary to remark publicly that the *Sacre* had not been heard in Russia in over thirty years, which infuriated the Soviets—particularly since there was some truth in that observation.* "There are two Stravinskys, and I love them both," exclaimed Bernstein, addressing a Moscow audience. "Impossible," replied a Soviet critic, "the traits of decay and creativity in music are incompatible."[17] Nevertheless, the public discussion engendered by Bernstein's remarks began to pave the way to an eventual reconsideration of Stravinsky's role in Russian music—a reconsideration that culminated in the master's visit to Russia three years later, in 1962.

Among the first American composers to visit the Soviet Union were Roger Sessions, Peter Mennin, Roy Harris, and Ulysses Kay in the autumn of 1958, and Aaron Copland and Lukas Foss in the spring of 1960. In exchange, five Soviet composers—Khrennikov, Shostakovich, Kabalevsky, Dankevich, and Amirov came to the United States in the autumn of 1959; they were accompanied by the musicologist, Boris Yarustovsky. These were but the first of many similar exchanges. Composers, theorists, critics, and historians went back and forth; from the Soviet Union came, among others, Shchedrin, Karayev, Khachaturian, Keldysh, Martynov, and Nestyev. The United States sent the musicologists Gustave Reese, William Mitchell, Nicolas Slonimsky, and Boris Schwarz, the composers Norman dello Joio and Benjamin Lees. This list does not include the mutual visits of virtuosi and smaller ensembles. Similar exchanges were made with Great Britain and France; in fact, there was hardly a country in Europe that did not participate.

It goes without saying that the composers chosen for these mutual visits were screened very carefully. Within the first group of American composers, one—Roy Harris—was "conservative", two (Mennin and Kay) were moderately modern, and only Sessions could be considered "advanced". However, the music selected for performances in the Soviet Union was such as not to offend the Soviet "realist" taste, and Sessions was represented by his "Suite from the Black Maskers", an early, non-problematic work dating from 1923; besides, it had the advantage of having been written as incidental music to a play by a

* The allegation was refuted in the Soviet press: *Sacre* was performed in Tallinn "as recently as last year". But in Moscow . . . ?

Russian writer, Leonid Andreyev. None of the other compositions performed in honour of the American visitors—Harris' Fifth Symphony, Kay's Overture *Of New Horizons*, and Mennin's Sixth Symphony—was musically controversial.

The American composers visited Moscow, Leningrad, Kiev, and Tbilisi—four cities freely chosen by the Americans "because of their variety of musical life". They attended rehearsals and performances, they visited music schools and conservatories, they discussed music with fellow composers, and listened to each other's scores. Meeting Mr. Kay, a Negro composer and an official of the influential organization BMI (Broadcast Music Incorporated) must have been an enlightening experience for the Soviets whose propaganda customarily exploited the disadvantaged position of the American Negro. Kay's impressions of contemporary Soviet music were of particular interest, "To my taste, there was an undesirable sameness and a lack of experimentation noticeable in most of the contemporary scores we heard. Undoubtedly, these qualities reflect some official view which the passing visitor can only speculate about. However, various trends seem to indicate a coming change of view . . ."[18] The "official view"—as Kay eventually discovered—was of course Socialist Realism which "pervades all musical education, performances, productions, and composition". The Soviet composers "appreciated our comments, (but) they seemed reluctant to discuss aesthetic matters". As to the "change of view" envisaged by Kay, he may have been thinking of some music by younger Leningrad composers. There was, for example, a Violin Sonata by Galina Ustvolskaya which Roy Harris described as "dissonant from beginning to end" and "kind of ugly".[19]*

Kay's statement was not permitted to go unchallenged. The Soviets, highly sensitive to outside criticism, sent forth their expert, Yarustovsky, to answer Kay's charge of uniformity. In the form of an open letter to Kay, Yarustovsky gives his own views on Soviet music —namely that, because of the multi-national culture of the Soviet Union, there is a "genuine wealth of creative diversity". In fact, Yarustovsky counter-attacks by saying that "it is far more difficult to distinguish between two dodecaphonic composers", as he observed at Harvard's music department where he found avant-garde music "distressingly monotonous".[20] The controversy shifted from the *Atlantic Monthly* (which had published Yarustovsky's essay) to the pages of *Sovetskaya Muzyka*.[21] Kay replied that although he had heard works by composers of many nationalities, he found uniformity; there was talent

* Harris does not name Ustvolskaya but merely identifies the work as by "a woman composer from Leningrad".

and skill, but the use of national material seemed outworn and poorly organized, and he quoted a remarkable sentence from a letter of Tchaikovsky addressed to Taneyev (13 June 1885), "In composing a programme symphony I have a feeling as if I were a charlatan swindling the public; I am paying, not in hard currency, but with worthless credit coupons."*

Yarustovsky was quick to reply that the same Tchaikovsky once said, "Broadly speaking, *all* music is programmatic." All composers in the Soviet Union are united in addressing themselves to a broad public while young American composers deny the need for a public. Naturally, the controversy led nowhere, but Yarustovsky, being a skilful professional writer, succeeded in sounding more convincing.

Roy Harris was visibly impressed by the organization of the arts in the Soviet Union. Compared to the United States, the Soviet cultural effort seemed stronger and more widespread, higher education was more highly prized and more prestigious. He found that Soviet life radiated a "dynamics of atmosphere" that imparts itself to the people. "Ballet, opera, drama are not only well supported by the State but enthusiastically received by large masses of the population. In Tashkent, in Central Asia, we found a city of 400,000 people with six or seven theatres, one of which gives 200 performances of ballet and opera each year to a consistently filled hall."[22] Such a situation made Harris think of the uncomfortable conditions of the arts in the United States where orchestras and opera houses go begging for private contributions year after year.

As for monetary rewards for composers, the American visitors found out that there was an established pay scale for musical works; for example, an established composer will receive 100,000 roubles** for an opera commissioned by the Bolshoi Theatre. In fact, this was nothing new; a creative "pay scale" was established as early as the 1930's. On the other hand, the American violinist Sidney Harth—also a visitor to the Soviet Union—was struck by the fact that the average weekly pay of a Soviet symphony musician was about fifty roubles a week, roughly one-fourth of what an American musician would receive. This may be true, but it is deceptive. The Soviet musician is paid on a yearly basis while most American symphony musicians have only seasonal employment. The Soviet musician pays very little rent, he has free medical services and pension as well as paid vacations, but he must give his full

---

* That same letter to Taneyev contains the sentence, "No! it is a thousand times pleasanter to write without any programme." Yet he composed a great many programmatic works. See p. 221.

** This is an inflated figure prior to the revaluation of the Soviet currency.

time to the orchestra, and rehearsal hours are unlimited. Harth found willing co-operation and much enthusiasm in Soviet orchestras, particularly with guest conductors, but the discipline was lax and the ensemble less than perfect.

It is useful to compare the Russian visit of the American composers with that of the Soviet composers to the United States in the autumn of 1959 (22 October to 21 November). The tour of the Americans was under the control of the Soviet Composers' Union and its various local affiliates. As Harris recalled, "I certainly was not prepared for the highly organized Composers' Union which was our host in Moscow, Leningrad, Kiev, and Tbilisi. Each chapter of the Composers' Union differed according to its regional customs and officials, but each chapter was . . . well able to plan and develop the long conferences, discussions, parties, and dinners which consumed our days so swiftly."[23]

The American tour of the Russians was in the hands of the U.S. State Department in Washington, but the organization was much less tight. "The five composers were exuberantly handed around from one hospitable group to another, and many last-minute adjustments were made for mutual convenience and enjoyment," wrote an American reporter.[24] If the reception was casual, there was certainly nothing casual about the tightly-knit group of the Soviet visitors. Khrennikov was the official spokesman, and they met every morning for briefing sessions. His power was demonstrated when he caused the cancellation of a radio appearance on *Face the Nation* over the Columbia network by the two most prominent members, Shostakovich and Kabalevsky. Although both had accepted, Khrennikov demanded that the entire delegation appear on the programme, whereupon the network withdrew the invitation. *The New York Times* remarked that "Khrennikov has been known to have prevented Soviet composers from talking freely with American music critics visiting the Soviet Union."[25]

Ultimately, Khrennikov had his way: a broadcast with the entire delegation took place, under NBC auspices, in November 1959. The American participants were the composers Harris, Kay, Howard Hanson, and Alan Shulman; the moderator was Nicolas Slonimsky. Kay repeated his "impression of sameness" with regard to Soviet music and added, "The question is, Does this condition grow out of the Soviet pre-occupation with national idioms in their work?" There is some truth in Kay's observation: while the basic musical material is varied, the impression of sameness arises because of the technical similarities of treatment and development. The twenty-odd conservatories of the Soviet Union provide the same "basic training", whether the budding composer is an Uzbek or a Tartar. Thus, two essentially different folk tunes might be harmonized according to Balakirev or orchestrated according to Rimsky-Korsakov, and of course subject to the ideology of Socialist Realism. As the national cultures grow more self-reliant and become increasingly aware of their indigenous heritage, the dependence on the Russian-type academic schooling will undoubtedly decrease, if such a development is deemed permissible by the Party authorities.

The multi-national aspect of Soviet music was emphasized in the choice of the Soviet Composers' delegation; two of the five delegates belonged to "minorities": Dankevich represented the Ukraine, Amirov his native Azerbaijan. The three other members—Khrennikov, Kabalevsky, and Shostakovich—were "Russians", as was the critic Yarustovsky. All made an excellent impression. Kabalevsky (the only one with some command of the English language) was found to be the "friendliest and most extrovert of the six, qualities also characteristic of his music". Shostakovich was described as "highly nervous, a chain-smoker with darting eyes and fidgeting hands, ill at ease most of the time".[26] Reporters recalled his 1949 visit to the United States as "peace" delegate when he had accused America of "warmongering". Shostakovich was asked by reporters whether his opinion had changed. He answered diplomatically, through an interpreter, that "he had always been friendly towards the United States" and the "talented American people".[27] The situation in 1949 differed from the one today, he added, and his critical remarks of ten years ago "cannot be related to the whole American people".

Khrennikov, as head of the delegation, seemed at times cold and officious, particularly when it came to politically sensitive situations. In personal dealings, however, he was friendly and co-operative.* The choice of Yarustovsky to represent Soviet musicology was a happy one, for he proved to be well-informed, articulate, and always ready to contribute intelligent comments. Amirov, the youngest of the group, seemed withdrawn and somewhat colourless, but Dankevich made up for it with his beaming smile, radiating good-will. As the composer of the opera *Bogdan Khmelnitzky*, censured in 1951 and rehabilitated in 1953, he seemed to represent a new era of mutual understanding. In fact, the American visit of the Soviet musicians was a love feast: the Americans overwhelmed the visitors with hospitality, both social and musical. Leading American orchestras—Philadelphia, Boston, New York, Washington among others—included works by the visiting composers on their programmes. As it so often happens, the provincial audiences proved more enthusiastic than the sophisticated capital cities.

* The author is indebted to Khrennikov for an introductory letter which greatly facilitated his initial musical contacts in the U.S.S.R.

In Louisville, the smallest city* visited by the Russians, the rapport between audience and visitors was most evident.[28]

Audiences and critics in the major cities were more discriminating and less easily pleased. It became soon apparent that the Soviet visitors had little of musical substance to offer. Only Shostakovich had brought something new—his Cello Concerto Op. 107, first performed in Leningrad on 4 October 1959 and given its première in Philadelphia on 6 November, with Rostropovich as soloist in both cases. Rostropovich also made a recording of the Concerto with the Philadelphia Orchestra under Ormandy, and the composer was present during the session. Fairly new was also his Tenth Symphony, played in the composer's presence in Washington. As for the other Soviet works presented on the tour, they were not new in terms of chronology and old-fashioned in terms of style. Khrennikov's First Symphony was his graduation piece of 1935, while he was still at the Moscow Conservatory, and his Incidental Music to *Much Ado About Nothing* dated from the same period. Somewhat more recent were Kabalevsky's Cello Concerto of 1949 and his Third Piano Concerto of 1954, but they belonged to the "youth concerto" series and were kept deliberately simple. Was there nothing more weighty, more challenging that the Soviet visitors could have brought across the ocean? Apparently not, for one must assume that these programmes were assembled after much deliberation.

The American music world gave a cordial reception to five Soviet composers, only to realize that Soviet music seemed to be caught in a cul-de-sac, that the much-vaunted Socialist art had little to offer to the West, that the Western listener could not relate to the distant world of, say, Kurdistan, even in symphonic disguise.

Not only was much of the music presented by the Russians found disappointing, but the exchange of ideas with the visitors was narrow in scope. This became evident in Los Angeles, during a forum dealing with music of young American (mostly local Californian) composers. The correspondent of *Musical America* vented his disappointment,

> "Shostakovich's views can best be described as cautious and non-committal . . . All six (Soviet) musicians exhibited a conformity of thought in discussions of representatively contemporary music. Questions about Stravinsky's later style, Berg, Webern, and their experimenting offshoots, while not put aside with ideological

* Louisville (population ca. 320,000) is the largest city in Kentucky and the seat of a university. Its orchestra is publicly supported and has acquired an international reputation by commissioning and recording contemporary music.

labels, were treated gingerly and evasively . . . In answer to a purported trend towards 12-tone music in Russia, Shostakovich stated flatly that 'there is none'. Another stock statement was that atonality and musical experimentation in general had been exhaustively exploited in Russia in the 1920's and 1930's. (This recalls similar observations made by members of the Bolshoi Ballet about abstract dance trends in America.)"[29]

In keeping with the Soviet policy not to show any astonishment at what was shown abroad, Shostakovich remarked, rather arrogantly, "You must not think that we learned anything about the musical life of your country we did not know before coming here."

At a luncheon given on 18 November (1959) by the Music Critics' Circle, the question of official criticism in the Soviet Union was raised. Kabalevsky had to admit that there had been some injustice in the past, but that these matters had been rectified and that the retractions had been given wide publicity. "We do not intend to say that our life and the life of our art is a development without any kind of contradiction. But we are never afraid to recognize unfairness. Life can never be developed without errors and exaggerations."[30] Shostakovich did not want to be drawn into any controversy; questioned on the matter of *Lady Macbeth*, he declined to comment because he was "too tired". Dankevich, on the other hand, adhered without hesitation to the Party line; the criticism of his opera *Bogdan Khmelnitzky*—he said—had "enabled him to improve the opera which has since been restored to favour". The musicologist Yarustovsky represented a critic's point of view. He said that critics should be free to write anything except "an untruth". This, of course, is a pompous platitude for no respectable critic will deliberately print lies. Yarustovsky failed to mention that, to speak the truth as he sees it, is not "without peril" for the Soviet critic.*

There is a basic difference between Western and Soviet criticism: whereas Western criticism represents the subjective opinion of an individual critic, Soviet criticism is a collective opinion expressed in the words of an individual critic. Particularly in Moscow and Leningrad (the "opinion makers" of the Soviet Union), there is a consensus of opinion that crystallizes rather subtly after the presentation of a new composition or the appearance of a new performer or ensemble. There is never any hurry to write a review since the Soviet daily papers, as a rule, do not carry instantaneous critical reviews, only summaries of important events. *Sovetskaya Kultura* or *Sovetskaya Muzyka* might delay reviews for weeks or even months. However, when there is no

---

* See the remarks of Khubov and Shostakovich, pp. 304 and 303.

clear consensus "at the top" of the establishment, critics might remain silent altogether, and no review will appear. Even a work considered outstanding today—the ballet *Spartacus* by Khachaturian—was greeted by a "chorus of silence" in the Soviet press. These conditions were well known to Yarustovsky when he spoke in New York in the autumn of 1959. In fact, the neglect of music by the daily and weekly publications in the Soviet Union had been a chief topic of complaint at the Moscow Conference on Musical Criticism which convened in Moscow in May 1958.

When Yarustovsky spoke of critical "untruths", he may have had in mind the frequent Soviet complaint that foreign visitors often published "distorted" reports about musical life in Russia. A case in question was Leonard Bernstein who visited the Soviet Union in September 1959, at the head of the New York Philharmonic. Bernstein, it was said, was full of praise about Russian musical life while he was in Moscow, but "changed his tune the minute he was out of the country".[31] Knowing Soviet sensitivity, it may well be that the "establishment" over-reacted to Bernstein's casual criticism. It often happens that whatever displeases Soviet officialdom is branded immediately as capitalist lies.

Accuracy was also on Khrennikov's mind when he promised, at the critics' luncheon in New York, that his account of the American visit of the Soviet composers would contain "not a word of untruth". The promised report appeared in *Pravda* on 11 December 1959 over the signatures of Khrennikov and Shostakovich, and it filled nearly three columns.[32] Praise and criticism were judiciously mixed. Clearly, the Soviet visitors were more impressed by the conservative characteristics of American music than by the ultra-modern trends. They attacked the practice and teaching of twelve-tone technique and asserted that this style had virtually no followers among the old and middle generation of American composers. Here, the authors were obviously in error which only proves that not every error is necessarily a deliberate lie. They simply lacked the information that older composers like Wallingford Riegger, Roger Sessions, Milton Babbitt, Aaron Copland, Ross Lee Finney and others were using (or had used) dodecaphonic techniques. The Soviet visitors were obviously stung by the frequent criticism that twelve-tone music was "banned" in the Soviet Union; their explanation was that "it is liked neither by Soviet audiences nor by musicians", hence it remained unplayed. In their opinion, the widespread use of the twelve-tone system by young American composers resulted in works "largely scholastic and without artistic merit". Yarustovsky reiterated, "I vote against the gloomy and stereotyped expressionism of some youthful followers of the contemporary musical avant-garde in America. Their sprinklings of sound, with all their apparent novelty, are distressingly monotonous."[33]

The Soviet visitors also failed to understand the American system of musical education, much of which is concentrated at colleges and universities, in contrast to the Soviet system which relies exclusively on the conservatories and secondary music schools. They could not understand that a student could enter college at the age of seventeen or eighteen and "elect" music as a major subject with comparatively limited professional preparation. Hence, the curriculum of a music school like the Juilliard made more sense to the visitors than, for example, the course of a "music major" at Columbia or Harvard.

I happened to be present when Kabalevsky visited the composition class of Professor Otto Luening at New York's Columbia University. At the piano sat young Charles Wuorinen, at the time one of the most talented young "rebels". Kabalevsky asked many questions. He wanted to know the extent of prior preparation in music theory before a student was admitted to Columbia's Music Department. "It varies," answered Luening. "And if the student is not sufficiently prepared?" inquired Kabalevsky. "He'll have to make up the deficiencies," parried Luening. "What happens if the preparation is still not satisfactory?" insisted Kabalevsky. "Then," said Luening with a wry smile, "we take him to the woodshed." Unsure of the colloquial answer, Kabalevsky and the interpreter exchanged puzzled glances. It took some time to disentangle the misunderstanding. During the same session, one Soviet visitor remarked critically that the young Americans were taught "techniques" without being taught when and how to use them. The Soviet visitors failed to understand that the "freedom of choice" was as essential to the American educational system as was the "guided choice" to the Soviet system.

Upon their return from the United States, the Soviet composers must have realized that—from the musical point of view—their journey had been a near-failure. No amount of hospitality, oratory, and good-will could disguise the fact that the music presented by the visitors was of little interest to American audiences, with the exception of Shostakovich. But even his Cello Concerto did not win approval as unanimous as the earlier Violin Concerto. And what happened to the younger generation of composers? What would be the future direction of Soviet music, now that the official strictures had apparently been relaxed? These were the questions asked not only in America but even in Communist Poland where, in 1956, the composers had been freed of the dogmatic shackles of Socialist Realism.

Soviet visitors to the Warsaw Autumn Festival—composers, performers, and critics—felt increasingly estranged from their Polish
comrades, and they expressed concern about the newest course of
Polish music. The Poles rejected all advice somewhat contemptuously.
Shostakovich, interviewed by a Polish publication in the autumn of
1959, said that he was "... very much worried that certain Polish composers, particularly the younger ones, cling to the 'revelation' of
dodecaphony, seeing in it the musical art of the future. I should sincerely
like to warn them away from this infatuation and advise them to dedicate themselves attentively and feelingly to the national tradition of
Polish music, the tradition of the great Polish classics, Chopin and
Szymanowski . . . The Western avant-garde music played at the
Warsaw Festival is contrary to human nature and to the lofty human
art of music."[34]
These words show Shostakovich's growing estrangement from
Western musical modernism which he opposed and denounced with
increasing intensity. On these matters he was in full agreement with
the guiding spirits of the Composers' Union—Khrennikov, Kabalevsky,
Khachaturian. They set up a barrier against any "liberalization" that
would move in the direction of dodecaphony or any other advanced
musical experimentation practised in the West. They held the line
against their own home-grown "avant-garde" for as long as possible.
As for the Polish composers, they were tired of gratuitous advice—
such as came from Shostakovich and others—and asserted their newly-
won independence. The Warsaw Festival, given each autumn since
1956, became a citadel of modern music. Already two major Polish
composers, Witold Lutoslawski and Krzystof Penderecki, have emerged in this new climate of cultural freedom, and more are to come.
Almost like a challenge to Shostakovich, the Warsaw Festival performed one of his early works still "banned" in Russia—the orchestral
suite from the opera *The Nose*. The Warsaw Festival programmes also
played host to younger Soviet composers who could not easily get a
hearing at home, among them Andrei Volkonsky and Galina Ustvolskaya.
At musicological meetings, the Poles also showed their independence
and were not averse to twitting their Soviet colleagues. Thus, Nestyev,
the foremost Russian expert on Prokofiev, was put on the defensive at a
joint session of Polish and Soviet musicologists held in Warsaw in
December 1959. The topic of the session was "Prokofiev", and Nestyev
spoke on "The Significance of Prokofiev in the Music of the Twentieth
Century". Polish musicologists submitted eight papers representing
various opposing views. It was the Prokofiev of *pre*-Soviet days, so one
Polish argument ran, who had made a truly significant contribution to

modern music—at a time when he was in conflict with surrounding society, not later when he conformed to Soviet environment. Some young Polish scholars dismissed Prokofiev disdainfully as an "academician" and denied his significance for our time. In rebuttal, Nestyev published an article in *Sovetskaya Muzyka* entitled "The Controversy about Prokofiev".[35] He took issue with the "aesthetic aberrations" of his Polish colleagues, many of whom he termed as admirers of such "liquidators of art" as Boulez and Stockhausen, and ascribed the adverse Polish reaction to Prokofiev to the fact that his late works were rarely performed in Poland. In his choice use of invectives, Nestyev shows himself as a past master, and there is no inkling of any "thaw" in his style or viewpoint.

The attack on Prokofiev by fellow Communists was only one more sign of the gradual erosion of Soviet prestige in the field of contemporary music. The more the Soviet composers thundered against modernism, the more the Western world became impatient with the hollow phraseology emanating from the headquarters of the Composers' Union. "Present-day modernism and national colour are incompatible!" declared Shostakovich[36]—a statement as true as it is outdated. The British critic Arthur Jacobs, who visited the Soviet Union early in 1960, summarized his muted impressions under the heading "Music and Myth in Moscow",

> "As composers, Soviet musicians are still straight-jacketed by ideology imposed from the top. Radical experiment is frowned on. Concerts . . . at which such fertilizing agents as serial music and electronic composition are allowed free play, are missing in Moscow. The group of middle-aged-to-elderly composers and musicologists who officially received me at the Composers' Union condemned all such radicalism as 'avant-gardismus'. This is the mythological monster created in Moscow to represent all non-tonal experiments from Schoenberg to Boulez . . ."[37]

The situation in Soviet music in the late 1950's was indeed somewhat paradoxical. In 1953, shortly after the death of Stalin, artists like Khachaturian and Shostakovich were among the first to plead for less "petty tutelage". However, within a brief time both had joined the tutelary authorities and became outspoken opponents of radical innovations. What was sorely lacking in the Composers' Union was bold, creative leadership; it could not come from the "middle-aged-to-elderly" composers who continued to control the "establishment". In 1958, Khrushchev had exhorted all artists to display "greater daring in their quest". But the composers could not agree as to how musically to express such "daring". They seemed to agree, though, that the young generation had to be protected from the "pitfalls" of Western-style modernism. If there was a change of policy, it merely consisted in making foreign scores and taped performances accessible for study purposes. For the intellectually curious, this was a welcome development: at union headquarters (particularly in Moscow and Leningrad) sessions were arranged to listen to the latest Western imports of musical modernism. But the warnings against imitating such "deviations" were redoubled.

At the Twenty-first Party Congress, which opened in January 1958, the arts were exhorted to contribute their full share towards the building of Communism,

> "The building of Communism . . . offers unexampled scope for the fullest, comprehensive development of all the creative potentialities and talents of man. Literature and the arts, which are actively helping to mould the man of Communist society, play an important part . . ."

Soviet science had been triumphant: the first sputnik was launched in 1957. Would the arts be equal to their task?

> "A big role will be played by our Soviet intelligentsia which— together with the working class and the collective-farm peasantry —will make a worthy contribution to the cause of building Communism."[38]

The flattering references to the arts intelligentsia were exposed in all their hollowness by the *Dr. Zhivago* "affair" in that same year 1958. Disagreement about Pasternak's novel had been smouldering since July 1956, when the author submitted his manuscript to the journal *Novyi Mir*. The letter of rejection was not published until 25 October 1958. In the meantime, the book had been published in Italian in November 1957, in English in September 1958. The Swedish Academy conferred the Nobel Prize on Pasternak in October 1958. His initial acceptance and eventual rejection of the prize created a world-wide furore. The abuse suffered by Pasternak at home exposed Soviet cultural policy in all its narrow-minded dogmatism; the incident did more to tarnish the cultural image of the Soviet State than anything that had happened since the Zhdanov purges. Pasternak died in 1960, and his literary reputation has been rehabilitated since then. But *Dr. Zhivago* remains unpublished in the Soviet Union.

Musically, the year 1958 did not bring forth any masterpieces. The chief contribution of Shostakovich was the operetta *Moskva-Cheremushki*, dealing humorously with the housing shortage in Moscow. It has no claim to immortality. When the Third Plenum of the Composers' Union's directorate convened in December 1958 to review the musical accomplishments of the year, no one seemed fully satisfied. Khrennikov sounded concerned, Kabalevsky was displeased. Among the many compositions of younger composers played at the Plenum, only a few good works stood out—by Shchedrin, Eshpai, Nikolayev, Pakhmutova. Much of the music, however, was afflicted by so-called "typical errors": pallor, pessimism, and inexpressive melodic language. What was lacking, in the opinion of Soviet critics, was a representation of true Soviet reality. The failures were attributed not only to the composers but also the weakness of musical criticism and the indecisive educational policies of the conservatories. Clearly, the leadership of the Composers' Union was uneasy. "None of our previous Plenums has taken place in such a tense atmosphere as the one this year. The Communist Party calls on us to perfect our art", exhorted Khrennikov.

The following year—1959—was marked by a huge success: the *Pathetic Oratorio*, on texts by Mayakovsky, composed by Georgi Sviridov. The work was awarded the Lenin Prize for 1959. More effective than profound, it is nevertheless a striking composition, "an enormously dynamic, vigorous, and inventive 'poem' of the Revolution and Civil War", in the opinion of Werth.[39] Sviridov will be remembered as the composer of the "Yesenin" cycle for voice and orchestra, a rather nostalgic work.* The *Pathetic Oratorio* captures the flamboyance of Mayakovsky's texts—inciting, declamatory, almost poster-like, full of the aggressive revolutionary spirit of the 1920's. Some of the movements are melodramatic and somewhat crude, others are introspective and moving. Of the seven movements, the sixth is—perhaps—the most interesting: entitled *Dialogue with Comrade Lenin*, it combines song, recitative, and speech in an ingenious manner. A male solo voice is juxtaposed to a full chorus which is an active participant—sometimes subdivided into male or female voices, sometimes thundering forth in massive outbursts. The *Pathetic Oratorio* is not "exportable"; it is wedded to the Soviet ideology. Its success depends on the complete receptivity of the audience, linguistically and ideologically.

Soviet critics were ecstatic about the new work. Kremlev called it ". . . a work full of optimism and tremendous conviction. A firm, unshakeable faith in victory and the joyous realization of the beauty

---

* See p. 294.

of the new world are the keynote of the oratorio. The *Pathetic Oratorio* is an innovational work. The author has striven for simplicity, clarity, and the true expression of the progressive ideas of his time."[40]

Fellow composers were equally impressed. Shaporin felt that Sviridov, after having been a "faithful pupil" of Shostakovich for so long, had now developed "a very original style of his own". Kabalevsky praised the "very contemporaneous" sound of the *Pathetic Oratorio*, ". . . not only because Mayakovsky's poem is directed towards the future, but also because in the whole music of that talented, masterly work, we feel the full-blooded pulse of contemporaneousness, its joyous breath and vital contemporary idiom."[41]

Sviridov's *Pathetic Oratorio* was performed at the Fifth Plenum of the Composers' Union which opened on 18 January 1960. Other new works heard on that occasion were new cello concertos by Shostakovich and Vainberg, and an effective violin concerto by Khrennikov, all completed in the year 1959. Eshpai's Symphony No. 1 was also well received; it is a comparatively short work in two movements that bears an epigraph by Mayakovsky, "One must tear the joy out of future days." A violin sonata by the Armenian Arno Babadzhanyan was a pleasant surprise because it broke away from the conventional "folkishness" and spoke in a fresh musical idiom.

The Fifth Plenum stood under the motto *Music and Contemporaneousness* and the key address, by Kabalevsky, was devoted to this topic.[42]

Kabalevsky was not concerned with musical technicalities but with the emotional climate of Soviet music, its topicality, its relationship to the contemporary Socialist viewpoint. He spoke against the "exaggerated idea of the importance of tragedy" and criticized the young composers who, without having experienced tragedy, produced "falsely tragic" works. An exception was Shostakovich "whose really tragic and amazingly powerful symphonies" reflect the "actual tragic conflicts of our time". But in general, Kabalevsky stated clearly that "tragedy is not the sphere of art adapted to the main features that are characteristic of our country's life and of the spirit of our people". Among the characteristic features he lists, first of all, strength—"the strength of ideological conviction, of intellect, feeling, and will." In second place comes optimism—"the firm belief in the future and revolutionary aspiration . . . born of the Socialist outlook".

Kabalevsky's thesis, his warning against the over-emphasis of tragedy, was directed primarily towards the younger composers who, perhaps, were infected by Shostakovich's Tenth Symphony. Kabalevsky is careful to assure us that "no limits are set to Socialist realistic art". But he qualifies the statement immediately by saying, "The people expect us to give them, first and foremost, works that are connected with the image of the contemporary man, his rich inner life, and clear optimistic outlook on the future." Of course, he means the Soviet man, in the "ideal human society—Communism".

From this prejudiced position, Kabalevsky proceeds to criticize a number of works which he finds "falsely tragic". Among them is the oratorio *Nagasaki* by Alfred Shnitke, the string quartets by Oganesyan ("In Memoriam A. Isaakyan") and Salmanov ("In memory of Comrades Killed in the War"), and the *Cosmic Symphony* by Ryaets. To the Western observer, Kabalevsky's evaluations are entirely unrelated to the quality of the music itself. One can only pity the Soviet composer whose self-expression is subject to such dogmatic and irrelevant limitations.

Kabalevsky's address reflected the official attitude of the Composers' Union. While any intent to "dictate" to the young composers was disavowed, there was certainly a desire to direct them. The musical establishment favoured a sort of orderly evolution, non-experimental and independent of any Western-style musical "extremism". But the days of this type of tutelage were numbered. While the Composers' Union was influential, it was not omnipotent. Its role in the choice of repertoire was, at best, advisory, and many orchestras, opera and ballet companies acted with considerable independence. Nor did the Composers' Union have any influence on the repertoire played by visiting ensembles and individual artists. But whenever the Composers' Union extended invitations to foreign composers, safe, middle-of-the-road composers were the favoured guests. When, in 1962, Stravinsky was invited, it was a "calculated risk" which proved highly successful.

Preceding this historic visit were several years of a gradual widening of musical horizons in the Soviet Union, mainly through an expansion of the modern repertoire. Not only were long-neglected works by Soviet composers re-introduced into the programmes, but foreign visitors performed music as yet unknown in the Soviet Union.

Among the Soviet compositions that re-entered the concert repertoire were the Second Symphony of Khachaturian and the Eighth Symphony of Shostakovich, both "war symphonies" and both neglected since the 1940's. Even more significant was the belated première of Shostakovich's Fourth Symphony on 30 December 1961. This work, it will be recalled, was completed in 1936, but the score was withdrawn by the composer on the eve of the planned first performance because he was embroiled in the *Lady Macbeth* controversy. Now, after twenty-five years, the Fourth Symphony was finally heard and proved to be a pivotal work in the evolution of Shostakovich. This première was followed, barely a year later, by the long-awaited revival of the opera *Lady Macbeth of Mtsensk*, presented in Moscow in December 1962, in a somewhat revised version as *Katerina Izmailova*.

Many rediscoveries were made in the Prokofiev repertoire. The opera *Semyon Kotko*—subjected to so much vicious criticism in 1940—was re-staged in Perm in 1960. The response was gratifying, and Marina Sabinina wrote in *Sovetskaya Muzyka*, "*Semyon Kotko* is an opera of the most brilliant individual characterizations and deep socio-historical conclusions . . . In the richness and unexpectedness of contrasts, in the abundance of the various 'layers' of action, *Semyon Kotko* surpasses all the mature operas of Prokofiev . . ."[43]

This was followed, also in 1960, by the vindication of Prokofiev's last opera, *The Story of a Real Man*, so crudely rejected in 1948. Yarustovsky reported on the production at the Bolshoi Theatre in Moscow, "The hit of the current season . . . is Prokofiev's last opera . . . It is written in simple language, but retains all of Prokofiev's original manner . . ."[44]

These belated accolades are all the more poignant if one recalls the agony and humiliation suffered by Prokofiev in connection with these two operas. They represented his affirmation of Soviet reality; he had planned them with particular care, he defended them with eloquence, and he was shaken, though unbowed, by the rejection.

Other works of Prokofiev reappeared, particularly those of the controversial Parisian period. Rozhdestvensky conducted the Second Symphony of 1925—perhaps the harshest-sounding work of that period, fashioned of "steel and cement"—and it was received with respect and interest. Gradually, Prokofiev assumed the stature of a modern classic, and the elaborate reservations made in Nestyev's biographical volume were invalidated one by one. By 1963, when the tenth anniversary of Prokofiev's death was commemorated, the acceptance of his greatness was complete. Nestyev himself edited a collection of articles dedicated to Prokofiev which opens with his essay, *The Classic of the Twentieth Century*.[45]

Not all revivals went so smoothly. Thus, the Second Symphony of Gavril Popov (one of the composers singled out for censure in 1948) was to be played in Moscow on 14 January 1958, after years of neglect, but the performance was suddenly cancelled. This provoked an angry protest from the old master, Shaporin, who wrote a letter to *Pravda* under the heading, "For a Respectful Attitude Towards Artists",

"The programme for the symphony concert at the Conservatory Hall on 14 January listed Popov's Second Symphony. This work by a Soviet composer, which in my opinion is interesting both in plan and execution, has not been performed for a long time. Hence the initiative shown by the conductor, U.S.S.R. People's Artist Nathan Rakhlin, in reviving a half-forgotten symphony, deserved high praise.

Imagine the surprise of the audience and the composer, who attended the concert, when his symphony suddenly and without explanations was replaced by another work. It seems to me that such a disrespectful attitude towards a work by a Soviet composer should be severely condemned."

Whether the reasons for the cancellation were artistic or political was never fully explained, nor did Shaporin's letter help Popov's career. But the fact that *Pravda* printed the letter indicated that artistic matters were not to be left to the whims of some minor officials.

The expansion of the Soviet repertoire was matched by an influx of foreign music and musicians. One must realize that the Soviet Union had been virtually cut off from Western music since the mid-1930's. Not only were Soviet musicians and audiences unfamiliar with foreign music composed since that time, but an entire generation of Russians had never enjoyed the opportunity of hearing foreign music composed since the First World War. From now on, there was an ever-growing demand to hear as much of the twentieth-century repertoire as possible —and permissible. As yet, not all contemporary foreign music was considered acceptable. For some inexplicable reason, Arnold Schoenberg (who had been so warmly received in Petersburg in 1912) remained on the "banned" list longer than anyone else, and with him the chief representatives of the dodecaphonic school.

Orchestras and solo performers who visited the Soviet Union under the cultural exchange agreements with Western nations greatly contributed to the propagation of hitherto unknown music. Thus, the pianist Glenn Gould played music by Webern, the violinist Isaac Stern brought works by Leon Kirchner, Robert Shaw conducted an early chorus by Schoenberg—and also reacquainted the Russian audiences with Bach's B-minor Mass. Foreign composers—singly and in groups —were invited to visit the Soviet Union as guests of the Composers' Union, and it was customary to honour the guests by performances of some of their works, be it orchestral or chamber music. The Soviet custom of observing anniversary dates was extended, in 1960, to the 100th birthday of Gustav Mahler who was commemorated by a jubilee concert, with Shostakovich and Igor Boelza as speakers. As a gesture towards the United States (and towards a composer very much appreciated by the Russians), Samuel Barber was honoured by a concert on his fiftieth birthday.

In addition, regularly scheduled auditions of recorded foreign music were arranged by the Composers' Union for its members. For example, the Union's Information Bulletin 1960:1 listed five programmes with music by the Americans Paul Creston (Symphonies Nos. 2 and 3), Copland (Appalachian Spring), and Peter Mennin (Symphony No. 6), as well as by Bartok and Hans Werner Henze. Other recorded programmes, presented twice weekly, included the names of Boulez, Schaeffer, Britten, Alban Berg, Honegger, late Stravinsky, and Barber. This is an amazingly diversified list, though one must remember that these were "closed" performances, accessible only to professionals. The Composers' Union took special care of its "musicological" wing by printing a quarterly digest of foreign musical opinions in Russian translation; this was particularly important since foreign journals are virtually unobtainable by individual Soviet citizens. Despite the conservatism of its directorate, the Union contributed significantly to the lifting of the musical barriers separating East and West.

All in all, the "information gap" that existed prior to 1960, narrowed within a short time. In the course of a visit to Moscow and Leningrad in the spring of 1960, I found that the leading critics and composers were well aware of musical trends and events abroad. The broad audiences, however, remained ignorant of modernist music. In fact, it is even questionable to what extent young music students were acquainted with it at the time. This point is brought out in the report of Aaron Copland, who visited the Soviet Union in March–April 1960, under the exchange programme: "I told the professors . . . that when I listened to the music of their students, I found it difficult to imagine whole areas of contemporary music, the very existence of which could hardly be suspected from the evidence their compositions supplied."[46]

The professors' feelings were hurt which only testifies to their naiveté. For it is true that, around 1960, much of Soviet music (and not only that composed by students!) remained strangely untouched by twentieth century trends. As Copland remarked, Soviet music considered "controversial" would come closest to pieces like the *Scythian Suite* (1914) by Prokofiev or other "dynamically propelled" music of the 1920's. (This would include also some early Bartok—an observation made by Stravinsky.) Such a style would be considered "old hat" in the West, said Copland—a remark that left his Soviet listeners incredulous. As an example of the limited information available to students, Copland cited the private complaint of a conservatory student that, in a one-year history course on Western music, only two hours were devoted to contemporary music of the West. (This information must however be evaluated in the light of the entire curriculum: specialized courses on twentieth-century music of the West are offered at the Moscow and Leningrad Conservatories).

Copland found signs of "active propaganda" to "discredit twelve-tone atonality and what is referred to as 'electronic noises' when composed as *absolute* music". He found, however, that any dissonance became permissible when its use seemed justified by some literary story content. This was confirmed by the composer Lukas Foss who was Copland's companion on the Soviet trip. "The dissonance of the explosion was all that one might have anticipated," wrote Foss in describing the oratorio by a young Moscow composer dealing with the first atomic bomb. But these were exceptions rather than the rule. In general, Soviet music preserved that typical "Russian" flavour, as Copland remarked, "I was hardly prepared . . . to discover to what degree Russian music is exclusively Russian. There is an extraordinary and all-pervasive unity of expressive ideal . . ."

And yet, there was a cautious groundswell of interest in Western modernist techniques. "Soviet composers", observed Foss, "are paralleling technical experiments in the West, and although serial music, electronic music and similar avant-garde movements are not current in Russia, they are known and studied privately." Publicly, however, none of it was noticeable around 1960. Soviet critics, whenever questioned on the absence of avant-garde performances, had a stock answer, "Our performers are not keen on studying this type of music, and our audiences are not interested in hearing it."

Copland and Foss spent four weeks in the Soviet Union on a cultural exchange tour. Copland was known as an old friend of the Soviet Union, and his activities within the American-Soviet Friendship Society during the Second World War were well remembered. Foss, then in his thirties, was not yet the "avant-gardist" he is today. Both composers conducted and played in Moscow, Leningrad, and Riga. The programmes consisted mainly of their own works though at least one Russian composition was performed at each concert.

All the performances were handled expertly by Soviet musicians, despite the fact that much of the music was written in an idiom that was strange and unaccustomed. The visiting composers were immensely pleased with the quality of the playing. They found the Leningrad Philharmonic especially impressive, not only for its accomplishment but also for its devotion to perfectionism. The composers were given five or six days of rehearsals, and some of the sessions lasted up to five hours. "At the end of such a five-hour session, the concertmaster was still not satisfied, so he took the strings through some passages again," recalled Foss.[47]

The American visitors were surprised by the existence of "jazz clubs", though their repertoire and playing style were imitative of American-type jazz. Copland heard a "Stan Kenton"-like band in Riga and some authentic American sound in Leningrad. The Soviets like to distinguish between "Rumanian" jazz, "Hungarian" jazz, etc., but when Copland was asked about the difference between Hungarian and American jazz, he startled the Soviet questioner by saying that fundamentally *all* jazz is American. The issue of jazz became a topic for heated controversy during the next few years. While Benny Goodman was permitted to give a series of concerts in the Soviet Union, the visits of other American jazz ensembles were politely declined. The question finally came to the boil with Khrushchev's denunciation of jazz in March 1963.

On 17 July 1960, the Soviet intelligentsia was once again honoured by a reception at the Kremlin. The atmosphere was described as one of "cordiality, unity, and elation".[48] There must have been considerable informality: one picture shows Khrushchev in shirt-sleeves. In another photograph, Madame Furtseva, the newly appointed Minister of Culture, is surrounded by leading composers—Shostakovich, Khrennikov, Khachaturian, and others. Among those invited were prominent writers—Sholokhov, Ehrenburg, Korneichuk, Fedin—and artists from other fields.

The main speech was given by Mikhail Suslov, the party ideologist. He stressed the necessity of developing those aspects that unify the cultures of the many peoples of the Soviet Union. Apparently, Suslov wished to reverse the priority of that old Stalin precept—"an art national in form, Socialist in content". From now on, the common denominator—Socialist content—was to receive prime attention. Suslov emphasized the common features "that are born of the relationships between the Soviet Socialist nations in the course of Communist construction".[49]

The musicians were ecstatic in their approval as can be gathered from comments by Khrennikov, Khachaturian, Taktakishvili, and others, that were reprinted in the official Information Bulletin of the Composers' Union. Khachaturian remarked, "Hitherto all attention was concentrated on the national form of music, stylistic, rhythmic, and so on. Content came after form. But that is wrong, because Socialist content is exactly that factor which makes the music of any Republic our own, Soviet music."[50] Theoretically, Suslov's speech could have meant a de-emphasis of the "folkish" national traits in Soviet music which had served as a crutch for so much mediocre composing. In practice, however, Soviet composers did not rush to abandon devices that had been found so convenient in the past.

The reaction of Shostakovich, who published an article in *Pravda*, is of particular interest. Because of his stature as the undeclared leader of

Soviet music, it was considered a major policy pronouncement, enhanced by its appearance in the official newspaper of the Communist Party. The date of the publication—7 September 1960—is intriguing, for it almost coincided with the approval of Shostakovich's candidacy for membership in the Communist Party which came up for discussion a week later, on 14 September.[51] It is strange to realize that Shostakovich—until the age of fifty-four a mere "fellow traveller"—decided at last to take that decisive step, notwithstanding his many brushes with the cultural guardians of the Party. Shostakovich may have felt that the new Party attitude towards the arts, initiated after Stalin's death and gathering strength under Khrushchev, promised a definite turn towards liberalization.

Whatever Shostakovich's inner reasoning, his article in *Pravda*, entitled "The Artist of our Time",[52] commits him to the Party. Never before had he spoken with greater devotion about Communist ideals, never had he sounded quite so much like the "composer laureate" of the Soviet regime. "Now that the country has entered the period of building the Communist society," he said, "the mission of the Soviet artist has become great and exalted." He expressed full agreement with the following sentence from a recent Party document, "It is their lofty Communist principles, their unbreakable ties with the actual work of Communist construction and the life of the people that enable the intellectuals more fully to perform their part in Soviet society."

Shostakovich took pride in the fact that the Party considered creative music as a means of educating the people, and he gave assurances that the musicians were united with the Party "in our views on the content, and on the main goal, of art". Then he took issue with foreign critics,

> "So when people abroad try to prove—out of purely political hostility or sheer childish naivety—that the principles of Socialist aesthetics are mere dogmas violating the artist's creative personality, one is tempted to ask such people, What musical 'creed' would they like to oppose to the principles of our art?"

This confession of loyalty was followed by a disdainful reference to aspects of Western art—"the groundless, crudely formalistic experiments totally unrelated to art"—and one of his strongest attacks on the twelve-tone system. In part, he repeated what he had said in Poland the previous autumn,

> "The history of music knows of no more dogmatic and barren system than the so-called dodecaphonic music. Based on mathematical calculations, artificially constructed, it has killed the soul of music—melody—it has destroyed form, the beauty of harmony,

the wealth of national rhythms . . . at the same time doing away with everything like content, the human quality of musical works. Dodecaphony has no future, nay, it has no present, for it is nothing more than a fashion which is already going out. Dodecaphony and the trends born of it, like pointillism, the electronic and concrete 'music' . . . have long over-stepped the bounds of art."

After ridiculing the "smug individualists" who cry about alleged "dogmatic Party guidance of Soviet culture" and the "pressures brought to bear upon the Soviet artist" supposedly deprived of the right to experiment, Shostakovich stated with frightening finality, "We do not conceal that we reject the right to fruitless formal experimentation, to the advocacy—in our art—of pessimism, scepticism, man-hating ideas, which are all the products of individualism on the rampage in the contemporary bourgeois world."

Here speaks, not the artist, but the Party member: not only is experimentation condemned, but the *right* to experiment is denied. Declaring that Soviet artists had abandoned, of their own free will, to be the "despicable purveyors of emasculated 'art' '', Shostakovich made another statement of faith, "Fighting with the Party for the ideological purity and artistic perfection of our music, we have taken the only true road of creating musical works of profound content, differing in style and comprehensible to the masses of listeners. This road was chosen not in compliance with a decree but with the dictate of our hearts . . ."

This signified Shostakovich's final conversion to Party orthodoxy. Coming from an artist who, more than anyone else, was subjected to the narrow dictates of Party hacks, it is a strange, puzzling phenomenon.

In the course of his article, Shostakovich took pains to explain that he did not dislike all contemporary Western music, "Modernism with its stillborn ideas and formal and technological dogmas levels down creative output and destroys artistic personalities . . . All the more worthy of respect are those Western composers who defy the prevailing musical fashion . . ." He specifically named Bartok, Britten, Honegger, Villa-Lobos, Milhaud, Wiéner, Auric, Poulenc, Durey, Orff, Barber, "and some others".

What a curious conglomeration! Durey and Wiéner make strange companions for Bartok and Britten. The list is even more remarkable for those it does not name, for example Hindemith and Krenek whom Shostakovich imitated in the 1920's. As for Stravinsky, he was found guilty of "complete divorcement from the true demands of our time and the cult of fashion unworthy of talent". Two years later, Shostakovich sat on the same dais with Stravinsky who had come to Moscow as the honoured guest of the Soviet Union. The entire list of composers

shows the retrospective mind of Shostakovich, for most of the names
were fashionable during the 1920's when Shostakovich himself was
young and adventurous.

One wonders how much of this article was political expediency, how
much of it artistic creed? Those who know Shostakovich believe him
to be completely sincere in his actions and words. Harrison Salisbury
writes, "You may disagree with Shostakovich strongly as I did . . . You
may regard him as naive as I did . . . You may believe him to be mis-
taken as I did . . . But you are in no doubt about one thing. He is
completely honest and completely sincere, and his mistakes come from
the heart and not from the mind."⁵³

Whether motivated by his "heart" or his "mind", Shostakovich
identified himself more and more closely with the cultural policies of
the Party. His opinions appeared in print, usually in *Pravda*, which lend
them an aura of authority and prestige. Following the Twenty-second
Party Congress (which began on 17 October 1961), Shostakovich wrote
an article entitled "The Composer and his Mission". It was published
in *Pravda* on 17 January 1962. After praising the Party's programme
for "the building of Communism in our land", he continued in flowery
style, "In this historic document which opens up grand and beautiful
prospects for universal happiness . . . great importance is attached to
culture. We musicians can draw from this programme many profound
thoughts and principles of the greatest value to the principles of our
art." And then asserted that none of that "universal happiness" was
available in the West,

> "The confusion of ideas that holds sway in the capitalist world
> today with its undercurrent of despair, fear, and overhanging
> doom, with its absence of positive ideas and clear aims in life, is
> responsible for the large number of trends in art, so far removed
> from the requirements of the people and in their very essence
> devoid of perspective . . . We cannot be too emphatic in stressing
> the fact that all these anti-humanistic trends are entirely alien to
> Socialist Realism."

Shostakovich, whose usual prose style is angular and artless, may not
have written this pretentious drivel, but he signed it and thus identified
himself with its propaganda content. Paul Henry Lang, the well-known
musicologist and critic of *The New York Herald Tribune*, has implied
that Shostakovich had submitted to the direction of "political wind".⁵⁴
It is true that, by nature, Shostakovich was not a fighter, and that his
recantations of 1936 and 1948 were docile and meek, more so than
necessary. But in 1962 he had reached the pinnacle of his fame and there

was no outward pressure, no visible reason for him to flatter the Party to such an extent. If these articles were a sincere expression of his beliefs at the time, he was rudely awakened later that year when, in December 1962, his Thirteenth Symphony was banned amidst a boorish outburst of Khrushchev's displeasure.

The changing attitude of Shostakovich, his repeated emphasis on the civic and ideological obligations of the composer, are discernible in his music. The true monuments to Socialist Realism are the Symphonies No. 11 ("The Year 1905") and No. 12 ("To the Memory of Lenin"). Their premières were planned to coincide with important events on the political scene: the Eleventh was ready for the Fortieth Anniversary of the October Revolution, observed in 1957, and the Twelfth was heard at the opening of the Twenty-second Party Congress in October 1961.

The composer designed these two symphonies as gigantic frescoes depicting Russia's revolutionary past. They were sufficiently programmatic to fire the imagination of the Soviet masses, and they were received with frenzied enthusiasm. In the West, however, the critical reaction was rather cool and condescending, at times even hostile. Clearly, a Western listener cannot respond with anything like the fervour displayed by Soviet audiences since he does not identify himself emotionally with the topics. The question arises whether Shostakovich's "revolutionary" symphonies can survive independently of their underlying programme, whether they have enough intrinsic musical values to evoke a universal response. This question has been answered in the negative by many Western critics—"the programme rather than the music has gained the upper hand" was one opinion. While the "pictorial" character of these scores was criticized by experts in the West, it was considered an asset by Soviet theorists. "The problem of 'mass appeal' in the symphonic genre was solved by Shostakovich in a brilliant and original manner by means of . . . letting the symphony be permeated by other mass genres . . .", wrote one Russian commentator. "One can say that the symphonic art of Shostakovich has experienced the influence of film music."[55]

This "cinematic" quality seemed to Western critics a decided drawback. "To the Western ear," wrote Martin Cooper, "its [the Twelfth Symphony] alternately drab and garish colours, and obsessive repetition of commonplace musical ideas are intolerable, while the naive ideological programme suggests that perhaps the work's true home might be the cinema."[56] In fact, the Twelfth Symphony, the "Lenin", received a disastrous drubbing by the critics when it was given its

Western première at the 1962 Edinburgh Festival. Peter Heyworth wrote in *The New York Times*, "Shostakovich is, of course, a notoriously uneven composer. But this new symphony has strong claims to be considered the worst of his major works. The majority of musicians and critics at Edinburgh were frankly aghast at its crudity and lack of interest."[57]

These lines were written by a critic who had reviewed rather kindly the previous—the Eleventh—Symphony, and who in the *Observer* in 1960, had defended Shostakovich's motives in writing a "programmatic" symphony. In his opinion. "the task of writing a symphony on the events of 1905 in his native city of Leningrad was not uncongenial" to Shostakovich. Heyworth ridiculed the almost automatic rejection of this type of composition by Western aestheticians, "Soviet critics have only to herald a work like the Eleventh Symphony . . . as a masterpiece of Socialist Realism, for some of their Western confrères to dismiss it with Dulles-like promptitude as a propaganda piece . . . To regard it as a sacrificial offering to the regime seems to me as silly and unsubtle as to describe Elgar's Second Symphony as a salute to British imperialism."[58]

When Shostakovich turned to writing two programmatic symphonies—the Eleventh and the Twelfth—he did so after much reflection. Of his previous ten symphonies, only the Seventh (the "Leningrad") could be called entirely programmatic. Of course there were also his two youthful works, the Second ("To October") and Third ("May Day"), where the final choral sections set the mood for the entire symphony, but these two works had disappeared from the Soviet repertoire and were disavowed by the composer himself.

Must we then conclude that all the other symphonies of Shostakovich are *non*-programmatic? Not necessarily. Shostakovich has very personal and rather unconventional ideas about programme music which he expounded in an article entitled "On Real and Alleged Programme Music" in 1951. An idea underlying a musical composition (such as the philosophical content of his Fifth Symphony) constitutes to him a "programme". Shostakovich admits that the technique of tone painting cannot be entirely dismissed—such as the invasion sequence in the first movement of the "Leningrad" Symphony or the battle sequence of his film *The Fall of Berlin*. But in general, Shostakovich rejects the concept of merely "descriptive music" whenever external pictorial factors are made to substitute for musical ideas. From this point of view, Shostakovich rejects a piece like the *Iron Foundry* by Mossolov as exactly such a "substitute". But he feels that Bach fugues, Chopin pieces, symphonies of Haydn, Mozart, and Beethoven are "programmatic" because of their "wealth of ideas and content". This, of course, runs counter to virtually all current definitions of programme music. While one is bound to disagree with him, one must accept his definition as valid at least for his own musical output. This is how he expressed it,

> "I identify programmaticism (i.e. the programmatic approach) with cogent content . . . And content in music consists not only of a subject stated in detail but also a crystallized idea or the sumtotal of ideas . . . In my personal case—and in the case of many other composers writing instrumental music—the programmatic conception *always* precedes the composition of the music."[59]

This was written in 1951, two years before Shostakovich composed his Tenth Symphony which was to arouse so much heated discussion in Moscow because of its prevailing gloom. If there was a "programme" in the composer's mind, he did not reveal it.

But the problem of a symphony with programmatic content was very much on his mind. Did he feel the challenge of such a task? Or did he, perhaps, realize that—regardless of some weakness—his last symphonic success was the programmatic "Leningrad" Symphony of 1941 (the Seventh) and that—despite his sincere efforts—his three subsequent symphonies, of a more abstract character, did not reach the people. And so, as a gift to the Soviet people on the Fortieth Anniversary of the October Revolution, Shostakovich created what Asafiev would have called a "musico-historical painting"—a portrait in music of the First Russian Revolution of 1905. Yet, one must not over-stress the programmatic content: in fact, it is more reflection *on* a theme than a description *of* a theme. True, there are some—though not many— "realistic" sections, but there are also long ideational musings and contemplations, an artist's sublimated evocation of events long past, yet still vibrantly alive. The extent to which a listener can share the composer's emotion depends, in this particular case, on the degree of his identification with the great revolutionary theme—a human rather than a Russian theme. When this music is exposed to antagonistic or indifferent ears, it will wilt, and loose its communicativeness.

Soviet critics have compared the Eleventh Symphony to the Seventh, the "Leningrad". His biographer Rabinovich wrote, ". . . Both compositions give the best and the most finished expression to the characteristic features of Shostakovich's music, the tones of the impassioned pamphleteer, of a musician with a lofty sense of civic responsibility. In both cases he gives us a faithful picture of periods that are exceptional in their significance in the life of the people . . ."[60]

The word "pamphleteer"—an unfortunate choice—is not used in the pejorative English sense but to convey the idea that Shostakovich is a "fighter for a cause". Shortly after the première of the Eleventh Symphony, Shostakovich wrote, "Creative activity is fruitless unless the writer, artist, or composer has very close ties with the life of the people. Only he who feels their heartbeats and the spirit of the times can truly express the thoughts of the people; no big work of realistic art is possible under any other conditions."[61]

After the tremendous impact created by the Eleventh Symphony, Shostakovich obviously felt encouraged to proceed further on the same path. While composing his next—the "Lenin"—symphony, he conveyed some of his thoughts in a speech to the RSFSR (Russian) Composers Plenum; they appeared in print early in 1961:

"The creative failures in the genre of programme symphony music are regrettable. The positive role of programme music in musical education is well known, for this music is understandable to mass audiences. One of the reasons for the setbacks in this genre is the standardization of the musical and dramatic designs which lead to a conservatism of expressive means and, as a result, to a weak artistic effect . . . Programme and textual genres have a special democratism. But this does not mean that we must neglect other genres of symphony and instrumental music. If a non-programmatic composition is imbued with the outlook of the new Soviet man, it is no less contemporary than a programme composition devoted to an urgent topic of the day. In Prokofiev's Fifth Symphony, for example, we hear the genuine living voice of our times . . ."[62]

Shostakovich's words had a didactic inflection which was fully justifiable since he addressed himself to fellow composers. As if anticipating a rush towards the "programme" symphony—now that he had formally espoused the genre—Shostakovich indicated that the *absolute* forms of music need not be neglected. In mentioning some "creative failures" in the programme genre (he listed a few recent examples by Lev Knipper and by younger composers like Alexander Kholminov and Alexander Flyarkovsky), Shostakovich blamed primarily the "conservatism of expressive means" and "flabby eclecticism". While aligning himself with progress and creative innovation, Shostakovich found it necessary to warn against the "danger of pseudo-innovation and of blind imitation of contemporary Western fashion" which he identified as "dodecaphony and concrete music". Obviously, Shostakovich envisaged a middle-of-the-road path for Soviet music, steering clear both of stale conservatism and experimental serialism. He stressed the spiritual attitude of the composer, "True realistic innovation

placed at the service of contemporary themes in music, the striving for
a natural, free and emotional expressiveness of music speech—such are
the characteristic features which determine to an ever greater extent the
creative quests of many Soviet composers."[63]

Shostakovich's goals were made clear not so much in his words, but
in his music. He demonstrated in Symphonies Nos. 11 and 12 his concept of "true realistic innovation". These two works represented a certain re-orientation of his symphonic thought towards pictorialism. One
Soviet historian described it as "a type of 'symphony-drama in four
acts' fused . . . with the picturesque-narrative tradition of Berlioz".[64]

Greeted as a revelation by the Soviets and an abomination by Western critics, Shostakovich's new symphonic style was neither that good
nor that bad. While frankly programmatic, the pictorial aspects of the
music were more suggestive than realistic, "*mehr Ausdruck der Empfin-
dung als Malerei*", as Beethoven said in his "Pastoral" Symphony.

Applied to the Eleventh and Twelfth Symphonies, one could say
that the music is more commentary than description. True, they are
topical works, and they deal with concrete historical events. But the
topicality is superimposed on a traditional four-movement pattern, and
the only clue given to the meaning of each movement is its sub-title.
In both works, symphonic form plays an important role; in fact, the
first movement of the Twelfth is a well-wrought "sonata allegro"—a
rarity among the opening movements of Shostakovich.

The Eleventh and Twelfth Symphonies are a diptych of the Russian
Revolution—just as the Seventh and Eighth were a diptych of the Great
War. The Eleventh is entitled "The Year 1905": the tragic events are
summarized in the sub-titles of the movements—"Palace Square",
"Ninth of January", "In Memoriam", and "Tocsin". All four movements flow into each other without separation; the over-all form of the
symphony is cyclic, and certain themes reappear, particularly in the
finale. The first movement pictures the vast square in front of the Winter
Palace in St. Petersburg, snow-covered and desolate. The second movement describes, often in realistic terms, the massacre of the "Bloody
Sunday". The third is a funeral dirge to the fallen heroes, the fourth a
militant promise of ultimate victory.

Into each of the movements, Shostakovich has woven authentic
music related to the revolutionary experience. Such "historical concreteness" was not a new procedure; it had been used by Russian
composers of the nineteenth century, and even more often by Soviet
composers. But, with very few exceptions, the insertion of authentic
themes had led to shallow musical results. The method was fraught
with danger: some composers used a potpourri-like technique, stringing
together well-known tunes without much personal imprint, while

others felt the need to adapt the folk material to their individual style, thus distorting the original idiom.

Shostakovich solved the inherent problems with mastery and impeccable taste. The themes never appear merely "quoted" but are fully integrated into the fabric of the symphony. By their manner of presentation and development, they miraculously acquire a distinctly "Shostakovian" profile. In the choice of the "borrowed" material, Shostakovich showed great discernment. The first movement is built on two nineteenth-century songs of political convicts—*Listen!* (Slushai) and *The Prisoner* (Arestant). In later movements, he uses songs of the 1905 Revolution: the proletarian funeral march *You Fell as Victims* (Vy zhertvoyu pali), *Rage, Tyrants* (Besnuytes, tirany), and the *Varshavyanka* (originally a Polish song). In addition, Shostakovich introduced two of his own themes from his *Ten Choral Poems on Revolutionary Texts* (Op. 88, 1951)*; they are taken from the sixth poem, entitled *Ninth of January* and transferred to the second movement of the Symphony which bears the same title. The first theme is the people's plea to the Tsar *Oh Thou, our Tsar, our Father* (Goy ty, tsar nash, batyushka), the second begins with the words *Bare your Heads* (Obnazhite golovy). At one point in the finale Shostakovich borrowed a theme from the musical comedy *Ogonki* (Sparks) by Sviridov (a former student of his) dealing with the life of workers in pre-revolutionary days.

All this—seemingly so disparate—musical material was welded by Shostakovich into a powerful evocation of the fateful days in January 1905. Lenin, shaken by the events of the "Bloody Sunday", wrote two days later, "The uprising begins . . . Fighting in the streets, barricades, salvos, cannons. In rivers of blood begins the civil war for liberty . . ."[65] Nineteen years later, Lenin—victorious—was buried to the strains of that old proletarian funeral march—*You Fell as Victims.*

As if to demonstrate that a "realistic" atmosphere could be achieved without quoting "authentic" material, Shostakovich abandoned this method in his next, the Twelfth, symphony which is based on freely invented themes. The inner relationship between the two symphonies is clear—in fact, so clear that one is often called a "sequel" to the other. Both are dedicated to great revolutionary events—the Eleventh to the year 1905, the Twelfth to the year 1917. But because of the lack of song associations, the Twelfth appears less descriptive, less programmatic, more sublimated in its content.

* Preceding the Eleventh Symphony by eight years, the *Poems* for *a cappella* chorus of mixed voices can be considered a spiritual "prologue" to the symphony itself. They show Shostakovich's early preoccupation with the revolutionary topic. The texts are by various revolutionary poets of the late nineteenth and early twentieth centuries.

Composed in 1961 and dedicated to the memory of Lenin, the Twelfth Symphony has the customary four movements, played without interruption. Each has a suggestive title, "Revolutionary Petrograd", *Razliv*, *Aurora*, "The Dawn of Mankind". Yet, the titles do not constitute a "programme" but merely a clue to the mood to be conveyed. "Revolutionary Petrograd" is assertive and agitated, with a flowing second theme that becomes the motto of the entire work.* The second movement, *Razliv*, is introspective and slow; the title can mean "The Rising Tide", but it can also refer to the hiding place of Lenin prior to the October Revolution. The third movement derives its title from the cruiser *Aurora* whose guns opened fire on the Winter Palace. The last movement shows the apotheosis of mankind, brought about by Lenin's victory.

As a symphony, the Twelfth follows the traditional form more closely than, perhaps, any of Shostakovich's previous symphonies. The first movement is a classical Sonata-Allegro; the second a pensive Adagio; the third an aggressive Scherzo (minus the "jest"); and the fourth a pompous Finale. While each of the movements has its own themes, there is much intertwining of themes through the technique of theme transformation and cyclic recurrence. What makes the musical idiom of the Twelfth Symphony so distinctive, however, is its closeness to the epic grandeur of Borodin, particularly his Second ("Bogatyri") Symphony. Never has Shostakovich sounded more Russian than in the first movement of his Twelfth Symphony. The Russianism is still present in the quiet contemplation of the second movement, and the aggressive activity of the third. Unfortunately, the Finale—the "Dawn of Mankind", is somewhat bloated and repetitious. Even Soviet critics admit the weakness of the final movement, but their criticism usually refers to its being "static"—a mild understatement.

The Twelfth Symphony was not played by any major American orchestra until 1970. Its West European première took place in September 1962, at the Edinburgh Festival, in the presence of Shostakovich to whom that year's festival was dedicated, and was a tremendous disappointment. Peter Heyworth did, however, add a significant afterthought to his damning criticism of the symphony itself:

"... For years the Western world has liked to think of Shostakovich as a victim of Stalinism, and the outstanding Violin Concerto and Tenth Symphony that emerged in the years after Stalin's death seemed to support this view. Today he may not be a 'free' composer in the Western sense, but he probably could, if

---

* There is an affinity between this "victory" theme and the finale of Prokofiev's *Alexander Nevsky*—the hero's victorious entry into Pskov.

he would, have considerable liberty of action. Why then does
this composer, who is capable of writing music of such splendid
and human warmth, such wit and sophisticated irony, waste his
time on monumental trivialities of this sort?"[66]

Indeed, why? Perhaps because the function of a Soviet composer is
sociological as much as artistic. His prime obligation is neither to Art
nor to the World, but to his audiences of compatriots and co-Leninists.
This music is a social message, and it only speaks to those who *believe*.
This kind of rapport is impossible in the West: there are too many
"non-believers".

The Twenty-second Party Congress, held in October of 1961, put a
touch of finality on the de-Stalinization begun in 1956 at the Twentieth
Congress: it was decided to remove Stalin's embalmed remains from
the Lenin Mausoleum on Red Square. The resolution, passed on 31
October, speaks of Stalin's breach of Lenin's heritage, his mis-use of
power, the mass repression against "honest Soviet people", and other
evil acts during the "cult of personality".

Dominating the Congress was the renewed drive to "build Communism". The speech of Madame Furtseva, minister of culture,
brought little comfort to those who were hoping for greater freedom.
She simply denied that there was any need for such freedom,

> "The reactionary critics of Soviet literature and art accuse our
> writers and artists of tying their creative work to the politics of
> the Party and thus allegedly limiting the 'freedom of creativity'.
> To this there is only one answer: we have a different concept of
> the freedom of creativity. Those people simply do not understand
> the incontrovertible truth that the Communist Party is the guid-
> ing spirit of our society . . . and that the Soviet artists, with deep
> inner conviction, serve the intersts of the people, the tasks of the
> Party."[67]

Iogansen, president of the Academy of Arts, was the spokesman for
artists, Sholokhov spoke as a writer, but there is no record that a composer was invited to speak. A few days after the Congress had ad-
journed, *Sovetskaya Kultura* printed an article by a secondary official of
the Composers' Union, Sergei Aksyuk. Under the aggressive title
"Forward March, Music!", he gave a tedious enumeration of Soviet
musical accomplishments. He mentioned compositions dealing with
contemporary topics like the Cosmonauts, Fight for Peace, Struggle

against Colonialism, and—of course—the ever-present Lenin. One notices a few new names among the composers; the Russians Alexei Nikolayev (Symphony No. 1) and Alfred Shnitke (*Songs of War and Peace*), the Estonians Jan Ryaets (*Ode to the First Cosmonaut*) and Arvo Pyart (*Path to Peace*). Aksyuk concentrated his displeasure on *Musica Stricta* by the "talented" Volkonsky who "for too long has remained in the stifling atmosphere of fruitless modernistic 'searchings'." Hinting at a modernist splinter group, Aksyuk said, "The youth of today gives hope and joy, tomorrow it will guide Soviet musical art. All the more regrettable are the rare but disagreeable creative failures, when one of the young permits himself be tempted by modernist bourgeois trends, dodecaphonic music, 'experiments' in the swamp, wallowing in the morass of dead dogmas and schemes."[68]

While Volkonsky was the only one so far mentioned by name, others joined him soon to challenge the monolithic resistance of the "establishment" against the inroads of musical experimentation.

This topic was brought up repeatedly at the Third All-Union Congress of Composers, held in Moscow from 26–31 March 1962. All the leading speakers referred to dodecaphony in a disparaging manner, coupling derision with a warning to young composers. Most emphatic was, of course, Khrennikov,

> "I must speak here of an exclusive small group existing in the backwater of the broad stream of musical life and engaged in formal searchings and fruitless experimentation. Their striving to deck themselves in other people's cast-off clothes is undoubtedly the sign of immaturity of some of our young composers . . . Our young experimenters should realize that there is a difference between freedom of creative searchings and lack of principles."[69]

It is always amusing to see how willingly the older composers are granting all sorts of freedom to the younger generation—provided that freedom remains within the bounds of tradition. Thus, Khachaturian proclaimed, "I see nothing alarming if certain young composers overdo sometimes. Danger arises only if these bubbling high spirits of youth lead them to seek novelty for its own sake, and if—in search for an individual style all his own—a young composer borrows the scheme of dodecaphony or serial music, worn threadbare from long usage."

Another stalwart of the establishment, Kabalevsky, seemed less concerned, "Certain young composers show an interest in twelve-tone music. Well, what about it? I am firmly convinced that if a composer has talent he will either ignore such music completely or, having tried his hand at it, discard it as have talented composers all over the world." Kabalevsky continued by expressing surprise that Stravinsky had "taken up dodecaphony"; however it has become clear that "even a great composer cannot produce anything valuable in accordance with its rules".[70]

Otar Taktakishvili of Georgia revived the old hoax about the alleged link between bourgeois ideology and dodecaphony, "Dodecaphonic and 'serial' music is associated with a clearly defined ideology, one that is disseminated assiduously, and which is supported by a good deal of money . . . So the struggle against dodecaphony and serial music is more than a struggle between styles: it is an ideological struggle and a very acute one at that."[71]

Shostakovich had already expressed his opposition against dodecaphony, electronic music, and the "primitivity" of *musique concrète* in an article published on 17 January 1962, "One must with all decisiveness emphasize once again that all these anti-humanistic tendencies are absolutely alien to Socialist Realism, alien to the needs of the Soviet people in general and to Soviet artists in particular. Our music is built on a different basis . . ."[72]

The fact that so many prominent speakers at the Composers' Congress ranted against modernism was an indication that more than a mere handful of young composers were involved in the dodecaphonic heresy. What had been, until recently, an "underground" movement was now coming to the surface. One composer in particular, the young Estonian Pyart, was singled out for castigation by Khrennikov, "A work like Pyart's *Obituary* makes it quite clear that the twelve-tone experiment is untenable. This composition is dedicated to the memory of the victims of Fascism, but it bears the characteristics of the productions of foreign 'avant-gardists': ultra-expressionistic, purely naturalistic depiction of the state of fear, terror, despair, and dejection."

While Khrennikov admitted that Pyart is "a talented composer", he considered his expressive media a failure, "So we see that the attempts to employ the expressive techniques of the avant-garde bourgeois music for the realization of progressive ideas of our time are discredited by the results they produce."[73]

How provincial is this self-righteous position that "bourgeois" means had been used to picture the resistance to Fascism, as if tonal music had a monopoly on being anti-Fascist. One shudders to explore the Soviet evaluation of the flaming anti-Fascist compositions by Dallapiccola or Luigi Nono, all written in a serial idiom.

But the discussion of dodecaphony provided only a fleeting "discord" in the triumphant survey of Soviet musical achievements during the years 1957-62, to which the Third Composers' Congress was dedicated.

"The five years between the Second and the Third All-Union Composers' Congress have been a most fruitful period in the history of Soviet music; indeed they may be characterized as a period of fresh efflorescence of the composers' creativity."[74]

And there was reason for pride if one considers the high points: the last two symphonies of Shostakovich, the oratorios of Sviridov, the ballets of Khachaturian and Karayev, the recent works of Khrennikov and Kabalevsky. In addition, a number of younger men had emerged who, without espousing Western modernism, had something fresh and appealing to say in a—basically traditional—idiom.

Much praise was lavished on a young Armenian composer, Eduard Mirzoyan (born 1921) whose Symphony for Strings and Timpani impressed the professional audience. Khrennikov spoke of its "optimism, irresistible drive, and bright plastic themes". It made a "tremendous impression" on Shostakovich who said, "This is a major success, both of the composer and of Soviet music as a whole." Kabalevsky called Mirzoyan's Symphony "remarkable".

It is indeed an engaging work, tinted with folkish Armenian coloration, full of life and vitality—yet essentially very old-fashioned. Robert Craft (who accompanied Stravinsky on his Russian visit in 1962), heard a taped performance of the Mirzoyan work and professed his disappointment, "It starts with a steppe-like *largo*, goes on to some *Schelomo* (equally profound, I regret to say), and concludes in a fast movement, which is half rhapsody, half Moscow two-step, and all *kitsch*."[75]

Alexei Nikolayev's First Symphony and the Fourth Symphony by Moissei Vainberg were found to be characteristic of the new trend in Soviet symphonism, stressing joyous or lyric moods in place of the "gloomy, brooding, and pseudo-tragic" attitudes of a few years ago.

Rodion Shchedrin added to his growing reputation: the Bolshoi Theatre gave the première of his opera *Not Love Alone* in 1961. He was highly praised for having discovered "fresh riches of the Russian musical imagery in the modern *chastushka*".[76] The libretto of the opera, an adaptation of several short stories by Antonov, depicts life in the Soviet countryside of today. The composer carefully preserved the engaging rhythms and melodies of the *chastushki*: he used them "to convey the general atmosphere, the emotions of the characters, and the relations between them".[77]

Another opera, by the older and far more experienced Ivan Dzerzhinski, was a major disappointment. *The Fate of a Man* was based on a story by Sholokhov who had provided the material for the composer's first success in 1935, *The Quiet Don*. One must assume that the work reached the stage of the Bolshoi in 1960 entirely on the strength of its libretto. The story is affecting and simple, the score is static and incompetent. Lack of inventiveness, a primitive use of leitmotive technique, and a thin orchestration hamper the unfolding of the drama to a point of utter dullness. His colleagues accused him of "professional carelessness", "creative irresponsibility", and "self-indulgence", which led him to "deliver to several theatres a half-baked work, granting them the right to do with it whatever they wanted to".[78] This was the last in a chain of disappointments for Dzerzhinsky who had never been able to duplicate his early successes of the 1930's, much as he had tried to ride on the coat-tails of Zhdanov.

A young Ukrainian composer, Leonid Grabovsky (born 1935) was highly praised for his *Four Ukrainian Songs* for chorus and orchestra. Shostakovich's opinion is friendly without being uncritical, "The *Ukrainian Songs* by Grabovsky pleased me immensely . . . His arrangements attracted me by the freedom of treatment and good choral writing. The only reproach I could make to the composer is his overly refined orchestral style; perhaps more simplicity would be in place here as the theme itself suggests greater modesty."[79] It is true that Grabovsky's orchestral garb was rather too lush for the simple texts. However, it proved to be a passing phase; at present, Grabovsky belongs to the growing group of Soviet avant-garde composers.

The Third Composers' Congress of 1962 showed the Composers' Union at the height of its power. The membership represented forty-two different nationalities, as Khrennikov pointed out with pride—"a truly fraternal union of workers of Socialist musical culture".[80] The Composers' Union enjoyed the esteem and friendship of the Party which was expressed by Suslov, the Party's ideologist, in a personal greeting to the Congress. Khrennikov, the Union's first secretary since 1948, had survived the delicate transition from Stalinism to Khrushchevism; he was re-elected again in 1962. Elected with Khrennikov was a board consisting of eighty-four members, forming a nation-wide representation. Of these, twenty-five served on the secretariat. By drawing some of the younger members into the work of the board, the directorate blunted any incipient criticism that the "old guard" was too domineering. Among the younger composers now on the board were Shchedrin, Sergei Slonimsky, Mirzoyan, Nikolayev, Pakhmutova, and Karen Khachaturian (the nephew of the famous Aram). They nominally shared the responsibility without being able to influence the course of events; the big names, the older generation still dominated.

Among those who attended the 1962 Congress were a number of

foreign guests. Foremost, of course, were the representatives of the "Peoples' Republics", meaning the countries within the Soviet orbit. China, Japan, and India attended, but neither North Korea nor Albania. Guests from the West included France, Belgium, Norway, Finland, and the United States. The American composer Samuel Barber spoke for his country; he sounded a note of caution,

> "Here I would warn against impatience in trying to create a Soviet contemporary style. As you well know, talent cannot be forced, and the extraordinary gifts of a young Shostakovich, who burst upon the world with his First Symphony, cannot be repeated so often. In the field of education you have done so much, and out of this great effort first-rate composers must surely spring. But there can be no five-year plan for talent, and too much interference as well as too much encouragement of composers can be unwise. Young composers will find their own styles and if they are too experimental, the public will not accept them anyway . . ."[81]

The presence of international representatives at the Composers' Congress testified to the changing Soviet position towards the musical world at large. What a contrast between the First Congress of 1948 which was xenophobic, the Second of 1957 which was strictly national, and the Third of 1962 with its international frills. Contributing factors to this development were the cultural exchanges between the Soviet Union and various countries, the international competitions of performing virtuosi, and the triumphant successes of Soviet artists around the world. Names like Gilels and Richter, Oistrakh and Kogan, Rostropovich and Vishnevskaya had become symbols of the highest artistry. True, Russian musicians had enjoyed international acclaim in Tsarist days, but it is to the credit of the Soviet educational system to have preserved the old standards of excellence and to have broadened the base of musical education to include every gifted child. With justified pride, Madame Furtseva in her speech at the Party Congress in 1961, said that, "In the last five years, thirty-nine international musical competitions were held. Soviet performers were awarded twenty-seven first prizes, thirty-five second and third prizes at these competitions."[82]

Khrennikov, in his speech to the Composers' Congress, made several references to international relations. He mentioned that, since 1957, the Composers' Union in Moscow had received 250 visitors from thirty countries; an equal number of Soviet composers and musicologists had visited, as members of delegations, various countries in Europe, Asia, Africa, and America. "The exchange of musical scores, recordings, periodicals, and books on music has intensified," he added. In 1960, the Composers' Union became a fully-fledged member of the UNESCO

International Music Council, with Kabalevsky and Vinogradov (a folk-lorist) as representatives. Not mentioned by Khrennikov, but equally important, was the fact that the International Musicological Society acquired two Soviet members, Yuri Keldysh and Ivan Martynov. They represented the Soviet Union at the International Musicological Congresses in New York (1961), Salzburg (1964), and Ljubljana (1967). However, all efforts to recruit individual Soviet musicologists as members of the IMS were rebuffed by the Composers' Union; obviously, the two official members were the permissible "quota" of co-operation. The Soviet Union was also slow in extending help to the international RISM (Répertoire International des Sources Musicales) that lists the rare holdings of the world's important music libraries.

In his speech, Khrennikov mentioned that foreign contemporary composers were receiving an increasing number of performances in the Soviet Union. He expressed hope for a further increase but upheld the vigilance against the "cosmopolite tendency characteristic of bourgeois art",

> "The stand of Soviet musicians concerning all types and trends of decadent bourgeois music is perfectly explicit. The struggle against bourgeois ideology in art is an integral part of the ideological struggle waged by our Party . . . We know that in the aesthetic conflict of the two worlds we are in the right . . ."[83]

Yet, Khrennikov had to admit that "we are not adequately studying the processes taking place in the musical art of the capitalist world". For this failing, he blamed the Soviet critics who "often lack stable principles in assessing some phenomena of twentieth century bourgeois art." In Soviet semantics, "stable principles" mean, of course, Marxist or Leninist principles. What Khrennikov really wanted was to see the critics denounce more vigorously the pernicious tendencies in Western music, instead of attempting to "whitewash certain modernist trends". The source for his anger became clear in the next sentences,

> "I mean the discussions held recently at the Institute of Arts History where some musicologists and art critics emphasized the alleged progressive and enriching influence of Expressionism on today's art as a whole, including our Soviet art. Such discoveries . . . lead us back to a stage Soviet music has long left behind."

What Khrennikov refused to acknowledge was that a re-evaluation of terms like modernism, impressionism, expressionism, etc., was long overdue. Certainly, the Institute of Arts History (at that time attached to the Academy of Sciences), with its staff of experts in all fields of the arts (including music) was ideally qualified to initiate such a re-evaluation. The discussion on Expressionism was a step in the right direction, though Khrennikov and other conservatives did not see it that way.

In the course of the debate at the Composers' Congress in 1962, the musicologist Keldysh[84] touched upon the topic of modernity. He asserted, quite rightly, "Modernity is not what it was twenty or thirty years ago." Or, according to Khrennikov, "Modernity is becoming the dominant theme in most of the musical forms." Upon closer examination, however, one realizes that the term "modernity" has a different meaning for the Russians: both Keldysh and Khrennikov seem to speak, not of a modern musical *idiom*, but of an up-to-date *topicality* or *attitude*. To Khrennikov, modernity in music means music dealing with subjects of Marxist actuality—labour heroism, the conquest of the Cosmos, the fight for peace, the struggle against colonialism, and so on. Keldysh, too, refers to changed conditions, "gigantic upheavals" that have taken place in the past two or three decades; millions of people have awakened to a "new life" that demands "changed themes and subjects in art, different imagery and expressive media". All the Soviet talk about modernity, at that time, concerned not the musical language, but the extra-musical circumstances that may influence the creation of music.

Nevertheless, neither Khrennikov nor Keldysh wished to be considered narrow-minded. Khrennikov asserted that "we are not ascetics or reactionaries in our attitude to modern music. Realizations of modern themes and images presuppose a search for new expressive means". And Keldysh explained, "We have become more tolerant in assessing the different creative trends, both in the works of Soviet composers and in modern foreign music which used to be classified as formalistic, often for little or no reason." But no sooner had Keldysh made this admission than he pointed to the inherent "dangers"—the possible "obliteration" of the "borderline between the art of Socialist Realism and certain phenomena in foreign art" though the latter may contain "some valuable and progressive elements".

There is one thought-provoking paragraph in Keldysh's statement where he seems to challenge the competence of the outside world truly to comprehend contemporary Soviet music,

"The art of our era—the era of the triumph of Socialism and Communism on a world scale—cannot be defined by the aesthetic categories borrowed from the complex of artistic trends that existed at the beginning, or in the second quarter, of the twentieth century and were the product of crisis and degeneration of the bourgeois culture (although they did contain certain elements of protest, e.g. expressionism)."

Is Keldysh altogether wrong? Is it possible that East and West have lost a common standard of values? Surveying the Soviet scene as a Westerner (and an avowed modernist), Robert Craft said in 1962, "My own feeling is that to the custodians of this outward-growing society, Anton Webern's music can only seem like the nervous tick of a moribund culture. I feel no need for it here, in any case, or correspondence between it and what I have seen of Soviet life . . ."[85] At the same time, Craft sees Soviet composers as "a school whose musical logic is at least a light year away, and whose emotional field is on the other side of the galactic field". The split seems complete.

Nevertheless, one can feel in Keldysh's tortuous prose, in his hesitant and tentative "concessions", that there were attempts to reassess such concepts as modernism, formalism, realism, and other encrusted "isms". There were forces at work, in that year 1962, ready to take a fresh look at the accumulation of outworn slogans and obsolete prejudices encumbering Soviet musical thought.

Less than six months later, Igor Stravinsky, the Russian-born octagenarian, arrived in Moscow after an absence of fifty years and shook up the establishment with some unvarnished truths. Speaking about dodecaphony to a group of young musicians in Leningrad, the old maestro turned to Khrennikov and said, "You, too, Tikhon Nikolayevich, will be trying it soon." And, as Craft (an eye witness) tells us, "everyone laughs at this and, most magnanimously, Tikhon Nikolayevich himself".[86] It was, we can be sure, the laughter of a polite host. Stravinsky did not convert Khrennikov who did not try "it"; but quite a few of the young Soviet composers felt greatly encouraged by Stravinsky's words and deeds.

During the autumn of 1962 I was in Moscow—a stay made possible by the cultural exchange agreement between the United States and the Soviet Union. These were exciting months, musically, artistically, politically. Prominent musicians and artists came from abroad—Igor Stravinsky, Yehudi and Hephzibah Menuhin, Robert Shaw and his Chorus, the New York City Ballet under George Balanchine. There were important festivals and premières, among them Shostakovich's controversial Thirteenth Symphony and the revival of his (once controversial) opera *Katerina Izmailova*. There was the great art exhibition at the Manège, showing paintings and sculptures long in hiding, and Khrushchev's vicious attack on modern art. There was the Cuban missile crisis which brought the two world powers to the brink of war. All this—and more—happened in the short span of three months, from October to December 1962. What I saw and heard during that time left an indelible impression. The next chapters, then, will be mainly a record of my personal observations in Moscow and Leningrad.

On 3 October, two days after my arrival, I was able to hear Stravinsky's last concert in Moscow. The programme consisted of a very early work, *Fireworks*, Op. 4 (1909), the Symphony in Three Movements (1946), the Capriccio for piano and orchestra (1929), and the 1947 version of *Petrushka*. The Large Hall of the Conservatory was filled with an expectant crowd which had come primarily to see and hear the legendary maestro in person. Stravinsky conducted only the last work on the programme, and the reception was demonstrative, both before and after the performance. As an encore, he conducted his arrangement of the *Volga Boatmen* which baffled the audience, perhaps because of its unusual harmonization. The first half of the programme, conducted efficiently by Robert Craft, produced only mediocre playing from the orchestra: its limited familiarity with the music was obvious and there was no conviction or fire in the performance. The Soviet pianist Tatiana Nikolayeva, a strong advocate of contemporary music, played the Capriccio brilliantly.

A few days after this concert, a press conference was called on behalf of Stravinsky, but the guest of honour did not appear, to the keen disappointment of a large crowd. No reason was given, but rumours were circulating that he had been asked to visit Khrushchev. This was indeed the case. The meeting seems to have been cordial though Stravinsky reported about it with characteristic dryness. Music was not discussed since "Mr. Khrushchev is not a musician". But the fact that this all-powerful man made a special effort to meet him somehow flattered the imperturbable maestro. Present at the meeting were Mrs. Stravinsky, Khrennikov (representing the Soviet composers), and Robert Craft.

One must recall the love-hate relationship between Stravinsky and his homeland in order to understand the full significance of his Russian visit. He had left St. Petersburg in 1912 and had returned in 1962. His dislike for the ruling Bolsheviks and their ideology was as strong as that of any emigré, and this dislike seemed to grow, rather than diminish, with the years. In 1925 he declined a personal invitation of Lunacharsky to conduct in Russia. During the 1920's, Stravinsky's works were played in Russia. Asafiev's *Book on Stravinsky* had appeared in 1929. As late as 1935, *Petrushka* was given in Leningrad, with published comments by Mikhail Druskin.

During the 1930's, the relations between Stravinsky and Russia began to deteriorate. An essay by Arnold Alshvang, published in 1933, opened with the sentence, "Stravinsky is an important and almost complete artistic ideologist of the imperialist bourgeoisie."[1] Stravinsky's autobiography, which appeared in French in 1935, contained some unflattering remarks about the Russian Revolution. This was followed by Stravinsky's "Charles Eliot Norton" lectures delivered at Harvard University during the academic year 1939-40.[2] The fifth lecture, "The Avatars of Russian Music," contained biting criticism of Sovie music and musical concepts. In turn, the vilification of Stravinsky in the Soviet Union reached a climax during 1948, the year of the Zhdanov purge. At that time, Khrennikov—Stravinsky's host in 1962—referred to him as the representative of reactionary bourgeois music.[3] The attacks increased in bitterness—"the shameless prophet of bourgeois modernism" (Nestyev in 1951)[4]—and they became scurrilous when Stravinsky embraced dodecaphony and serialism: old and new antipathies were compounded to form an insuperable barrier. A review of Stravinsky's *Canticum Sacrum*, under the title "Holy Cacophony", contained the sentence, "How ravaged, how emasculated must have been the soul of the composer capable of creating such dreadful

music?"[5] When Leonard Bernstein, during his 1959 Soviet visit with
the New York Philharmonic, put works by Stravinsky on the programme (the *Sacre* and the Piano Concerto), he had to be apologetic.
In the meantime, Stravinsky had not remained silent: he continued to
criticize Soviet music and musical aesthetics and in his *Thirty-five
Questions and Answers* (1957) we read that,

> "Russia's musical isolation—she will call it our isolation—is at
> least thirty years old . . . The Soviet virtuoso has no literature be-
> yond the nineteenth century. I am often asked if I would consent
> to conduct in the Soviet Union. For purely musical reasons I could
> not. Their orchestras do not perform the music of the three
> Viennese [he means Schoenberg, Berg, and Webern] and myself,
> and they would be, I am sure, unable to cope with the simplest
> problems of rhythmic execution that we introduced to music
> fifty years ago. The style of my music would also be alien to them.
> These difficulties are not to be overcome in a few rehearsals; they
> require a twenty- or thirty-year tradition . . ."[6]

Obviously, both sides—Stravinsky as well as the Soviet authorities—
had to soften their intransigeance towards each other in order to make
the historic visit of 1962 possible. The official invitation was transmitted in person by Khrennikov who visited Stravinsky at his home in
California.

Stravinsky himself was well aware of the animosity towards him that
existed in certain Soviet circles. On the eve of his departure for Moscow,
he stated with unsentimental candour,

> "Nostalgia has no part in my proposed visit to Russia. My wish
> to go is due primarily to the evidence I have received of a genuine
> desire or need for me by the younger generation of Russian musi-
> cians. No artist's name has been more abused in the Soviet Union
> than mine, but one cannot achieve anything with the Russians by
> nursing a grudge."[7]

Ultimately, the visit had certain nostalgic overtones, despite Stravinsky's disclaimer. But its significance went beyond the symbolic recon-
ciliation between the eighty-year-old master and his homeland after
fifty years of estrangement. Stravinsky's four-week visit made a lasting
impact on Soviet music—and this despite the fact that his concert programmes did not offer any of his later, "serial", compositions. But even
without serialism, there was enough to be learned from his scores:
suddenly, his *oeuvre* from the *Sacre* to *The Rake's Progress* (1951) was
revealed to a new generation of Soviet listeners. Even the ballet *Agon*

(1957) was heard in Moscow without a murmur of protest when it was presented by the New York City Ballet in the autumn of 1962.

The young generation of Soviet musicians flocked admiringly around Stravinsky—particularly in Leningrad. His open manner in discussing dodecaphony and serialism disarmed the old and the young; suddenly it was no longer "sinful" to discuss these subjects—serialism lost the aspect of a clandestine operation. At the time, the effect was intangible and incalculable, and though the ideological "screws" were tightened again a few months later, the progress made was permanent. It did not escape the experienced eye and ear of Stravinsky that the so-called "avant-garde" in the Soviet Union consisted of comparative beginners who were groping for guidance, struggling to absorb unfamiliar techniques. Stravinsky was reported to have called them "pathetic, untalented imitators". Whether he was quoted accurately is another matter; the quote was used by a high Soviet official to discredit the musical avant-garde.[8]

On the other hand, Stravinsky was also quoted (by the foreign press) as having made some unflattering remarks about the current crop of "official" Soviet music. "That was the real *fer rideau*," he told Craft after one such audition in Leningrad.[9] However, no such opinions found their way into the Soviet press which treated the old maestro with deference and even affection. Stravinsky, while on Soviet soil, was amiable and visibly touched by the emotional and musical impact of his visit.

The arrival of the American conductor Robert Shaw and his choral group provided excitement of quite a different nature. The Russians are used to a rich, rather massive choral style, and the limpid, exquisitely transparent sound of Shaw's chorus was a revelation. The singers —numbering only about three dozen—were spread across the stage, arranged not in the usual grouping according to vocal register, but in "solo" quartets. Each vocal quartet stood separately, yet blended with each other. The spatial separation, however, did not cause any loss of power when power was needed. The surprise and delight of the Moscow audiences was boundless, and there were wild ovations. Additional interest was provided by the programmes. I heard a performance of Bach's B-minor Mass on 16 October which, so I was told, had not been given in Moscow for a great many years. An added delight was the small group of "imported" instrumentalists supporting the Bach performance in impeccable style.*

* Robert Shaw's ensemble consisted of thirty-four singers and twenty-four instrumentalists. They gave thirty concerts in eleven cities. Bach's B-minor Mass was performed ten times; in Moscow alone there were four performances.

Somewhat later, on 19 November, I heard one of the final concerts of the Shaw Chorale. This time it was a mixed programme. It contained some music new for Moscow—Arnold Schoenberg's *Peace on Earth* (an early work dating back to 1907) and several works by the American composers Charles Ives and Norman Dello Joio. The enthusiasm of the audience demanded encores which were generously given, and here the accent was on "Americana": two scenes from *Porgy and Bess* by Gershwin and *Oklahoma* by Richard Rodgers, and three or four Negro spirituals. A Russian folksong (sung in Russian) was a gracious gesture to the hosts.

When Yehudi Menuhin arrived in Moscow in mid-November 1962, he was greeted as an old friend. Shortly after the Second World War, as soon as hostilities had stopped, Menuhin was the first foreign artist to visit the Soviet Union. This gesture of good-will remained unforgotten. Menuhin also had friendly ties with many Soviet artists who visited Western countries—among them Oistrakh, Barshai, Rostropovich—and these personal ties were much in evidence when he came in 1962, accompanied by his sister, the pianist Hephzibah. I had to miss the first concert—a sonata recital with one of the Bartok Sonatas on the programme—because it was impossible to obtain a ticket; even the usual sources—the American Embassy or the Ministry of Culture—proved of no help. On the afternoon of Menuhin's second appearance —it was 16 November—I wrote a personal note to Menuhin describing my ticket-less plight. We happened to stay at the same hotel—the "Budapest"—and I received an answer within the hour. He called on the house phone—"yes, join us, we'll go to the concert together." So we all piled into an "official" car—Yehudi, his wife Diane, Hephzibah, the manager, and some Russian aunts who had emerged from nowhere. The square in front of the Conservatory (where the concert was to take place) was cordoned off by police; hundreds of people milled around hoping, if not to hear, at least to see the artist. Menuhin and his party had to push their way through a good-natured crowd while I was at his side carrying his big square violin case; obviously I was indispensable. On that evening, Yehudi Menuhin played the Beethoven Concerto more beautifully than ever. During the intermission there were animated gatherings of violinists in the foyer, discussing the performance.

The Russian response to Menuhin's artistry was more than admiration—it was an emotional affinity to his concept of music, a spontaneous reaction to his radiant warmth, his humanism. No one quibbled about technical perfection because his art reached beyond mere mechanical accuracy. One performance remained particularly vivid in my mind—an evening of Bach and Mozart concertos with the Moscow Chamber Orchestra under Rudolf Barshai. The rehearsal began about midnight—immediately following a performance of Bach's complete *Art of the Fugue* by the orchestra. No other rehearsal time could be found, and so Yehudi Menuhin and the Russian musicians—tired but happy—settled down for a night of work. Such devotion to a cause will not be found easily anywhere else in the world.

Much has been written about the tumultuous reception given the New York City Ballet and its director, the Russian-born George Balanchine who had been away from Russia for thirty-eight years. One could say that his choreographic art was as far removed from the Russian ballet concept as Stravinsky was from his teacher Rimsky-Korsakov. Nor did Balanchine's choice of repertoire reach out for an easy success. On the contrary, choosing ballets set to music by Stravinsky (*Agon*) and Webern (*Episodes*) was a deliberate challenge, as was Prokofiev's *Prodigal Son*, not yet heard in the Soviet Union. Ballet without story, without scenery, without elaborate costumes was a novel departure for the Soviet audiences. But the New York Company conquered all obstacles—even such political obstacles as playing for 6,000 people at the Kremlin Hall while the Cuban Missile Crisis was at its height. (Incidentally, at exactly the same time—on 21 October 1962—the Leningrad Philharmonic Orchestra under Yevgeni Mravinsky made its début in New York; the reception was enthusiastic.)

An important delegation of French composers, Henri Sauguet, Raymond Loucheur, and Daniel Lesur, arrived in Moscow in late October and was given a cordial welcome. Georges Auric joined them somewhat later. On 29 October, an orchestral concert was given at the Conservatory Hall, devoted entirely to works by the French visitors: the *Phèdre* Suite by Auric, the Suite from the *Oedipus* ballet by Sauguet, the *Malagasy* Rhapsody by Loucheur, and the Overture *Andrea del Sarto* by Lesur. The music contained just enough modernism to titillate the ear without offending anybody; consequently, the success was great. Also on the programme was Ravel's Piano Concerto in G, easily the best piece on the programme, despite a somewhat heavy-handed performance by the Soviet pianist Yakov Zak. With the group of French composers came the musicologist Michel-R. Hofmann, a native Russian living in Paris, the author of numerous books on Russian and Soviet music, all published in Paris.

During October 1962, the Union of Soviet Composers also greeted two British guests, the young composers Stephen Dodgson and Kenneth Leighton. With Moscow flooded by prominent visitors, their two-week stay generated comparatively little public attention. Dodgson's perceptive observations of the Soviet musical scene were published in *The Composer* (Spring 1963), and many of his impressions parallel my own experiences.

But not all musical excitement was provided that autumn by foreign visitors. Among the important premières was Leonid Kogan's performance of the new *Concerto-Rhapsody* for violin and orchestra by Aram Khachaturian on 3 November. While the *Rhapsody* has more musical sophistication than Khachaturian's early Violin Concerto (1940), it lacks the spontaneity of the older work and sounds somewhat contrived. A few days later, the Second Symphony by Andrei Eshpai was played for the first time. There had been a good deal of favourable advance comments, including Khrennikov's personal praise. It proved to be a work of charm but little profile.

The conductor Abram Stassevich introduced two "semi"-premières, both arranged by him. A *Sinfonietta* in C-minor for strings and timpani by Shostakovich turned out to be the String Quartet No. 8, refurbished for a larger ensemble—a totally unnecessary exercise. Stassevich also presented his arrangement of a cantata drawn from Prokofiev's film score to *Ivan the Terrible*. Obviously, the arranger had hoped to accomplish for *Ivan* what Prokofiev himself had done for *Alexander Nevsky*. His hopes were not fulfilled: the new cantata resembled a pastiche without much inner coherence. Yet, to hear these Prokofiev excerpts without the distraction of the screen was a pleasant and occasionally moving experience.

A number of musical premières was presented from 20 to 30 November, under the heading "All-Union Survey of the Creative Work of Young Composers". Eleven concerts were given in Moscow—orchestral, choral, chamber music, and light music. They were called "concluding concerts"; in preparation, a first round of concerts had taken place in the capitals of the republics and other major cities in order to select the best works, worthy to be sent to Moscow. Under the rules, all members of the Union of Soviet Composers were eligible, in addition to students of music schools, and even amateurs; the age limit was thirty-five. It is reported that, in the course of the survey, over one thousand compositions were heard and evaluated. Although no new major talent was discovered, the experience was undoubtedly useful for many a young composer.

All the concerts were given at the customary big concert halls, before select critical audiences, performed by experienced artists and professional orchestras and choruses. Prizes were awarded, and the recipients —though within the age limit of thirty-five—were already known by reputation: Grabovsky, Shchedrin, Tamberg, Pyart, Pakhmutova, Oganesyan. There were no major surprises; in fact, the music heard at these concerts revealed a prevailing sameness of technical approach and a strange lack of musical adventurousness. It was "establishment" music, carefully screened by local officials and cleansed of all suspicious newness. The most notable feature, to the outsider, was the nation-wide representation of composers—a true cross-section of the Soviet Union. Whether the programmes presented in Moscow were truly the "best" is impossible to ascertain; certain compromises must have been made in order to achieve such a national balance. But the success of the project revealed, once again, the firm grip of the Composers' Union on the musical life of the nation.

As if to show that the Composers' Union was not dedicated exclusively to "serious" music, a plenary meeting held in Moscow in November (from the 12th to the 16th) was devoted entirely to what the West would call "popular" music. The Soviets have the term *estradnaya muzyka* (variety-stage music) which includes popular songs and jazz. In charge of this "popular" meeting was no less a musician than Shostakovich; among those participating in the discussion were composers like Kabalevsky, Khrennikov, and Muradeli as well as some of the leading "popular" composers like Matvei Blanter and Alexander Tsfasman—both of whom had been jazz pioneers in the 1920's.

Most of the debate centered on the question of jazz, especially the new type of improvisational jazz. What was performed at the demonstration sessions was "primitive" and amateurish by American standards, but the checkered history of jazz in the Soviet Union is an extenuating factor.

American-style jazz swept Europe during the 1920's, as an aftermath of the World War. Russia was not immune: in 1925, Sidney Bechet's Sextet paid a six-month visit and created a sensation. Russian musicians quickly absorbed and assimilated the new style; among them were Blanter, Isaak Dunayevsky, and Leonid Utesov who enjoyed enormous popularity. In 1929, the Russian Association of Proletarian Musicians (RAPM) succeeded in having jazz banned as "bourgeois decadence". Even a writer of the stature of Maxim Gorky spoke out against its capitalist connotations, in *Muzyka tolstykh* (Music of the Fat Ones,

1931). When RAPM was dissolved in 1932, jazz received a new lease on life. A boost to Soviet jazz was the film *Vesyolye rebyata* (Gay Young-sters), with music by Dunayevsky, and Utesov (originally a "popular" singer) in a leading role. In the years 1932 to 1938, Alexander Tsfasman —a gifted pianist—toured the Soviet Union with his jazz band which, in fact, was closer in style to Paul Whiteman's symphonic jazz than to a dance orchestra. Tsfasman's *pièce de résistance* was the *Rhapsody in Blue* by Gershwin. In 1938, an official State Jazz Band of the U.S.S.R. was formed which absorbed some of the best players from Tsfas-man's band and other organizations. In essence, it was an *estradnaya* orchestra—an ensemble playing "light" music—and the jazz element was strongly diluted. This "compromise" was not to everyone's liking, as a former member of the band reported, "The broad masses of listeners would not accept us because we were not much like the real jazz which they knew and loved. And we didn't please Stalin because there was nonetheless something of real jazz in us."[10]

The outbreak of the Second World War put an end to the State Jazz Band. Eventually, a new unit was formed which became the State Variety Orchestra of the Russian Republic under the direction of Utesov. During the Zhdanov era, Western-style jazz was, of course, sternly condemned, but in the more relaxed post-Stalin years musicians tried to find a *modus vivendi*—adjusting jazz to the popular demands of the young generation. Soviet jazz enthusiasts were limited, for a time, to copying their jazz from smuggled phonograph records or the clandestine "Voice of America" broadcasts. The Russian visit of Benny Goodman and his band focused once again the interest on American-style jazz. "We are not opposed to jazz, we are only opposed to 'Americanized' jazz," Khrennikov told me in 1962. "In time we shall develop a Soviet-style jazz. Take, for example, the waltz: it was born in Vienna, to be sure, but look how *our* composers have transformed the waltz, given it a Russian flavour. The same will happen to jazz."

The fact that Shostakovich was chairman of the "light music" meet-ing in November 1962, reminds us that—back in the 1930's—he had written several suites for jazz band (now known as suites for "variety orchestra") which were widely played by Tsfasman's touring band. In connection with this meeting, Shostakovich invited Khrushchev to attend a concert given at the Kremlin Large Hall at which some of the best Soviet bands were to appear. It was a calculated risk—Khrush-chev's conservative musical taste was known—and it misfired. A few days later, he said, "I don't like jazz. When I hear jazz, it's as if I had gas on the stomach."[11]

This extemporaneous comment was amplified in a major speech made a few months later, in which he also made disparaging remarks about the jazz concert he had attended in November. "The enthusiasm for jazz and jazz music . . . cannot be regarded as normal. It should not be thought that we are against all jazz music . . . However, there is a kind of music that gives you a feeling of nausea . . . For some reason, a jazz band appeared, then a second one, then a third one, and then all three at once. You feel unhappy when there is too much of a good thing. It was very hard to stand that salvo of jazz music and you couldn't hide, even if you wanted to . . . There is some jazz music that you can't understand and hate to hear."[12]

This was said at a time when chairman Khrushchev's word was law. Nevertheless, during a temporary *détente* in 1964, Shostakovich urged publicly a more flexible attitude towards light music and jazz since "young people cannot dance to classical music". At that time, it was Khrennikov who took a purist attitude and wrote in *Sovetskaya Kultura*, "We receive many complaints about the saturation of broadcast time with jazz." In reply, *Komsomolskaya Pravda* (with a circulation of five million!) charged Khrennikov with a lack of concern for popular music.[13] The whole controversy has now subsided, and a recent Soviet Music Encyclopaedia discusses the subject of jazz in a factual and dispassionate manner.*

A fascinating confrontation between conservative and liberal intellectuals took place at a three-day conference (26 to 28 November 1962) under the heading "Tradition and Innovation in the Art of Socialist Realism". It was co-sponsored by three academic institutions: the Institute of Arts History (affiliated with the Ministry of Culture), the Institute of the Theory and History of Art (a branch of the Academy of Arts), and the All-Russian Theatrical Association. The first day was given to a plenary session devoted to fine arts. The second day's agenda was subdivided into three sections—on theatre and cinema, on music, and on fine arts. A plenary session on the third day ended with a speech by the director of the Institute of Arts History, Kruzhkov.

The tone of the general discussion was revealing. Speaker after speaker arose to denounce the evils and the remnants of cultural Stalinism. Tempers flared, and any hint at regimentation was hissed. When the musicologist Yarustovsky—one of the most respected members of his profession—tried to demonstrate the "absurdity" of Western modernism by playing some recordings he had brought from Paris, the audience received him with such impatience that he had to cut short his prepared statement. The conservative painter Serov was interrupted by hecklers; a week later he emerged as the new president of the Aca-

* See the observations of Copland on Jazz in Soviet Russia on pp. 332-3.

demy of Fine Arts. As one musician remarked to me with concern, "It's fashionable today to blame the past—but what about the present and the future?"

Indeed, what about the present? On 26 November, the day the conference opened, a semi-private art show was held at the studio of art teacher Eli Belyutin. The canvasses exhibited—about seventy-five— were the work of Belyutin and his students, done in an abstract or semi-abstract style. Some of the sculptures by Ernst Neizvestnyi were also shown. A few days later, the Belyutin exhibition was transferred to the Manège, a huge exhibition hall where a major retrospective art show, "Thirty Years of Moscow Art", was in progress. However, separate rooms were reserved for the Belyutin show, which was not open to the public.

On 1 December, Khrushchev and his official entourage visited the Manège exhibition and were also shown the separate rooms housing the abstract art. Khrushchev's reaction was predictable; he launched into an ill-tempered tirade against the abstractionists, berated them as jack-asses and parasites, and accused them of having betrayed the trust of the State. At Khrushchev's elbow were the conservative painters Serov and Gerasimov who may have plotted the entire incident to check the growing boldness of the modernists. However, Khrushchev's fury was more than anyone had bargained for; he scolded Madame Furtseva (the minister of culture) and Leonid Ilyichev (the cultural affairs expert) for having been too permissive. "We are going to maintain a strict policy in art," Khrushchev said on the spot, and he vowed "no co-existence" in ideological matters.

Khrushchev's intemperate outburst—covering the front page of *Pravda*—was, as one expert wrote, "the signal for the most far-reaching crackdown on the creative arts in the Soviet Union since the Zhdanov purge of 1946–48."[14] A call went out immediately to the representatives of the arts intelligentsia to meet with Party leaders. On 17 December 1962, some four hundred artists, writers, musicians, film and theatre people assembled at the Kremlin. The main speaker was Ilyichev, the chairman of a newly formed "ideological committee" responsible to the Party's Central Committee.[15] For some strange reason, Ilyichev tried to minimize the crisis in the arts. "Nothing exceptional or extraordinary has happened," he said, "our Party is satisfied with the state of affairs in the sphere of culture." However, it soon became clear that a crisis situation did exist: under the guise of exposing Stalin's "cult of personality" there was allegedly a softening of Socialist resolve.

"We must not permit Socialist society, ideology, and culture to be shaken and weakened . . . The exposure of the 'cult' and the over-coming of the consequences should not weaken but rather streng-then our forces . . . There has not been and cannot be any peaceful co-existence between Socialist ideology and the ideology of the bourgeois world."

The brunt of Ilyichev's criticism was directed against abstractionist painters and sculptors. Literature and the cinema received some atten-tion; music was mentioned in just one brief paragraph,

"Formalist tendencies have unfortunately begun to spread not only in the fine arts but in music, literature, and the cinema as well. In music, for example, we observe—despite general progress—an infatuation with the outlandish howlings of various foreign—and not only foreign—jazz bands. This refers not to jazz music in general but to the cacophony of sounds with which listeners are sometimes assailed and which is dignified with the name of music only through a misconception."

But a week later, Ilyichev returned to the "incorrect tendencies" in music. On 26 December he said, "The preoccupation of some young composers with experiments in the style of dodecaphonic music bodes no good. In senselessness and ugliness this compares only with abstract art." It is here that Ilyichev quoted Stravinsky's low opinion of the "home-bred admirers of a formalist avant-gardism in Leningrad", and belaboured the point, "Well, in this case Stravinsky's judgment is valuable testimony. It should give pause to some young people who have exchanged great, meaningful art for cheap imitation, for a dubi-ous success with a certain part of music's hangers-on."[16]
After such a build-up, one would expect armies of dodecaphonists threatening the foundations of Soviet music. But Ilyichev reveals only one name, "One cannot fail to mention the position of composer Andrei Volkonsky, a gifted man who, for some reason, likes to don fashionable clothes off other people's back. What good does he see in locking himself up in a narrow little world of precious music confection that would arouse interest only among music snobs? After all, to judge by everything, he could gladden Soviet audiences with good music . . ."[17]
This sounds more in sorrow than in anger. Volkonsky had been a rebel since 1954 when, as a student, he was expelled from the Moscow Conservatory for "insubordination". Ilyichev's appeal for his return to the "establishment" was naive and fruitless.
So far, music was spared any large-scale condemnation because there

was really little to complain about: the tight control exercised by Khrennikov and the directorate had driven the few experimental composers underground. They were not given an opportunity to be heard and judged by the public. Writing in *Pravda*, Muradeli, a pillar of the musical establishment, urged vigilance, "True, except for the *Suite of Mirrors* by Volkonsky, we have not yet encountered on our concert stage any musical works of abstract tendencies. However . . . we have no guarantee against a stepped-up aggression of such anti-realistic tendencies directed against our realistic art."[18]

There can be no doubt that the information about the underground "danger" of experimental composers was fed to Ilyichev and Khrushchev by the directorate of the Composers' Union in order to elicit some warning remarks from official quarters, meant to scare any would-be rebels. For the time being, the one trapped in the cultural muddle of 1962 (aside from Volkonsky) was the most respected of composers—Shostakovich. After two triumphal performances on 18 and 20 December 1962, his new Thirteenth Symphony, a work based on texts by Yevgeni Yevtushenko, had to be withdrawn because some of the words were found objectionable. Thus, Shostakovich was caught through "guilt by association".

At the time, the twenty-nine-year-old Yevtushenko was eyed with suspicion by the conservative wing of the writers. His immense following among the young stirred the rebellious spirits. Yet, Party officials seemed lenient: only recently, on 21 October, two of his controversial poems had been published that caused a shudder among the hard-liners: the *Heirs of Stalin* and *Fears*. Both warned against the return of Stalinist oppression. His poem *Babyi Yar*, published in September 1961, had raised another unpopular spectre, anti-Semitism. He was known to have friends among the abstractionist painters, and he had the courage to speak up on their behalf. At the 17 December meeting, a—by now famous—dialogue took place between Yevtushenko and Khrushchev.

Y.: "We must have great patience with this abstract trend in our art
    . . . I know the artists in question, I know their work . . . I am
    convinced that several formalistic trends in their work will be
    straightened out in time."
K.: "The grave straightens out the hump-backed."
Y.: "Nikita Sergeyich, we have come a long way since the time when
    only the grave straightened out hump-backs. Really, there are
    other ways . . ."[19]

This dialogue happened to take place one day before the première of the Thirteenth Symphony of Shostakovich. The work is actually a symphonic cantata; each of the five movements is a musical setting of a poem by Yevtushenko for baritone solo, bass chorus, and orchestra. The poems were written at different times and do not form a preconceived "cycle" although one can discern an inner relationship—an oblique criticism (at times only an ironic inflection) of the Stalinist past. Whether the poems were chosen by Shostakovich personally or with the assistance of the poet is not known. Ultimately, the choice was the responsibility of the composer, not the poet, since musical considerations had to be the determining factor—the suitability for a musical setting, the necessary contrasts between the poems, and so on. All the poems used by Shostakovich were published previously, with the exception of *Fears* (used as fourth movement) which must have been known to him prior to its publication on 21 October 1962.

The titles of the poems were retained in the symphonic score: (1) *Babyi Yar* (the poet's outcry against anti-Semitism), (2) *Humour* (irrepressible, even by despots), (3) *At the Store* (a tribute to Russia's women who "mixed concrete, ploughed, and reaped" . . . and queued to feed the family), (4) *Fears* ("fears are dying in Russia like the ghosts of past years"), (5) *Career* (a good-humoured tribute to the nonconformist . . . "forgotten are those who cursed, remembered those accursed"). Shostakovich's musical settings alternate between solo voice, chorus, and orchestra. He underlines and intensifies every inflection of the text, giving impact to the drama and wings to the humour. The music is welded to the word; the chorus is used consistently in unison, within a narrow melodic range, and often creates the effect of choral recitation. The solo voice, too, tends to resemble a "speech-song". Though the mood of each movement is inspired by the poem, the music is by no means imprisoned by it. Shostakovich sets each poem within a firm musical framework provided by the orchestra, and the emerging design approaches a classical concept of form.

This is most noticeable in the first movement, *Babyi Yar*, which has three major theme groups: the introductory, dirge-like Adagio which reappears at the climactic restatement and as coda (a theme never sung); the aggressive "tormentor's" motive (twice as fast); and the lyrical "Anna Frank" episode (Allegretto). Through purely instrumental intensification, the shattering restatement is reached just before the poet repeats the opening line, "Nad Babyim Yarom . . .".

The second movement, *Humour*, occupies the traditional place of a Scherzo; it is sarcastic, grotesque, often deliberately crude, and very much in the Shostakovich manner. The music heightens the effect of the text through word repetitions and dialogue between solo and chorus.

The third and fourth movements (*At the Store*—Adagio and *Fears*—

Largo) are thematically related, played without interruption, and form a bi-partite slow movement. The ominous mood of the text is conveyed in a masterful way. Gradually, the fear dissolves into the serenity of the Finale, *Career*, an Allegretto of lilting charm and sly humour. In this movement, the purely instrumental sections outweigh the vocal parts, both in length and depth. The orchestration is transparent, making extensive use of solo instruments; only for one moment, in the central *fugato* section, is the orchestra used with full power. The instrumental coda is enchanting, and the movement trails off to the fairy-like sound of the celeste. Throughout the symphony, the chimes play an important, almost symbolic, role, and the work ends, as it began, with the ominous timbre of a chime.

The première of the Thirteenth Symphony was awaited in Moscow with intense anticipation. The excitement generated was not purely musical: people were aware of the artistic tensions behind the scene, of the meetings between the arts intelligentsia and the Party. The city was buzzing with rumours of a possible last-minute cancellation of the performance. The dress rehearsal was open to conservatory students and faculty members. A staff member of the Glinka Museum emerged from the dress rehearsal; my question about the music was waved aside, ". . . but the WORDS".

At the première, the government box remained unoccupied, and a planned television transmission did not take place. A listener approaching the Conservatory Hall on the evening of 18 December found the entire square cordoned off by police. Inside, the hall was filled to overflowing. The first half, consisting of Mozart's "Jupiter" Symphony, received a minimum of attention; no one cared . . . The intermission seemed endless; finally, the chorus filed on stage, followed by the orchestra, the soloist, the conductor Kyril Kondrashin. The tension was unbearable. The first movement, *Babyi Yar*, was greeted with a burst of spontaneous applause. At the end of the hour-long work, there was an ovation rarely witnessed. On the stage was Shostakovich, shy and awkward, bowing stiffly. He was joined by Yevtushenko, moving with the ease of a born actor. Two great artists—a generation apart—fighting for the same cause—freedom of the human spirit. Seeing the pair together, the audience went wild; the rhythmic clapping, so characteristic of Russian enthusiasm, redoubled in intensity, the cadenced shouts "Bra-vo Shos-ta-ko-vich" and "Bra-vo Yev-tu-shen-ko" filled the air. The audience seemed to be carried away as much by the music as by the words, although (contrary to custom) the texts were not printed in the programme distributed to the public.

The following morning, a one-sentence report appeared in *Pravda*, an absurd anti-climax for anyone who had witnessed the exciting evening. I rushed to the headquarters of the Composers' Union in search of a score or a piano reduction; I wanted to re-read the texts and evaluate their relationship to the music. My request was met with polite head-shaking and evasive excuses—the "only" available score was in the hands of a critic who had failed to return it . . . Needless to say it was never "returned", and all my efforts to have a glimpse of the score remained fruitless. Only later did I realize that this was no accident: there was an "embargo" on the score because of official dissatisfaction with certain sections of the work. No further performances of the Thirteenth Symphony were permitted until adjustments were made in the first movement, *Babyi Yar*. This seemed patently absurd: the poem had been printed, recited, and televised around the world since 1961, and the delayed censorship was as pointless as it was idiotic.

At issue were four lines towards the beginning of the poem (lines 6 to 10). Pressures were exerted on Yevtushenko and Shostakovich to agree to a change so that Jews were not pictured as the only victims at Babyi Yar. It is said that Shostakovich was the first to yield, but since the new lines preserve the metric structure of the original lines, Shostakovich's approval was merely one of principle. The change diluted the original meaning of Yevtushenko's words; now we are told that "Here / at Babyi Yar / lie Russians and Ukrainians, / They lie with Jews in the same Earth". Another substitution, at the end, exalts Russia's greatness. Incidentally, *Fears* was also subjected to a change of seven lines.

What confused an already muddled situation was an interview given by Yevtushenko to the French paper *Le Monde* and published on 14 February 1963. In it Yevtushenko denied that his decision to alter *Babyi Yar* was taken under duress, "No one asked me to change *Babyi Yar*," he asserted.[20] The question arises—if no one forced him, why did he do it? And why does he continue to recite the poem in the *old* version, as I have heard him do in New York in 1966? Are there now two versions—one for the Symphony, one for recitations? I personally believe that both Yevtushenko and Shostakovich are waiting for a change of "climate" so that the original version of the Symphony can be restored. Significantly, the score published in 1970 by Leeds Music (Canada) contains the *original* words though it may have been done without Soviet authorization. This version was used for the long-delayed American première on 16 January 1970 by the Philadelphia Orchestra under Eugene Ormandy.

Among the few performances of the "revised" Thirteenth Symphony in the spring of 1963 was one given in Minsk. On 2 April 1963, the newspaper *Sovetskaya Byelorussia* published a lengthy review, signed by Ariadna Ladygina.[21] Her status in the music world is not known to me; she is not listed in the 1960 directory of the Soviet Composers' Union (which also lists member-critics).

Miss Ladygina makes a distinction between the music—which she finds overwhelming—and the poems which, to her, seem "somehow faded, dimmed . . . petty, and of small significance"; in fact, she speaks of Yevtushenko's "childish coquetry" and "cheap sensationalism".

The attempt at separating words from music is clever but untenable, because the ultimate responsibility for choosing these "petty" poems belonged to the composer, Shostakovich. The Thirteenth Symphony, says Miss Ladygina, has been named by some "sceptic" the "Symphony of the composer's civic courage". She asks rhetorically—is it civic courage or merely the "loss of civic tact", and she concludes that it is the latter. The critic is displeased not only with *Babyi Yar* for its "lack of historical truth", but also with the "prosaic subject of the third poem, *At the Store*": here, a queue of women is raised to an event "just short of national tragedy". Miss Ladygina's reaction to the poems is a "thought of falsity" and an "irresistible feeling of inner protest". Even the parts that are ideologically correct acquire, in the total context, "some kind of ambiguity and an ironical undertone".

If such is the case, then the creative plan of Shostakovich and Yevtushenko succeeded to perfection. For there can be no doubt that each of the five poems aims at some vulnerable aspect, not only of the Soviet past, but also of the Soviet present. Though written "in different years, and for different reasons", the overriding mood is one of opposition to the encrusted *status quo*. The change of four lines may have appeased the petty minds, but it did not affect the over-all impact.

Miss Ladygina's article has become an historic document showing the uncertainty of critical judgement in a time of stress and transition. Since then, Soviet writers have analyzed the Thirteenth Symphony in depth, recognizing its artistic significance. Yet, a shadow seems to hang over the work, and it remains rarely performed. In the meantime, Shostakovich has joined hands again with Yevtushenko in creating the symphonic cantata *The Execution of Stepan Razin*.

That the première of the Thirteenth Symphony should come one day after the ideological meeting at the Kremlin was indeed a strange coincidence. Equally strange (and coincidental) was the timing of the revival of Shostakovich's opera *Katerina Izmailova*, the revised version of his *Lady Macbeth of Mtsensk*, silenced by Stalin in 1936. After years of planning, the revival took place at the height of the ideological debate, on 26 December 1962. It took place without prior publicity, almost surreptitiously.*

In Moscow's musical circles it was known that the rehearsals for *Katerina Izmailova* were in their final stages and that the première would take place sometime in December. However, in view of the tense situation on the ideological arts front, fears seemed to have arisen that some last-minute Party veto would be imposed. It was, therefore, important to enlist the full support and approval of Madame Furtseva, the minister of culture. Yet, as fate would have it, her position was suddenly weakened by Khrushchev's outburst at the art exhibition on 1 December where he had called her too permissive. Now, even her full support might not carry enough weight to prevent some bureaucratic interference. Be this as it may, at one of the last rehearsals, given in the presence of a small professional gathering, Madame Furtseva sat in the front section of the theatre, flanked by Khrennikov and Kabalevsky. The composer was in the hall but kept in the background. There was animated conversation between Madame Minister and her companions, but ultimately Madame Furtseva must have become convinced that the performance should go on as planned. Considering the ugly Party mood of that month, this decision took some courage, for *Katerina Izmailova*, despite some retouchings, remained a drama of violence, lust, and sadism. And Khrushchev's moral standards of 1962 were as Victorian as those of Stalin in 1936; there was no guarantee that he might not explode in indignation at the amoral happenings on the stage. A decision seemed to have been made to proceed cautiously, to test the reaction of the public before advertising a gala première.

And so, the Stanislavsky-Nemirovich-Danchenko Theatre announced its repertoire for the last week of December, with *The Barber of Seville* set for 26 December. Moscow art circles knew well in advance that, at the last moment, *Katerina Izmailova* would be substituted. A standing joke among musicians was, "See you at the Barber!" Tickets were at a premium. On the morning of the 26th, stickers were affixed to the large posters outside the theatre, announcing blandly a "change of performance". In the evening, the ticket controller would whisper discreetly, "Are you aware that there has been a change of programme? You may exchange your ticket." I did not see any rush for exchanges. But it is a fact that on that night of 26 December, the theatre was filled, not only by Moscow's cultural élite, but also by many people who had bought tickets to hear Rossini. I found myself to be

* The official date of the première of the revised *Katerina Izmailova* is given as 8 January 1963. However, the performance on 26 December 1962, was the first before an audience, both paying and invited. Khrushchev was represented by his son-in-law, Mr. Adzhubei.

seated next to Mr. Victor Hochhauser, the London impresario, who had come to Moscow to hear that première.

In view of the "mixed" audience, the success was doubly overwhelming. It was a blazing performance, perhaps not fully polished as yet, but sung with passion by a youthful cast, in the actor-singer tradition of the founders of the theatre. The staging and direction were ingenious, avoiding extreme naturalism, yet conveying all the raw passions of the libretto. The amusing scene in the police station (unfortunately omitted at the New York revival in 1965) served as an ironic reminder that, after all, police methods had not changed very much.

Time and again, all eyes in the audience turned to the composer who sat in the centre of the stalls; he seemed oblivious to the surroundings as he listened—fully absorbed—to the savage realism and impassioned surge of his youthful score. The ovation at the end was more than a tribute to a great composer; it seemed that every listener identified himself with this historic act of vindication. Shostakovich appeared on the stage in the midst of the applauding performers. His sensitive face was haggard and showed the emotional strain. He had won a battle—but at what price!

Much had happened since 1936 when the same work had been characterized as "Chaos instead of Music", or when a Western critic coined the word "pornophony" to describe the suggestive trombone slides in the orchestra during the bedroom scene. It is true that Shostakovich had made a few revisions (eliminating, incidentally, the "pornophony"). He himself described the changes as minor—a few retouchings in the orchestration, a polishing of the vocal tessitura, especially with regard to the extreme registers. He also composed two new orchestral interludes. The British conductor Edward Downes (who conducted the London performances in 1963 and also translated the text) is quoted in *Sovetskaya Muzyka* as having said that the new version represented "that improvement which a mature and very experienced composer would bring to his youthful work."[22]

But essentially, it is the same opera, and it is recognized today by Soviet critics as the first great *Soviet* opera—and perhaps the greatest Russian opera since *Pique Dame* of Tchaikovsky. Such comparisons are idle; after all, between *Pique Dame* of 1890 and *Lady Macbeth* lies virtually the entire operatic output of Rimsky-Korsakov—hardly a negligible *oeuvre*. But as a piece of effective musical theatre, *Katerina Izmailova* has few rivals in the twentieth century repertoire. It is sad to contemplate that the disastrous criticism of this opera in 1936 discouraged Shostakovich from composing the trilogy of operas he intended—and the time for such a project is irretrievably past.

In the autumn of 1962, I was assigned as an exchange scholar to the Institute of Arts History, a research centre, in Moscow. I had no teaching obligations because no teaching was done at the Institute.

I had visited the Institute briefly in April 1960. At that time, it was attached to the Academy of Sciences. The chairman of the music division was Dr. Boris Yarustovsky, an excellent scholar, whom I had met in New York during the 1959 visit of the Soviet music delegation. Yarustovsky and his colleagues received me with much cordiality, and I was impressed by the "community of scholars" and the unity of purpose in their work.

Returning to the Institute in 1962, I found certain changes. The most important, perhaps, was that the Institute had lost its affiliation with the Academy of Sciences; it had been transferred to the jurisdiction of the Ministry of Culture. To the outside observer, this transfer seemed a mere formality, but soon one gained the impression that the change was considered by some as a sort of "demotion". The chairmanship, too, had changed; the new chairman of the music division was Dr. Yuri Keldysh, one of the best scholars of the "middle" generation, who was one of the two Soviet representatives at the International Musicological Congress in New York in 1961. During my three months in Moscow I came to know Keldysh quite well, and my respect for his scholarship and his balanced judgment rose day by day.

My arrival at the Institute as an "exchange scholar" appeared to be a major surprise to almost everyone concerned. The Academy of Sciences, which had negotiated the exchange, was no longer in charge. No one knew what my function was to be; in fact, I had no function.

I could not possibly participate in the weekly meeting of the music division since they were concerned mainly with "work in progress", either that of individual members or collective projects. Such meetings were usually devoted to "communal" criticism at which outsiders were understandably unwelcome. I found out later that such critical sessions were quite sharp and pitiless; criticism was expressed without regard to personalities.

I was invited to attend open meetings of the music division, where I heard Yarustovsky give a report on a UNESCO meeting in Rome, and Shneerson (a non-member) describe the events at the Warsaw Autumn Festival. At one of the meetings I was asked to give an outline of my research on the history of Soviet Russian musicology. The project was found interesting since no specialized, separate study of Soviet musicology had ever been made. There was a lively round-table discussion, and I was given a number of helpful suggestions. One piece of advice—as I recall—was to concentrate on historical musicology and to avoid theoretical musicology, since the theorists were "confused". Needless to say, this advice came from a historian, but he was not far wrong.

The members of the Institute's music division showed no interest in American musical life and research. This lack of official curiosity seemed almost deliberate, as if to emphasize that the guest from America had nothing to offer that was new to the Soviet specialists. It was somewhat characteristic of the attitude of cool detachment, of standoffishness that permeated the Institute.

Since I could not participate in the work of the Institute's music division, I sought to have private interviews with the senior members. Some were frank, others were cautious—and understandably so. They all knew that I was gathering information, and they were careful not to express any criticism of existing conditions. All agreed that in the last few years things had changed enormously to the better: there was more freedom of expression, a renewed interest in foreign topics, a widening of research areas. Such subjects as expressionism, dodecaphony, jazz—black-listed until recently—could now be discussed with a certain dispassionate objectivity. One prominent member told me that while the principle of Socialist Realism remained valid, it was applied and interpreted with far greater flexibility. But this was before December 1962, when Khrushchev's attack on abstract art set the clock of "liberalization" back by a decade.

The better I became acquainted with the workings of the Institute of Arts History, the more I realized the strength and the weakness of its set-up. There can be no doubt that the basic concept of an Institute devoted to a study of *all* the arts—the cross-fertilization of ideas, the collective work—was an intellectual challenge. Yet, some of the musicologist-members were not entirely happy; they would have welcomed more subjects of a purely musical nature, and they also found some of the inter-disciplinary topics rather artificial. Here is an example of the projects "in progress" during the autumn of 1962; each was in charge of a committee of scholars selected because of their specialization.

Project

1. History of Music of the Soviet Peoples (5 volumes; 2 published by 1970).
2. The Theatre of the Peoples of the USSR.
3. History of Art and Architecture of the Peoples of the USSR.
4. Contemporary Art in the Capitalist Countries.
5. The Art of the Socialist Countries (of Europe).
6. Research in Old Russian Art.
7. Research in Foreign Classical Art and Art History (up to the mid-nineteenth century).
8. Theory and Aesthetics of Art.
9. History of the Cinema.
10. The Art of the Peoples of the Far East.
11. Study of Russian Art in the Early Twentieth Century.
12. Study of Decorative (applied) Art.

Project No. 1—a comprehensive music history of *all* the Soviet peoples—was begun after a similar project devoted only to the music of the Soviet *Russian* area had been concluded (five volumes, published between 1956 and 1963 under the imprint of the Academy of Sciences). Collective authorship does not exclude collective errors, and some of these previous volumes were roundly criticized.

Trying to profit from past mistakes, the present "History" is being written, not only with participation of all the music members of the Institute (and there are over twenty), but also by corresponding members and by specialists in each of the various republics and territories. The progress is painfully slow since each chapter, once written, is subjected to collective criticism and then rewritten. The first two volumes, under the editorship of Yuri Keldysh, are admirable—far better than the corresponding volumes of the *History of Soviet Russian Music*—and the entire project promises to set new standards of excellence.

The list of musical scholars who belong to the Moscow Institute, is indeed impressive. Here are their names and their field of individual specialization or research as of 1962. Since then many of the projects have resulted in published monographs.*

Alexeyev, Alexander (born 1913)   History of pianism
Bachinskaya, Nina (b. 1906)   Russian folk creativity
Belayev, Victor (b. 1888)**   Various national cultures of USSR

---

* By 1971, the number of musical scholars attached to the Institute had increased from 20 to 28. Among the new members are Victor Bobrovsky (b. 1906), Grigori Golovinsky (b. 1923), Olga Levasheva (b. 1912), Liudmilla Poliakova (b. 1921), and Daniel Zhitomirsky (b. 1906). E. Gippius, M. Brazhnikov, and Y. Ryzhkin are no longer listed as members.
** Died in 1968.

Brazhnikov, Maxim (b. 1904)	Russian church chant
Gippius, Yevgeni (b. 1903)	History of Russian working class in folk songs and revolutionary hymns
Keldysh, Yuri (b. 1907)	Russian music of the eighteenth century
Konen, Valentina (b. 1913)	American music
Levit, Sophia (b. 1910)*	Monograph on Yuri Shaporin
Listova, N. A. (Miss)	Monograph on Shebalin
Livanova, Tamara (b. 1909)	Bibliography of Russian periodicals of the nineteenth century
Nestyev, Israel (b. 1911)	Monograph on Bela Bartok
Popova, Tatiana (b. 1907)	Contemporary Sov.-Russ. folksong
Ryzhkin, Yosif (b. 1907)	Musical aesthetics
Sabinina, Marina (b. 1917)	Soviet music, especially Prokofiev
Stepanova, S. R. (Miss)	Early years of Soviet music
Tumanina, Nadezhda (b. 1909)**	Two-vol. work on Tchaikovsky
Tarakanov, Mikhail (b. 1928)	Symphonies of Prokofiev
Vasina-Grossman, Vera (b. 1908)	German *Lied*. Russian *Romance*
Vershinina, I. A. (Miss)	Stravinsky's early ballets
Yarustovsky, Boris (b. 1911)	Symphonies of War and Peace

Imposing though this list is, one cannot escape the impression of a certain one-sidedness. Most members are *historical* musicologists; there are no theorists among them. One or two can be classified as folklorists or ethnomusicologists, but no folklore project was in progress at that time. Noteworthy is the enormous preponderance of projects on Russian and Soviet music; apart from the topics "Bela Bartok" and "American music", there is barely any interest in foreign music though Yarustovsky's *Symphonies of War and Peace* is "international" in subject matter. The absence of "foreign" topics must not be interpreted as a lack of competence in non-Russian fields: Livanova's early publications, for example, included works on Mozart and a history of European music before 1789. One can assume that the choice of subjects is governed by set policies: each subject must be approved by a committee, and thus the choice can be controlled. The absence of research on the Middle Ages, the Renaissance, the Baroque shows the prevailing lack of interest in music of the "distant past".

Perhaps the Soviet musicologists realize that their libraries lack primary source material on Western music; they are strong in archival holdings in the field of Russian music; hence the concentration. As for the apparent avoidance of topics in the field of theoretical musicology, the Russians still hold to the—rather old-fashioned—belief that theoretical subjects are the domain of the conservatories: therefore, most books dealing with problems of theory and musical analysis are written by conservatory professors.

* Died in 1967. ** Died in 1968.

Almost all the members are middle-aged, apart from the two young "aspirants", who were seen but not heard. One needs a certain established reputation before being elected to membership. The two youngest members, Miss Sabinina and Mr. Tarakanov, are among the most articulate, and the most interested in the contemporary aspects of music: Miss Sabinina, who wrote her dissertation on Prokofiev's controversial opera *Semyon Kotko*, has also written on the early symphonies of Shostakovich. Tarakanov has recently published several "advanced" articles on modern (even avant-garde) Soviet music in the journal *Sovetskaya Muzyka*. Another younger member, Miss Konen, impressed me as extremely well informed and broad-minded. Her concentration on American music came to her naturally: she spent part of her formative years in New York, studied for some time at the Juilliard School, and has, of course, complete command of the English language.

As the name implies, the function of the Institute of Arts History touches upon all the arts—music, theatre, fine arts, and cinema (though not literature). Each of these divisions is staffed by recognized experts, on permanent appointments and yearly salaries. If a vacancy occurs, a new appointment is made by a committee from a list of candidates, after a thorough scrutiny of qualifications and publications. The title of senior member is "uchennyi sotrudnik" ("scholarly collaborator"). A few post-graduate students (aspiranty) are admitted who write their dissertation under the guidance of a senior member; in the autumn of 1962, there were only two in music.

Each scholar-member has individual as well as collective duties. Individually, he is required to produce a certain "norm" of finished work, i.e. scholarly writing; the minimum for a senior member is the equivalent of seven "listy". (Each "list" is equivalent to 16 printed pages or 40,000 imprints or characters; thus, a member is expected to produce 112 printed pages per year.) The requirements for junior members are somewhat less. If, during a calendar year, a member is engaged in research leading to a major book, his "norm" is adjusted. Since scholar-members receive a yearly salary as payment for creative work, they are not entitled to the usual fees, once the book (written under the sponsorship of the Institute) appears in print.

Apart from his individual research and writing, the scholar-member is also expected to contribute to the collective projects. Even though a member may not actively participate in the writing, he is called upon to contribute to the evaluation of work done by others.

The demands made upon the scholar-members do not seem excessive, and they have ample time for writing and research, unencumbered by any teaching obligations. Nevertheless, a number of the scholars in the music division teach in addition. In 1962 there was much talk about a government regulation whereby a scholar or teacher should not be permitted to occupy two paying positions—unless he were "irreplaceable". The purpose of this regulation was obviously to avoid the monopolization of important positions by older teachers wielding some influence, and to create opportunities for younger scholars. The regulation, however, was never enforced, and many of the older teachers seem to have proved "irreplaceable". Thus, Keldysh, Tumanina, Nestyev, and Yarustovsky, among others, teach at the Moscow Conservatory while being members of the Institute. True, they *are* scholars of high calibre and in their cases, at least, the exemption granted is valid.

The Institute of Arts History in Moscow is a comparatively new institution. It was founded in 1944, shortly before the end of the Second World War.* Among its charter members were Igor Grabar, the famous art historian (who died in 1960 at the age of eighty-nine) and the equally famous Boris Asafiev, musicologist and composer, the only full-fledged musician-member of the Academy of Sciences to which he was elected in 1943. (After Asafiev's death in 1949, his particular position—that of a musician-member—remained unfilled.)

In 1962 the Institute was housed in inadequate quarters on one of the upper floors of a building on Kuznetskyi Bridge; the ground floor was occupied by a savings bank. The Institute floor was primarily a meeting place; it did not provide any facilities or offices for the work of individual members. The reference library was small and certainly inadequate for any serious research in the musical field.**

In contrast to the Moscow Institute, the Leningrad Institute of Music, Theatre, and Cinema, is housed in a sumptuous palatial building in the heart of the city, on the square of St. Isaac's Cathedral. The Leningrad Institute has an uninterrupted history, a continuity of work, a heritage of tradition that lends it an air of established superiority. In a way, the scope of the Institute is more limited since it does not include the fine arts; but within the three division—and particularly in the field of theatre history and music—there seems to be greater depth. Less time is taken up with inter-disciplinary projects; each division concentrates mainly on its own research area, publishing the results of the research in collective volumes. Such collections containing musical materials came out in 1947 (in honour of the thirty-fifth anniversary of the Institute), in 1958, and in 1962.

Because the Institute has so much space, it can accommodate certain

* Hence, it is not directly connected with the Arts Institute of the 1920's that was transferred to Leningrad in 1933.

** According to information received in 1971, the Institute has recently moved to its own building at Kozitskii Pereulok in Moscow.

permanent exhibitions, such as the unique Museum of Musical Instruments, one of the finest collections in the world, particularly of folk instruments of the entire Soviet Union. Any instrument on exhibition is not only seen, but can also be heard. If a visitor wishes to hear a certain instrument, he presses a button next to the showcase; this activates a signal in a central phonograph room whereupon a recording of that particular instrument will be played immediately. It is a novel experience, and often a surprising one, since the visual appearance of an instrument in a glass case does not necessarily suggest the type of sound it produces. K. A. Vertkov, the director of the Instrument Museum, is also the chief editor of a recently published sumptuous book, *The Atlas of Musical Instruments of the Peoples of the U.S.S.R.*

The chairman of the Institute's music division, Yuli Kremlev (born 1908), is an extremely intelligent and well-informed scholar. Since he is also a sharp-tongued critic, he has more than the usual number of detractors, in Leningrad as well as in Moscow. Kremlev's negative evaluation of Shostakovich's Tenth Symphony, in *Sovetskaya Muzyka*, has not been forgotten and has brought him much enmity. Kremlev's special field is musical aesthetics. At the time of my visit he was working on a major book on Debussy; in fact, he was the Soviet representative at the 1962 conference on Debussy in Paris. An anthology in three volumes, entitled *Russkaya Mysl o Musyke* ("Russian Thought on Music"), edited and annotated by Kremlev, is a valuable source of scholarly information. Important, to Kremlev, is the *continuity* of Russian thought from pre-revolutionary to post-revolutionary times, the differences of opinions, the previous debates, in one word, the *tradition of dissent*.

Kremlev is surrounded by a group of some fifteen musical scholars who, though perhaps less famous than their Moscow colleagues, are no less verbal and often more productive. During my brief visit, I was extremely impressed by two younger men, Genrikh Orlov and Arnold Sokhor. Orlov (born 1926) has recently published two excellent books, *The Symphonies of Shostakovich* (1961) and *Soviet Russian Symphonism* (1966). He tries to break away from the stereotyped evaluations and approaches controversial subjects with a fresh, unfettered mind. Here is a new voice, unencumbered by the memories of past intellectual oppressions, ready to take a new look at old taboos. Sokhor (born 1924) has published a number of useful volumes devoted to Soviet folklore. Another member, Lev Raaben (born 1913), who also teaches at the Conservatory, has made Russian and Soviet chamber music his specialty. He has also written on the history of the violin and on various violinists (among them Leopold Auer).

The interesting cross-relationship between music and the theatre is demonstrated vividly in two extremely valuable books published under the imprint of the Leningrad Institute. The author is Abram Gozenpud (born 1908), the titles are *Muzykalnyi Teatr v Rossii* ("Musical Theatre in Russia", 1959) and *Russkii Sovetskii Opernyi Teatr* ("Soviet Russian Opera Theatre", 1963). The latter covers the period 1917–41; a second volume will bring the work up to date. Gozenpud possesses a wealth of information, and the Leningrad Institute, where music and theatre are housed side by side, is the ideal sponsor for such an enterprise.

In Leningrad, as in Moscow, one feels that the Institute holds itself aloof, that it does not wish to mingle too much with the Conservatory, nor with the hubbub of concert life and competitive pressures. The Institutes consider themselves in a class by themselves. This attitude creates a somewhat rarified atmosphere, a trifle removed from what is *really* going on in music. After having attended several talkathons about music, I turned with a sigh of relief to the Conservatories where one could *hear* music.

The Soviet conservatory is a college-level music school which provides a professional education to performers, theorists, musicologists, and future pedagogues. It takes five years to complete the conservatory course; normally, a student enters at the age of eighteen and receives his diploma at the age of twenty-three. The curriculum is unified and centrally controlled by the Ministry of Education, though minor deviations—dictated by local conditions—are permitted. One could compare this course of study with that of some professional music schools in the United States where the student, after four or five years of study, receives the degree of "Bachelor of Music" (B.M.) or "Bachelor of Science" in music (B.S.).

There are twenty-four conservatories in the Soviet Union. Most of them have an affiliated "Central Music School" where particularly gifted children, age seven to eighteen, can receive an integrated education of music and general subjects. Here is a complete list of the conservatories; those marked with ★ have an affiliated Central Music School:

Moscow: Conservatory★ and Gnessin Institute★

Leningrad★	Kazan★	Kiev★	Lvov★
Gorki	Sverdlovsk★	Kharkov★	Minsk★
Saratov	Novosibirsk	Odessa★	Tashkent★★
Alma Ata★	Kishinev★	Baku★	(*two* Central Music Schools)
Riga★	Tbilisi★	Vilnius★	Erevan★
Tallinn★			

Vladivostok (called Institute)
Astrakhan (established 1969)

There are also Central Music Schools in several cities not having conservatories: in Kaunas, Frunze, Kherson, and Dushanbe.

Post-graduate studies (*aspirantura*) are offered at eight of these conservatories: in Moscow, Leningrad, Kiev, Minsk, Tbilisi, Erevan, Riga, and Alma Ata, as well as at the Moscow Gnessin Institute. The three-year course leads to the degree of "candidate", comparable to the American master's degree.

Compared to the Institute of Arts History, there is less intellectual depth at the Conservatory, but far more musical activity. The official conservatory curriculum is designed for performers, composers, theorists, and musicologists. But in truth, the main effort is geared towards the training of outstanding performers. Of the eight hundred students enrolled in the Moscow Conservatory, about eighty to one hundred specialize in theory, composition, and musicology; all the others are performers.

To give musicologists a conservatory training is a peculiarity of the Soviet educational system; in the West, this responsibility is assumed by the universities. In the course of the curriculum reform in 1925, the training of musicology students was transferred from the Institutes to the Conservatories. At that time, Ivanov-Boretzky took charge of the music history department at the Moscow Conservatory while Asafiev assumed the same responsibility in Leningrad. There are advantages and disadvantages in this system. Undoubtedly, the young Soviet musicologist is a better *practical* musician than his university-trained Western counterpart; but he is sadly lacking in the intellectual breadth that only a university can impart. Within the Soviet conservatory curriculum, non-musical subjects are reduced to a minimum and geared to Partyline education. Required subjects are dialectical and historical materialism and a course in "The History of the Party". A student having completed the conservatory curriculum is primarily an accomplished musician, though in a somewhat narrow sense. His technical equipment is excellent, his musical taste leans heavily towards the nineteenth century, the methodology is deliberately conservative.

The teaching of piano, violin, and violoncello is superb. The presence on the faculty of the greatest Soviet virtuosi—Oistrakh, Kogan, Gilels, Rostropovich—insure the continuity of tradition. There is also a strong phalanx of supporting teachers—less famous, to be sure, but often more experienced as pedagogues. Every great Soviet musician considers it his civic duty to transmit his knowledge to the young generation. This applies also to the composers, all of whom occupy teaching chairs at the conservatories or music schools.

But the excellence of conservatory teaching is only a partial explanation of the Soviet success in training first-rate instrumentalists. We must remember that a student *enters* the conservatory with a full technical preparation; in all probability, he has attended a secondary music high school and, before that, an elementary music school; or he has completed one of the central music schools attached to the conservatories. Compared to this systematic development of the talented child, the preparation of a gifted youngster in Europe or America is decidedly haphazard and depends on the private initiative and insight of a parent.

The playing of wind instruments, on the other hand, is less highly developed among Soviet musicians, and Western standards are higher. This may be due in part to the inferior instruments used in Soviet orchestras, perhaps also to the limitation of repertoire and years of isolation. When the Moscow State Orchestra visited New York, the oboes and French horns were found particularly wanting in quality.

The Soviet public became aware of the difference in orchestral standards when the Boston Orchestra came on a visit in 1959, soon followed by the Philadelphians and the New York Philharmonic. Harold Schonberg of *The New York Times* quotes a Russian musician as saying, "It was a blow to our pride . . . The difference between Boston and our orchestra was so great it was insulting. We had meetings and decided to do something about it, about the calibre of playing, about the calibre of the instruments themselves."[1]

Vocal instruction is admittedly weak in Russia. One can hear it at every opera performance, especially among sopranos and tenors. Soviet officials are aware of it, and some promising young Russian singers have been sent to study in Italy.

The teaching of theoretical subjects was hampered, until recently, by the lack of up-to-date textbooks. The methods of Rimsky-Korsakov—in harmony—and of Taneyev—in counterpoint—are still basic, and even though newer books may be used, the approach remains essentially the same. In music history, the study of Russian music is emphasised out of all proportion, lately also the music of the Soviet peoples. General music history is covered in a conventional and abridged manner, judging by the teaching outlines and by the lectures I have attended. Much, of course, depends on the personality of the teacher: a lecture by Keldysh or Druskin, by Yarustovsky or Nestyev can still be exciting. But they are "part-time" teachers, and the supporting faculty of historians lacks stature, particularly since the death, in 1962, of Roman Gruber. His former students and assistants carry on "in his spirit", Alexei Kandinsky took over as chairman. But the teaching of music history at the Moscow Conservatory "always was, and still is, inadequate", as one prominent Institute member (and former student of the

Conservatory) told me in private: "in my time, pedagogues like Shaporin and Sposobin considered history with contempt while theory was the most important subject."

The historical curriculum is further diluted by courses especially tailored for the needs of the "performers": they contain a bare minimum of information. Composers and future musicologists study their history on a somewhat higher level though there does not seem to be a system of "elective" courses as in the American colleges and universities.

A comparatively new field which has interesting possibilities is the "History of Performance Art". Nothing is as elusive, as fleeting as a musical performance, especially prior to the invention of the piano roll or the phonograph record. Soviet musicologists attempt to reconstruct and preserve the art of great performers of the past, their style, their repertoire, their idiosyncrasies. "In the past, the history of musical culture was written exclusively in terms of the composer," said Dr. Lev Ginzburg, author of an important *History of Violoncello Playing*; "now, the performers are taken into consideration, and the importance of the interpreter-performer is stressed in many utterances of Russian and Soviet composers". Soviet historians are planning to transform the subject of musical performance into a serious branch of historical study, and many books and courses are devoted to this topic.

In the field of musical analysis, Moscow points with pride to Lev Mazel, recently retired from the Conservatory, who is considered one of the most original minds among Soviet theorists. His 1965 series of articles in *Sovetskaya Muzyka* indicates that his retirement is not a period of inactivity. With his associate Victor Zukkerman, Mazel is engaged in writing a three-volume work on Musical Analysis. Zukkerman himself is a creative mind; his book on the *Kamarinskaya by Glinka* is highly regarded. He owes much to his teacher Yavorsky—as do, in fact, many Soviet theorists. Books by two Western scholars, Ernst Kurth and Ernst Toch, have influenced Soviet writing, but the name of the theorist Heinrich Schenker is virtually unknown to Soviet musicians.

The chairman of the theory department at the Moscow Conservatory, Sergei Skrebkov,* has written a textbook on polyphony which is in use at the Conservatory. He is a man of wide knowledge though he has the reputation of being somewhat rigid in his views. He told me that he had a collection of thousands of polyphonic church pieces which could not be published under present conditions. Vladimir Protopopov is another specialist in polyphony, though his field is more the *history* of polyphony. Of a projected two-volume work on this

* Skrebkov died in 1967.

subject, the first appeared in 1962. It dealt, predictably, with the history of *Russian* polyphony.

The faculty of the Conservatory is expected not only to teach but also to write for publication. A certain balance is maintained between teaching and writing which is reflected in the annual "teaching load". A minimum of four "listy" (about sixty-four printed pages) is expected of a professor; those who have no urge (or no gift) to write, are given heavier teaching schedules. The teacher-pedagogue is committed to 1,440 hours during the academic year, of which 720 hours are for teaching and 720 for creative work. (The academic year consists of forty weeks: nineteen weeks for the first term, seventeen weeks for the second, and four weeks for examinations.) The teaching assignments vary somewhat according to the rank of the faculty member and other considerations; twelve to twenty hours per week seem to be the norm. Salary increases are granted every five years. There are three academic ranks: professor (highest), lecturer (called "dotsent"), and assistant.

The building which houses the Moscow Conservatory is in the narrow Hertzen Street. Shaped like an open rectangle with a small square at the centre, adorned by a statue of Tchaikovsky, it accommodates about sixty classrooms, the library, the acoustical laboratories containing all the recording equipment, and two concert halls, the "small" (of chamber music size, seating perhaps three to four hundred) and the "large" which serves for all important concerts in Moscow, acoustically perfect. Like so many older European concert halls, it is not over-large—seating slightly over one thousand. Originally there was also the Glinka Museum, which, however, has been moved to its own palatial building on Georgievskii Pereulok in 1965.

In 1962, the music library of the Conservatory was wholly inadequate for any type of serious work. The book shelves and the reading space were combined in one large room, separated by the issuing counter. The readers' section had spaces for fourteen readers; another ten could squeeze in if need be. No books or scores were within reach of the reader, not even reference books; a separate call slip had to be filled out for every item. When material is issued to a reader, his library card and a clearance slip (handed to him at the entrance) are retained at the issuing desk; both are returned to the reader when he hands back the borrowed material. The clearance slip, stamped by the librarian, is collected at the exit from the library. No material can be taken out; this section is exclusively for reference.

However, there is a circulating service for books and music. This service, called "abonnement", is handled in an ante-room, even more crowded, with the "subscribers" jostling each other, trying to balance the bulging card files. There is no space to put down a card file drawer;

a few shaky round tables are of little help. The cards are well organized but hand-written, and kept in rickety, ill-fitting wooden file shelves. A corner of the ante-room is set aside as work space for the chief librarian, and a few cubby holes are usable for conferences. At the exit is an elderly woman whose job it is to collect briefcases that cannot be taken inside; at the same time she applies her amateur talents to the gluing of some tattered music. The shortage of sheet music and the lack of multiple copies of scores is evident everywhere and hampers the work of the students. Undeterred, however, young people study and work.

In the vestibule of the Conservatory are several tables where books, music, and magazines are sold. There is also a book and music store facing Hertzen Street and accessible from the street level.

The collection of phonograph records is kept separately and is available to students only by special arrangement. Neither faculty members nor students are permitted to handle phonograph records. If a recording is needed for classroom demonstration, the following system is used:

Fifty of the sixty classrooms in the Moscow Conservatory are wired for sound and connected by direct lines with a central "playback" room. At the time (1962), this playback room was equipped with eight tape machines and three turntables so that eleven classrooms could be served simultaneously. Each of the fifty classrooms has a loudspeaker but no turntable. There is a telephone line from each classroom leading to the central playback room; each instructor carries a telephone receiver in his briefcase which he can plug in to speak to the playback room. Of course, the faculty member has to file his requests ahead of time—perhaps twenty-four hours—so that the material can be held in readiness. The system has obvious advantages: it saves the equipment from inept handling and it stretches the limited supply of recordings. But it is also very rigid: no last-minute changes can be made, no replay is possible, and human error is ever present.

Students wishing to listen to a certain recording must also file an advance request. Only three listening rooms are available, each seating several people. Here, too, the tapes or recordings are handled by a central attendant, and the sound is piped into the listening room which has a loudspeaker but no turntable. There is also a recording studio with a piano and a wealth of equipment. Tapes and recordings are stored in separate stacks, each under controlled temperature and humidity.

I visited the acoustical laboratory which is housed in a wing of the Conservatory building. It occupies three floors with space of "over four hundred square metres" as I was informed. The installations were obviously new; there is an abundance of equipment and machinery. The laboratory is divided into three units: sound reproduction, sound recording, and acoustics research.

The sound recording unit has a direct line to both concert halls of the Conservatory so that anything that is performed there can be put on tape. Some foreign artists refuse to grant permission because of contractual obligations with recording firms. However, whether such refusals are actually honoured is difficult to tell since the tapes are made for internal archival purposes. There is a shortage of foreign-made records; certain works not in the Russian repertoire are unobtainable.

The acoustical laboratory is not concerned with "electronic" music. The laboratory was established in 1932 by Professor Garbuzov who had been in charge of a similar unit in the GIMN (State Institute of Musical Science) during the 1920's. His picture hangs on the wall (he died in 1955), and the research staff continues his line of research. During my visit to the laboratory I was told that Lev Theremin, the engineer and inventor, had settled in Moscow in 1945 (he had been in America for a number of years), and that he worked as a physicist and electronics specialist. In April 1970, Theremin emerged from obscurity; he spoke at a musicological meeting in honour of Lenin and was introduced as "the inventor of the first electronic instrument brought to Lenin's attention".

All in all, the many hours I spent at the Moscow Conservatory were among the most interesting and enlightening of my three-month stay. Dean Alexander Nikolayev (not to be confused with Alexei Nikolayev, his son, who is a composer) was most generous in permitting me to visit any class and any lecture of interest to me. I attended dozens of class sessions—with Khachaturian, Kogan, Rostropovich, Tatiana Nikolayeva, Galina Barinova, Protopopov, and many others. I talked to departmental chairmen and individual pedagogues, and I came to admire their spirit and their dedication. True, there were shortages—of textbooks, music, recordings; the buildings are old, the pianos are worn, the classrooms poorly lit. There was occasional criticism, but no grumbling. Above all, there was enthusiasm and devotion in the bright and eager faces of the students, ambition and true comradeship.

I remember one evening when I was invited to hear a concert of the graduate violin students. I arrived punctually at seven o'clock—the usual hour for concerts—and I found myself faced with a programme that consisted entirely of works by Wieniawski and Szymanowski. After having heard three hours of this music—very well played indeed —I staggered out of the hall while the concert was still going on. The next morning, the elderly secretary asked me eagerly, "How did you like it, Boris Yosifich?" "I liked the playing," I replied, "but why so much Wieniawski and Szymanowski?" "Oh, didn't you know—this was our brigade rehearsing for the Wieniawski Contest in Warsaw."

Curiously, that year the Wieniawski Contest was won, not by a member of that well-trained brigade, but by an unknown young American, Charles Treger.

When I visited the Leningrad Conservatory in December 1962, the celebration of the 100th anniversary of that institution had just taken place. Everything was spick and span, new paint was in evidence; obviously, a general face-lifting had taken place for the centenary. This was in sharp contrast to the rather dilapidated appearance of the Moscow Conservatory. However, it is safe to assume that for Moscow's centenary in 1966, the same beautification process took place.

But even without the difference in outward appearance, the Leningrad Conservatory seems to be more spacious, better planned, less crowded than its Moscow cousin. There is more room everywhere—in the music library, in the cafeteria, in the cloakroom, in the director's office. The Conservatory building faces an imposing square, with the Kirov Theatre on the other side.

My first step was to pay a visit to the pro-rector of the Conservatory, Elena Orlova. (As in Moscow, the rector himself is rarely seen; all the administrative work appears to be done by the pro-rector.) Madame Orlova is a historian; at the time she was completing a book on Asafiev which was published in 1964. She is articulate, purposeful, full of energy and highly intelligent. (This impression was reinforced when I met her again, two years later, during her visit to New York.) Madame Orlova presented me with two volumes, containing the history of, and reminiscences about, the Leningrad Conservatory, published for the centenary.[2] The entire institution, so it seemed, was permeated with the pride of being the oldest of its kind in the country. Badges celebrating the 100th anniversary were worn by many faculty members and students.

Being the oldest institution had certain practical advantages, too. While the curriculum is standardized for all the conservatories in the country, the Leningrad Conservatory is permitted to experiment in curricular matters. A new instructional plan for musicologists was introduced in 1962, advancing seminar work to earlier years. Thus, the second year included a seminar in archival and bibliographical work, the third year offered a seminar in music criticism (including reviewing books, music, concerts, operas), the fourth year culminated in a history seminar. In addition, the student-musicologists were taught the techniques of publishing under the guidance of an editor of the State Publishing House (MUZGIZ/Leningrad).

At the Leningrad Conservatory the study of musicology has been reorganized in such a way that the average student can complete the entire course in four (rather than the customary five) years.

The four-year student leaves the conservatory with a regular diploma, and usually becomes a teacher. Only the outstandingly promising musicology students are retained for a fifth year during which they are prepared for special research projects or the post-graduate *aspirantura*. The cut in the length of study does not, however, affect the number of subjects covered by the curriculum, as one or two hours per week are added to the students' schedule.*

When I questioned the wisdom of "channelling" a student that early, Madame Orlova replied that there was no risk involved. She explained that the conservatory student, having gone through a secondary music school, was already well typed as to his major field of interest; those who showed an inclination towards musicology, toward the "humanistic" aspects of music, were screened more thoroughly (by means of an entrance examination) than were the performers.

Madame Orlova mentioned that Shostakovich taught a class of post-graduate composers at the Conservatory (which is his alma mater); he travels from Moscow about every two weeks and is very thorough and punctual in his work. One of his students was the highly gifted Boris Tishchenko (by now an established name among young Soviet composers).

The Leningrad Conservatory has a number of "non-resident" students, both on the undergraduate and post-graduate level. These are students who live in other cities; those on the undergraduate level take six years (instead of the regular five) to complete the course, while the post-graduates need four years instead of three. These non-resident students are required to come to Leningrad for personal instruction twice a year for one month, in January and in June, remaining on salary in their regular jobs. The non-resident students are mostly pedagogues already placed in teaching positions; they receive and return their lesson assignments by mail. Experiments with recorded lessons have also been made.

The system of non-resident music instruction—mainly by correspondence—(called "zaochnoye muzykalnoye obrazovanie") is fully accepted in the Soviet educational system; most conservatories and music institutes are giving such courses, following a centrally established curriculum. In Moscow, the Gnessin Institute is especially active

---

* A cursory comparison with a typical college plan in the United States shows that the Leningrad reform is more than justifiable. During an academic year, the Soviet student spends thirty-six weeks in the class room compared with a total of thirty weeks in an American college. Yet, the American student receives his B.A. degree after four academic years. The fifth year, given to the most gifted young Soviet musicologists, is a real bonus, and it seems only fair that this be reserved for the "cream of the crop".

in this field. This system is particularly important for people who cannot attend regular school sessions, or who live in towns which do not have college-level music schools. (Incidentally, this type of course is also available on a secondary level.)

A brief visit to the Leningrad Conservatory convinced me that, far from resting on its laurels as the oldest institution, it was most receptive to new ideas and fresh initiatives.

Because of my limited stay in Leningrad, I visited only a few classes in order to have more time for personal interviews. I remember an hour in Mikhail Mikhailov's class on Scriabin as a fascinating experience. Under discussion was Scriabin's late period, and the examples played in class demonstrated anew how far ahead of his time this master had been. Mikhailov traced Scriabin's relationship to Debussy; and though the older Soviet generation (especially Prokofiev and Shostakovich) was anti-Scriabin, Mikhailov felt a certain influence in the second movement of Shostakovich's First Symphony. Prokofiev even dedicated one of his early pieces to Scriabin. A satisfactory analysis of Scriabin's late period is still lacking, Mikhailov said, though Yavorsky's theories have contributed to his understanding.

A two-hour class on foreign music of the 1920's and 1930's proved to be surprisingly interesting. The lecturer, a spinsterish lady named Galina Filenko, had a thorough command of her topic—Germany between the two World Wars. In fact, she dispensed a mass of information and though the students took copious notes, the words without any musical illustration lost some of their meaning. Nevertheless her class was a first-rate musico-sociological exposé.

After the class, I stayed to talk to Miss Filenko. She obviously felt that her lecture without musical examples had not been fully effective. At any rate, she told me that the students, aside from listening in class, also had special listening sessions; so, for example, they recently spent three hours under her guidance listening to Berg's *Wozzeck*. Suddenly, Miss Filenko came to life, "Youth now rediscovers things which we, the older generation, know as a matter of course. Those of us who studied in the 1930's (and even more so in the 1920's) heard everything and everybody—how we adored Klemperer! Today, the young people —having been cut off for so long, are simply overwhelmed by things thirty years old which they hear for the first time. The young musicologists are still a bit cautious, they have to *talk* about things, be verbal. But the composers are absolutely entranced by it all, they simply do not want to listen when one cautions them or when one mentions 'weaknesses or drawbacks' . . . *Wozzeck* made a strong impression on the students; they studied it with score and recording. Schoenberg's system interests people, while in Webern they admire the workmanship." So much for Miss Filenko's monologue which I found very revealing and somehow touching.

Among the music historians of the Conservatory, Mikhail Druskin (born 1905) impressed me as the strongest personality. His bearing is a bit stiff, almost military, his speech is precise, his judgments razor-sharp. He did not remember our brief meeting in Berlin in the early 1930's where he studied with Artur Schnabel after having completed the piano course at the Leningrad Conservatory. Druskin belonged to the early Asafiev disciples who battled on behalf of musical modernism. When I reminded him of his first book on *New Piano Music* (1928), he smiled and said, "I got plenty for it in 1948". At present his interest has turned again to the contemporary scene. He has attempted a new periodization of contemporary music; the old one seemed too splintered to him. As for the future of dodecaphony in the Soviet Union, he said, "I am no prophet, but certain 'tonal' aspects of that technique are already being applied by some Soviet composers, for example Salmanov."

When I touched upon the subject of the rivalry between the historical schools of Leningrad and Moscow, Druskin said that today there was none; but that there had been a great deal of it in the 1920's and 1930's. Moscow's Ivanov-Boretzky had stressed the historico-cultural factors, while Leningrad's Asafiev combined the musico-historical with theoretical aspects. (There was no love lost between Asafiev and Ivanov-Boretzky). In general, Moscow was more "conservative". Moscow's Konstantin Kuznetsov was not a "professional" musician but a former business man though he wrote well about music. On the other hand, Leningrad had Sollertinsky whom Druskin praised in glowing terms. However, while Leningrad seems to have been stronger in history, Moscow was more important in matters of theory: Yavorsky, Alshvang, Mazel and Zukkerman—these were, and are superior, brilliant scholars. Leningrad's theorist Tyulin is competent yet without much personality, and, besides, sadly lacking in understanding for the twentieth century. His method of harmony is so conservative that students falter even if they have to analyze Mussorgsky, not to mention Debussy or more recent harmonies. Unable to cope with modern harmonic aspects, Tyulin refers the students to Druskin for "aesthetic" analysis, while Druskin maintains that it is a matter of theoretical technique. Incidentally, the historian Gruber—so Druskin said—was also totally alien to the twentieth century and therefore left no "school"; even his students (such as Sabinina and Poliakova) do not mention him as their *maitre*. (Gruber had taught at the Leningrad Conservatory until 1941 when he was transferred to Moscow.)

Concerning "sociological trends" in music history, Druskin said, "In the 1920's and 1930's, we were all guilty of 'vulgar sociology'—not only Braudo, but also Sollertinsky, Gruber, all of us. Today it's the turn of the East Germans; they are more 'left' than we are, going through all the infantile disorders . . . Look at Georg Knepler's *Music History of the Nineteenth Century*, for example."

Compared to Druskin, the other historians of the Leningrad Conservatory seem less forceful, but not necessarily less scholarly. Semyon Ginzburg—not to be confused with the Moscow historian Lev Ginzburg—is a highly respected member of the faculty. Like Druskin, he belongs to the earliest disciples of Asafiev whose "junior spokesman" he was in the early 1920's. Actually, Ginzburg's most valuable musicological contributions were made in the field of Russian and Soviet music. He was chief editor of a two-volume *History of Russian Music in Musical Examples* (vol. 1 in 1940) which rescued a great deal of early Russian music from total oblivion.* During the war, he was evacuated to Tashkent and became interested in the music of Uzbekistan. From there his interest broadened to include many other Soviet peoples. In the 1950's, Semyon Ginzburg edited three anthologies devoted to the "classical" music of the Ukraine, the Caucasus, and the Baltic States. He continued to write textbooks on the subject of the musical literature of the Soviet peoples, with particular stress on the secondary school level where—he felt—this area was unduly neglected. For a time, he collaborated with Victor Belayev; however, their approaches now differ: while Belayev stresses folklore, Ginzburg is more interested in the musical culture of *art* music and its history.

An entirely different area was discussed with Professor Georgi Tigranov, a kind, voluble man of Armenian descent, though educated in Leningrad. His dissertation had dealt with the *Operatic Dramaturgy of Verdi* and he has retained his interest in the general field of operatic stage problems. He told me that the Leningrad Conservatory had a new study area—to train operatic stage directors who are not "theatre" people but trained musicians, who can shape the staging of an opera from the score, not merely from the libretto. The new course for stage directors is, of course, tied closely to the vocal department and the opera studio. Leningrad is alone in teaching this type of opera direction; they also train opera directors at GITIS (State Institute of Theatre Art), but there the focal point is the text, not the music.

Our interview was interrupted by a student who arrived to discuss some dramaturgical aspects of Rimsky-Korsakov's opera *Pskovitianka* ("The Maid of Pskov") which he had seen at the Kirov Theatre. The

* A second enlarged edition was published in 1968.

student criticized certain aspects of the production, and discussed various dramatic needs and implications, demonstrating his points at the piano. Tigranov helped, clarified, and gave him a further assignment along the same lines. "We train our students for the practical life," Tigranov remarked with some pride, "when they criticize, they must *say* something; we expect opinions, challenges, intelligent summaries. But not everything must be for public consumption; as Tchaikovsky said, 'not every six-four chord needs to be published'."

In reminiscing about Asafiev, Tigranov called him "the greatest" but mentioned that he was not a good speaker ("I think with the tip of my pen," Asafiev used to say). His antipode was Sollertinsky who was a fascinating lecturer but left comparatively little in writing.

Among the theorists of the Leningrad Conservatory, I found the "grand old man", Yuri Tyulin, most impressive. At the time, he was near seventy, teaching a reduced sehedule, but still intense, warm, outgoing, and deeply involved in his subject. Tyulin's main field is harmony though at one time he has also taught form and analysis. He presented me with several of his textbooks, among them an early one dating back to 1937. He apologized for the washed-out colour, "it's my last copy, it went through the blockade of Leningrad". Tyulin mentioned that the old Rimsky-Korsakov text on harmony was meant as an elementary book, not designed for "spetz" (i.e. "specialists") courses; the most recent edition of this old text—the twentieth—is called an "academic edition" because it restores the original and eliminates many later additions of Rimsky's son-in-law, Steinberg. Lately Tyulin has had a younger collaborator, Nikolai Privano, with whom he has published several textbooks. (Privano joined us later during the interview.)

With regard to contemporary harmony, Tyulin felt that it should be studied and discussed—perhaps not so much taught as analyzed. (I remembered Druskin's rather negative comments on this subject.) The classical foundations—Tyulin felt—were still most important; he quoted Shostakovich as saying that, even if awakened out of a deep sleep, he (Shostakovich) could still play all the keyboard modulations he was taught at the Conservatory. (This affectionate bit of memorabilia contrasts sharply with what Shostakovich once said in the 1930's —"at the Conservatory, they kept us from composing"—a statement much resented by his former teacher of composition, Steinberg. Or— perhaps—all those modulation exercises *did* keep him from composing!)

Later on, Professor Tyulin sat at the piano and played a few of the "modulatory preludes" handed in by students. These were exercises based on a skeletal beginning provided by the teacher; the usual form seemed to be a standardized A–B–A, with a statement, digression, and a varied restatement, the whole ending with a forceful pedal point on the dominant. What I heard was harmonically often interesting, at times even advanced though not beyond the accepted norm. Tyulin smiled benignly at some of the dissonances.

With a forceful personality like Tyulin at the helm, the teaching of harmony occupied a more central position in the Leningrad curriculum than that of counterpoint. I met one of the professors in this field, Alexander Dolzhansky, but too briefly to form any impression. He was known to me mainly as a lexicographer, and we talked about the immense sales of his *Kratkii Muzykalnyi Slovar* ("Brief Musical Dictionary", 1959). "This little book has netted the State Publishing House one-and-one-half million roubles,* and I got a comparative pittance for writing it," he complained. At the time of our meeting, Dolzhansky was completing an analytical study of the "Twenty-four Preludes and Fugues" by Shostakovich which was highly praised after its publication in 1963. Dolzhansky died in 1966, at the age of fifty-eight.

While the firm structure of the conservatories, the unified curricula, the aura of time-honoured tradition, arouses the admiration of the outside observer, there is one inherent danger in all that solidity . . . something one could call "academic inbreeding". Too many of the faculty members have done their undergraduate and graduate studies at the institutions where they are now teaching. They spend their lives within the same walls, first as students, then as teachers. This is basically an unhealthy situation. While American and English colleges and music schools seek to attract a diversified faculty with different educational and regional backgrounds, the reverse seems to be the case in the Soviet system of higher education. In effect, differences of approach and method have virtually disappeared, to be replaced by grey conformity. The dissensions in music theory, for example, which were so violent in the 1920's, have become historical memories. In the present-day network of Soviet conservatories, differences of methods are minimized, except for certain folkloristic idiosyncrasies. The much-vaunted decentralization of culture is bound to remain a myth as long as the guidelines are issued in Moscow. This "inbreeding" is noticeable not only in musical education but also among composers and compositional schools, despite the stress on regional characteristics. It is the tutelage of Moscow's bureaucrats that impedes the freer development of Soviet music in all its aspects.

* Apparently Dolzhansky used the old "inflated" rouble valuation.

Moscow has a second institution of higher learning in the field of music—the *Gnessin Institute*. Its co-existence with the famed Conservatory is possible because the Gnessin Institute stresses the training of future pedagogues—it is a kind of "teachers' college". Originally it was a private music school, founded in the 1890's by the Gnessin family —the composer Mikhail Gnessin and his four sisters, all professional musicians. Eventually, the curriculum was expanded to include schooling on a "secondary" level; finally, in 1944, the Gnessin Institute became a "vuz", an institution of higher learning. However, with each "up-grading", the previous educational level was retained; thus, the same building houses the children's music school on the ground floor, the secondary music school on the second floor, and the "vuz" on the third floor. The adjoining intimate concert hall serves not only school purposes but is used generally as a chamber music hall. As a structure, the Gnessin Institute is impressive; it may have been a private mansion or government office in Tsarist days. The facilities are well maintained (by Soviet standards), the class rooms are airy and decorated with portraits of famous Russian composers. The library of books seemed extremely small.

The curriculum is geared, as we have said, to the training of competent teachers. This is already expressed in the official name "State Musico-Pedagogical Institute Named After Gnessin" (Gosudarstvennyi muzykalno-pedagogicheskii institut imeni Gnessina). Methods courses and practice teaching are emphasized, and pedagogical topics prevail in the "diploma" dissertations. Older students acquire experience by teaching in the elementary division, first as observers, then as assistants, finally on their own responsibility. Musicology students are trained to deliver lectures for laymen; they are required to prepare two lecture topics a year which they present at club meetings, cultural centres, to children's groups, and so on. The Gnessin Institute also teaches the playing of folk instruments (an area not covered by the Conservatory) and the techniques of folklore research.* Students go on summer expeditions to collect new folklore materials. Despite the widespread interest in folklore in the Soviet Union, there is no central folklore institute as yet; however, there were plans in 1962 to centralize all such research.

While less glamorous than the Conservatory, the Gnessin Institute is an efficient, well-integrated school. Within its walls, a young person, age seven to twenty-three, can receive a total musical education, from the beginning to mastery. For future teachers, the concentration of all educational levels under one roof is a unique advantage, in terms of of observation and practical experience. The intimacy of the Institute is

* At the Moscow Conservatory, a "folklore cabinet" was established in 1938.

an asset rather than a drawback. The Gnessin Institute is proud of its tradition of professional excellence, and among its former students are a number of distinguished musicians, for example the composer Aram Khachaturian. Mikhail Gnessin himself taught at the Institute only after it became a "vuz", from 1944 to 1951 (he died in 1957 at the age of seventy-four). Earlier, he had been a faculty member of the Moscow Conservatory (1925–35) and of the Leningrad Conservatory (1935–44); among his students were composers like Salmanov, Khrennikov, and Khachaturian. Although Gnessin could compose in a traditional Russian idiom and adjusted himself early to the Soviet trend (his *Symphonic Monument* of 1925 was one of the first compositions on a revolutionary topic), he is best known as an important representative of the Jewish wing of Russian composers. The fact that the Gnessin Institute retained *his* name after its nationalization testifies to the high regard he and his sister Elena Gnessina enjoyed in high Soviet circles.

In keeping with the pedagogical curriculum of the Gnessin Institute, the present faculty concentrates on the writing and publication of text-books, many of them for the secondary school curriculum. Some fifteen such texts were printed during the past years, among them one by Mikhail Pekelis on Soviet music, by Rozenshild on foreign music up to 1750, and by Levik on Western European music from 1750 to the present. Victor Berkov of the theory faculty contributed several books on harmony, including the volume *Harmony and Musical Form* (1962).

The outstanding scholar of the Gnessin history faculty is its chairman, Mikhail Pekelis, a man of impressive erudition and wide experience. Born in 1899, he taught at the Moscow Conservatory from 1924 to 1941 and joined the Gnessin faculty in 1948. Pekelis's two-volume *History of Russian Music* was published in 1940 but was violently attacked in 1948 as "too subservient" to Western influences.

Pekelis' life-long preoccupation is the life and work of the composer Alexander Dargomyzhsky; he published a study of him in the 1930's and followed it up in 1951 by a book, *Dargomyzhsky and the Folksong* (Dargomyzhski i narodnaya pesnia). In 1962 he was working on a definitive monograph of Dargomyzhsky. Pekelis also serves as one of the editors (with Kiselev and Danilevich) of the publication *Musical Heritage* (Muzykalnoye Nasledstvo). These are volumes containing essays and specialized studies on music and musicians of the Russian past. The first volume appeared in 1962* (an impressive volume

---

* In 1935, a volume also entitled *Muzykalnoye Nasledstvo* appeared under the editorship of Ivanov-Boretzky.

of over 600 pages), the second in 1968 (293 pages). Additional volumes are to appear at irregular intervals.

In our conversation, Pekelis pointed out how much had been accomplished recently in the exploration of Russian music. For example, the composer Alexander Alyabiev (1787-1851) had been known mainly for his song compositions; recently instrumental music by him was discovered, hidden during the war in cellars in Moscow. In the field of folk music, collectors of pre-war days concentrated mainly on songs; new research has unearthed much *instrumental* folk music. These are only a few examples out of many; one glance at the pages of *Muzykalnoye Nasledstvo* or similar publications shows the amazing activity of Soviet musicologists covering all aspects of their secular musical past.

Excellent though the Soviet conservatories and research institutes are, they are not necessarily better than comparable institutions in the Western world. "The Soviet education system presents a study in contrast. The most modern and the most obsolete teaching techniques exist side by side."[3] But the true secret of Soviet successes in music—particularly in training great instrumental performers—lies in the discovery of the gifted child *at an early age*. This discovery is followed up by most careful attention given to the guidance and systematic development of the child's talent. Soviet music derives its strength from the elementary and secondary musical education given to a child between the ages of seven and seventeen. The whole system is comparable to a broad-based pyramid, with the conservatory at the top.

A musical education, to be fully successful, must start in early childhood. This is an axiom accepted by educators everywhere, but only the Soviet musical system has drawn the appropriate conclusions. The Soviets have developed a gigantic network of music schools on all levels, spread over the entire country. The figures are staggering: 2,219 children's elementary music schools (primary level, enrolment in excess of 400,000);* 187 intermediate music schools (secondary or high school level, enrolment about 36,000 students); 24 Central Music Schools (combining elementary and secondary levels in an eleven-year curriculum for especially gifted children, enrolment in excess of 7,000 students); and 24 college-level conservatories, of which eight also offer post-graduate studies. State-approved correspondence courses leading to a diploma are given by most of the conservatories.

In addition, there are about 1,000 evening music schools where young people and adults can study music, usually as an avocation; here

---

* Actually, children's elementary music schools are an older Russian tradition: there were forty such schools in Tsarist Russia.

the enrolment is about 150,000. Last but not least, the Soviet educational system gives high priority to a musical education *for all*, and music is a required part of the school curriculum.*

A child showing musical talent can be enrolled in a Children's Music School (Detskaya Muzykalnaya Shkola) at the age of seven or eight. Here, only music is taught while academic subjects are taken at a regular school. After seven years of study in such a children's music school, the student proceeds to a specialized intermediate school where the curriculum includes both musical *and* general subjects; such a school is called *technicum* or *muzykalnoye uchilishche*. If this school is to be the student's terminal education, he remains for four years; the diploma he receives entitles him to teach at an elementary music school, unless of course he prefers some other musical activity. Obviously, after ten or eleven years of consecutive music study, the graduate of a *technicum* is—at the age of about eighteen—a solid instrumentalist with a good command of theoretical subjects. However, he is not obliged to become a musician. In fact, if his interest shifts, or if his early-discovered musical talent proves unsubstantial, he can switch to another school since his academic curriculum follows a normal pattern.

However, if his musical gifts are particularly promising, the student at the *technicum* is permitted, after only three years, to sit a competitive entrance examination for admission to a conservatory. Competition for admission is very keen since the capacity of the conservatories is strictly limited.

The exceptionally musical child has another, more direct and more fully integrated, way to reach the conservatory. This is through the admission to one of the twenty-four "Central Music Schools". Such music schools are usually affiliated with a conservatory**; some of the conservatory professors also teach at the music school which insures a high degree of continuity and professionalism.

A child, having qualified for admission to a Central Music School, will enter at the age of seven which is the normal starting age in the Soviet school system. The eleven-year curriculum is subdivided into the "elementary" level (grades one through eight) after which an examination is given; and a "secondary" level (grades nine through eleven) with a final examination. During the first eight (elementary) years, the academic curriculum parallels as closely as possible the courses in a

* The figures were given to me in 1962 by an official of the Ministry of Culture. The statistics published by the Composers' Union in 1966 were higher in a few instances, in which case the later figures are given. See also Kabalevsky's statement of 1968 (p. 490).
** See p. 379.

normal school so that a child wishing to transfer to a different type of school can do so without loss of time.

After a young musician completes the Central Music School at the age of about eighteen, he receives a diploma enabling him to teach at an elementary music school. Most of them, however, attempt to qualify for entry into a conservatory, a high honour indeed. Usually the conservatory, with its five-year course of study, is a "terminal" school: the finest graduates become soloists, others will be chamber music players, orchestra musicians, opera singers, conductors, teachers, musicologists. A very small number is admitted for post-graduate work, the three-year *aspirantura*, open in any field—performance, musicology, or composition.

By establishing the Central Music Schools and the Intermediate (secondary) Music Schools with their correlated curricula of musical and academic subjects, Soviet educators have solved the basic problem —the combination of a normal school curriculum with early emphasis on a specialized subject, in this case, music. I know of no other country where a musically gifted child is given such early professional attention.

In November 1962, Yehudi Menuhin and I were invited to visit the Moscow Central Music School. At the time, Menuhin had plans to establish a similar school in Great Britain (a plan he has since realized at Stoke d'Abernon), and he was eager to observe the Soviet approach.

What we saw and heard was delightful. The children who played for us (all violinists) were not "prodigies", their musical development had not been pushed beyond their years. What they showed was careful schooling, near-perfect intonation, fine musical memory, technical accuracy, and a musical perception that reflected their personality. No technical fireworks, no sensuous vibrato, no bursts of temperament. It was wholesome, normal, and touchingly beautiful. The repertoire selected for performance was within the musical horizon of the children, a concerto by Vivaldi or Mozart, a few student pieces . . . nothing that made unnatural demands in terms of depth or feeling. I remember one little violinist—his last name was Kogan. We were told that he was the son of Mr. and Mrs. Leonid Kogan. Both parents are violinists —the father, of course, the famous virtuoso, the mother née Elisabeth Gilels, the sister of pianist Emil Gilels. The boy had a serious face like all the children; perhaps they were a bit intimidated by the presence of the famous visitor, Mr. Menuhin.

We were told that the Central Music School in Moscow had been the first of its kind in the country. It started in 1932 when some fifteen gifted children were permitted to have their music lessons at the Moscow Conservatory. Because of outstanding talent, they were assembled into a "special children's group" to be taught together, not only music but also general school subjects. The initiative came from the famous piano pedagogue, Professor Goldenweiser, and other great teachers joined him—Neigaus, Zeitlin, Yampolsky, Igumnov. Out of these modest beginnings grew the present school, housed in its own beautiful building. In 1962, the school had 390 pupils—some 200 from Moscow, and about 190 from other cities. About 75 students are boarded at the school, an arrangement preferred by the administrators, the others live at home or with families. Classes are kept small; the average is about eighteen to twenty pupils in each. Some of them take their music subjects in the morning and their general subjects in the afternoon; for the others, the order is reversed. It keeps the pupils fresh, and the teaching staff is fully utilized. Instrumental practice is not supervised —unless it is done by parents at home.

In reading the roster of students who completed the Central Music School (usually to enter the Conservatory), one is amazed how many of the famous musicians of today—often children of famous musicians —went to that school. Here are a few names: the violinists Igor Bezrodnyi, Nina Beilina, Irina Bochkova, Eduard Grach, Leonid Kogan, Igor Oistrakh; the cellists Natalia Gutman and Mstislav Rostropovich, the pianists Vladimir Ashkenazy, Bella Davidovich, Yevgeni Malinin, Tatiana Nikolayeva; the conductors Gennadi Rozhdestvensky and Maxim Shostakovich, the composer Kyrill Molchanov, the entire Borodin String Quartet. And the Moscow school is only one of twenty-four such schools!

These children are fortunate not only in having expert guidance from the start, but an unbroken continuity of guidance. There are no changes of method or approach, no need to re-learn or retrace one's steps. Many of the children are taught almost from the beginning by truly great teachers who are able to guide them uninterruptedly to mastery; the entire schooling is based on established traditions and methods.

The thought, the care, and—last but not least—the financial investment that the Soviet government put into these (and many similar) schools has been repaid a thousandfold. In music—and particularly in musical performance—Soviet virtuosi enjoy unique international acclaim.

However, the true musical influence inside the Soviet Union is wielded, not by the performers (famous though they may be) but by the composers. It is the Union of Soviet Composers that is the power behind all musical decisions of the Soviet government. It is an amazing power wielded by the small directorate of a professional union. The Composers' Union can influence prizes (including the coveted Lenin Prize) and awards, commissions and publications. It can guide the repertoire of opera houses and philharmonic orchestras, of radio and concert programmes. The Union can send its members abroad on special assignments. It also holds the purse strings through control of MUZFOND, i.e. government funds for music and musicians.

A young Soviet composer—especially if he lives outside Moscow— can rise only through the regular channels of the Union; first, his work might be played at a local survey of new music, then, if successful, recommended for performance at a national plenum in Moscow. But first of all, he must please those in power—the older, established and (invariably) conservative composers. The Union can, and does, assist its loyal members in a variety of ways, from the copying of orchestral parts to a stay in a vacation home. In return for this bounty, the Union directorate demands absolute loyalty and conformity—mainly, adherence to the official cultural directives of the Party. "Rebels" are unwelcome, whether they dabble in serialism or grumble about the sterility of Socialist Realism. Khrennikov is quoted as having said, "Anybody is free to compose any kind of music . . . While a revolutionary may compose anything, that does not mean that he is necessarily entitled to the benefits of the Union of Composers."[4]

The membership of the Union—it must be remembered—is limited to composers and musicologists, the articulate musical intelligentsia. The Union controls two widely read publications—the scholarly monthly *Sovetskaya Muzyka* (founded in 1933) and the semi-monthly *Muzykalnaya Zhizn*, a more popular journal founded in 1957. In addition, members of the Composers' Union serve as critics for the entire Soviet press.

Actually, Moscow serves as headquarters not for one, but three Composers' Unions: the nation-wide organization headed by Khrennikov; the state-wide union of the Russian Republic (RSFSR) whose chairman, until recently, was Shostakovich, now succeeded by Sviridov; and the local Moscow chapter. Many Moscow musicians belong to all three, and there are complaints of over-organization and duplication of purposes. Nevertheless, each group serves its distinct aims. The nation-wide union is deliberately multi-national though the Russian members are most numerous and most influential; but in the interest of fairness, composers of the "periphery" are often given attention far in excess of their musical merit and numerical representation. For the sake of comparison, here are the membership figures as of 1960:

Russian Republic (RSFSR)   673 (including Moscow 399, Leningrad 125)
Ukraine   144
Estonia   55

Latvia	44
Lithuania	33
Armenia	69
Gruzia (Georgia)	81
Azerbaijan	54
Byelorussia	35
Tadzhyk	13
Moldavia	27
Kirghizia	8
Uzbekistan	51
Turkmenia	12
Kazakhstan	26
	1325

(By 1967, the total membership had risen to 1600; no breakdown according to republics is available).*

* See also p. 472.

In a speech in 1962, Khrennikov had said that "The membership of our Composers' Union consists of composers and musicologists. This is no accidental combination but is perfectly natural, just as natural as the tremendous role played by the aesthetic thought in the progress of creative practice."[5]

This "perfectly natural" combination does not, however, work always so harmoniously: critics are rarely welcome when they criticize, yet it is part of their function within the Union to offer constructive criticism. Notwithstanding the tensions, the role of the musicologist as critical observer and musical analyst is considered very important.

At the Composers' Union, it is customary for every composer, regardless of fame, to present newly written works (or works in progress) to a critical forum prior to public performance. Such advance auditions can be vital for the success or failure of a new composition. Shostakovich rarely fails to bring new works to the Union for discussion, and he is very sensitive to all comments. One perceptive critic told me, "One cannot call Shostakovich 'thin-skinned'—he has practically no skin at all. When his Twelfth Symphony was played at the Union in a four-hand arrangement, he suffered visibly because he felt that those present were not quite satisfied, that they felt a certain disappointment."

Another critic, equally prominent, said that one could not print an "objective" criticism about the Twelfth Symphony of Shostakovich, but that mouth-to-mouth criticism was sufficient to place it below the Eleventh. While Shostakovich's unique reputation may have saved him from outright criticism, other—less prominent—composers are often subjected to brutally frank critical discussions. More than one score has been rewritten after such a dismemberment at the Union.

To the outside observer, this type of "workshop" creativity might seem preferable to the intellectual isolation surrounding a composer in the West. On the other hand, the Soviet system has grave disadvantages: they include control over creativity and pressure for conformity which is particularly harmful in the case of truly creative and innovatory minds.

Incidentally, membership of the Composers' Union is not obligatory. Some avant-garde composers prefer to remain outside the Union. There are also musicologists—particularly historians—who feel no need to become involved in the activities of the Union. In fact, I was told in Leningrad that musicologists were not eligible for membership unless they had contributed some writings on contemporary Soviet music. To what extent this rule is enforced is hard to know; certainly there must have been flexibility in the past, otherwise an eminent historian like Roman Gruber (exclusively occupied with music of the past) could not have belonged to the Union. But the Leningrad regulation shows the pressure applied on musicologists to get "involved" in Soviet music, not to seek refuge in the past. Although the musicologists have a certain semi-autonomy within the Composers' Union (there is, for example, a special commission for musicology in Moscow), it is clear that the composers' wing is far stronger and the more influential. The musicologists are useful for providing a theoretical and aesthetic base for the music being written; beyond that, many of the composers are distinterested in the activities of the musicology wing, and some are even contemptuous.

The Moscow headquarters of the Composers' Union, with its far-flung affiliates, serves as a gigantic clearing house for new Soviet music. It is a unique centre of information for any visitor, out-of-town or foreign. Musicians from abroad in particular are steered immediately to the Union offices located on a quiet sidestreet a few steps off the majestic Gorky Street, separated from it by an arch. The unassuming corner building is in the heart of the city, five minutes from the Conservatory, within walking distance of the Bolshoi Theatre, yet isolated from noisy traffic in a sort of semi-private enclave.

In the immediate neighbourhood are several imposing apartment buildings which are owned co-operatively by actors, performing musicians, and members of the Composers' Union. The Composers' Union owns several other co-operative apartment buildings in different parts of Moscow. Since living space is at a premium, these co-operative buildings are of great help to the members of the Composers' Union. As most of them work at home, they are permitted additional living space, significantly more than the ordinary citizen is allotted.

I visited several of the apartments; those I saw had three rooms and a small kitchen, and each room had a convertible bed though during the day these rooms served as music room, dining room, or study. But the families living there had privacy, light and sunshine, and even luxuries like refrigerators. The whole set-up is highly comfortable, and the only complaints one hears are of the poor soundproofing. With a house full of musicians, this can be a problem. A story was going round at that time about a composer in this co-op building who was trying to write a cadential ending at the piano. He kept playing chordal sequences, one cadence, then another—trying and testing, still dissatisfied. Suddenly there was a banging on the ceiling, and from the apartment above he heard someone play four-five forceful chords while a stentorian voice exclaimed, "Here, take them, I give them to you, only finish!"

Surrounded by the new apartment houses the Union building looks rather shabby, but it is surprisingly spacious. The basement houses a large collection of scores sent to the Union from all over the world. The visitor, who enters on the ground floor, steps through a small vestibule into an immense room dominated by a very large rectangular table covered with green cloth. At the far end are two grand pianos, and one wall consists of bookshelves with the latest Russian publications on music. This is the meeting room where the members congregate, where auditions of new works are held, where foreign visitors are received. It is a homely and practical room, without any claim to distinction.

Adjoining are several smaller rooms, occupied by the chairman of the foreign commission and three secretaries who are mainly in charge of foreign contacts. One of them is the legendary Nina Petrovna, known for her charm and helpfulness to every foreign visitor. Her last name is Briussova, and she is a musicologist by profession.

The Union building, apart from these reception rooms, has of course many offices not known to the casual visitor, amongst them the inner sanctum—the office of the first secretary, Tikhon Khrennikov. The few contacts I had with him were very pleasant, and he was quite helpful to me in many ways. But I have seen his eyes become cold and forbidding when he is crossed, and I can imagine that he is a demanding "boss".

A visitor wishing to see new scores or hear recordings of recent Soviet music is immediately accommodated at the Union headquarters. Tape-playing equipment is available, all the latest recordings are on hand, and everything is handled in a most competent and friendly manner. I myself have spent many hours of undisturbed listening in that large room on Briussovskii Pereulok, and so have many other foreign visitors. The advantages of such listening sessions cannot be overestimated; within a few days, one can become acquainted with the musical highlights of a whole year. Because the choice of material is so large, the innocent foreigner must rely on the judgment of his hosts. Perhaps there are standing directives as to what is to be played for visiting capitalists. It cannot possibly be a coincidence that all the visitors from the West during the autumn of 1962—Stravinsky, Craft, Slonimsky, Dodgson, Leighton, myself, amongst others—were presented with more or less the same pieces—in Moscow as well as in Leningrad. Invariably we heard one of the cantatas by Sviridov, the Symphony for Strings and Timpany by Mirzoyan, a quartet by Salmanov in pseudo-twelve-tone technique, the violin sonata by Ustvolskaya, perhaps also Grabovsky's Ukrainian songs or something by Babadzhanyan or Shchedrin. Admittedly, the choice of composers emphasized names ordinarily not known to visitors from abroad; from this point of view it was certainly instructive.

While the Moscow home of the Composers' Union is modest and time-worn, the Leningrad affiliate lives literally in a palace. There are beautiful large rooms with sculptured woodwork, high ceilings, luxurious spaciousness. Yet, while the Moscow headquarters are usually full of life and bustle, the Leningrad affiliate seems almost dead, deserted. So much of Leningrad gives the impression of faded beauty, of past grandeur while life churns on in Moscow . . .

My conference with members of the Leningrad Composers' Union consisted of one hour of talk and two hours of listening to music. I was told that, during the year 1961–62, members of the Union published thirty-seven books. (This is a remarkable figure, considering that the Leningrad affiliate had only 125 members, composers and musicologists combined). Among the titles mentioned were some collective works— *Muzykalnaya Zhizn Leningrada* (Musical Life of Leningrad); a volume called *55 Sovetskikh Simfonii* (55 Soviet Symphonies), giving brief descriptions of representative symphonic works from Arutiunyan to Yuzelyunas (each essay written by a different author); the two already mentioned books dedicated to the history of the Leningrad Conservatory; a collection of theoretical and historical essays.

The Leningrad Union categorizes its musicologists neatly into authors, critics, folklorists, bibliographers, researchers, source explorers, and lecturers. The activity of lecturing on music (we might call it music appreciation) is considered very important, and its tradition dates back to the first years of the Revolution. But although the problem of "untutored audiences" is no longer acute (in fact, the audiences of Moscow and Leningrad are quite sophisticated), the tradition of explanatory lectures has survived. In Leningrad alone, hundreds of lectures, with musical illustrations, are given by experts in the "houses of culture", in clubs, in factories—during the one-hour lunch break—in military colleges, and in the "Universities of Peoples' Culture". The custom of "explaining" music to laymen has become a characteristic trait of Soviet musical life. In Moscow, in the spacious foyer of the Conservatory Hall, one can observe a music lecturer—prior to the concert and during the intermission—expounding his introductory remarks with great seriousness to an equally serious public. Or before some orchestral concert, a hefty woman lecturer in a mannish outfit may step on to the stage and give a well-prepared "popular" introduction to the programme. All this, of course, is not accidental but part of an over-all educational plan to raise the level of the concert-going public.

The more interesting part of my meeting at the Leningrad Union was the music. I heard works by Salmanov and Ustvolskaya, Leningrad composers whose advanced idiom is regarded as proof that modernism *can* survive and coexist with Socialist Realism. The truth, however, is that Salmanov's twelve-tone experiments are deliberately "tonal", and that Ustvolskaya's dissonant writing is counterbalanced by some perfectly charming pieces in the best Socialist-Realist tradition.

After having listened to several tape recordings, I was introduced to two "live" composers, Boris Tishchenko and Sergei Slonimsky. Both played their compositions for me: Tishchenko a piano concerto (accompanied on a second piano), Slonimsky a piano sonata.

Tishchenko (born 1939 in Leningrad) was at the time a post-graduate student of Shostakovich. He played with incredible verve and brilliance; here was a piano style that had been nurtured on the languor of Scriabin and Rachmaninov, the percussiveness of Bartok and Prokofiev, the polyphonic clarity of Shostakovich—all of them twentieth century masters who, to this twenty-three year old composer, represented the "tradition". He had assimilated them all (perhaps not quite fully yet), had retained what appealed most to him, and injected his personality and temperament into this conglomerate heritage. It was an exhilarating exhibition of a young talent reaching for the stars while his feet were still on the ground. This was in 1962. In the meantime, Tishchenko has made great strides as a composer. He has won recognition at home and attracted some attention abroad. Tishchenko is close to the "avant-garde" without belonging to it. He has a burning interest in what is going on in the musical West, and he urged me to send him recent publications on serialism.

Sergei Slonimsky, born in 1932 in Leningrad, is a more mature and more introspective artist. His piano style is imaginative, his feeling for form unusually developed. One could feel the intellect behind his innate musicianship. Slonimsky, seven years older than Tishchenko, was already a member of the theory faculty of the Leningrad Conservatory. He showed me an impressive list of completed compositions. Since that time in 1962, he has advanced significantly as a composer. His musical idiom is modern without being dogmatic, and he is gaining growing acceptance. In addition to composing, he has published a book on the Symphonies of Prokofiev and an interesting essay entitled "Mahler's *Lied von der Erde* and Problems of Orchestral Polyphony." His greatest success, so far, is the opera *Virineya*, staged in 1967.

While Leningrad has more than its fair share of adventurous young composers, the official musical life of the city impresses the visitor as less vital than that of Moscow. True, the Kirov Ballet has a unique reputation. But the Kirov Opera lacks the brilliance of the ensemble of the Bolshoi in Moscow. The performances I saw in Leningrad—Tchaikovsky's *Pique Dame*, Glinka's *Ruslan*, Rimsky-Korsakov's *Kitezh*—were generally uninspired, flaccid; the singing was second-rate (with one or two exceptions), the stage direction conventional to the point of silliness (as in *Kitezh*). A performance of *Coq d'Or* at the Malyi Opera was depressingly provincial. Even the famed Leningrad Philharmonic Orchestra, which I heard in its resplendent marble-columned hall, sounded hardly more than competent; perhaps the players were tired from their American tour.

In Moscow, the orchestral scene in 1962 was equally mediocre, and neither the Moscow State Orchestra nor the Philharmonic could measure up to a first-rate European or American orchestra. The winds produced a quaint sound, the intonation was not impeccable, and there was a lack of true "ensemble" in the woodwinds.

Perhaps the best orchestral musicians are saved for the orchestra of the Bolshoi Theatre, for here one can hear really first-rate playing. A performance of the integral *War and Peace* by Prokofiev under Melik-Pashayev (who died in 1964) remains an experience not to be forgotten. No less impressive was the production of Mussorgsky's *Khovanshchina* with its monumental stage sets and sumptuous costumes. The artistic directors of the Bolshoi are also responsible for the repertoire presented at the large Kremlin Hall which seats 6,000 people. Because of the immense space, the sound is electronically reinforced, but it is done in such a skilful manner that at no time is the listener aware of this fact. The grandness of the Kremlin Hall stage permits the movement of large masses of people, horses, battle wagons, and what not. The operas and ballets given there become spectacles which astound but do not warm the listener. At the Stanislavsky-Nemirovich-Danchenko Theatre—comparable to the Malyi Opera in Leningrad—one sees operas which need acting as well as singing, clarity of word projection, humour or drama. This is the perfect setting for operas like *La Duenna* of Prokofiev with its eighteenth-century wit, or *Katerina Izmailova* by Shostakovich. Interestingly enough, there is a version of Prokofiev's *War and Peace* given at the Stanislavsky-Nemirovich-Danchenko Theatre which stresses intimacy rather than pageantry; it holds its own next to the grander Bolshoi production.

The two most important libraries of Russia are the Lenin Library in Moscow and the State Public Library Saltykov-Shchedrin in Leningrad; in fact, they are among the great research libraries of the world.

In 1962 the Lenin Library celebrated its centenary. It was in 1862 that the collection of Count Rumyantsev (1754–1826), originally housed in St. Petersburg, was transferred to Moscow and established in its own building. Called the Rumyantsev Museum, it included not only books but a variety of collections, among them one of minerals. Its director, at that time, was the well-known author and music scholar, Count Vladimir Odoyevsky.

Although the Lenin Library possesses many rare editions and manuscripts of music, its "music department" as such was established as recently as October 1961. It is destined to become the central collecting point of all printed music, both Soviet and foreign; at present, it is still in a state of growth.

Gaining admission to the Lenin Library is no easy matter. The applicant must fill out a detailed Russian questionnaire, including his academic background. Depending on the scholastic status of the applicant, he receives a card for a certain reading room. Room No. 1 is reserved for professors, scholars, and those with doctorate degrees. It is a pleasant room of medium size, panelled in wood and with potted greenery in the corners that lend it an intimate character. The individual desks were well worn, and many of the lamps were not in working condition. In general, I found the lighting in the library rather dim, and I saw people reading in semi-darkness. The waiting time for a book is, by American standards, painfully long, well over an hour, though not necessarily longer than at the British Museum or the Bibliothèque Nationale. Safeguards against theft are sharper than in any library in Europe or America. Not only must one get a signed release from the librarian that all borrowed material has been returned, but at the exit one is examined by a stern militia man or woman in uniform.

One curious incident has stuck in my mind. I filed a request for the November 1962 issue of the journal *Novyi Mir* which contained the controversial story by Alexander Solzhenitsyn *One Day in the Life of Ivan Denisovich*, hotly discussed by everybody. After an interminable wait, I received a copy in the reading room, but the allotted reading time was two hours: the demand was so great that the journal had to be rationed. A month later, in London, I bought a cheap photostat reprint of the Russian original for a few shillings . . .

While conditions in the privileged Reading Room No. 1 were uncrowded, it seems to be different for the "ordinary" reader. According to Fred Hechinger, education editor of *The New York Times*, ". . . a Russian student may spend hours standing in line at the Lenin Library—first, until he is able to check his outer garments in the entrance hall, and then, until he actually is given his book . . ."

Conditions in Leningrad are no better, "Undergraduate reading space is so scarce that students buy tickets to the nearby Ermitage Museum and study in quiet corners in the galleries."

On the whole, Hechinger finds that "freewheeling research in politically sensitive areas is impossible. Undergraduate libraries are inadequate, and only graduate students are admitted to the excellent libraries of the Academy of Sciences."[6]

Compared to the Lenin Library, the State Public Library in Leningrad is less formidable. The building itself is old, the rooms high-ceilinged and large, and none too well suited for library purposes, the corridors endless and labyrinthine. Only books and rare materials (manuscripts, etc.) are kept in the main library; printed music and newspapers are housed in a separate building, on the Fontanka. In fact, the division of printed music was added comparatively recently, in 1930.

In the nineteenth century, the St. Petersburg Library was a rather stolid place until Vladimir Stasov joined the staff in 1854. For the next half-century (he died in 1906 at the age of eighty-three) this remarkable scholar devoted his immense energies to the betterment of the Library. Being passionately interested in music (he was the "godfather" of the group he named the "Mighty Five"), he saw to it that the Library acquired the manuscripts of Glinka, Balakirev, Mussorgsky, and the other members of the group, as well as Dargomyzhsky, Serov, and many others. After the death of Rimsky-Korsakov, his family transferred all his manuscripts and letters to the Public Library, and the composer's son Andrei catalogued the holdings. In 1938, Andrei Rimsky-Korsakov, who had joined the staff of the Library in 1918, published a Catalogue of the Manuscript Division of the State Public Library. However, I was told in 1962 that the catalogue was out of date, and that the Library had acquired much additional material since then, particularly on Franz Liszt. At the time of my visit, one of the chief administrators of the manuscript division was Anastasia Liapunova, the daughter of the composer-pianist Sergei Liapunov. The Library also has a famous collection of musical documents dating back to the eleventh century—music written in the (as yet not fully deciphered) "kryukovaya" notation.

Leningrad has a wealth of libraries and archives, and interesting discoveries are still being made, as for example, in the library of the former Maryinsky, now Kirov, Theatre.

My own searches for Beethoven manuscripts led me to the so-called Pushkin House or, to give it its full title, the "Institute of Russian Literature of the Academy of Sciences of the U.S.S.R.". It houses a comparatively young collection, started in 1908, and contains not only literature, but musical manuscripts of many famous composers of the eighteenth and nineteenth centuries, both Russian and foreign. At the Pushkin House, I was permitted to examine three manuscript letters of Beethoven, addressed to Schreyvogel, to Archduke Rudolph, and to an unknown recipient (probably Holz). My request for a microfilm of the latter was refused; the reason given was that a Soviet scholar was working on the same topic and had to be given preference. However, I obtained a photostat of this letter from other sources and published it for the first time in *The Musical Quarterly* in facsimile and decipherment.[7]

Further Beethoven research brought me to the Glinka Museum in Moscow or—as it is formally called—the "Central Museum of Musical Culture named after M. Glinka".* My principal reason for visiting the Glinka Museum in 1960 had been to see two of the rarest Beethoveniana —the so-called "Wielhorsky" Sketchbook of 1802-3 and the so-called "Moscow" Sketchbook of 1825. Previously in private possession, these sketchbooks became state property after the Revolution and were finally entrusted to the Glinka Museum. The "Moscow" Sketchbook was published by Ivanov-Boretzky in the Beethoven year 1927; the "Wielhorsky" Sketchbook was published in 1962.

When I returned to the Glinka Museum in 1962, I was received like an old friend. The director, Madame E. N. Alexeyeva, is a person of great energy and charm—a former member of the Bolshoi Opera, as I found out later. The museum collects everything pertaining to musical culture—books, music, manuscripts, photographs, memorabilia, instruments, lithographs, letters. At the time of my visit, it was housed in cramped quarters in one wing of the Conservatory building. In 1965, the Museum was moved to a new home in Georgievskii Pereulok,

* The Glinka Museum was established in 1943 and absorbed the holdings of the Nikolai Rubinstein Museum.

near the Kremlin—a building dating from the sixteenth or seventeenth century that was once the town residence of the boyar Troyekurov. Musical instruments are exhibited on the first floor, though they represent only a fraction of the 1,500 instruments in the possession of the Museum. Here, folk instruments stand side by side with a Florentine spinet of 1565, once owned by the Medici family. On the first floor is also the valuable manuscript collection with rare items by Beethoven, Liszt, Chopin, Brahms, Mahler, Debussy, and Benjamin Britten. The second floor is devoted to materials bearing upon the life and work of Russian and Soviet composers—manuscripts of the masters, various memorabilia (as for example the pianos used by Glinka and Borodin), autographed pictures, operatic stage designs, etc. Contemporary Soviet music occupies a special section. Microfilms, photostats, and recordings of rare music complete the collections of the Glinka Museum.

There is a useful research library and a small staff of young musicologists who catalogue and study the material. Occasionally, pamphlets and books are published under the Museum's imprint. The senior research member, Nathan Fishman, is recognized as an outstanding Beethoven expert. It was he who was responsible for the exemplary publication of Beethoven's "Wielhorsky" Sketchbook. The edition consists of three volumes: a complete facsimile, an edited decipherment, and a volume of commentary. Ordinarily, Beethoven's sketchbooks are published in decipherment only, with a few added facsimile pages. By making available the complete facsimile plus decipherment, the scholarly value of the Glinka Museum publication is enhanced immensely, for it enables the serious student to compare the master's jottings with the decipherment of an expert.

Another, more recent, publication of the Glinka Museum is a volume of *Reminiscences about the Moscow Conservatory* (Vospominanya o Moskovskoi Konservatorii), published for the centenary of the institution in 1966, under the editorship of Madame Alexeyeva.

Several visits to Soviet publishing houses provided some insight into the workings of the State-owned and State-subsidized "business" of publishing music and musical literature. The abbreviation MUZGIZ stands for the all-powerful "Muzykalnoye Gosudarstvennoye Izdatelstvo" (State Music Publication) which has an almost monopolistic grip on all publications pertaining to music. During the NEP era of the 1920's, MUZGIZ worked with the Universal-Edition in Vienna in order to secure copyrights for Soviet works; many compositions of the time were published simultaneously in Moscow and Vienna. Lately, in the 1960's, similar arrangements have been made to publish copyrighted editions of Soviet compositions in England (Boosey & Hawkes),

Germany (Breitkopf & Haertel), and America (MCA-Leeds). All this is necessary because the Soviet Union is not a member of any international copyright agreement (neither was Tsarist Russia, for that matter). Even prior to 1917, Russian composers were published abroad—by Belaieff in Leipzig, Rahter in Hamburg, Kussevitsky (Edition Russe) in Paris or Berlin. Despite these precautions, there is an enormous amount of Russian and Soviet music that is unprotected by copyright. Popular works like Prokofiev's *Peter and the Wolf* or the "Classical" Symphony can be bought in many Western editions, and every anthology of music contains well-known pieces by Kabalevsky, Khachaturian, and Shostakovich. On the other hand, MUZGIZ freely reprints foreign music and books regardless of any copyrights. Sometimes, strange things happen: for example, the pocket score of an American edition of Gustav Mahler's First Symphony turns out to be a photographic reproduction of a Soviet edition, complete with footnotes in Russian (but not in English)!

Certain business arrangements have also been made between the Soviet Union and several Western phonograph companies to process Russian tapes on Western labels. Still, there are many "pirated" recordings of Russian origin on the market. "Pirated" is, perhaps, the wrong word since, in the absence of legal safeguards, there is nothing "illegal" about the procedure.

When I visited MUZGIZ in 1962 (housed in the old building of the pre-revolutionary music publisher P. Jurgenson), I was met by the director, Konstantin Sakva. I had seen Sakva in New York as head of a delegation of musicologists, including Nestyev, Kremlev, Alexeyeva, and Vasina-Grossman. Sakva, a musicologist in his own right, is a man of high intelligence though he has the cold and calculating demeanour of a political commissar. In his office he showed me his own preface to a new edition of Mozart's *Requiem* and gave me some statistics about the workings of MUZGIZ.

A few weeks later, I was invited to see the editorial offices of MUZGIZ. The space seemed incredibly cramped. All the music editors sat in one large room and considered themselves lucky to have an individual desk. In another small room, the chief book editor, Tatiana Lebedeva, shared her office with two girls doing menial jobs, like pasting, cutting, and sewing bindings. Yet, the excellent results obtained by MUZGIZ show that glass-enclosed offices in skyscrapers are not a prerequisite for quality.

Madame Lebedeva told me that the Moscow office of MUZGIZ aims to publish about eighty-five books each year, but rarely exceeds sixty-five titles, including brochures and pamphlets. Sakva had given me the somewhat more optimistic figure of 200 titles a year (which may have included the Leningrad production).

MUZGIZ publishes its production plan a year ahead. I was given a catalogue of 260 pages entitled *Thematic Plan for 1963*, with a separate order book. This material was distributed in 1962 to every book store manager in the country, with a request to send in his orders. The catalogue itself contained a description of every piece of music and every music book to be published, with indication of price and the size of the printing. According to this catalogue MUZGIZ-Moscow planned to publish 812 titles of music, 49 music textbooks, 83 books on music; and its Leningrad affiliate 79 titles of music, 30 books on music. But the number of titles planned or published, is less indicative than the number of copies printed. The full score of Glinka's *Ivan Susanin* was to be printed in 700 copies, while the *Piano School* by Nikolayev had a printing of 200,000 copies. The size of the printing is based on advance estimates, and at times there are colossal miscalculations.

MUZGIZ takes particular pride in its "academic editions". These are definitive "Complete Works" editions of the great Russian masters from Glinka to Rimsky-Korsakov. Each volume is provided with critical annotations and a scholarly introduction. Some volumes contain several versions of the same work (as, for example, Tchaikovsky's *Romeo and Juliet*). All the operas are published in vocal scores and full scores. The following examples will illustrate the magnitude of the task: the Glinka edition consists of 20 volumes of 250 to 450 pages each; the complete Tchaikovsky will include 62 volumes of music and 17 volumes of letters and prose writings; the complete Rimsky-Korsakov is planned for 50 volumes (but actually 63 volumes because some of the opera scores are published in separately bound volumes). All of these editions are very near completion.

Furthermore, MUZGIZ publishes series of "Collected" or "Selected" Works by twentieth-century Russian composers; among them are multi-volume editions of Medtner, Miaskovsky, Rachmaninov, and Sergei Prokofiev. The art music of non-Russian peoples is not neglected; an edition of the Armenian composer Komitas has been started. In addition, there are scholarly anthologies entitled *Classical Music of the Peoples of the U.S.S.R.*, among them volumes of art music of the Ukraine, Transcaucasia, and the Baltic States. A wide range of folk music is also published in authoritative editions.

The musicologist Vassili Kiselev is the editor of the "academic editions". In order to make his editions as complete as possible, he is always looking for letters written by Russian composers to recipients abroad which may be in Western museums or private collections. Among Soviet editors and curators of archives and museums, there is a strong interest in assembling all available letters and all memorabilia concerning Russian musicians abroad—not necessarily the originals which are frequently unobtainable, but at least photostats or microfilms. Some archives have been repatriated (Chaliapin), others are kept abroad (Rachmaninov, Kussevitsky). Quite often, the heirs of Russian-born musicians are not eager to deliver or sell these materials to Soviet authorities for political or sentimental reasons. On the other hand, the Glinka Museum (chief among those interested) is often unable to offer any sizeable compensation for such materials because of foreign currency problems or budgetary limitations.

In the mid-1950's, MUZGIZ became so overburdened with its manifold responsibilities and ever-growing demands that Soviet composers and authors lost patience with the interminable delays. One can safely assume that the Composers' Union exerted some subtle pressure. At any rate, in 1956, a second publishing unit was established, devoted exclusively to contemporary Soviet composers and authors. It was named "Sovetskii Kompozitor" (The Soviet Composer), with the head office in Moscow and a branch office in Leningrad. However, the new enterprise, though very successful, lasted less than ten years: in 1964, MUZGIZ and "Sovetskii Kompozitor" were fused into one "super" publishing establishment, called "Muzyka" (Music).

When I visited the Moscow office of "Sovetskii Kompozitor", it was at the height of its success. The director was the composer Igor Ilyin who impressed me as articulate and sincere. He stressed the "profile" of the new house: the concentration on contemporary Soviet music and books, folklore, and mass enlightenment. MUZGIZ continues to publish the classical and pedagogical repertoire. Even a famous composer like Shostakovich—so Ilyin said with some pride—liked to entrust some of his works to "Sovetskii Kompozitor" while further editions (i.e. reprints) are handled by MUZGIZ.

At first, "Sovetskii Kompozitor" gave preference to Moscow authors —a policy that caused some protest, as Ilyin admitted; now, they strive towards nation-wide representation. Even foreign music is being considered for publication; as a first try, some Children's Pieces by the American composer Elie Siegmeister were published, with a preface by Kabalevsky who had brought them back from America.

When I questioned Ilyin about the difficulty of buying chamber music in parts (not score), he admitted that they were hampered by paper shortages. He said,

"If I am given the choice of publishing four scores by different composers or one string quartet in score and parts, I'd choose the first alternative. Frankly, how many people really need and buy chamber music in parts? How many professional string quartets are there in this country—ten, fifteen, twenty at most. The need is too small to print parts for every chamber music work; we limit ourselves to scores."

The actual truth, however, is that even in the case of quartets by Miaskovsky, Prokofiev, or Shostakovich, parts were virtually unobtainable in Moscow's retail stores.

Ilyin showed me his printed *Thematic Plan for 1963*. Though somewhat smaller (161 pages) than that of MUZGIZ, it was still impressive. There were 501 titles of music and 78 book titles. No subdivision was made between materials published in Moscow and in Leningrad; however, there was a Ukrainian section.

Just as we were parting, Ilyin introduced me to his technical director, Abram Goltzman. Later, I was told that Goltzman was extremely capable in his field, that he had developed advanced printing techniques for music, and that he was supervising the construction of a new printing plant.

A few months later, Goltzman was promoted to director of MUZGIZ as successor to Sakva, who had retired after a heart-attack. The following year, MUZGIZ and "Sovetskii Kompozitor" were merged and Ilyin became chief editor of the new "Muzyka". In mid-1967 the imprint of "Sovetskii Kompozitor" was re-activated though apparently on a smaller scale.

While in Leningrad in 1962, I also visited the Leningrad branch of "Sovetskii Kompozitor", run by two very able men, Victor Zaborsky, director, and Israel Guzin, editor. I was told that the Leningrad branch published about 100 titles a year including about 15 books and 85 selections of music, and could boast to have authors like Druskin, Kremlev, Ossovsky, Raaben, Dolzhansky, Orlova, Sokhor, Orlov and composers like Salmanov, Ustvolskaya, Slonimsky . . . There seemed to be a great deal of activity in the Leningrad branch; here, they were able to concentrate on the promotion of Leningrad musicians while the Moscow office had nation-wide obligations. Among the projects of the Leningrad branch are small, individual brochures about young Leningrad composers, attractively presented, with biographies, evaluations, and lists of works.

Yet, all the activity in the Leningrad "Sovetskii Kompozitor" could not conceal the fact that the important composers were in Moscow, or had moved to Moscow. The irresistible pull of the capital had attracted so many former Leningrad musicians—Shaporin, Miaskovsky, Prokofiev, Shostakovich, Sviridov, Asafiev, Gruber—many of them Leningrad-born and Leningrad-trained. Most faithful to his native city is Shostakovich who had dedicated his Seventh Symphony to Leningrad, who continues to teach at his alma mater, and who preferred in the past that his symphonies be first played in Leningrad under the leadership of his old associate, Mravinsky. But even this tradition has been broken in recent years. Three of Shostakovich's late symphonies have been given their premières in Moscow—the Eleventh under Rakhlin in 1957, the Twelfth under Ivanov in 1961, and the Thirteenth under Kondrashin in 1962. However, with the Fourteenth Symphony the primacy returned to Leningrad where Barshai conducted it on 29 September 1969. The Fifteenth was presented in Moscow on 8 January 1972 under the composer's son, Maxim.

The economics of Soviet publishing are puzzling to the outsider. In the Soviet Union, the author or composer is paid a set fee for his work, and he is remunerated again at (I believe) half the original fee if there is a second printing; but there are no royalty payments. Thus, MUZGIZ can make a profit of over a million roubles* on one small dictionary for which the author, Dolzhansky, was paid a moderate fee. But Dolzhansky was the first to admit that MUZGIZ was losing money on scholarly books. The reason is that book prices in the Soviet Union are extremely low, and scholarly editions are often small. For example, MUZGIZ would pay an author 300 to 400 roubles for one signature, i.e. sixteen printed pages, and these sixteen pages would be sold to the public for about five kopecks. Thus, in order to recoup the author's fee alone, some 6,000 copies of the book have to be sold. Yet, more often than not, only 1,500 to 2,000 copies of a scholarly book are printed (sometimes even less) so that a loss is inevitable. A book like Belayev's *Old Russian Music Notation* (Drevnerusskaya Muzykalnaya Pisemnost) was printed in only 820 copies, to the dismay of the author. On the whole, it seems that MUZGIZ balances its profits on popular items with the anticipated losses in the scholarly field. As for the musicologists and the composers receiving set fees (which, by the way, are often generous), they are certainly better off than if they were dependent on sales and royalties. A number of musicologists I met were free-lance authors, without a regular position, who derived a handsome income from writing and publishing.

But MUZGIZ's willingness to absorb losses or publish esoteric materials has its limits. When I spoke to Maxim Brazhnikov, the only Soviet scholar specializing exclusively in old church notation, he said not without bitterness, "You probably think that my list of publications is small. Yes, it is. But at home I have stacks of unpublished manuscripts

---

* "Old" roubles, before the revaluation of 10:1. See p. 392.

which I cannot get into print; some are accepted for publication, but there are interminable delays. And there is no serious student interested in my field, I have no one to whom I could pass on my knowledge . . ." In his efforts to decipher the old church notation, Brazhnikov worked out a statistical approach which, he said, aroused "derision". "I know more about these things than anyone else . . . but no one wants to learn . . . everything is directed towards contemporaneousness."

He was indeed a pathetic figure—a scholar of immense erudition, caught in an environment of total estrangement and indifference.

The confrontation between the Party and the arts community during the month of December 1962, resulted—as was to be expected—in a retreat of the intelligentsia. There was no abject submission, however; an attempt was made to reason with Khrushchev, to dissuade him from reinstating a reactionary arts policy. In his speech of 17 December, Ilyichev mentioned several letters addressed to Khrushchev, begging him to do everything in his power to prevent a return to the policies of Stalin's "cult of personality". Ilyichev quoted from one of these letters sent by a group of writers and artists; though no date was mentioned, it must have been written in the first half of December 1962. Here are excerpts as quoted by Ilyichev and published in *Pravda* on 22 December,

"Dear Nikita Sergeyevich!

We turn to you as to the man who, more than anyone else, contributed to the uprooting of Stalinist arbitrariness in the life of our country . . .

We have witnessed with joy the restoration, by the Party, of the spirit of Lenin: liberty and justice. The architects enjoy the opportunity of building contemporary houses, the writers—of writing truthful books; composers and people of the theatre breathe more easily . . .

An exhibition as the one at the Manège became possible only after the Twentieth and Twenty-second Party Congresses. We may have different evaluations of one or the other work of art represented at the exhibit. If we turn to you with this letter, it is only because we want to say in all sincerity that, without the possibility of coexistence of various artistic trends, art is doomed. We see now how your words at the exhibition are being interpreted by those artists whose style flourished exclusively under Stalin while others were not given a chance to work and even to live.

We deeply believe that you do not wish this to happen and that you are opposed to it. We turn to you with the request that in the field of fine arts you stop this return to past methods which are contrary to the whole spirit of our times."[1]

After having read this letter, Ilyichev said that another letter, of similar content, but signed by a different group, was received. This second letter went so far as to call for "peaceful coexistence" of all artistic tendencies. Ilyichev interpreted this as a call for peaceful coexistence "in the field of ideology". Hence, he felt compelled to issue a strong rebuttal,

"We must declare with utmost clarity:—There was not, and there cannot be, any peaceful coexistence between Socialist ideology and the ideology of the bourgeoisie. The Party opposed, and will continue to oppose, the bourgeois ideology and all its manifestations. Following the precepts of Vladimir Ilyich Lenin, the Party has advocated, and will advocate, the partyness in literature and the arts."[2]

Ilyichev mentioned with some satisfaction that the authors of the second letter preferred after some reflection, to withdraw it altogether.

The early months of the new year—1963—were relatively calm, aside from some press attacks on literary figures, particularly Ilya Ehrenburg. In February, the "affair" Yevtushenko stirred up considerable commotion because the young poet had permitted the serialization of his Autobiography in a French journal prior to Soviet publication —a grave breach of the rules.

Obviously, the Party leaders felt that stronger measures were needed to curb the simmering rebellion of the intelligentsia, especially among writers. During the December 1962 confrontation only Ilyichev had spoken, though Khrushchev's impromptu remarks had caught the headlines. A definitive statement by the Chairman was in order to clear the air of all lingering doubts.

Party and intelligentsia were called to the Kremlin for an important meeting on 7 and 8 March 1963. Preceded by a "warm-up" speech of Ilyichev on 7 March, Chairman Khrushchev delivered a two-and-a-half hour address on 8 March. It was, as one expert says, "the most sweeping statement on literature and the arts by a Soviet leader since Andrei Zhdanov's pronouncement of 21 August 1946 . . . His remarks, like those of Zhdanov, seventeen years earlier, bristled with military metaphors. If words were deeds, surely Khrushchev would have succeeded, as Zhdanov did, in putting Soviet artists back in uniform."[3]

His speech jolted the friends of liberalization, both in Russia and abroad. The opinions he voiced became the law of the land. Perhaps Khrushchev inspired less fear than either Stalin or Zhdanov, and artists still felt that they could reason with him. But essentially, Khrushchev laid down a hard line, he set a limit to cultural de-Stalinization, and he dealt a fatal blow to ideological coexistence. Until his departure from the political scene in October 1964, his speech of 8 March 1963 remained valid as a guideline for the arts.

As far as music was concerned, his position produced no surprise. His tastes were plain and simple, and though he assured his audience that "I do not, of course, claim that my knowledge of music should become some sort of standard for everybody," this is exactly what happened. Here is his credo,

> "We stand for melodious music with content, music that stirs people and gives rise to strong feelings, and we are against caco-phony . . . We cannot humour those who palm off cacophonous sounds as genuine music . . . Music without melody gives rise to nothing but irritation."
>
> " . . . You can meet young people who try to prove that melody in music has lost the right to exist and that its place is now being taken by 'new' music—'dodecaphony', the music of noises. It is hard for a normal person to understand what the word 'dodeca-phony' means, but apparently it means the same as the word 'cacophony'. Well, we flatly reject this cacophonous music. Our people can't use this garbage as a tool of their ideology."[4]

The saddest part of this diatribe is, perhaps, the "spontaneous" approval given to it in the hall by the *élite* of Russia's intelligentsia.

Once again, Lenin's authority was invoked to justify the intellectual repression, "Our policy in art, a policy of rejecting abstractionism, formalism, and any other bourgeois distortions, is a Leninist policy which we have been pursuing unswervingly and shall continue to pursue in the future."[5]

There is, as Walter Laqueur points out, an "unfortunate semantic confusion" in the use of such terms as abstractionism and formalism: " 'Abstractionists' and 'Formalists' have come to mean anything and anybody who does not conform to Socialist Realism, regardless of style or content . . . 'Abstractionism' is a mere red herring . . . The real issue at stake is the right of the writer to think for himself and to shape his creative work as he deems necessary and proper."[6]

To such a proposition, Khrushchev has an answer, "Some people can be heard talking about some kind of absolute freedom for the individual. I don't know what they mean, but I consider that never—not even under complete Communism—will there be absolute freedom for the individual . . . Under Communism, too, the will of one person will have to submit to the will of the collective." And in a summing-up paragraph, he asserts that "The Party's criticism of formalistic perversions is in the interests of the development of literature and art which play an important role in the spiritual life of our society . . . Society has a right to condemn works which are contrary to the interests of the people."[7]

The fact is, however, that Soviet "society" never had an opportunity of formulating a free opinion; the "interests" of the people were always determined by decree from above. In 1958, it was admitted that Stalin's personal tastes had influenced all adverse cultural decisions; in 1965, after Khrushchev's fall, it was implied that his individual tastes were too much in evidence when decisions in the arts were made. Time and again, Lenin is quoted as the one infallible source for the "right" decision. But as one thoughtful American critic recently remarked, "One cannot quarrel with Lenin's concept, 'Art must be for the people'. But why must *all* art be for *all* the people?"

By coincidence, the Khrushchev speech of 8 March was followed closely by a Plenary Meeting of the Board of Soviet Composers, held in Moscow from 23 to 30 March 1963. It was the first such plenary meeting since 1960. As usual, the agenda was divided into formal speeches, discussions, and performances of new music. There were three symphony concerts, three chamber music concerts, and one programme of works by students and post-graduate "aspirants" of the Moscow Conservatory. The stress was on works by young composers.

For the first time, the keynote address was delivered by a rising composer in his early thirties, Shchedrin. He was talented and articulate, yet "safe" from the ideological and musical point of view. Hence, his choice as key speaker was ideal as far as the "establishment" was concerned.

In general, Shchedrin did not disappoint the old guard. Dutifully, he traced all recent Party decisions affecting the arts to Lenin and his article of 1905, "Party Organization and Party Literature". With equal circumspection, Shchedrin stressed the multi-national aspects of Soviet music and enumerated new composers from Estonia to Kazakhstan. He acknowledged the indebtedness of the young generation to the older masters and emphasized the unity among generations,

> "There is no cleavage between the various generations within the Composers' Union . . . We have no music of the young existing separately. We have our Soviet Socialist musical culture, strong in its unity of ideas and ethical aspirations, embracing the creative achievements of acknowledged masters and the first victories of young musicians . . ."[8]

What an idyllic situation! No generation gap here—old and young composers creating in unison, firmly looking backwards. But how true was it? Technically, Shchedrin may have been right: the number of "rebels" within the Composers' Union was infinitesimally small—even in 1968 the "avant-gardists" hardly numbered a dozen, scattered in various cities, while the overwhelming majority of young composers wrote in the accepted style. Yet, if one stops to think that, in the 1860's, a group of five musicians succeeded in revolutionizing Russian music, one should not underestimate the power of a determined small group. There is a difference, however: in the nineteenth century, the "Mighty Five" rode the wave of a growing nationalism and found support in public opinion, while the avant-garde of the 1960's was for a long time an underground movement.

Shchedrin spoke with some contempt about young composers of mediocre talent who try to attract attention by "errors": the sharper the public correction, the more pleased the "errant" composers are. But when one deals with "real" talent—as in the case of Volkonsky— the question becomes more complex, as Shchedrin explained,

> "It has become almost trite to mention Volkonsky's name at every plenary session. By now it is obvious that his position of social indifference is deliberate. Deliberately he has estranged himself from the Composers' Union and isolated himself from public opinion, from friendly criticism, even from the public function of his music. I believe that Volkonsky's position is tragic and without future for a musician, and if he is a true artist, he must understand it eventually."

This mild rebuke refers more to Volkonsky's attitude than to his music. Volkonsky, convinced that his type of music was met with continued malevolent hostility by the tightly controlled world of Soviet music, became a non-composer: he shifted his main activity to the playing of harpsichord and the conducting of an old-music ensemble, "Madrigal", while keeping his own music to himself. Against such tactics the Composers' Union was virtually powerless, all the more since Volkonsky's avant-garde works attracted growing attention abroad, at the Warsaw Festival, in Düsseldorf, and elsewhere. He could afford to bide his time.

While Shchedrin's speech was full of worn-out clichés, it did contain a few new departures. It will be remembered that, a few years earlier, Shchedrin had raised the question about the scurrilous definition of Impressionism in the Soviet Encyclopaedia. Now he spoke up in favour of upgrading many of the modernists of the 1920's and 1930's, some of whom had actually become models for younger composers,

"In the last years great changes have taken place in our musical life. After the Party Resolution of 1958 . . . such figures as Hindemith, Bartok, Stravinsky, Britten, Honegger, Pouienc, Milhaud, Orff, and others not only entered the horizon of our composers but became the object of creative absorption. All this contributed to the enrichment of the musical language of our young composers."

This admission, though significant, requires careful scrutiny. The list of composers is familiar by now: these are the "classicists" of the mid-twentieth century who had become acceptable by Soviet aesthetic standards. But Arnold Schoenberg and his school as well as the more recent serialists remained as *un*acceptable as ever. Dodecaphony was still the bugaboo, but one could not ignore it entirely. "Some young composers not only use it but even argue for the inclusion of dodeca-phony in the conservatory curriculum." Shchedrin maintained the official position that dodecaphony was a blind alley and that it had not produced any great music in the forty years of its existence; time spent on its study would be a waste. Furthermore, Shchedrin pointed out (quite rightly) that the real Western *avant-gardist* had come to consider dodecaphony a "classical" device, already displaced by various mini-systems that have lost "all contact with art". Shchedrin exclaimed, "If we are guilty of anything, it is not of backwardness, but because we do not fight avant-garde tendencies with sufficient vigour." For this indifference, he blamed not only the composers but also the critics and musicologists.

Shchedrin's speech endeared him to the "establishment"—here was a *young* composer who talked sense! But how sincere was he? A few years later (in 1965), Shchedrin used some of the external trappings of avant-gardism—as for example aleatoric devices—in his Second Symphony. He became the "official modernist" of the Soviet musical establishment.

In June 1963, the Party's Central Committee felt the need to discuss, once again, the problem of literature and the arts. The dilemma was how to win the co-operation of the liberal-minded intelligentsia with a minimum of coercion. The method of public castigation had resulted in a few delayed and luke-warm recantations of the "guilty", but a hard core of resistance to official policies remained intact.

Khrushchev spoke on 21 June; he urged greater vigilance of censor-ship and centralization (which meant centralized control) of publishing. At the meeting, a proposal was made to abolish the system of separate unions for writers, composers, and artists, to be replaced by a single union of creative artists, presumably because such a union could be more easily dominated by Party stooges. Among those in favour of this proposal was not only Ilyichev but—strangely enough—Khrennikov as well. The proposal made no headway, however, because Khrushchev had no objection to the various unions as long as they obeyed Party directives.

Eager to show his compliance, Khrennikov called a meeting of the directorates of the Composers' Union (national, Russian, and the Moscow chapter) for 17 and 18 October 1963. The purpose was the implementation of Party guidelines.

One of the central issues of this meeting was, as Khrennikov phrased it, "the fight against enemy ideology in music". Once again the critics were blamed for not forcefully exposing "the formalist and abstractionist trends in modern music". Turning to the "internal" problem, Khrennikov said,

> "We all know that certain Soviet composers (true, there are very few) show a heightened interest in the twelve-tone gimmicks. Influences of the avant-garde music have wormed their way into the music of some Socialist countries, even becoming widespread there. This is a bad sign . . . We cannot ignore the notion of 'modern style' or 'the style of the twentieth century' which has found currency . . ."[9]

This sounds somewhat defensive. One by one, the Socialist countries —led by Poland—had become increasingly receptive to modernist influences. In contrast, the Soviet Union found herself on a par with Albania in being the most reactionary country in relation to modernism in the arts . . . a somewhat humiliating partnership.

Khrennikov thundered against Western critics who suggested that young Soviet composers were opposed to Communist ideology and the Party's policy towards the arts; he derided any such thought and ascribed the trend rather to a "temporary fancy". Khrennikov's speech was reprinted in *Pravda* which gave it added importance.

Shostakovich, chairman of the Russian Union of Composers, also spoke at the meeting. He, too, admitted, that "some artists with rather progressive convictions have succumbed to the baleful influence of avant-gardism". Condemning such experiments as "sterile", Shostakovich added, "The scholastics of serialism, the dry abstractions and monotony of pointillism, the formal tricks of *musique concrète* have deprived musical art of all that is alive and human, and have destroyed all logic, form, imagery, contrast, and emotion."[10]

The leaders of the Composers' Union were more perturbed than they were ready to admit. Not only were they unable to stem the growing tide of modernism at home, but they were aware of the unfavourable publicity abroad where many articles were published on the alleged backwardness of Soviet music. For the home front, Khrennikov could boast, "Our music is performed throughout the world. Millions of people in different countries applaud the works of Soviet composers."[11]

But he could not deceive the critics abroad. True, Prokofiev and Shostakovich, Khachaturian and Kabalevsky continued to be widely performed. But the music of the younger generation of Soviet composers, the music representing Socialist Realism, aroused little or no response in the West.

In fact, while Soviet virtuosi were widely acclaimed, the prestige of Soviet composers had declined sharply. In terms of "modern" music, Soviet composers were outsiders in the world of international music festivals. Even Shostakovich had his problems: while he was fêted generously at the Edinburgh Festival. of 1962, his latest work, the Twelfth ("Lenin") Symphony, was received with dismay. Most aggravating, perhaps, was the international success of Polish composers; indeed, the Warsaw Autumn Festival had become one of Europe's showcases for modern music. Not only did the Soviet participants play an obscure role, but all the dialectics of returning Soviet critics could not hide the real defeat of Soviet-oriented aesthetics. One need only read Nestyev's article "The Critics and Apologists of the Polish Avantgarde" in *Sovetskaya Muzyka* (April 1963) to realize the huge chasm between Polish and Soviet musicians.[12]

In the meantime, foreign observers—among them prominent musicians and critics—began to visit the Soviet Union in ever increasing numbers. They reported what they saw and heard; and while no one could deny the accomplishments of the Soviet regime in bringing literacy and culture to the people, the verdict on current Soviet music was generally negative. Outwardly calm and unruffled, the Soviet musical establishment was well aware of foreign criticisms. Once a sufficient amount of detrimental material was collected, a Soviet critic-polemicist was given the job of blasting the foreign fault-finders, of refuting the charges, and of accusing the foreign critics of bias and perversion.

The safest way to disarm a critic is, of course, to impugn his motives. And so, in *Sovetskaya Muzyka* of October 1963, one can read a blazing article written by Nestyev refuting a number of foreign critics. The title, "From the Position of the Cold War", implies, of course, that the adverse opinions of the foreign critics were motivated, not by valid personal observations, but by political considerations. Perhaps Nestyev seriously believed that a Western critic did not dare write approvingly of the Soviet Union in fear of impairing his position at home. Perhaps

Nestyev imagined that a Western observer, reporting favourably on the Soviet Union, would be subjected to the same vilification as was Victor Nekrasov in Moscow after he published his positive impressions of the United States. (Nekrasov, a former Stalin Prize winner, was blasted for his "bourgeois objectivity", and Khrushchev demanded his expulsion from the Communist Party.) But it is also possible that Nestyev—known for his skill as a polemicist—was simply given the "job" of answering the foreign critics and he did it in the best cold-war style.

Nestyev singled out Colin Mason of England, Boguslav Scheffer of Poland, Hans Stuckenschmidt and Fred Prieberg of the German Federal Republic, André Hodeir and Antoine Goléa of France, and Boris Schwarz of the United States. He could have added Robert Craft, Stravinsky's assistant, whose judgments about contemporary Soviet music were unfavourable, but obviously Nestyev did not want to disturb the tenuous truce between the U.S.S.R. and the redoubtable Stravinsky himself.★

Let us take the case of Colin Mason. Following a brief trip to the Soviet Union in the company of Benjamin Britten, Mason published two articles in *The Guardian* on 21 and 30 March 1963, entitled "Russia's Young Conservatives" and "Anti-Music in Russia". It seems that Britten warned his Russian hosts, "You must not judge the views of the British people by what you read in our papers." Nestyev clings to this statement while trying to discredit Mason by contrasting him with the "great . . ., honest and serious" Britten. As a correspondent for *The Guardian*—a paper "not distinguished by any particular sympathies for the U.S.S.R."—Mason was allegedly obliged to write as he did. Nestyev, filled with indignation, blames Mason for having come to Moscow with preconceived notions, and of basing his hasty conclusions on a superficial survey of the Soviet musical scene. What was Mason's opinion before he embarked on the journey? In his words, "It scarcely seemed possible that in all the Soviet Union not a single interesting

★ Nestyev attacked allegedly anti-Soviet opinions expressed in the following publications:

H. Stuckenschmidt, *Glanz und Elend der Musikkritik*, Berlin, 1957
A. Goléa, *La musique dans la société européenne depuis le Moyen Age*, Paris, 1960
A. Hodeir, *La musique depuis Debussy*, Paris, 1961
C. Mason, *The Guardian*, 21 and 30 March 1963
Boris Schwarz, "Soviet Music since Stalin", *Saturday Review*, New York, 30 March 1963
B. Scheffer, *The Classics of Dodecaphony*, Cracow, 1961
F. Prieberg, *Die Zeit*, Hamburg, 12 April 1963
Also *Ruch Muzyczny*, Warsaw, 1962, Nos. 4 and 9

composer had emerged since 1930." Upon his return he wrote, "I must admit that in the limited time available to me over there . . ., I did not find one."

Mason criticises the outmoded musical idiom, the ideological chauvinism, the intrusion of non-musical criteria, and—ultimately—the theory of Socialist Realism which he considers "fundamentally anti-artistic". He says, "It is this persistent fallacy, that art in Soviet society has taken on a new character, a function, that more than any restriction of vocabulary (though the two go hand in hand) is killing music in Russia today," and urges Soviet composers to turn from "Socialist Realism to artistic realities . . . Music is made not with ideas but with notes."[13]

One cannot expect Nestyev or, for that matter, any Soviet critic to take kindly to such blasphemous views which strike at the heart of Soviet aesthetics. But Mason is not alone in saying that Russia has not produced a significant composer since Shostakovich; this opinion is shared by many Western critics. What limits the international appeal of contemporary Soviet music is its concentration on Soviet topicality, on textual and descriptive music, on a folk-rooted accessible idiom— all of which are precepts of Socialist Realism. Nestyev knows it just as well as Mason, but to admit it would be professional suicide.

While Mason is berated for belittling Soviet achievements, the West German critic Fred Prieberg is taken to task for praising the wrong people—namely the small group of avant-garde composers. Actually, Prieberg was not alone to draw attention to this group. The first information appeared in the Polish journal Ruch Muzyczny (1962 No. 4). Shortly afterwards, on 1 May 1962, the same journal published a "Letter from Kiev" by Galina Mokreyeva, a Soviet musicologist, which contained a few details about the work of Ukrainian dodeca-phonists. As a result Miss Mokreyeva (at that time the wife of the Kiev conductor Igor Blazhkov) suffered discrimination in her professional career as a teacher.

Prieberg, a critic and author with many personal contacts in the Soviet Union, continued the campaign on behalf of Soviet avant-garde composers. His essay in the Hamburg journal Die Zeit (12 April 1963) is flanked by his two articles for the London journal Survey (January and July 1963). Basically, they contain the same information, though Nestyev only refers to Die Zeit, which he calls "that most reactionary Hamburg weekly". There is annoyance with Prieberg who was considered "a friend of Soviet music"; and the annoyance has become very shrill after the publication of Prieberg's book, Musik in der Sowjetunion (1965). Nestyev's strident reaction reflects the morbid hatred of dodeca-phony within the Soviet musical establishment.

It is significant, though, that—for the first time—a Soviet critic finds it advisable to mention the early Russian roots of serial experiments which actually can be traced to pre-revolutionary times. Nestyev speaks briefly of those musical pioneers, Efim Golyshev and Nikolai Roslavetz, and he remarks sarcastically, "Thus, we have a right to be 'proud': pre-revolutionary Petersburg produced not only the first 'abstractionist', Vassili Kandinsky, but also one of the ancestors of the notorious dodecaphony, Efim Golyshev."[14]

There *is* reason to be proud, and only the ideological straight-jacket prevents the Soviets from admitting it. The Russian composers who were pioneers in the use of a "tone row" deserve to be explored objectively, on the basis of purely musical reasoning and without ideological prejudices. Obviously, Soviet musicologists are not yet ready for such an exploration. Polish musicologists have worked on these problems— Zofia Lissa in *Geschichtliche Vorform der Zwölftontechnik* (1935) and Boguslav Scheffer in *The Classics of Dodecaphony* (1961).[15] Leading the rediscovery of Roslavetz are the American George Perle and the West German Detlef Gojowy.[16] The Russian pioneers worked not as imitators of Arnold Schoenberg, but independently of him. Schoenberg's "Method of Composing with 12 Tones" was not fully enunciated until 1924 although it was foreshadowed in his music a decade earlier. At the same time, however, Scriabin and Roslavetz, Lourié and Golyshev, among others, pursued their own theories in the field of non-tonal music and the use of the tone row. Had it not been for the premature death of Scriabin in 1915, Moscow might have become a citadel of atonality, side by side with Vienna.

The antagonism towards Schoenberg and his "twelve-tone system" is a curious remnant of Stalinist aesthetics. It began in the early 1930's as part of the campaign against Western "bourgeois degeneracy" and has continued unabated for over thirty years. When Stravinsky lectured before a group of young Leningrad composers on the "seriation principle" in the autumn of 1962, he was confronted with questions like "Doesn't it constrain inspiration? Isn't it a new dogmatism?" To which the old maestro (himself a recent "convert" to serialism) replied, "Of course it is a dogmatism, but don't dismiss it because of that. So was the old system constricting and dogmatic, to bad composers."[17] What the Soviet Russians fear in dodecaphony and serialism is the "levelling" effect, the loss of individuality, and—more importantly— the loss of a national musical idiom. But gradually, the discussion of twelve-tone music becomes less hysterical; one is more inclined to consider Schoenberg's system as a "classical" device of the twentieth century. More important than discussions are performances of twelve-tone music. A trend towards growing acceptance can be discerned in the fact that two works by the most important Schoenberg disciples were recorded in the Soviet Union in 1968: the Chamber Symphony Op. 21 by Anton Webern (by the Leningrad Philharmonic under Serov) and the Violin Concerto by Alban Berg (with Leonid Kogan as soloist).

Soviet historians forget all too easily that Arnold Schoenberg was well received in St. Petersburg as early as 1912 when he conducted his own orchestral work *Pelleas und Melisande*, Op. 5. Previously, his piano pieces Op. 11 and the Second String Quartet Op. 10 had been heard there. (Sergei Prokofiev remarks in his *Autobiography* that he had been the first in Russia to perform Schoenberg's piano music.) The *Gurre-Lieder* were performed in Leningrad in 1927. A monograph on Schoenberg appeared in 1934 under the imprint of the Leningrad Philharmonic.

When Hitler came to power in 1933, Schoenberg had to leave Germany, and there was some speculation that he might migrate to Soviet Russia. He turned for advice to his old friend, the conductor Fritz Stiedry who occupied an important position in Leningrad. In 1934, Schoenberg wrote to Stiedry, "Hanns Eisler asked me through my son whether I might come to Russia, and I sent him an outline for the establishment of a musical institute, to be submitted to the proper Soviet authorities. May I ask you to further this project, should the opportunity arise . . ."[18] However, Stiedry—aware of the reactionary trends in Stalin's Russia—discouraged Schoenberg from pursuing the Soviet project. Schoenberg moved to the United States and ultimately settled in California.

During the 1940's and 1950's, the Soviet attitude towards Schoenberg and his school hardened into an impenetrable hostility. In the 1960's, isolated attempts were made to treat him as a "historical" figure within the twentieth century. Grigori Shneerson's book *On Music, Alive and Dead* (O muzyke zhivoi i mertvoi) presents the facts in an objective manner though the evaluation of the twelve-tone school remains essentially negative. However, Shneerson takes cognizance of the growing Soviet interest in Schoenberg: he expands his chapter on "Schoenberg and his School" from thirty-seven pages in the first edition of his book (1960) to fifty pages in the second edition (1964).

Khrennikov's attempt, in October 1963, to use the meeting of the Composers' Union to impose new ideological restrictions was largely unsuccessful. No one was sufficiently scared by the oratory to desist from pursuing novel trends. But on the whole, the composers were a docile group, and even Chairman Khrushchev seemed satisfied, judging by his opinion expressed in June, "Speaking of music, we think that it is developing in the right direction. True, certain composers had a fling now and then, but we drew attention to such doings in time, and now things seem to be going well."[19]

While the musical scene was comparatively calm, there was a bitter controversy in the literary field, centering mainly around Solzhenitsyn. For a time it seemed that *One Day in the Life of Ivan Denisovich* might be nominated for the Lenin Prize. But he had become a symbol of de-Stalinization, and even Khrushchev—who had initially authorized the publication—could not (or would not) force the issue. The list of winners was published in April 1964; Solzhenitsyn was not among them. During the next years he was to be subjected to a campaign of systematic denigration.

By the spring of 1964, it became apparent that the Party leaders, for political reasons, were willing to make concessions to the intelligentsia in order to win broad support. At meetings held on 15 and 16 May 1964 Ilyichev promised "to be more liberal towards the arts and literature in return for support . . . in the ideological struggle with the Chinese". While the May meetings did not signify a fundamental change in the Party's attitude, they seemed to "indicate a more flexible approach designed to develop Soviet culture into a more viable independent force on the world scene."[20]

Despite the ideological flair-ups the years 1963-64 were a lively period in music. They were marked by the "jubilees" of several older composers—the sixtieth birthdays of Khachaturian in 1963 and of Kabalevsky in 1964, and the fiftieth birthday of Khrennikov in 1963. Each was celebrated with warm tributes printed in *Sovetskaya Muzyka*, with much oratory and many full-length concerts. Their latest works received much attention: Khrennikov had written an operetta, *One Hundred Devils and a Girl*; Khachaturian's new Concerto-Rhapsody for cello and orchestra was given its first performance by Rostropovich; Kabalevsky made an important contribution with his *Requiem*. Each of these works received fulsome praise, but the music was predictable, the style was established, and surprises were neither expected nor were they forthcoming.

Kabalevsky's *Requiem*, conceived as a memorial to those who died in the Second World War, is a non-liturgical work. The text was written by the thirty-year-old poet Robert Rozhdestvensky who had received a mild reprimand by Khrushchev in 1963 and had recanted volubly. The *Requiem* consists of three long movements subdivided into eleven episodes. As one critic says, "The work develops not so much on the principle of dramatic contrast between the movements as on the evolution of one leading idea which grows from episode to episode. The idea is the call *Remember!*"[21] The performing forces consist of two choruses (one of mixed voices, the other of children's voices), two vocal soloists, and orchestra. The monumental work, some ninety minutes in length, was received with respect and interest at its first performance in February 1963; but certain sections were found to be over-extended, slow-moving, and lacking in dramatic pulse. The lively and somewhat impish talent of Kabalevsky, endearing but not profound, does not seem ideally suited to create a work of such dimensions and emotional demands.

The Nestor of Soviet composers, Shaporin, presented a new work on 19 January 1964—the oratorio *How Long Shall Soar The Kite* (Dokole korshunu kruzhit). It was to be his last major work: he died in 1966, at the age of seventy-nine. The title is derived from a line of Alexander Blok's poem *The Kite*. Once again, Shaporin turns to a patriotic theme of his homeland. The work is conceived as a trilogy: the first part is based on two poems by Blok and entitled "The Years 1914–1918"; the second uses texts by Konstantin Simonov and treats "The Years 1941–1945"; the third and last, named "The Post-War Years", is a setting of verses by Mikhail Izakovsky. Within the seven movements there is much variety of musical means employed—a bass solo with women's chorus, a mezzo-soprano with male chorus, a symphonic interlude, a full chorus. All this is carefully planned to create contrasts. The culmination is the fifth movement, a Requiem to the Fallen. Shaporin's musical idiom is intensely "Russian" and personal in its conservative character; at one point he does not hesitate to introduce a folk song, "Revela burya, grom gremel" (The storm howled, the thunder roared). Though his is a retrospective art, one must admire his masterly skill in setting a mood and sustaining a grand line. But such a work needs an audience which is emotionally attuned to this type of fusion between poetry and music. It is not "exportable".

Shostakovich faced the same problem with his major work of 1964, the symphonic cantata *The Execution of Stepan Razin* on words by Yevtushenko. It is set for bass soloist, mixed choir, and orchestra and was first performed on 28 December 1964. Yevtushenko's opinion (which he expressed to me in New York in 1966) was quite enthusiastic; he considered it a finer work than the Thirteenth Symphony. But this may be an author's opinion; he had shaped *Stepan Razin* as an entity while the Thirteenth Symphony merely used five of his poems at random.

Stepan Razin is a rather straightforward setting of a somewhat melodramatic text. With poetic licence, Yevtushenko transforms the Cossack rebel, the leader of a peasant uprising, into a revolutionary hero who dies for the people. The scene is set for the execution on Red

Square. The bass soloist acts as narrator and also impersonates Razin; the chorus comments, emphasizes, repeats. Razin is led to the gallows, through crowds of people, rich and poor. He is spat upon, and his bitter thoughts are, "Very well, spit, spit . . . You people always spit on those who wish you well." He looks up, and "among those mugs, snouts, muzzles" he sees *faces*—and he knows that he is not dying in vain. The execution itself is pictured musically in the Berlioz-plus-Strauss tradition, with rolling drums. There follows a weird celebration dance, ordered by the Tsar's henchmen. But "Red Square cringed . . . even the buffoons were silent". And then the ghastly ending: the chopped-off head of Razin "began laughing at the Tsar".

The entire text is set with the utmost simplicity; every word is clearly heard. The orchestral interpolations are terse, concentrated, the instrumental timbres are used with cutting realism. The musical effects are rather obvious, particularly in the percussion—and yet, the entire work carries a strong emotional impact for a Russian audience to whom Stepan Razin is a folk hero. Shostakovich's musical idiom stresses "Russianism", with a pronounced affinity to Mussorgsky.

One more work of 1964 should be mentioned—Muradeli's opera *October*, given for the first time in Moscow on 22 April 1964, in memory of Lenin's ninety-fourth birthday. Lenin appears on the stage which is not a new departure; but in this opera he not only speaks but sings: at one point he intones the folk song *Kamushka*, another time he is heard in the *Internationale*.

The composer Muradeli owes his fame mainly to the 1948 purge when his opera *Great Friendship* was annihilated. Critical opinion about the new opera, *October*, crystallized rather slowly. Apparently, a consensus of views had to be reached as to how to evaluate this patriotic production. A detailed review did not appear in *Sovetskaya Muzyka* until eleven months after the première. In the meantime, the original production, staged in the immense Kremlin Palace Hall, had been refurbished and moved to the Bolshoi Theatre. It enjoyed considerable success, mainly due to a superb performance of the actor Eizen in the role of Lenin.

By March 1965 however, the novelty had worn off. That month, *Sovetskaya Muzyka* published a detailed criticism by a young Leningrad musicologist, Mikhail Byalik. The reviewer stated that the patriotic subject of the opera did not make it immune to criticism and should not be used as an excuse to hide the shortcomings of its realization, that the musical idiom was stereotyped, intentionally "accessible", and needlessly simplified. The "intonational" possibilities were not fully exploited by the composer, not even by the standards of classical Russian opera. It must be remembered that Muradeli is one of the leading figures within the Composers' Union which makes the criticism all the more remarkable.*

The trend towards expanding the Soviet concert repertoire by greater emphasis on twentieth century foreign music was continued. Works thirty or forty years old, which had been withheld from Soviet audiences for decades on pseudo-ideological grounds, made their appearance (or reappearance) on concert programmes. In the case of one neo-classical composition of the 1920's, a critic wrote impatiently, "Why did we have to wait forty years to hear this?" Early Stravinsky was rediscovered, undoubtedly as a result of his 1962 visit. Thus, his opera *La Rossignol* was given in concert form in 1963. It is safe to assume that no one in the audience remembered an earlier performance of this work—in May 1918, in Petrograd, staged for the Maryinsky Theatre by Meyerhold and conducted by Albert Coates. Also played in the 1960's were Stravinsky's *L'Histoire du Soldat* and his Violin Concerto, performed by David Oistrakh. Other twentieth-century works heard in Moscow in the early 1960's were Bartok's Violin Concerto No. 2, Hindemith's *Sinfonia Serena* and his *Symphonic Metamorphoses on Themes by Weber,* and Copland's trio *Vitebsk*.

Zoltan Kodály came to Moscow in December 1963—it was his first visit since 1947—and an entire concert of his works including *Psalmus Hungaricus* and *Háry János* was given in his honour. Kodály's folk-oriented musicianship struck a responsive chord among Soviet musicians, and he was received with much affection, particularly since his visit coincided with his eighty-first birthday. The occasion was combined with a joint session of the Soviet and Hungarian Unions of Composers, held in Moscow.

Many American artists came to the Soviet Union that year, mostly under the cultural exchange agreement, and again their performances contributed to the widening musical horizon of the Soviet audiences. An ensemble like the New York Pro Musica, with its repertoire of medieval and Renaissance music played on authentic instruments, was a revelation to Soviet musicians (not to mention the public). The group —six vocalists and thirteen instrumentalists directed by Noah Greenberg—travelled as far south as Tbilisi and Baku.[22]

But the true excitement, in Moscow, was provided by the *Festival of British Music* which took place from 6 to 19 March 1963. There were two symphony concerts and five chamber music concerts. Norman Del Mar was the principal conductor, leading the U.S.S.R. Symphony Orchestra. With him came Benjamin Britten, Peter Pears, the French

* Muradeli died on 14 August 1970 at the age of sixty-two.

horn player Barry Tuckwell, the harpsichordist George Malcolm, and the Amadeus String Quartet. Headlines like "Our British Friends" greeted the visitors.

Britten was very much the centre of attraction,* and the programmes were built around his works—the Sea Interludes and Passacaglia from *Peter Grimes*, the Sinfonia da Requiem, the Serenade for Tenor and Horn, songs interpreted by Pears, and the new Cello Sonata, dedicated to, and played by, Rostropovich. Also heard were Walton's First Symphony, the "Ritual Dances" from Michael Tippett's *The Midsummer Marriage*, and *The Planets* by Gustav Holst. Music by old English masters—Purcell, Gibbons, Farnaby, and Byrd—completed the "British" aspect of the festival which (as one critic surmised) was a gesture of reciprocity for the 1962 Edinburgh Festival dedicated to Shostakovich.

Britten's views on music were given wide publicity, all the more since they seemed to coincide with those of the Soviet musical establishment. Whether all the quotes attributed to Britten are accurate is another matter, for they were translated into Russian and retranslated into English; at times, Britten himself may not have recognized his own words. According to Soviet sources, he said that he had "no use" for dodecaphony[24] and that he was opposed to the "notorious ivory tower where the artist walls himself in from the world of reality". He was further quoted as saying,

> "I think in general that there can be no art for art's sake. A chief social duty of an artist is to shape, educate, and develop the aesthetic taste of the people. I do not recognize the division of audiences into 'the select' and the rest . . . The important thing is, not the choosing of the recipient for one's work, but having something to say to the people."[25]

Britten's opinion about current Soviet music was not recorded—at least it was not reported in Soviet publications. But during the two weeks he spent in the Soviet Union in the spring of 1963, he charmed all who came in contact with him. It is not surprising, therefore, that Britten's fiftieth birthday—which occurred in November—was observed by concerts devoted to his works. The programme in Moscow, played by the U.S.S.R. State Symphony conducted by Boris Gusman, consisted of his Variations on a theme of Frank Bridge, the Serenade for Tenor, Horn, and Strings, excerpts from *Peter Grimes*, and the Variations on a theme by Purcell. Leningrad had an even more festive

* A year earlier, in 1962, the English composer Dodgson observed in his *Russian Journal*, ". . . again I was impressed (and delighted) with the great regard and curiosity that Britten's music aroused all over the Soviet Union."[23]

offering—two concert performances of *Peter Grimes* given with different casts. The conductor was Dzhemal Dalgat who led the Leningrad Philharmonic, the Radio Chorus, and soloists drawn from Moscow, Leningrad, and Riga. The opera was sung in Russian, in an "excellent translation of literary quality", according to a Soviet critic. "The première had a signal success and was a major event in Leningrad's cultural life," reported the Information Bulletin of the Composers' Union.[26] Britten missed the opera performances by only a few days. He had come to the Soviet Union to conduct the world première of his Symphony for Violoncello and Orchestra, composed for Rostropovich, but did not stay for the opera performances.

Britten's Cello Symphony was originally planned for the Aldeburgh Festival in 1963, but the performance was postponed because of Rostropovich's health. The world première in Moscow, on 12 March 1964, took place within the framework of the monumental cello cycle presented by Rostropovich which included some forty concertos. Moscow's critical response to Britten's concerto was not entirely favourable, despite Rostropovich's obvious enthusiasm for the work.[27] But it did not dampen the general admiration and affection displayed towards the composer.

Benjamin Britten is without doubt the best known and the most widely performed contemporary foreign composer in the Soviet Union. His reputation is enhanced by his personal appearances. His cycle with the Covent Garden chamber opera ensemble in 1964 which included *Albert Herring*, *The Turn of the Screw*, and *The Rape of Lucretia* was much admired. His friendship with Soviet artists—Shostakovich, Vishnevskaya, Rostropovich—is well known and well publicized. In August 1965, he was invited to spend a month in Soviet Armenia, at the Composers' Home for Creative Work in picturesque Dilizhan. Here he wrote a vocal cycle of Six Romances on texts by Pushkin which he dedicated to Galina Vishnevskaya and Rostropovich.

Britten's opera *A Midsummer Night's Dream* was staged at the Bolshoi Theatre in Moscow on 28 October 1965, conducted by Rozhdestvensky. Somewhat earlier that year, the Leningrad Conservatory gave the Soviet première of the *War Requiem*. It took a year's study until the students mastered the "rather complex contemporary style". But once it was accomplished, they were filled with enthusiasm. "Whenever you entered the Conservatory," wrote Byalik, "you could hear—in the corridors and on the staircases—fragments from the fugue in *Libera Me*."[28]

Britten also contributed articles and interviews to *Sovetskaya Muzyka*, clarifying his thoughts and intentions—so, for example, in March 1965, when he spoke on the chamber opera in general and the work of the

Covent Garden chamber ensemble in particular.²⁹ All in all, he has become a familiar figure to the Russians—personally, musically, and intellectually—far more than any other living foreign composer.

Two other British composers visited the Soviet Union in the autumn of 1963—Alan Bush and Alan Rawsthorne. With the composers conducting, the U.S.S.R. State Symphony performed the Second Symphony (Pastoral) and the Concerto for Strings by Rawsthorne as well as Bush's Festive Overture and Second Symphony ("Nottingham") in Moscow and in Yerevan. Alan Bush is well known as a champion of Soviet music, and his works are played frequently in the Soviet Union; in fact, this was his seventh visit to Moscow. Again he was warmly received, and his symphony was especially applauded. Rawsthorne (whose name presented great problems of transliteration) was also quite successful with his Pastoral Symphony.

Preceding all the British artists named above was Sir Malcolm Sargent who was guest conductor of two major Moscow orchestras—the State Symphony and the Philharmonic—in October 1962. This was Sir Malcolm's second visit (the first had taken place in May 1957), and he won the wholehearted approval and admiration of critics and audiences. Among the British scores conducted by Sir Malcolm were the Overture *The Wasps* by Ralph Vaughan Williams and the Serenade for Strings by Elgar.

The musical exchange between the Soviet Union and Great Britain continued to be lively. The Soviet Armenian composer Mirzoyan and the musicologist Kukharsky made "an interesting journey to Britain where they studied musical life and had many friendly meetings with their British colleagues", as the Composers' Bulletin reported in Moscow in 1964.³⁰ In exchange, the British composers Geoffrey Bush and John Gardner visited Moscow, Leningrad, Tbilisi, and Yerevan in September–October 1964.³¹ There can be no doubt that these cultural exchanges create much good will on both sides. Whether those selected to make the visits are always the most characteristic representatives of their respective countries is another matter. The Soviet comments with regard to "our English friends" are in general unusually friendly. The British visitors are equally warm and appreciative in reporting on the outgoing hospitality of the Russians.

By 1964, the Soviet arts intelligentsia had established a *modus vivendi* with the Khrushchev regime. Despite the controversies of 1962–64, writers and artists had been treated with a certain consideration by the Party. Khrushchev himself had made many personal contacts among the artists; he was jovial, outspoken, and accessible. His opinions on art were well known and widely publicized. An exchange of opinion was possible; those who had argued with him—Dudintsev, Ehrenburg, Yevtushenko, and others—were at liberty and active. As Alexander Werth remarked after a trip to Russia in 1964, "The abolition of fear is certainly the greatest thing that has happened in Russia in the last ten years, and the intelligentsia appreciates it more keenly than anyone else."[32]

The speeches of Khrushchev contained not so much restrictions as exhortations; he appealed to the Socialist conscience of the artists to adhere to the old Leninist principles, as he interpreted them. Whatever the arts intelligentsia thought of Khrushchev as a "critic", there was a feeling of appreciation for a measure of greater freedom. The musicians had little reason to complain: Khrennikov was a great favourite of Khrushchev, and the Composers' Union derived many benefits from its politically advantageous position. The Minister of Culture, Madame Furtseva, was flexible, and as for Ilyichev, his bark was worse than his bite. Thus, Werth was right when he said that the feeling prevalent among artists was, "For God's sake, let Khrushchev stay; anyone else might be *much* worse." And this feeling was shared widely throughout the world.

Within a few weeks after these words appeared in print, the Soviet power structure underwent a violent shake-up. On 14 October 1964, the startled world was informed that Chairman Khrushchev had "resigned". His place was taken by a group of high Party officials, formerly associated with Khrushchev though little known abroad. The two leading men were Alexander Kosygin, who became chairman of the Council of Ministers, and Leonid Brezhnev, the new first secretary of the Party. The Khrushchev era had ended; a collective leadership took the reins.

Part V

COLLECTIVE LEADERSHIP 1964-70

To what extent was the Khrushchev era an era of "liberalization"? Some experts take a dim view of this label. Robert Conquest, for example, decries "the indiscriminate use of the word 'liberal' with regard to Communist (and particularly Soviet) politics". He divides the Soviet ruling circles into "repressionists" and "concessionists", but the latter are merely "concessions to reality" and should not be confused with genuine liberalism. That special Soviet breed of Party bureaucrats—the *apparatchiki*—continue to rule with singular inflexibility; there is "an insensitivity at the core of the Party mind, even at its most 'liberal', which cuts it off from the essential aspirations of any new generation". And, as Conquest points out, "the intellectuals provide the focus of *all* resentments against dictatorship, besides being the standard-bearers of the desire for intellectual liberty and an end to petty Party control by Party hacks".[1]

In music, one of the earliest protests against petty bureaucratic rule had been voiced by Khachaturian as early as November 1953—the year of Stalin's death and long before Khrushchev played any significant role.[2]

Khrushchev himself started undoubtedly as a "concessionist". Only when he realized that his concessions generated demands for more concessions did he balk and become "repressive". One can blame Khrushchev for a lack of consistency in his treatment of the intelligentsia, but there were times when he had to appease the neo-Stalinist wing. Ultimately, the arts were governed by political, not aesthetic, considerations.

Yet, all in all, the arts prospered during the years of Khrushchev's leadership as they had not since the 1920's.

For several months following Khrushchev's removal from power there was watchful silence on the arts front. No one was certain of the attitude of the new leadership, and no one cared to expose himself without some official hint. The journal *Sovetskaya Muzyka* turned suddenly non-political. Only recently the journal had published (in its April 1964 issue) a resplendent photograph of Khrushchev, conveying to him, "the true Leninist", the warmest wishes of Soviet musicians on the occasion of his seventieth birthday. Only recently, Khrushchev's speeches on art—published under the title *The High Mission of Literature and Art*—provided material for lengthy editorials as the "voice of the Party". Suddenly, *Sovetskaya Muzyka* and its editors were afflicted with a case of complete amnesia. Not a word was said about the political changes. The editorials examined with great intensity the problems of the musical theatre and the forthcoming plenary session on that subject. The first issue of 1965 was to contain a brief essay by Khrennikov, entitled "Our Soviet Power" (Sovetskaya nasha derzhava); but though it is listed in the table of contents, the page was eliminated from copies reaching the United States.

Finally, on 9 January 1965, almost three months after the change of regime, *Pravda* published an editorial on the arts and reiterated the well-worn phrase (a favourite of Khrushchev's) that coexistence did not extend into the ideological field. There was renewed warning against "so-called progressive trends" in art, against "formalism" and "digression from realism". It would seem that Ilyichev was still in his old post as arts expert.

But it soon became obvious that matters affecting the arts were under intense discussion; apparently, there was a behind-the-scenes struggle. At any rate, a few weeks later—on 24 January—*Pravda* hinted at a shift, "We must guard here against dashing from one extreme to another, first crude shouting, then flinching and 'amnestying' of serious errors." Though Khrushchev was not mentioned by name, it was clear who was meant. *Pravda* criticized the method, but the ultimate aim remained unchanged—ever "greater ideological orientation of young artists and writers along Party lines". There was dissatisfaction with the conduct of some of the young poets who liked to pose as "unrecognized". For a time, this was where matters were left.

Finally, a month later, on 21 February 1965, *Pravda* published a significant statement entitled "The Party and the Intelligentsia", signed by its new editor-in-chief, Alexei Rumyantsev. It signalled a return to Leninism, to certain principles enunciated by the Party in 1925. Rumyantsev quoted the forty-year-old Resolution, "Communist criticism must rid itself of the tone of literary command. The Party must in every way eradicate attempts at homebred and incompetent administrative interference in literary affairs . . ."[3] Rumyantsev declared this to be "the most important Party principle in matters of artistic creation". Progress in any field, be it science or art, demanded "the existence of different schools and trends, different styles and genres competing with one another". He declared himself opposed to interference with creative search and experimentation before a "considered judgment of their actual value can be made". In this connection, Rumyantsev displayed particular impatience with "attempts to impose one's subjective evaluations and personal tastes as the yardstick of artistic creation, particularly when they are expressed in the name of the Party". Rejecting the trend towards anti-intellectualism under Khrushchev, he said that "genuine creativeness is possible only through search and experimentation, free expression and clashes of viewpoint". All this sounded highly promising to hopeful liberals, were it not for the qualification that the creative possibilities would have to conform to the principles of Socialist Realism.

To what extent was the statement of Rumyantsev a "liberalization"? His criterion as to whether or not a work of art was consonant with the interests of the Party was rather vague: he defined it as "all-round free development of the personality of every member of society". But at least he promised an end to the aesthetic judgments by a "single leader, confident in his own outlook". This oblique reproach could, in fact, apply to Stalin as well as to Khrushchev: Stalin's interference in the arts was openly admitted in the Party document of 1958, while Khrushchev's crude criticism and abysmal ignorance had made him a butt of ridicule among the intellectuals of the world.

Rumyantsev's statement evoked a rather optimistic response among Western "Kremlinologists". *The Times Literary Supplement*, in an editorial entitled "Stop and Go"[4] thought that Rumyantsev was merely "paying lip service to the old Stalinist slogan of Socialist Realism" while returning to the Party's position of the mid-1920's. Rumyantsev's statement that "truly creative work . . . cannot be stimulated by orders and does not tolerate an officially bureaucratic approach" could lead, in the opinion of *The Times Literary Supplement* to a "change in the relationship of Soviet and Western intellectuals from the present rather forced politeness to a proper, but not uncritical mutual respect". Many Western liberals and Marxists (like the East German Professor Robert Havemann) shared the hope that the Soviet Communist Party would eventually abandon the outworn concept of Socialist Realism and stop its interference in matters of aesthetics. It was a vain hope, as future developments proved.

The editorial in *The Times Literary Supplement* aroused some controversy. It was pointed out that the 1925 Party Resolution was never intended as a "liberalizing" measure but rather as a step to restrain certain left-wing factions claiming to speak in the name of the Party. In the broad context of Rumyantsev's statement, however, it was clear that he intended to erase the traces of both Stalinism and Khrushchevism in order to return to true Leninism. This was the reassuring aspect of Rumyantsev's statement.

A month later, in March 1965, one of the last symbols of Khrushchev's arts policies disappeared: Ilyichev was transferred to the Ministry of Foreign Affairs. The ideological commission, of which he had been chairman since its inception in November 1962 was dissolved. Madame Furtseva remained in her previous post as minister of culture; perhaps she owed her retention to the fact that Khrushchev had scolded her for having been "too lenient" in her policies.

As the year 1965 progressed, it became apparent that there were disagreements within the Party hierarchy as to how much freedom the artists should be granted. Rumyantsev, the *Pravda* editor, became again the spokesman for a more flexible interpretation; he even engaged in a public argument with *Izvestia*—a rare occurrence in the monolithic Communist set-up. *Izvestia* had criticized as 'nihilistic" the tendency of certain writers to depict the seamier aspects of Soviet life. Rumyantsev saw nothing wrong in such a trend since, by exposing such drawbacks, the authors endeavoured to correct them. In a lengthy article published in *Pravda* on 9 September 1965, Rumyantsev defended the authors, "It is unrealistic to expect from every writer an absolute balance" in describing Soviet life.[5] He went so far as to say that some people "devoted to the ideas of Communism" felt no need for Party control of arts and literature. As defined by Rumyantsev, the present attitude of the Party was "to defend the artist's freedom to choose theme and subject, style and manner of execution".

As a result, the year 1965 proved an exciting one for music. The temperate stand of the new political leaders and the abolition of the odious watch-dog commission with its verbose chairman, Ilyichev, released creative energies in Soviet music that had been dammed up since 1962. An unidentified Soviet composer confided to the American journal *Newsweek* in June 1965, "Almost by default we are currently in the freest period of Soviet culture we have known since the days of Stalin. There's simply no strong man who can or is yet inclined to dictate as Khrushchev did. There's no hand at the wheel. What could be better?"[6] And indeed, things changed rapidly.

As recently as March 1964 a Soviet avant-garde composer preferred to remain anonymous when one of his works was played in New York at a concert sponsored by the International Society for Contemporary Music.[7] Even in early 1965, the position of Soviet avant-garde composers was not an enviable one. In March of that year Paul Moor wrote that

"One hears more and more of younger Soviet composers who write ... 'for their desk-drawers', but the prevalent atmosphere [in Moscow] remains such that the Western visitor does them only a disservice by calling attention to them . . . The result of this situation is that anyone relatively well informed about the field of Soviet composers finds himself in a position of not being able to report very much publicly without harming the individuals he would most like to help and encourage."[8]

As the year 1965 progressed, the musical scene began to expand; it acquired a wider spectrum and more exploratory zeal. The pace setter was Leningrad where, in Moor's words, "many musical things are possible which are unthinkable in Moscow". The Leningrad Philharmonic Orchestra had two young assistant conductors, Serov and Blazhkov, both interested in all kinds of new music. Within a subscription cycle, "Countries of the World"—each concert being devoted to the music of a different country—Blazhkov had, in 1964, conducted the Leningrad Philharmonic in an all-American programme including William Schuman's Third Symphony, Samuel Barber's Piano Concerto, and Gershwin's *Porgy and Bess* in Bennett's symphonic arrangement. Blazhkov, too, had the initiative to revive, in 1965, Shostakovich's Third Symphony ("May Day") that had been in limbo for over thirty years; suddenly, this heretofore "formalistic" work was rediscovered as an important step in the composer's continued effort to master a "revolutionary topic". Shostakovich was so impressed by young Blazhkov that he entrusted him with the performance of his *Five Fragments for Orchestra*, Op. 42, never played before because they belonged to his experimental period.

Blazhkov's most daring enterprise, perhaps, was the première of an outright avant-garde composition, *The Laments of Shchaza* by Andrei Volkonsky for soprano, violin, viola, English horn, vibraphone, and harpsichord, the latter played by the composer. The performance took place in the spring of 1965, but suffered a typical "burial by silence"; *Sovetskaya Muzyka* did not report the event but *Musical America* did.[9] Volkonsky is said to have had no public performances of his works for some five years; the public knew him primarily as a harpsichordist and conductor of old music. *The Laments of Shchaza* was composed in 1962.

It is a sensitive and intensely expressive work revealing the influence of Webern and post-Webern developments, not all fully assimilated, yet showing a certain personal style. In the meantime, the work has been performed, among other places, in New York and London. It must be said that the setting of the London première in August 1967, at one of the Promenade Concerts in the Albert Hall, was unfortunate for this delicate, almost fragile work. In fact, *The Sunday Times* called the conductor, Pierre Boulez ,"cruel" for having "these stammering and etiolated *Laments*"[10] followed by their musical antithesis, Stravinsky's *Les Noces*. Peter Heyworth in the *Observer* called it "by far the most individual and interesting avant-garde work I have heard by a young Russian composer" though he found "Volkonsky's persistent habit of punctuating each phrase with a pronounced pause mannered."[11] *The Times* (Joan Chissell) also objected to the "fragmented, disjoined vocal line that did not shed much light on the work" though the "very delicate strokes of instrumental colour" were praised.[12] The comment of the *Daily Telegraph* was very perceptive:

> "The music is often moving and always striking, showing an extremely practised hand in the use of up-to-date compositional techniques. Or more precisely, the techniques of just a decade ago, for it has fewer affinities with what is happening in the West at the present moment than with Boulez' *Marteau sans Maître*, from which in its innate lyricism and tiny 'closed' episodes it reveals a direct line of descent."[13]

The problem of being "up-to-date" is a real one for Soviet avant-garde composers. They operate in a vacuum, in an immense isolation booth—without the benefit of public performances, hence unable to gauge the reactions of audiences, without the stimulating interrelationship with other arts, without trend or response . . . No wonder their ears are cocked toward the West, eagerly trying to comprehend what is going on in music, and why. More than once, Soviet composers must have looked with envy toward Poland or Hungary where modernism was not considered subversive.

Yet, slowly but surely, modern devices—such as serialism and aleatory (i.e. "chance" music)—won converts among Soviet composers. Not only did such young composers, as Slonimsky and Tishchenko, move closer to the avant-garde, but established composers like Shchedrin and Karayev began to spice their conservative musical idiom with novel devices.

Kara Karayev, the leading musician of Azerbaijan, and Rodion Shchedrin, Moscow's rising star, had visited the United States during 1964 under the cultural exchange programme. The following year—in April 1965—they presented two symphonic scores that displayed a degree of modernity not previously associated with their musical style. They set out to explore new musical vistas, each in his own way, and the critical reaction in the Soviet press was so intense that the Moscow correspondent of *The New York Times* cabled a report opening with the startling sentence, "The musical world has been stirred by the official approval given to two musical forms denounced by N. S. Khrushchev—twelve-tone music and jazz."[14] This correspondent, obviously no musical expert, had based his report on recent articles in *Pravda* and *Izvestia*. His sensational deduction was over-optimistic: at best, one could detect a greater tolerance toward new musical techniques, but certainly none of the drastic reversal of previous positions announced in *The New York Times*. Nevertheless it is interesting to examine the Russian sources that led to such a startling report.

First of all, one must separate twelve-tone music from jazz: they have nothing in common except that they both were reviled by Khrushchev in his speech of 8 March 1963. It so happened that *Pravda* and *Izvestia*—independent of each other—carried articles on these topics almost simultaneously which induced *The New York Times* correspondent to lump them together.

The topic of jazz was explored in the weekly supplement *Nedelya* of *Izvestia* (16/22 May 1965). The title of the essay was "Jazz at a Turning Point", the author a well-known specialist in the field, Medvedev. He gave a brief history of Soviet jazz but carefully avoided any reference to the Afro-American elements though admitting that jazz had come from the West. While the old Soviet jazz style was related to the popular mass song and hence called "song jazz", the new style leaned toward a larger instrumental idiom approaching the big symphonic forms, and serious composers like Eshpai, Babadzhanyan, Petrov, Gordeli were writing for jazz bands. As Medvedev says, "Jazz is a complex, multifaceted, controversial phenomenon whose essence and artistic principles are difficult to contain in a simple formula."

The article by Medvedev was prompted by a three-day jazz competition—actually auditions closed to the public in order to select a few of the best ensembles. Fourteen jazz groups competed, many of them non-professionals. The composer Muradeli acted as chairman of the jury, and there were heated discussions. "We heard enormously gifted musicians, but there was also dilettantism and poor taste, evidenced in weak imitations of the jazz 'fashion'; this was harshly criticized," wrote Medvedev. The best of the jazz was "improvisational, and improvisation is a great art." The author concluded, "A new Soviet jazz style is being created slowly but surely. We understand that we must create our own, homegrown idiom. Let us search!"

What actually happened is that a development toward a "Soviet" jazz—temporarily interrupted by Khrushchev's distorted attack in late 1962—was resumed in 1965. The term "improvisational", used by Medvedev in a laudatory fashion, indicates that American influences were at work, though not openly acknowledged. But, in the words of Medvedev, "there is strong, serious inclination of our youth toward jazz". With the departure of Khrushchev, aesthetic opposition to jazz seems to have disappeared.

The interest in jazz continued to be encouraged. The composer Muradeli published an article in *Komsomolskaya Pravda* in which he called for more jazz concerts and recordings and recommended special courses to teach jazz techniques. *Komsomolskaya Pravda*—which represents Soviet youth—sponsored a contest for jazz ensembles which was shown on Moscow television. The winners were to participate in an East European contest later that year. It will be remembered that, only a year earlier, *Komsomolskaya Pravda* was engaged in a controversy with Khrennikov whose attitude toward jazz was found too rigid.

On 11 and 13 April 1965, the conductor Rozhdestvensky—always a champion of the new—performed Shchedrin's Second Symphony. On 21 April the Moscow Chamber Orchestra under Rudolf Barshai gave the première of Karayev's Third Symphony. "Both works were a signal success," reported the Bulletin of the Composers' Union, but neither was immediately discussed in the pages of *Sovetskaya Muzyka*.[15] Instead the two symphonies were made the subject of several critical essays in *Pravda* and *Sovetskaya Kultura*, thus reaching a much wider audience.

Shchedrin found a sympathetic critic in Alexandra Pakhmutova, a gifted young Leningrad composer.[16] We learn that the Second Symphony was completed early in 1965, the result of three years' work. (Thus, the composition was begun well before Shchredin's trip to the United States and finished after his return to Moscow). The Symphony is subdivided into twenty-five "orchestral preludes", but an over-all design of five movements is discernible. The basic theme is Peace and War, Life and Death. For the realization of this theme, the composer chose an original path—"the infinite world of sound surrounding man." Peace has its own sound—a bell, the rustle of a forest—just as War has the noise of battles and planes, and funereal stillness. It is important to realize that the sharp, contemporary sounds in Shchedrin's Symphony do not appear as the ultimate aim but are necessary "to reveal the inner world of a hero, to reveal life and its rich inner polyphony". In the critic's opinion, there is no intrinsically "good" or "bad" musical idiom: "musical language is a means for expressing artistic ideas".

While Miss Pakhmutova is obviously carried away by Shchedrin's ability "to peer into the most important aspect of our life and to express it brilliantly", another critic—Dmitri Blagoi—is somewhat more detached.[17] He describes the Second Symphony as a "very interesting" work in which a certain "cinematic influence" can be felt—the quick changes of musical "frames" expressed in the twenty-five sections (or preludes). Blagoi points out the sharply dynamic finale. "Where will

Shchedrin go from here," the critic asks, "is he threatened by the danger of 'purely technological manufacture'?" A third critic, Yuri Levitin, finds the Symphony in part over-long, too calculated in design, and rather uniform in its technical procedures.[18]

Karayev's Third Symphony was reviewed sympathetically by a fellow Caucasian, the composer Karen Khachaturian.[19] The Symphony has the traditional cycle of four movements which are unified by thematic material and intonational ties. The two corner movements are described as "dynamic" but less expressive than the middle movements. In second place stands a beguiling Scherzo whose complex rhythms are close to the capricious accents of Azerbaijan folk music. There follows a deeply expressive slow movement. Karayev often uses "bold and sharply expressive means". Yet they are not an end in themselves but are always subordinate to the work's idea. They appear as the result of prolonged creative thought and searching. The innovational means, so the critic maintains, enable the composer to reveal the positive content of the Symphony.

Nowhere in any of these reviews is there any mention of serialism or twelve-tone technique; yet, the words "sharp, contemporary sounds" or "bold and sharply expressive means" suggest that both composers have abandoned the idyllic sounds of conventional realism, socialist or otherwise. But—as Aaron Copland already observed in 1960—virtually any dissonance is permissible in Soviet music as long as it is motivated by some topical need. Certainly, the implied programme of Shchedrin's Symphony justified the "sharp" means employed. No such "justification", however, can be found in Karayev's Symphony which is non-programmatic. Evidently, the critics were still hesitant to admit the unvarnished truth—namely that two established composers had left the security of traditionalism to explore novel means of musical expression, heretofore considered the domain of the "avant-garde". The reluctance to discuss these matters soon yielded to open debate, as we shall see.*

Though the symphonies of Shchedrin and Karayev aroused so much interest and discussion in Moscow, they do not seem to have been played widely at the time. A letter from Leningrad, published in the August issue of *Sovetskaya Muzyka*, complained that neither of the two works had been heard in Leningrad. The same letter (by a well-known critic) objects to the delays in bringing new works by Moscow composers to Leningrad. One wonders what the reason might be. Has the critical opinion of Leningrad become so unimportant—or is the Leningrad Philharmonic so busy with its own composers that Moscow composers have to wait? The traditional rivalry between the two great cities might have something to do with it.

* See p. 458.

The reports reaching the West concerning the state of Soviet music were puzzling and contradictory during the first half of 1965. To get some clarification, I addressed a direct inquiry to Grigori Shneerson, the Soviet critic and author, with whom I had maintained personal contact. His reply, dated 20 June 1965, contained the following description of the musical scene,

> "With regard to the general direction of the explorations of our young composers, I can say that there is indeed at present a greater tolerance toward dodecaphonic experiments, though on the whole this school remains unacceptable. Free devices of twelve-tone writing, i.e. the 'tone row', are used (though without strict method) in some compositions which aim at expressing a certain nervous tension, an expressionistic atmosphere . . . There are quite a few disputes about it, but in a 'peaceful' manner . . . From the enclosed article in *Pravda* of 20 June 1965 by Yuri Levitin, dealing quite objectively with the young and middle generations of our composers, you can see that there is absolutely no switch in viewpoint concerning dodecaphony. And I hope there never will be . . ."

The keywords of this letter are "tolerance . . . but no acceptance" of dodecaphony. Shneerson, whose aversion to an advanced musical idiom is amply demonstrated in his book, *On Music, Alive and Dead*, sticks to his guns. He represents the opinion of the directorate of the Composers' Union.

The *Pravda* article by Levitin (a composer in his fifties) is revealing not only because of the names mentioned but also because of those omitted. The survey begins by listing the recognized masters of Soviet music—Prokofiev, Shostakovich, Khachaturian, Khrennikov, and Kabalevsky. It ends with a brief mention of Sviridov, Karayev, and Karen Khachaturian—brief because their works had been discussed recently in the press. The author concentrates on the young and middle generation of composers: they are destined to carry on the work of their teachers and older *confrères*. The choice of the composers and works discussed in this article reflects the established viewpoint of the Composers' Union. They are the standard-bearers of official Soviet-style modernism—a "third force", as it were, standing between the stalwart conservatives and the rebellious avant-gardists. Harold Schonberg, chief music critic of *The New York Times*, gave an apt description of this middle group after a visit to Moscow,

> "By far the largest amount of present-day Soviet music comes from a middle group that is trying to make a synthesis of old and new techniques. They are not avant-gardists, and they are reluctant to give up their traditions of folk material. All of them write tonal music, generally with a good deal of the kind of dissonance that was popular in the 1930's. On the whole their music gives the Western listener a feeling of *déjà vu*. But they are cautiously feeling their way into the international idiom of the West. In this they now have official sanction . . . Stronger representatives of the middle group are pushing hard and will be the Establishment tomorrow. Most talked-about is Shchedrin . . . the 'official' modernist . . ."[1]

All of the composers listed by Levitin belong to that "middle group". Most prominently discussed are Rodion Shchedrin, Moissei Vainberg, Andrei Eshpai, Arno Babadzhanyan, and Boris Tchaikovsky. An additional paragraph merely lists a number of younger composers who had recently achieved "significant successes"—Boris Tishchenko, Sergei Slonimsky, and Benjamin Bassner of Leningrad, Eino Tamberg, Jan Ryaets, and Arvo Pyart of Estonia, Alfred Shnitke, Alexei Nikolayev, Alexander Chugayev, and Alexander Pirumov of Moscow. "Their talented and original works gave much joy to the audiences," writes Levitin.

Finally come two paragraphs dealing with the "untouchables",

> "However, we have a few unhealthy phenomena which must be mentioned. An insignificant number of our young composers follow at times a thoughtless enthusiasm for avant-garde devices, for serial music. In my opinion, it is not even enthusiasm but merely a tribute to fashion. It is pleasant to march among the alleged progressives, the unappreciated, to create, so to speak, for the future. I am not inclined to exaggerate this danger. I think that these young composers will soon have to understand and rethink much, and that they will join the broad road of genuine true art that reflects the life and the feeling of people.
>
> Out of curiosity, the audiences will listen once or twice to these abstract works, resembling one another like two sheets of dry plaster. They, too, will listen as a tribute to fashion. But they will

immediately forget the senseless hammering, the dry scholastic note-spinning, and they will prefer the lively, full-blooded, talented, and hence always diversified music . . ."[2]

Within the avant-garde group no names are mentioned: did the critic wish to spare their reputation or did he not want to give them free publicity? Whichever the case, their names are well known in musical circles, and they number less than a dozen.

To dismiss Levitin's article as reactionary prattle would be a grave error. Serious students of Soviet music must acknowledge that Soviet music is undergoing a slow process of evolution and that Soviet composers are showing a growing awareness of Western compositional techniques. But there is no corresponding evolution of Soviet musical taste, all the more since the vast audiences are not exposed to any kind of musical experimentalism, be it foreign or indigenous. No radical break with established musical policies (such as occurred in Poland) can be expected in the Soviet Union in the foreseeable future, judging by the stiffening ideological stance of 1970. It is important that the Western critics evaluate without prejudice the music written by that "middle group" of Soviet composers because they *are*, for better or for worse, the representatives of contemporary Soviet music. These young Russians are neither "primitive" nor naive. They are not averse to playing around with some of the new devices—a bit of aleatory, of atonality, of pointillism or some electronic effects. But using a technical device of avant-gardism does not imply acceptance of its aesthetics. The Soviet composers still write music for people to play and for people to enjoy; the latest Western affectation—contempt for the listener—is as alien to them as the computerized approach to musical composition.

So far, these "middle-group" Soviet composers have received more praise at home than abroad. Western critics react rather coolly to their "official modernism". Rodion Shchedrin is the best known. He came to the attention of a wider American audience in the spring of 1965 when two orchestras—the visiting Washington National Symphony and the New York Philharmonic—played his *Mischievous Ditties* (Ozornye chastushki) in New York. It is a superficially amusing piece which is making its way into American concert programmes. Shchedrin's standing within Soviet music was considered high enough to award him a commission for the 125th anniversary of the New York Philharmonic Orchestra. The completed composition was named *The Chimes* (Zvony)* and received its world première under Leonard

* The subtitle is "Concerto No. 2 for Orchestra". The *Mischievous Ditties* are presumably "Concerto No. 1".

Bernstein on 11 January 1968. The *Programme Notes* of the New York Philharmonic printed the following commentary by the composer,

> "Throughout Russian history chimes have always been very important to our people. Their sound was associated with joys and sorrows, feasts and tragedies. The chimes of ancient Russia represent a very particular feature of old Russian civilization with an ancient tradition, its own terminology, its special ABC, and so on. Some of the principles of Russian chimes are used, in a very free way of course, in my composition, as well as some elements of the old Russian way of writing down music without staves—the so-called 'crooks' or 'Znamenny neumes' (the most ancient form of Russian music notation used for the traditional church chants).
>
> Some of the musical pages of *The Chimes* were inspired by the art of the greatest Russian painter: the creator of Russian ikons, Andrei Rublev (ca. 1365–1430).
>
> My composition is in one movement and it is based on two constructions of six notes. This main feature may be heard at the very beginning in piccolo and flute."

The composer's comments make several interesting points. Unusual for a Soviet artist is the reference to the old church chants and the admission that the composition had been inspired, in part, by ikon paintings. The mention of the "Znamenny" notation can be taken as an explanation (if not apologia) for the use of aleatoric devices since the "Znamenny neumes" (not as yet fully deciphered) gave only an indication of the *direction* of the melodic line but not its accurate pitch; hence, an element of improvisation was justified.

Whatever the composer's stated intentions, he did not succeed in their full musical realization. At least not in the opinion of Harold Schonberg of *The New York Times*:

> "*Chimes*, a concerto for orchestra, has a certain amount of skill, notably in a colourful orchestration. It also has some biting sounds that would have been inconceivable coming from a Soviet composer only a few short years back. There even is a flirtation with serial techniques and aleatoric-sounding devices. But the avant-garde techniques are used in a rather half-baked manner. Shchedrin thinks tonally, and his atonal textures sound superimposed and calculated."[3]

Boris Tchaikovsky, born in 1925 and considered a strong hope for the future, did not fare much better. Rostropovich introduced his Cello Concerto in Moscow in 1964, and Levitin wrote in *Pravda*, "The depth of intent, the bright themes, the admirable understanding of the cello's nature, the faultless logic of form, the real sweep and temperament—all this permeates the new concerto."⁴ But when the same work was played by the same soloist in New York in October 1965, the *New York Times* disagreed, "The Boris Tchaikovsky Concerto was a dismally academic piece whose four movements unwound in more than thirty minutes. Not even Rostropovich's supreme dedication saved the work from being banal."⁵

Undeterred, Rostropovich brought Boris Tchaikovsky's Partita for cello, harpsichord, piano, electric guitar, and percussion* to New York where it received its first performance ("in the West") on 5 March 1967.** The composer tried quite obviously to be up-to-date, but he only succeeded in sounding contrived and pretentious, at times even sophomoric in his striving for effects.

As a rule, Soviet performers who come to the United States for guest appearances, present rather unadventurous programmes. Rostropovich, of course, is a shining exception. But usually, the tacit obligation to play at least one Soviet work is fulfilled by including some composition by Prokofiev or Shostakovich. (It must be admitted that American artists visiting the Soviet Union are equally unadventurous as far as American music is concerned.) In the rare instances when a new work by an unknown Soviet composer appears on the programme, the response of critics and public is lukewarm, for example, when Barshai and the Moscow Chamber Orchestra introduced a work by Jan Ryaets or the Komitas Quartet played a string quartet of Mirzoyan. Yet the same critics are indignant when the programmes of visiting Soviet ensembles are too stereotyped.⁶ The result is that Soviet as well as American audiences live in abysmal ignorance of each other's contemporary music.

The difficulty of a Soviet avant-garde composer under present-day conditions is exemplified by the case of the talented Ukrainian Leonid Grabovsky. Grabovsky is by no means an "unknown": he had been highly praised for his early *Four Ukrainian Folksongs* for chorus and orchestra (1959), but when his musical idiom became more "adventurous", his works began to meet with official disapproval. In the spring of 1965, a Plenum of Ukrainian Music was held in Kiev, and *Sovetskaya Muzyka* printed the following report by its critic, Malyshev,

* Timpani, cymbals, small bells, xylophone, and vibraphone.
** World première in Moscow on 10 January 1967.

"The attitude of the Union of Ukrainian Composers towards a large group of youthful composers is beyond understanding. In its time, one has written much, and enthusiastically, about L. Grabovsky's work. In 1963, it was even said that one could not gain a true impression of Ukrainian musical culture without knowing Grabovsky and Kolodub. Yet, how can one gain this impression if not a single work by Grabovsky was performed in Kiev, Kharkov, Odessa, Donetsk? His recently completed work, *Symphonic Frescoes* . . . is known in Moscow, Leningrad . . . but not in the Ukraine. It would seem natural that a work that has produced heated discussions would have been included in the programme of the Plenum, but this was not the case. It would seem natural that the Plenum would also listen to a number of works by young composers whose names have appeared in the press, usually accompanied by unflattering epithets or boundless enthusiasm . . . This, too, has not happened. How does youth fare in the Union of Ukrainian Composers? Perhaps one should arrange a Plenum on that subject, with performances and a creative discussion? Such a Plenum would not lack an audience . . ."[7]

The last sentence was meant ironically because there had been complaints that the Plenum concerts were poorly attended by the public; there must be something "repellent" about our music, said one commentator.

Obviously, the Union of Ukrainian Composers is dominated by a hard core of conservatives to whom the small but active group of Kiev avant-gardists is an abomination. This is described amusingly by the critic Schonberg of *The New York Times* who travelled to Kiev in 1967 for the specific purpose of meeting the group of Ukrainian avant-garde composers. He was met by some twenty old-school composers, with none of the young composers in sight. "Do you really like this new kind of music?" Schonberg was asked. Ultimately, the four avant-gardists—Grabovsky, Silvestrov, Zagortsev, and Godziatsky—arrived, and Schonberg succeeded in hearing some taped performances of their works. Compared to Western models, and even to the "more polished" Moscow and Leningrad avant-garde, the Kiev group "could possibly be described as modern primitives, in the art-history sense of the word". They are mainly autodidacts in the realm of serial technique, but they know what is going on in the outside world of experimental music and are in close contact with the Polish avant-garde headed by Penderecki. "While their music may be somewhat crude," says Schonberg, "it has vitality and enthusiasm. It is also a mishmash. Everything is jumbled together—serial technique, aleatory, extra-musical sounds (such as rappings on the cello with knuckle or bow), explosive tonal outbursts, extreme dissonance, an exploitation of extreme and uncomfortable instrumental registers."[8]

Judging by the scores that have reached the United States and have been performed at various university concerts,* Grabovsky emerges as the most accomplished of the Kiev group. Silvestrov is talented and adventurous, while Zagortsev appears as yet rather unsure in the handling of new devices. Godziatsky (according to Schonberg) is "the only one of the four who experiments with electronic music", though he lacks equipment and must work with home-made tools.

Schonberg's opinion about the Moscow avant-gardists is cautious: they are "a polished and careful group without the strength and profile of the Leningrad or Kiev composers. They work in the accepted international style. Their music illustrates a modern kind of academism."[9] Admittedly, the Moscow composers have greater experience in orthodox twelve-tone writing and post-Webern serialism. Such works as Denisov's cantata *Sun of the Incas* (1964), Shnitke's *Music for Piano and Chamber Orchestra* (1964) and his Second Violin Concerto (1966), Volkonsky's *The Laments of Shchaza*, as well as the *Polyphonic Symphony* of the Estonian Pyart, are written with assurance and technical expertise. In fact, one perceives a "Russian" flavour in the vocal lines of Denisov and Volkonsky; it is not all that "international". It may be true that some of this music (as Gerald Abraham puts it) is "rather tame by comparison with the damnedest our young men can do".[10] But this is not necessarily a disadvantage.

Among the Leningrad composers, Slonimsky and Tishchenko are considered the most talented. But they are not true "avant-gardists"; they can be called border-line cases. They are modernists without flaunting their avant-gardism. Both are familiar with avant-garde devices and have used them occasionally. Nevertheless, they are accepted by the establishment, and their creative development points towards a *modus vivendi* with officialdom. It may well be that composers of this calibre are destined to build the necessary bridges that will

---

* Symposia and concerts dealing with Soviet avant-garde music were given, among others, at Indiana University (20–21 February 1967), at the State University of New York at Buffalo (27–29 January 1967), at Sarah Lawrence College (24 May 1967), and at City College of New York (11 May 1968). The last-named was sponsored by the American Musicological Society, Greater New York Chapter. The performances included works by Volkonsky, Grabovsky, Silvestrov, Denisov, Shnitke, Zagortsev, Slonimsky—and of older "avant-gardists" Roslavetz, Lourié, and Hershkovits. Most of the scores were obtained by Joel Spiegelman, a young American musicologist and composer, who spent a year as exchange student in the Soviet Union.

enable Soviet music to move forward without breaking with the past.

Some flexibility will be required on all sides. The Soviet avant-garde will eventually realize that the mere imitation of Western-style devices is essentially unproductive unless they are made to serve a creative design. On the other hand, the conservative leadership of the Composers' Union will come to realize that serialism is not synonymous with counter-revolution and that Soviet music cannot remain encased, cannot flourish in splendid isolation. Perhaps these conservative leaders underestimate the staying power of Russian traditionalism. When, in the nineteenth century, Wagnerism swept European music, the Russian composers were attentive but aloof. When, in the early twentieth century, French Impressionism became the fashion, Russian composers did not succumb; in fact, Debussy and Ravel learned more from the Russians than vice versa. Today's Soviet academics are willing to learn from Bartok and Hindemith, but not from Schoenberg and Webern. This is one of the reasons why they admire Benjamin Britten so much: his unquestionable newness is not dogmatic.

Slonimsky, Tishchenko, Shchedrin and others of that generation of Soviet composers are also non-dogmatic: they are pragmatists. Certainly, Slonimsky had to control his avant-garde leanings to have his opera *Virineya* performed simultaneously in Moscow and Leningrad, or to have his *Songs of Freedom* recorded. Tishchenko's Cello Concerto, Shchedrin's Second Piano Concerto, and Karayev's Third Symphony are among the works of strongly modernistic tendencies recently recorded under the official *Melodiya* imprint. No one claims the avant-garde label for these compositions; yet, they are aeons removed from anything resembling Socialist Realism.

Tishchenko's Third Symphony seems to be no less advanced. Schonberg of *The New York Times* heard a rehearsal of the work in Leningrad in April 1967, and had the following revealing comments,

"Tishchenko has the reputation of being . . . representative of the new wave, something even of a wild man . . . If anybody in the hall had entered with the idea that the Tishchenko Third Symphony was going to be the usual imitation of Shostakovich of only a few years back, any such notions were dispelled with the opening notes. Here was the world of the post-Webern experimentalist period. The score was not serial, though serial devices were used. So was aleatory. The ending of the second movement was a wild, dissonant mass of purely orchestral improvisations . . . Nobody looked shocked; far from it. And it struck the visitor that times indeed have changed.

Only a short time ago any writing of this kind would have been inconceivable. Now quite a few composers are completely contemporary ... Only the middle-aged or veteran composers adhere to the old manner, and they are completely ignored by the new wave. All but Shostakovich ..."[11]

It would seem that Khrennikov and the old guard at the Composers' Union have over-played their hand in painting the dangers of dodecaphony in the darkest possible colours. Youth ceased to listen and refused to be frightened.

There is so much talk about the "decadence" of dodecaphony that one is tempted to ask—how dangerous, or on the other hand how vital, is dodecaphony for the future of Soviet music? Actually, the issue has been exaggerated out of all proportion, partly because of the ferocious and short-sighted resistance of the conservatives within the Composers' Union. These opponents should realize that the true danger for Soviet music lies in the colossal inbreeding, the stale conformity which is inhibiting the spirit of creative adventure. If today's standards had been applied in 1912, Prokofiev, Scriabin, and Stravinsky would have been booted out of the Union. It is not dodecaphony *per se* which is important to the future of Soviet music, but the freedom to explore, to experiment, to learn by trial and error—a freedom that is essential to all artists and that should not be denied to young composers. The time when musical exploration among Soviet composers was virtually an "underground" operation seems to have passed. There is more open and reasoned discussion, notably in the pages of *Sovetskaya Muzyka*. There is a willingness by Soviet performers to take chances with scores considered unacceptable only a few short years ago. Rostropovich, Rozhdestvensky, Leonid Kogan, Igor Oistrakh, the Borodin Quartet have included "controversial" works in their repertoire; younger artists like the conductors Eduard Serov and Igor Blazhkov have done their share in breaking down musical prejudices. Visiting ensembles—such as the B.B.C. Orchestra under Barbirolli and Boulez in January, 1967—felt uninhibited in presenting bold programmes which included Schoenberg, Webern, Berg, and Boulez as well as other twentieth-century composers. At that time, all the signs pointed towards gradually increasing tolerance in musical matters. However, the stiffening attitude in the literary field—sparked by the trials of Sinyavsky and Daniel and the defection of Kuznetsov—was to have repercussions in music, as we shall see.

Beginning in 1965, *Sovetskaya Muzyka* showed greater awareness of the problems of contemporary music. In the past, Western-style experimentalism was usually discussed in negative, and often insulting, terms. Now, articles began to appear that approached the problems of "modern" music in a scholarly and objective manner. Though the results were often equally negative, at least they were reached, not through polemics, but through thoughtful research. Perhaps the most important contribution was made by Lev Mazel, a highly respected theorists and, until recently, professor at the Moscow Conservatory.

Mazel's essay, entitled "The Paths of Evolution of the Language of Contemporary Music" (O putyakh razvitia yazyka sovremennoi muzyki) was of such length that it had to be published in three instalments (*Sovetskaya Muzyka* 1965, Nos. 6, 7, 8). The first is a general introduction; the second is subtitled "The Crisis of Harmony at the Beginning of the Century and Further Developments"; the third (and most important) deals with "Dodecaphony and Later Avant-garde Trends". In his process of reasoning, Mazel came to a rejection of Schoenberg's dodecaphonic system. However, he believed that certain principles of twelve-tone technique could be used—without Schoenberg's "dogmatism"—in a free serial style, not necessarily atonal. To liberate such a style from the stigma of such compromised terms as dodecaphony and avant-gardism, Mazel proposes a new terminology which is virtually untranslatable—"composition with a preselected intonational complex" or, for short, "complexional variant" or "variant-complexional composition".*

There has been no rush to adopt these cumbersome terms. A young composer like Tishchenko prefers to call himself a "post-Webern serialist". But regardless of terminology, Mazel's essay served as an important reminder that the free manipulation of the twelve tones of the chromatic scale within a widened tonality was used by composers of the nineteenth and early twentieth century, long before Schoenberg formalized his system and, in fact, quite independent of him.**

Encouraged by Mazel's persuasive reasoning, musicologists of the younger generation approached the task of analyzing recent works by young composers which resisted "traditional" analytical methods. First in line was Mikhail Tarakanov (born in 1928), a graduate of the Moscow Conservatory where he taught theory from 1955 to 1964. During my Moscow stay in 1962, I had noticed Tarakanov as an outspoken and persuasive participant in various theoretical debates.

The first two issues of 1966 of *Sovetskaya Muzyka* carried a lengthy

---

* "Kompozitsia s zaraneye izbrannym intonatsionnym kompleksom"; "kompleksnaya variantnost"; "variantno-kompleksnaya kompozitsia".[12]

** At one point Mazel speaks of the "atonal dodecaphonic system". It should be remembered that Arnold Schoenberg himself disassociated his twelve-tone system from atonality.

essay by Tarakanov entitled "New Images, New Means". His contribution was placed prominently, but under a cautious general heading, "Reflections and Disputes", as if to indicate the controversial nature of the subject.

Tarakanov's topic was a detailed professional analysis—with lengthy musical examples—of two recent Soviet symphonies: the Third by Karayev and the Second by Shchedrin. The author bowed politely towards Mazel whose views on dodecaphony he acknowledged to be "in many ways close to his own". He also disclaimed sympathy for the excesses of the "avant-garde" which he placed outside the sphere of music.[13]

Having thus secured his flanks, Tarakanov plunged into his subject. He dispensed with all belletristic prose and verbal acrobatics (so amply present in the reviews in *Pravda* and other papers)* which tried to find ideological justifications for the novel procedures used by the composers. By way of musical examples, Tarakanov demonstrates that Karayev and Shchedrin operate with a "full (twelve-step) chromatic system" in which the tonal centre is often "extremely obscured" or at times "practically non-existent". He continues,

> "This reminds one of certain principles of dodecaphonic-serial technique about which so much ink has been spilled in our critical literature . . . For me, there is no doubt that, whenever really talented composers use elements of this technique, a certain objective logical evolution of the musical language takes place, which it would be wrong to ignore."[14]

Even without the perceptive analysis, the musical examples illustrating Tarakanov's essay must have been eye-openers for the professional readers of *Sovetskaya Muzyka*. For here were stretches of atonal music, dissonant counterpoint, and bold harmonic combinations, all culled from the works of two composers who, until recently, were among the stalwarts of Socialist Realism. At the time Tarakanov's essay appeared in print, the scores of the two symphonies in question were not yet published, nor were they heard outside Moscow. Thus, *Sovetskaya Muzyka*, distributed each month in 18,000 copies to professional musicians throughout the vast country, carried the first visible proofs of musical heresy.

The following month, the journal continued its exploratory policy by publishing an article on music in Estonia where a strong avant-garde group is active. The authors were Nestyeva (the daughter of the veteran musicologist Nestyev) and Fortunatov, the title "Youth

* See pp. 446-7.

Searches, Doubts, Finds"; again (as in Tarakanov's case) the general headline was used, "Reflections and Disputes".[15]

The two young Russian visitors to Estonia were impressed by that country's reputation as "the singing land". Of each 100 Estonians, 15 to 18 belong to some choral organization. Everybody sings, so it seems: children and oldsters, blue- and white-collar workers, professionals and non-professionals. Nor is instrumental music neglected. The composers' school of Tallinn has an old and strong tradition, pre-dating the Soviet take-over of the country. The article merely mentions some of the older generation—Kapp, Tamberg, and others; the emphasis is on four young Estonians—Jan Ryaets (born 1932), Arvo Pyart (born 1935),* Velio Tormis (born 1930), and the "very young" Kuldar Sink. Of the four, two have a more conservative bent—Ryaets (nicknamed "the Estonian Hindemith") and Tormis, apparently a post-Impressionist. The other two are mentioned most often in connection with avant-garde trends. Pyart got into trouble with Khrennikov as early as 1962 for his *Obituary*. Sink's music (together with that of Denisov and Pyart) had been performed at the 1967 Biennale in Zagreb. It almost seems as if Soviet authorities tolerate "avant-garde" music in order to export it to foreign festivals while withholding performances at home.

Unlike Tarakanov's essay, the Nestyeva-Fortunatov article lacks musical examples. Thus, we are limited to verbal descriptions of the exploratory nature of the music by Pyart and Sink. Pyart's Symphony (later named "Polyphonic Symphony") uses "rather consistently the devices of dodecaphonic writing", though the authors hurry to explain that, perhaps, Mazel's new terminology might be more applicable. Young Sink likes to explore the coloristic possibilities of small instrumental ensembles, as in his Divertimento for four violins, three French horns, and two trombones.

Again it was left to Tarakanov to nail down the issues with concrete examples without pussyfooting on terms or hidden meanings. In his article "New Life in an Old Form", published in *Sovetskaya Muzyka* in June 1968, Tarakanov discusses three major new Soviet compositions —Pyart's "Polyphonic Symphony", Tishchenko's Third Symphony, and Shnitke's Second Violin Concerto. Of these, the first and the last are outright dodecaphonic compositions. It is startling to see the musical examples, complete with tone rows (neatly numbered), and to read about the structural principles of their elaboration. In the opinion of Gerald Abraham,

"Our Western avant-garde would smile pityingly at their idiom

* Estonian spelling: Rääts, Pärt. Orchestral works by these two composers were released in 1969 on two *Melodiya* records.

[i.e. orthodox twelve-tone], which appears to be that of a quarter of a century ago, but for the Soviet Union it is an advanced idiom and the mere fact that works written in it can be discussed openly and not unsympathetically in an official publication represents a great breakthrough."[16]

It is indeed a "breakthrough". For once, dodecaphonic devices are discussed dispassionately and professionally, without reference to "bourgeois decadence" or equally faded Stalinist invectives. The Shnitke Concerto (of which I have heard a taped performance) has enough novelty to make an ordinary listener squirm in his seat. One can almost visualize the dismay of a violinist weaned on the Tchaikovsky Concerto when confronted with the Cadenza from the Shnitke. Again, each musical example is worth a hundred words: suddenly, the Soviet reader is confronted with excerpts that shatter his conventional concept of music.[17]

Pyart's "Polyphonic Symphony" consists of two movements—(1) Canons, (2) Prelude and Fugue. However, since the "Prelude" contains elements of both a slow movement and a Scherzo, one could conceive it as a traditional four-movement cycle. The first movement, however, has none of the attributes of a sonata-allegro; "its rich mosaic of polyphonic combinations exhausts, so it seems, all the inherent possibilities of the preselected intonational complex". At one point, Tarakanov describes the cumulative force, the "thickening" of the texture by the successive entrance of voices until a culmination is reached where everything flows together in a massive stream of sound. It is interesting to recall that young Shostakovich in his controversial Second Symphony ("To October", 1927) used a similar cumulative device by letting thirteen instrumental "lines" enter successively. Judging by the above-mentioned recording, Pyart has abandoned all national musical ties in favour of an advanced atonal idiom.

In appearance, the Tishchenko Symphony is more traditional. Dedicated to his teacher Shostakovich, the work is subdivided into five movements. The first four, called "Meditations", are interrelated, while the last, "Post Scriptum" forms a strong contrast.* No dodecaphonic devices are used, says Tarakanov in his analysis; the thematic invention is diatonic and has a certain Russian flavour. (The same, incidentally, can be observed in Tishchenko's more recent Cello Concerto). The treatment of the orchestra stresses transparency of ensemble rather than mass effects; this is already manifest in the sparing use of instrumentalists: each instrument is represented by only one player.

* This is the Symphony heard by Harold Schonberg of *The New York Times*, during his visit to Leningrad in the spring of 1967. See p. 455.

This puts the quintet of string instruments at a disadvantage; but since the symphony has long stretches of dialogues (or "trialogues") in which only two or three instruments participate, the balances are maintained.

Tarakanov continued his crusade in the October 1968 issue of *Sovetskaya Muzyka*. This time, his careful analysis dealt with a new Violin Concerto by Kara Karayev whose Third Symphony he had reviewed two years earlier. The première of the new work was given in Moscow on 28 April 1968 at a special concert celebrating the fiftieth birthday of Karayev. His—still controversial—Third Symphony was also played* and Tarakanov uses this occasion to discuss it again:

> "For those who are used to the colourful decorative idiom in the previous works of the Azerbaijan composer, much in this symphony seemed unexpected. Various apprehensions were voiced . . .most importantly,—what did he gain by his turn to twelve-tone technique? Yet, so persuasive is the music of this symphony that there were even voices saying, 'What are we talking about, there is no serial technique in this work at all . . .' "18

Since then, the disputes have lost their edge, says Tarakanov; "by now we know that in effect there are no isolated 'forbidden' means; all depends on the talent and mastery of the composer."

The subsequent analysis of the new Concerto makes it clear that it follows in the footsteps of the Third Symphony. "The Concerto has even fewer purely external traits of a national style than the Symphony"; in fact, they are non-existent. The work opens with a twelve-tone row:

However, the arrangement of notes has certain harmonic implications: for example, the first three or the last three notes form a definite triad (or its inversion). At this point, Tarakanov reminds the reader of the tone row in the Violin Concerto of Alban Berg which is dominated by a sequence of thirds. (The Berg Concerto was composed in 1935 and is considered a classic of its kind in the free use of twelve-tone technique. Leonid Kogan was the first Soviet violinist to include this work in his repertoire and to introduce it to Moscow audiences in 1966, followed by a recording in 1968.)

* The violin soloist was Kogan, accompanied by the State Symphony under Svetlanov. The Third Symphony was played by Barshai's Moscow Chamber Orchestra.

There is no need to follow Tarakanov's analysis of Karayev's Violin Concerto through all its three movements. Suffice it to say that the new work confirmed the composer's emancipation from the tenets of Socialist Realism.

In fact, nowhere in these important essays dealing with new Soviet music is there any mention of Socialist Realism. Does this mean that the issue is dead? Not at all. It only means that it is considered permissible to discuss music of a more esoteric kind in an objective manner. At the same time, Soviet theoreticians are trying to evolve a new terminology, less dependent on Western models. This is not as impossible as it would seem; after all, Russia has her own history of non-tonal music reaching back to 1913, the First Violin Sonata of Roslavetz, and her own vocabulary of analyzing this kind of music.

Significant though these essays on new departures in Soviet music are, they must not blind us to the fact that of the 1,200 composers active in the Soviet Union, less than a dozen are inclined to "experiment". The remaining ninety-nine per cent continue to write in the accepted musical style. This does not necessarily indicate stagnation; even within traditional bounds there can be a gradual evolution, a widening of scope and technical procedures. Yet such processes work very slowly, almost imperceptibly.

There are also indications that there may be more debate on avant-garde music (both domestic and foreign), but no lessening of resistance. A vast majority among Soviet composers and musicologists remains opposed to musical "modernism", and this extends even to the—by now classical—technique of dodecaphony. Though reluctantly, the Western observer must reach this conclusion after reading the speeches and editorial comments in connection with the Theoretical Conference of December, 1965. The Conference, called by the Composers' Union in collaboration with its musicological commission, was held in Moscow and lasted four days. There were thirty-six speakers, composers as well as musicologists, from Moscow, Leningrad, the Ukraine, and other parts of the country. The basic "position paper" was the three-part essay by Lev Mazel, published by *Sovetskaya Muzyka* in the summer of 1965.*

Sovetskaya Muzyka was rather late in reporting on the Theoretical Conference. A first instalment was published in May, 1966; it contained four speeches—three on the conservative side, one favouring a more adventurous approach (by the composer Shnitke). The following

* See p. 457.

month (June), three more speeches were published, essentially conservative. This was followed by a nine-page "postscript" entitled "From the Editors". Here, speeches were summarized and—whenever they did not coincide with the conservative views of the editors— severely criticized. This happened, for example, to the speech of the composer Denisov. Somewhat amusing is the indignation of the editorial board about the "tactless" remarks of a young, virtually unknown composer-musicologist named N. Martynov.* He addressed himself to certain unnamed "Musical fathers" who—he said—"do not trust the solidity of their aesthetic platform and the level of their mastery, being afraid that youth might escape their influence". And further, Martynov said, "It seems to me there is no need to rush to 'help' the youth at all cost in their search. Youth is tired of that 'help'. To start with, let's at least have no obstruction. That's the best thing that we can hope for at present."[19]

The editors were furious, " 'We!' Who is that? In whose name is Martynov preaching? And where do 'they' get that snobbism—'we' don't need the opinion of the organization? . . ."

But, as a reassurance to would-be rebels, there is the statement by Khrennikov, made at the Conference and also at the Fifth Plenum of the Directorate,

> "It has been said on this platform that there are allegedly some interdictions of some devices, of some procedures in creative work. This . . . does not correspond to reality. For us Soviet composers, there are no forbidden means, no forbidden devices of compositorial work whatsoever. Everything that has been created before us, and all that can purposefully serve our intentions, must enter into the arsenal of Soviet music, and into the creative arsenal of any composer . . . All depends on the results of creativity, all depends . . . on that conception which can truly determine the profile of Soviet music."[20]

There is a certain ambiguity in this statement. Who is to determine the "profile of Soviet music", who is to select the means that will serve its future "purposefully"? In his speech, the wise and conciliatory Mazel made a gentle remark,

> ". . . When I hear the advice given to our composing youth—'yes, one must study the new devices, but be careful and don't get carried away'—with this kind of advice I cannot fully agree. To be careful is a very good thing, but to give an artist the advice not

* Not to be confused with the veteran musicologist Ivan Martynov.

to be 'carried away' by his work—such advice can be only given by people who do not understand the nature of real art."²¹

Sometimes "avant-garde tendencies" find more tolerance among the older composers. This is illustrated by a report on a "creative discussion" of new compositions held at the Composers' Union in the autumn of 1965. Among those present were Shostakovich, Khrennikov, Mazel, Eshpai, Shchedrin. Under discussion was, among other works, the cantata *The Sun of the Incas* by Denisov, a work with avant-gardist tendencies. The older composers were not unfriendly towards it, and Shostakovich urged one (or even several) public performances of the work to gauge the reaction of the public. Mazel called the work "neo-impressionist". The one to come forth with a furious denunciation of Denisov was young Shchedrin; he called him essentially an "imitator" of modernistic devices and doubted his creative gifts. (We have seen in the meantime that Shchedrin himself is not averse to "imitating" certain effective devices.) Another young composer, Eshpai, warned against hasty judgments about "talent" but essentially agreed with Shchedrin's evaluation.²²

This type of "creative discussions" must have caused much dissension and bitterness in the ranks of Soviet composers. On the other hand, Russian composers are used to public criticism. We may recall how venomously Khrennikov attacked his confrères (including Shostakovich) in 1948 and how fraternally they worked together in later years.

Turning from theoretical discussions to musical realities, one must say that the Soviet musical scene was as rich and varied as ever in 1965 and the succeeding years. Foreign artists enlivened the picture. The Cleveland Orchestra under George Szell came in the spring of 1965, with the pianist John Browning as soloist. Some rather "tame" American music was played—by Gershwin, Copland, Barber, Elwell, Grant Still, and Peter Mennin. The latter's Third Symphony was found by one critic to be influenced by—Miaskovsky, a discovery that surprised the critic as much as it must have surprised Mennin himself.²³ In June, Leonard Bernstein's *West Side Story* was given in Russian at the Moscow Operetta Theatre. In October Benjamin Britten's *Midsummer Night's Dream* was staged at the Bolshoi Theatre. He returned again in December 1966 to give concerts with Peter Pears. While Moscow greeted foreign visitors, the Moscow Philharmonic played abroad—in Great Britain, Canada, the United States, Mexico, and Cuba.

On the domestic scene, there was a large-scale "Festival of Leningrad Music" held in Moscow between 24 November and 2 December 1965.

No fewer that eighty-four concerts were given, and 600 performers from Leningrad participated, in addition to various Moscow organizations. The Leningrad Philharmonic Orchestra arrived with its five conductors—Mravinsky and Yansons as well as three young assistants—Blazhkov (who fared best), Serov, and Alyev. Two other conductors from Leningrad, Dalgat and Eliasberg, directed Moscow orchestras. Among the performing guests were also the Academic Glinka Choir, a Russian Folk Orchestra, a Popular Music Orchestra, a Children's Choir, Radio and T.V. ensembles, the Taneyev String Quartet, instrumental and vocal soloists, musicologists, composers . . . Nothing was neglected to stress that Leningrad was a leader in cultural affairs, and the lesson was not lost on the Muscovites. Among works by contemporary Leningrad composers performed at the festival were Salmanov's Third Symphony and the oratorio *The Twelve* (after A. Blok), the Second Symphony by Yevlakhov (born 1912), the Violin Concerto by Arapov (born 1905), and the Partita for Piano and Strings by Bogdanov-Berezovsky. The younger generation was represented by the Piano Concertos of Ustvolskaya and Tishchenko, the vocal-symphonic *Songs of Freedom* by Slonimsky, the symphonic cycle *Songs of our Days* (based on epigraphs by Soviet poets) by Andrei Petrov, and the oratorio *Poem of Leningrad* (on verses by the poet Olga Berggoltz) by young Gennadi Belov (born 1939). Correlated with the concerts was a huge exhibition of books and articles written by Leningrad musicologists (more than 500, all told).

It is noteworthy that while Moscow—being the capital city—accepts her leadership role in cultural affairs as a matter of course, Leningrad fights for her own pre-eminence. The Moscow Festival of Leningrad Musical Art was one such effort; similar festivals had been held previously in Saratov (1964) and Yaroslavl (1965). There are at least three current books dealing specifically with the Musical Culture of Leningrad. No other city in the Soviet Union has made any comparable efforts, and in fact no other city can dispute Leningrad's historic leadership in the arts.

The year 1966 was one of anniversaries, all observed in true Russian fashion. There was the 190th anniversary of Moscow's Bolshoi Theatre which was founded in 1776. There was the centenary of the Moscow Conservatory, the second-oldest in the country. The seventy-fifth anniversary of Prokofiev's birth was commemorated in April of that year, and Shostakovich was fêted on the occasion of his sixtieth birthday in September.

The memory of Prokofiev was honoured by the première of a work that, during the composer's lifetime, was considered unworthy of even a single performance: the Cantata for the Twentieth Anniversary of the October Revolution (1937), based on texts drawn from the "classics" of the Revolution. Described as "little more than an unsuccessful experiment" in Nestyev's biography of 1957, it was now rediscovered as a unique masterpiece, in the words of the same Nestyev. At the belated première, two of the ten movements were omitted —"Stalin's Vow" and "The Constitution". Investigating this matter somewhat further, we find that Prokofiev's work catalogue lists as authors Marx, Lenin, and Stalin; when the Cantata was recorded in 1967 the listing in the Soviet catalogue read: "Text arranged by the author [Prokofiev] from the works of Marx, Engels, and Lenin." In the recording, as in the performance, the two "Stalin" movements are eliminated.

The year's most important celebration was, of course, the sixtieth birthday of Shostakovich. A Kremlin decree conferred on him the title of "Hero of Socialist Labour", the Order of Lenin, and the "Gold Hammer and Sickle" Medal. Madame Furtseva, minister of culture, sent her congratulations, and messages streamed in from all parts of the world. At a gala concert on 25 September, Shostakovich's son Maxim conducted his father's First Symphony, and Rostropovich gave the first performance of the new Second Cello Concerto. Another new work, belonging to the same period, is his String Quartet No. 11, dedicated to the memory of Vassili Shirinsky, one of the founding members of the Beethoven Quartet—an ensemble close to Shostakovich for several decades.

The significance of Shostakovich in his homeland far surpasses that of an important composer. Unlike Prokofiev and Miaskovsky, who were essentially non-political, Shostakovich is a public figure, an artist who has accepted civic responsibilities. He is a deputy to the Supreme Soviet, representing his city of birth—Leningrad—and his public pronouncements on the duties of a Soviet artist have carried great weight, particularly during the 1960's. True, his music had produced some ideological disputes—in 1936, in 1948, in 1962—but even while under a political cloud, he did not shy away from representing his country, as he did in 1949 at the New York "Peace" Conference. He has been reproached at times for having accepted public castigation too submissively and for having admitted "errors" too willingly. With all his flexibility, he preserved more than anyone else the dignity of his art, and his personal dignity as an artist. Whatever reservations one may have about Shostakovich's creative career, one cannot doubt his absolute artistic sincerity and integrity. I, for one, do not believe that he ever wrote music to assuage any political ideology. There are other, more subtler, reasons why his musical style, after the "Storm and Stress" of the late 1920's and early 1930's, did not develop in the direction of

Western modernism. As a creative artist, he was sensitively attuned to the needs and responses of his country and his countrymen. His "Russianism" is not of the flamboyant kind (though he does not lack flamboyance when it is needed). It is, rather, an imperceptible affinity that permeates so much of his writing. No doubt, had Shostakovich lived abroad, his talent would have developed differently. But no one can say whether it would have been more significant.

The Leningrad Spring Festival of 1966 deserves brief mention because younger composers, regardless of "direction", were given ample opportunity to be heard. Galina Ustvolskaya's Symphony was performed after a ten-year delay. She is a composer of strongly modern, though not dodecaphonic, leanings, and the unusual sonorities as well as performance problems may have delayed the première. It is a three-movement work of which the two outer movements are purely orchestral while the middle movement uses children's voices. Originally written for two boy soloists, they were replaced by a children's chorus singing backstage. This vocal movement consists of eight miniature poems, set to texts describing the "joyless life of children in capitalist cities". These rather ascetic words produced a rather ascetic score which did not meet with unanimous approval.

Slonimsky and Tishchenko were represented with two works each, showing that their standing in the composers' community did not suffer by their "leftist" musical tastes. Slonimsky's Concerto buffo—an advanced work by Soviet standards, with sections of controlled aleatory—won the audience by its freshness and perky impertinence; it was conducted by young Serov. Tishchenko's major contribution was his Third Piano Sonata which uses bold sonorities, including playing with the elbows. Such "tone clusters", however, are not exactly an innovation: the American composer Henry Cowell used similar devices in the 1920's.[24]

The Third International Tchaikovsky Contest was held in Moscow in June, 1966. Thirty-eight countries had sent contestants—altogether 342 performers. For the first time, singers were to compete, in addition to pianists, violinists and cellists. The jury was international, although, of course, Soviet adjudicators predominated. In fact, even some of the American experts were Russian-born, like Zimbalist and Piatigorsky.

Among the pianists, the Russians won the first, third, and two fourth prizes, while the Americans were awarded second prize (Mischa Dichter) and two fifth prizes (Edward Auer and James Dick). That the youngest of the contestants, sixteen-year-old Grigori Sokolov, should have come out as first-prize winner is a near-miracle. He had not yet reached the conservatory and was still a ninth-grade student at the Central Music School attached to the Leningrad Conservatory.

The winner of the violin contest was Victor Tretyakov whose talent has recently been confirmed in his performances in New York with the Moscow State Orchestra. The second and third prizes were divided— each between a contestant from Japan and one from Russia. The two Japanese girl violinists, incidentally, are both Russian-trained: Masuko Usioda studied in Leningrad with Vaiman, Yokko Sato with Kogan in Moscow. (Miss Usioda also studied with Szigeti.) The fourth-prize winner, Nicolas Chumachenko of Argentina, was a student of Zimbalist in Philadelphia.

Among the cellists, the winners were Karin Georgian of the U.S.S.R. (first prize) and Stephen Kates of the United States (second prize).

The big surprise, of course, was the winner of the vocal competition for women: the virtually unknown Jane Marsh (U.S.A.) won the first prize; among her arias was the "Letter Scene" from Tchaikovsky's *Eugene Onegin*, sung in Russian which she had learned phonetically. To have conquered a Russian audience with this most Russian of all arias is miraculous. The second prize went to the gifted American Negro soprano, Veronica Tyler. On the other hand, both first winners in the men's vocal division were Russians, followed by the American Negro Simon Estes.

Thus, the Third Tchaikovsky Competition became history. The previous victories of Western instrumentalists—Van Cliburn, John Ogdon —were not repeated.* Although the Russian contestants, playing "at home", under familiar conditions, have an advantage, one must concede that their superior showing under stress is due not only to talent but to superb and consistent schooling. The twenty-year-old Tretyakov, for example, had but one teacher through the Central Music School and the Conservatory—Professor Yuri Yankelevich; there was never any need for relearning, for time-wasting changes in technical procedures. Compared to such consistency, the instrumental education of a child in a Western country appears almost haphazard. Ultimately the "home atmosphere" is not a decisive reason for the success of young Soviet artists: they are successful wherever they compete, be it in Brussels, Genoa, Montreal, or Fort Wayne.

The same musically so rich year saw the revival in Moscow of Stravinsky's *Oedipus Rex*, unplayed since the 1920's, the first performances of

*However, at the next Tchaikovsky Competition in 1970, the British pianist John Lill shared the first prize with the Russian Vladimir Krainev.

Britten's *War Requiem* (previously heard in Leningrad) and of Honegger's *Jeanne d'Arc au Bûcher*. In the autumn, Svetlanov conducted Stravinsky's *Symphony of Psalms* while Rozhdestvensky introduced the Violin Concerto by Alban Berg with Kogan as soloist. Anton Webern's *Five Pieces for String Quartet*—composed in 1909 yet still controversial from the Soviet point of view—were performed by the Borodin Quartet, but the same ensemble had to postpone the planned première of the string quartet by Shnitke until 1968.*

*See p. 478 and 478n.

For the jubilee year 1967—the fiftieth anniversary of the October Revolution—the Soviet musical world mobilized its full strength. All branches of the Composers' Union had held special meetings throughout 1966 to plan appropriate events.

Moscow, as the capital of the federation of republics, played host to arts ensembles from all parts of the country. Orchestras and choruses, opera and ballet ensembles, folk dancers and individual performers were heard and seen in Moscow by audiences numbering in excess of one million. The festival, called "Art of the Fraternal Republics", extended over four months; seventy-two ensembles representing various republics and regions gave 360 concerts; 285 "Meet-the-Composer" parties were given. Whether the artistic results were commensurate with the enormous effort and expense involved cannot be judged by outsiders. Actually, there was nothing particularly new in such artistic visits to Moscow by national ensembles; similar festivals had been given before and after the Second World War. But the festivities of the jubilee year dwarfed all previous occasions.

Following the May Day celebration, the tourists were regaled with a special festival week (5–12 May) called "Moscow Stars". It offered an opportunity to display such marvellous artists as David Oistrakh and Sviatoslav Richter, the Moiseyev Dancers, the Armenian Song and Dance Ensemble, and various orchestras. The programmes were essentially traditional.

In the meantime, Leningrad proceeded with its third Spring Festival, given from 23–29 April. Here the accent was on new music, not only by Leningrad composers but also by their neighbours from the North —Soviet Karelia. Much of the music was composed for the jubilee year, and there were the usual cantatas on patriotic texts—Belov's "Thus Commanded Ilyich" and Kravchenko's "October Wind". (The Soviet consumption of such works seems unlimited.) Young Tishchenko had two works performed: his Third Symphony whose "linear" style aroused much controversy; and a new Violin Concerto in a more "melodious" idiom which was found to be a welcome change. Actually, the Concerto was the revision of an older work originally composed eight years earlier during Tishchenko's conservatory days. This may explain a certain disparity of style which was criticized when the work was played in Moscow later that year.

Leningrad—the birthplace of the Revolution—was appropriately chosen as host city for a solemn meeting of the Russian branch of the Composers' Union in late September. Khrennikov opened the meeting in the historic Smolny Institute where Lenin had proclaimed the birth of the Soviet State. The key address was delivered by the musicologist Ivan Martynov, who spoke on "Soviet Music over the Fifty Years". The delegates were engulfed by a flood of musical events: forty concerts and stage performances within eight days.

Sergei Slonimsky's first opera, *Virineya*, produced almost simultaneously in his home town of Leningrad on 30 September and in Moscow on 4 November, was the outstanding event of that season. The libretto is based on a well-known novel (later dramatized) by Lydia Seyfullina, first published in 1924. The heroine is a peasant woman emancipated by the Revolution. In keeping with the subject, Slonimsky has used a musical idiom close to folklore, and his skill in choral writing made the mass scenes particularly impressive. Tarakanov, who had reviewed the opera before it was staged, traced influences of the Mussorgsky folk drama; nevertheless he found that there was no contradiction between Slonimsky's previous style of writing and the idiom employed in the opera.[1] Be this as it may, *Virineya* became enormously successful.

In October, Leningrad staged an arts festival, "The Dawn of October". The inaugural concert, on 25 October, took place in a newly built auditorium, appropriately named "October", with a seating capacity of 4,000.

Not to be outdone, Moscow had its own Soviet Music Week in October. Presented were Miaskovsky's Symphonies Nos. 17 and 27, the "Festive Overture" by Glière, the "October" cantata by Prokofiev, a symphony by Anatol Alexandrov,* some arias by Khachaturian, the Second Symphony by Boris Tchaikovsky, the Second Piano Concerto by Shchedrin, the Second Violin Concerto by Shostakovich and his new overture "October", Tishchenko's Violin Concerto, Kabalevsky's Second Cello Concerto and Khrennikov's Violin Concerto. An impressive new song cycle by Shostakovich on words by the poet Alexander Blok,** was superbly sung by Galina Vishnevskaya. Several inevitable cantatas rounded out the programme which was found unrepresentative by many critics.

The announcements of the Lenin Prizes for music—usually made in

* A recent work by the eighty-year-old composer.
** With accompaniment by piano, violin, and cello.

the spring—were awaited with particular interest. In June 1967 *Sovet-skaya Muzyka* announced two winners—the composer Kara Karayev and the choreographer Iogr Moiseyev. Karayev received his award for the musical score to the ballet "The Path of Thunder" which dated back to 1958. Perhaps it is significant that Karayev's award-winning work was an older composition, written in a folkloristic style, not his much-discussed, rather controversial Third Symphony. Yet it is also significant that his recent "conversion" to serial techniques was no deterrent to his being chosen a recipient of the coveted prize.

Another list of winners was published in the December issue of *Sovetskaya Muzyka*; this time it was called the "State Prize" for 1967 (Gosudarstvennaya Premia). Three composers were honoured: Khrennikov for his "cycle of instrumental concertos", specifically those for violin and for cello*; Otar Taktakishvili, a prominent composer from Georgia; and Andrei Petrov, a thirty-seven-year-old composer from Leningrad and, for the past few years, first secretary of the Leningrad branch of Soviet Composers. Incidentally, Khrennikov was rounding out his twentieth year as first secretary of the Union of Soviet Composers—a position he had assumed in 1948—and the award of a government prize at this juncture was well timed.

It was Khrennikov who had built the Composers' Union into a tightly controlled, politically active organization. Khrennikov's basic conservatism, with an occasional concession to "liberal" demands, earned him the confidence of Khrushchev and of the present political leaders, including Madame Furtseva, the powerful minister of culture. Under Khrennikov, the Union of Soviet Composers became the official voice of all Soviet music, and the award of the "Order of Lenin" to the Union in 1968 was the Party's recognition of that dominant role. Numerically, the Composers' Union was never strong, and it was not meant to be numerous because of its exclusivity. Here are the membership statistics, published in October 1967:**

(1932—organization of Union; number of members not reported)
1948—First Congress of Soviet Composers—about 1,000 members
1957—Second Congress—1,220 members (964 composers, 256 musicologists)
1962—Third Congress—1,390 members (1,067 composers, 323 musicologists)
1966—1,537 members (no subdivision given)
1967—1,600 members (1,170 composers, 430 musicologists)

It should not be overlooked that these figures include all the branches in the various republics, cities, and regions of the Soviet Union. It is indeed a small, exclusive "club" which provides its members with a multitude of benefits. These are distributed mainly with the help of

---

* London première: 3 July 1965.　　** See pp. 399–400.

MUZFOND, the Music Fund controlled by the Composers' Union. The Union Bulletin describes its functions as follows,

"The U.S.S.R. Music Fund (founded in 1939 with branches in every republic of the U.S.S.R.) concerns itself with the welfare of members of the Union of Soviet Composers. The Music Fund is an economically independent organization; its activities are directed by a Board appointed by the Secretariat of the Union of Soviet Composers. Its budget is made up of the entrance fees and dues of its members, of royalties from public performances of musical compositions, of prescribed deductions and royalties from publishing houses, theatres, concert-giving and other organizations, and so on. The U.S.S.R. Music Fund has opened, and runs, Homes for Creative Work in the most picturesque parts of Armenia, the Ukraine, Karelia, Latvia, and in the environs of Leningrad and Moscow. A composer or musicologist wishing to concentrate on his work is provided, upon application, with a cottage containing a piano, and full board at one of such homes. Facilitating the copying of music, the tuning and repair of the pianos, providing medical aid, constructing houses and sanatoria, running summer health camps for children—these are a few of the many functions of the Music Fund."[2]

The expression "economically independent" means apparently that the Music Fund functions without government subsidy; it derives its income from "prescribed" deductions and royalties paid by every institution connected with music.

When Madame Furtseva gave a press conference in October 1967, to summarize the cultural accomplishments of the Soviet State in the past fifty years, the composers and their Union received high praise from the minister of culture. After having dispensed some staggering statistics in all fields of culture, Madame Minister said,

"It would seem that music is not a proper subject to discuss in terms of figures, yet in a brief account of the achievements of Soviet culture over the half-century we cannot altogether dispense with figures. Only four years have passed since the U.S.S.R. Ministry of Culture and the U.S.S.R. Union of Composers announced a country-wide competition for the best production by musical theatres, and here we have the new staging of 28 operas, 23 ballets, and 31 musical comedies."[3]

Impressive though these figures are, they reveal only quantity, not quality. To make a proper evaluation, one would have to know how many of these new works survived the première, how many entered the permanent repertoire, how many were shown at more than one theatre. Madame Furtseva also revealed that "within the current five-year period we plan to open 92 new theatres and to reconstruct the buildings of 80 active theatres".* (There were 508 professional theatres in the Soviet Union in 1967.) Yet, Moscow musicians complained that the Affiliate of the Bolshoi Theatre was without an adequate building, and that none was foreseen while "forty-nine circus buildings are to be constructed". In the field of recorded music, Madame Furtseva mentioned with pride the centralized recording firm *Melodiya* established in 1964: "since then the number of recordings issued has increased fifty per cent and will exceed the 180,000,000 mark in the current year," she said.

The statistics merely confirm the well-known fact that the Soviet Government has supported, and is supporting, all cultural endeavours on an enormous scale. Unavoidably, government patronage on such a scale entails government planning and controls. In a country where ideology is all-important, such controls can, as we have seen, become repressive.

Nor can centralized planning be expected to solve all the problems. At the Twenty-third Congress of the Communist Party in 1966, several prominent musicians spoke with concern of certain flaws in the Soviet musical structure. Kabalevsky, for example, criticized the state of provincial orchestras: of thirty-eight professional orchestras in the country,** twenty-seven were seriously understaffed, especially with regard to string instruments. Speaking on the same subject, the musicologist Vinogradov (a specialist in Far-Eastern music) remarked that some of these orchestras—while having a full wind section—play with only two violas or six violins, with lamentable results: such ensembles "cannot give satisfactory performances of even the most uncomplicated works".

Other criticism voiced at the same session included the lack of qualified music teachers, lecturers, and radio personnel; the faulty planning of concert tours which neglect certain areas of the country; the low level of concert programmes and entertainment music. Said Kabalevsky,

* The opening of the 38th opera house—in the Georgian town of Kutaisi— took place on 31 December 1969.

** In comparison, the United States has many more professional symphony orchestras—one hundred and twenty-four according to 1969 statistics. However, the Soviet Union is far ahead in the number of resident professional opera and ballet companies.[4]

"Each year we hear statistics, but these are mere figures . . . of course it is good to know that 'millions' of people go to concerts, but what kind of music do they hear at these concerts? . . . There are many more variety concerts than philharmonic concerts, and the programmes of these variety concerts very often contain some of the lowest trash . . ."⁵★

Another speaker, the critic Yuri Korev, deplored the bureaucratic apathy with which justified criticism is being received—and ignored. "Some ten years ago," he said, "the journal *Sovetskaya Muzyka* drew public attention to the unenviable fate of 'mini-philharmonics'★★ and proposed to combine and strengthen some of them . . . Only recently, the Ministry of Culture came to the same conclusion."

An army bandmaster, I. Petrov, complained about the decline of band playing and the shortage of qualified young players. "For every 100 pianists there is only one wind player" in the conservatories and schools of the Russian Federation, Petrov said; "in the Georgian Republic, the ratio is 100:0.5. Out of 500,000 children enrolled in Russian music schools, only 3,500 play a wind instrument." And he warned that, if this trend continued, there would be no professional wind players in fifteen or twenty years. Already now there is a shortage of qualified wind instrument teachers.

Of course, such complaints and shortcomings are not limited to the Soviet Union; they can be found in most Western countries. The only difference is that, in the West, governments are unconcerned since the dispensation of "culture" is usually not considered a government responsibility—for better or for worse. But even "planned" culture can have its pitfalls, as the Soviet example shows.

★ Nevertheless, the statistics are impressive: "Our concert-giving bodies (nearly 130) and over 180 major performing groups unifying 24,000 musicians give more than 350,000 concerts a year" said Khrennikov in 1969.⁶

★★ In Soviet terms, a "philharmonic" is not an orchestra but a regional organization responsible for arranging all kinds of musical events for the public.

After the intense, almost hectic, musical activities of the jubilee year 1967, came a period of sobre reflection and consolidation. Past errors were examined and plans were made for the future. As usual, the forums for such discussions were various meetings of the Composers' Union, regional and national. Most important among them was the Second Conference of the Composers' Union of the Russian Federation (RSFSR) in May 1968, and the Fourth All-Union Congress of Soviet Composers in December of that year.

But discussions also took place in rather intimate circumstances, and they proved often more revealing and fruitful than the large-scale meetings. One such round-table discussion was initiated by the editorial board of *Sovetskaya Muzyka*, and a rather full stenographic report was published in the January 1968 issue. The principal topic was the "Soviet Music Week" presented with much fanfare in Moscow in October 1967, and found disappointing and unrepresentative by many informed observers. But the debate reached much deeper and revealed some basic disaffections in the musical establishment. Among those who took part were the musicologists Nestyev, Marina Sabinina, Moissei Grinberg, and Yuri Korev; and the composers Yakov Solodukho, Sergei Balasanyan, Roman Ledenev, and Karen Khachaturian. Not the greatest names, perhaps, but quite a representative group, covering a wide age span.

The important point brought out by Nestyev and others was that not enough *new* Soviet music was heard in public, and that much new music remained ignored or neglected. The debate revealed that discrimination was practised against certain composers, particularly those with avant-garde tendencies. Said young Ledenev,

"Take the case of Edison Denisov. In my opinion, the Philharmonic has declared a 'cold war' against him since it denies the use of the stage to any group wishing to perform his works (even the early ones). Yet . . . *The Sun of the Incas* [by Denisov] is often played abroad . . . as if [it] belonged there. Is this normal? It is time . . . that we give the audiences the opportunity to hear and to evaluate such music, because no 'round table' . . . can and should make a decision on behalf of millions of listeners for whom, it may be said, this music is written."[1]

Karen Khachaturian spoke in the same vein,

"For some time there has been talk that there is no spirit of renewal in the work of our section . . . Year after year, the same three to five people meet and stew in their own juice . . . We professional musicians often don't know the music of our colleagues. We travel abroad . . . and are confronted by questions based on such detailed information that we are embarrassed. For example, I have never even seen the young Kiev composer Silvestrov.* His music is not heard. It is not a matter of choice—it is a matter of obligation that we know each other. New music—bad or good—must be judged without hysterics, without hysterics of approval and without hysterics of disapproval . . . One must play all, because one must know all—and if not in the large halls, then at least 'at home', in the composers' circle . . . "[2]

To hear young composers speak in this manner may not be surprising, but the veteran critic, Nestyev, said essentially the same. He, too, protested against the narrow choice of new music, against the exclusion of certain composers. Among those not performed he mentioned Alfred Shnitke and Andrei Volkonsky, both belonging to the avant-garde. Nestyev continued,

". . . we hear much less than what is actually being composed. I am concerned because a great many works are not played at all in our country, and some are played abroad before they are played in Moscow . . . If there is a controversial work, nevertheless it must be played . . . and evaluated seriously, professionally. It is necessary that the authors of such controversial works should not withdraw within the narrow circle of like-minded persons, but should develop in an atmosphere of discussion, factual disagreements, and divergences of opinion. Then only can we expect a more normal creative and ideological growth. At present, these composers exist, in essence, outside of criticism. I think that, among them, there are talented people. And even if they take a course somewhat more 'left' than we like, it might well be that the friendly criticism could help them find a more correct path."[3]

All three speakers stressed the same point: whether experimental or not, *all* new music should be exposed to public hearings.

* Silvestrov is a special case: until recently he did not belong to the Composers' Union in order to avoid hostile criticism. See also p. 487.

One of the participants, Balasanyan—who had served on the selection committee—objected to the allegation that Shnitke was "excluded" without sufficient reason. Actually, the committee had heard two of his works, the Second Violin Concerto and the String Quartet. The latter was found to be a "curious and experimental, rather than a valuable, opus". At any rate, it was not considered worthy of presentation at the Fiftieth Anniversary*. Balasanyan continued, "We are surprised that Shnitke ignores the traditions of our national music and turns to the doubtful experiments of Western avant-gardists. We told this to the author, but he answered that the Germans heard much in his music that was Russian."[4] Balasanyan was incensed that "foreign musicians" should be called as witnesses to determine the "Russianism" of Soviet music. Nevertheless, it is true that Soviet avant-garde music—despite its Western-oriented technique—often displays an undefinable "Russian" colouration which belies the repeated assertions that "all" serial music sounds alike.

There was also controversy around a non-controversial composer —Shchedrin. Miss Sabinina was captivated by his Second Symphony and his Second Piano Concerto, both of which use a mixture of very novel and traditional (or "traditionalistic") techniques. Balasanyan, too, felt that the Piano Concerto was a "continuation of Prokofiev traditions". Others expressed regret that, while pursuing novel effects, Shchedrin had lost some of his Russian identification. These effects were not particularly "organic" in the Concerto: "the material is dry, the square rhythm is étude-like; even the bits of jazz . . . sound dried-up", in the opinion of Ledenev. On this point, Nestyev made an interesting observation,

> "Listening to the Second Concerto of Shchedrin and other works, it came to my mind that, lately, our composers are trying to resurrect the style that, during the 1920's, was called *Sachliche Musik* in Germany ('objective', matter-of-fact music)—a style that was represented, in those days, in the scores of Krenek, Hindemith, Kurt Weill, and others. It is a style of 'workman-like' intellectualism, harsh linear combinations, swift 'perpetuum mobile' with elements of atonal anarchy, cleverly planned dynamic constructions, behind which one does not always feel a diversity of emotion and wealth of soul."[5]

---

* Shnitke's Quartet received its delayed Moscow première on 1 February 1968. A few weeks later, on 6 March, it was played in New York where a critic described it as "the work of a good academician who wished to exploit up-to-date ideas without really posing as a radical".[4]

This is an apt description of a certain trend in Soviet music, particularly where the piano is involved—motion in place of emotion. There are motoric rhythms and driving energy, but also much percussive clatter and mechanical sequences. Used creatively by Bartok, Prokofiev, and Hindemith more than forty years ago, it sounded fresh and new; resurrected by Shchedrin, Tishchenko, and others, it is curiously outdated, despite some "modern" trimmings.

This round-table discussion succeeded in drawing attention to a vast amount of new Soviet music, unperformed for a variety of reasons. Some composers were considered too "experimental", others failed to get a hearing because they lived in the provinces or lacked the necessary connections and personal contacts among those who influenced the repertoire. The Soviet musical scene showed signs of saturation: more music was written than could possibly be performed in Moscow and Leningrad. Quite rightly, Balasanyan pointed out that the Moscow Philharmonic was over-burdened, that new music began to encroach on the great cycles of classical music, that other cities with good orchestras should present more premières. Yet, Moscow—like Paris, London, or New York—remains the "show case" where a musical career must receive its stamp of approval, and the competition among young composers to receive a hearing in the capital becomes increasingly keener.

One such composer, Nikolai Sidelnikov (mentioned by Nestyev as unjustly neglected) spoke up in May 1968, at the Second Meeting of the Composers' Union of the Russian Federation (RSFSR). He complained that the secretariat of the Composers' Union made too little effort to present works of composers not yet widely known. And Sidelnikov asked a rhetorical questions, "Aren't we developing that same type of composer whom, twenty years ago, Khrennikov aptly named the 'composer-dignitary?' " This was indeed an acid remark. What Sidelnikov implied was that in 1968 an encrusted hierarchy of favourite composers had emerged, similar to the one in 1948, ousted from power by Khrennikov's broadside attack. (In those days, Khrennikov—barely thirty-five—was outside the select circle). Sidelnikov, whose major works were totally ignored during the jubilee performances of 1967 (though he had written a few specially for the October celebration), said with some bitterness, "In such cases, one tries to console oneself by remembering that Schubert, for example, never heard one of his symphonies during his lifetime . . . One could assume that even the great Schubert would willingly exchange the posthumous fame of his symphonies for a performance during his lifetime . . ."[6]

Andrei Petrov—a successful composer and the first secretary of the Leningrad Union—complained as well. Not only did many interesting new works remain unperformed, but important compositions were laid aside after just one hearing: he mentioned the Third Symphony of Eshpai and the Cello Concerto of Tishchenko. Turning from the home-front to the subject of Soviet music abroad, Petrov criticized, and with full justification, the policy of limiting the choice of foreign perform-ances to just a few Soviet composers,

> "True, they are very great masters, not only of Soviet but of world music. But, by limiting our presentations to their works we unwillingly confirm the bourgeois propaganda—namely that all Soviet music consists of a few world-famous names of some twenty years ago. More then once I witnessed in Moscow and Leningrad how foreign artists, exploring our music, discover with surprise a quantity of new names, new talented works which completely change their wrong impression of us."[7]

The strongest possible support for struggling young composers came from Shostakovich, the most influential voice among Soviet musicians. During a press interview, Shostakovich declared flatly, "Young com-posers are little known and little played." And when he was asked, "How do you explain this unfair attitude towards composers?" he burst out, "Explain it! I absolutely do not understand it, nor do I con-done it . . . It is simply vitally necessary that young composers learn what it is like to have an audience. But how are they to learn this if . . . they have almost no contact with audiences? Symphony orchestras play their works very rarely . . ."[8] To remedy the situation, the Composers' Union planned at one time, Shostakovich said, to create "an orchestra especially for performing today's music . . . by young composers". But the idea was abandoned because it was feared that this would merely relieve the regular orchestras of their responsibility to perform new music. They would, Shostakovich remarked, " 'with a clear conscience' play the approved classics without 'all those experimental things'."

Soviet composers, then, want to see more new music by young composers performed within the regular programmes of the concert-giving organizations. This problem is as acute in Moscow, apparently, as it is in Western capitals. All too often, performances of modern compositions are limited to special festivals, for special audiences—a kind of musical "quarantine"; and only rarely does a new work enter the regular repertoire of "subscription" concerts. The Soviet Com-posers' Union recommends new works for performance, but it cannot force acceptance. Ultimately, the opera theatres, the philharmonics, the radio and television stations make their own decisions—to the distress of the slighted composers.

Apart from venting these grievances, the Composers' Congress of the

Russian Federation served several important purposes. It elected Georgi Sviridov to the post of first secretary, replacing Shostakovich who had asked to be released because of poor health. Shostakovich's farewell address reaffirmed the importance of the *Russian* contingent within the Composers' Union. His words also reflected the stiffer ideological directives of the Central Committee of the Communist Party, issued shortly before the Composers' Conference opened.

A Western reader might find it curious that the Russian Federation was the last to organize a Composers' Union: it was formally established in 1960. Perhaps, the need for such an organization was not felt too keenly because Moscow had always been the headquarters for the national Union of Composers of the U.S.S.R. But the Moscow secretariat became increasingly involved in running a "multi-national" organization. Thus, the composers of the Russian Federation began to realize the need for their own organization, on a par with those of the other constituent republics. After all, the Russian contingent was the largest within the national Union, and they wanted their voice to be heard.

It should not be assumed, however, that the grouping within the "Russian" Union was homogeneous; quite the contrary. While it included the city unions of Moscow, Leningrad, Gorky, Rostov, Saratov, and Sverdlovsk, it also included Siberia and the autonomous republics of Bashkir, Buryat, Chuvash, Daghestan, Karelia, Mari, Northern Ossetia, and Tatar as well as other minorities. At the time of its formation in 1960, the Composers' Union of the Russian Federation had 673 members of whom 524 were concentrated in Moscow and Leningrad. In the words of Shostakovich,

> "The musical culture of Russia is a broad and capacious concept. In the gigantic expanse of the Federation, dozens of national musical 'languages' and 'dialects' resound . . . peoples, large and small, many of whom before the Revolution had no professional music whatsoever, but have now successfully developed their own distinctive art in the stream of the single Socialist culture. Year by year the musical ties and reciprocal influence of the various musical schools are growing stronger—this is the actual embodiment of the principles of Lenin's nationalities policy."[9]

At the same time, Shostakovich felt obliged to take cognizance of the hardening ideological line issued by the Party. He did so in the following sentences,

> "The decisions of the April plenary sessions of the Party's Central Committee have made it incumbent on us to take an

active stand against attempts to smuggle into individual works of literature and art views alien to the Socialist ideology of Soviet society.

"In this connection, I should like to touch upon the question of so-called 'avant-gardism' in music (the term . . . usurped by a small group of musicians occupying a definite position in Western art). At the base of this militant trend lies a destructive principle in relation to music . . .

"'Avant-gardism' is a deliberate attempt . . . to achieve a new quality in music merely through the repudiation of historically evolved norms and rules. This is a gross theoretical error . . .

"We Soviet artists resolutely reject 'avant-gardism'."[10]

Shostakovich speaks of the "wretchedness and poverty of content of 'avant-garde' opuses" and points to Prokofiev as the supreme example of "innovation springing from the base of tradition". And he closes with an appeal to "create music worthy of our great people, who are building Communism".

It will be noticed that Shostakovich only applies the term avant-garde to a "small group" active in *Western* art. But implied is the warning to Soviet composers to keep away from the compromising label. Shostakovich's distaste for dodecaphony has apparently subsided, perhaps because this technique was no longer a threat, having been superseded by far more "outrageous" musical experiments.

But there are "nuances" in Shostakovich's public utterances which deserve attention. While he spoke rather sternly in his official capacity as retiring first secretary of the Russian Composers' Union, he sounded much more relaxed and willing to compromise in a personal interview granted to the monthly *Yunost* (Youth) which appeared at the same time. In reply to the question, "In connection with experiments, what is the situation in regard to quests for new means of expression in music?", Shostakovich answered,

". . . As for the use of strictly technical devices from such musical 'systems' as, say, the twelve-tone or the aleatory . . . everything is good in moderation . . . The use of elements from these complex systems is entirely justified if it is dictated by the idea of the composition . . . Please understand that the formula 'the end justifies the means' to some extent seems right to me in music. Any means? Any, as long as they convey the goal."[11]

This statement is a far cry from the inflexibility displayed on other occasions by Shostakovich. Significant, too, is the fact that, among the

"classics of the twentieth century", he named not only Mahler, Proko-
fiev, Miaskovsky, Stravinsky, and Bartok—but also "the Austrian
Alban Berg". True, Berg is the least "dogmatic" of the Schoenbergian
Twelve-tone School; yet his inclusion as a "classic" of our century is a
significant concession. No doubt Shostakovich had admired Berg's
Wozzeck in the 1920's; now, at last, he is ready to admit his admiration.

In the same context, Shostakovich pays a touching tribute to the art
of Benjamin Britten whom he calls "a very important composer". And
he continues,

> "I would like a few more Brittens—Russian, English, and German
> . . . What attracts me to Britten is the force and sincerity of his
> talent, his outer simplicity and the depth of emotional effect . . .
> Britten has an extraordinary effect on me in all his creative work
> . . . Everyone who seriously likes music should get a little more
> closely acquainted with Britten's compositions . . ."[12]

The Central Committee's decision, to which Shostakovich referred in
his speech to the Russian Composers' Union, was formulated during a
two-day meeting of the Kremlin leaders on 10 and 11 April 1968. In
fact, Shostakovich lifted an entire sentence *verbatim* from the resolution
—namely the warning against "smuggling views alien to Soviet society's
Socialist ideology into individual works of literature and art". An intensive ideological campaign was to be launched to combat so-called
"subversive efforts" by the West. There had been warnings to Soviet
intellectuals that "they faced retaliation if they continued a wave of
protest over the recent trial of critics of the regime and other grievances". The political reform movement in Czechoslovakia and a certain unrest in Poland contributed to the tenseness of the Kremlin
hierarchy. At the April meetings, Leonid Brezhnev was the main
speaker; the others were Madame Furtseva and G. M. Markov,
secretary of the Soviet Writers' Union.

The Composers' Union did not participate actively in these meetings;
there was no need, since the Party's main quarrel was with dissident
writers. The conflict had begun with the arrest and convictions of
Andrei Sinyavsky and Yuli Daniel in early 1966 and continued with the
agitation of Pavel Litvinov, Larisa Daniel, and others protesting
against the convictions. But the musical scene was not unaffected: in
July 1968, the gifted junior conductor of the Leningrad Philharmonic,
Igor Blazhkov, was removed from his post because his programmes
showed his consistent interest in musical modernism and the avant-
garde. He was prevented from obtaining any other conducting

assignment and returned to Kiev where, for a time, he lived in straitened circumstances. The composer Denisov, an avant-gardist, was suddenly dismissed from the faculty of the Moscow Conservatory; he was reinstated eventually.

That Soviet intellectuals were not entirely cowed was revealed in the essay *Thoughts on Progress, Peaceful Coexistence, and Intellectual Freedom* by Andrei D. Sakharov which reached the West in July 1968.[13] Sakharov, a member of the Academy of Sciences and a nuclear physicist, spoke out against the "influence of neo-Stalinists in our political life". Mentioning the "passionate and closely argued appeal against censorship by the outstanding Soviet writer A. Solzhenitsyn", Sakharov said,

> "The crippling censorship of Soviet artistic and political literature has again been intensified. Dozens of brilliant writings cannot see the light of day," ... "Today the key to a progressive restructuring of the system of government in the interests of manking lies in intellectual freedom. This has been understood, in particular,by the Czechoslovaks and there can be no doubt that we should support their bold initiative, which is so valuable for the future of Socialism and all mankind."

What happened next is a matter of history. The Soviet leaders, unable to curb the Czech reform movement by persuasion, resorted to armed intervention. On 20 and 21 August 1968, Czechoslovakia was occupied by Soviet troops.

For intellectuals on either side of the frontier, it was a traumatic experience. Traditionally, the musical ties between the Russians and the Czechs had always been very close, in Tsarist days as well as after the Revolution. There were times when new Russian or Soviet music was performed in Czechoslovakia before it was heard at home; a noted example is Prokofiev's ballet *Romeo and Juliet,* given first in Brno after it had faced endless delays in Leningrad. The Czechs, being more liberal in artistic matters, took particular interest in Soviet avant-garde music; the best book on this subject was written by a Czech, Vaclav Cucera, and published in Prague in 1967.

There were courageous Soviet intellectuals who staged public protests against the invasion of Czechoslovakia; they were immediately arrested, tried, and convicted in October 1968. Since then, a great silence has descended upon the literary scene. Reports from Moscow speak of a "tightening of controls in all areas of culture". Yevtushenko and Voznesensky faced delays in the publication of their latest poems. Solzhenitsyn became virtually a "non-person", and his name was not mentioned in the press except in a defamatory way. Mark Slonim reported,

"This course, commonly called 're-Stalinization', aggravates the already pessimistic feelings among the members of the literary community. The split between the 'liberals', struggling for freedom of expression, and the 'apparatchiki', actually part of the huge Party machine, is sharper than ever . . . Censorship grows more obnoxious every day . . ."[14]

In this climate of political tension and intellectual frustration, the Fourth All-Union Congress of Soviet Composers convened in December 1968. Six years had elapsed since the last Composers' Congress, and the periodic review of successes and failures was due.

Just prior to the opening of the Fourth Congress, the Composers' Union received a signal honour—it was awarded the Order of Lenin. The citation, dated 13 December 1968, read,

"For meritorious services in the development of Soviet musical art, embodying the ideas of the Great Socialist October Revolution, and for the active participation of Soviet composers in the building of Communism, the Union of Soviet Composers is herewith rewarded with the Order of Lenin."[15]

In a covering statement, published on 17 December simultaneously by *Pravda* and *Izvestia*, the Central Committee of the Communist Party congratulated the Composers' Union and expressed confidence that "Soviet music will continue to play an ever increasing role in the Communist education of the people". The lengthy statement addressed the composers as "Dear Comrades" and contained the following paragraphs,

"The musical art of Socialist Realism is developing on the basis of the principles of Party spirit and kinship with the people. It counterposes its ideological purposefulness and its human spirit to the decadent culture of the contemporary capitalist world.

"Today, in a period of sharp aggravation of the class struggle between Socialism and Capitalism, the workers of Soviet music are called upon to come forth even more actively against bourgeois ideology, to convey even more consistently the ideas of Socialist humanism, Soviet patriotism, and proletarian internationalism . . .

"It is important to develop comradely criticism of shortcomings to fight more actively against the various kinds of formalist distortions in music, to achieve a further rallying of the composers and music scholars to the positions of Socialist Realism, to train them in the spirit of the great ideas of Marxism-Leninism . . ."[16]

The statement was more than a greeting; it was a clear policy directive, and the convening composers had little choice but to endorse it. Noteworthy is the repeated reference to "Socialist Realism". Without having been discarded, the term was used rarely during the past few years; in theoretical writings it was often replaced by a reference to "musical realism". Now, Socialist Realism had returned with all its implications, its barbed opposition to "bourgeois" art.

All this was reflected in the key address of Khrennikov, delivered to the Congress on 16 December.[17] He spoke with the confidence of a man who had been at the helm for twenty years. In 1948, he had assumed the leadership of a frightened, demoralized, disorganized group of composers who had crumpled under the vicious attack of politicians, who had witnessed the public humiliation of their most famous *confrères*. Ten years later, in 1958, Khrennikov had presided at the rehabilitation of his Union and of the slandered composers. Another ten years later he experienced the supreme satisfaction of seeing the Composers' Union, more influential than ever, receive the highest recognition of the land. The Order of Lenin was, above all, a tribute to Khrennikov's astute political leadership, a reward for exemplary Party discipline and ideological loyalty during periods of political and intellectual tension. The Kremlin leaders had every reason to be pleased with the co-operativeness of the musicians.

Khrennikov warned against the "camouflaged methods" of capitalism in attacking the Socialist camp and in "trying to bolster the forces of internal counter-revolution that have not been put down completely". The principal propaganda aim is to *de-ideologize* art, to achieve its complete "freedom" from politics and social problems, to demand that the artist take no interest in the events occurring in the world around him. Such "views alien to the Socialist ideology of Soviet society" have to be fought, in accordance with the Party's directives, said Khrennikov.

Returning to a favourite topic, Socialist Realism, its art "has been engendered by the most progressive ideas of our century, the ideas of Revolution and Socialism". The opposing trend is "militant individualism. To an individualistic artist, 'everything is permitted' . . . Voluntarism [meaning permissiveness] has become a fundamental philosophic principle of decadent bourgeois art."

Khrennikov scorns some of the avant-garde practices which, he says, resemble "circus stunts rather than works of music", as for example in the works of John Cage. He contrasts "the aesthetics of the extreme leftist (*sic*) trends of modern music" and its revival of "the old worn-out catchword of 'art for art's sake', an art intended . . . for a small handful of artistic snobs", to the Leninist slogan "Art is the Property of the Working People". Yet, he has to admit that some foreign composers "holding progressive ideological and political views" (meaning, of course, Marxist views) take interest in avant-gardism. Here, he mentions the Italian Luigi Nono, but he may also have thought of the Polish and Czech avant-garde composers.

Significantly, there is no reference to the Soviet musical avantgardists: they are buried in silence, a fate perhaps worse than an open attack. However, there is one lengthy paragraph in Khrennikov's speech in which he berates the monthly journal *Yunost* for having published an interview with a Soviet avant-garde composer whom Khrennikov churlishly refuses to name. He asks rhetorically, "On what grounds does our most popular mass youth journal disseminate such a *credo* in a printing of two million copies?" The unnamed composer turns out to be Valentin Silvestrov (born 1937) whose avant-garde "credo" is told with startling frankness to a perceptive interviewer, Natalia Gorbanevskaya.*[18] Silvestrov, a member of the Kiev avantgarde group, is very little known at home, though Blazhkov conducted his *Spectres* for chamber orchestra in Leningrad. But his works have been played abroad, in Prague, Zagreb, Berlin, Paris, Copenhagen, and (anonymously) in New York.** In 1967, Silvestrov obtained a commission from the American Kussevitsky Foundation for an orchestral score, *Eschatophony*, which was first performed in Darmstadt under Bruno Maderna on 6 September 1968. His gods are Schoenberg and Webern. He defines avant-garde music as a "mutiny against the inertia of compositional thought". Khrennikov is very much annoyed by this new "aesthetic" position and quotes Silvestrov out of context, making him sound rather foolish. It is obvious that this interview with Silvestrov was initiated by the editors of *Yunost* without consultation with the musical establishment which made it doubly offensive. "Why has there been no open criticism of this matter in the Composers' Union or its printed organs?" asks Khrennikov.***

In spite of Khrennikov's fervour on behalf of Socialist Realism he realizes that the musical idiom is expanding and a "sensible search for new expressive means and methods" is justified. In fact, "all and every method, however daring, is good if it helps the composer to give the fullest possible and profoundly true expression of the progressive ideas, imagery, and conflicts of our time". This sounds rather "per-

* Early in 1969, Miss Gorbanevskaya, a gifted poet and writer, was committed to a mental hospital after having been accused of anti-Soviet slander . . . a shocking political chicanery.[19]

** At a concert of the ISCM in 1964 his Suite for Piano was played. See p. 442.

*** The *Yunost* interview appeared in September 1967; Khrennikov spoke in December 1968.

missive". And Khrennikov ends the first part of his speech by saying that, "While strenuously opposing the fashionable 'avant-garde' infatuations, we should not lose sight of another dangerous trend, sometimes encountered in our music. I mean creative stagnation, smug academicism, colourless craftmanship which are now and again passed for realism."

In his analysis of recent Soviet music, Khrennikov is actually far more tolerant of new trends than his speech would indicate. He bestows approval on certain works by Pyart, Karayev, Tishchenko, and Shchedrin which—at least to Western ears—have severed their ties with Socialist Realism by their advanced musical idiom. But this new-found Soviet modernism might indicate, not a "break" with Socialist Realism, but rather an *expansion* of the concept itself which, according to Khrennikov, "gives full scope to the creative imagination of the artist and embraces an immense variety of individual styles".

A hint towards a broader interpretation of "national" elements in music was given in another part of Khrennikov's speech. He condemned the "conservative" approach to the national element in art "whose main criterion in assessing a new piece is whether it contains familiar folk tunes and to what extent canonized modal and rhythmic formulas are used". This is likely to lead to "patent simplification, to downright negation of the wealth of musical form developed in world music". Khrennikov welcomed the fact that many of the national schools had "an influx of young, well-trained composers" who were mastering "some forms and genres new to a given national school".

An important section of the speech was devoted to musicology and criticism. Khrennikov pointed with pride to the accomplishments of Soviet musical scholarship, guided by the principles of "Marxist-Leninist aesthetics". Much has been achieved in the field of Russian music of the eighteenth, nineteenth, and early twentieth centuries. "We have a right to say that the science of the history of Russian music has been created in Soviet times." At present, Khrennikov saw the "principal goal of musicology in the critical study of Soviet creativity". A prime example was the multi-volume *History of Music of the Soviet Peoples* of which the first volume (edited by Yuri Keldysh) had appeared in 1966.

Urging "studies viewing Soviet music as an important part of the musical culture of the world; studies that would juxtapose our, and foreign, creativity", Khrennikov cited Yarustovsky's *Symphonies of War and Peace* as an example. Perhaps he did not realise how difficult, if not impossible, such comparative studies are as long as the artificial division between "socialist" and "bourgeois" music is maintained. Yet he expected such studies to yield even greater insight into the "roots and idiosyncrasies of our Socialist art". In fact, Khrennikov does not care for narrow technical analysis or, as he says, "theory for theory's sake". Important is, not *how* a piece of music is put together, but its *content*. What are the goals of the composer, aside from purely technical application? With these questions, Khrennikov revived the issue of "form versus content" that has plagued Soviet musical analysis for decades. He revived it at a moment when young Soviet musicologists (as, for example, Tarakanov) seemed to abandon the method of dialectics in favour of objective technical analysis. It will be interesting to see to what extent Soviet musicologists will fall into line.

Khrennikov also favoured a rapprochement between musicology and sociology. "So far there is no science of sociology of music, but there is need for it," he declared. (Incidentally, the International Musicological Society devoted an entire session at its 1967 Ljubljana Congress to "Sociology of Music".) Coming from a Soviet Russian, the call for sociological methods in musicology is curious because, in the 1920's, Soviet musicologists were in the forefront of evolving a sociological approach. Their extreme zeal was later belittled by their own confrères as "vulgar sociology", and little effort was made to develop this trend. In a way, the Soviets are not discovering, but *re*discovering the importance of sociology in music.

There are certain contradictory features in Khrennikov's speech which reflect his dual position as a Party official and a musician. He echoed the Party's call for "an offensive war against bourgeois ideology" by saying, "Our music is a weapon in the implacable war between the ideologies of two worlds—Socialist and capitalist". This is a meaningless slogan, designed for the use of politicians who know nothing about music. The West will continue to play "socialist" music by Prokofiev and Shostakovich, while Soviet audiences will continue to enjoy the "capitalist" music of Britten and Copland, and no one is expected to win this "war".

Similarly, the revival of the spectre of Socialist Realism is a concession to Party directives: it can please only the ultra-conservative elements among the composers. In practice, modern Soviet music has moved far afield, even discounting the experiments of avant-gardists. Recognized composers—even Lenin Prize winners—use techniques embodying serialism, aleatory, atonality, pointillism, and dissonant counterpoint. By praising composers who have used such devices, Khrennikov accepted the broadening of the Soviet musical idiom as a *fait accompli* and sanctioned "all methods, however daring" if they helped express the "progressive ideas of our time". (Here is the word "progressive" again, meant perhaps as an escape clause?) Every Western observer of the Soviet musical scene is aware of the impressive "modernization" of the musical idiom of younger Soviet composers which is matched by the growing sophistication of the audiences. At the time—in 1968—there was nothing in Khrennikov's speech that would indicate a forced reversal of this evolutionary trend. Yet, within the next two years, his attitude was to stiffen considerably.

The second major address at the Fourth Composers' Congress was given by Dmitri Kabalevsky; his topic was "Mass Musical Education".[20] Kabalevsky's life-long interest in youth music is well known; he has enriched the children's music repertoire with special concertos and many charming pieces. His report centered on the efforts of the Composers' Union to assist in the aesthetic education of the people and to bring more music into the school curriculum. The problems facing the schools are summarized in the following questions, "What should be the correlation between science, art, and manual work in the system of school education and instruction? What part is art to play in this system and what should be its place in school curricula? What should be done to insure that the school give all pupils a sound aesthetic education?" How to balance science and art in the curriculum is a problem that is not limited to the Soviet Union where the question is under intense study. However, the Communist Party has gone on record as wishing to "ensure that the people are educated aesthetically", and that this effort should be concentrated on the secondary schools.

Kabalevsky's statistics concerning the growth of children's choruses in Georgia or Latvia are impressive but not unique. What is unique in the Soviet Union is the organization of children's music schools and the specialized schooling available to gifted children which has been discussed earlier. Kabalevsky announced that at present (1968) there were more than 4,800 children's music schools in the Soviet Union, both daytime and evening. Not all of the children enrolled will become professional musicians, but a receptive attitude towards music will remain with them through life. Just as illiteracy has been eliminated in the country through a gigantic educational effort—"That is one thing we did do—we made readers out of them," remarked Ilya Ehrenburg —so has the musical awareness of the people been developed by a continuing process of musical mass enlightenment. This was facilitated by the innate musicality of the Russian people; even the illiterate peasant could sing or play the balalaika or the "garmoshka" (accordion). Nor were the educational efforts limited to "art" music; there was just as much encouragement in the field of folk music, orchestras of folk instruments, "samodeyatelnost" ("do-it-yourself" activity). The efforts on behalf of the "aesthetic education" of the population are continuing. It is to the credit of the Composers' Union that its comparatively small membership is deeply involved in guiding (or attempting to guide) all music dispensed to the Soviet people—through radio, television, cinema, concert, opera, records, and other channels. Whether such centralized controls are possible, or even desirable, is another matter. One can imagine the uproar on both sides of the Atlantic if a committee of "classical" musicians attempted to decide whether The Beatles or *Hair* were "aesthetically good" for the people. In fact, this kind of tutelage is not particularly appreciated by Soviet youth. It will be remembered that Khrennikov was bitterly attacked by *Komsomolskaya Pravda*, the influential youth newspaper, for "opposing the promotion of light music and jazz for young people". That was in 1964. In August 1968, a group of young Ukrainians defied the music curbs by writing an open letter to *Pravda Ukrainy*, the official Communist newspaper, protesting against the paper's backward and conservative attitude towards young peoples' cultural tastes, "In our country people go almost into hysterics when they see a young man with hair à la Beatles, and with a guitar as well".[21]

The year 1969 proceeded in a mood of watchful tension among intellectuals. Harrison Salisbury, who revisited Moscow in May, reported that the liberals "are preparing to wait out an indefinite period of harassment and restriction".[22] Yet, a return to Stalinist terror practices was doubted. Another *New York Times* correspondent, writing in late June, saw the cultural scene in Moscow as an "officially sanctioned balance between conservatives, apparently favoured by the Communist Party, and liberals, on whom the Party seems unwilling to crack down". However, most liberals "believe the balance is to their disadvantage", and "there has been little change in the rather strict controls in the art and music world, where virtually no experimentation is allowed."[23]

Sovetskaya Muzyka seemed quite unruffled by it all. Its pages do not reflect any particular tension. Foreign visitors arrive according to plan —John Ogdon, Badura-Skoda, the Sarah Lawrence College Choir . . . The critic Romadinova reports on her impressions of New York concert life. The new Violin Sonata by Shostakovich, written for David Oistrakh's sixtieth birthday, is heard at the Composers' Union on 8 January 1969 and arouses much praise. And so musical life goes on as usual, on the surface at least.

The defection of the writer Anatol Kuznetsov in July 1969, and his revelations about the intolerable psychological pressures on intellectuals, and writers in particular, made it clear once again how deceptive the surface calm can be. Later that year, in November, Alexander Solzhenitsyn was expelled from the Writers' Union. The campaign of vilification directed against him acquired new stridency when he was awarded the Nobel Prize in 1970.

In September 1969, Arthur Miller published a lengthy essay about his experiences on a Russian visit during the preceding winter months.[24] His interests are concentrated in the field of literature, but there are many perceptive observations that can be applied to music. At one point he says, "There is nothing wrong with Socialist Realism as an aesthetic theory, only provided that the artist is indeed a Socialist Realist. If he is not, the theory especially when it is administered as law and enforced by censorship, is a crippling thing." This is as true in music as it is in literature. Ultimately, it is sincerity that matters, not style.

If one searches for an analogy in music to Arthur Miller's evaluation of Tolstoy: "the roots of Socialist Realism, the official Soviet credo of all art, are in Yasnaya Polyana", it is the creative genius of Mussorgsky that springs to mind. He is the true ancestor of a "people's" music, when he writes in 1873 to a fellow artist, the painter Ilya Repin,

> "What an *awful* (in the true sense of the word) richness there is in the people's speech for a musical figure . . . What an inexhaustible mine in which to find the genuine, the whole life of the Russian people! Just choose—one could dance for joy—if one is a genuine artist."[25]

Mussorgsky died in 1881, at the age of forty-two—the half-wasted life of a great artist, with many projects abandoned or unfinished . . . The full recognition of his greatness came after the Revolution, in the 1920's and 1930's, when the original versions of his works were re-evaluated and published. Even at a time when proletarian cultists belittled the classical heritage (including Tchaikovsky), Mussorgsky's glory remained untarnished. Today, the highest praise that can be bestowed on a new work is that its concept is "Mussorgskian". There is, in his music, that bold mixture of "tradition and innovation" which is the elusive dream of Socialist Realism.

The spirit of Mussorgsky—and particularly his *Songs and Dances of Death*—influenced Shostakovich's latest symphony, the Fourteenth. In both cases the leitmotive is death. Shostakovich wrote a work of anguish and pessimism, relieved occasionally by sardonic humour or pensive lyricism. It is also a work of protest, defying every established tradition. The entire concept is non-symphonic: a vocal cycle of eleven songs, using two voices and a chamber orchestra of string and percussion instruments, without firm symphonic architecture or strong musical cohesion. Equally challenging is the composer's selection of the poems: all but one are by West European poets—Apollinaire, Rilke, Garcia Lorca—and all are aeons removed from the psyche of the Soviet listener. The tortured imagery of the Western poets is captured by Shostakovich in a musical language of bleak colours, dissonant atonality, and surcharged emotionalism. Significantly, the only lyric interlude in the work is provided by the lone Russian poet, Wilhelm Küchelbecker, a schoolfellow of Pushkin. Küchelbecker, who spent the last twenty years of his life as a political prisoner because of his involvement in the Decembrist Revolt, addresses his poem to a fellow poet, Delvig. His words are quietly defiant, "What comfort is there for talents among villains and fools?" He castigates the "power of tyrants" and extols the immortality of "brave, inspired deeds" and freedom-loving art. This particular section—it is the ninth poem of the cycle—serves as point of repose and introspection.

To what extent does Shostakovich identify himself with these lines or, for that matter, with any of the poetry he has chosen? We do not know; all we know is that he created a musical score of intense self-revelation that denies and defies every tenet of Socialist Realism. The Fourteenth Symphony represents Shostakovich's new credo—*all* means are justified if they serve the idea of the musical composition.

Considering the present climate of intellectual repression in Moscow, such a work could have provoked critical censure. Strangely enough, this was not the case. The first performances of Shostakovich's new symphony, given in Leningrad on 29 September and in Moscow on 6 October 1969, were received with respect and critical acclaim.* Shortly after the première, the work was recorded, making it available to a nation-wide audience. What is the explanation? Has Shostakovich finally reached the plateau of the "untouchable" artist whose creative genius can do no wrong? Did the Soviet hierarchy, battling against the international criticism for its treatment of Solzhenitsyn, wish to avoid another world-wide outcry in defence of artistic freedom? Or is the Fourteenth Symphony to be used as prime exhibit to prove to the world that Soviet composers are free to create without official restraints?

---

* Performed by the Moscow Chamber Orchestra under Rudolf Barshai; vocal soloists, Galina Vishnevskaya and Mark Reshetin. On the recording, the singers are Margarita Miroshnikova and Yevgeni Vladimirov.

Be this as it may, the favourable critical reaction in Moscow was confirmed by the critics in London and New York.[26] Such critical unanimity is rare, and particularly noteworthy in the case of a work that is decidedly controversial. The first performance of the Fourteenth Symphony outside of Russia was given on 14 June 1970 at the Aldeburgh Festival under the direction of Benjamin Britten to whom the score is dedicated. The United States première took place on 1 January 1971 in Philadelphia under Eugene Ormandy, followed by a performance in New York (by the same Philadelphia Orchestra) on 5 January.

But while the Moscow approval of the latest Shostakovich opus may reflect a measure of "tolerance", no such trend can be discerned in the latest statement of Khrennikov who continues to be the official spokesman for Soviet music. His militant words, published in *Pravda* on 10 December 1970, were flashed immediately to *The Times*,[27] and Western observers became concerned about the renewed rigidity towards "advanced" music. Referring to musical experimentation, Khrennikov emphasized that the Composers' Union would take a "very serious view of such matters". He urged the Soviet critics to "overcome the spirit of 'liberalism' still prevailing in our midst". In general, Khrennikov viewed all modern music as a Western plot to subvert the listener, to fill his soul with pessimism, and to divert him from the true goal of fighting for social progress. "In our drive against hostile bourgeois ideology and inimical aesthetic theories, we shall continue our tireless effort to carry forward the fine traditions of Soviet music, the traditions of the art of Socialist Realism." Significantly, the name of Shostakovich is mentioned by Khrennikov only in passing among many other composers having contributed music for the Lenin Anniversary.

Such strong language had not been heard since the Khrushchev diatribes in 1963 and might even conjure the memory of Zhdanov. But Khrennikov's statement can also be viewed as a political move with an eye towards the approaching XXIV Party Congress in 1971: he is strengthening the defences of the Composers' Union by building a position of conservative illiberalism, in keeping with the Party's mood towards the intellectuals. What the ultimate outcome will be, no one can foretell. But it is clear that no blustering statements can eradicate the decades of musical progress in Soviet music, bleak though the present outlook may be.

Indeed, the gap between the musical idiom of Soviet composers and their Western colleagues has narrowed considerably. This is the case not only within the realm of "avant-garde" but, more significantly, among the established composers. Some day—hopefully soon—the isolation of the "avant-garde" will end, and Soviet composers will write neither vanguard nor rearguard music, but simply music to express the challenge and the torment of our times. The leaders of Soviet music are too intelligent not to realize the danger of stale conservatism. "We are not ascetics or reactionaries in our attitude to modern musical idiom," said Khrennikov in 1962 and reiterated the same thought in 1968. But many composers fear and mistrust the avant-garde. Their feelings are similar to those of the writers about whom Arthur Miller says, "The conservative Russian writer—the honest one anyway—is moved by the fear that the high communal aims of the Communist state will be . . . ultimately destroyed by the vanguard."[28]

Western critical opinion concerning new Soviet music is often ambiguous and vacillating. There is an almost automatic rejection of music that suggests Socialist Realism, folklorism, or programmatic content. On the other hand, "advanced" music of Soviet composers is usually evaluated by the yardstick of the latest Western fashion; hence, it is often found either out of date or "imitative" of Western models.

All too often, Western critics of the Soviet scene overlook the positive aspects of the musical set-up in the Soviet Union. In matters of musical education for children (professional and non-professional), the Soviet system is supreme. In the performance and publication of new music, the production of scholarly books, the search for new talent, the Soviet organization (though bureaucratic) offers distinct advantages. Composers and musicologists are in the mainstream of musical life, not—as so often in the West—totally isolated from a potential public. Strangely enough, some Western composers consider the non-audience a desirable state of affairs. But if composition is musical communication with people, then the Soviet composer is in an enviable position. Prokofiev felt it when he recrossed the line from West to East in the 1930's, when he was faced with new audiences and had to redirect his musical thought,

"The time is past when music was written for a handful of musical aesthetes. Today vast crowds of people have come face to face with serious music and are waiting with eager impatience."[29]

In the past fifty years, Soviet music has made gigantic strides. It has strengthened its ties with the life of the country and its people. It has brought enjoyment and musical literacy to millions. It has preserved its musical past and explored the wellsprings of folk-music. It has educated (perhaps too stringently) a generation of composers to be mindful of the cultural needs of the masses. Once the young composers are given free rein to search and experiment, once the restrictive concept of Socialist Realism is revised to fit the increasingly sophisticated needs of Soviet society, Soviet music will undoubtedly regain full acceptance in the mainstream of music in the Western world.

Part VI

DEVELOPMENTS AND EXPANSIONS 1970–81

1970

Nineteen seventy was a year of festive commemoration—the centennial of the birth of Lenin and the bicentennial of the birth of Beethoven. To a Russian intellectual, this coincidence was significant. In his days Lenin had responded warmly to Beethoven's music, and a framed reproduction of the painting *Lenin Listening to the Appassionata* could be found in many Soviet homes. The Russian veneration of Beethoven began early in the nineteenth century; among Beethoven's admirers were many Russian noblemen and musicians. Beethoven responded with dedications to Russian aristocrats, from Tsar Alexander to Razumovsky and Galitzin. The *Missa solemnis* received its first complete performance anywhere on 26 March (7 April) 1824, at the Philharmonic Society of St. Petersburg. The enthusiasm for Beethoven continued unabated after the Revolution of 1917, particularly since Soviet authors (among them Anatol Lunacharsky, Lenin's first cultural commissar) portrayed Beethoven as an ardent republican and a revolutionary spirit. The Beethoven Centennial of 1927 brought forth a spate of Soviet publications, and the year 1970 was equally productive in terms of Russian Beethoveniana.

But the Lenin Centennial took precedence in the minds of Soviet musicians. Just as the Communist Party rededicated itself to Leninism, so the Soviet composers poured their loyalty into music—songs, oratorios, symphonies, operas. Official celebrations do not necessarily produce great music, and only a fraction of all the works composed for the occasion will survive the jubilee. Nevertheless, the Lenin Centennial preempted all the creative energies of Soviet musicians during 1970. Not only music flowed from the pens of leading Soviet composers; solemn statements of loyalty and devotion to Leninism and its ideals also appeared. An editorial in the journal *Sovietskaya Muzyka*, "The Holy Leninist Banner", quoted the "prophetic" words of Lenin about

the future of Socialist literature—words that were extended by the
editors to embrace all the Soviet arts and music in particular,

> "It will be a free literature . . . because it will be imbued with
> the ideas of socialism and compassion toward the working
> people, which will attract new and newer forces to their ranks
> . . ."1

One wonders what happened to this illusory "freedom", which
has forced Mandelshtam into death, Pasternak into submission,
and Solzhenitsyn into exile.

Under the cloak of Leninism, the editors succeeded in inserting
a crude attack against Israel and Zionism. This is particularly regrettable, for anti-Semitism was never part of Lenin's policies.
The wave of repression during the 1970's swept thousands of Jews
and non-Jews into the stream of discontented Soviet citizens wishing to leave their homeland. The reasons for leaving, given by
many emigrants, were the curtailment of personal and artistic
freedom and the oppressive thought control, while religious restrictions or Zionism played a secondary role. We shall return to
this point when discussing the emigration of Rostropovich and
other prominent artists.

The summer of 1970 was eventful in the musical life of Moscow.
In June, the Fourth International Tchaikovsky Contest took place;
in July the International Society for Music Education (ISME) assembled for its Ninth Conference. Both events attracted a strong
international representation.

An unprecedented number of performers—almost 200—
arrived for the Tchaikovsky Contest. Shostakovich served as
chairman of the organizing committee, while the various juries
were headed by prominent Soviet musicians: Emil Gilels (piano),
David Oistrakh (violin), Mstislav Rostropovich (cello), Alexander
Sveshnikov (voice). The first prize for piano was divided between
Vladimir Krainev (U.S.S.R.) and John Lill (Great Britain). The
first prize for violin went to Gidon Kremer and the second to
Vladimir Spivakov, two young Soviet artists. Among the vocal
winners were Elena Obraztsova (mezzo-soprano) and Yevgeni
Nesterenko (bass). What a remarkable array of talent!

In the following decade, each of these artists won international
acclaim, and deservedly so. Obraztsova is now a "star", equally
admired at the Bolshoi, at La Scala, and at the Metropolitan Opera. She is a singing actress with an opulent voice and histrionic

versatility who can portray the title role in *Carmen* as well as the aged countess in *Pique Dame*. Kremer and Spivakov represent a new breed of Soviet violinists: their formidable technique is secondary to their musical projection; their approach is leaner, more intellectualized. Their programs are consistently interesting, for they search out forgotten music and champion contemporary composers. Spivakov is elegant, aristocratic, and somewhat reserved; Kremer is impetuous and imaginative, with an inquisitive mind. Both must be ranked among today's top violinists.

The topic of the ISME meeting was "The Role of Music in the Life of Children and Young People." It was attended by 1,100 delegates from forty countries and chaired by Frank Callaway of Australia. The keynote speaker was the veteran Soviet composer Dmitri Kabalevsky, long known for his creative interest in youth music. He reiterated the Soviet educational philosophy, "Music, as a profession, should of course be taught only to children with a high degree of musical talent . . . but a general musical education must be made available to absolutely *all* children".[2] Kabalevsky conceded that pop music "creates many difficulties in the field of music education and confuses the minds of young people" and that these harmful influences had reached Soviet youth. But "we do not intend to capitulate to these influences or to give up our ideological esthetic and our pedagogical position". Kabalevsky used the occasion to extol the superiority of Marxist-Leninist esthetics.

Another Soviet educator, the Georgian Givi Ordzhonikidze, took issue with the statement of an American participant, Sidney Fox, who was quoted as saying,

> "Many young people who do not accept the school programs and the methods of teaching, discover for themselves the great composers by way of *rock,* where classical music is quoted without embarrassment."

The Soviet argument was that jazz transformation of the classics fostered estrangement, not rapprochement.

> "A prepared Bach is a negation of the real Bach. The ear, used to the 'rock 'n' roll' variant of Bach's music, will react to the real Bach as a kind of anomaly."[3]

Actually, the Soviet educators are fighting a rear-guard action against the inroads of pop music. There are complaints among

Soviet youths that not enough dance and entertainment music is to be heard. Recordings of foreign jazz and rock are the most-prized possessions of Soviet teenagers.

More impressive than the discussions were the actual perform-ances of visiting groups of children and adolescents, who appeared as choruses, in orchestras, and in folk dances. They ranged from elementary school to college students. They came from Budapest and Quebec; from Bulgaria and Finland; from Japan and the United States; from France, Sweden, and Switzerland. Young Hungarians trained in the Kodály method excelled in music by Bartók and Kodály. Among Soviet performers, the Boys Choir from Lithuania aroused particular admiration with the oratorio *Do Not Touch the Blue Globe* by the Lithuanian Eduardas Balsys.

Shostakovich contributed his share to the Lenin Jubilee with the choral cycle *Vernost'* (Loyalty) Op. 136. It consists of eight ballads for unaccompanied male chorus on texts by E. Dolmatovsky. The first performance was given on 5 December 1970 in Tallinn by the Estonian Male Choir. It was followed a week later (13 December) by the première of Shostakovich's Thirteenth String Quartet.

Within the context of the Lenin Year, Prokofiev's cantata Op. 74, *To the 20th Anniversary of October,* was examined anew by his biographer Israel Nestyev.[4] The cantata had been rejected in 1937 and remained unperformed until 1966, when it was declared a masterpiece.[*] Nestyev retraced the genesis of the work and em-phasized the point that Prokofiev conceived the idea as early as 1933–34, while he was still commuting between Paris and Mos-cow. He was assisted at first by Pierre Souvtchinsky, a Russian music critic living as an emigré in Paris, and also received some advice from the veteran French Communist Jacques Sadoul. On 26 June 1935 Prokofiev signed a contract with the Soviet State Radio for the composition of an anniversary cantata, to be com-pleted by autumn 1936. But his work on the ballet score *Romeo and Juliet* kept him so busy that the cantata was not finished until May-June 1937; the actual scoring was done by Pavel Lamm in accordance with the detailed particell of the composer. Prokofiev struggled with the textual material of the cantata; he discarded the suggestion of broadening the scope by including some of Pushkin's poetry. Ultimately, Prokofiev relied on his own judg-ment ("for better or for worse", as he said), using prose sections from Marx, Engels, Lenin, and Stalin. This innovational "documentary" approach was rejected by the Committee on the Arts, which found the selected texts unsuitable for musical settings. The audition was a complete fiasco; an eyewitness reminisced, "Prokofiev sang very badly though he played the piano excellently". The chairman, a well-meaning Marxist *littérateur* without much musical background, seemed bewildered. "Why did you select these texts, which are part of the people's heritage, and set them to such incomprehensible music?" The musicians present, among them the conductor Alexander Gauk, did not offer any rebuttal. Obviously, the recent attack on Shostakovich's *Lady Macbeth* and modernism in general had frightened everybody. Prokofiev did not live to hear the rehabilitation of his work.

As 1970 neared its end, there was a noticeable trend toward ideological tightening in the sciences and the arts. On 13 November *Pravda* published a report emphasizing the need to step up the struggle against bourgeois ideology. The journal *Khudozhnik* (The Artist), the official organ of the Union of Russian artists, was taken to task for being too lax. "Party spirit and the class viewpoint in life are inseparable from the creative method of Socialist Realism [which has] epochal significance."[5] This call to battle was a clear premonition of the approaching XXIV Congress of the Soviet Communist Party, planned for March 1971.

Under these circumstances, Tikhon Khrennikov's militant speech before the Directorate of the Composers' Union in December 1970 should come as no surprise.* He defended Socialist Realism, rejecting the "false" assumption that it was a dying concept, somehow kept alive by decrees. He ranted once again against the New Viennese School, against Schoenberg and Webern,

> "Of course one cannot object to the study of the works of these composers. But can we, as representatives of Socialist art, face uncritically the musico-technical constructivism of this school, which is totally estranged from life itself in its subjectivistic esthetic principles? No, we cannot . . . It is important that we differentiate between tendencies which strengthen Socialist Realism and those which weaken it."[6]

It was a desperate attempt to revive a dogma which was indeed dying and which was openly flouted by most major Soviet composers, with Shostakovich in the lead. At the end of his diatribe, Khrennikov announced that, prior to the Party Congress, there

*See p. 494.

would be a month of Soviet music in all the republics—a demonstration of the composers' devotion to the ideals of the Party and their indestructible unity with the people. This promise was kept.

1971

In preparation for the XXIV Party Congress, the Composers' Union displayed an almost frantic activity during the early months of 1971. It seemed as if the Directorate wanted to compile a record of "service to the people" that would stand up under the scrutiny of the Party bureaucrats and would justify the enormous investment of funds and efforts being channelled into the arts. Through its regional chapters, the Composers' Union arranged 2,500 concerts of all kinds throughout the vast country: choral, symphonic, and chamber music, and "meet-the-composer" events. Composers and performers traveled to cities, towns, and villages; they visited factories and *kolkhozes;* they met with students and the armed forces. Each chapter of the Composers' Union was responsible for its own territory, but there were also many exchange visits to distant regions.

The Moscow chapter alone gave seventy-five concerts during February and March 1971, visiting industrial and rural areas. Let us remember that the members were composers, not professional performers; the emphasis was on new music, not virtuosity. The Soviet composer is not allowed to live in a vacuum; it is considered his civic obligation to meet his public face to face. This may be mutually satisfying—depending on the personality of the composer and the patience of the public. But the amount of contemporary music (much of it second-rate though ideologically pure) that is being force-fed to the population might be counterproductive. How many Lenin cantatas, how many victory oratorios can one absorb?

Nevertheless, the results were satisfying, as can be seen in the greeting extended by the Party's Central Committee to the Composers' Union,

> "The musical art of Socialist Realism develops on the basis of partyness and folkishness. Its ideational direction, its humaneness, are in stark contrast to the decadent culture of the contemporary capitalist world."

And the editors of *Sovietskaya Muzyka* responded with remarkable modesty,

"Our music is the art of great thoughts and deep feelings, leading humanity in its spiritual development."[7]

Opening the Party Congress on 30 March, Chairman Brezhnev mingled praise with criticism,

"In the past five-year period, our literature and music have given the Soviet people much that is new, interesting, and talented . . . However . . . a good many works still appear that are shallow in content and inexpressive in form . . ."

Here Brezhnev pointed an accusing finger at the critics:

"Shortcomings would have been eliminated faster if our literary and arts criticism had pursued the Party line more vigorously and had acted with greater devotion to principle, combining exactingness with tact, with a solicitous attitude toward the creators of artistic values . . ."

Brezhnev cautioned against any attempts "to whitewash phenomena of the past that the Party had subjected to resolute and principled criticism . . .", in other words, he was warning against so-called revisionists. Finally,

"The Party and the people will not tolerate attempts . . . to blunt our ideological weapons . . . If a writer slanders Soviet reality and helps our ideological adversaries . . . , he deserves public scorn."[8]

His words were greeted with stormy applause. Brezhnev then reaffirmed his belief in Socialist Realism, which contributed the "diversity and richness of forms and styles . . ." He also reiterated the principle of Party guidance of art and artists, with the aim of "making the artist a convinced and active participant in the transformation of society on communist principles".

If there seemed to be a slight lessening of party pressures in the late 1960's, the XXIV Congress certainly reversed any such trend. "Implacability against everything that impedes our progress" became a key attitude.[9] "Our literary and arts critics must pursue the Party line", decreed Brezhnev.

Such pronouncements have the force of law, and the Composers' Union swung into action to implement the Party's recommendations. At the Fourth Plenum of the Directorate (10−17 May 1971), Khrennikov outlined the course of action in a speech entitled "The XXIV Party Congress and the Tasks of Composers' Organizations".[10] Here are some of the high points:

> "The ideo-political education of young composers is of paramount importance . . . to serve the people, to create works filled with the ideas of communism, of realistic content and life-affirming spirit. But the stronger our positions, the stronger are the efforts of the apologists of capitalism to undermine them. The battle of ideas is raging. To be victorious, we must strictly follow the party line and lead the youth."

After that, Khrennikov lashed out against homegrown avant-gardists:

> "Listening to pieces of certain young composers, one begins to think—they seem to have forgotten that Soviet music is heir to the greatest, most sublime and most human art of the past!"

Some of these works, Khrennikov said, somehow found their way onto the programs of Western avant-garde festivals, where they were being touted by the U.S.S.R.'s ideological foes, giving Western listeners a totally false impression of Soviet music.

For the future, Khrennikov foresaw a growing influence of the Party on the activities of the Composers' Union.

> "We are asked to perfect a system of cultural services to the people by creating 'Houses of Culture' in all population centers. We must strengthen our contacts with the workers in the villages and help them fulfill their own musical aspirations. We must write music that reflects agricultural topics—the Kolkhoz and the Sovkhoz. We must create cadres of qualified teachers and improve the educational work in our schools. We must stimulate the manufacture of musical instruments. The XXIV Congress of our Party opened up vistas of grandiose proportions to guide us forward."

The immediate result of these exhortations was a redoubled effort on behalf of the Composers' Union to reach into remote areas, to initiate musical exchange visits among the republics and regions, to create musical activities where none had existed before. Regional composers received more attention and encouragement. The pages of *Sovietskaya Muzyka* are filled with reports of festivals in faraway places, with exotic names of new composers. Through the exchange visits, composers and listeners acquired a greater awareness of various national cultures. The term *multi-national* was used consistently to describe the essential character of Soviet music. There was a certain cross-fertilization among nationalities, which led to a debate on whether one could speak of a supra-national *Soviet* musical idiom.

Characteristic of the 1970's was the increasingly active role played by the regional composers in the musical life of the Soviet Union. For over half a century, the Soviet regime had pursued a broad-based cultural policy, building a network of theatres and concert halls, opera and ballet companies, choirs and orchestras, conservatories and music schools, folk music centers and research institutions. Now the time had come to reap the harvest. The Composers' Union was entrusted with a twofold task—to produce a worthwhile repertoire of Soviet music and to involve the people in these cultural achievements. Khrennikov's speech was a call to action.

In conjunction with the 1971 Plenum, the Directorate listened to a great many performances of new Soviet music. More than eighty composers were represented, and the choice was not easy. The selection committee screened the works recommended by the regional chapters and made further eliminations. There had to be an even-handed distribution, geographic as well as by genre. Young composers tended toward symphonic and chamber music, neglecting theatre and vocal music. There was a dearth of music dealing with "contemporary" topics, with revolutionary and patriotic themes. "It is not the first time that this fact worried us," remarked the composer Andrei Eshpai, a member of the Directorate. "Two years ago we addressed the same reproach to the young composers." This complaint is, in fact, a perennial one, dating back to Andrei Zhdanov in 1948.

As for the geographic distribution, it is not surprising that the ethnic Russians were in a minority. The list of composers was far-ranging. A large group came from Central Asia and Kazakhstan, regions that were considered underdeveloped in terms of musical professionalism as recently as 1958. Strongly represented were the Baltic republics, the Ukrainians, and the Trans-Caucasians, as well as Byelorussia and Moldavia. Among the composers singled out for praise were a few new names that went on to acquire significance during the 1970's. One was Giya Kancheli, a Georgian composer born in 1935 in Tbilisi, whose First Symphony was warmly received at the Plenum. By that time he had already completed his Second Symphony, and within five years he was to attract international attention with his *Michelangelo* Symphony (No. 4).*

Other compositions commended by the jury were a Violin Concerto by Miroslav Skorik (Ukraine); a Partita by Tigran Mansurian (Armenia); *Küi,* ** for violin and orchestra, by Mansur Sagatov (Kazakhstan); Lak Folk Songs by Shirvani Chalayev (Daghestan); *Makom†* by the Tadjik T. Shakhidi; and Variations, for strings and timpani, by the Uzbek T. Kurbanov. Kurbanov also submitted a Fugue for orchestra which was not performed on that occasion, but it was admired by Eshpai because it treated a "native" theme (an Uzbek *Makom*) in a Bachian polyphonic style.

Best known among the ethnic Russians was Boris Tishchenko. His *Sinfonia Robusta* was described as a one-movement work of structural strength but somewhat short in expressiveness. Other Russians mentioned with varying degrees of approval were Vladimir Pikul, Tatiana Chudova, Yuri Butsko (for his opera *The White Nights*), and Kyrill Volkov†† (for his *Vocal-Symphonic Pictures,* for mezzo-soprano and orchestra).

The last-named work provoked some pointed comments from Eshpai.[11] "He related Volkov's composition to the "New Folkloristic Wave", a novel and more sophisticated manner of dealing with folk material. One of the innovations was to write new music to old texts, that is, to utilize the folk *texts* but to discard the melodies. A few such attempts were judged successful— Sergei Slonimsky's *Pesni volnitsy* (Songs of Free Men; 1961) and Valery Gavrilin's *Russkaya Tetrad'* (Russian Notebook; 1965), but the fashion spread and Eshpai voiced disapproval. In Volkov's case there is no denying the composer's talent, but his musical realization of the folk texts is often at odds with the inner rhythm and imagery of the words. "Such a procedure requires a very special sensitivity", warned Eshpai.

Some interesting comments were made by the young Ukrainian Skorik.[12] To him, the "New Folkloristic Wave" represents the contemporary absorption and rethinking of the folk song. Now

---

*See p. 593.
**Küi:* originally a Kazakh folk piece played on the plucked *dombra.*
†*Makom (maqam)*: a mode in Tadjik or Uzbek traditional professional music.
††Not related to Solomon Volkov.

there are new principles of quotation, new realizations of folkish or stylized idioms through new procedures of modal harmonizations, colouristic sounds, and formal shapes. There emerge more complex relationships between compositional concepts and folklore: the discovery of hidden modal and structural phenomena of folk melos, and especially the discovery of the musical practices of folk musicians who achieve interesting effects through intentional digressions from the tempered scale.

Skorik's attitude can be summarized in four words: innovation—*yes,* avant-garde—*no.* He admits that certain modern techniques—new sonorities and aleatory effects or the method of *collage*—can be found in works by young Soviet composers. He is not in favor of these techniques and also rejects dodecaphony, which is by now a dead issue. Skorik shows his ignorance by asserting that Schoenberg and Webern "deny the previous musical experience". This misconception is widespread among Soviet composers, who parrot old and outworn slogans. If they only knew how Schoenberg and Webern cherished musical tradition! Skorik is typical of a young breed of Soviet composers who are torn between enlightenment and conventionality. The dividing line is fluctuating, and there are signs of cracks in the protective wall.

Several anniversaries occurred in 1971. The most important were Nikolai Miaskovsky's ninetieth birthday and Prokofiev's eightieth. The stature of Miaskovsky has shrunk since his death in 1950, and his music is rapidly disappearing from the Soviet repertoire—a fact noted with sadness by his prominent students Khachaturian and Kabalevsky. The appreciation of Prokofiev, on the other hand, has grown steadily, to the point where he is now proclaimed the "classic" of the twentieth century by Soviet musicologists. In fact, Prokofiev's fame is worldwide; he is one of the most frequently performed composers of our time. In addition, the Prokofiev repertoire is being expanded by the rediscovery of hitherto neglected works—not so much "neglected" as studiously ignored, even maligned, in his own country for assorted "ideological" reasons.

In 1971, there appeared an essay by Israel Nestyev[13] which is a kind of *peccavi* (an admission of guilt), for it was Nestyev's biographical volume of 1957 that helped perpetuate the myth about Prokofiev's "inferior" Parisian period. Nestyev now admitted that he had shown Prokofiev his first version of a biography in 1941 and that Prokofiev had disputed certain viewpoints in it. Prokofiev had taken issue with the opinion that his foreign period was less significant. "I shall always dispute it", he said. "Without it the next period would have been of lesser quality." He strongly denied Nestyev's contention that Diaghilev was "insensitive to human relations" or that Koussewitzky was "business-minded". He disputed Nestyev's negative evaluations of compositions like the Cello Concerto Op. 58, the opera *Semyon Kotko,* or the early ballet *Chout.* Prokofiev also vented his anger against the choreography of *Romeo and Juliet* done by the admired Lavrovsky, who "often choreographed against the music".

Nevertheless, when Nestyev's biography finally appeared in Russian four years after the composer's death, it was marred by picayune criticisms and wrongheaded attitudes. Printed in a small edition of 5,000 copies, it quickly became outdated in terms of both biographical details and "esthetic-musicological conclusions", to quote the author. He admitted to a change of mind because he studied many heretofore unknown documents hidden in the archives. This seems like a subterfuge: it is more likely that his old prejudiced opinions had become untenable and unacceptable. Nestyev, the master of the ideological switch, became one of the leaders in the ongoing reappraisal of Prokofiev. In 1963 he edited a volume commemorating the tenth anniversary of Prokofiev's death, contributing an important article; and in 1973 he brought out the second edition of his Prokofiev biography, entirely revised and rewritten. Before and after, he acted as the prime spokesman for a revival of Prokofiev's neglected works; as late as 1979 he pleaded the cause of the opera *The Flaming Angel,* which had never been seen in the Soviet Union.

Another activist on behalf of Prokofiev was the conductor Gennadi Rozhdestvensky. Among other works, he revived the Second Symphony and the Quintet Op. 39; he conducted the Soviet première of *The Gambler* in 1963 in a radio performance which was later released on *Melodiya* records. It paved the way for the triumphant first staging at the Bolshoi in 1974.* Rozhdestvensky made some revealing comments in 1971, accusing the leading Soviet ballet companies of falsifying Prokofiev's orchestrations:

"It is known, for example, that such masterpieces as Prokofiev's three last ballets have never been given on our stages in their original version. In *Romeo and Juliet* the entire second act was reorchestrated, and in the last act the scene in Mantua

*See p. 555.

is not in the composer's original version—it has been added. *Cinderella* (in the staging by Zakharov) has also been completely reorchestrated . . . and the meaning of the Finale has been turned literally upside down . . . In *The Stone Flower,* too, the author's score has been subjected to severe changes."[14]

This confirms my previous assumption that Prokofiev's orchestration had undergone some tampering.* In 1979, the choreographer Grigorovich restaged *Romeo and Juliet* for the Bolshoi and brought the new production to New York in August of that year. He incorporated some scenes and numbers that were eliminated in the course of the Lavrovsky production; in fact, Grigorovich asserts that his present staging is close to Prokofiev's original intent. We know that Prokofiev and Lavrovsky had bitter fights about the music—not only about the orchestration. Whether the Grigorovich version would have pleased the composer is an open question; at any rate, it did not please the New York critics.

Rozhdestvensky also voiced his objections to the Rimsky-Korsakov version of Mussorgsky's *Boris Godunov,* a version enshrined in Soviet tradition. He attacked another taboo when he advocated a Soviet production of Alban Berg's *Wozzeck* (last seen in Leningrad in 1926), "which would have had an enormous response on our stages". It was a cry in the wilderness.

An important cultural event was the Seventh Congress of the International Music Council (attached to UNESCO), which took place in Moscow 4–9 October 1971. It was the first time that the Council was meeting in a Socialist country. At the previous Congress, in 1969, the violinist Yehudi Menuhin had been unanimously elected president of the IMC, and his reelection for another two-year term was expected. In a rare case of unanimity, the Russians nominated him and the Americans seconded the motion. But behind the scenes there was a bitter struggle. Menuhin, known the world over as a humanitarian and an idealist, delivered a speech on 4 October (in Russian) which touched certain sensitive spots in Soviet circles. In an unusual snub, the speech was ignored in both *Pravda* and *Izvestia. The New York Times* picked up the ball and published the speech on the editorial page. Two Moscow correspondents of the *Times* interviewed Menuhin, who seemed unconcerned. "The word will get around", he commented; "already

*See pp. 156, 241.

there were some private comments and they were heart-warming".[15]

There were two paragraphs in the speech that the Soviets found objectionable. One was meant as a tribute to the host country:

> "The size, power and depth and meaning of musical and poetic utterances, as those of a Shostakovich, a Solzhenitsyn, a Yevtushenko and many others are an indication of the vision and the greatness of men and women evolving in this vastest of lands."

This praise was received in stony silence. Solzhenitsyn was "neither a great Russian nor a great writer" and did "not deserve to be free", according to the Ministry of Culture. Yarustovsky came to the airport to see Menuhin off and said mournfully, "If only you hadn't said that!" Menuhin was neither apologetic nor repentant.

The second offensive paragraph produced the following head-line in *The New York Times:* "Menuhin, at Moscow Congress, Calls for Open Emigration".[16] His actual statement was, "May we yet live to see the day when every human being can dwell where his heart calls, whatever his creed, race, or occupation". It was made clear to Menuhin that "Soviet officialdom was deeply angry" with him. On his previous visit to the Soviet Union in 1962 he was feted with unusual warmth. But circumstances had changed, as he explained in his memoirs,

> "My outspoken regret when the screws of censorship were tightened, when the Russians invaded Czechoslovakia, and when Jews lost their jobs for applying to emigrate to Israel, incurred displeasure, especially that of the late Madame Furt-seva, the minister of culture . . ."[17]

Undaunted, Menuhin continued to make his influence felt on be-half of Russian friends and artists. He has not returned to the Soviet Union since that memorable visit in 1971.

The Congress proceeded as if nothing had happened. Delegates from thirty countries attended and were feted in official receptions and musical performances. The Glinka Museum showed a special exhibit, "The Musical Culture of the Soviet Republics". Khren-nikov spoke on behalf of the Composers' Union,

"In our days there is much talk about freedom of creativity. This is one of the basic principles governing Soviet musicians. But freedom is not an abstract concept. Freedom of creativity entails service in the cause of peace and social progress."[18]

Earlier that year, Khrennikov was more direct when he addressed his composers:

"Soviet composers undividedly subordinate their talent to the interests of our Socialist society."

One of the principal speeches was delivered by Boris Yarustovsky, the official Soviet delegate to the IMC.[19] He reiterated Lenin's theory of the two cultures in a class society—that of the democratic forces and that of the ruling classes. With a clever twist, Yarustovsky equated the latter with the "elitist" avantgarde, which he juxtaposed to the "pseudo-democratic Pop-Art". Rejecting this "bifurcated art", he offered as an antipode "the democratic musical culture of the world, the art about mankind and its spiritual existence". Then the Soviet delegate presented a list of composers "truly admired" by the lovers of modern music, a selective list which is amusing by its selectivity:

"Prokofiev and Britten, Shostakovich and Orff, Bartók and Khachaturian, Stravinsky and Berg, Hindemith and Honegger, Szymanowski and Enesco, Eisler and Pipkov."

Pipkov? Yes, Lyubomir Pipkov is a Bulgarian composer (1904–1974), a Hero of Socialist Labor, a member of the Bulgarian Communist Party, though not exactly a household word outside Sofia.

On that list are five or six composers who were on the Soviet blacklist in 1948; that can be considered progress. Surprisingly, Americans are excluded, though Gershwin, Copland, and Barber are quite popular in the Soviet Union. This was a bit of politicking by Yarustovsky, a great Soviet functionary.

Another Soviet speaker, Kabalevsky, was given much prominence. His topic was "The Education of a Composer and Contemporary Music".[20] After describing the bewildering welter of modernistic trends, he asked in mock dispair, "How can you teach the future composer in such a stylistic kaleidoscope?" He quoted Hindemith, "Don't teach composition in the usual way.

Teach music." Good. But how can one do it with samples from the newest works, written outside the laws of musical grammar and syntax, which can only be deciphered with the help of the author's instruction sheet? *Musica negativa* leads to *Pedagogica negativa,* which is, in essence, the negation of all pedagogy. Of course, Kabalevsky, an experienced pedagogue, gave advice on solving the problem.

Among the papers given by foreigners, those of Zofia Lissa (Poland) and Kurt von Fischer (Switzerland) were reprinted in full in *Sovietskaya Muzyka.* The foreign visitors sent glowing thank-you letters, which were quoted, including one by Menuhin. What a shame the journal did not reprint his beautiful and moving speech!

During the Congress, the delegates were offered much music by contemporary Soviet composers. An American delegate, the musicologist William Austin, circulated a private report after his return. Here are a few of his observations and comments.

> "A. Eshpai, Concerto for orchestra (1967). In this one-movement piece the concertino, comprising trumpet, piano, vibraphone, and bass, propels a great variety of ideas toward an unconventional synthesis."

(Eshpai also composed the fanfares that opened and closed the Congress.)

> "A memorable newcomer was 35-year old Shirvani Chalayev of Daghestan, who sang his own cycle of seven Lak Folk Songs with chamber orchestra accompaniment, winning the audience's enthusiastic response."

(That year Chalayev was named People's Artist of the Daghestan Republic.)

Austin mentioned two other Moscow composers—Nikolai Sidelnikov (b. 1930), whose effective *Suite of Russian Tales* is scored for chamber ensemble with percussion and vibraphone; and Vladimir Terletsky, whose Violin Concerto incorporates Jewish themes. The Ukrainian Skorik was represented by a Recitative and Rondo for piano trio. Gavrilin's *Russian Notebook* was heard—by then it was the classical example of the "New Folkloristic Wave".

In Tbilisi, Austin heard an early work by Kancheli, Largo and Allegro, for piano, strings, and timpani (1963), "which includes some ingenious contrapuntal and rhythmic developments of ideas along with elusive chordal passages"; and Nodar Gabunia's *Basnia* (Fable), a suite for reader, three male voices, and seven instruments (1964), "a brilliant, subtle, delightful work, worthy of a comparison with Stravinsky's *Renard* which it challenges". (Gabunia was born in Tbilisi in 1933.)

The operatic novelty performed for the delegates was *Virineya* by Sergei Slonimsky in its 1967 version (a second version appeared in 1976).* Topically and musically, *Virineya* represented traditional modernism, Soviet style. In this work, Slonimsky tempered his non-conformist tendencies and achieved a notable success.

On 20 October 1971, *Izvestia* published an article by Shostakovich in which he praised the Moscow Philharmonic Orchestra on its twentieth anniversary. He paid tribute to Samuil Samosud (d. 1964), the "outstanding Soviet conductor and ardent propagator of Soviet music" who was its first conductor, and mentioned the "fruitful" years under Nathan Rakhlin, who succeeded Samosud. Shostakovich continued,

> "As a composer, I think with special gratitude and enthusiasm of the orchestra's interest in, and receptivity to, present-day music—a quality undoubtedly instilled by the conductor Kyril Kondrashin . . . Work with contemporary music is difficult . . . One must be not only a talented conductor, but first of all a musician of great scope and broad views; one must recognize one's duty and civic responsibility to one's contemporaries. The artistic director of the Moscow Philharmonic Orchestra possesses all these qualities in full measure . . ."[21]

Shostakovich commended Kondrashin for bringing back Mahler (including the Soviet première of the Ninth Symphony), Bartók, Ravel, Hindemith, Britten, and many others. He had reintroduced Beethoven's *Missa solemnis,* which had not been heard in Moscow for many years. Kondrashin also conducted many important premières of Soviet music, including Prokofiev's *October* Cantata, Shostakovich's Thirteenth Symphony (*Babyi Yar*), and his cantata *Stepan Razin.*

In 1978, the unthinkable was to happen: Kondrashin chose to become an exile.

*See p. 586.

1972

The new year started auspiciously: On 6 January a concert in Moscow honored the centenary of Scriabin's birth; on 8 January the world première of Shostakovich's Fifteenth Symphony was given; and on 18 January a new lyric stage, the Moscow Chamber Opera, opened.

Another important cultural event was the inauguration of the Rimsky-Korsakov Museum in Leningrad, at No. 28 Zagorodny Prospekt, in the flat occupied by the composer and his family from 1893 until his death in 1908. The living quarters were restored to look as they did during Rimsky-Korsakov's lifetime. On display were many documents, photographs, letters and manuscripts, as well as personal memorabilia. (A Rimsky-Korsakov Museum has been in existence in the composer's birthplace, Tikhvin, since 1944.)

At the Scriabin concert—the first event in a worldwide observance of the anniversary—the composer Rodion Shchedrin was the main speaker. He read a statement by Shostakovich, the chairman of the Scriabin Centenary Committee, entitled "Praise of Scriabin". It was probably the work of a ghost writer, for Shostakovich was not known for flowery pronouncements or for any particular admiration for Scriabin. When he was young, he denounced Scriabin as an "enemy" of the new generation; in later years, he called all of Scriabin's symphonic poems "gibberish".[22]

During the Soviet era, the esteem for Scriabin fluctuated because his genius could not be classified. He died in 1915 and so could not be claimed by the Revolution, but that problem was solved when Lunacharsky interpreted Scriabin's music as a "premonition" of the Revolution. In 1922 a Scriabin Museum was established in Moscow; however, the younger generation soon turned to more robust models like Stravinsky and Prokofiev. Nevertheless, the honors bestowed on Scriabin in 1972 were fully justified, for he is one of the architects of the modern musical idiom and certainly a prophetic innovator.

At the anniversary concert, Yevgeni Svetlanov conducted the *Poem of Ecstasy* and Stanislav Neigaus played the Piano Concerto. Shostakovich's presence at this concert is not recorded.

However, Shostakovich was very much present two days later when his son conducted the première of the Fifteenth Symphony at the Great Hall of the Moscow Conservatory. It was the first time that Maxim, a rising conductor, was entrusted with such an important task. The ensemble was the Symphony Orchestra of

Radio and Television, which was not considered first-rate, but the performance went surprisingly well. Obviously, father and son had worked together on the preparation, and the resulting recording (on *Melodiya*) bears the stamp of authenticity.

News of the Moscow première was flashed to American newspapers. Robert Kaiser, the correspondent of *The Washington Post,* wrote a colorful review under the headline "Shostakovich Gets Ovation in Moscow".[23]

> "The 15th Symphony received a tumultuous and emotional first-night reception . . . The audience for this world première, stylish and gay by Moscow's dull standards, applauded and shouted approval for nearly ten minutes at the end of the performance . . . Shostakovich, now 65, took bow after bow with his 33-year-old son Maxim . . . It was an emotional moment for Moscow's musical public, which has known for months that Shostakovich has been seriously ill . . . He walked with a limp tonight, and friends said that he was still not fully recovered . . . On stage he kissed his son . . . and shook hands with all the musicians within reach . . ."

Kaiser—who is not a music critic—described the music as "full of melody, spirit, and humor". *The New York Times* quoted Khrennikov, head of the Composers' Union, as saying, "This is one of Shostakovich's most profound works. It is filled with optimism, affirmation of life, and trust in man's inexhaustible strength."[24]

While the work is profound, Khrennikov's statement is not; in fact, it is a rather superficial evaluation of music that tends more toward morbidity than optimism. The Soviet critics were clearly puzzled: after four symphonic works that were programmatic or text-connected, Shostakovich had produced a "pure" symphony, a piece of absolute music with hardly a hint as to its content. The quotations from Rossini and Wagner added to the puzzlement. Shostakovich had returned to his first love—a four-movement symphony, purely instrumental and without captions. He offered only one hint: the playful gaiety of the first movement represented the spirit of a "toy shop". The Soviet critics noticed other things, too: the occasional use of twelve-note series in a tonal context, or the colorful and delicate display of the percussion section. But they could not equate it with the funereal and depressive mood of much of the music.

After the Fourteenth Symphony, which dealt with the fear of death, the Fifteenth appears much more resigned as it depicts the nearness of death, the individual's desperate loneliness in the face of the inevitable end.

Before the Fifteenth Symphony could reach the West in a live performance, the British Broadcasting Corporation (BBC) presented a tape of the Moscow première on 16 April 1972. It was reviewed by several critics, among them Jeremy Noble. His perceptive essay closed with the following judgment,

> "Shostakovich's new symphony is a disquieting work, for all its passages of wry humour and serene lyricism. Its preoccupation with mortality is made quite explicit in the last movement, and it offers no consoling panaceas . . ."[25]

After the New York première by the Philadelphia Orchestra under Eugene Ormandy on 4 October 1972, Harold Schonberg of *The New York Times* found the work "weak", "unconvincing", and "in a way, a pastiche".

> "The big trouble with Symphony No. 15 . . . is its pseudo-profundity. Those slow themes and noble-sounding brass chords cover up an exercise in banality. Shostakovich, that great technician, has nothing much to say here. Everything sounds forced and tired."[26]

The line between profundity and "pseudo-profundity" depends on the observer; it is a very personal judgment. To me, the brass chords opening the second movement are indeed noble and moving. Shostakovich's symphonic testament requires time before one can penetrate its lighthearted façade.

The opening of the Moscow Chamber Opera was an important event. For years Soviet composers had complained about the unwieldy operation of the Bolshoi, and even the smaller Stanislavsky-Nemirovich-Danchenko Opera Theatre was not flexible enough. What was needed was a small experimental stage that could afford to take risks with new, forgotten, or neglected works. The artistic director was Boris Pokrovsky, a sixty-year-old theatre expert affiliated with the Bolshoi Theatre but also experienced in training young artists. The performing ensemble was deliberately small, twenty-seven voices and eighteen instruments: a string quintet; a woodwind quartet; a brass quartet consisting of two horns, trumpet, and trombone; harp; percussion; and keyboard. There was neither chorus nor ballet; the ensemble took care of all such needs. The performers, recent graduates of theatrical and music institutions, had little or no experience, but much talent and enthusiasm. "We need versatile young people who can play old music today, new music tomorrow, and a Haydn quartet in-between", said the conductor, Vladimir Delman. The physical set-up was cramped. The diminutive downstairs theatre lacked a regular stage, wings, orchestra pit, and overhead props. A low platform served as a stage, and the musicians were reseated for each production, perhaps on either side of the stage or alongside the audience. The young ensemble viewed its undertaking as synthetic theatre, which does not separate vocal skills from fine acting and which places immense importance on musical stage action. The scenery, costumes, and lighting were all spartan but vivid. As one critic said, "The Chamber Opera should not be termed totally experimental. It is purposefully building a road by combining tradition with new searchings."[27]

With this in mind, the repertoire of the first years was deliberately eclectic: Rossini, Mozart, and Schubert; the Russian pre-classics Vassili Pashkevich and Dmitri Bortnyansky; but also modern works by Shchedrin, Khrennikov, Shostakovich, and Alexander Kholminov. The hope was that young composers would write works especially for the ensemble.

The opening bill was *Not Love Alone* by Shchedrin, first staged in 1961 on the monumental stage of the Bolshoi, where it had had a short life. And not surprisingly so, for Shchedrin's opera demands more intimate surroundings. Pokrovsky's young group needed three months to prepare the work. It opened on 18 January and was a big success. The next production, *Much Ado about Hearts* by Khrennikov, was staged in March. The greatest achievement of the early years was Shostakovich's *The Nose,* given under Rozhdestvensky in September 1974. It had not been seen in the Soviet Union since 1930, when it had a run of fourteen performances at the Malyi Theatre in Leningrad. For over four decades *The Nose* was on the "formalistic" blacklist, and even performances abroad were rare because of the difficulties of staging and translation.* It required a new breed of acting singers, a new orchestral approach, and a new scenic concept. Pokrovsky and Rozhdestvensky solved all the problems and revived a shunned masterpiece of the Russian lyric stage. Shostakovich participated

---

*German performances took place in Düsseldorf (1963), Frankfurt/Main (1966), East Berlin (1969), and Munich (1971). They followed the publication of the score by Universal Edition in Vienna in 1962.

in the rehearsals and was so delighted that he made all necessary adjustments; he also agreed to a very effective new ending — voices from the audience speak sentences from Gogol's original version. A recording of the opera made by the original cast is now available internationally. In 1978, Pokrovsky achieved a similar success with Stravinsky's *The Rake's Progress,* which had also been proscribed for many years by Moscow.

When the Bolshoi Opera visited New York in 1975, Pokrovsky received little attention, though he directed Prokofiev's *War and Peace* and *The Gambler.* But in Moscow he enjoys ever-growing prestige. Operatic stagecraft was never at a high level in Russia until the art of Stanislavsky and Nemirovich-Danchenko brought about a reform movement. When the Moscow Chamber Opera opened, Pokrovsky made it clear that he intended to continue where the great Stanislavsky left off. "We have different tasks and different ideals from the Grand Opera," he declared. "We are not merely an opera on a 'small scale' but one with different esthetic views."[28]

Pokrovsky's ideas crystallized when he taught stage direction at the Institute of Theatre Arts, where he was active for two decades. He considered the stage director the "slave" of the composer. The musical score must serve as a basis for the director's work, he felt. Though it has its independent function, the director's art is secondary.

> "Don't compose for the composer, don't conduct for the conductor, don't sing for the singer. Your job is to translate the ideas of the composer into the needs of a scenic realization. Analyze the score as your point of departure; to take the libretto as your starting point is a mistake . . ."

These are some of the ideas Pokrovsky taught to his students and applied in his own work.[29]

In the Western operatic world, where the stage director is king at the expense of both composer and librettist, Pokrovsky's ideas may seem old-fashioned to some, refreshing to others. But they are certainly different from what is done (or perpetrated) on the stages of Central Europe and America.*

Pleasurable though it is to deal with purely artistic problems, the Soviet reality always asserts itself by raising the spectre of ideolog-

---

*In April 1981, Pokrovsky's leadership of the Bolshoi Opera was publicly criticized by one of the star singers, Elena Obraztsova.

ical vigilance. In January 1972 the Central Committee of the Party issued a resolution entitled "On Literary and Art Criticism". It was summarized in *The New York Times* under the headline "Kremlin Warns Literary and Art Critics on Ideology".[30]

Actually there was nothing new in the resolution, merely a re-affirmation of the decisions of the XXIV Party Congress. Once again there is a condemnation of "conciliatory attitudes toward works that are ideologically and artistically defective". There is too much "favoritism" toward one's friends. Criticism is not vigorous enough "in asserting the revolutionary, humanistic ideals of Socialist Realism, in exposing the reactionary essence of bourgeois 'mass culture' and decadent trends, and in combating various trends of non-Marxist views . . . and revisionist esthetic concepts."

What caused this flurry of repetitive rhetoric? Hedrick Smith, the well-informed *Times* correspondent, connected it with an effort to stem the popularity, among Soviet youth, of imported jazz, folk, and rock music, and of foreign broadcasts in general.[31] In January there were crackdowns against dissidents, with searches and arrests. While Yekaterina Furtseva was visiting Washington to sponsor a Soviet art exhibit, American Congressman James A. Scheuer was detained in Moscow for the "crime" of visiting a Jewish family and eventually expelled from the Soviet Union. *The New York Times* took a strong editorial stand, particularly in view of the twelve-year sentence inflicted on the dissident Vladimir Bukovsky: "If today's Soviet regime wants to be considered cultured, it would best begin by behaving in a cultured and humane fashion."[32]

Among Soviet intellectuals, the new resolution was greeted with humility. The Writers' Union, in a published statement, declared,

"In all conscience, we must admit that criticism nowadays is not so much sharp-toothed as smooth surfaced, vegetarian, and complimentary. It is criticism characterized by being un-demanding of quality and indifferent to the esthetic features of the work."[33]

The Composers' Union was equally humble but also aired some grievances. It demanded a broader forum for musical criticism. Shchedrin became its spokesman, claiming that since the daily newspapers (mainly *Pravda* and *Izvestia*) rarely printed musical commentary, then at least a cultural newspaper like *Sovietskaya*

Kultura (published three times a week) should open its columns for discussion. As for *Sovietskaya Muzyka* (a monthly publication), the time-lag was intolerable: it took one month to write a criticism, three to four months to get it into print, and another three to four months if the "victim" wished to reply. Shchedrin quipped, "Some 'discussion' . . . ." The young Ukrainian composer Skorik saw a real need for music coverage in the daily press. Some progress had been made in Kiev, where the evening paper had weekly reviews. But there was general demand for more cooperation from the daily press as well as from radio and television. The profession of music critic was unattractive to young musicologists because there were not enough outlets. In April, the editors of *Sovietskaya Muzyka* presented an important demand: an additional musical newspaper since *Sovietskaya Kultura* did not meet the musical needs of the country.[34]

On 25-27 April the Directorate of the Composers' Union convened to discuss the official resolution on criticism. Khrennikov opened the procedures. He admitted that the Union had not given enough attention to the musico-critical activities. "There has to be a decisive change: The Composers' Union must become the true focal point of critical thought." He gave as an example the fact that Socialist Realism—for half a century the guiding force of Soviet music—had not yet been explored in depth. Foreign opponents of Soviet esthetics, "the ideologists of the bourgeois world", should be rebuffed more vigorously. There was no influx of young musicologists into the Composers' Union; the graduates of the conservatories were not choosing the critical profession. "It is not surprising that the median age of the musicology members of the Composers' Union is nearly fifty", Khrennikov exclaimed with scorn.[35]

The keynote address was given by Yarustovsky, the most influential musicologist member of the Composers' Union.* His speech seemed interminable, stretching over forty-four columns in *Sovietskaya Muzyka*.[36] One thing became clear: the musicology wing of the Composers' Union (and that included the critics) had not received fair and equitable treatment. After more than forty years of "co-existence" with the composers, the musicologists and critics were finding themselves on the lowest rung of the ladder. The original plan of equal status with the composers was not being achieved. Yarustovsky provided statistics: rarely, if ever, were musicologist critics given prizes and honors. The

---

*For years there had been antagonism between Khrennikov and Yarustovsky.

musicologists were the only group among the arts writers who had never received the Lunacharsky Prize. Only one Glinka Prize was ever awarded to a musicologist, to Konstantin Vertkov for his *Atlas of Musical Instruments.*

"If you want more and better critics, you have to give them an incentive", said Yarustovsky. He accused the Composers' Union of making little effort to obtain recognition for its musicologist members; for example, the musicologists' share of the title "honorary worker of the arts" was only 7% in the Ukraine and 15% in the Russian Federation, but 30% in Georgia and 36% in Armenia. The geographic distribution of musicologists was poor: of a total of 490 members, 130 were concentrated in Moscow, 45 in Leningrad, and a good number in Transcaucasia. But there was only one musicologist critic per republic in Kirghizia, Tadzhikistan, and Turkmenia, and only one in the big city of Dnepropetrovsk. There were none in the Far East, and even in Odessa the musicologists had died out. All this proved that the Composers' Union had little influence on the geographic distribution of its critic members. There had been hardly any growth in the musicological wing: in 1970, twenty members joined the Composers' Union, and their median age was forty-three! In 1971 there were twenty-six applicants with the same median age. Of some 500 musicologists, only thirty-six were younger than thirty-five, and only four of those were in Moscow! Although some thirty musicologists graduated from the Moscow Conservatory alone, they showed no interest in working as critics.

Things were much better in the 1930's, concluded Yarustovsky. He, too, blamed the dearth of outlets for musical criticism. Music critics had no forum: while literary critics had fifteen newspapers and eighty-five journals at their disposal, musicians had only three journals and a minimal number of provincial newspapers which occasionally printed music materials. In the 1930's there had been a music newspaper; unfortunately it had merged with a general arts paper. In the 1970's *Sovietskaya Kultura* was supposed to cover the arts, but it neglected music. Yarustovky said, "As a minimum, we need another weekly newspaper, perhaps a publication combining Music and Theatre; without it, music criticism fights a losing battle".

Reports of the discussion on musical criticism continued through several issues of *Sovietskaya Muzyka*.[37] There were many perceptive comments by senior critics—Druskin, Martynov, Keldysh, Mazel, Sokhor, Medvedev—and one younger one, Liana Genina. (In fact, Genina was the first recipient of a newly established prize for music critics in 1973.) The speech by Arnold Sokhor pointed up the moral dilemma of the Soviet critic and the need to investigate the way in which critical evaluations are reached.

> "We must confirm the *active* role of the critic in forming public opinion. At present the situation is such that the critic, writing for a publication, must express the opinion formulated by the editorial staff, which is then presented to him (the critic) as 'public opinion'."[38]

There were cases (and Sokhor cited one) where the critic had the choice of changing his opinion or tearing up his article. In other words, the critic was merely the spokesman for a prefabricated opinion. What a humiliating position! At times, important works were killed by silence because no "consensus" could be reached. This was a sore spot in Soviet criticism.

The discussion was concluded in the September 1972 issue of *Sovietskaya Muzyka*. All the speakers were critical of existing conditions: lack of information among those who were in charge of dispensing information, lack of discussion, lack of understanding new trends (for example, the issue of pop music, which engulfs young people who are in need of guidance not scorn).

At the end came Vassili Kukharsky, voice of the boss from the Ministry of Culture. Kukharsky's statement was strong though polite: he did not name any names, he did not accuse any individuals, but he clearly said that the Party was not satisfied with the musicological wing of the Composers' Union. He criticized the Union, the conservatories and their curricula, the quality of teachers and students. At the conservatories, he complained, the field of musical criticism occupied third place in the curricular structure. There was a need for seminars for critics and an obligatory apprenticeship system at various journals and newspapers. There would be competitions for gifted young musicologists for the best papers on Soviet multi-national music.

Kukharsky wanted the qualifications for teachers raised. Of fifty-seven chairmen in all twenty-nine conservatories, only five had doctoral degrees. Eleven departments were chaired by pedagogues with no degrees. Over 70% of the teaching staffs of the conservatories had no scholarly degrees. He announced a five-year plan to raise the scholarly qualifications of the teachers. Kukharsky rebuffed Sokhor (without naming him) with regard to the formation of critical opinion: it was a fact, he contended, that criticism, even by the most talented critic, was still the opinion of an individual. According to Kukharsky, this was a dangerous situation: "Criticism must crystallize and be defended in discussion, especially today when there is a lack of clear-cut positions— ideological, esthetic, theoretical. Unfortunately, in musicology there is a certain licence of views which tends toward a significant oblivion of Marxist-Leninist esthetics and a, by far not innocent, flirtation with modish foreign trends."[39]

The final results were decisions with the following goals: strengthening the ideo-organizational role of arts criticism in the battle for Socialist Realism; improving the work of the musicological commission of the Composers' Union; requiring yearly reports of the editors of *Sovietskaya Muzyka* and *Muzykalnaya Zhizn;* establishing a weekly arts journal; improving the ideo-professional preparation of young musicologists; instituting country-wide discussions among the directorates of the Composers' Union about new works, under the widest possible participation of society.

In the tradition of Anglo-Soviet friendship, there was an English music festival in Moscow and Leningrad in the spring of 1971 and a Soviet music festival in England in the autumn of 1972.

Representing Britain were the London Symphony Orchestra under its permanent conductor, André Previn (who also appeared as piano soloist), the composer Benjamin Britten, the tenor Peter Pears, the pianist John Lill (a prize winner at the Tchaikovsky Contest), and the Allegri String Quartet. Two eminent Soviet performers—the pianist Sviatoslav Richter and the cellist Mstislav Rostropovich, both personal friends of Britten—lent their art to the English programs. The repertoire was predictably Anglo-Russian: music by Britten, Walton, Vaughan Williams, Tippett, Elgar, and Holst, as well a gesture toward the old master Purcell. Rachmaninov was represented by his Second Symphony and his Piano Concerto in C minor. Britten, always a favorite in Russia, must have felt particularly honored by the superb performances of his Piano Concerto (by Richter) and his Cello Symphony (by Rostropovich). But on the whole, the reviews published in *Sovietskaya Muzyka* were rather perfunctory and lacked the warmth displayed on previous occasions.[40] The best review was written by Shchedrin, who discovered a kinship between the musical idioms of Purcell and Britten, noticeable perhaps only to Russian ears. Much praise was lavished on the London Symphony Orchestra, "its high professional inspiration", and its rare balance of orchestral choirs.

When the contingent of Soviet musicians arrived in London for the return visit in November 1972, they could not complain of indifference. The English critics relished the opportunity of discussing each event at great length. The opinions of London's most respected critics—including Sadie, Noble, Greenfield, Cooper, Shawe-Taylor—ranged from warm approval to ironic ridicule: no false politesse here, no undue respect for foreign sensitivities, no hiding behind initials. The reviews were written in the best English tradition of honest, hard-hitting criticism.

The Soviets brought their own chorus, which was indispensable for the vocal works, but relied on English orchestras—the London Philharmonic and the London Symphony. The conductors were Yevgeni Svetlanov and Maxim Shostakovich; the soloists were violinist David Oistrakh and pianists Emil Gilels and Vladimir Krainev (the latter a recent Tchaikovsky Contest winner), the Glinka String Quartet, and a few vocalists. As to repertoire, the visitors played only their own music, Russian and Soviet.

The most important event was the London concert première of Shostakovich's Fifteenth Symphony. Maxim's conducting was termed "superb". The work, already known through the BBC's taped performance, received overwhelmingly favorable reviews. The public success was genuine; the orchestra was on its feet, joining the audience in paying tribute to the composer, who bowed from the Royal Box in Festival Hall.

Another significant success was the concert offered by the Glinka Quartet, an ensemble established under this name in 1968. The critics were delighted with the unhackneyed program as well as the faultless performances. Three London premières were on the program—string quartets by Sulkhan Tzintzadze (b. 1925 in Georgia), Karen Khachaturian (b. 1920 in Moscow), and Shostakovich (his Thirteenth). In addition, the rarely heard Second Quartet by Tchaikovsky was played.

The Soviet organizers failed to provide any information about the first two composers, and the public was left guessing as to what it heard. Unbeknownst to the London critics, Tzintzadze had composed seven string quartets. Whether they heard the Sixth (successfully performed in Paris in 1969) or the Seventh (composed in 1970) cannot be ascertained. One critic was impressed by the "strong and cultivated feeling for the medium".[41]

A string quartet composed in 1969 by Karen Khachaturian (a nephew of the famous Aram), which had been recorded by the Glinka Quartet, was undoubtedly the piece played in London. It was praised for its "adventurous language, spectral and demonic", and for containing "tougher, more exciting ideas than newer Russian music is usually credited with".[42]

The London première of the Thirteenth Quartet by Shostakovich, given by the Glinka Quartet, coincided with performances of the same work by the Fitzwilliam Quartet in Harrogate and York. This British group earned Shostakovich's personal approval with its performances of his late quartets.[*]

However, other Soviet composers were treated rather roughly by the London critics. Tikhon Khrennikov appeared as soloist in his own Second Piano Concerto, a work recently premièred in Moscow. London did not share Moscow's predictable enthusiasm. One critic described it as a

> "15-minute piece of coarse, loud, banal pianistic jumble, in a relentless sub-Prokofiev idiom . . . No coherent development, no orchestral argument . . . the composer thundering away at the piano . . ."[43]

It was a calculated risk to present politically conditioned choral works. Shchedrin's *Lenin Lives in the Heart of the People* (composed in 1970) is "not easy to swallow as a whole" for a non-Russian— such "instant hagiology may seem simple-minded, even repugnant to us", wrote Jeremy Noble. He had a better impression of Shchedrin's Second Symphony of 1965,

> "Shchedrin seemed to be using a relatively advanced idiom to genuinely personal ends, substituting for the approved 'epic' model of Soviet symphony something more of a collage of vivid musical images."

But this "dazzling display of invention" might "conceal a lack of capacity for sustained musical thought", warned Noble. He cleverly compared Shchedrin to a "kind of Yevtushenko, licensed to take liberties which in others were still frowned on".[44] Actually, Shchedrin's Second Symphony aroused quite a bit of controversy when it was first given in Moscow in 1965.

Georgi Sviridov's *Pathetic Oratorio* fared less well. Apparently, it was over-amplified, resulting in a "deafening onslaught", more appropriate for the White City Stadium than Festival Hall, com-

---

[*]Since 1976 the Fitzwilliam Quartet has presented complete cycles of all fifteen Shostakovich quartets in five cities, including London (1979), Montreal (1980), and New York (April–May 1982).

plained one critic.[45] But the London public seemed to have been captivated by the swagger and brilliant sound of the presentation.

Sviridov's *Folksongs from Kursk* was misunderstood by the critics as being merely an "arrangement". Actually it is a totally original work in the style of the "New Folkloristic Wave," using folk idioms in a novel way. One critic heard overtones of Orff's *Carmina burana,* "rather too slickly strung together with obvious contrasts between moods and voices".[46] Much praise was given to the Yurlov Choir, particularly the quality of the contraltos and the basses, while the sopranos were occasionally found "reedy" and the tenors at times "aggressive".

"The style of singing is either intensely dramatic or dreamily romantic, with a strong emphasis on color rather than line, a preference for heavy staccato and for sudden sforzati followed immediately by pianissimo."[47]

Music of the eighteenth-century Russian composer Dmitri Bortnyansky proved the highlight of that program—"a feast of rich choral tone perfectly balanced and integrated and moving effortlessly from fortissimo to pianissimo". Other lighter numbers ("quasi-pop") by Sviridov, Alexander Davidenko, and others were performed in "execrable taste"—sentimental solos, humming accompaniments, and some "sickening" texts. But the British public loved it, showing all its "gullibility."[48] And there were ovations for the "sure-fire pop-Russian music" conducted by Svetlanov, like Glinka's *Ruslan* Overture, Borodin's Second Symphony, and Tchaikovsky's *Capriccio italienne.* Svetlanov's conducting was lively but at times coarse; "he has a tendency to blow music up more than life-size".[49] The soloists, Gilels and Oistrakh, were in top form. All in all, the British visit of the Soviet artists was a great success, despite some criticism. Thirty-two concerts were given—twelve in London and twenty in other cities, such as Birmingham, Bristol, Liverpool, Manchester, and Leicester.

Shortly before greeting the Soviet visitors, London paid its own tribute to the greatest of Soviet-Russian composers, Prokofiev. Early in October 1972, *War and Peace* was staged at the Coliseum by the Sadler's Wells Opera Company. The English translation was by Edward Downes; the conductor was David Lloyd-Jones. The version offered was the most complete ever, even more so than the Bolshoi Theatre's. Every effort was made to make the sequence of events clear to a public not necessarily familiar with

Tolstoy's narrative. Placards were used to indicate time, place, and content of the ensuing scene.

Few opera houses outside the Soviet Union have attempted to stage *War and Peace*. The London press devoted an unbelievable amount of space to discussing the production and to providing background information about the genesis of this monumental work. The flaws were not concealed, but praise was given where praise was due. The staging (under Colin Graham) made much use of back projections in order to free the stage for the mass scenes. The performance took four and a half hours with one intermission—fourteen scenes, seventy-two principal roles—an impressive effort of theatrical and musical art.

Despite the tensions and increased pressures on the so-called dissidents within the Soviet Union during the year 1972, the artistic exchanges with the Western countries proceeded smoothly. Among the visitors from abroad were the Vienna State Opera, the New York City Ballet, the San Francisco Orchestra, and various other American ensembles and individual artists.

The Vienna Opera was received with rapt attention in Moscow. Opera is the lifeblood of the Russian musical scene, and there was much that could be learned from the tradition of the unique Viennese ensemble, which brought *Der Rosenkavalier, Tristan und Isolde,* and *Marriage of Figaro.*

Der Rosenkavalier, not currently in the Soviet repertoire, was a revelation in terms of style and atmosphere. Josef Krips conducted; the Marschallin was sung by Leonie Rysanek. *Tristan* (conducted alternately by Karl Boehm and Heinrich Hollreiser) was considered the climax of the Viennese visit; the soloists were Jeff Thomas and Berit Lindholm. Neither Strauss nor Wagner is given often in the Soviet Union, and the critic in *Sovietskaya Muzyka*[50] dealt with both works in the sort of detail usually accorded premières.

Figaro was more familiar; nevertheless the Soviet critics discussed at length the social significance of Beaumarchais and Mozart. Boehm and Hollreiser alternated in the pit; the stage direction, which was highly praised, was in the hands of Leopold Lindtberg. The orchestra was called ideal, discreet without ever sounding subdued. Such unanimity of enthusiasm is rare indeed.

After an absence of ten years, the New York City Ballet under George Balanchine returned to the Soviet Union in September-October 1972. The visit included Leningrad, Moscow, and Tbilisi in Georgia, the ancestral country of Balanchine. The performances were sold out and the excitement was great, but the same controversies arose: "It's too far from ballet, too abstract, too modern." Some critics felt that the choice of repertoire was less adventurous than in 1962. Stravinsky's *Violin Concerto* was praised as effective yet somewhat pretentious and artificial. The Balanchine ballets *Tchaikovsky Third Suite* and *Symphony in C* received rapturous applause, as did the jolly setting of Gershwin's *Who cares?*. Jerome Robbins's *Dancers at a Gathering* was well liked, but his *Goldberg Variations* seemed rather abstract. The technical mastery of the dancers was highly praised though it was achieved at the expense of "soul and personality." One writer spoke of "collective artistry".

"The visit of the New York City Ballet forces us to rethink and to discuss the evolution of choreography within the contemporary musical theatre. One can expect that these discussions will be fruitful since they are based on such high artistic examples as demonstrated by Balanchine's company, which has achieved world-wide recognition."[51]

The San Francisco Symphony under Seiji Ozawa visited Moscow, Leningrad, and Vilnius. The soloists were concertmaster Stuart Kanin and the pianist André Watts. The repertoire included some American works: the Fourth Symphony of Charles Ives, the Sinfonietta (1928) of Henry Cowell, and Leonard Bernstein's *Candide* Overture and Serenade for violin—not very adventurous choices. The classics were represented by Beethoven, Brahms, Berlioz, and Dvořák. Ozawa risked playing some Russian selections (Tchaikovsky's Fourth, Prokofiev's *Romeo and Juliet* Suite) and he lost. "I don't mind so much if Ozawa diverged from our tradition, but I do mind that he offered no satisfying substitute in its place", growled the critic, a retired professor of conducting.[52] His prejudices showed throughout his review: he liked best what he knew least. Though recognizing Ozawa's enormous talent, he felt that the conductor was hindered by

"what we used to call 'Americanism': i.e., technical brilliance over content, though actually it can be found any place. Yet it seems that such an approach flourishes on American soil."

The same "Americanism" may have worked against André Watts, who played the Tchaikovsky First Piano Concerto as a "show piece". At the end, the critic offered some revealing observations:

he discussed the reasons behind the enormous public response to the Ozawa concerts and ascribed it to the fact that Ozawa's programs were joyous, like holiday events, while "our [Soviet] concerts are often grey and dull". The critic blamed Soviet programming, which induced the conductor and the orchestra to perform works they did not care to play. Rabid cultural nationalism tends to force Soviet performers to give preference to the Russian and Soviet repertoire containing much second-rate music. This excessive patriotism may be killing the joy of Soviet audiences attending their own philharmonic concerts.

The return engagement of Van Cliburn, the unforgettable winner of the First International Tchaikovsky Contest in 1958, aroused particular interest. The young Texan is a legend in Russia. Internationally, Cliburn never achieved the adulation that he enjoys in the Soviet Union. His concerts are not reviewed but rhapsodized about. He played his old repertoire—the concertos of Grieg and Tchaikovsky, the same selections by Chopin and Liszt. While there were isolated objections—slow tempi, excessive subjectivity—one could always feel the deep affection of the critics and the public for this gifted foreigner, whom the Russians have adopted as their own.[53]

Musically rewarding was the visit of two American chamber groups that interacted in their performances: the Composers Quartet and the New York Wind Quintet. Their programs offered a clever mixture of old and new, of pure strings and pure winds with an occasional joining of forces. An example of the latter was Schubert's Octet. American composers were represented by the string quartets of Samuel Barber (Op. 11) and Elliott Carter (No. 1; 1951) as well as Ingolf Dahl's Allegro and Arioso for wind quintet. Other twentieth-century works were Hindemith's *Kleine Kammermusik* Op. 24 No. 2 for winds (1922) and Alban Berg's String Quartet Op. 3 (1910). This repertoire is rarely heard in Soviet concert halls, and it was duly appreciated.[54]

The merits of visiting ensembles bringing contemporary music to the Soviet public cannot be overestimated. These are the "windows to the West" so desperately needed in a country where the repertoire is still censored by bureaucrats in the State Concert Office or the Ministry of Culture. How this is done was told by Rostislav Dubinsky, for thirty years first violinist of the Borodin Quartet, until he decided to emigrate to Holland. His story[55] begins with the objections raised to the programming of Haydn's Op. 51, the *Seven Last Words of Christ on the Cross*. The bureaucrats suggested that the title be shortened to "Seven Words" or, even better, simply "Opus 51". The next hurdle was a program that included two quartets by the "Second Viennese School" — Arnold Schoenberg's Second, Op. 10 (1907), and Berg's Op. 3 (1910). The program was considered "too concentrated", and permission was refused unless one of those works was dropped. Further negotiations: substitute Shnitke for Schoenberg. Further objections: what kind of music is Shnitke? And why the Berg? "We await other proposals", was the decision of the *apparatchiki*. There were more pressures: the Borodin Quartet would be denounced to the Central Committee for "anti-Soviet activities and ideological diversion". This led to dissension among the quartet members. Finally Dubinsky accepted the consequences and applied for emigration for himself and his wife, the pianist Lyuba Edlina. It was a hard decision. He was called a "bastard and a cheat".

> "We applied for visas. During the three months we had to wait for them, all our friends stopped talking to us. No one phoned. We couldn't play in public. We had become enemies of the Soviet Union."[56]

There is nothing unusual about this tale of woe. Soviet artists are in bondage to Goskontsert, the State Concert Office. Bureaucrats decide what and where and with whom the artist plays, and how much of a fee he is permitted to retain. We hear the same from Rostropovich, Vishnevskaya, Kondrashin, Davidovich, Egorov, Ashkenazi. Concert dates are annulled, exit visas are cancelled, lies are spread about the artists' "health", and programs are censored. Chicanery runs rampant.

When Stravinsky died in April 1971, *Sovietskaya Muzyka* carried a half-page obituary,[57] calling him "one of the grand Russian artists of the twentieth century, the patriarch of contemporary music". His "deep nostalgia" for his homeland was mentioned, despite his absence of five decades, but he was "in many ways the typical representative of the bourgeois esthetics of our time". Shostakovich's *Testimony* contains a funny passage about Stravinsky's visit to Moscow in 1962,

> "The invitation to Stravinsky was the result of high politics. At the very top it was decided to make him the 'number 1' national composer, but this number didn't work. Stravinsky hadn't forgotten anything—that he had been called a lackey

of American Imperialism and a flunky of the Catholic church—and the very same people that had called him that were now greeting him with outstretched arms.

"Stravinsky offered his walking stick instead of his hand to one of these hypocrites, who was forced to shake it, proving that he was the real lackey.* Another kept hanging around but did not dare come up to him. He knew that he was at fault, so he stayed in the foyer the whole time, just like a lackey."[58]

The references here are to Yarustovsky (whose 1961 biography of Stravinsky was full of critical Soviet clichés) and to Grigori Shneerson or Israel Nestyev, who had written negative comments on Stravinsky. In fact, Shostakovich himself had changed his opinion on Stravinsky. He said in *Testimony,* "Stravinsky is one of the greatest composers of our time and I truly love many of his works". He remembered that, as a youth of twenty, he had played the second piano part at the Leningrad première of *Les Noces* (December 1926).[59]

To commemorate Stravinsky's ninetieth birthday, a special concert was arranged in Moscow on 19 June 1972. Svetlanov gave an introductory speech and conducted the USSR State Symphony and the Radio Chorus. On the program were the ballet *Orpheus,* the Piano Concerto (played by Nikolai Petrov), and the *Symphony of Psalms.* Another commemorative concert, conducted by Dmitri Kitayenko, offered an imaginative chamber program, including the Wind Octet (1923) and the Septet (1953), the latter one of Stravinsky's first "serial" compositions. At the end, *Renard* was performed in the Russian version (*Baika pro lisu*) with singers from the Stanislavsky-Nemirovich-Danchenko Theatre. Also worthy of mention is a radio performance of Stravinsky's *Mavra*—a comic opera after Pushkin—conducted by Rozhdestvensky. Previously blasted as a distortion of a great Russian classic, *Mavra* was now treated as a legitimate musical experiment, and Rozhdestvensky was praised for his skill and imagination.[60]

In October 1972, *Sovietskaya Muzyka* picked a fight with Aaron Copland, one of the oldest and staunchest friends of Soviet music. The bone of contention was a postscript in the revised edition of

---

*Extending his cane for help was never meant by Stravinsky as an "insulting" gesture, according to Robert Craft (in *The New York Review of Books,* 24 January 1980).

Copland's book *The New Music* (1968), which angered the Soviet editors:

> "As far as can be judged from the admittedly scarce evidence that reaches us, musical creativity in the U.S.S.R. has been stultified. The revolutionary fervor of the war years, exemplified in the Shostakovich works of that period, degenerated into a mere conformism . . . Where are the adventurous youngsters who can hold their own with their counterparts in Western Europe or Japan or America? . . . If they do exist, they are not being exported . . ."[61]

As a footnote, Copland had added three young Soviet composers—Andrei Volkonsky, Edison Denisov, and Valentin Silvestrov—who had been performed recently in America. But he pointed an accusing finger at the "Russian cultural authorities" for not giving the West "a complete picture of the state of Soviet composition today".

The Soviet reply was furious, "Is that all that Mr. Copland is able to say about Soviet music of the post-war period? And why base a statement on 'scant evidence'?" After listing names of recent Soviet composers, the Soviet journalist concluded, "It is impossible to assume that Mr. Copland did not know all that. For that reason, any unbiased reader must see in his statement, not a lack of information, but a deliberate tendentiousness." And he expressed regret that "the aging Mr. Copland" had now joined the ranks of narrow-minded anti-Soviets.[62]

The abusive response merely shows that Copland had touched a sensitive nerve: complaints about not being adequately presented abroad have been voiced by various Soviet composers of the younger generation. Recently, the Composers' Union established a Bureau for the Dissemination of Soviet Music, but it works more internally than internationally. Whatever support is given does not apply to the non-conformist composers, who continue to operate under wraps.

Two important musical premières took place in Moscow early in the summer of 1972. The first was a work by Sviridov, the second by Shchedrin.

On 7 June the Yurlov Choir presented the first performance of *Spring Cantata* by Georgi Sviridov, based on texts by the nineteenth-century Russian poet Nikolai Nekrasov. The vocal movements are based on Nekrasov's best-known work, *Who Is*

Happy in Russia, published in 1873. It is a description, in folk style, of the wanderings of seven peasants and their encounters with various classes of society. The literary style is vigorous and satirical, and Sviridov, the master of text-connected music, ingeniously captures the spirit of the Russian peasantry and countryside. Framed by three choral movements is an instrumental interlude: we hear the pastoral sounds of two oboes, sounding like old reed instruments, against a background of bells, celesta, vibraphone, and harp. Each of the choral movements is a gem—the exuberant "Spring Song", the pensive "Tell Me Why . . .", and the forceful finale "Mother Russia".

Less than a year after this première, Alexander Yurlov, the conductor, suddenly died at the age of forty-five. Sviridov expressed his sorrow in a gripping work for wordless chorus entitled *Concert in Memory of Yurlov.* The three-movement composition was performed and recorded under the direction of Yurlov's successor, Yuri Ukhov.* The work is full of choral effects, intense and unconventional, and extremely difficult to perform.

The Shchedrin première was a big event. *Anna Karenina,* a new ballet on "motives" from Tolstoy's famous novel, was given at the Bolshoi on 10 June. The heroine was danced by Maya Plisetskaya, who was also producer and choreographer. The orchestra was led by Yuri Simonov, the Bolshoi's principal conductor. There was great excitement before the première, and the line for tickets, even for the dress rehearsal, extended for blocks around the theatre and into the adjoining underground stations. Rumors were flying that Shchedrin had used excerpts from Tchaikovsky, that the music was not really his own.

The extent to which Rodion Shchedrin had used Tchaikovsky became a subject of controversy among the critics. As to quoted themes, Mikhail Tarakanov wrote, "In a refined and unobtrusive way Shchedrin subjected them to contemporary retouchings, be it by use of original timbres or by the application of heightened harmonic coloration".[63] To which Liana Genina replied, "Retouchings—of course. But the issue is that there are *no* themes by Tchaikovsky in Shchedrin's ballet . . . only initial hints, shadowy reminiscences . . ." (with one exception: the F minor theme from the Andante of the Second String Quartet, which is quoted more fully). Yet, even Genina conceded that much of the music was in the mood, if not the manner, of Tchaikovsky.[64] Shchedrin himself spoke of "two musics", his own and the bor-

*Columbia/*Melodiya* M 34525

rowed influence, and explained his approach. His procedure was quite subtle—he guided and controlled the interplay. Some musicians reproached Shchedrin for not subjecting the "borrowed" music more forcefully to his own treatment; after all, they recalled, Stravinsky had used Tchaikovsky for *Le baiser de la fée,* but every measure bore Stravinsky's imprint. According to Khrennikov's review of the new ballet,

> "Some episodes strike one as skillful stylizations. And yet, Shchedrin's own creative personality, expressive and abounding in daring contrasts of sounds and dynamics, is felt throughout the work."[65]

In 1972, the Soviet Union celebrated the fiftieth anniversary of its legal existence. It was the treaty of 22 December 1922 which created the Union of Soviet Socialist Republics. The concept of federalism was established and cemented by the Constitution of 6 July 1923. Other republics joined the Union in due course, voluntarily or by annexation. But 1922 remained enshrined as the birth year, and 1972 was marked by massive commemorative observations.

At the Joint Plenum of all the creative unions of the U.S.S.R., Khrennikov spoke on behalf of the Composers' Union on 29 November 1972. Tracing the historic growth of multi-national musical cultures in the Soviet Union, he remembered the significant help given by Russian composers who worked and taught in remote regions. Reinhold Glière had been active in Azerbaijan and Uzbekistan, Vladimir Vlassov and Vladimir Feré in Kirghizia, Yevgeni Brusilovsky in Kazakhstan, to mention but a few. By 1972, all the republics and regions had their own master composers. "The basis for this powerful development of musical cultures was exclusively the wealth of folk creativity."[66]

Yuri Keldysh (chief editor of the multi-volume *Music History of the Soviet Peoples,* 1966–1974) pointed out that "minority" composers needed to collaborate with experienced Russian or Ukrainian composers who would provide the technical expertise to shape the extant folklore into acceptable form.[67] We may add at this point that quite a few of such "collaborations" proved to be fraudulent because most of the work was done by the mentor. Such frauds were known and ignored by the Composers' Union, which was eager to fulfill its "quota" of native composers. Shostakovich (in *Testimony*) speaks of outright plagiarism and of compositions being ghost-written for money, not only in remote regions but right in Moscow.

"Take the astonishing rise of Mukhtar Ashrafi, famous composer, and not only in his native Uzbekistan . . . He even has the order of Lenin . . . He turned out to be a shameless plagiarist and thief. I was chairman of the commission that smoked him out . . . He was expelled from the Composers' Union . . . But recently, Ashrafi was granting an interview. He was in power again . . ."[68]

True or false, Ashrafi is indeed listed in the Soviet *Musical Encyclopedia* (1973), even with a photo.

Of course, Keldysh did not refer to any of the scabrous aspects of "collaboration", nor did any of the other speakers. A meaningful discussion was begun by Sokhor under the heading "Multinational, International".[69] (A better word would have been "supra-national" since he meant the interchange of national elements *within* the Soviet Union.) He warned, "For the time being it seems to me premature to assert that a certain unified international [i.e., supra-national] system of Soviet music has emerged".

On this point, Yarustovsky contradicted Sokhor in an article entitled "There Is a Soviet Intonational System!"[70]

"The Soviet intonational system is the fruit of the dialectic union of national and international elements which arose from a common socialist foundation, the result of the common effort of those who are active in socialist musical culture."

Yarustovsky showed instances of interaction between various national strands on Soviet soil, in simple songs as well as in large forms like operas or symphonies. He saw a Soviet thematicism, a Soviet stance characteristic of the new Soviet man. He drew parallels with the era of the French Revolution, which produced a certain style of revolutionary music. Some composers of national minorities (Yarustovsky warned) were so preoccupied with preserving their own national heritage that they neglected the larger aspects of internationalism (that is, Sovietism). Others had become so fascinated with archaic folkloristic devices that they, too, forgot the most treasured aspect of the current Soviet culture.

Yarustovsky's article, though persuasive, elicited negative responses. Young minority composers in particular, on the threshold of shaping their own nationally idiomatic music, were not willing to dilute or abandon their recent achievements to pursue the chimera of "Soviet" music. In fact, Yarustovsky—being a theorist, not a composer—spoke rather glibly about all the creative aspects involved. *Sovietskaya Muzyka* printed various answers during the year 1973; no one supported Yarustovsky, and there were some decisive rebuffs.[71] In his final word, Yarustovsky reiterated the formula that defines the essence of Soviet culture: "Socialist in content, national in form, *international in spirit*".[72] The last three words were added during the fiftieth jubilee year of the U.S.S.R., and not accidentally: in the half-century of Socialist environment, the Soviet people in all fields, including the arts, acquired much that was the result of interaction among the Socialist nationalities, transforming their life in a truly international spirit. Therefore, Yarustovsky maintained, we *can* speak of an intonational sphere of Soviet music in its totality. Soviet music, in its best creative examples, has proven the effectiveness of dialectic ties between the generalized all-Soviet idiom and the individualized national idiom.

The discussion did not settle any issues, yet it helped clear the air. The emphasis on "national" elements had become obsessive and, to some, limiting and oppressive. This might explain the flight of some composers into the "new folklorism", which Khrennikov, at one point, called "escapism".

The elder statesmen of the Composers' Union displayed an element of suspicion toward the "New Folkloristic Wave". They dared not condemn it outright because folklore is the unshakable foundation of Soviet musical esthetics. But time and again they warned against "excesses". What are the basic ingredients and the motivation of the new movement, which arose in the 1960's and stretched well into the 1970's? In the words of one expert, Solomon Volkov,

> "Common to the composers of the 'New Folkloristic Wave' is the heightened interest for the archaic layers of folklore: the ancient incantations, the ritual dances, the funereal laments, and—broadly speaking—music of rites and ceremonies. One began to value the genuine folk tunes, unspoiled and undistorted by canonized arrangements. From there sprang the new and heightened interest in folk performances and techniques, such as the sliding glissando, the cut-off words, the unstable structures, the improvisational style. These—one may say—*maximal* characteristics of the folklore were examined in the light of contemporary compositional systems."[73]

In turning with renewed vigor to folk song, the young Soviet composers seemed eager for a rapprochement with the Soviet mass audiences. One of them, Valery Gavrilin (who received the Glinka Prize in 1967 for his *Russkaya Tetrad'*) said,

> "Our popularity acquires meaning only when our art serves not only the 'white collar' but also the 'blue collar' strata of our society . . . We must deal with audiences of enormous numbers and great variety . . . living people whom we cannot disregard. And we must work and shape them just as they shape us."[74]

Volkov saw a connection between cause and effect,

> "There can be no doubt that the slogans and the creative practices of the 'New Folkloristic Wave' arose as an answer to the demands and expectations of the potential audiences."

Whether the "New Folkloristic Wave" really accomplished its goal of attracting more audiences to art music cannot be answered unequivocally; actually, the new techniques are rather sophisticated and far less accessible than the "old" manner of prettied-up quotations of folk tunes in rhapsodies and fantasies.

The trend toward increased "Sovietization" (that is, national unification) of musical styles also played a role in the growing interest in folklorism, old or new. Fears were expressed among composers and commentators that old folk traditions might be devalued or even forgotten. The process of "levelling" produced a counter-process of re-emphasizing national moods and trends. "In search of the lost national authenticity, the national intelligentsia now turns to cultural treasures once discarded as no longer needed", remarked Volkov. At times, the reactions against the "levelling" process became extremely powerful as far as the cultural sphere was concerned. Lenin himself was opposed to what he called "reactionary nationalism" but preached a cautious and sensitive approach to the problem of nationalities. The official Soviet policy in music is undoubtedly dedicated to the careful preservation of national identities while encouraging a maximum circulation of ideas among the nationalities through mutual visits and musical exchanges.

A revival of religious moods seems to be working in favor of the "New Folkloristic Wave". According to official Soviet statistics, the number of believers in the country may be 25% to 30%, though allegedly limited to the elderly and less educated. A recent sociological study among Leningrad students—obviously young and educated—provides the surprising result that one out of every four participates in some religious ceremony; these students also admitted to keeping religious books and ikons at home. Volkov concluded,

> "The interest in ceremonial customs is obviously not accidental; it corresponds to the interest in ceremonial music evident among composers of the 'New Folkloristic Wave'."

Call it religion, mysticism, or a fascination with medievalism, the fact is that Soviet composers are interested in reviving some of the religious rites. There also seems to be a relaxation of official taboos against music connected with religious subjects: Maxim Brazhnikov's research in medieval church notation received encouragement, Sergei Skrebkov's collection of polyphonic church music was partly published, Handel's *Messiah* and Beethoven's *Missa solemnis* were performed in Moscow, the church music of Tchaikovsky and Rachmaninov is heard, Rimsky-Korsakov's *Russian Easter* Overture is played again under its old name *Svetlyi Prazdnik* (Bright Holiday). Politically the state is atheist, but church-connected music seems alive.

1973

On 27 February 1973 the Soviet government took an important step toward the normalization of relations with the international publishing world: it formally notified UNESCO of its intention to adhere to the Universal Copyright Convention, effective 27 May. Thus, the Soviet Union became the sixty-fourth member state. This decision put an end to the unlicenced reprinting of foreign materials in the Soviet Union as well as the unlicenced publication of Soviet materials abroad. The Soviet Union went so far as to change its own copyright laws to bring them in line with international practice. However, the copyright agreement was not to be retroactive, and no composer or author, foreign or Soviet, could reap a sudden windfall profit in delayed royalties.

Opinions were divided as to the mutual benefits of the new copyright agreement. On the whole, Western publishers were pleased about the protection extended to their authors and the collection of royalties. However, dissidents within the Soviet Union pointed out that the Soviet government acquired the legal right to control the foreign publication of works by Soviet authors; they saw the Soviet step as an attempt to cut off the flow of dissident writings published in the West. Established Soviet authors and composers must negotiate foreign publication projects through a centralized Soviet agency called VAAP.* But there is actually no way the Soviets can control the smuggling of clandestine material to the West. What they are trying to control is the publication of such material by Western publishers. Yet there are apparently ways in which the copyright agreement can be circumvented; witness the publication in New York in 1979 of *Testimony: The Memoirs of Dmitri Shostakovich* "as related to and edited by Solomon Volkov". Protests by the Soviet government and by the Shostakovich family were of no avail.

Shostakovich, who had not visited the United States since 1959, decided to accept an invitation in 1973. The occasion was the awarding of an honorary doctorate at Northwestern University, in Evanston, Illinois. With his wife, Irina, he arrived in New York by boat on 11 June and returned to Europe the same way on 30 June. He had no time to waste. In Chicago he gave a reluctant half-hour press conference (he disliked reporters intensely!), and an interview with Stephen Rubin of *The New York Times* did not go much better.[75] Shostakovich sounded like an official of the Composers' Union: he praised the solicitude of the Union, the working conditions for composers, and the excellent pay scale for commissioned works. He declined any queries of a personal nature, saying, "I am unable to characterize myself". To a leading question, "Are there any disadvantages for a composer working under the socialist system?" the answer was a dry and predictable *nyet*. "Do you enjoy the works of Western avant-gardists?" was answered with a diplomatic "Not everything". But he sounded sincere when he spoke of his own motivation for composing. "The reason I compose a current work is because I'm unhappy with my previous one. If I'd say, 'Well, this is composed beautifully', I'd be finished as a composer".

An interview with Royal Brown for *High Fidelity*[76] was friendlier because the questions submitted showed the interviewer's familiarity with the master's work. Asked about his occasional use of dodecaphony in his late works, Shostakovich replied,

*Acronym for *Vsesoyuznoye agentstvo po okhranenie avtorskikh prav* (All-Union Agency for the Protection of Authors' Rights).

542   DEVELOPMENTS AND EXPANSIONS 1970-81

"I did use elements of dodecaphony in these works [the Twelfth Quartet and the Violin Sonata]. Of course, if you take a theory and solely use this theory, I have a very negative attitude towards this kind of approach. But if a composer feels that he needs this or that technique, he can take whatever is available and use it as he sees fit. It is his right to do so . . ."

When asked whether he composed at the piano or away from it, he said, "I can work at the piano, but I prefer not to. I don't compose manually but mentally."

The conversation turned to the various versions of the opera *Katerina Izmailova* (Lady Macbeth . . .)—the original of 1932, the revised version staged in 1962, and the filmed version. Brown's assumption that the film used the original version was corrected by Shostakovich. "The film, by the way, does not use the entire original version but rather a revision of it." (In 1979, the original 1932 edition was recorded by Rostropovich, with Vishnevskaya in the title role. It is a blazing musical document and in many ways stronger than the revision.)

While in New York, Shostakovich met with composer-colleagues he knew from previous visits—Schuman, Mennin, Luening, Kay, Gould, Crumb, and the Russian-born Alexander Tcherepnin. Shostakovich was described as very animated and intense though highly nervous and showing signs of his recurrent illness. The use of his right hand was impaired; he gesticulated with his left hand as he spoke. His voice was described as "high, somewhat sibilant . . . [it] comes out in fast, almost youthfully enthusiastic bursts that are highly accentuated." He emanated warmth and an "enormous inner strength". Brown taped the interview with Shostakovich. After the master's death in 1975, it was released on a recording in Moscow.

What a strange coincidence: while Shostakovich was stating blandly in New York that there were *no* disadvantages for a composer working under the Socialist system, a younger colleague of his, Andrei Volkonsky, arrived in Vienna as an emigré from Moscow—a living rebuttal of Shostakovich's statement. The fact that Volkonsky, the scion of an old aristocratic family, was given an exit visa for Israel only underlines the hypocrisy of the Soviet emigration policy. (In order to be "eligible", Volkonsky entered into a *pro forma* marriage with a Jewish woman followed by a prompt divorce, once he was abroad.)

Speaking to a *New York Times* correspondent in June 1973,[77] Volkonsky said that he had "fought for twenty-five years to establish and preserve his artistic individuality" in Moscow before requesting the right to emigrate in December 1972.

"The next day I was expelled from the Union of Composers. All my concerts were cancelled. The record company was instructed not to issue the recordings I had just made . . ."

Five months of suspense and unemployment followed, during which Volkonsky sold most of his belongings, including scores and books, to keep himself afloat. He hounded the passport office.

"The Soviet authorities finally had the intelligence and wisdom to allow a composer to go away who was of no use to them in their fulfillment of their musical five-year plans because he could not compose the kind of music that alone can be played in the Soviet Union . . . I was just a speck of dirt in the grand marble palace of Soviet culture."

In the meantime, Volkonsky has settled in his native city of Geneva★ and his music is heard occasionally in the West. The readjustment will take time.

The centennials of two great Russian musicians, Sergei Rachmaninov and Fedor Chaliapin, were observed in 1973. Both were early emigrés: Rachmaninov left in 1917, Chaliapin in 1922, and both died abroad without revisiting Moscow. By now, their transgression of having abandoned their country has been forgiven, and both are treated by Soviet historians with the respect and admiration they so fully deserve.

Rachmaninov was honored with a gala concert on 2 April at the Great Hall of the Conservatory. Yevgeni Svetlanov conducted the *Symphonic Dances,* Elena Obraztsova sang some Romances, and a cycle of choruses for women's voices was given its Soviet première. On 20 April the Stanislavsky-Nemirovich-Danchenko Theatre sponsored a concert of Rachmaninov's music under conductor Kitayenko. In eight programs during 1973 the USSR State Symphony performed all of Rachmaninov's works that employ an orchestra: symphonies, concertos, operas, and cantatas. Not to be outdone, the Bolshoi Theatre presented concert performances of his operas *Francesca da Rimini* and *Aleko,* while the ballet *Paganini*

★See pp. 296–97.

was shown as choreographed to Rachmaninov's *Rhapsody on a Theme of Paganini.*

All the musico-historical institutions and conservatories in Moscow and Leningrad arranged musicological sessions devoted to Rachmaninov. The Glinka Museum mounted a large exhibition of memorabilia. *Sovietskaya Muzyka* published interesting new material in the April and June issues. *Melodiya* Records released series of recordings played by Rachmaninov, as well as Richter's interpretation of all the Piano Preludes. The opera *Aleko* was reissued on records. The book *Rachmaninov and His Time* by Yuri Keldysh appeared in 1973, one of many publications. Rachmaninov's letters and literary reminiscences have been kept in print (the latest volume, *Literaturnoye Nasledie,* came out in 1978). A memorial museum was opened in Novgorod, the region where Rachmaninov was born. Concerts of his music were held in many Soviet cities, to coincide with his birthday on 1 April. On that day, flowers were laid at the memorial plaque on the Moscow building where he had lived from 1905 to 1917. Yet, it annoys the Soviet cultural authorities that a number of Rachmaninov's musical manuscripts are kept in perpetuity at the Library of Congress in Washington, according to his wish and that of his family.

Rachmaninov and Chaliapin were good friends in their younger years. The friendship cooled when Chaliapin withdrew from two roles that Rachmaninov had conceived for him when he composed *Francesca da Rimini* and *The Miserly Knight.* That was in 1906; at the time Rachmaninov was conductor of the Bolshoi Theatre and Chaliapin the much-admired bass at the Imperial Theatres of Moscow and St. Petersburg.

While Rachmaninov's musical heritage is in print, Chaliapin's is evanescent; his art was that of an interpreter and the memory is fading with time, kept alive only through descriptions by contemporaries. Of course there is the recorded sound of his voice, but Chaliapin's art was not purely vocal; it was also histrionic: he recreated a role in its totality, aurally and visually. He added touches of characterization to the roles of Boris Godunov or Ivan Susanin, Mefistofele or Don Quixote, that have become part of the Russian tradition. It has been said that he became the "co-author" of a role. He was a natural, intuitive artist, yet he was also an excellent sightreader with a brilliant musical memory. Maxim Gorki, to whom he dictated his autobiography, said of Chaliapin,

> "He is a symbolic image. People like him are created to remind all of us: so strong, so beautiful, so talented are the Russian people."

Unlike Rachmaninov, Chaliapin lived through the early and bitter years of the Revolution, staying with his people. He sang at mass concerts and contributed his art and his presence to the revolutionary struggle. Even abroad he remained the symbol of the great Russian artist. He always sang in Russian because that language was part of his art. He frequently sang *Boris* in Russian while the rest of the cast used another language, but audiences did not mind because they were mesmerized by his impersonation.

Attempts were made in Russia in 1952 to reconstruct Chaliapin's interpretations in musical notation on the basis of his phonograph records. The efforts of a certain Lev Lebedinsky were reported in *Sovietskaya Muzyka* by the opera expert Elena Grosheva.[78]

Two major figures in Soviet music celebrated significant birthdays in 1973 — Aram Khachaturian turned seventy and Tikhon Khrennikov was sixty.

Khachaturian was feted in music, words, and print. It was evident that he had no enemies, only friends, and everybody wished him well. Nobody expected this ruddy master to die within five years, in 1978.

The celebration for Khrennikov was of more musico-political significance. He had ruled Soviet music since 1948, and his stewardship of the Composers' Union was shrewd, expert, and strong-fisted. He was reelected periodically and unanimously; only during the period of "the thaw" was there a feeling that someone less tainted by Stalinism should take over the leadership. But Khrennikov survived Stalin and Khrushchev, and he prospers under Brezhnev. Was he really the opportunist that Shostakovich described in his memoirs? Khrennikov cleverly followed the zigzag course of Soviet cultural policy. The members knew that it was his political maneuvering that made the Composers' Union so powerful. But the position he holds also enhances and inflates his own career as composer.

Khrennikov is played, printed, and recorded; the theatres perform his operas and ballets; he travels as delegation head throughout the world; he plays his piano concertos at every occasion; he receives Lenin Prizes and awards. Since the deaths of Shostakovich and Khachaturian, certain sycophantic critics are trying to elevate Khrennikov to chief Soviet composer, but in vain; there is simply not enough originality in his works.

For a time, Khrennikov produced little because of the administrative demands of his job. But in the 1970's he became more active as a composer, obviously searching to modernize his essentially conservative style. His Second Piano Concerto (premièred on 8 February 1972) has a studied artificiality. It begins with a twelve-tone theme that falters on the thirteenth note. He adopts a *secco* piano style and a pseudo-Baroque texture that leads to a hymn-like theme; there is an arid sonata as centerpiece and a bit of folklorism in the final Rondo. The stylistic discrepancies between the movements are disconcerting. All these heterogeneous elements do not fuse into a personal statement. Even Khrennikov's supporters were taken aback by his "new" profile. This uneasiness was evident in the labored and lengthy review by Genina; she even risked some mild objections but quickly retracted them.[79] One fashion in contemporary Soviet music juxtaposes ultra-modern devices with conventional sections—clusters of modernism without integration. So here was Khrennikov, who had fought modernism all those years, suddenly joining the experimental crowd—but not too much, just in spasms.

Khrennikov's *Much Ado about Hearts* is a chamber opera written for Pokrovsky's new stage and first performed in March 1972. The music is based on the incidental music of 1935-36 which he wrote for the Vakhtangov production of *Much Ado about Nothing*. Obviously, additional music had to be composed, both vocal and instrumental. One reviewer described it as "irresistibly dynamic, bubbling over with high good humor and optimism".[80] The same material was used for his ballet *Love for Love* in 1975.

Shortly after his Second Piano Concerto Khrennikov composed his Third Symphony Op. 22. One critic spoke of the "close and intimate links" between the two works, but in fact there is no link whatsoever. In his new symphony Khrennikov fell back on his old, well-tried idiom: it is lively, colorful, entirely traditional in terms of harmony and texture, and effectively orchestrated. It is reminiscent of his spirited First Symphony of 1933/35, his graduation piece, which he composed as a conservatory student in Vissarion Shebalin's class.

In fact, Shchedrin, who delivered the congratulatory speech, mentioned Khrennikov's First Symphony as a "seminal" work of the 1930's, side by side with works by Prokofiev, Shostakovich, Khachaturian, and Yuri Shaporin. This comparison was a bit of jubilean exaggeration! Shchedrin also spoke of Khrennikov's "theatrical" musical talent, his diplomatic skills, and his ability to continue his career as a composer while under the daily pressures of his job as head of the Composers' Union. Within months of that speech, Shchedrin was elected chairman of the Russian chapter of the Composers' Union, clearly becoming the heir apparent, should Khrennikov ever decide to retire.

Two television productions were dedicated to Khrennikov: one dealing with his music for films, the other a live transmission of a gala concert of his compositions at the Kremlin Palace hall (where all 6,000 seats were filled). We have no way of judging his film scores, but it may well be (as O. Feltsman wrote) that his melodic gifts are particularly effective for the screen. As for the concert program, it was a mixed bag: the finale of his Second Symphony, two choruses on words by Nekrasov, and the final movement of his Second Piano Concerto (by far the most effective part of the work). Then came vocal excerpts from his stage works (*Much Ado about Nothing, The Mother, In the Storm*) and finally some of his songs, which enjoy great popularity throughout the country.

There were a number of other jubilarians in 1973. The veteran composer Lev Knipper turned seventy-five. He is perhaps best known for his song "Meadowland", but he was actually a leader in music during the 1920's and 30's and the composer of twenty symphonies, many concertos, some string quartets, and stage music. He composed to the end of his life (he died in 1974) without making much impact. Another composer whose fame was in the past was Yuli Meitus, who turned seventy. His opera *Molodaya Gvardia* (The Young Guard; 1947/50) was considered one of the best to come out of World War II, though his youthful "industrial" piece *Dneprostroi* is best forgotten. His thirteen operas all deal with patriotic or revolutionary topics.

Alexander Mossolov—once famous, then denounced, now forgotten—died in 1973 at the age of seventy-two. In the late 1920's he had represented his country at the festivals of Frankfurt and Liège. His orchestral piece *The Iron Foundry* was an international sensation, but he fell from grace in 1936 and never regained much status.* An article in *Sovietskaya Musyka* explored his spectacular early career.[81]

Many honors were bestowed on Yevgeni Mravinsky, the greatly admired conductor of the Leningrad Philharmonic, on his seventieth birthday (and even more when he turned seventy-five in 1978). When Mravinsky took *his* orchestra to Vienna in 1974, he earned the highest critical praise not only for his interpretations but also for the quality of the orchestra, which he had shaped since 1938. One critic called it "the basso profundo among the top orchestras of the world", with a sound dominated by dark colors—velvety yet with a firm metallic base. "Mravinsky wants everything—except to be conspicuous", was a critic's remark on

*See pp. 85–86.

his leadership, which is as self-effacing as it is authoritative. On the program were Prokofiev's Sixth Symphony and Beethoven's Fifth. The Viennese critic had to admit that he had never heard the pianissimo transition from the Scherzo to the Finale in the Beethoven played with such "sculptured tenderness". This was an amazing tribute from one of Vienna's toughest critics![82]

The Soviet press did not lag behind in its praise for the maestro. Mravinsky had always been supportive of Soviet composers whenever he recognized true talent. His strongest encouragement went to Shostakovich ever since he conducted the memorable première of the latter's Fifth Symphony on 21 November 1937, which "rehabilitated" the young composer after his downfall in 1936. After that Mravinsky conducted the world premières of Shostakovich's Sixth, Eighth, Ninth, and Tenth symphonies (all in Leningrad), and the friendship between conductor and composer remained close. Among the articles written about Mravinsky for his seventieth birthday was one by the composer Vadim Salmanov, whose three symphonies Mravinsky had conducted; it is overflowing with the enthusiasm of a creative artist who felt himself fully understood by an interpreter. Another was by Viktor Liberman, for many years Mravinsky's concertmaster in Leningrad and a fine artist in his own right, who is now living in the West. He spoke of the conductor's ability to extract from the orchestra a maximum of accomplishment, and then to raise the level time and again by setting the goals even higher. Mravinsky is as demanding of others as he is of himself—a "thinker" among conductors, erudite, broadly educated, and with a firm grasp of the international repertoire. For decades he was the only Soviet Russian conductor of world stature.[83]

Toward the end of 1973, meetings were held in all the chapters of the far-flung Composers' Union, in preparation for the All-Union Congress planned for April 1974. The most important of the regional meetings was that of the Russian Federation (RSFSR), which was held in Moscow on 13–16 November 1973. It was attended by 291 delegates representing all regions of the Russian Republic. The keynote address was given by Georgi Sviridov, the chairman of the Russian composers. He concluded with the words,

> "Our creative and social position is determined by our close association with the people and their heroic labor exploits. We must do our best to have our music carry an important message. It should be filled with lofty ethical content. It

should be comprehensible to those for whom it is composed. To compose for the people means loving the people, loving our great Motherland."[84]

There is a fundamentalist tone in these words, a return to Lenin's basic concepts. A similar trend can be detected in other speeches summarized under the title "Moscow Composers for the Working People". A new crusading spirit seemed to engulf the composers.[85]

On the other hand, Andrei Petrov, chairman of the Leningrad chapter, called for innovations and daring searches. Even the chairman of the Buryat Composers' Union (membership three) spoke of "novel expressive media" needed to depict contemporary subjects. However, the chairman of the Tatar Composers' Union warned against measuring "the modernity of a composition solely by the criterion of the complexity and novelty of its musical idiom". He gave the delegates a timely reminder, "We value highly the striving for what Prokofiev termed 'a new simplicity': this, too, is innovation". Clearly, the need and concept of "innovation" is not the same on both sides of the Ural Mountains.

At the end of this meeting, Sviridov stepped down as chairman. Rodion Shchedrin was elected to the post, with Andrei Eshpai as first secretary. A younger generation was taking over.

1974

Nineteen seventy-four was to be a crucial year for the arts in the Soviet Union: two eminent personalities, Solzhenitsyn and Rostropovich, left their homeland to live and work in the West.

There is no need to recount the heroic struggle for intellectual freedom by Alexander Solzhenitsyn, winner of the Nobel Prize for literature in 1970, who was hounded out of his own country. On 14 February 1974 the Soviet authorities forcibly put him on an airplane and sent him to West Germany. His family was permitted to join him shortly thereafter. He now lives in seclusion in the State of Vermont, in one of the loveliest regions of the United States.

The case of Mstislav Rostropovich and his equally famous wife, soprano Galina Vishnevskaya, was somewhat different. The fact that Rostropovich had offered shelter to Sozhenitsyn contributed to the official disfavor but was not decisive. Early in February 1974, Rostropovich declared that he and his wife were under a virtual "quarantine" imposed by the Soviets, unable to fulfill engagements abroad. On 29 March the two artists appealed directly to Leonid Brezhnev:

> "In recent years an intolerable atmosphere of persecution has been created around our family. Our artistic activity has been shamefully limited and our art ignored.
> "We have written to you many times with requests for help, but have received no reply.
> "Since we see no way out of this tragic situation, we request you to permit us and our two children to go abroad for two years."

This appeal to the head of the state was granted one half-hour after it was received. On 26 May Rostropovich landed at London airport, accompanied by his cello and his pet dog. His family joined him two months later. During the next few years, Rostropovich's career as cellist and conductor expanded dramatically. London, Paris, Vienna, New York—all acclaimed him. Together with Vishnevskaya he made memorable recordings of the operatic and vocal repertoire. He signed a three-year contract as principal conductor of the National Symphony in Washington. Artistically and financially, his success was fabulous.

Still, there was no open talk of permanent emigration. The Rostropovich visas were renewed by the Soviet authorites in 1976 and 1977, each time for one year. It is true that Rostropovich declared openly in Paris in October 1974 that he did not intend to go back unless "full artistic freedom" was established in the Soviet Union. "As artists, we must be able to play *what* we want, *where* and *when* we want, *with whom* we want." Simple as this statement may sound, it is virtually an artistic "declaration of independence" and certainly unacceptable to the Soviets, particularly since they have always denied the existence of any restrictions.

True enough, when Rostropovich applied for a three-year extension of his passport early in 1978 the answer was delayed. On 15 March it was announced that he and his wife were stripped of their Soviet citizenship. The following day, the newspaper *Izvestia* published a brief article under the headline "Ideological Degenerates", announcing the expatriation decree on grounds that "Rostropovich and Vishnevskaya systematically commit acts harmful to the prestige of the Soviet Union and incompatible with Soviet citizenship."[86] A second statement, filled with slanderous accusations against the two artists, was distributed by TASS on 22 March.[87] The detailed rebuttal made public by Rostropovich and

Vishnevskaya was to no avail. There is a thick file of charges and counter-charges. But stronger than all legalistic talk rings the voice of Galina Vishnevskaya in her "Reply to TASS" (26 March 1978):

> "The Soviet Government has shown that in the Soviet Union people's fate is decided not by the Law but by the persons who control the Law. I do not recognize the right of these persons to deprive me forcefully of the soil which has been given me by God . . . I have given to my people the greater part of my life. I have borne and brought up two children. And I will not allow anybody to order my family about as if we were slaves."

Vishnevskaya's indignation was deep-seated. Later in 1978 an interview in *The Observer* revealed that she had been the victim of vicious intrigues by her colleagues at the Bolshoi, who had denounced her and Rostropovich to the authorities. A recording of *Tosca* in Moscow had been rudely interrupted and cancelled while it was in session. One well-known Soviet conductor is alleged to have written to the Culture Ministry in 1974, "Rostropovich is a political and musical gangster. We Soviet people are cleaner when he leaves."[88]

While the drama of Rostropovich's departure was unfolding behind the scenes, the musical bureaucrats of Moscow conducted business as usual. Rostropovich had been scheduled to perform at the 1974 Spring Festival, but his name was scratched. He was replaced as chairman of the cello division of the forthcoming International Tchaikovsky Contest by Daniel Shafran. According to plan, the Fifth All-Union Congress of the Composers' Union opened on 2 April. Rostropovich and Vishnevskaya were never mentioned.

Shostakovich read the opening remarks; they were brief and very much Party-oriented.[89] We must ask ourselves, he said, how does our music affect the Soviet citizen, his world views, his moral stance—in short, how does our music contribute to the building of Communism? Art should not be turned into pure entertainment nor music composed for a small elite—"such theories are amoral and absurd". Genuine art is created by man for mankind, to give joy and hope. "Marx once said that the happiest individual is the one who gives happiness to most men." This, said Shostakovich, should be our device. He closed with assurances to "our dear Communist Party" and to the Leninist Central

Committee of continued loyalty to these ideo-artistic principles. One is inclined to doubt Shostakovich's sincerity in reading this prepared text; surely he must have known how the "dear Party" was treating his friend Rostropovich and other associates.

Khrennikov's keynote address[90] had the task of summarizing five years of accomplishments of the Composers' Union (since the last Congress in December 1968). Khrennikov had just received the highest honor of the land, the Lenin Prize, in recognition of his Second Piano Concerto, and he was at the height of his fame and power. On the whole, he sounded less pugnacious and aggressive than in the past. His attacks on avant-gardism were comparatively mild. The references to Socialist Realism were hardly more than dutiful. He had to admit that Soviet composers and critics had learned the "devices" of avant-gardism though they did not subscribe to any "system". Actually he had no choice but to be more flexible; it was impossible to ignore the powerful movement toward rapprochement with Western modernism which was evident in Soviet music. To do otherwise would have been foolish.

In his summary, Khrennikov stressed the internal expansion of the Composers' Union, the well-planned support given to hitherto underdeveloped regions. The musical horizon was being broadened, in keeping with Party policy. More and more, the Composers' Union of the U.S.S.R. and its official organ, *Sovietskaya Muzyka,* were assuming a multi-national role, and it was Khrennikov's job to keep a careful balance among the regional chapters and to give them a feeling of importance even though all the decisions were made in Moscow. From this point of view, Khrennikov and his Directorate are quite successful. Once a talented composer emerges in a faraway region, he or she receives far more attention than would normally be the case. Clearly, a new opera in Tadjikistan is of more importance to the Muscovites than the première of *Lulu* in Paris. The *Information Bulletin* of the Composers' Union is filled with new names and exotic places, with festivals and premières, with exchange visits and mutual tributes. The solidarity extends to the Socialist-bloc countries. Even the relationship with Polish musicians, which was somewhat cool since Poland abandoned ideological restraints a decade earlier, has been normalized and intensified, though the "Warsaw Autumn" remains an irritant to the Soviet establishment. Prokofiev said in the 1930's that the danger for the Soviet composer to become "provincial" was real. In the 1970's this provincialism had become a matter of national policy.

The transcript of Khrennikov's speech occupied twenty-three printed pages in *Sovietskaya Muzyka*. It was followed by three days of discussion.[91] Actually, there were no differences of opinion; the speakers, representing all the regional chapters, merely elaborated on certain points. Andrei Petrov of Leningrad emphasized the efforts of his colleagues to establish close contact with the city's industrial workers by way of lecture-concerts and introductory talks, so that "they may enter the world of great music". (Such efforts are nothing new—they date back to the first years of the Revolution—but obviously there is a never-ending need to build new audiences.) Shchedrin, chairman of an ad hoc committee to strengthen ties with television and radio, described progress in this field. The importance of *Melodiya* Records in terms of mass music education was stressed by many speakers. The speech by Natalia Sats, the seventy-year-old director of the Children's Opera in Moscow, was received with particular interest. Active in the field of children's theatre since 1920, she became director of the world's first Musical Theatre for Children, in Moscow, in 1964. Here she started special shows (operas, ballets, fairy tales) with music by contemporary Soviet composers, among them Kabalevsky, Khrennikov, Koval, and Rubin. Sats's merits were recognized by a government prize in 1973 and the title "People's Artist" in 1975. In her speech Sats mentioned the close ties between her theatre and the composers who worked for it. Sats's influence extends far beyond Moscow; many Soviet opera houses copied her special shows for children.

Alexandra Pakhmutova, a successful song composer, described the Soviet song as a "true mirror of the people's life", which should carry a civic message and which deserves to be treated with special care by composers. The "civic responsibility" of song writers was also stressed by Serafim Tulikov, chairman of the Composers' Union Moscow chapter.

The musical exchanges among the various Soviet republics and regions were the topic of many speakers. The Kazakh composer E. Rakhmadiyev stressed the importance of making the music of each Soviet nationality interesting to all Soviet people, thereby facilitating an exchange of national and supra-national elements in music. Andrei Shtogarenko of the Ukraine told of exchange visits with Georgia, Byelorussia, Turkmenia, Estonia, and Lithuania. Contact between composers and audiences was estabished in "meet-the-composers" events.

Andrei Eshpai of the Mari Soviet Republic, a high functionary in the Union of Russian Composers, discussed the traditional relationship between composer, performer, and listener, to which he added a fourth element, the critic. "He may not be a creative artist, but he must be a talented musician, keenly attuned to the thoughts and ideas of the composer." Soviet musicology in general and its relationship to musical criticism was discussed by Lev Mazel, Yuri Keldysh, and Lev Danilevich. The young critic-musicologist Liana Genina spoke up.

Among the foreign guests of the Composers' Congress, the representatives of the Socialist-bloc countries were the most visible. They came not only from Eastern Europe but also from Cuba, Vietnam, Bangladesh, and even Yugoslavia. Other countries represented included France, Switzerland, Canada, Japan, Spain, Finland, and Turkey. From the United States came Peter Mennin, president of the Juilliard School in New York. Reminiscing about his previous visit to Moscow sixteen years earlier, he praised the advantages of cultural exchanges. Another return visitor was the veteran composer Roy Harris, an old admirer of the Soviet musical scene.

The participants of the Congress were regaled with much Soviet music, mostly new. Among the premières were the ballet *The Enlightenment* by Yuri Butsko and *Illumination* (a "choreographic novelette") by Alexandra Pakhmutova. The Moscow Philharmonic premièred the Second Symphony by Khayam Mirza-zadze of Azerbaijan and the Third Symphony by the fast-rising Giya Kancheli of Georgia. New chamber works heard were the Fourth String Quartet by Boris Tchaikovsky and Recitative and Fugue for two pianos by Aram Khachaturian. Much admired was a new cantata, *Hymn to Friendship,* by Kara Karayev.* Other compositions using vocal forces were Otar Taktakishvili's *Gurian Songs* and Petrov's vocal-symphonic fresco *Peter I.*

In keeping with the emphasis on a wide geographic range, the program included compositions from Kazakhstan (*Kudasha Küi* by Rakhmadiyev), Kirghizia (*Happy Youth* by Kaly Moldobasanov), Armenia (Violin Concerto by Lazar Saryan), Ukraine (*Carpathian* Concerto by Skorik and *Kiev* Symphony by Shtogarenko), Azerbaijan (the symphonic "mugam" *Gulistan Bayati-Shiraz* by Fikret Amirov and *Two Miniatures* by Akshyn Ali-zadeh), and Estonia (Seventh Symphony by Jan Ryaets). Almost lost in this multinational array was the Russian Boris Tishchenko, with his Concerto for flute, piano, and chamber orchestra. There was a concert

---

*Karayev won the Lenin Prize in 1979.

of Russian folk instruments balanced by a program of Kazakh folk instruments. Topping everything in national variety was a song concert representing over thirty Soviet composers from various regions.

At times, the range of these programs showed more concern for ethnic equality than for musical quality. Such congresses are showcases for the achievements of the entire Soviet Federation. It is useful to remember that the Russian ethnic representation has shrunk to 52% of the entire population—still a majority, but a slim one. Quite naturally, the Composers' Union tries to distribute its favors as even-handedly as possible, though Moscow remains the focal point.

Musically, the most important event of the Congress was the opera *The Gambler* by Prokofiev at the Bolshoi, a première delayed since 1917, when the soloists of the Petrograd Maryinsky Theatre refused to study the modernistic score. A revised version was prepared by Prokofiev in 1927 for Leningrad, but the project was abandoned. The première took place in Brussels in 1929 (in French), and a Russian radio performance was conducted by Rozhdestvensky in 1963. The Bolshoi gave the first staged production in Russian on 7 April 1974, using Prokofiev's revised version of 1927. The conductor was Alexander Lazarev, the stage director Boris Pokrovsky. It was done in the expressionistic style of the 1920's, which is well suited to the frantic action of the libretto and the biting modernism of the music. Pokrovsky said about his task,

> "As time goes by, Prokofiev stands out more and more as a modern artist congenial to us in spirit and artistic expression . . . With its combination of satirical, lyric and dramatic elements, *The Gambler* is a very complicated work . . . The cast had to study hard to master the subtleties of Prokofiev's score; the stage interpretation was determined by the dynamism of the music . . . ."[92]

When the Bolshoi brought the new production to New York in 1975, the critics took note of the unusual modernism of the staging and gave Pokrovsky full credit for a "night of brilliant theatre, . . . reaching a fantastic intensity in the last act's gambling scenes, with sets rotating like roulette wheels". It was "a striking example of how to deal with that latter-day form of opera, the play in which the music deliberately refuses to sing".[93]

Indeed, Prokofiev's intentional avoidance of cantabile or aria style and his reliance on a rapid recitative where the understanding of the words is essential proved so unattractive to the New York audiences that the last performance had to be cancelled. But this does not diminish the remarkable initiative of Pokrovsky, who, that same year, tackled another "problem" opera, Shostakovich's *The Nose.*

The Gambler remains a remarkable—almost unique—work in the Russian repertoire, because it defies every operatic tradition. Perhaps its time has come, after half a century.

The efforts to explore Prokofiev's musical heritage led to several projects of varying interest. On 14 May 1974, the incidental music to Pushkin's *Eugene Onegin*—composed by Prokofiev in 1936 for a Moscow production that was not realized—received a performance by students at the Gnessin Institute in Moscow. The score was prepared by the musicologist Yelizaveta Dattel in a setting for narrator, symphony orchestra, wind band, harpsichord, and chorus.

On a grander scale was the creation of a ballet based on *Ivan the Terrible,* Eisenstein's film with Prokofiev's score. (In 1962 a cantata had been extracted from the film by A. Stassevich.*) The arrangement for the ballet score was entrusted to Mikhail Chulaki (b. 1908), an experienced theatre composer. Chulaki expanded the film score by adding three sections from Prokofiev's Third Symphony (the one based on *The Flaming Angel*) as well as other fragments. One may call it a "scissors and paste" job, but it was skillfully done and served the needs of the choreographer Grigorovich. The idea of a dancing tsar did not set too well with some critics. Grigorovich's explanation (if not defense) was,

> "Since the emphasis will be on the shaping of the Russian national character, the civic spirit, heroism, and high morals of the Russian people, the tsar will be allotted a secondary role."[94]

The ballet *Ivan* was given four times at the Bolshoi early in March 1975 and then shipped to New York for the visit of the Bolshoi Ballet at the Metropolitan Opera House. Clive Barnes, *The New York Times* expert, was impressed though not convinced. He compared Grigorovich's "operatic" approach to a similar one in Eisenstein's film (Part I).

*See p. 359.

"At the end we have a scene ambiguously called in the synopsis: 'The Triumph of the Russian People'. Certainly the story is a tribute to their resilience, but their triumph? Possibly Mr. Grigorovich was identifying Ivan with Stalin. He would not be the first to do so."[95]

Barnes called it "a grand and important ballet which only new-fangled minds will dismiss as old-fashioned. It is a work in the great Russian ballet tradition . . . unaffectedly bold, brash, and spectacular." Other American critics were less friendly, and one went so far as to say "Ivan *is* terrible!"[96]

The Fifth International Tchaikovsky Contest ran in Moscow from 11 June until July. As usual it promoted the careers of some talented young artists and proved disappointing to others. There are recurring complaints that the judges' decisions are politically motivated and that some promising Western contestants are deliberately downgraded. But time has a way of correcting any misjudgements: no unworthy winner has ever made a career while some who were overlooked have risen to the top. Be this as it may, the Tchaikovsky Contest is considered one of the most important competitions for young artists.

In the violin division, no first prize was awarded. The second prize was divided between the American Eugene Fodor and two Soviet contestants.

While Fodor was praised by Soviet critics as a "first-class virtuoso", his performance of the Tchaikovsky Concerto was described as "not in very good taste".[97] American critics have confirmed the judgment that Fodor's musicianship is not on the same level as his virtuosity, and his career has yet to unfold.

In the piano division, a Russian, Andrei Gavrilov, won first prize and deservedly, as his international success has shown, until the Soviets curtailed his foreign travels for unexplained reasons. The second prize was divided between the Russian Stanislav Igolinsky and the American-trained Korean Myung Whun Chung, a student at the Juilliard School who has since turned to conducting. In an instance of misjudgement the third prize was given to Yuri Egorov, whom one Soviet critic described as "perhaps the strongest talent among Soviet participants".[98] Egorov defected to the West and is fast rising to the top of his generation.

Later in 1974, *Melodiya* released six records presenting all fifty-nine prize winners, each playing a short selection.

While mutual visits between the Soviet Union and the Socialist countries are almost routine, cultural exchanges with Western Europe are high on Moscow's priority list. England has gained in importance, but it is still France that tops the list in cultural matters. It was Paris that first gave international approval to Russian music in the late nineteenth century, and the Parisian festivals of Russian music and art in the first decade of this century paved the way to world recognition. The Soviets continue to cultivate their friendship with France.

In June 1974 a large group of Soviet artists appeared not only in Paris but also in Nantes and Angers with programs of Russian and Soviet music. The return visit of the French came in November-December 1974.

The premières offered by the Soviet musicians were Prokofiev's *October* Cantata, Shchedrin's cantata *Lenin Lives in the People's Hearts,* the Fifteenth Symphony by Shostakovich, the Second Piano Concerto by Khrennikov, and Sviridov's vocal cycle *In Memory of Yesenin.* These programs combined musical conservatism with political leftism. The audience response was highly appreciative.[99]

The French programs were more sophisticated; they contained orchestral and chamber music but no choral works. Concerts were presented in Moscow, Leningrad, Kiev, Minsk, Vilnius, Riga, Tbilisi, Yerevan, and Baku. The Strasbourg Orchestra under Alain Lombard brought two programs—one of twentieth-century "classic" composers (Debussy, Fauré, Ravel), the other more advanced: *Intégrales* by Edgard Varèse, Twenty-four Preludes for orchestra by Marius Constant, *Cinq Métaboles* by Henri Dutilleux, and the *Bacchus et Ariadne* Suite by Albert Roussel. A third program was played by the Moscow Philharmonic Orchestra under the French conductor Charles Bruck: music by Jacques Bondon, Antoine Tisné, and Gilbert Amy. In addition, the famous Percussion Ensemble of Strasbourg electrified a professional audience at the Soviet Composers Club with works by Varèse, Ballif, Miroglio, and the Pole K. Serocki. The Piano Trio of Paris offered music ranging from Milhaud to Jolivet, Martinon, and Messiaen. With the French performers came a delegation of French composers—Auric, Dutilleux, Bondon, Constant, and Gallois-Montbrun. They participated in their own works and exchanged views with their Soviet colleagues.

There was more contemporary music on these programs than any French city outside of Paris is likely to hear in a decade. Only one name was conspicuously absent, Pierre Boulez, whether by the artist's choice or by Soviet-inspired exclusion cannot be ascertained. But Boulez had visited the Soviet Union in 1967 as conductor and composer, with no visible damage to Moscow's morale.

While the Soviet establishment is obviously unwilling to export the music of its own avant-garde composers, it seems slightly more tolerant toward internal performances. There is also more fairness in discussing the music of non-conformist composers. In October 1974, *Sovietskaya Muzyka* devoted fourteen pages to various opinions on the première of Alfred Shnitke's First Symphony. It took place not in Moscow but in Gorki—an indication that the musical authorities wanted to avoid the limelight of the capital for a work that was likely to arouse controversy. Though the orchestra was a provincial one, the conductor was one of Russia's best—Gennadi Rozhdestvensky. Some critics traveled to Gorki, others had to judge the work from a tape. The latter were at a distinct disadvantage because the Symphony, described by one critic as "instrumental theatre", involved certain visual effects. Perhaps exceptional treatment was accorded Shnitke because Yuri Korev, the editor of the journal, was a long-standing admirer of Shnitke's creative talent. Korev did not hear the actual performance but only the tape.

The coverage by *Sovietskaya Muzyka* included reprints of two provincial reviews, one favorable, the other opposed;* statements by the composer and the conductor (the latter very enthusiastic); four essays by selected critics; and a lengthy summary by Korev. Though opinions *pro* and *con* were voiced, the tone of the entire presentation was friendly and encouraging.

Shnitke used aleatory and collage techniques as well as visual effects (such as musicians coming and going). There are sections of jazz improvisations and a parodistic funeral procession. But the Symphony is not "Mahlerian"; rather it is a composition of our time. One writer implied a domination of intellectualism over emotionalism: Shnitke works, not from "heart to heart" but from "thought to thought". The Symphony is an audacious experiment, innovatively planned. It makes broad-stroked, poster-like use of heterogeneous devices and handles them with professional mastery and artistic conviction. Korev called the score "unique,

---

*Behind the scenes at the Composers' Union, Yarustovsky is reported to have worked against Shnitke's First Symphony, while Khrennikov was in favor of giving it a chance to be heard and discussed.

unlike any other in contemporary music". But he also voiced reservations: he was perturbed by a certain kaleidoscopic quality that interfered, to his ears, with musico-intonational development. In fact, the method of development seemed to him less musical than montage-like and often paradoxical. But Korev concluded,

> "I've watched Shnitke's development for some fifteen years, since the oratorio *Nagasaki*. I still prefer his old *Songs of War and Peace* [1959]; from then on I believed in the emotional capacity of his inner world, in the fact that he is *talented*."

It appears strange that a score accorded such attention was not chosen for further performances inside or outside of Russia. What happened to Rozhdestvensky's enthusiasm? Perhaps the conductor had second thoughts about the work. But on 26 April 1980, Rozhdestvensky performed Shnitke's Second Symphony in London, reaffirming his belief in Shnitke as the most talented among the younger composers of Russia.*

On 29 September 1974 *The New York Times* published an article by its chief music critic, Harold Schonberg, entitled "Is Anyone Writing Serious Music in Russia Today?" It was written as a reaction to the news that on 15 September an outdoor exhibit of nonconformist art in Moscow had been dispersed by brute force. "Something unhealthy is going on there . . . the reaction to modern art is only an indication", remarked Schonberg. What had happened to the so-called avant-garde school in music—those "doughty figures" he had met in 1967?** "Today they seem to have disappeared." Well, not quite, but things were in flux. Volkonsky had emigrated in 1973, and Pyart was to apply for emigration in 1979. Slonimsky and Tishchenko have made certain concessions in order to enter the mainstream of Soviet music. Denisov and Shnitke get occasional performances. Nodar Mamisashvili (b. 1930) became a functionary in the Georgian Composers' Union. The Kiev group—Leonid Grabovsky, Valentin Silvestrov, Vladimir Zagortsev, and Vitali Godziatsky—struggle on but receive little attention even though since 1975 there has been a rejuvenation within the Ukrainian Composers' Union. Schonberg was pessimistic:

*See p. 631–34.
**See p. 453.

"Things seem to be as bad as ever . . . In this day and age there still are no Western publications freely available in the USSR. Painters still cannot paint the way they want to; musicians cannot compose according to their own dictates . . . Many talented young people who would like to compose turn instead to performance . . . The result is artistic sterility. Soviet culture means virtually nothing to the world today . . . The Solzhenitsyn affair revealed deep-rooted dissatisfaction . . . How long can the Soviet ideologists sit on their creators and intellectuals? What are they afraid of?"

That was the picture in 1974, Solzhenitsyn's expulsion was a thing of the past, but the banishment of Andrei Sakharov to Gorki was just a few months old. In the meantime, the wave of emigration and defection continued unabated. Thousands of talented people could no longer bear the insidious pressures, artistic and political.

Yet, musical creativity is surviving in the Soviet Union. Western technical devices characteristic of the foreign avant-garde find their way into Soviet compositions, and even middle-of-the-road composers are inclined to experiment. Non-conformist composers find ways and means of bringing their works to the attention of Western festivals, where they are performed and applauded. Within the Soviet Union, the Baltic republics are hospitable to new ideas. And *Sovietskaya Muzyka,* as we have seen, is willing to open its pages to discussions representing opposing views.

All this indicates that composers with non-conformist leanings are given more leeway in the Soviet Union, despite occasional grumblings from the older generation of critics like Keldysh or Yarustovsky or threatening gestures from Khrennikov. The point has been reached where no Soviet composer feels too frightened to experiment. The dividing line between "establishment" composer and "experimental" composer is becoming blurred. Perhaps the time has come to drop the term "avant-garde" and substitute "non-conformist". In fact, today there are Soviet composers in high positions who choose at times to be "non-conformist". They can point to Shostakovich's late works, where everything seems permissible as long as it serves an artistic purpose. Their aim is to expand their musical vocabulary, to try novel devices.

There is also a new generation of "non-conformist" critics, who are sympathetic to the new aspirations of their comrade-composers. Their professional reviews and essays are highly literate and show remarkable familiarity with the world beyond the Soviet borders, a type of information which is hard to obtain in

Moscow. Such articles have appeared in a yearbook called *Muzyka i Sovremennost'* (Music and Contemporaneousness). Its editorial policy revealed a specific interest in modernism and reflected the personality of Tatiana Lebedeva, its chief editor, whom I met and admired in 1962 for her frankness. In 1971, after having published her seventh yearbook, Lebedeva was dismissed, probably because of her "liberal" leanings, though she was a Party member. Her successor was a young musicologist, Dmitri Frishman, who was apparently no less liberal but who had fewer enemies. Frishman managed to publish three excellent volumes (Nos. 8, 9, and 10; 1974–76) but ran into trouble with No. 11, which was edited but not published. With Frishman's emigration to the United States in 1978, his post became vacant. It is rumored that his successor will be the critic Dora Doragan, but No. 11 has not yet appeared and is years overdue.

The authors and critics who contributed to the yearbook *Muzyka i Sovremennost'* and occasionally to *Sovietskaya Muzyka* represent the elite of today's musical intelligentsia. They are articulate, well-informed, open-minded, inquisitive, and obviously sympathetic to the aspirations of the non-conformist movement at home and abroad. As critics, their career is as difficult as that of the non-conformist composers. Their names deserve to be recorded: Mikhail Tarakanov (mentioned repeatedly in this book), Yuri Kholopov, Valentina Kholopova, Maya Elik, Yosif Kon, Svetlana Savenko. Genrikh (Henry) Orlov belonged to this group until his emigration to America in 1976.

On 24 October 1974, the musical world was saddened by the news that David Oistrakh, Russia's greatest violinist, had suddenly died in Amsterdam at the age of sixty-five.[100] Oistrakh was in the midst of a Brahms cycle with the Amsterdam Philharmonic. He had conducted six concerts and had appeared as soloist in three of them when death overtook him. He was widely beloved, not only for his artistry but also for his rare human qualities. His colleagues were his greatest friends. Said Isaac Stern, "I feel as if I had lost a brother; in all the years I knew him I never heard him say an evil word about anyone". And Menuhin referred to him as "my greatest musical colleague and my closest friend".

Oistrakh was a violinist in the Russian tradition but with a modern grasp of stylistic differentiation. In his early years he tended to approach all music with the same violinistic aplomb, but these "elements of provincialism" (to use Schonberg's phrase) disappeared as he moved to the forefront of the world's great violinists. His international career came late: though he had won the prestigious Ysaÿe competition in Brussels in 1937 (at the age of twenty-nine), he did not begin to travel widely until the 1950's. His debut in New York in 1955 was a sensation; at that time he introduced the First Violin Concerto by Shostakovich at Carnegie Hall under Mitropoulos.

Just as Auer and his disciples Elman and Heifetz represented the older, pre-Revolution Russian violin school, so did Oistrakh represent the newer Soviet school. Oistrakh was trained in Odessa by Stolyarsky; he never studied with Auer, and his approach was more contemporary. He settled in Moscow in 1928 and was appointed to the Conservatory in 1934. For four decades he taught his classes and shaped a number of outstanding violinists. He must be considered the fountainhead of the Soviet violin school, the model for a whole generation. Oistrakh exerted his influence not only through teaching but also through his own playing, which grew in power and scope over the next decades. Soviet composers were quick to recognize his sensitivity to new music, his willingness to explore a new repertoire. Concertos and sonatas were written especially for him, by Miaskovsky, Prokofiev, Shostakovich, Khachaturian, and many others. He gave countless premières of major and minor works, always willing to put his art at the disposal of composers. His imprint on the Soviet violin repertoire is a lasting one. Yet at heart he was not a modernist, and he left it to his son, Igor, and his student Gidon Kremer to explore the newest repertoire of Berg, Bartók, and Shnitke. Oistrakh also presided with unfailing fairness over the violin sections of the Tchaikovsky Contests.

Side by side with Oistrakh's obituary appeared that of Yekaterina Furtseva, the long-time Minister of Culture, who died on 25 October. She rose to her important position during the Khrushchev era and was an effective spokesperson for the vacillating cultural policies set by the Central Committee. At the time of her death, her influence was fading, and she was not reelected to the Supreme Soviet in 1974. Her successor in the Ministry of Culture was Pyotr Demichev, described as "the Party's chief watchdog over cultural affairs".[101]

In December 1974, the seventieth birthday of Dmitri Kabalevsky was observed with considerable fanfare. As usual on such occasions, the panegyrics inflated his merits. Throughout his life, Kabalevsky was a sane and conciliatory influence on the musical life of his country. His compositions are traditional and expertly crafted. During the "purge" of 1948, he was not on the list of censored composers, though he did belong to the Composers' Directorate, which was dismissed. But no one really wished him ill, and he was spared the humiliation experienced by Prokofiev, Shostakovich, Miaskovsky, and others. With Khachaturian and Shostakovich, Kabalevsky belongs to the early "Sovietized" generation of composers. He served his country loyally since the 1920's. His most positive contribution, perhaps, was his consistent and creative interest in the musical education of children and adolescents, and he had a strong say in the revision of the music curricula.

At the XI Conference of the International Society for Music Education (ISME) held in Perth, Australia, in August 1974, the Soviet delegation was headed by Kabalevsky. (Indicative of the organization's esteem for Kabalevsky was his election, in 1972, as Honorary President of the ISME, succeeding Kodály.)

In the course of his speech in Perth,[102] Kabalevsky outlined his method of introducing children to music. He had set up a pilot program in twenty-five Soviet schools "in cities and towns, in the country, and in workers' settlements". He himself took over a first-grade class (that is, of seven-year-old children), giving them one forty-five minute session each week. The results exceeded his expectations: the children learned how to listen attentively, they could put their impressions into words, they could grasp the structure and the imagery of the music. They learned to sing traditional songs ordinarily reserved for nine-year-olds. Kabalevsky stressed the need of learning how to speak to children—not so much for the "explanation" of the music but for tuning the audience to an "emotional wave length". He told of his next project, a book entitled "How to Tell Children about Music", embodying his own experiences; it would also serve as a guide to what music to choose—good music, well performed, seriously taken, with belief in its spiritual strength.

Kabalevsky's speech, filled with social idealism, was clearly directed to the delegates of the developing countries, who needed guidance and concrete ideas to take home to their governments. In the meantime, Kabalevsky's pioneering efforts within the Soviet Union were watched with anticipation and affection.

One cannot bid farewell to the year 1974 without recalling certain political events which affected Soviet-American relations. In July, the summit meeting between Nixon and Brezhnev in Moscow spread a glow of goodwill between the two great countries, made possible (so Nixon assumed) because of "a personal relationship established between the General Secretary and the President of the United States".

On 8 August Nixon resigned his office under threat of impeachment. His successor, Gerald Ford, signed the Vladivostok agreement on arms limitation in November. Détente still seemed possible though with reservations on both sides.

1975

The high point of the cultural exchange between the Soviet Union and the United States was reached with visits to New York by the Bolshoi Ballet in April-May and by the Bolshoi Opera in June-July 1975. For the ballet company it was the fourth visit to America, where it was known and admired. But it was the opera ensemble's first visit and a crucial test: Russian ballet had long been recognized as the best in the world, but Russian opera had no such reputation. It had to be judged on its merits.

Even for the Bolshoi Ballet, the five-week engagement at the Metropolitan Opera House was fraught with problems. "Is the Bolshoi Ballet a victim of the past?" asked one critic rhetorically.[103] During a recent London season, criticism had been voiced and people had spoken of a "decline". But the oversensitive Soviets had rejected all such comments; "the Bolshoi Ballet, instead of profiting from public criticism, was inclined to attribute all unfavorable comments to political motives". However, in New York the reception was decidedly friendly, thanks mainly to Clive Barnes, *The New York Times* critic. Four of the five ballet productions had been choreographed by Yuri Grigorovich, who was very much the center of attraction. He reasserted his belief in a "synthesis of choreographic and dramatic expressiveness" and in the story-telling ballet, but he admitted that he was not unalterably opposed to plotless ballets.[104] In the repertoire was *Spartacus* (music by Khachaturian) in a new version by Grigorovich, which was a triumphant success, danced in "one great burst of energy and passion".[105] But the other novelty, *Ivan the Terrible,* to music by Prokofiev, provoked divided critical opinion* although it was still "formidable". The other ballets shown in New York were *Sleeping Beauty, Swan Lake,* and the Lavrovsky choreography of *Gisèle,* a "beautifully studied version".

*See pp. 556–57.

The visit of the Bolshoi Opera had something gargantuan which appealed to the American "Barnum & Bailey" circus spirit: 350 tons of scenery; 80 mammoth crates of costumes and props; 460 members of the company, including an orchestra of 110, a chorus of 125, sixty soloists, and five conductors; plus managers, technicians, librarians, wardrobe mistresses, and a throat specialist.

The opening *Boris Godunov* was not an unqualified success: critics questioned the use of the Rimsky-Korsakov edition. New York, at the moment, preferred the "original" version. Yevgeni Nesterenko was found too stolid in the title role. But Yuri Simonov's conducting was acclaimed, and the chorus was found superb.

Next came Prokofiev's *The Gambler,* to which the public reacted in a lukewarm fashion: the Russian "parlando" idiom was incomprehensible to a foreign audience.* The biggest successes were the two Tchaikovsky operas, *Pique Dame* and *Onegin;* one critic called the performances "mood-drenched". Young Elena Obraztsova was sensational, Vladimir Atlantov was equally exciting, but Tamara Milashkina as Liza was found "uneven". There was criticism of the stage direction—"awful" in *Pique Dame* and hardly better in *Onegin,* "with moments of inept lighting and surprisingly clumsy dancing". Still, the overall impression was unforgettable, "the kind of authenticity that only Russian artists can bring to sung Russian".[106]

What was planned as the climax of the visit, Prokofiev's uncut *War and Peace,* proved to be a major disappointment to many New Yorkers. Those who had seen the performance in Moscow found that the transferral to New York left much to be desired. Some of the stage effects did not come off, and some of the scenery did not fit the Metropolitan stage. Besides, inexplicable cuts in the final scene weakened the dramatic effect. The staging was found "terribly old-fashioned"; it belonged "to another world, another philosophy of stagecraft".[107] This was Boris Pokrovsky's responsibility.

The ultimate defeat of the Bolshoi visit was the new opera *The Dawns Are Quiet Here* by Kyril Molchanov (b. 1922). He was known chiefly for his operas on patriotic themes. Since 1973 he had been the artistic director of the Bolshoi. The production was unfortunate—"beneath contempt. It is cheap, sentimental, cynical Soviet art at its worst", fumed Schonberg in the *Times,*[108] in what may have been an overreaction. Another American critic, Robert

---

*See pp. 555-56.

Jacobson of *Opera News,* had seen the Moscow première on 11 April 1975 and had called it a "Triumph of Tears".[109] The opera had been written to commemorate the thirtieth anniversary of the end of World War II (called by the Soviets "The Great Patriotic War"). Jacobson explained,

> "This is not an opera in the conventional sense. Using popular melodies of the times as well as folk music, the work commemorates an important event for the Russian people during the dire years of German occupation, and Molchanov has intended his opera to be a tribute to the women who perished in the war."

The music is directly related to an earlier film, based on a book by B. Vasiliev, for which Molchanov had written the score. "The opera is also highly cinematic in the series of brief scenes and in the dreamlike childhood remembrances of the girls as they pass the evenings in the barracks." The girls are members of an anti-aircraft company, and they are killed in a German ambush, as is the only man in the cast, a sergeant. The staging carried out Molchanov's concept of "lyrical stylization" without shooting or violence, "only frozen action and flashing red lights at the moment of death". The work was, in Jacobson's words, "the latest manifestation in the U.S.S.R. of an operatic social realism". He continued,

> "*The Dawns Are Quiet Here* is not only a fascinating example of what is happening theatrically and musically at the moment in the Soviet Union, but a touching musical drama about a small corner of the world at an important time in this century."

But even the sympathetic Jacobson had to admit that "the sugary finale . . . stretches one's credibility". The tearful reaction of the Moscow public was understandable, but to bring such a tendentious work to New York was surely a miscalculation.

It must be said that the New York debacle hastened Molchanov's departure from the Bolshoi: on 4 November 1975 it was announced that his two-year tenure was terminated "for reasons of health". While in New York, Molchanov had appeared ebulliently healthy and full of plans for the forthcoming 200-year jubilee of the Bolshoi Theatre. He stayed on the job only long enough to see the first event, on 25 September, the indestructible *Boris Godunov.*

The New York visit of the Bolshoi was a financial disaster and hastened the demise of the American sponsor, Hurok Management. Sol Hurok, the Russian-born founder of the firm, had hoped to bring the Bolshoi Opera to New York, but he died on 5 March 1974 and never saw the realization of his plan. It was Hurok's skill and imagination as impresario which made the cultural exchanges with the Soviet Union into glittering events of artistic significance.

The efforts of the Composers' Union to publicize the works of its composer-members were channelled through a newly established Bureau for the Dissemination of Soviet Music. An effective method was the format of "meet-the-composer" concerts, which helped to attract and involve an audience through personal contact with selected composers. In another series, called "Monographic Concerts", all attention was concentrated on one or two composers. The philharmonic societies (which sponsor not only orchestras but all kinds of concerts) were persuaded to allow more space to Soviet music. Admittedly there were failures and miscalculations—some concerts were poorly prepared, others were cancelled at the last moment. Complaints were about the lack of qualified directors to run the various philharmonics. Nevertheless, the collective effort on behalf of living composers has been admirable, in contrast to the official indifference the Western world exhibits toward a composer.

The Composers' Union arranged "Monographic Concerts" not only for little-known members but also for those with established names. Older composers appeared next to newcomers, and reviews were printed of all the works performed. Beginning in 1975, two composers were often placed on the same program. For example, the instrumental chamber music of the Armenian Edgar Oganesyan was combined with Sergei Slonimsky's vocal compositions. Another concert paired the Muscovite Yuri Levitin and the Armenian Edward Mirzoyan in a program of vocal and instrumental chamber music. An entire program was given to the Estonian Velio Tormis, who had received a State Prize in 1974 for his choral works.

Compositions by the popular Rodion Shchedrin also filled an entire program during the Moscow Stars Festival of 1975. The concert consisted of his *Symphonic Fanfares,* First Symphony, Third Piano Concerto, and excerpts from the ballet score to *Anna Karenina.* Yevgeni Svetlanov conducted, and the composer played the solo part in the Piano Concerto. Actually, the Concerto was a year old, having been played for the first time on 5 May 1974. At that time, there were so many perplexed critics with raised eye-brows that *Sovietskaya Muzyka* decided to have a round-table dis-cussion to deal fairly with the new work. The discussion printed in the February 1975 issue was a collection of six opinions, includ-ing those of the musicologist Tarakanov, the composer Shnitke, and the critic Genina. Tarakanov, as usual sympathetic toward modernism, wrote,

"A perfectly natural unexpectedness—that is how this music impressed me. This new work is marked by the same searchings and experimentation combined with a clarity of purpose, the expedient and thought-out construction which characterizes the Second Piano Concerto."

Shnitke was deliberately vague in his evaluation,

"The Concerto strikes me as a concentrated expression of the musical conception encountered in works like *Anna Karenina* and *Poëtoria,* the dramatic perception of life with its con-tradictions."

Genina, an old admirer of Shchedrin, admitted that the Third Concerto presents problems for the listener, but her belief in the composer was unshaken,

"Knowing the work of this master, one may unhesitatingly assert that if there is something in his music that you don't understand you had better wait and see. A short time passes, he produces a new work, and in it you find the key to the preceding opus."

Shchedrin's work catalogue is well balanced between accessible and advanced music. His early successes were flashy and folkish, but beginning with his Second Symphony (1965) his idiom be-came more searching and adventurous. When he presented his Second Piano Concerto in 1966, there were critical moans about his having abandoned the lucid national Russian style of his First Concerto (1954). Far from discouraged, Shchedrin continued on this path with his Third. (He is planning to write his Fourth for the American pianist James Dick.)

In the Third Concerto, he completely abandons the traditional Russian concerto style. It takes the unusual form of "Variations and a Theme", thirty-three variations followed by the theme at the end. Obviously, at first hearing the structural logic cannot be perceived. What one hears is a rich variety of sound combinations, stressing extreme contrasts of range and dynamics, a flow of music often fragmented and abrupt, non-thematic, at times aleatory (improvisational). This interplay is punctuated by powerful accents or by occasional wailing slides, as if in lament. The orchestra and the solo piano are cleverly intertwined, but there are also long stretches of pianistic cadenzas. The orchestration is scintillating. There is not a single consonance in the piece nor is there any feeling for tonality; the writing is freely dissonant and nontonal (but not "serial"). After some eighteen minutes of intense listening, one suddenly perceives the chordal theme played by the piano; it comes almost as a relief but it is cut short by a clangourous percussive cluster that is repeated in diminuendo until the sound dissolves into nothingness.

Despite its break with tradition, Shchedrin's Third Concerto has received repeated performances, proving that an established composer can take liberties and pursue non-conformist paths that are closed to newcomers. The key to the success of Shchedrin, Slonimsky, and a few others is eclecticism; they are flexible enough that they can occasionally write music in an accessible idiom and thereby earn the privilege of going their own way when the creative need arises.

Another composer of the same generation, Boris Tishchenko, was subjected to a similar kind of multiple evaluation. His ballet *Yaroslavna* was brought to Moscow by the visiting Leningrad Malyi Opera Theatre in the summer of 1974. It provoked conflicting opinions in *Pravda* and *Sovietskaya Kultura*. It was discussed at the Ministry of Culture and at a conference of musicians and theatre experts in Leningrad. Finally, the musicologist Tarakanov summed up the issues in *Sovietskaya Muzyka* of April 1975 under the conciliatory title "On the Path to Mutual Understanding". Under fire was not only the music but the scenario and the entire production.

Yaroslavna deals with the same material as Borodin's *Prince Igor*: both are based on the ancient saga *The Lay of Igor's Campaign*. While Borodin's version is idealized and romanticized, Tishchenko's is more faithful to the original tale. The personages of Igor, Yaroslavna, and the Polovtsy tribesmen appear in a different light. No longer is Prince Igor portrayed as a shining hero but as a rash and arrogant leader, though full of courage, His antagonists, the Polovtsy, are not languid or sensuous but evil and awe-inspiring. Yaroslavna becomes the living symbol of Russia, whose image inspires Igor to break out of his captivity. His return represents the rebirth of the hero, who has perceived his guilt toward his homeland embodied in Yaroslavna. She is portrayed as being aware of her patriotic destiny. She is lyrical yet not idealized; earthy, passionate, yet fluttering like a bird of the Russian steppe. This characterization is carried into the choreography.

A contrasting epic element is the chorus, which acts as a classical commentator. The words of the chorus, half-sung, half-recited, express the thoughts of the anonymous author of *The Lay*. The music is deliberately archaic, stylized, and primitive; set in unison or two-voiced, often moving in parallel fourths or seconds. It serves less as an illustration than as a commentary on the action. A certain static quality is, perhaps, the principal weakness of the composer's concept, which in turn makes the choreographer's task difficult. Listening to the recording of the score, one is struck by the non-balletic character of the music—the long instrumental solos without rhythmic profile; the lack of propulsive motion except in short spurts; and the absence of light, sunshine, and sensuousness.

In 1977 the folklorist Izali Zemtsovsky defended the score to *Yaroslavna,* declaring that Tishchenko's music must be considered in its relationship to original folklore. In pages of musical examples, he compared motives employed in *Yaroslavna* with ancient folk incantations. Tishchenko used "Asian horizons" to depict the world of the Polovtsy. There are similarities of techniques and procedures—voices moving in parallel motion, glissandos, and metric liberties. Only the initiated listener can hear these affinities. There is no use looking for "quotes" or "sources" in *Yaroslavna;* one must hear the intonational content behind the notes, said the author. He quoted Tishchenko's ideas on folklore:

> "Listening to the original ancient folklore, one enjoys it without thought that this tune could be reworked or re-arranged. No, one must not rework it, each tune is a 'thing in itself' . . . A true artist does not 'utilize' anything, he only perceives poetry where others do not see it and knows how to make others notice it, after having absorbed some 'sparks of truth' and converted them into a single solid 'structural' truth."[110]

These meaningful words were written by a composer who had explored folklore since his student days. He too belongs to the "New Folkloristic Wave".

The Soviet balletomanes were offended by the rough-hewn images in *Yaroslavna*. The stage director Lyubimov was castigated for his

> "attempt to adapt the 'achievements' of 'pop culture' to a subject of Russian history . . . It is no accident that *Yaroslavna* was well received in Avignon in 1976. The audience was filled with hippies who recognized themselves on the stage and were ecstatic to find out that Russians could also be filthy, barefoot, unkempt ragamuffins (this is how Prince Igor and his retinue were 'dressed' in *Yaroslavna*)."[111]

The year 1975 was designated by the Soviets for the commemoration of the thirtieth anniversary of the victory in the Great Patriotic War. Music played an important role in this celebration. The twelfth Moscow Stars Festival (the Festival is usually held for a week in May) stressed programs with patriotic subject matter. The Bolshoi gave two of Molchanov's operas, *The Dawns Are Quiet Here* and *The Unknown Soldier*. Two ballets by A. Spadavecchia and S. Tzintzadze, offered at the Stanislavsky-Nemirovich-Danchenko Theatre, also glorified Soviet fortitude. Major vocal-symphonic works performed during that week were Sviridov's *Pathetic* Oratorio, Kabalevsky's *Requiem,* and Prokofiev's *Alexander Nevsky*. The "Leningrad" Symphony by Shostakovich was conducted by Kondrashin. Song and dance ensembles performed—Beryozka, the Yurlov Choir, the Uzbek Bakhor Ensemble, the North Ossetian Alan Dance Group, and the Lithuanian Trinitas Band. Soviet compositions written during the war were featured. This particular festival attracted 25,000 tourists from thirty-seven countries, including veterans' groups and resistance fighters.

Similar festivals, though on a smaller scale, were held in many parts of the Soviet Union. Among them was the Transcaucasian Musical Spring Festival in Tbilisi: some 1,300 performers assembled to perform about 200 musical works, not necessarily connected with the war. Musicologists of the region published a volume, *Music of the Transcaucasian Republics,* edited by the Georgian Givi Ordzhonikidze. Just in time, the six-volume *Music History of the Soviet Peoples* was completed and published in 1974–75. It covers the period 1917 to 1967 and presents for the first time a cohesive picture of the musical cultures that developed since the Revolution. The chief editor was Yuri Keldysh.

A rather nostalgic sidelight of the victory celebration was an attempt to pay tribute to the young composers who had lost their lives during the war. A concert in their honor was given at the Moscow Conservatory, and the Glinka Museum has an archive of relevant documents and letters. Some of the more memorable compositions are now being published and recorded. One particularly gifted composer who died in the war was Benjamin Fleishman, a student of Shostakovich. He left an opera, *Rothschild's Violin* (based on Chekhov), which Shostakovich completed and orchestrated. It was staged only once, in April 1968, at the Experimental Studio of Chamber Opera in Leningrad. Maxim Shostakovich attended; it was a "rousing success", according to Volkov.[112] But the censors thought otherwise and it was closed, to the distress of Shostakovich. In 1975, Shostakovich was quoted officially as saying,

> "Fleishman was a composer with a wonderful talent; his was the penetrating mind of a great artist. He had a complete mastery of orchestral writing, his refined score is rich in invention."[113]

The first International Day of Music was set by UNESCO for 1 October 1975, to be observed throughout the world in honour of an art that is truly international. To greet the day, Shostakovich wrote an Open Letter:[114]

> "This day must be a true feast of music, of an art that is especially communicative, an art that travels all over the world without a visa and requires no translation into other languages."

This was to be Shostakovich's last public statement. He died on 9 August 1975, on the eve of his sixty-ninth birthday. There was much sorrow throughout the world, but to the Soviet people, especially to the citizens of Moscow and Leningrad, his death was shattering. Shostakovich had been a vital part of the musical scene; young and old had turned to him for advice and encouragement. Since the death of Miaskovsky in 1950, Shostakovich had assumed the mantle of "the musical conscience of Moscow".

The official obituary[115] called him "a true son of the Communist Party, a prominent statesman and public figure, a civic-minded artist". He played this role to his last day, though much of it repelled him. His musical creativity remained unimpaired

until the end, and première followed première—the Fifteenth
Symphony in 1972, the Fourteenth Quartet and the *Tsvetayeva*
Songs in 1973, the Fifteenth Quartet in 1974, the *Michelangelo*
Cycle in 1975. Posthumously, on 1 October 1975, his last com-
pleted work, the Viola Sonata Op. 147, was heard. What a wealth
of communication, of fresh ideas! He had said in his Open Letter,

> "Music . . . is going through a difficult period in our days; it
> is looking for new means to give expression to our troubled
> and glorious epoch . . . It is absolutely imperative to master
> new ways. If an art stopped developing, that would spell its
> end as a creative effort."

But he warned, "Only those ways hold promise for the future
that grow out of the great classical traditions".

Shostakovich was given a dignified official funeral on 14 August. Thousands filed past the open flower-covered coffin in the
Great Conservatory Hall, which had been the scene of so many of
his triumphs. The body was dressed black, the hands folded across
the chest. Selections from his music were played on the balcony.
A black-bordered picture of the composer was placed to one side
of the coffin, and the stage was covered with wreaths. Uniformed
soldiers stood shoulder to shoulder along the center aisle to form a
path for the mourners.

The burial took place at the Novodevichy Cemetery under a
heavy, rain-threatening sky. Some 250 mourners attended, held
back by barricades. There were graveside speeches by Khrennikov
and Khachaturian, among others. Following the speeches, a Red
Army band played Schubert's *Unfinished Symphony* and Chopin's
Funeral March. In the Russian custom, each family member kissed
the departed on the forehead before the coffin was closed. Maxim,
his son, wept openly. At the end, the Soviet national anthem was
played. And so, a great epoch in Soviet music came to an end.

In anticipation of Shostakovich's seventieth birthday, many books
had been planned in the composer's honor; they now became
memorial volumes. A volume edited by Grigory Shneerson had a
musical appendix of short pieces by thirteen composers* on the

---

*The countries represented are the U.S.S.R. (A. Eshpai, K. Karayev, M.
Skorik, S. Slonimsky, and B. Tishchenko), East Germany (Günter Kochan, Sieg-
fried Matthus, and Ernst Hermann Meyer), France (Daniel Lesur), Great Britain
(Alan Bush and Ronald Stevenson), Spain (Carlos Palacio), and U.S.A. (Nicolas
Slonimsky).

motto theme DSCH, Shostakovich's initials. Various official measures were taken to honor his memory: a monument was to be erected at his graveside, two scholarships at the Moscow and Leningrad conservatories were established in his name, the Leningrad Philharmonic was named "after Shostakovich", and a postage stamp bearing his image was to be released in September 1976. In 1979, a string quartet was permitted to assume the name "Shostakovich Quartet": it was an ensemble of Moscow Conservatory graduates that had been in existence for twelve years under a different name. A Collected Works Edition in forty-two volumes was initiated, and publication began in 1977. Of immediate interest was the release of a series of Shostakovich records, starting with all fifteen symphonies under Kondrashin. Four records of Shostakovich as pianist were released, as well an interesting disc entitled "Shostakovich and Oistrakh", containing the Second Violin Concerto and a phone conversation between the two (Shostakovich could not attend the première because of illness). All this testifies to the undiminished admiration and affection for the great and unforgotten master.

All the more shocking to the Soviet citizenry was the news that filtered through in 1979: a volume of alleged memoirs by Shostakovich had been smuggled to the West in 1976 by a former editor of *Sovietskaya Muzyka,* Solomon Volkov. He brought the material to the United States, where an English translation was prepared. The original title, "Testimony of Guilt", had been changed to *Testimony: The Memoirs of Dmitri Shostakovich,* "as related to and edited by Solomon Volkov". It was published in New York in the autumn of 1979, and has since been translated and published in ten languages.

The Soviet authorities made every effort to stop the publication on legal grounds; having failed, they proceeded to discredit Volkov and to brand the book as a falsification. On 14 November 1979, *Literaturnaya Gazeta* published an official repudiation. First came an open letter signed by six well-known Soviet composers who were students and friends of the late master—Bassner, Karayev, K. Khachaturian, Levitin, Tishchenko, and Vainberg— expressing their "pain and indignation" over the fabrication of the alleged memoirs. (Whether the signatories acted voluntarily cannot be ascertained; a prominent name, Sviridov, is missing.)

Next came a detailed editorial rebuttal branding Volkov as a forger and refuting point by point the "false" image of the "revered master" as reflected in *Testimony.* Appended was a brief dossier documenting the protests filed by VAAP (the Soviet copyright agency) with the American publishers. There were also printed protests by the Shostakovich family—the composer's widow, Irina, and his grown children, Galina and Maxim. In an interview with *The New York Times,*[116] Irina denied that there had been any close contact between her late husband and Volkov. Maxim refused to discuss the book until he had read it in Russian, but he said simply, "My father's relationship to the 'cult of personality' is no secret". (This is the Soviet euphemism to describe Stalin's terror.) And he added quickly, "My father was a man who was surrounded by many evils . . . He tried to express his protest against evil by his music." Eighteen months later Maxim defected to the West, taking along his only son, Mitya.

Testimony is a gripping book, in turn shocking and amusing, critical and ironic, accusing and self-revealing. Its documentary value is hotly disputed.[117] Even close friends of the late composer disagree sharply: Kondrashin, for example, was convinced of its veracity, while Rostropovich expressed reservations. The text is based on interviews, conversations, and question-and-answer sessions between Shostakovich and Volkov, jotted down by the latter and subsequently reconstructed into a continuous first-person narrative.[118] Whether every word attributed to Shostakovich in *Testimony* was actually said by him cannot be verified, but the overall impression is persuasive. Certain sections have a particular ring of authenticity—Shostakovich's discussions of Glazunov, Meyerhold, and Zoshchenko; or his chilling descriptions of his mental anguish during the Stalin terror. On the other hand, there are passages of petty criticism that seem alien to the noble and generous image we have of Shostakovich. His unflattering remarks about Prokofiev have aroused objections, but, in fact, the dislike was mutual.

Testimony contains some revealing statements about Shostakovich's music; for example, the comment about the "exultant" Finale of his Fifth Symphony;

> "I think it is clear to everyone what happens in the Fifth. The rejoicing is forced, created under threat, as in *Boris Godunov*. It's as if someone were beating you with a stick and saying, 'Your business is rejoicing . . . ', and you rise, shaky, and go marching off, muttering, 'Our business is rejoicing . . . ' What kind of apotheosis is that? You have to be a complete oaf not to hear that. Fadeyev heard it . . . that the finale of the Fifth is irreparable tragedy . . ."[119]

As editor, Volkov was not able to reconcile the occasional contradictions in the text. For example, Shostakovich is quoted as saying that he wrote his Seventh ("Leningrad") Symphony very quickly, "I wanted to create the image of our country at war . . . From the first days of the war, I . . . started work."[120] On the next page he contradicts himself, "The Seventh Symphony had been planned before the war . . . and cannot be seen as a reaction to Hitler's attack". Most people would prefer to believe the war-inspired genesis of the work. As for the Scherzo of the Tenth Symphony being a "musical portrait of Stalin" (posthumously drawn!), that sounds plausible; the music has a biting quality, with shades of the *Dies Irae* hovering in the background.

In the gigantic struggle between Shostakovich and Stalin, between creative freedom and Party-imposed limitations, the ultimate victor was Shostakovich. When he was forced into the defensive in 1936 and again in 1948, he did not argue. But through the strength of his creative genius he widened and finally broke the confines of Socialist Realism to the point where it no longer inhibited his musical creativity. By claiming him as their model, other Soviet composers succeeded in arguing for the same freedom. One can say that by outwitting Party bureaucracy, Shostakovich contributed decisively to the liberation of Soviet music from outmoded ideological fetters.

In the pages of this book we have traced the creative career of Shostakovich, from his exuberant First Symphony of 1925 to the death-haunted Fourteenth Symphony of 1969 and the enigmatic resignation of the Fifteenth Symphony of 1971. We are used to thinking of Shostakovich as primarily a symphonist, but in his last years he confided his musical thoughts to small, intimate ensembles, instrumental and vocal. The urge to write word-connected music is especially characteristic; there are the choral ballads *Loyalty,* the *Tsvetayeva* and *Michelangelo* cycles, the *Captain Lebyadkin* songs, and—last but not least—the vocal cycle of the Fourteenth Symphony, which consists of eleven settings. All this was done between 1969 and 1975. Shostakovich wanted to make the meaning of his music absolutely clear; he was tired of being misinterpreted. In his younger years, he preferred to let the music speak for itself, but late in life he changed his mind, as we read in *Testimony:*

"Yet in recent years I have become convinced that the word is more effective than music. Unfortunately, it's so. When I

combine music with words, it becomes harder to misinterpret
my intent . . . Words are some protection against absolute
idiocy, any fool will understand when there are words. There
is no total guarantee, but a text does make the music more
accessible."[121]

Indeed there is no "guarantee", as he found out when some of
his friends criticized the vocal Fourteenth Symphony, much to his
distress:

> "They read this idea in the 14th Symphony, 'Death is all-
> powerful'. They wanted the Finale to be comforting, to say
> that death is only the beginning. But it is not a beginning, it
> is the real end . . . You must look truth right in the eyes
> . . ."[122]

In the same vein he said on another occasion,

> "The entire 14th Symphony is my protest against death.
> Composers such as Mussorgsky have written calm works
> about death, works that have a soothing effect upon the lis-
> tener. My intentions were just the opposite. That is also why
> I chose the texts I used which I have known for some
> time."[123]

Shostakovich identified himself deeply with his texts. His out-
cry against oppression, imprisonment, and execution rings out.
"Stalin is gone but there are more than enough tyrants around."
Shostakovich was unforgiving.

The six poems of Marina Tsvetayeva (who committed suicide
in 1941) are highly personal utterances, introverted and intimate.
Shostakovich captured their tenderness, irony, and fortitude with
particular sensitivity. He boldly contrasted tonal and atonal
concepts—the sinuous and intense twelve-tone phrase of the first
song ("My Verses") next to the ingratiating tonal refrain of the
second ("Whence Such Tenderness"). At the end stands the poem
"To Anna Akhmatova", the poet who suffered so much insult in
the 1940's from the boorish Zhdanov. Shostakovich knew and
admired Akhmatova, and although he never set any of her words
to music, his feelings reflect Tsvetayeva's lines. When the name
"Anna Akhmatova" is pronounced, the warm, luminous chords
are more expressive than any words could be.

The *Tsvetayeva* cycle, originally written with piano accompaniment, also appeared in a version with chamber orchestra,

which adds a range of timbres and heightens the expressivity. There are also two versions (piano or orchestra accompaniment) of the *Michelangelo* cycle.

Shostakovich selected eleven texts from among the almost 200 sonnets and poems of Michelangelo, in a Russian translation by Anatol Efros. Michelangelo wrote his poetry at various stages of his life, some at the height of his career, some when he was old and disillusioned. He expressed anger and rebellion, passion and sensuality, and at the end he was death-haunted and God-seeking. One can sense Shostakovich's affinity for every mood and every phrase as he selected the poems to be set to music. How timely are some of Michelangelo's sentiments—his rage against the artistic oppression of the pope; his disgust with a world full of "infamy and crime"; his invocation of Dante, who had been cruelly exiled. Shostakovich's cycle is a work of symphonic proportions, almost forty minutes in length. The composer is fully immersed in every word of the poet, and the musical idiom is often close to Mussorgsky. It is Shostakovich's farewell to life, but it is not a sad farewell. The last poem, "Immortality", is set to childlike, naive music, disappearing in the distance, *morendo al fine* ("dying out to the end"). The words fit the mood,

> "But I am not dead, although laid in the earth,
> I live in you, whose plaints I listen to . . .
> I live with thousands of others in the hearts
> Of all those loving ones, and thus, I am not dust
> And in death, decay will not touch me . . ."[124]

Shostakovich's late instrumental works—the Fifteenth Symphony, the last quartets (Nos. 13, 14, 15), and the Viola Sonata—are more difficult to classify. In fact, we must reach further back, to the works composed in 1968—the Violin Sonata and the Twelfth String Quartet—to understand the common denominator: a free coexistence of tonal and atonal elements, of astringent dissonances and traditional harmonies, of ingratiating melodic turns and twelve-tone themes (though without "serial" connotations).

This stance of creative freedom led to an astounding expansion of Shostakovich's musical vocabulary during his last period. Shostakovich skirted atonality; but his roots with tradition kept him from making the ultimate break, and in the end he always returned to a tonal affirmation. This polarity—tonal versus atonal—was not an entirely new facet of his creative personality;

such elements can be found in his early works—his Second Symphony, First Piano Sonata, *Aphorisms,* and *The Nose.* In a conversation around 1960, Shostakovich said,

> "Much time had passed since the 1930's. Some artists grow and change. As for myself, I do not see any stylistic changes in my creative biography. I am not the same as thirty years ago. Yet, man remains the same whether he lives thirty or one hundred years. He just ages and acquires more experiences."

In the 1970's, with his physical strength ebbing, Shostakovich spoke a musical language fully his own, without concessions, without compromise. His deeply moving last String Quartet (No. 15), an elegiac work in six continuous adagio movements, conveys a mood of brooding grief. In contrast, the Viola Sonata Op. 147, his last completed work, consists of three beautifully balanced movements that sustain an atmosphere of subdued serenity. The veiled timbre of the viola is the prevailing color. The most substantial of the three movements is the final Adagio. Its theme is a mysterious reminiscence of Beethoven's "Moonlight" Sonata, fleeting but unmistakable; the dotted motive reappears in the course of the movement with varying intensity. At the center of the Finale stands a long and difficult cadenza, exploring the viola's chordal and polyphonic possibilities. Eventually the initial mood of introspection returns, and the movement ends almost inaudibly on a sustained note in the viola while the piano barely moves in the background, in the clear key of C major. It represents Shostakovich's farewell—an intense philosophical meditation, emotion without sentimentality, resignation without bitterness, a closing worthy of a great artist.

In 1974 and 1975, the Soviets paid a significant tribute to the Gnessin family, a remarkable group of Russian-Jewish musicians—four sisters and one brother. Best known were Elena (1874–1967), Yevgenia (1870–1940), and Mikhail (1883–1957). Their private music school, established in 1895, is now Moscow's second conservatory, stressing the training of future teachers. Khrennikov, who had been a pupil of the Gnessin Institute at one time, honored the memory of the Gnessin family, which symbolized "selfless dedication to music, setting a glorious example of moral purity for all musicians to follow".[125] These were meaningful words, particularly in view of the prevailing anti-Semitism of the 1970's. Tangible expression of the general esteem was a new multi-story building for the Gnessin Institute, erected next to the old structure on Vorovsky Street. It was opened in 1975, exactly eighty years after the first Gnessin school was founded. At present the Institute has 1,200 students (day-time and evening) and a distinguished faculty of 240. It continues to teach all levels of music—elementary, secondary, and college.

Mikhail Gnessin, the creative member of the family, died in 1957. He was highly respected but was essentially unfulfilled as a composer. He had hoped to create an original style by fusing his Russian education as a student of Rimsky-Korsakov with his Jewish heritage. He seemed to succeed during the 1920's, but political developments during the Stalin era forced him to retreat from his Jewish roots. He broadened his folk song research to include various nationalities, and that in turn enriched his teaching. Replying to an inquiry in 1945, Gnessin answered, "The immersion in Jewish folk music helped me to understand folk art in general, and I became more 'democratic' as an artist".[126] Khachaturian, once his student, had this to say in an essay "About My First Teacher":

> "Gnessin was one of the first to assert that a national character is one of the basic principles of musical creation . . . It is no accident that composers who subsequently occupied a significant place in the musical life of the national republics came precisely from his classroom."[127]

The list of Gnessin's students includes such distinguished names as Eshpai, Salmanov, Kliuzner, and Stepanyan, in addition to Khrennikov and Khachaturian; they all pursued his ideal of a folk-related compositional style. Gnessin must be considered one of the most influential teachers of his generation.

A final political footnote on the year 1975: On 30 July thirty-five nations assembled in Helsinki for the Conference on Security and Cooperation in Europe, and the so-called Helsinki Agreement was signed on 1 August. Having achieved its supreme goal, the legalization of Europe's post-war map, the Soviet Union was in no hurry to fulfill other parts of the agreement with regard to human rights and "free movement" of ideas and people. Complaints were exchanged in both directions, and the Soviet Union charged the Western powers with violating the Agreement and meddling in its internal affairs. Soon thereafter, Andrei Sakharov, who had been awarded the Nobel Prize for Peace in 1975, was prohibited from going to Norway to receive the Prize. When "watchdog" committees were set up within the Soviet Union to monitor compliance with the Helsinki Agreement, the Soviet authorities initiated repressive measures.

1976

The XXV Party Congress opened on 24 February 1976. It did not produce any fireworks. Chairman Brezhnev was in a mellow mood; he stated that the criticism with regard to literature and the arts, expressed at the previous Congress in 1971, had been "completely correct". He seemed satisfied with the progress,

> "Soviet writers, artists, composers, and workers in the theater, films, and television—all those whose talents and professional skills serve the people and the cause of communism—deserve our deep gratitude."[1]

This statement was greeted with applause. But no relaxation was in sight, "After all, democracy is inconceivable without discipline and a sound social order". *The New York Times* summarized the proceedings of the Congress,

> "The resistance to any new radical concepts goes beyond blind ideological faith. It also reflects the hardening conservatism of an aging Politburo. Stability has long been a Kremlin byword."[2]

Tikhon Khrennikov spoke a few days later, on 28 February.[3] He had reason to be pleased. "We musicians have attempted to respond [to the criticism] in a worthy manner." He stressed the efforts of the composers to establish closer contact with the people, that is, "with those for whom they create their works".

> "Creative meetings at factories, on collective farms, and at nearby and distant construction sites of communism have become habitual and necessary events for composers. In the last three years, the Composers' Union has organized about 20,000 such meetings . . . They are exerting a profound life-giving influence on our composers' new creative thinking . . ."

Khrennikov did not fail to emphasize anew the ideological differences between East and West,

> "The art of Socialist Realism is counterpoised to the elitist, abstract, decadent art of bourgeois society, as well as to its so-called mass musical culture, which corrupts the artistic tastes of young people and mutilates them morally."

The warning came too late: right in Leningrad and Moscow, rock music was being composed, performed, and acclaimed by vast audiences, who did not seem "mutilated" in the least by the experience. Nor was it done surreptitiously. The May issue of the journal *Yunost'* (Youth) contained a detailed report of the première, in Leningrad, of the first Soviet rock opera. *Orpheus and Euridice,* by the twenty-nine-year-old composer Alexander Zhurbin, had been presented by the "Singing Guitars". The libretto was a mixture of styles, pitting antiquity against contemporary life. The plot began where the ancient myth ended, with the death of Euridice, amid heavy-handed symbolism.

Surprisingly, the show found favor with the distinguished composer Andrei Petrov, chairman of the Leningrad Composers' Union. He saw it as a "new step" for musical drama and praised the music "as a triumph for the young composer". "The original drama, the brilliant direction, and the masterful singing and acting of the 'Singing Guitars' have been fused into a brilliant production." Other critics, however, found that the show catered to low-class public taste and offered nothing but outdated commonplace clichés.[4] The article in *Yunost'*—actually a year late, as the opera had been shown in the summer of 1975—summarized the facts.

> "Rock music, viewed fifteen years ago as devilment or charlatanry, has now become a rather stable musical tradition in our country. The 'Singing Guitars', formed in 1966, was one of our first so-called 'vocal-instrumental ensembles', the term that has come to be used for groups performing in the rock style . . . With its strong expressiveness and theatricality, rock music performed on electric guitars lends itself naturally to musical drama . . . Visually, the production presents a bright array of colors . . . it reflects young people's strong attraction to the carnivalization of life itself and a challenge to the dreary grayness of standardization that one sometimes encounters in our life . . ."[5]

A month later, the same journal published an article on the singing group "Arsenal", led by Alexander Kozlov, who pioneered so-called jazz-rock. The group consists of Kozlov's alto sax, vocalists, electric organ, electric violin, electric guitars, and a brass and percussion section. The group was founded in 1970 but rehearsed for three years before making any public appearances. Nine of the members are conservatory or institute graduates. "The music combines the rhythm of rock, the arrangements of jazz, and the compositional devices of chamber music." In the 1960's Kozlov was a leading jazz performer but was looking for new modes of self-expression. As he explained,

> "Initially, 'Arsenal' borrowed and learned from such groups as 'Blood, Sweat, and Tears' or 'Chicago'. But now our repertoire consists almost exclusively of our own music—most of which I write . . . In our arrangements and improvisations we make use of old, genuinely Russian harmonies that one can hear today only in the most remote villages."[6]

The combination of "Chicago" and the "remote Russian village" seems incongruous. It is but another sign that the much-despised "mass culture" has caught up with Russian youth.

On a more elevated plane, the Bolshoi Theatre in Moscow celebrated its 200th jubilee all through 1976. The actual date of its founding is a matter of some dispute. Not so long ago the birth year was assumed to be 1825, when a beautiful new theatre was inaugurated. But Boris Asafiev, dean of Soviet musicologists, protested the celebration of a "building". "Why do we musicologists dismiss from the history of the Bolshoi Theatre a half-century of Russian comic opera, national ballet, and Western Classics . . . ?"[7] And so, after additional studies of old documents, it was decided that the true birth of the Bolshoi occurred on 17 March 1776, when Prince Urusov was granted a monopoly by the Tsarist government to operate a theatre in Moscow. He promptly hired a clever English entrepreneur, Maddox, and performances started that year, first privately, then beginning in 1780 in the Petrovsky Theatre. There were several fires and wartime dislocations before the Bolshoi settled in its magnificent neo-classical building in 1825. Miraculously it survived the Revolution of 1917 (though Lenin viewed it as a relic of Tsarist culture). Today it is the pride of the Soviet Union and the model for dozens of regional theatres.

The artistic policy of the Bolshoi Theatre has always been conservative, in contrast to Leningrad's more adventurous Maryinsky (Kirov) Theatre. The truly progressive stages were run by Stanislavsky and Nemirovich-Danchenko in Moscow, by the Leningrad Malyi Opera, and today by Pokrovsky's Moscow Chamber Opera. Nevertheless, the list of contemporary premières at the Bolshoi is not insignificant; at present, with Pokrovsky as stage director and Grigorovich as choreographer, it has the best men available for the job. Among the composers who received "world premières" at the Bolshoi were Ivan Dzerzhinsky, Vano Muradeli, Herman Zhukovsky, Dmitri Kabalevsky, Tikhon Khrennikov, and Sergei Prokofiev, and more recently Kyril Molchanov and Rodion Shchedrin. Side by side with opera, the Bolshoi has also given a number of ballet premières.

The Soviet system of theatre administration makes the Bolshoi virtually immune to box office considerations; the house is sold out regardless of what is presented. However, this situation does not make it any easier for an unknown composer to gain entrance into the staid repertoire, which is dominated by the Russian classics and a few carefully selected Western European works of established popularity. We may mention in passing that the Bolshoi runs a repertoire of opera and ballet not only in its own house but also in the enormous Kremlin Palace Assembly Hall. Because of the unwieldy aspects of a Bolshoi première, some provincial opera houses have taken the lead in presenting premières, for example, the excellent opera in Perm, an old industrial city near the Ural Mountains.

The Leningrad composer Sergei Slonimsky received considerable exposure during 1976, mainly through second and improved versions of two of his earlier works—the opera *Virineya* and the ballet *Icarus*.

Virineya, the cornerstone of Slonimsky's success, was first staged in 1967 and was highly acclaimed. However, it disappeared from the repertoire sooner than expected. The libretto was considered dramatically weak, but a contributing factor was the appearance of a play and a film based on the same subject. In February 1976, the Leningrad Malyi Opera staged a revised version of *Virineya*, which strengthened the work as a lyric drama. The original three acts were tightened and reduced to two acts (six scenes). At the same time, certain lyric aspects were expanded so that the opera became more of a personal drama. The review in *Sovietskaya Muzyka* (which appeared almost a year later) was extremely laudatory.[8]

The ballet *Icarus* was first produced on 30 May 1971 at the Kremlin Palace Assembly Hall under the auspices of the Bolshoi Theatre. Vladimir Vasilyev, who danced the title role, was also making his debut as choreographer. Slonimsky's musical concept was complex and presented certain problems for the choreographer. The entire production was not an unqualified success, though it strengthened the composer's reputation.

For a new staging in 1976, significant changes were made in the choreography and scenario, though the same choreographer, Vasilyev, was responsible. The score was somewhat expanded: Slonimsky restored several sections previously cut, composed an epilogue, and inserted new episodes in scenes 2 and 5. He also revised the orchestration to create more contrast in sound. Musically, the most important innovation was that the entire score was pre-recorded and played electronically during the performances. One critic remarked with surprise that the music gained in brilliance and impact by this novel treatment.[9] One reason was that the volume could be adjusted to fill the immense Kremlin Palace with quadraphonic sound. The new version was acclaimed as a "triumph".

As a composer, Slonimsky is not easy to classify because he is extremely versatile and eclectic. He can produce an avant-garde score using all the latest compositional devices, yet turn out a folkish chorus in the best Mussorgsky tradition. It can be said that he achieved his present recognition without compromising his artistic convictions. Only once did he fail to get a finished work produced: in 1970–72 he composed a chamber opera based on Mikhail Bulgakov's *The Master and Margarita,* a long-suppressed novel of the 1930's.* Though he had informal assurances that the controversial libretto would be passed, he was forced to withdraw the work after a closed audition for the Composers' Union. He has kept the score in his desk drawer, waiting for a more propitious time. In March 1981, it became known that the Polish composer and conductor Penderecki had expressed interest in producing Slonimsky's opera in Warsaw. However, the present crack-down in Poland makes such a project highly unlikely.

Nineteen seventy-six, the year of the American Bicentennial, saw several important cultural exchanges. In June, a group of prominent Soviet musicians appeared with the Philadelphia

---

*A dramatization of Bulgakov's book, staged in 1977 by Yuri Lyubimov at his Moscow Taganka Theatre, was sharply criticized in *Pravda.*

Orchestra—the conductor Svetlanov, the composer-pianist Khrennikov, and the father-and-son team of Leonid and Pavel Kogan, both violinists. The first program featured two works by Khrennikov, his Second Piano Concerto and his First Violin Concerto, and Tchaikovsky's Fifth Symphony. The second opened with the Double Concerto by Bach, followed by the Beethoven Violin Concerto and Shostakovich's First Violin Concerto. On his return, Svetlanov spoke warmly about the Philadelphia Orchestra—"one of the best, if not the best, in the world"—the rhythmic clapping of the audience of 15,000, and the "marvelous" reviews in the papers.[10] Certainly, Khrennikov got the lion's share of the visit, having appeared both as composer and as soloist.

In September 1976 the entire New York Philharmonic Orchestra came for a tour of eight concerts in Moscow and Leningrad, with four different programs in each city. The conductors were Erich Leinsdorf and Thomas Schippers. The orchestra had appeared in the Soviet Union once before, in 1959, and had created a sensation under the charismatic direction of Leonard Bernstein. This time the visit was accorded little official attention, perhaps because its principal conductor, Pierre Boulez, did not participate. At any rate, *Sovietskaya Muzyka* did not publish a major report on the concerts of the New York guests; only the house bulletin of the Composers' Union gave a brief resumé. From it we learn that the programs contained works by Mozart, Beethoven, Haydn, Brahms, Mahler, Bartók, Richard Strauss, Ravel, and Stravinsky.

> "Of particular interest proved the vivid, though brief, panorama of American music (Roy Harris, Bernstein, Barber, and Copland). The orchestra's encores were Rimsky-Korsakov and Prokofiev. Pianist Emil Gilels and violinist Vladimir Spivakov appeared as soloists with the New York Philharmonic, as did the first clarinetist Stanley Drucker."[11]

To limit Russian music to encores was rather cautious, to invite two Soviet soloists a political move. The choice of American repertoire was conventional. But there can be no doubt that the Philharmonic gave its customary excellent performances and that the visit was of mutual benefit. The orchestra's newsletter reported,[12]

> " 'A fantastic experience' say our returnees . . . The Russian tour . . . was planned to be a real reach into Soviet musical life. There were open rehearsals, workshops, lectures, master

classes, and discussion meetings led by orchestra members and conductors for every level of Soviet musicians. And there were informal get-togethers as well, with many Philharmonic members finding mutual languages for conversing with their Soviet counterparts far into the night. A trunkload of gifts, including books, records, scores, and tour buttons proved useful in accelerating friendships as well as needed services."

The photographs accompanying this article showed the Composers' Union receiving a gift of scores, Philharmonic musicians John Schaeffer (double bass) and Sol Greitzer (viola) demonstrating musical matters in a Moscow classroom, Leinsdorf at an open rehearsal, and Schippers giving a speech at the American Embassy. All in all, it was a satisfying experience from every point of view.

A major musical exchange with the German Democratic Republic took place late in 1976. The East Germans traveled to twenty-six Soviet cities, including Moscow, Leningrad, Kiev, Alma-Ata, Yaroslavl, and Ulyanovsk (Lenin's birthplace). The Berlin Komische Oper brought Felsenstein's productions of *Figaro* and Kodály's *Háry János*. The Berlin Symphony played music by East German composers Ernst Hermann Meyer and Fritz Geissler as well as two symphonies by Shostakovich (Nos. 8 and 10) and various German classics. In addition, a delegation of East German composers and musicologists came to Moscow to meet with their Soviet counterparts. The "creative ties between musicians of the GDR and the USSR" and the "unity of ideological positions" were emphasized.[13] In fact, the East Germans have a set-up patterned after the Composers' Union, with composers and musicologist-critics united in the same organization.

The Soviet visit was called "Days of Soviet Musical Culture in the GDR", and the East Germans were smothered by the bearlike embrace. No fewer than 200 concerts were given; compositions by fifty-five Russian and Soviet composers were played. The older Soviet composers were represented by Prokofiev, Shostakovich, Khachaturian, Miaskovsky, Khrennikov, Kabalevsky, and A. G. Novikov; the younger ones by Shchedrin, Eshpai, Taktakishvili, Tishchenko, Slonimsky, Shnitke, Pyart, and Denisov. The second group includes a surprising number of non-conformist composers, perhaps in response to the more sophisticated German taste in music.

The geography of the visit included large and small cities. Berlin gave the Leningrad Philharmonic under Yevgeni Mravinsky a rousing welcome. Khrennikov offered a program of his own music. Soviet guest artists were sent into the smaller towns of Thuringia. The East German journal *Musik und Gesellschaft* dedicated a great deal of space to these massive visits.[14]

Soviet successes abroad were not limited to the Socialist countries. Khachaturian was much in demand as guest conductor of his own works, especially during his seventieth birthday year, when he appeared in West Germany, France, and England. The West German city of Saarbrücken arranged a festival of Soviet Georgian music; Khrennikov appeared in Italy; Kabalevsky's *Requiem* was given in Louvain; Shchedrin's *Anna Karenina* was shown in the West. The number of Shostakovich performances in Europe and America in two months during the spring of 1975 was truly astounding. Under the heading "Soviet Musicians on the Stages of the World", the journal *Sovietskaya Muzyka* devoted six pages to listing performances of Soviet music abroad, as well as guest appearances of Soviet virtuosos and composers.[15] Soviet instrumentalists have always been welcome guests in the West, but in recent years Soviet vocalists and conductors have also been acclaimed. With so much talent, the Soviet Union does not seem to suffer too much from the drain of emigrés and defectors in the arts.

Toward the end of 1976, the Party's Central Committee issued a new directive, *Working with Creative Youth*,[16] which was an outgrowth of the XXV Party Congress. Obviously the Politburo (overage though it was) realized that the creative unions in the arts were dominated by an equally overage entrenched bureaucracy while a young talented generation was kept waiting at the gates.

The wording of the directive was repetitive but emphatic. It stated that there still were serious drawbacks in various institutions teaching the arts. More professional mastery, more attention to the students' Marxist-Leninist views, and more stress on absorbing Soviet and world culture were necessary. Also needed were highly skilled pedagogues in science and culture who could stimulate young people to social activism and shape their distinctive creative personalities. The physical facilities of educational institutions needed improvement. Young workers in the arts were to be encouraged to participate in editorial boards, arts councils, and exhibition committees; more attention was to be paid to recent graduates who were not yet members of a professional union. It was essential that young creative intelligentsia be drawn into the work of the creative unions. The procedure of admitting them to the ranks of the Party had to be improved. Authoritative masters in literature and the arts were to be enlisted to work with young people. Theory seminars, creative conferences, and discussions had to be expanded. Instructions were issued to review the regulations of admission to educational arts institutions on secondary and college levels, and to establish instructional theatres, opera studios, exhibition halls, and art studios. The paper directed that facilities for art exhibits be expanded, artists' studios be constructed in the major cities, and the best works of young writers, composers, and artists be published (in reproductions). It was decided to resume publication of the journals *Young Artist* and *Literary Studies*.

The directive included, among other measures, an increase in annual appropriations for commissioning and acquiring works by young artists, composers, and dramatists. Gold and silver medals were to be awarded to deserving graduates of institutions of higher learning in the arts.

This directive had the force of law. Suddenly there was frantic scurrying about by the old guard: *youth* became the magic word. Young musicologists, critics, and composers were searched out. A debate arose—who is young? under thirty? Never mind, just get rid of the moss-covered critics. *Sovietskaya Muzyka* opened its pages to recent graduates, attaching capsule biographies of those authors who were totally unknown. The Composers' Union redoubled its efforts, through regional auditions and trial concerts, to discover young composers and perform their works. The drive to expand was so successful that by 1979 fully one-fourth of the membership of the Composers' Union consisted of recently admitted members. Years of complaints by neglected composers could not achieve what this single directive accomplished—to open the doors to the young generation. One may ask why it took decades to discover the calcification and cliquishness in the Composers' Union, particularly in the Directorate.

In surveying the vast panorama of Soviet music, one can see that a major effort has been made to raise the standards throughout the land, concentrating on the more distant regions in the interior and the Far East. At a recently opened cultural institute in Khabarovsk, in northeastern Siberia, a competent body of performers is being trained. The Arts Institute at Vladivostok, with its Territorial Orchestra, has shown much improvement. The *Information Bulletin* of the Composers' Union has been filled with reports of activities in the regional branches. Countrywide preparations were made for a celebration of the sixtieth anniversary of the October Revolution, to be observed in 1977.

There were also many exchange visits between various republics and regions—the Transcaucasian Festival in Baku (comprising Armenia, Georgia, and Azerbaijan), Russian composers in Georgia, Armenian composers in the Ukraine, Ukrainian composers in Byelorussia, and so forth.

And in the Ukraine, a noticeable rapprochement between old-line composers and the Kiev group of non-conformists took place in 1975 and 1976. There had been an estrangement within the Ukrainian Composers' Union in 1967.* Now, under the impact of the XXV Congress, efforts were made to heal the breach. In 1975, a Kiev branch of the Ukrainian Composers' Union was established under active cooperation of the disaffected composers. Late in 1976, the First Plenum of the Kiev branch took place, with active participation by Party and government representatives, composers, and the public. The motto was the "Creative Youth" resolution of the Party. It was announced that the Kiev group had a membership of eighty composers and forty-three musicologists, making it the largest chapter in the Ukraine. The return to active participation of Leonid Grabovsky, Valentin Silvestrov, and Vitali Godziatsky was noted with satisfaction. Grabovsky (whose name is spelled "Hrabovsky" by nationalist Ukrainians) was once the great hope of Ukrainian music. His contribution to the Plenum was a *Symphonic Legend* based on one of his film scores, a Suite rather than a Symphony, music of "cool refinement" interlaced with folkish themes of Ukrainian roots. The score was described as a new step in his evolution as a composer (perhaps not so new if one remembers that he first came to attention in 1962 with his *Four Ukrainian Songs***). A string quartet by Silvestrov received warm approval—a remarkable fact since he is known for his experimental idiom. Godziatsky's contribution was found encouraging, especially since he had not been heard of as a composer for quite some time.

All in all, the compositions played at the Kiev Plenum embraced a wide range of musical idioms and proved that the Ukrainian compositional school was reinvigorated and purposeful.

The State Prizes for 1976 were awarded to five composers: Andrei Eshpai for the cantata *Lenin Is with Us,* Karen Khachaturian for the children's ballet *Cippolino,* Andrei Petrov for the opera *Peter I,* Kaly Moldobasanov (Kirghizia) for the ballet-oratorio *The Mother's Field,* and Giya Kancheli for his *Michelangelo* Symphony.

Petrov (b. 1930) is the chairman of the Leningrad Composers' Union. His opera *Peter I* was composed in 1972–75 and received

*See pp. 452–54.
**See p. 348.

its première at the Kirov Theatre in Leningrad in 1975. The conductor was Yuri Temirkanov. It is a traditional score of monumental proportions; the action takes place in the years 1689 to 1703 and centers on the heroic figure of Peter the Great. There are three acts, each subdivided into several "frescoes". The tenth and last fresco depicts the victorious battle against the Swedes; the opera ends with a hymn to Russia and to the Russian army. There is also an oratorio-like version for concert performances. As historical drama it is undoubtedly effective but it does not break new ground.[17]

Kancheli (b. 1935) was the youngest recipient to be awarded the State Prize in 1976. The *Michelangelo* Symphony, his Fourth, was performed for the first time by the Georgian Philharmonic in Tbilisi on 29 May 1975. The first American performance, in Philadelphia in 1978, also under the baton of Temirkanov, aroused much interest, particularly since the name of the composer was virtually unknown outside his homeland. Though Georgian nationalism shaped Kancheli's early style, there is hardly a trace of it in his Fourth Symphony. The single-movement work (twenty-three minutes in length) is prevailingly slow and meditative, punctuated by sudden, sharp dynamic contrasts. At times, several layers of sound are superimposed: high decibels in the foreground against a continuing pensive mood in the background. Bells and celesta are used effectively, perhaps indicating the influence of Shostakovich, but otherwise the work is free of visible models or folkloristic ties. It is a colorful piece in a freely dissonant idiom, showing an excellent command of orchestral techniques.*[18]

We have seen repeatedly how sensitive the Soviets are to criticism of anything Russian or Soviet, particularly from a foreigner. Indignation runs high—"How dare they?"—and printed recriminations appear, full of sarcasm and injured pride. We have seen how Copland was taken to task. Another case is that of the English author and musicologist David Brown, whose biography *Mikhail Glinka* (published in 1974) was taken as a case of *lèse majesté*. Even granted the Russians' adulation of Glinka, the exaggerated rebuff in *Sovietskaya Muzyka* seems puerile.[19] The critic,

---

*Kancheli's Sixth Symphony received its successful première in October 1981 at the All-Union Festival of Soviet Music in Tbilisi, conducted by Dzanshug Kakhides. Shortly thereafter, a repeat performance took place in Leipzig at the inaugural concert of the New Gewandhaus Hall under Kurt Masur. It was praised for its "epic diction, broad display of sound, and emotional intensity" (*Musik und Gesellschaft*, January 1982, pp. 41–42).

hiding behind the pseudonym "Journalist", managed to insult not only Brown (whose book is very objective) but also Brown's teacher, the eminent Gerald Abraham. "Journalist" claimed that Abraham had spent a lifetime belittling Glinka, the founding genius of Russian music. The anonymous reviewer went on,

> "There is that strange tendency in English musicology: the enthusiasm of Rosa Newmarch (not even mentioned in Brown's bibliography) has been stifled by the efforts of Calvocoressi, Abraham, and now Brown."

Congratulations to Brown: he is certainly in good company. As for Newmarch, her "enthusiasm" appears somewhat dated today. The whole incident had further implications: Abraham took offence and cancelled an impending visit to Moscow, though several Soviet musicologists expressed regrets.

The Soviet bureaucrats are not only petty but also provincial. Glinka's masterpiece *A Life for the Tsar* was not given for twenty years until the libretto was rewritten with a different slant and a new title. For decades the *Russian Easter Overture* by Rimsky-Korsakov was banished for its religious connotations. The most amazing and barefaced falsification can be found on a *Melodiya* recording* of the *Overture 1812* by Tchaikovsky, conducted by Svetlanov in 1974. The original score ends with the well-known quotation of the tsarist hymn. On this particular recording, the hymn is excised and replaced by a Russian tune that happens to fit the harmonic scheme. When I expressed my amazement, I was told that this version was "not for export", only for the "domestic market". How incredible that after six decades the mighty Soviet State was still afraid of the tsarist hymn! And how incredible that an artist of Svetlanov's stature would lend his name to such a blatant fraud!

Under the heading "The Legacy of Prokofiev", *Sovietskaya Muzyka* published additional biographical excerpts that had not

---

Melodiya C10–05904(a). USSR Academic Symphony Orchestra.

been included in his autobiography (published in 1973 in Russian as edited by M. Kozlova[20] and in an English translation entitled *Prokofiev by Prokofiev* in 1979[21]). Prokofiev actually wrote two autobiographies; they overlap but neither is complete. One leads up to the year 1936, when he definitely resettled in Moscow. It has been in print in Russian and English since the late 1950's as part of a volume of Prokofiev materials edited by S. Shlifstein.[22] The other (edited by Kozlova) is more detailed but breaks off much earlier, in 1909, when the eighteen-year-old Prokofiev left the Conservatory. Parts of it were dictated to Mira Mendelson, his second wife, during the 1940's. Included in this volume is Prokofiev's description of his budding friendship with Miaskovsky, who was ten years his senior—a friendship that was to last a lifetime. Those who wish to pursue this subject will find absorbing material in the *Correspondence between Prokofiev and Miaskovsky*, published in Moscow in 1977.[23] It is a volume of prime importance, though allegedly it is somewhat expurgated where political or artistic judgments are concerned, particularly with regard to Shostakovich, for whom Prokofiev had limited esteem. (The dislike was mutual, as we can see in Shostakovich's *Testimony*.)

Delays in first performances are not always easy to explain. We know of course that Shostakovich withheld certain works from performance (the First Violin Concerto, the Jewish song cycle, the Fourth String Quartet) because he felt that the musico-political climate of the late 1940's was not auspicious for this type of composition. But how does one explain the delay in the Moscow première of Shchedrin's *The Bells* (Zvony)? The work was commissioned for the centenary of the New York Philharmonic and was first conducted by Leonard Bernstein in 1968.[*] But the Moscow première did not take place until eight years later, at an all-Shchedrin concert in 1976 conducted by Temirkanov.[24] Perhaps it was thought that the Moscow public needed time to become attuned to Shchedrin's more advanced idiom. Even longer was the delay in the première of Tishchenko's choral symphony *Marina*, based on five poems by Marina Tsvetayeva. It was composed in 1962–65 but not performed until 1976 in Leningrad.[25] Possibly the choice of texts was the cause of the delay. It is interesting to note that in 1974 Shostakovich used a number of poems by Tsvetayeva for a song cycle which undoubtedly helped her posthumous rehabilitation.

[*]See pp. 450–51.

"Alban Berg is one of the most striking and original personalities in the music of the twentieth century." This is the opening sentence of Shchedrin's preface to *The Musical Theatre of Alban Berg* by Mikhail Tarakanov, published in Moscow in 1976. It is said that Shchedrin's recommendation was helpful in getting the book published. Indeed, in the eight-page preface Shchedrin reveals his liberal attitude toward modern Western music in general. Tarakanov's book—a 558-page volume in large format with many musical examples—deals exclusively with *Wozzeck* and *Lulu*. It is an analysis in depth with very little reference to Berg's life or personal experiences. At the time Tarakanov had no access to the unpublished parts of the third act of *Lulu*—"such opportunities are not offered to a Russian scholar", he remarked with some resentment. The text is difficult reading for the unprepared Russian, though *Wozzeck* had been performed in Leningrad in 1926. True, Berg is far more acceptable to Soviet esthetics than either Schoenberg or Webern; his music is actually played in the Soviet Union, though rarely. One occasionally hears the Violin Concerto, the *Lyric Suite,* and other chamber music; and excerpts from his operas were given on Soviet radio as part of a cycle called "Panorama of Twentieth-Century Opera". As Shchedrin said, "The interest in Berg's oeuvre is active, and his music has proven to be viable".* The fact that Tarakanov's book was published in an edition of 4,000 copies indicates a broadening of musical acceptance in the Soviet Union. *Sovietskaya Muzyka* printed a favorable review of the book in March 1977.

Random notes for the year 1976: The violinist Julian Sitkovetsky was remembered; he would have been fifty had he lived. He died in 1958 at the age of thirty-two. His short career was most promising: he was a prize winner in the Wieniawski Competition in 1952 and in the Queen Elisabeth Contest in 1955. He was married to the pianist Bella Davidovich. Their son Dimitri emigrated to America in the 1970's to study the violin at the Juilliard School. In 1978, he was the first winner of the new Fritz Kreisler Competition in Vienna; he now lives in the West, as does his mother, who is a successful concert artist.

"There is no monument over Babyi Yar" are the opening words of Yevtushenko's famous poem, used by Shostakovich for his Thirteenth Symphony. On 23 June 1976, *Pravda* reported that a "magnificent monument" had been erected, with the inscription

---

*But Rozhdestvensky's suggestion for a staged revival of *Wozzeck,* made in 1971, was ignored (see p. 511).

Here in 1941–42 German fascist invaders executed over 100,000 citizens of the city of Kiev and prisoners of war. There was not a word about the fact that the overwhelming majority of those executed were Jews, whom the Nazis had vowed to exterminate. The poem by Yevtushenko speaks only of Jewish victims; for this reason in 1962 Khrushchev had forbidden further performances of the Thirteenth Symphony until the text had been altered. But the Yevtushenko poem remains in print unchanged; only the words in Shostakovich's score have been "adjusted".*

Toward the end of 1976, two personalities in the arts left the Soviet Union—the dissident writer Vladimir Bukovsky, and the orchestra conductor Rudolf Barshai.

On 18 December Bukovsky was formally "expelled" from the Soviet Union after having spent twelve of his thirty-five years in Soviet prisons and mental hospitals. The official announcement in *Izvestia* on 26 December read, "The criminal Bukovsky has been expelled from our country . . . He is awaited in Chile." The article does not reveal that Bukovsky was actually exchanged for a prominent Chilean communist. Bukovsky said about his release,

> "We had conducted a desperate war against this regime of utter scum. We were a handful of unarmed men facing a mighty state in possession of the most monstrous machinery of oppression in the entire world. And we had won."[26]

On 21 December Rostropovich declared that dozens of other "Bukovskys" in the U.S.S.R. should be set free, and he repeated his complaints against Soviet regimentation of art and artists.

On the same day that Rostropovich released his statement Barshai was given an exit visa for Israel, for which he had applied in August. For some time before making the application, he had not been permitted to accompany his Moscow Chamber Orchestra on foreign tours, while Goskontsert invented flimsy pretexts to cover his cancellations. Interviewed in London on 28 January 1977, Barshai bitterly denounced the machinations of Goskontsert: a Soviet artist was not sure until the last minute whether he would be permitted to fulfill foreign engagements nor did he have any choice where he was sent. "I am not a politician, I am a musician", Barshai said, as had so many other emigré artists.[27] He conducted his last concert with the Moscow Chamber Orchestra

*See p. 368.

at the Great Conservatory Hall on 3 October 1976, though it was known then that he planned to leave. His successor is the violinist Igor Bezrodnyi. After his emigration, Barshai became chief conductor of the Israel Chamber Orchestra; at present he has a post in West Germany.

1977

As a doctrine, Socialist Realism seems inviolate and indestructible. It is reaffirmed periodically as the artistic law of the land. In music, however, an increasing number of composers seemed to disregard its principles during the 1970's, and they were doing it with impunity. The Party bureaucrats called for stricter application of criticism but the voices of the critics were a cry in the wilderness. The veteran musicologist, Boris Yarustovsky admitted that modernism was winning the battle:[28]

> "We are already familiar with a good many specific examples of certain (not mechanical!) devices of so-called free serial technique, sonorities, the deformation of genres and associative imagery in the works of R. Shchedrin and S. Slonimsky and even in the last works of Shostakovich and works of certain other composers."

Among the "certain other composers" are distinguished names like Karen Khachaturian and Tishchenko, Karayev and Kancheli, not to mention the "established" avant-garde like Denisov and Shnitke or several Baltic composers. The esteemed Grigori Shneerson continued his attempts to discredit the avant-garde, but he repeated himself and no one was frightened:

> "Avant-gardism is not so much a complex of artistic means as a false idea of art, a distorted snobbish attitude toward reality. Profiting by some material support from powerful quarters, this movement serves to propagate irrationalism, deflecting the attention of the artists from the great socio-ethical problem of our time."[29]

In general, literary critics discuss Socialist Realism with more depth than do musicologists. The academician D. Markov wrote in an article entitled "Socialist Realism as an Open Doctrine":[30]

> "Revisionist theoreticians . . . have come out against the esthetic narrowness of Socialist Realism and argued for

broadening its platform. The problem, however, is that they see this broadening lying in a convergence of Socialist Realism and Modernism. They try to blur and distort the ideological and philosophical foundation of Socialist Realism . . ."

Markov obviously believed that Socialist Realism and Modernism are incompatible. However, he admitted past errors, for example, the assumption that "non-realistic equals modernistic". This led to a summary dismissal, in Soviet Russia, of poets who are now valued highly (Alexander Blok, Verlaine, Baudelaire). These thoughts on literature can be applied to music. For example, the early denigration of French musical Impressionism has been reversed, and certain aspects of Expressionism have been recognized as valid influences.

In August, *Sovietskaya Muzyka* picked up the topic and published an article by the anonymous "Journalist" entitled "On a Few Aspects of Socialist Realism". It complained that the problems of Socialist Realism had not been investigated in depth by musicological research. In the 1970's, only two books of moderate size had appeared on that subject—*Theory of Realism and Problems of Musical Esthetics* (Leningrad, 1973) by A. Farbshtein, and *A Few Traits of Socialist Realism in Soviet Music* (Moscow, 1971) by In. Popov. According to "Journalist", neither offered any new viewpoints. A few articles in *Muzyka i Sovremennost* and other publications were useful, he said, but the entire subject needed further discussion. Paraphrasing Lenin, the author stated that Socialist Realism was not merely an aspect but the *essence* of the art of our time.

One unsolved problem was how to "prove" the existence of Socialist Realism in non-programmatic instrumental music? In fact, the question was under discussion since the 1930's, when the doctrine was first proclaimed. "Journalist" had no easy answer but he recommended the study of the intonational theories of Boris Asafiev.[31]

One suspects that the revival of theoretical discussions centred on Socialist Realism was designed to counteract the growing restlessness among Soviet composers who were opposed to ideological dictates. Shostakovich had shown the way, and the younger generation was reaching out for the same freedom.

As a collective body, however, the Composers' Union pursued an orthodox Party line, as was to be expected. "The ideas of the

Party give us wings", proclaimed an editorial in *Sovietskaya Muzyka*.[32] The praise bestowed by the XXV Party Congress on the creative intelligentsia continued to be a source of deep satisfaction. Musicians received the highest awards of the land—Elena Obraztsova won the Lenin Prize, Emil Gilels was named "Hero of Socialist Labor", and five composers had received the 1976 State Prizes.* In gratitude, the Composers' Union pledged to work actively on the "Theory and Methodology of Music of Socialist Realism" as well as the ideological and methodological functions of musicology as a social science. The principles of Marxist theory were to be followed and stressed. Thus, the year 1977 stood— musically speaking—under the sign of implementation of the resolutions of the XXV Party Congress. The pages of *Sovietskaya Muzyka* were filled with topical articles and reports, for example, "Musicology as a Social Humanitarian Science"[33] or "Ethical Education and Music".[34] They all dealt with the heightened role assigned to literature and the arts by the Party Congress in the ethical (i.e., communist) education of the people, particularly the working population. *Sovietskaya Muzyka* published photos of composers performing for factory workers during lunch breaks, in improvised settings. It was a missionary zeal reminiscent of the early years of the Revolution, when artists took their art "to the people". Nor were the contributions of composers limited to music; they spoke in support of social objectives, fulfilling their civic obligations. Two such pronouncements were published in *Sovietskaya Muzyka*—"The Great October Opened New Horizons" by Shchedrin, and "To Extol the Ideals of Communism" by Petrov.[35]

Undoubtedly, the motivation for all this political fervor was the approaching sixtieth anniversary of the October Revolution of 1917. The closer the date of the actual celebration the more ardent became the pronouncements. Under the headline "Dedication to Revolution" composers of various Soviet nationalities and age groups declared their loyalty and promised great deeds.

On 19 October 1977 a solemn assembly of all the creative unions took place at the Kremlin Palace. The participants included famous writers, theatre and film workers, composers, painters, sculptors, architects, and editors of newspapers and journals. The topic was "On the Achievements of Literature and the Arts in Sixty Years". Khrennikov spoke on behalf of music.[36] Taking his cue from a statement by Lenin, that "Our workers and peasants

*See p. 592.

deserve something better than mere spectacles: they have earned the right to truly great art", he expounded,

> "For the first time in history the artist has a full-fledged place in society, an honorable and responsible place . . . Nowhere in the world have composers and artists such a wide field to display their talents, such a grateful and sensitive audience, and finally such conditions for work . . . Now we enjoy the harvest of the Leninist Cultural Revolution."

Khrennikov referred with scorn to the new fashion abroad of meddling in internal Soviet affairs. He proclaimed that "those who truly know Soviet reality know that in our land our creative spirit is set free. New creative talents of all nationalities grow and flourish."

He mentioned with pride the recent winner of the Karajan conducting competition, Valery Gergiyev from Caucasia, and the diploma recipient T. Abdrashev from Central Asia—"shining examples of the success achieved within a historically brief period of time by the various peoples of our land". And he added disdainfully, "This is exactly that atmosphere of genuine freedom, that 'creative oxygen', that is lacking for some time in bourgeois art, which suffocates in the grip of business".

Here we have again the simplistic juxtaposition of capitalism "interfering" with art while Marxism does not; again the barefaced lie about "creative freedom" in the Soviet Union while works of art are being destroyed, books confiscated, manuscripts printed underground, and composers intimidated. At least Brezhnev had the honesty to admit that mistakes had been made (though he spoke only of the distant past):[37]

> "We know, comrades, that some years after the adoption of the current constitution [of 1936] were darkened by illegal repressions, violations of the principles of socialist democracy, Leninist norms of Party and state life. This was done in contravention of the constitutional provisions. The Party has resolutely condemned this practice and it should never be repeated."

Moscow was host to the International Book-Fair, which opened on 6 September 1977 "to expressions of delight from Russian booklovers and complaints of censorship from some American and British exhibitors".[38] No books were for sale. Fifteen hundred publishers from sixty-three countries were represented. A number of English-language books with politically sensitive titles were seized by the censors, and some publishers were denied visas. But three Israeli publishers reported no particular problems with customs, and one British publisher asserted that there was less censorship in Moscow than at the Warsaw Book-Fair. Announcements of emigré literature were confiscated. An American publisher specializing in Russian-language literature reported that thirty display copies were spirited away by booklovers in the first few days. In view of the fact that the Russian version of *Dr. Zhivago* was published in Michigan but not in Moscow, the eagerness of the Russians is easily explained. But one must not exaggerate the intellectual curiosity of the hosts: the biggest crowds of young Russians could be found around the books on sports.

Earlier in the year, the Soviet poet Bella Akhmadulina visited the United States. On 18 May 1977 she was made an honorary member of the American Academy and Institute of Arts and Letters. Upon her arrival she said,

> "I don't believe I'm here . . . I've always had a passion for America, for the freshness of life, for the youth of the people, for this grandiose space where you can exercise your soul."[39]

Yevgeni Yevtushenko, her former husband, once said of her, "Akhmadulina is one of the few women who write poems, and who possess the full right to be called a poet and not a poetess".

The Leningrad Symphony Orchestra under Yuri Temirkanov visited the United States in the spring of 1977 and gave two concerts at New York's Carnegie Hall on 4 and 5 March.[40] The conductor was at pains to explain the difference between his orchestra and the more famous Leningrad Philharmonic under Yevgeni Mravinsky. Before the 1950's, the Leningrad Symphony was known as the Radio Orchestra, serving the Leningrad region. As such, it remained in besieged Leningrad during the cruel 900 days of Nazi encirclement and blockade, though it had been decimated by hunger and death. The Radio Orchestra (then under Karl Eliasberg) continued to give concerts and maintain the morale of the population. It was for this orchestra that Shostakovich conceived the heroic "Leningrad" Symphony, which was played in that besieged city on 9 August 1942, with extra players drawn from front-line soldiers. With considerable pride, Temirkanov and his orchestra performed "their" *Leningrad* Symphony at Carnegie Hall. Two young Soviet soloists appeared on the programs—the violinist Victor Tretyakov, who was already known in New York, and the pianist Eliso Virsaladze, a lovely artist, who chose to play the Schumann Concerto. Temirkanov was no stranger to America: he had conducted the visiting Moscow Philharmonic in 1970. He was born in the Caucasus and educated in Leningrad. He won first prize in a Soviet conducting competition in 1968, at the age of twenty-nine. His home base is Leningrad, where he also conducts at the Kirov Opera. He is obviously interested in contemporary Soviet music; he conducted the première of Kancheli's Fourth Symphony (*Michelangelo*)* and had a tremendous success with Shchedrin's complex opera *Dead Souls* at the Bolshoi in Moscow.

The world première of *Dead Souls* opened the 1977 autumn season in a most auspicious way. "The Bolshoi Theatre has won a glorious triumph", wrote Kondrashin, conductor-turned-critic, in his review in *Literaturnaya Gazeta* (16 November 1977).[41] The composer himself had performed the difficult task of writing the libretto, after Gogol's masterpiece. According to Kondrashin, "as far as plot is concerned, *Dead Souls* has no conclusion and it lacks the love interest traditional for opera . . . Gogol's narrative has no positive characters . . . The true positive hero is The People."

The libretto was conceived on two levels and the stage was subdivided: the upper part showed the "boundless expanse" of Russia while the lower one provided the setting for the appearance and disappearance of grotesque characters. The action switches back and forth between the two levels; plot episodes alternate with Russian songs played by the orchestra. The songs are based on folk texts, yet the music is freely composed without quotations. The violins in the orchestra pit are replaced by a chorus which serves as commentator, accompanying the action and emphasizing the psychological accents.

Shchedrin's approach to Gogol's material was described as "complex and interesting"; it required a "sophisticated musical and scenic realization", which was handled superbly by conductor Temirkanov and stage director Pokrovsky.

Kondrashin commented that "Shchedrin's musical language utilizes every means in the arsenal of the contemporary composer, but is based on the undying traditions of Mussorgsky". That

*See p. 593.

influence might have been subconscious, for the score reveals a thoroughly modern melodic line, often jagged and atonal, employing certain twelve-tone procedures. Shchedrin uses traditional forms and all kinds of ensembles, from duets to massed choral scenes; yet the characters retain their individuality despite the multi-level action. Each protagonist is associated with a specific instrumental timbre: only Chirikov, the main character, has no motive of his own but adapts himself to whomever he talks with, expressing himself in a "florid" way (as Gogol envisaged him).

The critic Tarakanov[42] described Shchedrin's vocal idiom as part recitative, part sung—a vocal melody in the modern sense of the word, initiated by Prokofiev, Stravinsky, and Berg. There is also buffoonish quick-talk, especially in the ensembles. The orchestra is often used as "prompter", beginning a phrase which is continued by a voice. During the pantomime scenes (one in each of the three acts) the orchestra assumes particular importance.

Tarakanov, who analyzed the opera in depth, appeared satisfied with the scenic concept of Shchedrin's libretto, which preserves Gogol's original book though it redistributes the material. But did Shchedrin preserve Gogol's original *meaning?* On this point, the critic Dora Romadinova registered a strong *no.*[43] She contended that Gogol's message of "alarm" and "pain" over the suffering of the Russian people had been diluted by Shchedrin by a twist of optimism. The libretto avoided "this miserable tragic question about Russia's fate" and replaced it with a positive image,

> "the image that the Russian people will decide in the very near future all the problems of the country which the government in Gogol's time didn't want, or was unable to decide . . . This idea is expressed very clearly in the score and was underlined in the première at the Bolshoi."

Romadinova assumed that it was

> "a difficult compromise for Shchedrin which brought him to substitute the main idea of Gogol's work . . . [but] he was obligated . . . he had to pay a price for recognition."

This was a harsh judgment. The implication was that Shchedrin had yielded to pressure in shaping the libretto with an ideological twist. Romadinova spoke as a Russian who cherished the heritage of her literature; at the same time her admiration for Shchedrin as *composer* was undiminished—an awkward situation.

In all fairness to Shchedrin, his reinterpretation of Gogol may have been sincere. Gogol left *Dead Souls* unfinished; he burned the second half in a fit of madness. Can one blame Shchedrin for taking (in Kondrashin's words) "his own modern approach"? He gave a contemporary answer to Gogol's anguished question, posed almost 150 years earlier. What prompted Shchedrin to do so, no one can tell.

Whatever the literary objections, it must be said that the production of *Dead Souls* was a triumph. Scenically and musically, there was "complete immersion" in the new style of contemporary opera, with all its sophistication. "The viewer cannot fail to share the enthusiasm of all the performers", concluded Kondrashin.

Musical education is an area of particular accomplishment and considerable pride in the Soviet Union. Under the title "Sixty Years of Musical Education" *Sovietskaya Muzyka*[44] published a summary of past achievements written by L. Ilyina. She also provided some updated statistics with regard to music schools, which showed a normal growth:*

	as of 1 September 1977	as of 1973
Music institutions of higher learning (VUZ)	32	27
Secondary specialized music schools	over 250	238
Children's music schools	ca. 6000	4743

In accordance with the recent party directive "Working with Creative Youth", Ilyina outlined certain improvements in admission procedures to the VUZ, for example, to exempt young people with high marks (4.5, or A−) from a few onerous examinations. Plans had been made to activate youth, to lead them to independent work, to organize more seminars, to demand more papers and more course work. In the past, according to Ilyina, the emphasis in teaching music history had been on the lecture method. But it was no longer acceptable to learn mere facts; the student had to read the source literature and learn how to analyze historic events. Lecturing, she wrote, is too dry, too detached from life.

The intentions were sound but very belated. Such curricular improvements were long overdue. In fact, recommendations for

*Compare earlier statistics on pp. 379–80, 395–96, and 490.

curriculum changes had been made periodically, but with little impact. This time, the Party criticism seemed to have shaken up the establishment.

Ilyina pointed to the tradition of artist-teachers in the Soviet conservatories. On the faculties of the vocal departments were such outstanding performers as Irina Arkhipova, Yevgeni Nesterenko, Elena Obraztsova, and Tamara Milashkina. Student orchestras were conducted by Kondrashin and Rozhdestvensky. While Sviatoslav Richter did not teach piano, he organized student ensembles and gave concerts with them; in this manner he fulfilled his "civic duties".

1978

"Problems of the Musical Theatre" was to be the topic for discussion during the early part of 1978. In preparation for a full-scale debate in May by the Directorate of the Composers' Union, *Sovietskaya Muzyka* published a position paper in its January issue, listing twelve points that needed improvement. None of the problems were particularly new: some had been brought up during the Zhdanov controversy, in 1948; others had been mentioned at the last symposium on musical theatre, in 1965. The following were some of the most important issues:

Composers had weak contacts with literary people and so were having difficulties obtaining librettos. [This was an old problem!]

Stage directors specializing in opera had weak qualifications, and actor-singers were insufficiently prepared to deal with modern repertoire.

The theatres' policy on repertoire was limited. The press lacked interest, and too many superficial laudatory reviews were being printed.

The distribution of out-of-town visits by the theatres was poorly planned.

Opera was poorly promoted on television and radio. A revival of opera in concert form was needed.

Most important: The scope of contemporary opera was too narrow. It was too naive, and the dramatic conflicts were anemic. From the compositional point of view, there was too much preoccupation with recitatives. [This controversy went back to the late 1930's.]

There was still a lack of strong personalities among conductors. [The exceptions listed were Temirkanov, Svetlanov, and Rozhdestvensky.*]

The distribution of operatic masterworks was still spotty. For example, among works by Prokofiev, *Semyon Kotko* had been given in three theatres (in Moscow, Odessa, and Perm), *War and Peace* in two (in Moscow and Leningrad), *Story of a Real Man* in two (Leningrad and Tallinn), *The Duenna* in two (in Leningrad and Moscow), and *The Gambler* in only one (in Moscow). This could not be called "distribution", the editorial exclaimed: four productions in Moscow, three in Leningrad, and only three in the provinces! (Silence surrounds the fact that *The Flaming Angel* has never been given in the Soviet Union.)

In 1965 a Soviet musician had complained: why is it that America can see our best opera and ballet companies every year while Kazakhstan has never seen any of our major companies? Bad planning? No, economics. The American tour brings hard dollars while the Kazakh tour costs soft rubles. While Khrennikov belittles "music as business", Goskontsert exploits Soviet artists who are successful in the West by withholding most of their fees. When making recordings abroad, Soviet artists are pegged to a ridiculously low pay scale; as an inducement, Western record companies make secret deals with the artists, who are only too happy to accept money "under the table" to keep it out of the hands of the Soviet bureaucrats.

The editorial lamented the problems of opera as one sign of the sad crisis in bourgeois culture in general. On the other hand, the flourishing of opera and ballet in the U.S.S.R. testified to the vitality of Soviet culture, its humanistic character, its "democratic direction". One may well ask, if everything was going so well, why call a plenary session on the "problems" of the musical theatre? In fact, the editorial provided a list of twenty-four successful Soviet operas and ballets, which would seem to negate all the complaints.

There is indeed a problem with opera in the U.S.S.R., as there is everywhere in the world. The specific Soviet problem is the narrow nationalist or ideological appeal. Soviet opera, except for Prokofiev or Shostakovich, is not exportable, as was proven by

---

*There was no mention of the excellent conductors on the Bolshoi staff: Mark Ermler, Yuri Simonov, and Alexander Lazarev, who were highly praised during the New York visit in 1975.

Molchanov's fiasco in New York.* The stage direction is staid and old-fashioned. Progressive though Pokrovsky or Grigorovich may be, it takes more directors with vision to remove the entrenched traditionalism in the Soviet lyric theatre. All the "classic" operas need restaging, but that is not going to happen. The opera as a genre is losing adherents, customers, and admirers; even the bureaucrats admit that. A single tiny experimental opera in Moscow will not create a renaissance: "one swallow maketh not summer".

The week of 11–17 May brought the plenary session of the Directorate. The participants sampled several new productions: the operas *Dead Souls* (Shchedrin), *The 12th Series* (Alexander Kholminov), and *The Rake's Progress* (Stravinsky); and the ballets *Tenderness* (Vitali Gubarenko) and *Stepan Razin* (Nikolai Sidelnikov). Some earlier successful ballets were also shown: *Love for Love* (Khrennikov), *Cippolino* (K. Khachaturian), and *Angara* (Eshpai). Somewhat incongruously Verdi's *Otello* appeared, a work likely to dwarf all "problems". Shown also were three operettas, five productions for children, a film ballet, and a musical show. Quite a schedule for one week!

During the day there were speeches and discussions. The keynote address by Khrennikov was a lengthy recitation of past achievements.[45] Once again he stressed the multi-national Soviet art that had developed into a single notion—the Soviet musical theatre. (Nevertheless, Khrennikov adheres to national subdivisions.) To bolster his assertion of undiminished public interest, he reported that during 1977–78 four and a half million listeners attended the musical theatre. Opera accounted for 60% of the repertoire; the remaining 40% was presumably divided among ballets, operettas, and musical shows. More than one-third of the operas had been written by Soviet composers, indicating that a very large percentage of the repertoire was fairly contemporary. Khrennikov mentioned proudly that the titles of almost 150 Soviet operas could be seen on the playbills of Soviet musical theatres each year.**

*See p. 566–67.
**These statistics seem spurious. I doubt whether there are 150 viable Soviet operas ready to be shown every year. Perhaps Khrennikov meant 150 "performances" of Soviet operas per year not 150 different titles. His statement seems at odds with the complaint about "spotty distribution" of contemporary operas on p. 607.

As for their subject matters, an increasing number of operas and ballets are based on significant literary works, not only the classics (e.g., Gogol) but also the writings of contemporary Soviet authors. Historic themes are important, particularly for the "minority" composers, who draw on their own national heritage—composers from Chuvashia, Daghestan, Kirghizia, Turkmenia, Tadzhikistan, and other regions. There has been an enormous increase in contributions from remote areas, which have been handled with growing technical skill.

Khrennikov praised the advances made in operetta and musical comedy. These forms also provide outlets for national idioms and popular songs. The Soviet operetta is fundamentally a "new genre"; while essentially humorous, "it can and should raise serious problems, and esthetically elevate and educate the listener" (no mention of that lowly word "entertain").

There was very little criticism in what Khrennikov had to say. He contrasted certain musical theatres, which willingly collaborated with composers, to others which showed a lack of cooperation. Occasionally aggressive producers interfered too much with the work of the composer. Finally Khrennikov expressed the hope that television and radio would promote and popularize the art of the musical theatre.

On 16 May, at the end of the plenum, the Directorate unanimously passed a fifteen-point resolution covering two pages.[46] An important statement of principles had emerged from the discussion.

While the problems of the musical theatre were being discussed on a theoretical plane, a practical problem exploded. At the center of the controversy was *Pique Dame*, Tchaikovsky's opera based on a Pushkin novella (also known as "Queen of Spades"). In March, *Pravda* published an indignant letter by a conductor of the Bolshoi Theatre, A. Ziuraitis, which read in part,[47]

"A monstrous action is being planned! The victim is a masterpiece by a genius of Russian music, P. I. Tchaikovsky . . . The pretext is that the libretto does not follow Pushkin . . . What demagoguery! If one were to adopt the viewpoint of these pseudo-Pushkinists, it would be necessary to bring suit against all librettists of all operas! . . . The whole opera has been twisted out of shape, entire numbers and dozens of pages have been thrown out . . . The text has been rearranged . . . New music has been written for it . . . Where

Tchaikovsky called for singing, the new version does not;
where the orchestra played alone, there is now singing. A
new instrument, a harpsichord, has been added to the orchestra . . . The question of *Pique Dame* is serious and disturbing. It goes beyond the bounds of innocent experimentation. . . . It is a deliberate action to destroy a monument of
Russian culture . . ."

The whole enterprise was allegedly planned to serve "petty interests of cheap foreign advertising". The production was to be
staged in Paris under the direction of Yuri Lyubimov, with
Rozhdestvensky conducting and the composer Shnitke serving as
musical adapter. But the public uproar in Moscow was such that
the project was dropped.

Lyubimov's attempt to rework *Pique Dame* was not isolated.
Yarustovsky, an expert on Russian opera, reported in 1977 on a
new production at the respected Stanislavsky-Nemirovich-
Danchenko Theatre.[48] The time of the action had been transferred
to the reign of Tsar Alexander I (early nineteenth century), in accordance with Pushkin's original. Of course this change nullified
certain of Tchaikovsky's artful devices in recreating the eighteenth
century and the period of Empress Catherine II. Another innovation was the omission of the opening scene with the children in
the park, about which Tchaikovsky himself had doubts. Thus, the
action began with Chekalinsky's phrase "How did the game end
yesterday?" (A similar approach was taken at the 1972–73 revival
at the Metropolitan Opera in New York.)

The Soviet theatre, though not free of censorship, is one of the
most interesting aspects of Russian cultural life. A group of American theatre experts who visited Moscow and Leningrad in May
1977 were exceedingly enthusiastic: "The best theatre I've ever
seen in my life"; "It was like seeing a goal that we're always aiming for."[49]As a result, a plan was worked out whereby Soviet directors would stage plays (in English) at selected American
theatres in 1977–78. I saw Anatol Efros's staging of Gogol's *The
Marriage* at the Guthrie Theatre in Minneapolis in October 1978;
its vitality brought back memories of the 1920's, of the "unchained theatre" of Meyerhold and Taïrov.[50]

At home in the Soviet Union, however, the stage directors and
choreographers are carefully watched, not only for ideological
deviations but also for departures from the classical tradition. The
prolific young choreographer Oleg Vinogradov has the reputation
of bold reformer and "destroyer of obsolete" canons of ballet. He

was taken to task in 1978 for tampering with Prokofiev's *Cinderella*, shifting numbers freely from one act to another. "Tastelessness and eclecticism reigned supreme on the stage", and the influence of "foreign models" was detected. Even worse, in his staging of Prokofiev's *Romeo and Juliet*, Vinogradov completely eliminated the character of Juliet's nurse, "the ballet's sole representative of the people", on the grounds of her "uselessness". The critic's indignation ran high,

"Vinogradov borrows the device of spoken dramatic dialogue from Béjart and from the American film *Jesus Christ Superstar*, which is one of the ideological standard bearers of Western Avant-Garde. There are also imitations of Robbins's *West Side Story* and Joffrey's *Trinity*. In the duets, the movements are contrived, cold, and inexpressive."[51]

This type of criticism is typical of Soviet narrowness. Ever since the 1930's it has been considered a mortal sin to admit any Western influences in Russian or Soviet arts, and the whole view of music history was readjusted in order to expunge any such references.

An important première took place on 18 September 1978 at the Leningrad Philharmonic Hall: the unfinished opera by Shostakovich, *Igroki* ("Players" or "Gamblers"), was given a concert performance under Rozhdestvensky, with orchestra and soloists drawn from the Moscow Chamber Opera. Shostakovich composed the work in 1942, using Gogol's dramatic sketch; he completed eight scenes, or about one-third of Gogol's twenty-five scenes. The playing time of the music is about one hour. Gogol's prose texts seem to be fated for non-completion: just as Mussorgsky abandoned *The Marriage* and *The Fair at Sorochinsk*, so Shostakovich broke off his attempt. Rozhdestvensky had found the incomplete manuscript in the archives. In his review, Sergei Slonimsky described the fragment as a tragi-comedy with musical style akin to that of Shostakovich's Eighth and Ninth symphonies. The première of the rediscovered work was described as a highlight of the season.[52] A recording of the performance is available.

Early in June, some 280 virtuosos (age sixteen to thirty) from all parts of the world assembled in Moscow for the Sixth International Tchaikovsky Contest. Seventy-two contestants came from America, while only thirty-two were Soviet citizens. But the

Soviet system of screening all its entrants through regional auditions before admitting them to the big competition virtually guarantees finalists. The Americans, on the other hand, enter on their own initiative as long as they can raise the plane fare, and disappointments among the inexperienced are unavoidable. Most hotly contended was the piano competition; of the seventy-two pianists who showed up the first day, twenty-two were Americans. But the Soviet school proved superior, and Mikhail Pletnyov received the gold medal. A Canadian, André Laplante, shared the second prize. The great surprise came in the string divisions. The American Elmar Oliveira was co-winner of the first prize with the Russian Ilya Grubert; it was actually the first time an American had won a gold medal in the violin division. The seventeen-year-old Dylana Jenson, another American violinist, shared the second prize. Even more convincing was the victory of the American Nathaniel Rosen, who was sole winner of the first prize for cello. Curiously, both Oliveira and Rosen studied with teachers of Russian background: the first with Rafael Bronstein (once an Auer pupil), the second with Gregor Piatigorsky.

Medal winners Pletnyov, Oliveira, and Rosen later appeared as an ensemble; they played and recorded the Tchaikovsky Trio in New York and also appeared at the Newport Festival in Rhode Island. Theirs was an extremely polished performance, immaculate as to instrumental control and tonal beauty, but not quite attuned as an ensemble. Pletnyov seems to be a major virtuoso and a thoughtful, intelligent musician.

Ilya Grubert gave a less-convincing performance when he was soloist in the Tchaikovsky Violin Concerto with the Moscow Philharmonic under Dmitri Kitayenko at Carnegie Hall on 31 January 1979. It was a small-scaled interpretation, tidy and sweet, but without much élan or imagination. Grubert received little support from the lackluster accompaniment of Kitayenko, who seemed very detached from the music he conducted. He also led a competent performance of Prokofiev's Third Symphony (based on *The Flaming Angel*), but it communicated little of the feverish excitement of the score. His minimal motions conveyed temperamental restraint or affectation. The Moscow Philharmonic sounded sturdy but showed weaknesses of ensemble.[53] It was rumored that fifteen percent of the orchestra members were last-minute replacements for regular players who were not permitted—for reasons of "unreliability"—to make the trip abroad. Incidentally, Kitayenko himself was a late replacement for Kondrashin, who had been the permanent conductor of the Moscow Philharmonic since 1960 but defected to the West in December 1978.

The Soviet musical world lost several significant personalities in one year. The composer Aram Khachaturian died on 1 May, on the eve of his seventy-fifth birthday.[54] He was the oldest of the "first" generation of Soviet composers, the other two being Shostakovich and Kabalevsky. All three were educated under the Soviet system and rose to prominence during the heyday of Socialist Realism. Except for a brief eclipse in 1948, Khachaturian was successful all his life. The style of his music—colorful, vibrant, tinged by Caucasian exoticism—was easily accessible and noncontroversial, glowing with the exuberance and warmth of his personality. His career as conductor of his own works added to his success, nationally and internationally. His creativity seemed to have slackened during the last years of his life, particularly after the death of his wife, Nina Makarova, in 1976. Among his last works are three unaccompanied solo sonatas, one for cello (1975), one for violin (1976), and one for viola (1977). The first is the most pictorial, the second the most lyrical, the third the most dramatic. Shchedrin said of these works, "One can easily recognize the composer's distinctive style—his indomitable temperament, his original active interpretation of the folk tradition."[55] Having been a cellist at one time, Khachaturian knew how to write idiomatically for strings, but his inspiration was faltering.

The theorist Yuri Tyulin died on 8 May at the age of eighty-five. He was the grand old man of harmony, having devoted most of his long life to teaching the subject at the Leningrad Conservatory, beginning in 1925. He also wrote authoritative textbooks on harmony, assisted in later years by Nikolai Privano. He took great pride in the fact that, during the 1920's, Shostakovich had been a student in his harmony class. He enjoyed the affection and admiration of all who met him.

The death of the musicologist Boris Yarustovsky on 15 July at the age of sixty-seven was unexpected, though it was known that he had a heart ailment. He was the highest ranking musicologist in the Composers' Union, and, like Khrennikov, he came to power and influence in the troublesome year 1948. It is said that he was a close advisor to Zhdanov during the "purge" and that he retained his links with the Central Committee of the Party. Yarustovsky was well known and highly respected internationally, for he usually represented his country at important congresses, looking every inch the suave diplomat. He wrote and spoke with great fluency, and his books show intelligence and scholarship. He occupied many high positions during his lifetime, but his obituary in *Sovietskaya Muzyka* was rather dry and unceremonious.[56] Perhaps he had few friends because he was a critic (his relationship with Khrennikov was known to be tense), but those who knew him personally remember his genuine charm and worldliness, as well as his sharp mind.

The defection of Kyril Kondrashin took place on 4 December 1978, while the conductor was on a concert tour in Holland. He asked for political asylum on the ground that his artistic freedom was being stifled at home.[57] At the age of sixty-four, Kondrashin was one of the most honored of Soviet artists. He had been a Party member since 1941, and his loyalty had never been in question. He had won Stalin prizes, and he had been named People's Artist of the U.S.S.R. in 1972. His conducting assignments were of the highest rank—at the Bolshoi Theatre and at the Moscow Philharmonic, which he built into the best Soviet orchestra during his almost twenty years of leadership. Kondrashin was the first Soviet conductor to come to the United States (in 1958); it was he who accompanied Van Cliburn at his prize-winning performances of Tchaikovsky and Rachmaninov. He is probably the most widely recorded Soviet conductor. For a time he was close to Shostakovich, and he conducted the premières of the Thirteenth Symphony and *Stepan Razin*. Kondrashin was a towering figure in Moscow's musical world, and his defection came as an unexpected blow to Soviet pride.*

The year 1978 saw the spectacular rise of yet another defector, the twenty-four-year-old pianist Yuri Egorov. He had won a third prize in the Tchaikovsky contest of 1974, but some considered him the most gifted of the contestants. While on an Italian concert tour in 1976, he decided not to return home and headed for Amsterdam. His reasons?

"In Russia I was not able to do what I wanted to do. You do things because you have to do them—not for yourself but for the government, or for the Russian system. Everything. One year, for instance, I was very interested in the Russian Orthodox Church. But I was not able to express it openly. I had

*The West received Kondrashin with open arms; he was appointed guest conductor of the Amsterdam Concertgebouw and chief conductor of the Bavarian Radio Orchestra. I heard him conduct in New York on 4 November 1980, when he led the visiting Philadelphia Orchestra in a searching interpretation of Shostakovich's Tenth Symphony. He died on 7 March 1981, when he was sixty-seven, after a concert in Amsterdam. In Kondrashin's memory, an international conducting competition is being organized.

to keep it a secret. I could not read certain books. I could not play certain music . . ."⁵⁸

Egorov entered the Van Cliburn Competition in Fort Worth, Texas, in 1977 but did not reach the final round. (It was rumored that the jury withheld the prize from a "defector" in deference to the Soviet Union.) American admirers of Egorov were enraged to such a degree that they raised the money for his debut in New York in January 1978. The recital was a sensation. Now Egorov is in the forefront of his generation.

By now, the fate of the many gifted emigré musicians has become a matter of international attention. Sooner or later they all play in New York because it is there that great careers are made. *The New York Times* commissioned a major article on the subject, "The Sound of Russian Music in the West".⁵⁹ The author, a young pianist-critic named Joseph Horowitz, interviewed some of the more successful artists—violinists Nina Beilina, Boris Belkin, and Rostislav Dubinsky; and pianists Lyuba Edlina (Dubinsky's wife) and Mark Zeltser. But Horowitz also mentioned Ashkenazy, Rostropovich, and Barshai, as well as the four Russians who have joined the prestigious Boston Symphony. He spoke of the New Russian Chamber Orchestra and the young Russian students who have entered the Juilliard School. Some have found teaching positions at schools or universities, some play menial engagements, some have joined smaller orchestras. The adjustment has not been easy, even for those who have been successful. "Their artistic triumphs have been mixed with emotional trauma." It is even more difficult for those trained in musicology or criticism: the lack of language communication is a barrier. Yet, Henry Orlov, Dora Romadinova, and Solomon Volkov are making their way in the United States while many gifted musicians—performers, composers, and musicologists—are carving out careers in Western Europe and in Israel.

1979

Sovietskaya Muzyka started the new year with a summary of the discussion on Soviet opera that took place in 1978. The editors noted as a positive sign the fact that the Bolshoi Theatre had never had so many contemporary Soviet operas and ballets in its repertoire. They singled out the recent productions of *An Optimistic Tragedy* by Kholminov, *The Abduction of the Moon* by O. Taktakishvili, and *Dead Souls* by Shchedrin, as well as the ballets *Angara* by Eshpai and *Love for Love* by Khrennikov. All over the country, opera was forging ahead, even in a region like Kazakhstan, which was not previously known for operatic activity. (This comment was made in connection with a remarkably successful visit to Moscow of the Kazakh Opera.)

Though seven years had elapsed since the Central Committee's 1972 resolution on criticism, music criticism was still a problem. The journal *Sovietskaya Muzyka* and its role were also under attack. Much remained to be done.

Sovietskaya Muzyka printed a brief but significant report by the young Soviet violinist Vladimir Spivakov, who served on the jury of the Carl Flesch Competition in London (currently chaired by Yehudi Menuhin). There Spivakov joined experts from Austria, France, England, and Japan. It was a happy idea to invite him even though there were no Soviet contestants for the award.[60] (For reasons known only to Moscow bureaucrats, the Flesch Competition is not on the schedule of Soviet contestants. When I discussed this matter with officials of the Moscow Conservatory in 1962, I was told that the faculty wished to limit participation in contests because they interfered with the educational curriculum.) Spivakov filled his jury assignment capably; as it happened, a young Rumanian trained in London, Eugene Sarbu, won first prize, and a Japanese the second.

The unforgotten David Oistrakh was honored at a memorial concert in Moscow on the occasion of his seventieth birthday. His son, Igor, was one of the performers, as was his little grandson Valery (Igor's son), who played a Mozart duet with his father. Thus, the Oistrakh "dynasty" is assured of a successor. Even now, Igor Oistrakh assumes more and more of his late father's duties—at the Conservatory, as chairman of the violin division of the Tchaikovsky Contest, and elsewhere.[61]

To pay more attention to the cultural needs of the rural population was one of the decisions taken by the Party in July 1978. The leaders of the Composers' Union discussed the matter late in 1978, and as a follow-up *Sovietskaya Muzyka* published an article entitled "The Need to Promote the Flourishing of Culture in the Villages".[62] The goals, outlined by Khrennikov, were to portray the countryside in composing music; to popularize music among rural listeners through active participation of composers and musicologists; and to create works reflecting the image of the contemporary peasant-farmer. As a good example, Khrennikov mentioned *The Song of the Forests* by Shostakovich. (This work, written in 1949, was one of the few "concessions" that Shostakovich made to satisfy Zhdanov's demands.)

To match this internal Socialist fervor, the attacks on the ideology of the West continued. *Sovietskaya Muzyka* carried a special section under the heading "Crisis of Bourgeois Culture". In an article by A. Farbshtein (remembered as the author of the 1973 book *Theory of Realism*) we read,

> "In the sphere of ideology there is no, and cannot be, any compromise between socialist and bourgeois ideologies. This refers to the sphere of musico-esthetic consciousness which interests us."[63]

This is an almost verbatim repetition of the drivel that Khrushchev used to dispense in 1963, ranting against ideological "coexistence". It does not make sense in music. Nonetheless, there is even a yearbook entitled *Crisis of Bourgeois Culture and Music* (1972, 1973, etc.), which parades all the old canards under the editorship of the musicologist Lev Raaben.

The alleged contempt for bourgeois culture does not diminish the desire of Soviet composers and artists to perform before the "decadent" bourgeois audiences in the West. More and more the name of Tikhon Khrennikov tops the list. When the Bolshoi Ballet visited France and Switzerland in February 1979 it took only one ballet on tour, Khrennikov's *Love for Love*. It received forty performances, always before full houses, in Paris, Cannes, Orleans, Dijon, Lyon, Besançon, and Lausanne. In all fairness it must be said that this spectacular work draws full houses in Moscow, too. The music is vintage Khrennikov, based on his 1936 incidental music to Shakespeare's *Much Ado about Nothing*. Curiously, the chief male dancer in Khrennikov's ballet was Alexander Godunov, whose defection in America later in the year aroused so much public excitement.

Another ballet with music by Khrennikov, *The Hussar's Ballad*, was produced early in April at the Kirov Theatre in Leningrad. The choreographer was Oleg Vinogradov, described as "talented" by the composer, despite his recent castigation in *Pravda* as a bold experimenter with no regard for the classical tradition. The action is set during the Napoleonic War of 1812; the music is based on Khrennikov's film score of the same title (1962), which goes back to his incidental music to the play *Long, Long Ago* by A. Gladkov (1942). Again we see how carefully Khrennikov managed his inspiration, reworking music that he had written decades before.

In July 1979 Khrennikov and Kara Karayev were named recipients of the Lenin Prize. This honor came to Khrennikov for the second time within a few years; in 1974 he had received it for his Second Piano Concerto. One could think of several other Soviet composers more deserving of that prize, but Khrennikov's position of power was irresistible. The speeches and articles produced on that occasion were full of exaggerated praise. How can one seriously describe Khrennikov as "one of the most prominent and competent musicians of our time", his Second Symphony as "one of the summits of the whole of Soviet music"? Is he really the "founder of the contemporary Soviet opera, alongside Prokofiev and Shostakovich"? Only toadying "critics" could produce such prose.[64]

Karayev, the other recipient, began his career as a "nationalist" composer rooted in his native Azerbaijan. In the mid-1960's he made a creative change with his Third Symphony and his Violin Concerto (1965–67). Among his later works are the mono-opera *Tenderness* (after Barbusse, 1972), the musical *The Fiery Gascon* (after Rostand, 1973), the oratorio-placard *Lenin* (1970), and the *Hymn to Friendship* for chorus and orchestra (1972). His talent for illustrative music is shown in more than twenty scores for film and theatre. Karayev is consistently interesting as a composer and always in search of new means of expression.[65]

On 9–13 April 1979, the Composers' Union of the Russian Federation held its Fourth Conference. Five years had elapsed since its last meeting, and Rodion Shchedrin had to account for his stewardship of the Russian chapter, the largest and most powerful component of the All-Union Composers' Union.

In analysing Shchedrin's speech,[66] one must differentiate between what he *had* to say and what he *intended* to convey. There were the obligatory tributes to the Party and Comrade Brezhnev, to the masters who had recently died (Shostakovich and Khachaturian), and to the senior composers still alive (Kabalevsky and Khrennikov—the latter "can on firm ground be described not only as the head but also as the soul of the Soviet Composers' Union"). Interspersed were a few paragraphs which illuminate Shchedrin's thinking. For example, he warned his audience not to deprecate non-programmatic (that is, absolute) music and not to conceal creative poverty behind flamboyant topics.

"The influence of concrete events in our lives on music is not always straightforward, and today nobody can deny the

significance of non-programmatic works which are not linked
to the word . . . We also know that the striking claim to a
topical theme does not determine the quality of the music. It
cannot salvage a composition that is cold and devoid of impressive imagery . . ."

Shchedrin suggested three general topical areas characteristic of
Soviet music—the revolutionary making of Soviet society, the
battle against the fascist plague, and the reflection through music
of the image of contemporary mankind. (Curiously his own Third
Piano Concerto does not seem to belong in any of these
categories.)

Shchedrin surveyed a wide spectrum of works—operatic, symphonic, choral, and chamber music. About the last-named genre,
he cautioned,

" . . . There are disquieting symptoms in chamber music
which should not be ignored. Sometimes one hears music for
the most incredible, even unthinkable combinations of instruments . . . not always prompted by artistic necessity but
by the desire to be conspicuous, following the whims of
changing fashions . . ."

Shchedrin praised "the sharp rise in the standards of music
within the autonomous republics. They now have . . . real masters with high professionalism . . ." In a rather pensive mood, he
summarized,

"We are on the threshold of the twenty-first century, and we
know that our century has been marked by manifold trans-
formations of the artistic means of music . . . It can be said
that almost everything has been tested that human thought
can perceive at the present stage of our art. It seems to me
that we now have another objective—a search for the synthesis of all the accumulated achievements . . . The problem
of tradition and innovation is ever-present in musical creativity. Traditions are sacred to us . . . Meanwhile we sometimes
forget that traditions are established by innovators, since only
that which is new and talented can perpetuate and assert itself
in life . . ."

Referring to the Party resolution on "Working with Creative
Youth", Shchedrin—himself only in his mid-forties—said
thoughtfully,

"Work with young composers requires great tact . . . Sometimes we, like clucking mother hens, demand that the young
ones should not swim in deep waters, not noticing that they
are already far from the shore. Such over-protective attitudes
lead to creative stagnation, a blind following of traditions
without enriching them, merely admiring their archaism.
Such tendencies, unfortunately, are present among some of
our creative youth . . ."

This speech by Shchedrin—given here only in skeletal form
—is far above the banal talk of party functionaries. It is as
thoughtful and courageous as can be expected from a person in an
official position. His intelligence shows not only in his words but
also in his music, his is an eclectic mind, to be sure, but he is
nimble, inventive, and open to innovation. This impression is
reinforced in a face-to-face meeting, where his personal charm and
incisive mind come into play.

Shchedrin's address was followed by speeches by thirty-four
delegates from every part of the Russian Federation,[67] which
comprises a vast geographic area and a wide variety of nationalities. The speakers came from the Tatar, Bashkir, Udmurt, Kare-
lian, North Ossetian, Daghestan, and Mari ASSR (Autonomous
Soviet Socialist Republics); and new branches of the Composers'
Union were established in the ASSR of Tuva, Komi, and Mordovia
(all within the Russian Federation). The delegate from Tuva reported with pride that there were now eighteen functioning music
schools in his republic. On the other hand, one must not overes-
timate the significance of the establishment of a new "branch" of
the Composers' Union in a remote region. To qualify for membership, three composers and/or musicologists can band together
and get an affiliation from the Moscow headquarters. Indeed,
there are several chapters with only three to five members.

Of course there were also speakers from the old established
chapters in Moscow, Leningrad, Saratov, and Gorki. The ethnic
Russians still prevail; in fact, the Moscow chapter alone accounts
for almost 25% of the *entire* national membership of the Composers' Union. But the "minority" chapters are treated with
greater care and consideration than ever before.

All during the year there was feverish activity in chapters of the
Composers' Union throughout the land in preparation for the
Sixth All-Union Congress of Composers, held under the chairmanship of Khrennikov on 20–26 November 1979. The assembly
place was the Kremlin Palace in Moscow, "from where the historic decision of our Party, our people radiate like sunrays

throughout the whole boundless land of the Soviets". These
flowery words were spoken by Dmitri Kabalevsky, the veteran
Soviet composer, who made the introductory remarks. The
Congress was attended by 713 delegates, representing all the chapters of the nationwide Composers' Union, plus guests from
twenty-three foreign countries.

In his keynote address,[68] Khrennikov gave an accounting of the
previous five years. He gave assurances of the Union's total compliance with the recent Party resolutions, namely "Working with
Creative Youth", "Further Improvement of Cultural Services for
the Rural Population", "Further Development of Amateur Activities", and "Further Improvement of Ideological and Political
Educational Work". He assured the politicians that these documents "largely helped perfect the activities of the Composers'
Union".

As for the state of the Composers' Union, it was healthy: it had
new chapters (already announced by Shchedrin), larger membership, and more creativity within the regional chapters, and it was
contributing to the "treasure-house" of Soviet music. Theatre and
concert attendances had grown by 50%, each year up to 150
operas and 100 ballets, as well as some 130 operettas, were being
produced. New theatres and concert halls were being built, and
there were new audiences "with immeasurably enhanced cultural
standards". A contributing factor was the

> "participation of the Soviet artist in social life, his direct con-
> tacts with the toiling people in town and country . . . Most of
> our members do not limit themselves to armchair activities;
> they visit factories, farms, educational establishments, mili-
> tary units. During these past years, dozens of composers and
> musicologists visited the Baikal-Amur-Mainline projects . . .
> and other major construction sites."

Khrennikov stressed the efforts of the composers to reach out to
the people. Culture and politics are interrelated; for example
Brezhnev's visit to Siberia and the Far East "gave rise to a new
upsurge of creative life in that mighty area".

Khrennikov enumerated the creative achievements of the past
five years, listing dozens of genres and hundreds of composers
who had contributed. These statistics might seem tedious, but
they were meaningful to the composers involved: a mere mention
of one's name implied recognition while an omission might indicate a rebuff.

Khrennikov continued to be unalterably opposed to the avant-garde and predicted its demise abroad because it "inevitably is losing its listeners".

> "A very brutal crisis is now being experienced by the musical avant-garde . . . this crisis is most closely linked with the general crisis of bourgeois culture and social life . . . Composers brought up in an atmosphere of the avant-garde boom are striving to reconsider . . ."

Still, the avant-garde has its "influential though depleted circle of supporters". Khrennikov's simplistic explanation was,

> "This is not only the result of non-spirituality of the contemporary bourgeois society but also the direct consequence of capitalist domination . . . Indeed, the isolation of life from art and art from life is the tendency of modern bourgeois society . . ."

But alas, all was not well at home, either. Some of the Soviet music Khrennikov heard produced a "very dismal impression". It was music written only

> "for the sake of unusual sonoristic combinations and eccentric effects in which musical thought—if at all present—drowns in a torrent of frenzied noise, harsh outcries, or unintelligible mutterings . . . And all that is passed off as innovation in art."

Khrennikov objected to the inertia of the critics,

> "Our critics frequently overlook these unhealthy phenomena, believing that they are isolated cases. Such liberalism is harmful both to the composer and to the forward movement of Soviet music as a whole . . ."

While Khrennikov did not consider such manifestations characteristic of Soviet music, there were "ideological opponents" abroad who stressed the negative aspects and distorted the true image of the Soviet musical scene.

> "Those who organize all sorts of avant-garde festivals, having received, by hook or by crook, some newly written scores from some of our sensation-seeking composers, put them immediately on their programs and present them as the last

word in Soviet music. These composers (incidentally, members of our Union whose music is played in our country more frequently than it deserves) are declared 'unofficial composers', allegedly oppressed in the Soviet Union."

At this point, Khrennikov attacked a festival held in Cologne in March 1979 with the "pretentious" title "Encounter with the Soviet Union". On the program were compositions by emigrés of the 1920's, Arthur Lourié and Joseph Schillinger, and by the recent emigré Andrei Volkonsky. "Are these the people to represent our country, our music?" fumed Khrennikov. But worse was yet to come. "Soviet composers, mainly young ones, found themselves in that unenviable company by the will of the organizers." By making the organizers responsible for the grouping, Khrennikov seemed to exonerate his young colleagues but at the same time to reprimand them by mentioning their names. It is clear that some of these composers had found ways to transmit their scores to the organizers of the festival; such direct contacts are frowned upon by the Composers' Union. What Khrennikov had to say on this point is not convincing,

> "We have always advocated that Soviet music, *including works by young composers* [italics mine], should be played abroad as often as possible in all parts of the globe. But we continue to advocate that the foreign listener should hear all the best, in all its diversity, that has been accumulated by Soviet music, the most characteristic of its past and present days."

Ultimately that meant that the officials of the Union would select the material to be presented abroad, and in such selections the non-conformist composers have only a minimal chance of being considered. As one German critic reported,

> "Obtaining the music for performance [at the Festival] caused many difficulties . . . The music custodians around the Kremlin consider part of their treasures unsuitable for public consumption."[69]

However, the young Soviet composers have friends and patrons abroad.[70] One important link is the West German music publisher Hans Sikorski of Hamburg, who is able and willing to provide information and new scores, even by composers frowned upon by Khrennikov.

Of the seven composers Khrennikov singled out for criticism, two were not so young nor were they unknown: Edison Denisov (b. 1929) appears on every list of Soviet avant-garde composers. Since 1960 he has been on the faculty of the Moscow Conservatory. He is also chairman of the modern music series at the House of Composers in Moscow, which is given for small, invited audiences. Performed at the 1979 Cologne festival were his *La vie en rouge* (1974/75) for voice and instrumental ensemble, with texts by Boris Vian; *Song of the Birds* (1969) for prepared piano and tape; and Double Concerto for flute, oboe, and orchestra (1978, world première).

Sofia Gubaidulina (b. 1931) completed her post-graduate studies in 1962 under Shebalin at the Moscow Conservatory. She is at her best writing for smaller ensembles and chamber groups; she has particular sensitivity to sonorities. Her work catalogue is considerable but her idiom lies outside the mainstream of Soviet music. Her *Five Etudes* (1965) for harp, double bass, and percussion and her String Quartet (1971) were performed at Cologne. She has also written an electronic work, *Vivente—non vivente* (1970), realized at the electronic studio of the Scriabin Museum in Moscow.

The remaining five composers were all much younger: Vyacheslav Artyomov (b. 1940) studied physics and music. He likes to experiment with sonoric effects. He has written for various ensembles, including music for stage and film. *Elegy* (1977) for violin solo, percussion ensemble, and nine additional violins ad libitum was given in Cologne.

Viktor Suslin (b. 1942) studied composition with Nikolai Peiko in Moscow. He is said to be influenced by Cage and Stockhausen. His *Ave Marcus* (1977) for percussion solo was performed at Cologne.

Alexander Knaifel (b. 1943) studied first at the Moscow Conservatory and then transferred to the Conservatory at Leningrad, where he now lives. He studied cello with Rostropovich and composition with Boris Arapov. He looks to Xenakis as his model. Performed at Cologne was his *A prima vista* (1972), a collective improvisation of four players on five sets of percussion instruments.

Dmitri Smirnov (b. 1948) completed his composition studies at the Moscow Conservatory under Sidelnikov and Denisov. He prefers to write for small ensembles in chamber music genres. *Solo* for harp (1976) was performed at Cologne.

Elena Firsova (b. 1950) studied composition at the Moscow Conservatory with Alexander Pirumov. She has been a member of the Composers' Union since 1976. Her works include a chamber opera; concertos for cello, violin, and flute; the solo cantata *Sonnets of Petrarch;* and chamber music. Her Sonata for solo clarinet (1976, published 1978) was given at Cologne.

It is hard to understand why Khrennikov chose to name these seven composers. There were other Soviets whose works were performed at the Cologne festival who could also have been classified as "non-conformist": Sergei Slonimsky (b. 1932)— *Merry Songs* (1971); Alfred Shnitke (b. 1934)—String Quartet (1966); Arvo Pyart (b. 1935)—*Arbos* (1977, instrumental version), *Missa* (1977/79, version for vocal ensemble and instruments), *Fratres* (1977, instrumental version), and *Cantate domino canticum novum* (1979, Psalm 95, for vocal ensemble and instruments); Valentin Silvestrov (b. 1937)—Second Symphony (1965); and Andrei Volkonsky (b. 1933, no longer a "Soviet" composer since his emigration in 1973)—*Quodlibet* (1978, text from the fifteenth-century *Glogauer Liederbuch,* for four vocalists). Towering above all of course was Dmitri Shostakovich (1906–1975)—Second Violin Concerto (1968).

Rounding out the Cologne programs was Soviet music of the 1920's, now mostly forgotten: Alexander Mossolov—*The Iron Foundry* (1928, for orchestra) and String Quartet (1926); Arthur Lourié—String Quartet (1915) and various piano pieces (1915–1936); Joseph Schillinger—*Excentriade* (1924); Boris Alexandrov—Two Piano Pieces Op. 1 (1928); Nikolai Roslavets—Song Cycles (1913/14) and *Nocturne* (1913, for harp, oboe, two violas, and cello); and Vladimir Deshevov—Scherzo (1922, for piano).

From Khrennikov's point of view, the Cologne festival was totally unrepresentative of Soviet music. Shostakovich was the only major composer included; the rest were repudiated composers of the 1920's or non-conformist composers of the 1960's and 1970's. But to the sophisticated West German public, it was precisely the "non-conformist" angle that was most attractive. The program was designed by Detlef Gojowy, a West German expert on Soviet music with a particular interest in the 1920's. There were six concerts in three days (23, 24, and 25 March 1979) sponsored by the West German Radio, thus insuring a wide audience on the air. There were no fewer than twenty-six German premières, among them "discoveries of the first order". The critic of the journal *Musica*[71] was particularly impressed by Denisov's Double Concerto, a work of "extreme difficulty and vast wealth of content . . . containing many cadenzas, some glitteringly colorful, some shaped like micro-melodies, contrasted with the rich orchestration". (The Concerto was composed especially for the flutist Aurèle Nicolet and the oboist Heinz Holliger, who played the world première.) Denisov's song cycle *La vie en rouge* revealed "biting sarcasm, mourning nostalgia, inner calm, and legendary fortitude". The Sacred Pieces by Arvo Pyart were stark and medieval in mood, while Volkonsky's *Quodlibet* was secular and tonal.

Khrennikov was angered by the realization that he could not control the export of Soviet avant-garde music. Such music appears regularly at the Warsaw Autumn Festival, in Darmstadt, and elsewhere. Unexpectedly, *Gradations* by the Soviet Ukrainian composer Vladimir Zagortsev (b. 1944) was played by the New York Philharmonic under Zubin Mehta in January 1980. The work had been composed in 1966 but had never been performed in the Soviet Union; in fact, the composer admitted that he had never heard any of his orchestral music in performance "because of its difficulty". Needless to say, Zagortsev was unable to attend the New York performance, which he described in a letter as "one of the most important events in my life". Zagortsev belongs to the so-called Kiev Avant-Garde, and his chamber music is performed occasionally.

Even inside the Soviet Union, the Moscow Directorate is not always able to control the spread of avant-garde music. The Baltic republics, particularly, with their own highly developed music tradition, often go their independent way. A good example is the Tallinn Festival of Early and Contemporary Music held in November 1978.[72] It was organized by the Estonian State Philharmonic under its conductors T. Koldits and B. Parsadarian. One of the chief initiators was Andres Mustonen, conductor of the Hortus musicus of Tallinn, an early music ensemble of four singers and ten instrumentalists. Also participating was the Vilnius Chamber Orchestra under S. Sondeckis. The programs were modern and daring by Soviet standards—Western avant-garde music by Stockhausen, Cage, Xenakis, Webern, and Henze side by side with works by Soviet non-conformist composers,

Much attention was given to the Estonian Arvo Pyart* (b. 1935). After years of dodecaphonic writing, Pyart has recently simplified his style and turned for inspiration to medievalism with religious connotations (as exemplified by some of the works played at Cologne). Heard at Tallinn were Pyart's *Missa* for voices

*The Estonian spelling Pärt is now generally used outside the Soviet Union.

and old instruments; *Tabula rasa* for two violins, prepared piano, and strings (1977), played by the duo-violinists Gidon Kremer and Tatiana Grindenko; and a Double Concerto for violin and cello premièred by Oleg Kagan and Natalia Gutman. According to late information, Pyart has emigrated and lives in West Berlin.

The Moscow composer Vladimir Martynov is—like Pyart—an artist with deeply held beliefs. He is said to resemble the monk Rasputin, with deep-set burning eyes and a pointed black beard. Martynov lives in total isolation from the world and draws his inspiration from the distant past. One of his new works, *Albumblatt,* was played at Tallinn and described as follows,

> "It opens with a small group of notes on the piano which are rotated within the compass of a major third. Organ, violin, and guitar provide a radiant background . . . Suddenly Martynov breaks into rock and conjures up the turmoil of apocalypse with electric guitar and drums. In comparison with the heavenly music of the opening . . . the contrast is effective in theory, but actually less enjoyable to listen to."

Viktor Suslin (one of the young composers cited by Khrennikov) was represented at Tallinn by his Trio for violin, harpsichord, and double bass, which was described as more consistent but less interesting than Martynov's piece. It was performed by a group of Moscow musicians led by the versatile Alexei Lyubimov, who plays piano, harpsichord, and organ. Lyubimov was also involved in the performance of Denisov's *Song of the Birds,* which involved some visual "hoopla":

> "the infinite variety of forest sounds provides a fine background to a strange-looking creature, dressed like Papageno in feathers and a bird mask, who plays on a prepared piano with obvious professionalism."

Lyubimov and his Moscow group proved that they had mastered the avant-garde idiom of the West by giving a splendid realization of Stockhausen's complex *Setz die Segel zur Sonne.*

Some stage play was also involved in the performance of a composition called *Drama,* by Valentin Silvestrov of Kiev.

> "Violent outbursts . . . are followed by a simple stroke . . . When the pianist has finished playing furioso on the keys and has wedged the loud pedal down with his hands and feet, the violinist strikes a match and then immediately blows it out."

Undoubtedly, some symbolism is intended with this gesture—perhaps the creative spark is extinguished by a higher force.

Life for non-conformist composers in the Soviet Union is far from easy. They are at the mercy of the officials of the local Composers' Union. Performances and publications can be delayed or denied simply by bureaucratic means. As the Finnish critic Heikinheimo described it,

> "Most of the non-established Soviet composers live a Spartan existence in tiny flats surrounded by their children and relatives . . . They are the scene of heated discussions, usually at night . . . and there the worthwhile compositions are written . . . Soviet music should be given more performances abroad. But in order for this to happen, people must go on foraging expeditions to the Soviet Union. The music which comes out through the normal channels is rarely the best."

Casual visitors to Moscow are not likely to hear avant-garde music in the usual concert halls; the musically initiated can find it at gatherings often disguised as "Creative Evenings". Such concerts are held in the tiny auditorium of the House of Composers, off Gorki Street. Admission is by invitation only, and the fifty to one hundred people who attend are usually musical specialists. The composer Denisov is in charge, though the programs are chosen by a repertoire committee to ensure "balanced" programs. It was here, in the summer of 1979, that works by Alfred Shnitke were premièred, including his Four Hymns for solo cello, double bass, harp, harpsichord, clarinet, and percussion. Appearing on the same program was music by Tigran Mansurian (b. 1939), whose idiom is quite advanced though it is rooted in ancient Armenian tradition.

Concerts of advanced music are also given at the Moskvorechiye House of Culture on the southeast outskirts of Moscow. Here, in 1979, Alexei Lyubimov played avant-garde pieces by John Cage, as well as some of his own electronic music, with help from the composer Martynov behind a synthesizer console.

In the basement of the Scriabin Museum in Moscow, young Soviet composers produce and perform electronic music on rather simple equipment. For a time the studio was sponsored by the Scriabin Museum, but the cost became too burdensome. Since the Composers' Union refused to help with the financing, Melodiya Records came to the rescue and took over the studio.

Somehow, experimental jazz fits into the picture. Many Soviet musicians consider modern music and jazz—both unconventional and improvisational—a precious taste of Western freedom. Jazz has had a checkered history in Soviet Russia. Popular in the 1920's, suppressed by Stalin, disliked by Khrushchev, belittled by Khrennikov, jazz has managed to survive and grow in popularity. Western jazz became known mainly through radio broadcasts from the West. Willis Conover's "Jazz USA" programs on the Voice of America, now in their third decade, have made jazz tunes so popular to millions of Soviet listeners that they applaud in recognition when they hear the first bars. In May 1979, at the invitation of the Soviet authorities, Elton John, the British singer and pianist, and Ray Cooper, the percussionist, gave a series of concerts in Moscow and Leningrad; they were wildly successful. Then, early in June, the first Soviet Jazz Festival—performed entirely by Soviet musicians—was presented. It opened with the big-band jazz orchestra of Oleg Lundstrem, who had been active in Soviet jazz since 1935 but really popular since 1956 as the leader of the variety orchestra Rosskontsert. At this festival, Baltic groups were the biggest hits—the Ganelin Trio from Vilnius and Saarsalu's Estonian group (which includes a violin). For a time it seemed that the limits of the permissible had been pushed back to the point where (in the words of a Western reporter in August 1979) "music may now be the least restricted of the arts" in the Soviet Union.[73]

Since then, the atmosphere has become much more strained, both internally and internationally. In August 1979, when the Bolshoi Ballet visited America, the high expectations were not quite fulfilled. True, the dancers' quality was admired, but Grigorovich's productions of two Prokofiev classics, *The Stone Flower* and *Romeo and Juliet,* were harshly criticized, the first as "pure kitsch", the second as "chaotic".[74] Then came the bombshells of defections by star dancers Alexander Godunov and Leonid and Valentina Kozlov. There was also the strange case of the ballerina Lyudmila Vlasova (Godunov's wife), who wished to return to Moscow but was detained at Kennedy Airport until an investigation was completed. Public recriminations were near-hysterical on both sides, Soviet and American. The entire structure of "cultural exchanges" became endangered when Soviet authorities suddenly cancelled the American visit of the Moscow Symphony Orchestra with conductor Maxim Shostakovich. The cancellation was announced on 28 September 1979, eight days before the five-week tour was to begin. The reasons for this action were never made entirely clear, but it was assumed in New York that the fear of defections was paramount.[75] This reasoning is not quite convincing because the Soviets permitted the Moscow Pops Orchestra to proceed with its American tour in October. There must have been a more cogent reason. It may well be that the Moscow Symphony tour was cancelled because it coincided with the publication of *Testimony* by Dmitri Shostakovich, a publication bitterly contested by Soviet authorities. If Maxim had been permitted to travel through the United States at that particular time, he would have been exposed to intensive, possibly embarrassing questioning by reporters. As it was, he stayed home and joined the family protest against his late father's "memoirs".

1980–81

Late in 1979, a few isolated Soviet artists visited New York, including Emil Gilels and Oleg Kagan. In January 1980 the Soviet authorities halted all future visits of their performers pending negotiation of a new agreement on cultural exchanges. The old accord had expired on 31 December, but a renewal had been expected so that there would be no interruption. Instead, the American music scene was plagued by cancellations of long-planned performances by Soviet artists—pianists Lazar Berman, Grigori Sokolov, Andrei Gavrilov, Mikhail Pletnyov, Alexander Toradze; violinists Vladimir Spivakov, Victor Tretyakov, and Gidon Kremer; conductors Yevgeni Svetlanov, Gennadi Rozhdestvensky, and Yuri Temirkanov; and mezzo-soprano Elena Obraztsova, who had been scheduled to appear at the Metropolitan Opera. Cancelled also was the exchange visit of the musical *A Chorus Line* (going to Moscow) and the Moscow Art Theatre (coming to New York).

In February 1980, two more ballet personalities connected with the Bolshoi, Sulamith Messerer and her son Mikhail, defected in Tokyo and made their way to the United States. Fortunately, this development did not affect the career of Maya Plisetskaya, the ballerina, who was close to the Messerers. She went on to choreograph the new ballet *The Sea Gull* by her husband, Shchedrin.

This period was a turbulent one in the relations between the Soviet Union and the Western world, particularly since the United States took the lead in condemning the invasion of Afghanistan and in boycotting the Olympic games. Under such

political tensions there is no hope for a normal "cultural exchange".

There are also internal tensions within the Soviet Union which
affect the cultural climate. Khrennikov's speech in November
1979 before the Composers' Congress was interpreted by
informed circles as a warning to potential dissidents among composers. Certainly, the castigation by name of seven non-
conformist composers seemed like a revival of previous strong-
arm tactics. The choice of these seven was arbitrary; it did not
include all known avant-gardists. Not mentioned, for example,
was Alfred Shnitke, currently the best known among the non-
conformists. During an interview in his Moscow apartment on 17
May 1980 he said,

> "My relations with Khrennikov are strained. The effect [of
> the speech] is to deprive those he attacked . . . of the oppor-
> tunity for having their works performed as frequently here as
> before. I hope this will be only temporary."[76]

Shnitke's own career at home does not seem to have suffered. In
April 1980, his *Requiem Mass* was performed at Moscow's
Tchaikovsky Hall under the direction of Valery Polyansky. Composer and performers received an ovation from the overflow audi-
ence. Shnitke used the traditional sections of the Requiem and the
Latin text but added the Credo as an additional movement. He
composed the work in 1975, in memory of his mother, who was a
devout Roman Catholic, and it was first performed in Budapest.
When asked about his own religious beliefs, Shnitke answered, "I
am not a practicing believer, but I am not an atheist either". His
Jewish father (who spelled his name "Schnittke") was born in
Frankfurt and settled in the Soviet Union in 1926. His mother was
of Volga-German descent. After World War II, the older
Schnittke was stationed in Vienna as translator and interpreter
with the Soviet Army. It was here that Alfred, then twelve years
old, began to study music seriously. He was admitted to the Moscow Conservatory in 1953, where he studied with N. Rakov.
Shnitke is now on the faculty of the Conservatory.

The Requiem Mass is written in a modern but tonal idiom. The
composer claimed, "It's not typical of my later work. My Second
Symphony, for instance, is more dissonant".[77] He was referring
to a new orchestral work that had been commissioned by the
British Broadcasting Company on the recommendation of

Rozhdestvensky, the current conductor of the BBC Orchestra. (It was Rozhdestvensky who had conducted the première of Shnitke's First Symphony in Gorki under difficult circumstances.) The new symphony, subtitled *St. Florian,* was first performed in London's Festival Hall under Rozhdestvensky on 23 April 1980.

Shnitke was denied permission by Moscow to attend the London première, in retaliation for some British cancellation of an exchange visit. He commented,

> "The exchange with the West is much less intense now. We in this country have begun to do our own things. But now the political situation makes exchanges more difficult, and it's too bad. Fewer people in the West will hear us now, and we will hear less of them."[78]*

Shnitke's Second Symphony received widespread coverage in the London press. In the eight articles I have seen the critics are far from unanimous. One called it "gently affecting, neither a challenge nor a masterpiece" and even "rather old-fashioned";[79] another praised the "bold but successful mingling of styles" and the "urgency of his inspiration".[80] One critic found it "strangely grey and static" with a "paucity of rhythmic interest or variety",[81] while another was impressed by the "outstanding artistic and intellectual format".[82] Another commented, "Shnitke's music is introspective, pessimistic rather in the manner of late Shostakovich, but with a definite and unexpected religious slant".[83] But one thing stood out clearly,

> "Alfred Shnitke has over the last few years proved himself the most striking of Russian composers at work today, a man who like Prokofiev and Shostakovich before him can keep to his Soviet brief while saying something unexpected and original."[84]

The *St. Florian* Symphony has an intriguing background. Shnitke was commissioned to write a thirty-minute work to be paired on a program with Bruckner's Mass in E minor. He delivered a fifty-three minute work which he described as *missa invisibilis,* a mass embedded in a symphony. It was inspired by the

---

*An all-Shnitke program was performed at New York's Tully Hall on 9 January 1982, by the Continuum ensemble, directed by Joel Sachs.

composer's visit to St. Florian, where Bruckner had worked as organist and where he is buried. Shnitke entered the cathedral while a mass was in progress and could hear, but not see, the celebrant; the work is a sublimation of that memory. It is conceived in six movements following the Ordinary of the mass. The chorus and the four vocal soloists are placed within the orchestra. Each movement begins vocally, with the Latin text intoned in plain-chant; then the orchestra takes over and elaborates the musical material. The orchestration is huge, including a large brass section, an army of percussion, organ, piano, harpsichord, celesta, and two electric guitars; not surprisingly, the texture is often dense and blurred. Shnitke makes effective use of contrasts between massed instruments and vocal simplicity.

> "The Gloria culminates in a sustained, Messiaen-like explosion of noise, ecstatic and tumultuous, which abruptly stops, leaving a single fortissimo note on the brass, followed by a mysterious whisper on the double bass, and then the clean, austere sound of the Credo chant."[85]

Shnitke's score is not free of "fashionable modernistic elements"[86] (mentioned as influences are Ligeti, Lutoslawski, Messiaen, Britten, and even Orff) and "occasionally it lurches dangerously in the direction of Hollywood soundtrack — chanting monks and tubular bells". But in its best moments it attains "effects of vibrant grandeur . . . most memorably perhaps in the overwhelmingly baleful slow march which heralds the Crucifixus".[87]

Does it deserve the name "symphony" or is it a "sonic montage" was the rhetorical question of one critic.[88] By whatever name, the work is sufficiently interesting (and controversial) to justify the clamour for a repeat performance at the Proms in Albert Hall or in a cathedral.

Several critics raised the question of Moscow's reaction to Shnitke's *St. Florian* Symphony. Can the Union of Soviet Composers ignore it? (After all, Shnitke's First Symphony was side-tracked to Gorki and never reached Moscow!) But times have changed, as one London critic remarked,

> "The risk went out of 'modernism' in Soviet music quite a few years ago. Many composers, judging by the scores I see, have adopted the armory of yesterday's European avant-garde, even if they lack Shnitke's skill in using it."[89]

The *St. Florian* Symphony was described as follows by Paul
Griffiths,

> "Thus although the work might seem to bow to official mu-
> sical standards in its very appealing surface, its judicious
> balancing of Ligeti and Shostakovich, the deeper meaning of
> the music is unquestionably subversive, for here Shnitke
> proclaims the strength of spiritual activity carried out in se-
> cret. In a work lasting almost an hour, the constant repeated
> message is one of sureness in the power of prayer."[90]

Shnitke is not alone; there has been a resurgence of religious
spirituality in other Soviet composers: Pyart, Sviridov, Martynov,
and some of the "New Folklorists".

Rozhdestvensky's activity in London* sparked increased interest
in modern Soviet music, particularly on BBC Radio. Prior to the
première of the Second Symphony, Shnitke's Piano Quintet
(1976) and Third Violin Concerto (1978) had been performed. The
reception had been mixed. The Quintet was described as a "dour
Shostakovian"[91] piece and "curiously inert . . . though its tone is
quite individual".[92] The Violin Concerto was praised for its
"sombre, glowing color and its rich neo-romantic expressiveness".[93] Indeed it is far mellower and more ingratiating than either
Shnitke's Second Violin Concerto or his Second Violin Sonata.

On 20 May 1980 the BBC offered Soviet chamber music by
Denisov, Shnitke, and Sergei Pavlenko. No information is available on Pavlenko, whose *Homage to Valery Popov* (c. 1978) for
bassoon and string quartet was described as "a completely forget-
table string of mild and substanceless 'efforts' ".[94] Denisov, who
is known abroad as one of the leading non-conformists, was represented by his *Romantic Music* for oboe, harp, and string trio,
written in 1968 for Heinz and Ursula Holliger. For its time, it was
an advanced piece by Soviet standards, with its "tender, Bergian
lyricism and the delicately pointillistic scoring".[95] In the same
year, Shnitke wrote his *Serenade for Five Musicians* (clarinet, violin,
double bass, piano, and percussion); "mostly fast and noisy, it is
one of those crazy pieces . . . stuffed to the gills with quotations
. . . punctuated by clangourous bells and inside-of-piano noises,
and not so much ending as sputtering out of exhaustion". But the
critic noticed a "truly Russian relish in its own grotesqueries, a

---

*His contract with BBC has not been renewed.

goblin energy and humor",[96] which set it apart from its "stillborn Western contemporaries". Whichever is the case, it is obvious that Shnitke, Denisov, and others of that Soviet generation absorbed much of the fashionable trends of the late 1960's, but "now we do our own things", as Shnitke remarked.

While modern Soviet music flourished in London, it led a rather dutiful existence in Moscow. The Composers' Union continued to be preoccupied with the campaign of popularizing Soviet music among the masses. This meant an emphasis on a more accessible type of music. Innumerable concerts and music meetings were arranged for factory workers, rural communities, students of all ages, and the armed forces. Composers went into the field to meet their audiences in person, and the reactions of "ordinary" listeners were carefully collected and publicized. The missionary zeal to "reach out" is reminiscent of the early years of the Revolution, when new audiences had to be attracted; in 1980, it was motivated by Party directives to bring culture to every region of the land. Ever alert to the winds of politics, Khrennikov and his Composers' Union, with its nationwide network of affiliates, mobilized all its forces to fulfill the Party's mandate.

Nineteen eighty was a politically sensitive year. It was the 110th anniversary of Lenin's birth and the thirty-fifth anniversary of the victory in the Great Patriotic War. It was also the year of the summer Olympics and of the preparation for the XXVI Party Congress (planned for early 1981). All this made it obligatory for Soviet music to make the best possible showing.

To emphasize the significance, on 3 February *Pravda* published a front-page editorial entitled "Music and Contemporaneousness". It opened with the sentence "Today there is no art more popular than music" and continued with a quote from Chairman Brezhnev, "The closer the ties of the artist with the entire many-sided life of the Soviet people, the surer is the path toward creative achievement and success". *Pravda* praised the activities of musical festivals and competitions and welcomed the participation of the new generation. But it also gave a veiled warning: it was "no secret" that some of the young composers were inclined toward formal experimentations, yielding to the spell of "avant-garde" infection. To guide creative youth toward the great realistic traditions was the responsibility of the institutions of higher learning and the creative Composers' Union. Without belittling the importance of *all* musical genres, said *Pravda*, special attention should be given to propagandize the mass song in order to satisfy the needs

of *all* listeners. Pointing toward the historic significance of the
year 1980, *Pravda* concluded,

> "More than ever, Soviet music occupies an important place.
> The bourgeois ideologists, helped by contemptible renegades,
> are trying to inhibit its growth and obscure its accom-
> plishments. These ideological enemies deserve the decisive
> rebuff of the Soviet musicians. We must not weaken in our
> vigilance . . . We must lend all our soul and talent to the cre-
> ation of works deeply concordant with our great epoch."[97]

This editorial was considered of such importance that the Directorate of the Composers' Union hurried into session to discuss its
implications. Music became politicized as never before.

During the month of April, the Lenin idolatry reached its culmination. The Leningrad Spring Festival, 1–10 April, was dedicated to Leniniana in music. It was followed on 17–22 April by a
gigantic festival of Soviet Music Days in Ulyanovsk, the region
where Lenin was born. Eighty concerts were given on thirty special concert platforms and attended by 70,000 listeners. The programs gave a panorama of recent Soviet music, performed by
three orchestras (a symphony orchestra, one composed of folk instruments, and a light-music ensemble), academic and folk choirs,
dance groups, chamber ensembles, and soloists. Many well-
known Soviet composers were present, and they participated
whenever possible in the performance of their own works. By
mixing art and folk music, song and dance, "serious" and
"entertainment" music, the Soviet organizers were able to attract
all strata of the population, thus satisfying the Party directives. In
addition, two plenary sessions were devoted to a discussion of
"Lenin and Musical Culture". Not satisfied with such a national
observance, the countries of the Socialist orbit were drawn into
the Lenin cult: they met in Moscow on 3 April and discussed
"Lenin's Ideas in the Creativity of Contemporary Composers".
The representatives from Bulgaria, Czechoslovakia, Cuba, the
German Democratic Republic (DDR), Hungary, Mongolia, Poland, Rumania, and Vietnam dutifully recited their prepared
speeches, while Khrennikov chaired the meeting and made his
own contribution.

During the month of May, the thirty-fifth victory celebration
coincided with the Moscow Stars festival, which served as a preview for the cultural "Olympics 80". Foreign performers from
twelve countries appeared in Moscow. Operas and ballets alter-

nated with symphonic concerts and folkloristic dance-and-music ensembles.

The Moscow Autumn '80 Festival was planned as a showcase under the motto "To Meet the XXVI Party Congress" (which was still several months away). The programs were reserved for Muscovite composers of various ages and different musical styles, from conservative to non-conformist, in a rare display of peaceful coexistence. There was so much musical material at hand, that parallel concerts had to be planned and no single critic could possibly cover all the events. To facilitate a critical evaluation, four round-table discussions were set up. *Sovietskaya Muzyka* covered the festival in several articles, and the critic V. Zaderatsky, particularly, seemed open-minded.[98] Evaluating the seven large-scale symphonies performed at the festival, he had special praise for the Fourteenth by Moissei Vainberg and the Ninth by Revol Bunin, while Yuri Levitin's "Olympic" Symphony was somewhat lacking in "olympic ideas".[99] In a footnote, Zaderatsky mentioned orchestral works by two well-known non-conformist composers, Shnitke's ballet music *Labyrinth* (1971)—"a very interesting score demanding further study"—and Denisov's symphonic piece *Painting* (Zhivopis, 1970). Among chamber symphonies, Zaderatsky was intrigued by the experimental character of the *Sinfonia da camera No. 3* (1978) for flute, oboe, vibraphone, marimbaphone, and strings by Vladislav Shoot (b. 1941, Moscow). Three concertos for string instruments—for violin by Yu. Ter-Osipov, for viola by M. Ermolayev, and for cello by R. Ledenev—had neo-Romantic traits in common, according to Zaderatsky. Among chamber music composers, several newcomers were singled out for their creative audacity: Sergei Pavlenko for his Piano Trio, V. Lobanov for his Piano Sonata (brilliantly performed by the composer), and I. Kefalidi for his vocal cycle *Russkie poteshki* (Russian Mockeries) in the style of the "New Folklorism". But the greatest praise was reserved for Sofia Gubaidulina—known as a non-conformist—and her music for cello and organ (untitled in the review but apparently identical with "In croce", 1979, in her work list). Zaderatsky was deeply moved by her sonorous imagination, the "cosmic space" of her music. The work produced a lively controversy during one of the round-table sessions. The festival program was rounded out by the customary festive cantatas and a few popular repertoire pieces by Shostakovich and Khrennikov. The Moscow Autumn Festival was a significant achievement, presenting a rich panorama of the creative forces at work in the Soviet capital.

The XXVI Party Congress opened on 23 February 1981 with a long statement by Leonid Brezhnev but nothing new in terms of cultural policies. Music was not specifically mentioned. "The spiritual life of Soviet society becomes increasingly diverse and rich, which is the undisputed merit of our cultural activists, of our literature and art"; this is the way Chairman Brezhnev expressed his satisfaction, but he warned, "The Party cannot and will not be indifferent toward the ideological direction of our art . . . Here we are implacable."[100]

Khrennikov, a member of the presidium of the Party, gave a brief speech from the rostrum, which was reprinted in *Sovietskaya Muzyka*. Entitled "To Create Music of Great Social Significance", it was a summary of Soviet musical achievements during the previous Five-Year Plan.[101] "Our ranks have been filled with talented youth!* Following the decrees of the XXIV and XXV Party Congresses, we have worked on the education of youth." Khrennikov recounted the efforts to bring music to *all* the people, to activate remote regions, to further multi-national cultures. He gave as an example a grandiose festival in Uzbekistan, where 2,500 composers and performers took an active part. "Such enterprises can only be presented with the help of the Party on all levels." This assistance extended to financial support: new opera theatres in Dnepropetrovsk and Krasnoyarsk; the funding of new music ensembles, music schools, concert halls, palaces of culture, and clubs; and the new Children's Musical Theatre in Moscow, the first such theatre in the world.

> "We composers are responsible to the people, to the Party, for carrying out . . . all the directives concerning cultural stimulation . . . But not all our tasks are solved. For our gigantic audiences, we must create music that reflects contemporaneousness. There are still too few such works. The contemporary theme, the image of the hero—the builder of communism and his spiritual life—that's our most important goal."

Khrennikov also admitted some administrative shortcomings and outright incompetence of some philharmonic organizations, "leav-

---

*The membership of the Union of Soviet Composers had increased significantly; as of 1980 there were 2,156 composers and musicologists listed as members of the national organization, according to *Muzykalnaya Entsiklopedia*, vol. 5, col. 233.

ing our concert halls empty and unused". He promised speedy improvements.

With understandable pride, Khrennikov pointed toward the international recognition of Soviet music.

> "In the past five years, some 7,000 works by Soviet composers were performed abroad. Soviet artists are received enthusiastically everywhere. But they also meet hostility, sometimes even terrorist acts. Our performers abroad need not only mastery but also courage."

In closing Khrennikov pledged that "Soviet artists will continue to be true helpers of the Communist Party of the Soviet Union, true propagandists of Leninist ideas".

Khrennikov's speech before the XXVI Party Congress exuded self-confidence and satisfaction with the accomplishments of his Composers' Union: collectively they had faced up to the criticism of the two previous congresses and had achieved improvements that were impressive in terms of statistics—attendance figures, frequency of performances, national and international growth. The members of the Congress were politicians, not music experts; they were neither able nor interested in judging the *quality* of the music produced, only the *quantity* mattered, and they liked the figures they saw. Khrennikov's influence never loomed larger; after thirty-three years of continued rule over his composers, he was at the peak of his power.

In the course of his speech, Khrennikov mentioned an international music festival to be held in Moscow in May 1981, for which the planning had already started. On 13 February 1981, just prior to the opening of the Congress, *Pravda* had published an interview with Khrennikov, as chairman of the planning committee, under the headline, "We Await You, Music". More than twenty countries were to participate in this "stereopanorama" of twentieth-century music. Such surveys, according to Khrennikov, were almost non-existent in the capitalist world: there, such festivals are more often devoted to the so-called avant-garde and geared to narrow specialists, not to the broad masses of music lovers. "We define the name 'festival' as a mass celebration." Obviously, Khrennikov's idea of a contemporary festival was no avant-gardism, no experimentalism, only establishment music. His idea prevailed. The result was a strange assortment of programs presented in the guise of "contemporary" music—programs "more astute than adventurous", in the words of the London *Financial Times*.[102]

The International Music Festival in the U.S.S.R. took place in Moscow on 5-11 May 1981, with the somewhat pretentious motto "Music for humanism, for peace and friendship between nations". It was planned to coincide with a meeting of the International Music Council, which was attended by delegates from about forty countries. Eleven concerts were presented: eight of symphonic music and three of chamber music, including a recital of piano music by Prokofiev.

The programs concentrated on music of the twentieth century—"something almost unthinkable just a few years ago", asserted the *Financial Times* with some exaggeration. The correspondent, Nigel Osborne (a British composer whose music was played at the festival), interpreted the programs as a sign of gradual rapprochement between Soviet and Western music: the Soviets had become more tolerant of innovation, the Western composers less abstract. "The musical cultures of East and West have rarely been so close together", wrote Osborne.

That much-vaunted "closeness" was achieved by simply eliminating all advanced or experimental composers from both East and West. A bizarre decision by the Soviet Composers' Union was the exclusion of *all* living Soviet composers. What was the reasoning behind it? Obviously it eliminated a lot of internal squabbles as to who should speak for the native land; dead composers were safe and no longer controversial. Thus, the U.S.S.R. was represented by Miaskovsky, Khachaturian, Shostakovich, Prokofiev, and Stravinsky. This evasive move deprived living Soviet composers of the opportunity to be heard by an international forum.

Other East European countries followed the Soviet example: Hungary was represented by Bartók and Kodály, Rumania by Enescu, Czechoslovakia by Martinu, and Bulgaria by Pipkov, all no longer alive. Only Poland had the courage and the vision to put forward two advanced living composers who enjoy international renown: Penderecki and Lutoslawski. Both conducted their own works and were enthusiastically acclaimed in Moscow. Penderecki's Violin Concerto (originally written for Isaac Stern) was played by the Soviet violinist Gregory Shislin and the Latvian Symphony Orchestra. Soloists in Lutoslawski's Double Concerto for oboe and harp were the incomparable Swiss artists Heinz and Ursula Holliger, for whom the work had been composed.

Western Europe and the United States were represented by distinguished composers of conservative leanings, among them Walton, Auric, Dutilleux, Jolivet, Mennin, and William Schuman. The two Germanys were represented by Carl Orff and Hans-Werner Henze for the BRD and Ernst Hermann Meyer for the DDR. Several masters of the past were remembered—Britten, Gershwin, Samuel Barber, and Villa-Lobos. Other countries represented were Italy, Spain, Cuba, Norway, Finland, Yugoslavia, and Japan. "Third World" countries—India, Iraq, Mongolia, Vietnam—were given their own forum at the Moscow Festival. But totally missing were composers representing the advanced wing of modern music. Obviously the programs were a triumph of compromise for which Khrennikov was chiefly responsible. He was rewarded with a special message from Chairman Brezhnev and intense coverage by the Soviet press and news media.[103]

In contrast, the Western press all but ignored the Moscow Festival. Perhaps it reflected a certain dissatisfaction with the limited range of the programs; one wonders whether the various countries were consulted about the choices. In fact, there was some polite criticism. In his parting statement, Peter Mennin said, "It would be desirable if, in the future, there would be more initiative shown in the discovery of new names and works".

The *Financial Times* noted with naive satisfaction that performances of two compositions by Shostakovich took place "irrespective of Maxim's recent departure . . . the Soviets are in no mood for small-mindedness in such matters". Leaving aside the question of Soviet "small-mindedness" (which can be harassing at times), it would be the height of foolishness for the Soviets to dethrone the father Shostakovich because the son decided to defect. The entire edifice of Soviet music would collapse if Shostakovich's contributions were removed. "Shostakovich is the mirror of the soul of our country, and the son's defection is a tremendous occurrence", was the reaction of Rostropovich, himself a recent emigré.[104] No one had expected such a dramatic turn of events.

On 12 April 1981, a news flash from Bonn informed the startled music world that Maxim Shostakovich and his son, Dmitri, had requested political asylum in West Germany. In Fürth (Bavaria), the Soviet Radio Symphony Orchestra, under its conductor, Maxim Shostakovich, had just given the final concert of its tour. Nineteen-year-old "Mitya" had been the soloist in his grandfather's Second Piano Concerto. A post-concert party had been planned to bid farewell to the visiting orchestra. Suddenly someone asked, "Where is the director?" A frantic search soon revealed that Maxim and Mitya had quietly slipped out, eluding the KGB surveillance. The party was cancelled, and the orchestra returned hurriedly to Moscow.

Before the foreign tour, Maxim Shostakovich had been forced to "purge" his orchestra, removing five of his best players because they were considered politically unreliable. Despite these precautions, a harpist disappeared during the tour, and Shostakovich knew that he would be held responsible for this defection, possibly even deprived of the opportunity of traveling abroad with his son. (When going on a foreign trip, Soviet citizens must leave behind a close family member as "hostage" to insure their return. Maxim is divorced from his wife, who is remarried and has a new family. The permission to travel with his son was a rare privilege under these circumstances.)

While Maxim had pondered emigration for some time, he realized in Fürth that it had to be then or never. His son was in full agreement. Once they had escaped the security agents, things happened fast. Within three days, it was announced in Washington that father and son Shostakovich could enter the United States as refugees. On 23 April they were both in Washington, facing a press conference. At their side was an old friend of the family, Mstislav Rostropovich, conductor of the National Symphony in Washington since 1977, who said proudly, "I now have an important part of my spiritual family with me".[105] He immediately announced that Maxim would conduct the National Symphony in May, at a special Memorial Day concert, and also during the week of 22 September, in commemoration of Dmitri Shostakovich's seventy-fifth birthday. Thus, Maxim's new career was launched.

At the press conference, Maxim spoke through an interpreter, weighing his words carefully. A prepared statement was read for him, explaining his reasons for leaving his native land.[106]

> "No matter how difficult it was to leave, it would have been even more difficult for me to stay . . . Our departure is a profoundly conscious step, a sign of protest, a *sign of disagreement* . . ."

His protest was directed against the "debasing of human dignity, the steady violation of human rights, the manifestations of explicit anti-Semitism", and the isolation or expulsion of great people (he mentioned Solzhenitsyn, Rostropovich, Vishnevskaya, and his "never-to-be-forgotten father"). Like all the other musicians who preceded him into emigration, he wanted to escape the iron-fisted

Soviet cultural policy, which stifles artistic expression and controls all musical activities. What he wanted was "the feeling of true freedom". In describing the situation in the Soviet Union, Maxim said, "The isolation of all arts there manifests itself by the total lack of information about the arts in the life of the rest of the world". Maxim settled in New York and applied for American citizenship for himself and Mitya because the United States "pays the most attention to the rights of man". A few months later he declared, "I have never lived in such a happy atmosphere . . . There is no such thing in the West as a composition that is not allowed—and that is wonderful."[107]

After several weeks of silence, the Soviets finally conceded publicly that Maxim Shostakovich had defected.[108] They called him a "conceited egotist" who was lured away by Western agents with promises of gold and glory. At a news conference in Moscow, Khrennikov declared that Maxim's defection was a personal matter, which would not change the Soviet attitude toward his father.

It is self-delusion for the Soviets to blame greed and avarice for the defection of such personalities as Rostropovich, Kondrashin, Ashkenazy, or Maxim Shostakovich. These artists were rich and pampered; all their material needs were satisfied. ("I could fill bathtubs with vodka", Maxim remarked with irony.[109]) But "man doth not live by bread alone". The hunger for freedom of expression made these artists decide to leave for the West, often at the risk of their lives.

There is a basic difference between the wave of emigration of the 1920's and the present defections. In the 1920's, the economic conditions inside Russia were wretched, with little hope for the arts, and Russia's artistic elite left in depair. No such conditions exist in Soviet Russia today: ideological pressure, not material need, creates the disillusionment among Soviet artists and intellectuals.

The present cultural estrangement between East and West is politically motivated. No one can foretell how long this international freeze will last. But it cannot permanently inhibit the rapprochement between the musical esthetics of the Soviet Union and the Western world. Khrennikov admitted it himself; "Many new devices elaborated by the world's compositional practice in the twentieth century have entered the arsenal of Soviet music." Indeed they are being used by Soviet composers of all schools and nationalities. This is the great forward step of the past twenty-five years. There is tough talk in Moscow about the "incompatibility" of East and West; but in practice the walls are crumbling. Despite temporary reverses, this rapprochement cannot and will not be stopped. It cannot come too soon.

Appendix: Conversation with Maxim Shostakovich

In June 1981 Maxim Shostakovich invited me to visit him at his New York apartment for a morning chat. He was noticeably pleased when he found out that we could speak Russian together.

Maxim lived on the twenty-second floor of a new apartment house near Lincoln Center, with a view of the Hudson River.* The building was only partly finished, and his apartment, modest in size, smelled of fresh paint. He and Mitya had moved in just two or three days before. I entered through a windowless foyer, where Mitya sat at a folding table. He was a bright-looking fellow, looking younger than his nineteen years. He wore a modish American T-shirt with a red heart on the front. Maxim ushered me into the living room, still sparsely furnished: a couch in front of the large window, a folding chair, a large television set in the corner, a built-in bookshelf. One empty wall was reserved for the piano, where Mitya (soon to be a student at the Juilliard School) would practice. Maxim looked around the smallish room. "That's enough for the time being; some day I'll have larger quarters . . . apartments are hard to get." He expected to travel a lot: on his shelf was a six-year appointment calendar, which he consulted when I asked him the date of his New York debut. "October 1982" he answered with a smile. In the summer of 1981 he was scheduled to guest-conduct in Santa Barbara and Honolulu, in September in Washington, and then in London, with Mitya as soloist. He seemed unconcerned about his future.

Maxim's light hair was combed forward, and he looked very much like his father. He wore tinted glasses and smoked several cigarettes during the hour we spent together. His motions were quick and youthful (he was forty-two, but didn't look it). He seemed restless at times and got up to walk around while speak-

*Since then he has moved to Connecticut.

ing. He was dressed in an open-necked long-sleeved shirt, jeans, espadrilles without socks (it was 79° outside). He spoke in a controlled, well-modulated voice, expressing himself with style and elegance.

About his emigration he said, "It was an act of protest, a sign of disagreement". Did his father ever consider emigration? I asked. Maxim hedged. "My father had family obligations. I was still young. It was not easy." Then he reached impulsively to the almost bare bookshelf and opened a volume by Anna Akhmatova, reciting the epigraph from her *Requiem*,

> I was with my people in those hours,
> There where, unhappily, my people were.[110]

He added, "My father was a patriot of his people, which is not the same as a Soviet *apparatchik*". This, of course, is clear to anyone who has read *Testimony*, the controversial volume of memoirs edited by Solomon Volkov.[111] Maxim had expressed his reservations about *Testimony* in several previous interviews. It is understandable that he had objected to the book while he was still in Moscow, but it is surprising that he still railed against it after his emigration. It would have been easy for him to endorse *Testimony*, which portrays his father as a victim of oppression and the Soviets (particularly Stalin) as bloodthirsty despots. In fact, Maxim did not question the facts, only the authenticity of the *words* put into his father's mouth. "It pictures him as far less generous and more vindictive and bitter than he really was", he said. "These are not my father's memoirs. This is a book by Solomon Volkov about Shostakovich." (Others disagree and feel that the book rings true; Kondrashin, for example, gave it a strong endorsement.)

When I questioned Maxim more closely about *Testimony*, he said that many statements ascribed to his father had possibly been made over a cup of tea, in the course of a casual conversation, and should not be taken as absolute truths. Yet, he said, "if the book accomplished one good thing, it is that it revealed for the first time the tragedy of the *mask of loyalty* that my father had to wear all his life". He underlined these words with a sweeping gesture from face to waist. "And all those official pronouncements", he continued with a frown, "I never saw my father write down any speeches or statements. They were brought to him all prepared from the Composers' Union, and he just signed them or delivered the speech as written for him."

This conversation only confirmed my own impression that the official statements made by Shostakovich on various occasions were pompous platitudes, which did not reflect his personal opinions. Maxim elaborated, "You know, he did not like to talk about his own music. Sometimes he just agreed in order to get rid of a bothersome interviewer." When I asked Maxim about the alleged program of the Fifteenth Symphony—the toyshop story in the first movement—he just laughed.

"My father did not write program music in the realistic sense—except in films, of course. There you have a fire and you write fire music. But otherwise his programs were idealized. He did not write about *this* war or *that* revolution, but about *war* and *revolution* in general, the state of mind and emotion, not facts."

And the *Leningrad* Symphony? I asked. "True, the *Leningrad* Symphony was written under the impact of events, it was not preconceived—on this point, *Testimony* is wrong—every movement is dated. Still, it is a description of the horrors of war *in general*."

I asked Maxim whether he had a favorite among his father's symphonies. "Not really. I love them all—some perhaps less, like the Second and Third, but then my father did not care so much for them either. He told me, 'Don't conduct them!'" Maxim smiled, remembering his father's advice. I asked him about the metronome markings in the scores, since different interpretations vary considerably. "The metronome markings are correct as they stand in the scores", replied Maxim, "and they should be observed. Of course there is room for individual tempo deviations." "Who among conductors is your favorite as interpreter of your father's music?" I asked. Without hesitation Maxim replied, "Mravinsky. He is the closest to my father's thoughts."

We talked briefly about the avant-garde composers in the Soviet Union. "They have little chance to become known, they are so rarely played. One could say, 'they don't live, they exist'. Still, musicians have it easier than writers: the word is more compromising. Look at the trouble the Thirteenth Symphony had just because of the texts!" Maxim said he had conducted some new Soviet music: he performed Tishchenko's Fifth Symphony in Germany; he also recorded two symphonies by Moissei Vainberg and music by R. Bunin. "What kind of repertoire will you conduct in the West?" I asked him. "Oh, I want to conduct a wide repertoire, but naturally there will be a certain concentration on Shostakovich." And Mitya? I asked "He played his grandfather's Second Piano Concerto on tour in Germany, the one he wrote for me in 1957." A smile played on Maxim's face. "You see, there is the continuity of tradition."

I showed Maxim one of the volumes of the new Collected Works of Dmitri Shostakovich—the third volume, which contains two symphonies. He looked pensively at the title page, where his (Maxim's) name was printed among those of other prominent musicians on the editorial board. "Will it remain there, do you think?" I asked. He smiled wryly, "They will scratch it out in time, just as they are trying to scratch out every reference to Rostropovich, that great artist who was so close to my father". But Maxim showed no regrets about leaving his homeland and giving up his citizenship. He quoted Vasily Aksionov, a dissident writer now in Washington, D.C. When deprived of his citizenship, he said "I deny that they—the Soviets—have a moral right to take away something that is my birthright". We parted with a handshake. He left a strong impression with me—controlled, collected, confident, weighing each of his words because he knew he would be quoted, but at the same time conveying sincerity and conviction. "My grandchildren will be free . . . I bring the blood of Shostakovich to freedom!"

Addendum: New Dates

Soviet musicians mentioned in the original volume who have died since 1971:

Grigori Bernandt, 1905–1978
Valerian Bogdanov-Berezovsky,
 1903–1971
Vadim Borissovsky, 1900–1972
Maxim Brazhnikov, 1904–1973
Revol' Bunin, 1924–1976
Alexander Chernov, 1917–1971
Oles Chishko, 1895–1976
Ivan Dzerzhinsky, 1909–1978
Yakov Flière, 1912–1977
Lev Ginzburg, 1907–1981
Kara Karayev, 1918–1982
Aram Khachaturian, 1903–1978
Boris Khaikin, 1904–1978
Lev Knipper, 1898–1974
Leonid Kogan, 1924–1982
Kyril Kondrashin, 1914–1981
Marian Koval, 1907–1971
Yuli Kremlev, 1908–1971
Boris Levik, 1898–1976
Anastasia Liapunova, 1903–1973
Nina Makarova, 1908–1976
Alexander Mossolov, 1900–1973

Lev Oborin, 1907–1974
David Oistrakh, 1908–1974
Mikhail Pekelis, 1899–1979
Gavril Popov, 1904–1972
David Rabinovich, 1900–1978
Nathan Rakhlin, 1905–1979
Konstantin Rozenshild, 1898–1974
Vadim Salmanov, 1912–1978
Semyon Shlifstein, 1903–1975
Grigori Shneerson, 1901–1982
Dmitri Shostakovich, 1906–1975
Arnold Sokhor, 1924–1977
Alexander Sveshnikov, 1890–1980
Alexander Tsfasman, 1906–1971
Yuri Tyulin, 1893–1978
Mikhail Vaiman, 1926–1977
Konstantin Vertkov, 1906–1972
Boris Volman, 1895–1971
Israil Yampolsky, 1905–1976
Yuri Yankelevich, 1909–1973
Boris Yarustovsky, 1911–1978
Yakov Zak, 1913–1976
Herman Zhukovsky, 1913–1976

Notes on Sources

Abbreviations used:
CurDig—*Current Digest of the Soviet Press* (weekly), New York, 1949–.
InfoBull—*Information Bulletin,* Union of Soviet Composers, English-language edition (monthly), Moscow, 1960–.
IMN—*Istoria Muzyki Narodov SSSR,* 5 vols., Moscow, 1966–74.
IRM—*Istoria Russkoi Muzyki,* 3 vols., Moscow, 1957–60.
IRSM—*Istoria Russkoi Sovietskoi Muzyki,* 5 vols., Moscow, 1956–63.
SovMuz—*Sovietskaya Muzyka* (monthly), Moscow, 1933–.
L—Leningrad; M—Moscow; N.Y.—New York

PART I

Chapter 1

1. Klara Zetkin, *Reminiscences of Lenin,* London, 1929, p. 14. Quoted in Russian in V. Lenin, *O Literature i Iskusstve,* M, 1957, p. 583.
2. Quoted in IRM, vol. 1, p. 236.
3. *The Musorgsky Reader,* transl. J. Leyda and S. Bertensson, N.Y., 1947, p. 215.
4. V. Yastrebtsev, *N. A. Rimsky-Korsakov, Vospominania,* L, 1959–60, vol. 2, p. 327–28.
5. Ibid.
6. *100 Let Leningradskoi Konservatorii,* L, 1962, p. 79.
7. N. Rimsky-Korsakov, *My Musical Life,* transl. J. Joffe, N.Y., 1923, p. 319.
8. Ibid., p. 320.
9. Yastrebtsev, op. cit., vol. 2, p. 321.
10. Yuri Keldysh, *Istoria Russkoi Muzyki,* M, 1954, vol. 3, p. 251.
11. Gerald Abraham, *Rimsky-Korsakov,* London, 1945, p. 122.
12. IRSM, vol. 1, p. 10.
13. Ibid., p. 12.
14. S. Prokofiev, *Autobiography, Articles, Reminiscences,* transl. R. Prokofieva, M, ca. 1956, p. 99.
15. Ibid., p. 33.
16. Ibid., p. 36.
17. Nikolai Malko, *A Certain Art,* N.Y., 1966, p. 135–36.
18. John Reed, *Ten Days That Shook The World,* N.Y., 1960, p. 13.
19. Prokofiev, op. cit., p. 46.
20. I. Nestyev, *Prokofiev,* tranl. Florence Jonas, Stanford, 1960, p. 135–36.
21. B. Asafiev, *O sebe,* quoted in E. Orlova, *B.V. Asafiev,* L, 1964, p. 69.

Chapter 2

1. Reed, op. cit., p. 156.
2. Malko, op. cit., p. 136.
3. A. Lunacharsky, *V Mire Muzyki*, M, 1958, p. 8.
4. *Lenin i Iskusstvo*, in Lenin, *O Literature i Iskusstve*, M, 1957, p. 589.
5. Klara Zetkin, ibid., p. 584.
6. Malko, op. cit., p. 137.
7. Quoted in E. Grosheva, *Bolshoi Teatr SSSR v Proshlom i Nastoyashchem*, M, 1960, p. 39.
8. A. Gozenpud, *Russkii Sovetskii Opernyi Teatr*, L, 1963, p. 19.
9. Ibid.
10. IMN, p. 49.
11. Lunacharsky, op. cit., p. 124.
12. Gozenpud, op. cit., p. 26.
13. Ilya Ehrenburg, *People and Life, 1891–1921*, transl. A. Bostock and Y. Kapp, N.Y., 1962, p. 287.
14. Ibid., p. 286.
15. Lenin, op. cit., p. 591.
16. Lenin, op. cit., p. 397 (8 October 1920).
17. To Klara Zetkin, op. cit., p. 583.
18. Quoted in Reed, op. cit., p. 342.
19. Ibid., p. 287.
20. IMN, p. 65–66.
21. B. Asafiev, *Chto Delat*, 31 December 1918 in *Zhizn Iskusstva*, quoted in IMN, p. 65.
22. Quoted in *V Pervye Gody Sovetskovo Muzykalnovo Stroitelstva*, L, 1959, p. 19.
23. *Muzykalnyi Leningrad*, L, 1958, p. 23.
24. IMN, p. 51.
25. F. Chaliapin, *Pages from My Life*, transl. H. M. Buck, ed. K. Wright, N.Y., 1937, pp. 310, 308.
26. A. Grechaninov, *My Life*, transl. N. Slonimsky, N.Y., 1952, p. 125.
27. E. Grosheva, op. cit., p. 39.
28. C. Stanislavsky, *My Life in Art*, transl. J. J. Robbins, London, 1967, p. 507–08.
29. Ibid., p. 511–12.
30. IMN, p. 50.
31. Stanislavsky, op. cit., p. 512.
32. Ehrenburg, op. cit., p. 416.
33. Klara Zetkin, quoted in Louis Fischer, *The Life of Lenin*, N.Y., 1964, p. 490.
34. Prokofiev, op. cit., p. 50
35. IMN, p. 46–47.
36. Speech "The Tasks of the Youth Leagues", transl. in V. Lenin, *New Economic Policy*, N.Y., 1937, p. 471.
37. Ibid., p. 484–85, "Proletarian Culture".
38. From Lunacharsky's *On Popular Education*, quoted in Reed, op. cit., p. 286.
39. A. Glazunov, *Issledovania, Materialy . . .*, L, 1960, vol. II, p. 427.
40. Ibid., p. 423.

41. Ibid., p. 424–25.
42. *100 Let Leningradskoi Konservatorii*, op. cit., p. 105.
43. Ibid., p. 108.
44. Excerpts quoted in *V Pervye Gody* . . . op. cit., p. 82–83.
45. H. G. Wells, *Russia in the Shadows*, London, 1920, p. 35 (Am. ed. p. 45).
46. Stanislavsky, op. cit., p. 514–15.
47. Ibid., p. 518.
48. Quoted in Gozenpud, op. cit., p. 41.
49. A. Lourié, *S. Koussevitzky and his Epoch*, N.Y., 1931, p. 160–61.
50. Wells, op. cit., p. 43 (Amer. ed. p. 53).
51. Glazunov, *Issledovania* . . ., op. cit., II: 23.
52. Wells, op. cit., pp. 38, 45, 47. (Amer. edition pp. 48, 57–59.)
53. Ibid., p. 137–38. (Amer. edition p. 161–62.)

PART II

Chapter 3

1. Quoted in Ehrenburg, *People and Life*, op. cit., p. 381.
2. Wells, op. cit., pp. 10, 11. (Amer. ed. p. 17.)
3. Quoted in Adam B. Ulam, *The Bolsheviks*, N.Y., 1965, p. 476.
4. Ehrenburg, *Memoirs: 1921–1941*, transl. T. Shebunina and Y. Kapp, London, 1963, N.Y., 1964, p. 66.
5. Ulam, op. cit., p. 477.
6. Fischer, op. cit., p. 496.
7. In Lenin, *O Literature i Iskusstve*, op. cit., p. 583.
8. Ibid., p. 455.
9. Lenin, *New Economic Policy*, op. cit., p. 274–75.
10. 17 October 1922. Quoted by Keldysh, *Sovetskaya Muzykalnaya Kultura* (privately printed), p. 6.
11. Joseph Szigeti, *With Strings Attached*, N.Y., 1947, pp. 220, 222.
12. Bruno Walter, *Theme and Variations*, transl. J. A. Galston, N.Y., 1947, pp. 256, 277.
13. Ibid. (German original), Stockholm, 1947, p. 379 (*Thema und Variationen*).
14. "Kunst und Volk im neuen Russland," in *Die Musik*, XVIII, No. 4, January 1926, p. 284.
15. Willi Reich, *The Life and Work of Alban Berg*, transl. C. Cardew, London, 1965, p. 69.
16. D. Milhaud, *Notes Without Music*, N.Y., 1953, p. 189.
17. Cf. Boris Schwarz, "Schoenberg in Soviet Russia", in *Perspectives of New Music*, Princeton, N.J., Fall-Winter, 1965, p. 88.
18. Prokofiev, *Autobiography*, op. cit., p. 69–70.
19. H. Gil-Marchex, "Back from a trip to Russia", in *The Chesterian*, VIII, No. 60, January-February 1927, p. 115–21.
20. Leon Trotsky, *Literature and Revolution*, N.Y., ca. 1924, p. 14.

21. Cf. Edward J. Brown, *The Proletarian Phase in Russian Literature, 1928–32*, N.Y., 1953, p. 235–40.
22. Title of the series: *Novaya Muzyka. Sborniki Leningradskoi Assotsiatsii Sovremennoi Muzyki*, 1927, 1928.
23. Lunacharsky, *V Mire Muzyki* (op. cit.), p. 210 (comment originally published in 1926).
24. "Oktyabr i Novaya Muzyka", issue No. V of *Novaya Muzyka* (see note 22). Transl. by N. Slonimsky in *Journal of the American Musicological Society*, Autumn 1950, p. 237 ("The Changing Style of Soviet Music").
25. In *Sovremennaya Muzyka*, VI, No. 32 (March 1929).
26. Shebalin, "O Proidennom Puti", in SovMuz, 1959: 2, p. 76.
27. *Anbruch*, 1931, XIII, p. 23.
28. Roslavetz, "O Sebe i Svoyom Tvorchestve", in *Sovremennaya Muzyka*, V: 1924, pp. 137–38.
29. In *Muzykalnaya Kultura*, 1924, No. 1, p. 50. The article is signed by "Dialecticus", probably the pen name of Roslavetz.
30. Ibid., pp. 9, 11.
31. Detlef Gojowy, "N. A. Roslavec, ein früher Zwölftonkomponist", in *Die Musikforschung*, 1969: 1, pp. 22–38.
32. IMN, p. 163. RAPM platform: 1st version in *Muzykalnaya Nov*, 1924, No. 12; 2nd version in *Muzyka i Oktyabr*, 1926, No. 1; 3rd version, English transl. in N. Slonimsky, *Music since 1900*, N.Y., 1937, pp. 549–55.
33. *Muzyka i Oktyabr*, 1926, Nos. 4–5.
34. Lunacharsky, *V Mire* . . . (op. cit.), pp. 308–11.
35. Brown, op. cit., p. 31.
36. *Sovremennaya Muzyka*, March 1929.
37. Partially quoted in IRSM, vol. I, pp. 64–65, and IMN, vol. I, p. 174.

Chapter 4

1. In *Zhizn Iskusstva*, 3 January 1922.
2. Lunacharsky, op. cit., pp. 142, 145.
3. *K Novym Beregam*, 1923, No. 1.
4. *The New York Times*, 20 December 1931.
5. Stanislavsky, op. cit., p. 505.
6. A. Gozenpud, *Russkii Sovetskii Opernyi Teatr*, L, 1963, p. 104.
7. Ibid., p. 101.
8. Ibid., p. 134.
9. Ibid., p. 142.
10. Ibid., p. 143.
11. Ibid., p. 145.
12. IRSM, vol. I, p. 165.
13. Gozenpud, op. cit., p. 147
14. Ibid., p. 147.
15. Ibid., p. 148.

16. *Izvestia,* 11 November 1927 (S. Boguslavsky), quoted in Gozenpud, op. cit., p. 149.
17. IRSM, vol. I, p. 186.
18. Gozenpud, op. cit., p. 162.
19. Quoted ibid., p. 160 f.
20. See V. Seroff, *Dmitri Shostakovich,* N.Y., 1943, pp. 167–71.
21. Ibid., pp. 169, 170–71.
22. L. Poliakova, *Soviet Music,* M, ca. 1950, p. 101 (in English).
23. IRSM, vol. I, p. 185.
24. Herbert Graf, "Oper im Neuen Russland", *Anbruch,* XI: 6 (June 1929), pp. 238–50.
25. IRSM, vol. I, p. 205.
26. Ibid., p. 216.
27. D. Rabinovich, *D. Shostakovich,* M, 1959, p. 31 (in English).
28. B. Asafiev, *Izbrannye Trudy* (Selected Works), M, 1957, vol. 5, p. 78.
29. G. Mahler, *Briefe,* ed. Alma Mahler, Berlin, 1924, p. 296.
30. N. Miaskovsky, *Avtobiografia* in *Statii, Pisma, Vospominania,* M, 1960, vol. 2, pp. 15–16 (originally in SovMuz, 1936: 6, pp. 5–12).
31. T. Livanova, *N. Miaskovsky,* M, 1953, pp. 119–20.
32. SovMuz, 1936: 5, pp. 38–39.
33. IRSM, vol. I, pp. 254–55.
34. IMN, vol. I, pp. 258–59.
35. G. Orlov, *Russkii Sovetskii Simfonism,* M-L, 1966, p. 67.
36. *The New York Herald Tribune,* 4 January 1933.
37. Gerald Abraham, *Eight Soviet Composers,* London, 1943, p. 18.
38. *Musical America,* 10 January 1933 (W. R. Murphy).
39. Ibid.
40. Rose Lee (see note 4).
41. Abraham, op. cit., p. 90.
42. Asafiev, op. cit., vol. 5, p. 79.
43. Quoted in IMN, vol. I, p. 169.
44. ISRM, vol. I, p. 41.
45. *Muzykalnaya Kultura,* 1924, No. 3.
46. E. Braudo in *Die Musik,* XX:7 (April 1928), p. 553.
47. Cf. Detlef Gojowy, op. cit.
Also George Perle, *Serial Composition and Atonality,* Berkeley, 1968.

Chapter 5

1. Asafiev, "Nash Dolg" in *Proshloye Russkoi Muzyki,* L, 1920. Quoted in E. Orlova, op. cit., pp. 83–84.
2. See *Anbruch,* "Russland-Heft", März 1925, articles on Musicology in Russia by M. Ivanov-Boretzky and S. Ginzburg. Also in *Union Musicologique,* The Hague, Bulletin 1925 (vol. 5, No. 1). Five-year reports on work done at OTIM- Leningrad and GIMN-Moscow in *De Musica,* issue I (1925)

and issue 2 (1926). Cf. *Muzykalnoye Obrazovanie* (Music Education), journal, м, I: 5–6, 65 f. (January 1926).
3. Lunacharsky, *V Mire Muzyki* (op. cit.), pp. 204–29 ("Odin iz sdvigov v iskusstvovedenii").
4. Boris Schwarz, "Beethoveniana in Soviet Russia", in *The Musical Quarterly*, 1961: 1, pp. 4–21.
5. Quoted in *Moskovskaya Konservatoria 1866–1966*, м, 1966, p. 295.
6. *100 Let* . . . (op. cit.), p. 113.
7. *V Pervye Gody Sovetskovo Muzykalnovo Stroitelstva* (op. cit.), p. 170 (note).
8. *100 Let* . . . (op. cit.), p. 113.
9. Lenin on 28 March 1922, at the XI Congress of the Party.
10. *Moskovskaya Konservatoria* (op. cit.), p. 298 f.
11. A. Glazunov, *Issledovania, Materialy* . . ., op. cit., vol. 2, p. 29 (note).
12. In *Muzyka i Revolutzia*, 1928, No. 2.
13. *100 Let* . . . (op. cit.), p. 120.
14. Asafiev, *Kniga o Stravinskom*, L, 1929, p. 7.
15. *V Mire* . . . (op. cit.), p. 183.
16. *100 Let* . . . (op. cit.), p. 144.
17. *Moskovskaya Konservatoria* (op. cit.), pp. 321–22.
18. *100 Let* . . .(op. cit.), p. 144.
19. Ibid., p. 146.

PART III

Chapter 6

1. Ilya Ehrenburg, *Memoirs, 1921–1941*, transl. T. Shebunina and Y. Kapp, London, 1963, p. 221.
2. Ibid., pp. 225–26.
3. English translation of the Resolution in Brown, op. cit., pp. 200–1.
4. A. Zhdanov, *Essays on Literature, Philosophy, and Music*, N.Y., 1950, pp. 7–15.
5. Ehrenburg, op. cit., pp. 270, 272, 273.
6. SovMuz, 1933: 3, p. 132, transl. by Slonimsky, op. cit., p. 347.
7. Ibid., pp. 106–08 (article "Istoricheski God").
8. From "Statutes of Composers' Union", quoted in *Entsiklopedicheskii Muzy-kalnyi Slovar*, ed. B. Steinpress and I. Yampolski, 2nd ed., м, 1966, article "Sotsialisticheskii Realism".
9. I. Nestyev, *Prokofiev*, transl. Jonas, op. cit., p. 278.
10. Prokofiev, *Autobiography* . . ., op. cit., p. 99.
11. I. Nestyev, *Sergei Prokofiev, His Musical Life*, transl. R. Prokofieva, N.Y., 1946, p. 103.
12. Prokofiev, *Autobiography* . . ., op. cit., pp. 99–100.
13. Ibid., p. 106.
14. Ibid.
15. I. Nestyev, transl. Jonas, op. cit., p. 241.

16. Prokofiev, op. cit., p. 197.
17. SovMuz, 1933: 6. Quoted in Gerald Abraham, op. cit., p. 25.
18. Victor Seroff, op. cit., p. 197.
19. Quoted by Nicolas Slonimsky in *Musical Quarterly*, 28: 4 (October 1942).
20. Virgil Thomson in *Modern Music*, XII: 3, pp. 123–26 (March-April 1935).
21. Gerald Abraham, op. cit., p. 25.
22. In *New York Sun*, 9 February 1935.
23. In *The New York Times*, 6 February 1935. Reprinted in *Olin Downes on Music*, N.Y., 1957, pp. 197–201.
24. In *The New York Times*, 1 September 1935.
25. Quoted in Seroff, op. cit., p. 200.
26. R.-Aloys Mooser, *Regards sur la Musique Contemporaine*, Lausanne, 1946, pp. 219–39. Quoted sentences on p. 237.
27. Translated in Seroff, op. cit., pp. 204–07. Also in N. Slonimsky, *Music since 1900*, N.Y., 1937, pp. 402–03.
28. SovMuz, 1936. Moscow discussion in March issue, Leningrad discussion in May issue.
29. Ibid., 1936:5 (May), pp. 38–39.
30. Ibid. Reprinted in B. V. Asafiev, *Izbrannye Trudy*, op. cit., vol. 5, pp. 116–119.
31. SovMuz, 1936: 5 (May issue, Leningrad discussion), pp. 40–45.
32. Mikhail Druskin, *Novaya Fortepiannaya Muzyka*, I, 1928, pp. 88–90.
33. *Entsiklopedicheskii Muzykalnyi Slovar*, op. cit., article "Formalism".
34. *Pravda*, 13 February 1936, quoted in Seroff, op. cit., p. 218.
35. Quoted in *The Times Literary Supplement*, London, 13 April 1967.
36. Gerald Abraham in *Horizon*, VI: 33, September 1942, p. 243.
37. *Tempo*, (London), Autumn 1966, p. 1. Article "Shostakovich at the Cross-roads" by Tim Souster, pp. 2–9.
38. *The New York Times*, 20 December 1931, "D. Szostakovitch" by Rose Lee.
39. Ibid. (cf. chapter 4, notes 4 and 40).
40. *Tempo*, loco cit.
41. SovMuz, 1935: 6. See also Siegmeister's "My Creative Path", ibid., 1934: 11 and Aaron Copland's song, "Into the Streets, May 1st", published as musical appendix in SovMuz, 1934: 7 (with words by Alfred Heiss).
42. Gerald Abraham, *Eight Soviet Composers*, op. cit., p. 90.
43. Prokofiev, *Autobiography* . . ., op. cit., pp. 253, 261.
44. Ibid., p. 114.
45. *Literaturnaya Gazeta*, 10 April 1939. Quoted by N. Slonimsky in *Musical Quarterly*, op. cit., p. 442.
46. D. Rabinovich, op. cit., pp. 41–42.
47. Ehrenburg, op. cit., p. 427.
48. Ibid., pp. 423–4.
49. IRSM, vol. 2, M, 1959, p. 8 (N. Tumanina).
50. Ehrenburg, op. cit., p. 498.
51. Ibid., pp. 507–08. Also A. Werth, *Russia at War*, London, 1964, p. 159.

Chapter 7

1. Nestyev, transl. Jonas, op. cit., p. 277.
2. Seroff, op. cit., pp. 249–55 (translation of complete essay by Shostakovich, "About My Opera". Quoted sentence on pp. 250–51.).
3. A. Gozenpud, op. cit., p. 298.
4. *Leningradskaya Pravda*, 15 October 1935, quoted ibid., p. 298.
5. Asafiev, "Opera" (1944), *Izbrannye Trudy*, op. cit., vol. 5, pp. 67–68.
6. Appeared in *Pravda*, 21 January 1936.
7. *Leningradskaya Pravda*, 24 January 1936. See N. Slonimsky, "The Changing Styles of Soviet Music", op. cit., p. 245.
8. IRSM, op. cit., vol. 2, p. 226.
9. Asafiev, op. cit., vol. 5, p. 71.
10. SovMuz, 1933: 3, p. 99, quoted in IRSM, vol. 2, p. 273.
11. Prokofiev, *Autobiography* . . ., op. cit., pp. 117–20.
12. Gozenpud, op. cit., pp. 336–37.
13. Ibid., p. 338.
14. Kurt London, *The Seven Soviet Arts*, London, 1937, p. 212 ff.
15. L. Poliakova, op. cit., p. 132.
16. Faubion Bowers, *Broadway, USSR*, N.Y., 1959, p. 31.
17. *Pravda*, "Ballet Falsehood", 6 February 1936. Quoted in IRSM, vol. 2, p. 192.
18. The reminiscences of Galina Ulanova and Leonid Lavrovsky are printed in the volume Prokofiev, *Autobiography, Reminiscences* . . ., op. cit., pp. 221–28 and pp. 269–81. The subsequent quotations are taken from this source.
19. Nestyev, transl. Jonas, op. cit., p. 268.
20. Prokofiev, *Autobiography* . . ., op. cit., p. 275.
21. Bowers, op. cit., pp. 37–39.
22. Most of the discussion is reprinted in SovMuz, 1935: 4–6.
23. SovMuz, 1934: 4, pp. 3–4 (D. Kabalevsky, "O Sovetskoi Tematike, Stile i Muzykalnoi Kritike".)
24. SovMuz, 1935: 4, p. 33.
25. Ibid., 1933: 3, p. 115 (G. Popov, "K Voprosu o Sovetskom Simfonisme").
26. The statement, made in 1937, is quoted in G. Orlov, *Russkii Sovetskii Simfonism*, op. cit., p. 80.
27. SovMuz, 1935: 5, p. 35.
28. Ibid., 1935: 6, p. 6.
29. Ibid., 1935: 4, p. 32.
30. Ibid., 1934: 9, p. 61–62.
31. G. Orlov, op. cit., p. 87.
32. Miaskovsky, op. cit. (Ch. 4, note 30). Quotation in vol. 2, p. 18.
33. Prokofiev, *Autobiography* . . ., op. cit., p. 104.
34. Miaskovsky, op. cit., vol. 2, p. 18.
35. Ibid., vol. 1, p. 329 (G. Shneerson, "Vstrechi s N. Ya. Miaskovskim").
36. Ibid.
37. Ibid., p. 331 (letter written in the autumn of 1942).
38. Nestyev, transl. Jonas, op. cit., p. 264.
39. Ibid., p. 298.

40. SovMuz, 1956:9, pp.9–15 (D. Shostakovich, "Dumy o Proidenom Puti").
41. Paul Bekker, *Die Sinfonie von Beethoven bis Mahler*, Berlin, 1918, p. 17.
42. SovMuz, 1948: 2, p. 61, (M. Koval, "Tvorcheskii Put Shostakovicha").
43. D. Shostakovitch, "Moya Rabota nad Leninskoi Simfoniyei" (My Work on the Lenin Symphony) in *Literaturnaya Gazeta*, 20 November 1938. Quoted in G. Orlov, *Simfonii Shostakovicha*, L, 1961, p. 104.
44. Virgil Thomson in *The New York Herald Tribune*, 4 December 1940, following the New York première. The American première had been given on 29 November 1940 in Philadelphia by the Philadelphia Orchestra under Stokowski. A more favourable review appeared in *Musical America* on 10 December 1940.

Chapter 8

1. Quoted in A. Werth, *Russia At War*, London, 1964, p. 119.
2. Ibid., p. 232.
3. V. Bogdanov-Berezovsky and I. Gusin, editors, *V Gody Velikoi Otechestvennoi Voiny* ("In the Years of the Great Patriotic War", Reminiscences, Materials), L, 1959, pp. 45–46.
4. Werth, op. cit., p. 410.
5. VOKS Bulletin, M, 1942, Nos. 3/4, p. 83.
6. Ibid.
7. Quoted by Werth, op. cit., p. 297. Cf. H. E. Salisbury, *The 900 Days*. N.Y., 1969.
8. Bogdanov-Berezovsky, op. cit., p. 46.
9. Ibid., p. 130.
10. *Sovetskoye Iskusstvo*, 9 October 1941.
11. Bogdanov-Berezovsky, op. cit., pp. 133–142.
12. Ibid., pp. 146–47.
13. VOKS, 1942, Nos. 7/8, p. 49 (statement by Professor K. Pavlov).
14. L. Danilevich, *Kniga o Sovetskoi Muzyke*, M, 1962, pp. 236–37.
15. Prokofiev, *Autobiography . . .*, op. cit., p. 125.
16. Bogdanov-Berezovsky, op. cit., p. 41.
17. Boris Yarustovsky, *Simfonii o Voine i Mire*, M, 1966.
18. Quoted ibid., p. 28.
19. VOKS Bulletin, 1942, issue 1/2, pp. 55–56.
20. From the composer's annotations for the première performance. Quoted in Yarustovsky, op. cit., p. 30, footnote 6.
21. D. Shostakovich, "O podlinnoi i mnimoi programmnosti", SovMuz, 1951, No. 5, pp. 76–78.
22. Ehrenburg, *War Memoirs 1941–45*, transl. Shebunina and Kapp, N.Y., 1964, p. 123.
23. Werth, op. cit., p. 411. See also ibid., p. 272.
24. Review of 18 October, 1942. Reprinted in V. Thomson, *The Musical Scene*, N.Y., 1945, pp. 101–04. Thomson is not much kinder toward the Eighth Symphony; see ibid., pp. 104–05 (Review of 3 April 1944).

25. SovMuz, 1956: 9, pp. 9–15.
26. Andrew Porter in *Financial Times*, London, 26 September 1960, and *The Times*, London, 30 August 1962.
27. G. Orlov, *Russkii Sovetskii Simfonism*, op. cit., pp. 175, 187.
28. D. Rabinovich, quoted in Orlov, *Simfonii Shostakovicha*, op. cit., p. 208.
29. SovMuz, 1957: I, p. 151.
30. Quoted in Nestyev, transl. Jonas, op. cit., p. 342.
31. Ibid., p. 374.
32. Prokofiev, *Autobiography* . . ., op. cit., p. 134.
33. Nestyev, op. cit., p. 399.
34. Prokofiev, *Autobiography* . . ., op. cit., p. 135.
35. Nestyev, op. cit., p. 366.
36. Quoted ibid., p. 371 (original in *Music News*, 11 January 1946).
37. *New York Times*, 14 February 1946. Reprinted in O. Downes, op. cit., pp. 338–40.
38. Nestyev, transl. Jonas, op. cit., p. 371 (also Translator's note). Original in *Musical America*, 25 November 1945, following New York première.
39. Quoted ibid., p. 401.
40. Prokofiev, *Materialy, Dokumenty, Vospominaniya*, M, 1956, p. 453, note 26.
41. Nestyev, op. cit., p. 398.
42. Ibid., p. 401.
43. *Musical America* (Robert Sabin), 15 December 1949
44. Letter to V. I. Petrov dated 18 May 1942; quoted in T. Livanova, *Miaskovsky*, op. cit., p. 181.
45. Letter dated 22 March 1942; quoted in Yarustovsky, op. cit., p. 175.
46. Orlov, *Russkii Sovetskii Simfonism*, op. cit., p. 211.

Chapter 9

1. A. Werth, *Russia at War*, op. cit., pp. 1044–45.
2. I. Ehrenburg, *Memoirs: Post-War Years, 1945–54*, transl. Shebunina and Kapp, N.Y., 1967, p. 43.
3. Translated in George S. Counts and Nucia Lodges, *The Country of the Blind: The Soviet System of Mind Control*, Boston, 1949, pp. 80–81.
4. Zhdanov, *Essays*, op. cit., p. 22.
5. Counts, op. cit., pp. 119–20.
6. Ehrenburg, *War Memoirs*, op. cit., p. 122.
7. Counts, op. cit., p. 128.
8. A. Werth, *Musical Uproar in Moscow*, London, 1949, p. 74.
9. Transcript of plenary session in SovMuz, 1946: 10, pp. 2–89.
10. Werth, op. cit., p. 67.
11. L. Danilevich, *Kniga o Sovetskoi Muzyke*, op. cit., p. 278.
12. SovMuz, 1946: 10, p. 58.
13. N. Cardus in *Manchester Guardian*, 28 January 1961.
14. D. Rabinovich, *Shostakovich*, op. cit., pp. 96–97.
15. Ibid., p. 99.

16. Livanova, op. cit., p. 200.
17. Rabinovich, op. cit., p. 116.
18. Werth, op. cit., p. 56.
19. Werth, op. cit., pp. 24–25.
20. Orlov, op. cit., pp. 248–49.
21. Werth, op. cit., p. 47.
22. Slonimsky, *Music since 1900*, op. cit., p. 601.
23. Werth, op. cit., p. 26.
24. Werth, op. cit., p. 86. (See SovMuz, 1948: 1, pp. 9–13 for original transcripts).
25. Original text in SovMuz, 1948: 1, pp. 3–8. English translation in Slonimsky, op. cit., 3rd ed., pp. 684–88.
26. Edward Crankshaw, *Khrushchev's Russia*, London, 1959, p. 101.
27. Ehrenburg, *Post-War Memoirs*, op. cit., p. 44.
28. Abridged original transcripts in SovMuz, 1948: 1, pp. 9–102.
29. Werth, op. cit., p. 56. All subsequent quotes in Werth's translation.
30. Zhdanov, *Essays*, op. cit., pp. 76–96.
31. Werth, op. cit., p. 69.
32. D. Rabinovich, op. cit., p. 114.
33. Zhdanov, op. cit., p. 87.
34. Ibid.
35. Resolution of 1948, transl. Slonimsky, op. cit. (See note 25).
36. Werth, op. cit., pp. 60–61.
37. Resolution (See note 25).
38. Khrennikov's entire speech in Slonimsky, *Music since 1900*, op. cit., pp. 691–99. All subsequent quotations are taken from this translation. Russian text in SovMuz, 1948: 1, pp. 54–62.
39. SovMuz, 1948: 2, pp. 12–22, reprinted Asafiev's statement under the title "For a new musical aesthetics, for Socialist Realism."
40. Elena Orlova, *B. Asafiev*, L, 1964, p. 392.
41. Werth, op. cit., p. 97
42. Ibid., p. 56.
43. Reprinted in Asafiev, *Izbrannye Trudy*, op. cit., vol. 5, pp. 93–94.
44. Werth, op. cit., pp. 98–99.
45. *Sovetskaya Muzyka na Podyome*, ed. Grosheva, Sakva, Shaverdyan, "Sbornik Statyei" (Collection of essays), M, 1950. German translation as *Die Sowjetische Musik im Aufstieg*, Halle, 1952.
46. SovMuz, 1949: 1, pp. 23–37.
47. Slonimsky, op. cit., p. 625.
48. SovMuz, 1948: 10, p. 5.
49. Werth, op. cit., p. 92.
50. SovMuz, 1948: 1, p. 69.
51. Ehrenburg, op. cit., p. 233.
52. SovMuz, 1948: I, pp. 66–67, transl. Slonimsky, op. cit., p. 705.
53. Prokofiev, *Autobiography* . . ., op. cit., p. 106.
54. Ibid., p. 199.
55. Ibid., p. 206.

56. Vernon Duke (V. Dukelsky), *Passport to Paris*, Boston, 1955, p. 314.
57. Quoted in M. Calvocoressi, *A Survey of Russian Music*, London, 1944, p. 112.
58. Slonimsky, op. cit., p. 706. (See note 52.)
59. In *Preface* to printed piano score of the opera, Moscow, 1962
60. Quoted in Fred Prieberg, *Musik in der Sowjetunion*, Cologne, 1965, p. 179. Critique by W. Goettig in *Abendpost*, Frankfurt/Main, 19 February 1962.
61. Olin Downes in *The New York Times*, 22 and 26 April 1953.
62. Nestyev, transl. Jonas, op. cit., p. 435.
63. Prokofiev, op. cit., p. 219.
64. Nestyev, op. cit., p. 428.
65. Prokofiev, op. cit., pp. 133–36.
66. Ibid., pp. 219–20.
67. Werth, op. cit., p. 61.
68. Prokofiev, op. cit., p. 137 ("Creative Plans").
69. Ibid., p. 220.
70. Ibid., p. 280.
71. Ibid., p. 220.
72. Ibid., p. 281.
73. Nestyev-Jonas, op. cit., p. 444.
74. Prokofiev, op. cit., p. 178.
75. Ibid., p. 64. The English translation reads "the first time"; however, in the Russian original the key word is "yedinstvennoye", meaning in this context "only".
76. Gleb Struve, *Soviet Russian Literature*, Oklahoma, 1951, p. 343.
77. Werth, *Musical Uproar . . .*, op. cit., p. 62.
78. Cf. SovMuz, 1948: 1, p. 78.
79. Letter to Khrennikov, cf. Slonimsky, op. cit. (See note 52).
80. Rabinovich, op. cit., p. 120.
81. Werth, op. cit., p. 40.
82. *The New York Times*, 24 and 27 March, 1 April 1949.
83. Ibid., 27 May 1949.
84. Ibid., 28 May 1949.

Chapter 10

1. SovMuz, 1949: 2, pp. 7–15 (complete Russian text).
2. I. Nestyev, *Prokofiev*, transl. Prokofieva, N.Y., 1946.
3. I. Nestyev, *Prokofiev*, M, 1957, transl. Jonas, Stanford, 1960.
4. SovMuz, 1949: 2, p. 19.
5. Ibid., p. 26.
6. Ibid., p. 32.
7. Ibid., 1939: 5, pp. 89–90.
8. Struve, op. cit., p. 343.
9. SovMuz, 1949: 2, p. 27.
10. Ibid.

11. T. Livanova, *Russkaya Muzykalnaya Kultura XVIII Veka*, M, 1952, I: 23.
12. SovMuz, 1949: 2, p. 25.
13. Ehrenburg, *Post-War Memoirs*, op. cit., pp. 240-41.
14. SovMuz, 1950: 4, pp. 48-54.
15. Ibid., p. 49, transl. A. Olkhovsky, *Music under the Soviets*, N.Y., 1955, p. 64.
16. SovMuz, loco cit., p. 54 (Olkhovsky, op. cit., p. 65).
17. SovMuz, 1952: 3, quoted in L. Danilevich, op. cit., p. 284.
18. Danilevich, op. cit., p. 283.
19. Lenin, *Party Organization and Party Literature*, M, 1966, p. 15.
20. SovMuz, 1953: 4, p. 17.
21. Werth, *Musical Uproar . . .*, op. cit., p. 69.
22. Ibid., p. 50.
23. Ibid., p. 60.
24. SovMuz, 1951:1, pp. 15-16; ibid., 1951: 3, pp. 25-34; *Sov. Iskusstvo*, 31 March 1951.
25. Prokofiev, *Autobiography . . .*, op. cit., pp. 117-18.
26. Reprinted in SovMus, 1953: 3, 4, and 5.

PART IV

Chapter 11

1. Ehrenburg, *Post-War Memoirs*, op. cit., pp. 301, 308.
2. Georg von Rauch, *A History of Soviet Russia*, transl. P. and J. Jacobsohn, 5th ed., N.Y., 1967, p. 425.
3. Translated in *Music Bulletin*, August 1954, Society for Cultural Relations with the U.S.S.R. (abbreviated SCR), London, pp. 3-4 (also p. 7).
4. Gleb Struve, *Geschichte der Sowjetliteratur*, Munich, ca. 1960, (updated version of *Soviet Russian Literature*, op. cit.), pp. 483-84.
5. Crankshaw, op. cit., p. 110.
6. SovMuz, 1953: 11. Translated in SCR *Music Bulletin*, op. cit., January 1954.
7. Ibid., August 1954 (original in SovMuz, 1954: 4).
8. Ibid., pp. 5-7 (original in SovMuz, 1954: 1).
9. Ibid., pp. 7-11 (original ibid.).
10. All quoted in Struve. op. cit., (German ed.), p. 502.
11. Rabinovich, op. cit., p. 132.
12. SovMuz, 1954: 6, p. 120. Translated in SCR *Music Bulletin*, August 1954, pp. 12-13.
13. Robert Schumann, *Gesammelte Schriften*, Leipzig, 1888, vol. 1, p. 38.
14. David Lloyd-Jones, "Shostakovich and the Symphony" in *The Listener*, 15 September, 1960, p. 445.
15. Robert Layton in *The Symphony*, ed. Robert Simpson, London, 1967, vol. 2, pp. 213-14.
16. *New York Times*, quoted in O. Downes, op. cit., pp. 426-28.
17. SovMuz, 1955: 5, p. 47 ("Diskussiya o Sovetskom Simfonizme"). Quoted in Orlov, *Simfonii Shostakovicha*, op. cit., p. 250.

18. SovMuz, 1954: 6, p. 119 ff. See also SCR, op. cit., August 1954, p. 12.
19. SovMuz., 1955: 5.
20. The same material, presented somewhat differently, is contained in the book by Harrison Salisbury, *American in Russia*, N.Y., 1955, pp. 250–53.
21. All quotes from *New York Times* Magazine section, 8 August 1954, pp. 9 and 44.
22. Translation in SCR *Music Bulletin*, August 1954, pp. 4–5.
23. SovMuz, 1954: 4, pp. 25–26.
24. Ibid., 1955: 7, pp. 15–17.
25. SovMuz, 1955: 10, p. 13.
26. Ibid., 1955: 7, pp. 7–14. Ibid. the following two quotes.
27. SovMuz, 1956: 7, pp. 6–7. For a previous brief comment, see ibid. 1955: 12, p. 90 (by M. Sabinina).
28. G. Abraham, *Eight Soviet Composers*, op. cit., p. 98.
29. *New York Times*, 3 and 14 July 1968.
30. Robert Craft in *Encounter*, London, June 1963, p. 44 ("Stravinsky's Return, a Russian Diary"). Incorporated into *Dialogues and a Diary* by Stravinsky and Craft, N.Y., 1963.
31. SovMuz, 1949: 1, p. 28.
32. "Music and Myth" in *New Statesman*, 21 May 1960.
33. SovMuz, 1956: 5, pp. 50–51 (Kukharsky) and 1956: 6, pp. 20–24 (Sabinina).
34. Ibid., 1958: 12, p. 11.
35. Werth, *Russia under Khrushchev*, N.Y., 1962, p. 266. (Published in Great Britain as *The Khrushchev Phase*).

Chapter 12

1. Bertram D. Wolfe, *Khrushchev and Stalin's Ghost*, N.Y., 1957, pp. 88–252.
2. Werth, op. cit., p. 37.
3. Khrennikov's speech in SovMuz, 1957: 5, pp. 24–51. English translation (condensed) in *Current Digest of the Soviet Press*, N.Y., IX: 14, pp. 11–13.
4. Shepilov's speech in SovMuz, ibid., pp. 6–23. English translation in *Current Digest*, op. cit., IX: 13, p. 15f.
5. Shostakovich's speech in SovMuz, 1957:7, pp. 63–66; in *Sovetskaya Kultura*, 2 April 1957. English translation in *Current Digest*, IX: 16, pp. 11–12.
6. Khubov's speech in SovMuz, 1957: 6, pp. 29–56.
7. SovMuz, 1957: 5.
8. *Kommunist*, No. 10, July 1957. Translation in *Current Digest*, IX: 33, pp. 3–6.
9. 16 July 1957. Translation in *Current Digest*, IX: 30, pp. 8–9.
10. English translation in *Current Digest*, IX: 35, 9 October, 1957, pp. 3–10. Original in *Kommunist*, No. 12, August 1957, pp. 11–29; *Novyi Mir*, September 1957; *Pravda*, 28 August 1957.
11. *Pravda*, 9 February 1958. English translation in *Current Digest*, X: 6, 19 March 1958.
12. Ibid.

13. *Pravda*, 8 June 1958. Translation in *Current Digest*, X: 23, 16 July 1958. Summary in Werth, *Russia under Khrushchev*, op. cit., pp. 263–65.
14. *Pravda*, 13 June 1958. Translation in *Anglo-Soviet Journal*, op. cit., 1958: 3, p. 5.
15. *Pravda*, 9 June 1958.
16. SovMuz, 1958: 6, p. 88.
17. *Sovetskaya Kultura*, 27 August 1959.
18. *The World of Music* (Bulletin of the International Music Council), May 1959, reprinted from *Hi-Fi Review*.
19. Roy Harris, "The State of Music in the Soviet Union", in *American Music Lover (American Record Guide)*, May 1959, pp. 576–79 (interview with Herman Newman).
20. *Atlantic Monthly*, June 1960, pp. 96 ff.
21. SovMuz, 1961: 9, pp. 115–20.
22. Roy Harris, "Contrasting attitudes toward Musical Life in the USA and USSR", *International Musician*, March 1959, p. 11f.
23. Ibid., December 1959, p. 3.
24. Ibid., p. 10.
25. *New York Times*, 5 November 1959.
26. *Musical America*, 1 December 1959.
27. *New York Times*, 24 October 1959.
28. See *International Musician*, December 1959, p. 10.
29. *Musical America*, loco cit.
30. *New York Times*, 19 November 1959.
31. Ibid., 18 December 1959.
32. Summary in *New York Times*, 18 December 1959.
33. *Atlantic Monthly*, op. cit., p. 100.
34. Quoted in the *Guardian*, 14 January 1960 ("Shostakovich assesses dodecaphony" by Arthur Jacobs). See original in SovMuz, 1959: 11. Excerpts also in Werth, op. cit., pp. 267–69.
35. SovMuz, 1960: 3, pp. 160–68.
36. Quoted in *Music Journal*, March 1964, p. 92.
37. *New Statesman*, 21 May 1960.
38. *Pravda*, 28 January 1958. Translation in *Current Digest*, XI: 3, p. 10.
39. Werth, op. cit., p. 267.
40. *Information Bulletin*, Union of Soviet Composers, 1960: 1.
41. Ibid. (original in *Pravda*, 15 February 1960).
42. Ibid., full text of address by Kabalevsky.
43. *Information Bulletin*, op. cit., 1960: 2, p. 7.
44. *Musical America*, June 1961, p. 28 (Report from Moscow). Première on 8 October 1960.
45. I. Nestyev and G. Edelman (eds.), *Sergei Prokofiev, 1953–1963, Statyi i Materialy* м, 1962.
46. *New York Herald Tribune*, 8 May 1960.
47. *Musical America*, May 1960.
48. *Information Bulletin*, op. cit., 1960: 3, p. 1.
49. SovMuz, 1960: 9 contains speech by Suslov.

50. *Information Bulletin*, op. cit., p. 3.
51. Fred Prieberg, *Musik in der Sowjetunion*, Cologne, 1965, p. 305.
52. Translation in *Information Bulletin*, op. cit., 1960: 3, pp. 38–47.
53. See chapter 11, notes 20 and 21.
54. *New York Herald Tribune*, 22 April 1962, section 4, p. 6.
55. IRSM, vol. IV, part 2, M, 1963, p. 163.
56. Martin Cooper in *Daily Telegraph*, 29 November 1962.
57. *New York Times*, 6 September 1962.
58. *Observer*, 31 January 1960.
59. D. Shostakovich, "O Podlinnoi i Mnimoi Programmnosti", SovMuz, 1951: 5, pp. 76–7.
60. D. Rabinovich, op. cit., p. 154.
61. Ibid., p. 155 (originally in D. Shostakovich's essay "Closer to the People", *Izvestia*, 8 January 1958, subtitled "On the use of folk melodies in compositorial creativity").
62. *Information Bulletin*, op. cit., 1961: 2, pp. 4–5.
63. Ibid., p. 2.
64. G. Orlov, *Russkii Sovetskii Simfonism*, op. cit., p. 309.
65. Lenin, *Revolutzia v Rossii*, essay published on 11 January 1905 (Coll. Works, vol. 8, p. 53). Cf. Orlov, *Simfonii Shostakovicha*, op. cit., p. 303.
66. *New York Times*, 5 September 1962.
67. *Pravda*, 22 October 1961.
68. *Sovetskaya Kultura*, 4 November 1961.
69. *Information Bulletin*, op. cit., 1962: 1, p. 11.
70. Ibid., pp. 36, 39–40.
71. Ibid., p. 44.
72. *Pravda*, 17 January 1962.
73. *Information Bulletin*, 1962: 1, p. 11.
74. Ibid., pp. 4–5.
75. *Encounter*, op. cit., June 1963, p. 44.
76. *Information Bulletin*, loco cit., pp. 6–7.
77. Ibid., 1961, No. 4, p. 1.
78. Ibid., 1962, No. 1. pp. 7–8.
79. Ibid., p. 32.
80. Ibid., pp. 15–16.
81. Ibid., pp. 70–72.
82. *Pravda*, 22 October 1961.
83. *Information Bulletin*, loco cit., pp. 2–24. (Original in SovMuz, 1962: 6, pp. 3–26).
84. Ibid., pp. 45–46 reprints the speech of Keldysh. All quotes taken from there.
85. *Encounter*, op. cit., p. 44.
86. Ibid., p. 46.

Chapter 13

1. Arnold Alshvang, "The Ideational Path of Stravinsky", SovMuz, 1933: 5.
2. Published as *Poetics of Music*, 1942 (in French), 1947 (in English), both Cambridge (Mass.).

3. See chapter 9, note 38.
4. I. Nestyev, "Dollar Cacophony", *Izvestia*, 7 January 1951.
5. I. Nestyev, "Holy Cacophony", SovMuz, 1958: 2, pp. 132 f.
6. Published originally in *Encounter* though Soviet critics usually quote from the German translation in *Melos*, June 1957; February 1958. Incorporated into the *Conversations* by Stravinsky and Craft, N.Y., 1958. (London, 1959, p. 114). See also Boris Schwarz, "Stravinsky in Soviet Russian Criticism", in *Musical Quarterly*, July 1962.
7. *Newsweek*, 21 May 1962.
8. Speech by L. Ilyichev, 26 December 1962 in *Sovetskaya Kultura*, 10 January 1963; transl. in *Current Digest*, XV: 2: 7.
9. *Encounter*, June 1963, p. 44.
10. Juri Jelagin, *Taming of the Arts*, transl. N. Wreden, N.Y., 1951.
11. *Encounter*, April 1963, p. 102.
12. Speech of 8 March 1963. Reprinted in *Encounter Pamphlet 9*, "Khrushchev on Culture", p. 30.
13. Cf. *The New York Times*, 5 June 1964.
14. Priscilla Johnson and Leopold Labedz, *Khrushchev and the Arts*, Cambridge (Mass.), 1965, p. 101.
15. Ibid., pp. 105–20, reprints the entire speech of L. Ilyichev in English translation (original *Pravda*, 22 December 1962).
16. See note 8.
17. Ibid.
18. *Pravda*, 17 December 1962.
19. *Commentary*, N.Y., December 1963. Reprinted in Johnson and Labedz, op. cit., p. 121.
20. Johnson and Labedz, op. cit., p. 41, note 140.
21. Reprinted and translated in *Russian Study Series No. 40*, Russian Language Specialties, Chicago (Ill.).
22. SovMuz, 1964: 4, p. 123.

Chapter 14

1. *The Soviet Union: The Fifty Years*, ed. H. Salisbury, N.Y., 1967, p. 188, paperback edition 1968, p. 234.
2. *100 Let Leningradskoi Konservatorii*, L, 1962. *Leningradskaya Konservatoria v Vospominaniakh*, L, 1962.
3. *The New York Times*, 5 October 1967 (Fred Hechinger).
4. Quoted by H. Schonberg in *The Soviet Union: The Fifty Years*, op. cit., p. 190 (paperback edition p. 236).
5. *Information Bulletin*, Soviet Composers' Union, 1962: 1, p. 17.
6. *The Soviet Union: The Fifty Years*, op. cit., p. 111.
7. Boris Schwarz, "More Beethoveniana in Soviet Russia", in *Musical Quarterly*, April 1963, pp. 143–49.

Chapter 15

1 Johnson and Labedz, op. cit., pp. 113–14 (different translation).
2. Ibid., pp. 114–15 (different translation).

3. Ibid., pp. 147–48.
4. *Encounter*, Pamphlet No. 9, op. cit., pp. 29–30.
5. Ibid., p. 32.
6. Ibid., pp. 2–3.
7. Ibid., pp. 32–35.
8. SovMuz, 1963: 6, pp. 9–24 (complete speech by Shchedrin).
9. *Information Bulletin*, op. cit., 1963: 2, p. 11.
10. SovMuz, 1964: 2, (*New York Times*, 14 November 1963).
11. *Information Bulletin*, loco cit., p. 12.
12. SovMuz, 1963: 4, p. 118. See also ibid., p. 4.
13. *The Guardian*, 30 March 1963, p. 5.
14. SovMuz, 1963: 10, p. 128.
15. Z. Lissa in *Acta musicologica*, 1935, pp. 15–21; B. Scheffer, *Klasycy Dode-kafonii*, 2 vols., Cracow, 1961, 1964.
16. See chapter 3, note 31, and chapter 4, note 47.
17. *Encounter*, June 1963, op. cit., pp. 45–46.
18. Boris Schwarz, "Arnold Schoenberg in Soviet Russia", *Perspectives of New Music*, Autumn–Winter 1965, pp. 86–94.
19. Johnson and Labedz, op. cit., p. 224 (different translation).
20. *New York Times*, 24 May 1964.
21. A. Medvedev, quoted in *Information Bulletin*, op. cit., 1963, No. 2, p. 24.
22. SovMuz, 1964: 12, pp. 115–16. See also Noah Greenberg, "A Soft Sound in the U.S.S.R.", in *High Fidelity*, N.Y., May 1965.
23. Stephen Dodgson in *Composer*, London, Spring 1963, p. 7.
24. "Britten razkazyvayet" (Conversation with Britten), SovMuz, 1963: 6, pp. 100–03 (esp. p. 102). Also ibid., pp. 97–99 (review by I. Nestyev of British Music Festival: "Moscow applauds".)
25. *Information Bulletin*, op. cit., 1963: 1, pp. 22–24 (esp. p. 24).
26. Reviewed in SovMuz, 1964: 9, pp. 81f. Also *Information Bulletin*, op. cit., 1964: 2, p. 18.
27. SovMuz, 1964: 8, pp. 66–71, review by V. Vlasov (esp. p. 69). See also ibid., 1964: 5, pp. 129–30.
28. Ibid., 1965: 8, p. 113.
29. Ibid., 1965: 3, pp. 63–64.
30. *Information Bulletin*, op. cit., 1964: 2, pp. 26–27.
31. Ibid., 1964: 3, p. 23. See also Geoffrey Bush, "Russia 1964", *Composer*, London, April 1965, pp. 12–13.
32. *The Nation*, N.Y., 5 October 1964, pp. 183–88.

PART V

Chapter 16

1. Robert Conquest, *Russia after Khrushchev*, London, 1965.
2. SovMuz, 1953: 11, op. cit. (see Chapter 11, note 6).

3. *The New York Times*, 22 February 1965. This and following quotes cited in *The New York Times* translation.
4. *The Times Literary Supplement*, London, 18 March 1965.
5. *The New York Times*, 10 September 1965.
6. *Newsweek*, 14 June 1965.
7. The concert took place on 13 March 1964, at the New School for Social Research. Cf. the review by Eric Salzman in *The New York Herald Tribune*, 14 March 1964.
8. *High Fidelity-Musical America*, March 1965.
9. Ibid., July 1965.
10. *The Sunday Times*, London, 3 September 1967 (Felix Aprahamian).
11. *The Observer*, 10 September 1967.
12. *The Times*, London, 29 August 1967.
13. 29 August 1967 (R.L. H.).
14. *The New York Times*, 24 May 1965. See also *Newsweek*, 14 June 1965.
15. SovMuz reviewed the Shchedrin Symphony in September 1965 (B. Yarustovsky). This work, as well as the Karayev Symphony, are discussed at length by M. Tarakanov in SovMuz, January and February 1966.
16. *Pravda*, 25 April 1965, p. 3.
17. *Sovetskaya Kultura*, 18 May 1965.
18. *Pravda*, 20 June 1965.
19. *Pravda*, 14 May 1965.

Chapter 17

1. *The New York Times*, 12 October 1967.
2. *Pravda*, 20 June 1965.
3. *The New York Times*, 12 January 1968.
4. *Pravda*, 20 June 1965.
5. *The New York Times*, 18 October 1965.
6. *Newsweek*, 1 November 1965.
7. SovMuz, 1965: 7, pp. 106–11.
8. *The New York Times*, 12 October 1967. Reprinted in *The Soviet Union: The Fifty Years*, op. cit., pp. 226–27.
9. Ibid.
10. *The Daily Telegraph*, London, 17 August 1968. ("Russia's 'Underground' Composers").
11. *The New York Times*, 30 April 1697.
12. SovMuz, 1965: 8, p. 18.
13. Ibid., 1966: 1, pp. 9 and 10 (footnotes).
14. Ibid., p. 10.
15. Ibid., 1966: 3, pp. 17–25.
16. *The Daily Telegraph*, 17 August 1968.
17. SovMuz, 1968: 6, pp. 54–62.
18. Ibid., 1968: 10, pp. 31–37.
19. Ibid., 1966: 6, p. 31. See also ibid., No. 5, p. 22f.

20. Ibid., 1966: 6, p. 30.
21. Ibid., 1966: 5, p. 31.
22. Ibid., 1966: 1, pp. 29–32.
23. Ibid., 1965: 7, p. 104.
24. Ibid., 1966: 10, pp. 25–33.

Chapter 18

1. SovMuz, 1967: 10, pp. 11–21 (article on Sergei Slonimsky).
2. *Information Bulletin*, Union of Soviet Composers, 1967: 9–10, p. 44.
3. Ibid., 1967: 11–12, pp. 3–8 (esp. p. 6).
4. Newsletter, American Symphony League Inc., April–May 1969, vol. 20, No. 2, p. 11. The United States orchestras are subdivided into "Major Orchestras"—30; "Metropolitan Orchestras"—65; "Urban Orchestras"—29.
5. SovMuz, 1966: 6, p. 5. The entire discussion, ibid., pp. 5–12.
6. *Information Bulletin*, op. cit., 1970: 2–3, p. 18.

Chapter 19

1. SovMuz, 1968:1, p. 23.
2. Ibid., p. 29.
3. Ibid., p. 17.
4. Ibid., pp. 24–25. Cf. *The New York Times*, 7 March 1968 (D. Henahan).
5. Ibid., p. 17.
6. Ibid., 1968: 8, pp. 16–17.
7. Ibid., pp. 9–10.
8. *Yunost*, 1968: 5, May. Interview with Natalia Lagina. Condensed English translation in *Current Digest of the Soviet Press*, XX, No. 24, p. 15.
9. *Current Digest . . .*, XX, No. 20, p. 21 (original in *Pravda*, 18 May 1968).
10. Ibid.
11. *Yunost*, loco cit., *Current Digest*, XX, No. 24, p. 16.
12. Ibid.
13. Published in *The New York Times* on 22 July 1968, pp. 14–16 (written by Sakharov in June of that year). The following quotes are from *The New York Times* translation.
14. *The New York Times*, 15 December 1968 (Book Review section).
15. SovMuz, 1969: 1, p. 3.
16. Ibid., pp. 2–3.
17. Ibid., 1969: 2, pp. 4–18 (original speech). Abridged English translation in *Information Bulletin* of Composers' Union, 1969, No. 1.
18. *Yunost*, 1967, No. 9, September, pp. 100–01.
19. "Dissident Poet tells of Days of Terror in a Soviet Mental Hospital", *New York Times*, 10 July 1970 (dispatch of *The Times*, London).
20. Original text in SovMuz, 1969: 3, pp. 2–14. Abridged English translation in *Information Bulletin*, op. cit., 1969, No. 2.

21. *The New York Times*, 13 August 1968.
22. Ibid., 27 May 1969.
23. Ibid., 27 June 1969. Cf. ibid., 10 August 1969, Magazine section ("Brezhnev sets the clock back" by Henry Kamm).
24. *Harper's Magazine*, N.Y., September 1969, pp. 37–78.
25. J. Leyda and S. Bertensson, *The Musorgsky Reader*, op. cit., p. 215.
26. *Daily Telegraph*, 15 June 1970 (Martin Cooper); *The New York Times*, 7 January 1971 (H. Schonberg).
27. *The Times*, London, 11 December 1970 (David Bonavia), reporting on Khrennikov's speech (*Pravda*, 10 December 1970). Cf. *The New York Times*, 3 January 1971, section 2 (H. Schonberg).
28. In *Harper's*, op. cit., p. 42.
29. S. Prokofiev, *Autobiography* . . ., op. cit., p. 106. Statement dated 1937.

PART VI

Chapter 20

1. SovMuz, 1970: 4, p. 4.
2. Ibid., 1970: 9, p. 16.
3. Ibid., 1970: 10, p. 86.
4. Ibid., 1970: 4, pp. 93f.
5. CurDig, XXII: 46.
6. SovMuz, 1971: 2, pp. 7–8.
7. Ibid., 1971: 3, pp. 5–7.
8. CurDig, XXIII: 14.
9. Ibid., XXIII: 17, p. 27.
10. SovMuz, 1971: 8, pp. 2–8; CurDig, XXIII: 25, p. 13.
11. SovMuz, 1971: 8, pp. 15–16.
12. Ibid., pp. 21–22.
13. SovMuz, 1971: 4, pp. 48ff.
14. Ibid., 1971: 5, pp. 32–36.
15. *The New York Times*, 11 October 1971.
16. Ibid., 8 October 1971.
17. Yehudi Menuhin, *Unfinished Journey*, N.Y., 1976, pp. 282 and 285.
18. SovMuz, 1971: 11, p. 5.
19. Ibid., pp. 6–15.
20. SovMuz, 1972: 1, pp. 37–43.
21. CurDig, XXIII: 42, p. 27.
22. *Testimony: The Memoirs of Dmitri Shostakovich,* as told to Solomon Volkov. N.Y., 1979, p. 40.
23. *The Washington Post*, 9 January 1972.
24. *The New York Times*, 10 January 1972.
25. *Financial Times* (London), 17 April 1972.
26. *The New York Times*, 4 October 1972.

27. CurDig, XVIII: 52, pp. 18–19.
28. SovMuz, 1972: 4, p. 135.
29. Ibid., 1972: 1, pp. 59–71. See SovMuz 1972: 10, pp. 41–48.
30. *The New York Times*, 27 January 1972.
31. Ibid.
32. "Welcome to Miss Furtseva" (editorial), *The New York Times*, 19 January 1972.
33. CurDig, XXIV: 4, p. 6 (*Literaturnaya Gazeta*, 2 February 1972).
34. SovMuz, 1972, Nos. 3 and 4.
35. Ibid., 1972: 6, pp. 2–5.
36. Ibid., 1972: 7, pp. 2–23.
37. Ibid., 1972, Nos. 3–9.
38. Ibid., 1972: 8. p. 63.
39. Ibid., 1972: 9, p. 58.
40. Ibid., 1971: 8, pp. 88–91.
41. *Sunday Times* (London), 3 December 1972.
42. *Daily Telegraph*, 28 November 1972.
43. *Financial Times*, 9 November 1972.
44. *Sunday Telegraph*, 26 November 1972.
45. *Financial Times*, 29 November 1972.
46. Ibid., 27 November 1972.
47. *Daily Telegraph*, 15 November 1972.
48. *The Observer*, 3 December 1972.
49. *Sunday Times* (London), 3 December 1972.
50. SovMuz, 1972: 5, pp. 38–49.
51. Ibid., 1973: 6, pp. 48–51.
52. Ibid., 1973: 11, pp. 72–78.
53. Ibid., 1972: 10, pp. 78–84.
54. Ibid., 1972: 10, pp. 84–87.
55. *High Fidelity/Musical America*, November 1977 (*MA* p. 10).
56. *The New York Times*, 7 June 1977.
57. SovMuz, 1971: 7, p. 151.
58. *Testimony*, op.cit., p. 34 and 34n.
59. Ibid., p. 32.
60. SovMuz, 1972: 3, pp. 90–91.
61. Aaron Copland, *The New Music*, N.Y., 2d ed., 1968, pp. 84–85.
62. SovMuz, 1972: 10, pp. 129–30.
63. *Sovietskaya Kultura*, 15 June 1972.
64. SovMuz, 1972: 10, pp. 18–32.
65. InfoBull, 1972: 6, pp. 20–21.
66. SovMuz, 1973: 2, p. 2.
67. IMN, vol. 5/2, pp. 307–308; abridged chapter in SovMuz, 1972: 10.
68. *Testimony*, op.cit., p. 175.
69. SovMuz, 1972: 12, pp. 4ff.
70. Ibid., 1973: 3, pp. 28–31.
71. Ibid., 1973: 9, pp. 23–25.
72. Ibid., 1973: 11, pp. 44–47.

73. "The 'New Folkloristic Wave' in Contemporary Soviet Music as a Sociological Phenomenon", International Musicological Society, *Report of the 12th Congress, Berkeley, 1977*, Kassel, 1981, pp. 49–50.
74. Ibid., p. 50.
75. *The New York Times*, 24 June 1973.
76. *High Fidelity*, October 1973, pp. 86–89.
77. *The New York Times*, 5 June 1973.
78. SovMuz, 1973: 2, pp. 64–71.
79. Ibid., 1972: 6. Reprinted in L. Genina, *Muzyka i Kritika*, м, 1978, pp. 139–48.
80. InfoBull, 1972: 2–3, p. 6.
81. SovMuz, 1976: 12, pp. 77–87.
82. Karl Löbl, *Kurier* (Vienna) 8 October 1974.
83. SovMuz, 1973: 6, pp. 53–55.
84. InfoBull, 1973: 11–12, pp. 7–8 (SovMuz 1974: 2, pp. 8–27).
85. SovMuz, 1973: 9, pp. 8–16; 1973: 10, pp. 2–8.
86. *Izvestia*, 16 March 1978. See also *The New York Times*, 16 March 1978.
87. *Golos Rodiny*, 1978, No. 13.
88. *The New York Post*, 11 July 1978.
89. SovMuz, 1974: 6, pp. 2–3.
90. Ibid., pp. 4–27.
91. Speeches in SovMuz, 1974, Nos. 7, 8, and 9. Partly summarized in InfoBull, 1974: 5, pp. 3–14.
92. InfoBull, 1974: 6, pp. 8–9.
93. *The New York Times*, 3 July 1975.
94. InfoBull, 1974: 6, p. 9.
95. *The New York Times*, 30 April 1975.
96. *Time*, 12 May 1975.
97. SovMuz, 1974: 10, pp. 41–45. See also D. Oistrakh in *Pravda*, 4 July 1974.
98. SovMuz, 1974: 11, pp. 12–26.
99. Report by I. Martynov in SovMuz, 1974: 11, pp. 119–21.
100. See obituary articles in *The New York Times*, 24 October 1974.
101. Hedrick Smith, *The Russians*, N.Y., 1976, p. 556.
102. InfoBull, 1974: 10, pp. 3–13.
103. *The New York Times*, 20 April 1975 (report from London).
104. Ibid., 22 April 1975 (Anna Kisselgoff).
105. Ibid., 23 April 1975 (Clive Barnes).
106. Ibid., 6 July 1975 (H. Schonberg).
107. Ibid., 11 July 1975.
108. Ibid., 27 July 1975.
109. Ibid., 4 May 1975.
110. SovMuz 1977: 9, pp. 23–34.
111. *Nash Sovremennik*, June 1978, No. 6 (CurDig, XXX: 33, p. 1).
112. *Testimony*, op.cit., pp. xiii–xiv and 225.
113. InfoBull, 1975: 5, p. 10.

114. InfoBull, 1975: 10, pp. 3–7. (SovMuz 1975: 8.)
115. G. Shneerson, ed., "D.Shostakovich", *Statii i materialy*, м, 1976, pp. 4–6. Also in InfoBull 1975: 9, pp. 3–6 (English translation).
116. *The New York Times,* 13 November 1979.
117. Partial listing in Laurel E. Fay, "Shostakovich vs. Volkov, Whose *Testimony?" The Russian Review,* 39: 4, p. 486n11.
118. Inserted into the text are several quotes attributed to Shostakovich and previously printed in Soviet sources (but not credited by Volkov). Fay (ibid., pp. 488–89) identifies seven such passages.
119. *Testimony,* op.cit., p. 183.
120. Ibid., p. 154.
121. Ibid., pp. 183–84.
122. Ibid., pp. 181–82.
123. *High Fidelity,* October 1973, p. 89.
124. Translated by Felicity Ashbee, London, 1977 (*Melodiya*/Columbia recording M2 34594).
125. InfoBull, 1975: 1, p. 16.
126. M.F. Gnessin, *Statii, vospominanya, materialy,* ed. R. Glezer, м, 1961, p. 207.
127. Ibid., p. 232.

Chapter 21

1. CurDig, XXVIII: 8, p. 2 (*Pravda,* 25 February 1976).
2. *The New York Times,* 10 March 1976.
3. CurDig, XXVIII: 13, p. 14 (*Pravda,* 29 February 1976).
4. SovMuz 1976: 11, p. 27.
5. CurDig, XXVIII: 36, p. 14 (*Yunost',* 1976: 5).
6. CurDig, XXVIII: 39, p. 12 (*Yunost',* 1976: 6).
7. SovMuz, 1976: 3, p. 50.
8. SovMuz, 1977: 1, pp. 80–81.
9. SovMuz, 1977: 9, p. 130 (A. Medvedev). Cf. CurDig, XXVIII: 51, p. 22.
10. SovMuz, 1976: 10, p. 126.
11. InfoBull, 1976: 10, p. 12.
12. *Quarter Notes,* Newsletter of the New York Philharmonic, September 1976.
13. InfoBull, 1976: 10, pp. 19–21. Also SovMuz, 1977: 1.
14. *Musik und Gesellschaft,* December 1976, pp. 733–36; January 1977, pp. 20–22.
15. SovMuz, 1977: 11, pp. 134–40.
16. SovMuz, 1976: 12, pp. 9–11.
17. SovMuz, 1976: 1, pp. 37–47 (D. Romadinova).
18. SovMuz, 1976: 10, pp. 13–29 (essay on G. Kancheli by G. Ordzhonikidze).
19. SovMuz, 1976: 4, pp. 127–28.

20. S. Prokofiev, *Avtobiografia*, ed. M. Kozlova, M, 1973. Excerpts reprinted in SovMuz, 1976: 5, 7, 8.

21. *Prokofiev by Prokofiev: A Composer's Memoir*, trans. G. Daniels, N.Y., 1979.

22. S. Prokofiev, *Autobiography, Articles, Reminiscences*, ed. S. Shlifstein, London, 1960; 2d ed., M, 1961, in Russian.

23. S. Prokofiev and N. Miaskovsky, *Perepiska* (Correspondence), M: Sovietski Kompozitor, 1977.

24. SovMuz, 1977: 9, p. 45; 1978: 5, p. 52.

25. SovMuz, 1976: 8, pp. 24–27.

26. Vladimir Bukovsky, *To Build a Castle: My Life as a Dissenter*, N.Y., 1977, p. 435.

27. *The New York Times*, 29 January 1977; also 5 October 1976.

28. *Sovietskaya Kultura*, 13 and 16 April 1976.

29. SovMuz, 1971: 1, pp. 106–17. See also SovMuz, 1976: 1, pp. 106–11. (G. Shneerson).

30. CurDig. XXIX: 19, p. 8 (*Voprosy Literatury*, January 1977).

31. SovMuz, 1977: 8, pp. 16–28. Reference to B. Asafiev, *Intonatsia*, M, 1947; 2d ed., 1963, pp. 272 and 269.

32. SovMuz, 1977: 1, p. 3.

33. SovMuz, 1977: 5, pp. 36–48.

34. Ibid., 1977: 4, pp. 5–12.

35. Ibid., 1977: 7, pp. 11–26.

36. Ibid., 1977: 12, pp. 2–5.

37. *The New York Times*, 4 June 1977 (speech of May 24).

38. Ibid., 7 September 1977.

39. Ibid., 25 April 1977.

40. See Ibid., 4 March 1977.

41. CurDig, XXIX: 46, pp. 9–10.

42. SovMuz, 1977: 10, pp. 85–97.

43. "Live and Dead Souls", *The World of Opera*, I: 3 (1978/79), pp. 11–19.

44. SovMuz, 1978: 1, pp. 12–17.

45. InfoBull, 1978: 6–7, pp. 4–17 (SovMuz, 1978: 8, pp. 5–23).

46. SovMuz, 1978: 9, pp. 6–7.

47. CurDig, XXX: 10, p. 2 (*Pravda*, 11 March 1978).

48. SovMuz, 1977: 9, p. 131.

49. *The New York Times*, 25 September 1977.

50. Reviewed in *The New York Times*, 14 November 1978.

51. CurDig, XXX: 33, pp. 1 and 2 (*Nash Sovremennik*, 1978: 6; *Pravda*, 3 December 1978; *Sovietskaya Kultura*, 1 December 1978).

52. InfoBull, 1979: 1; SovMuz 1979: 1, pp. 75–77 (S. Slonimsky).

53. Reviews in *The New York Times*, 2 February 1979; *The New York Post*, 1 February 1979.

54. Obituary in *The New York Times*, 3 May 1978. See also SovMuz, 1978: 6 and 8.

55. InfoBull, 1979: 5, p. 5.

56. SovMuz, 1978: 10, p. 143.
57. Dora Romadinova, "Kiril Kondrashin: Why He Defected", *High Fidelity/Musical America*, October 1979, pp. 26–27, 40. *The New York Times*, 5 December 1978; and 9 March 1981 (obituary).
58. *The New York Times*, 15 December 1978.
59. Ibid. (Sunday Magazine), 11 June 1978. See also Samuel Lipman, "The Russian Wave", *Commentary*, February 1980, pp. 68–73.
60. SovMuz, 1979: 1, p. 130.
61. See Viktor Juzefovich, "Oistrakh and the Present", SovMuz, 1979: 1, pp. 78–91.
62. SovMuz, 1979: 2, pp. 4–10.
63. SovMuz, 1979: 1, pp. 114–23.
64. InfoBull, 1979: 7, pp. 4–12.
65. Ibid., pp. 13–19.
66. InfoBull, 1979: 5, pp. 3–21. SovMuz, 1979: 7, pp. 2–21.
67. InfoBull, 1979: 5, pp. 22–27.
68. InfoBull, 1979: 11, pp. 7–73. SovMuz, 1980: 1, pp. 2–29.
69. *Musica*, 1979: 4, pp. 364–65.
70. See "Musik in der Sowjetunion", *Neue Zeitschrift für Musik*, March–April 1981. This issue is very informative.
71. *Musica*, loco cit. (H. von Lüttwitz).
72. Report by Seppo Heikinheimo, transl. J. Parsons. Privately circulated.
73. *The New York Times*, 14 August 1979 (Craig Whitney); and 23 March 1980 (Harlow Robinson).
74. *Newsweek*, 27 August 1979.
75. *The New York Times*, 27 September 1979.
76. Ibid., 18 May 1980.
77. Ibid.
78. Ibid.
79. *The Times* (London), 23 April 1980 (W. Mann).
80. *The Guardian*, 23 April 1980 (E. Greenfield).
81. *Financial Times*, 23 April 1980 (R. Crichton).
82. *Daily Telegraph*, 25 April 1980 (P. Stadlen).
83. *The Observer*, 27 April 1980.
84. *The Guardian*, 23 April 1980 (Greenfield).
85. *Sunday Times* (London), 27 April 1980.
86. *The Observer*, loco cit.
87. *Sunday Telegraph*, 27 April 1980 (B. Northcott).
88. Ibid.
89. *The Listener*, 29 May 1980 (C. MacDonald).
90. *Musical Times*, June 1980, p. 394.
91. *Sunday Times*, loco cit.
92. *The Observer*, loco cit.
93. *Sunday Times*, loco cit.
94. *The Listener*, loco cit.
95. Ibid.

96. Ibid.
97. *Pravda*, 3 February 1980.
98. SovMuz, 1981: 3, pp. 4–12; 1981: 5, pp. 21–27.
99. Ibid., 1981: 3, p. 10.
100. *Pravda*, 23 February 1981, pp. 2–9.
101. SovMuz, 1981: 4, pp. 1–3.
102. *Financial Times*, 9 June 1981. *Musik und Gesellschaft*, August 1981, pp. 490–92.
103. *Pravda*, 6, 9, and 11 May 1981.
104. *Newsweek*, 27 April 1981.
105. *Symphony Magazine*, June–July 1981, p. 78.
106. Ibid., p. 79. See also *The New York Times*, 24 April 1981.
107. *Newsweek*, 19 October 1981.
108. *The New York Times*, 10 May 1981.
109. *Newsweek*, 19 October 1981.
110. Anna Akhmatova, *Requiem and Poem without a Hero*, transl. D. M. Thomas, Athens, Ohio, Ohio University Press, 1976, p. 23.
111. *Testimony*, op. cit.

Selected Bibliography

1. Books in English, German, French, and
   Italian (including translations)

Abraham, Gerald. *Eight Soviet Composers.* London: Oxford University Press, 1943.
Asafiev, Boris. *Russian Music from the Beginning of the Nineteenth Century.* Translated by A. J. Swan. Ann Arbor, Mich.: Edwards, 1953.
Austin, William W. *Music in the 20th Century.* New York: Norton, 1966; London: Dent, 1967.
Bakst, James. *A History of Russian-Soviet Music.* New York: Dodd, Mead, 1966.
Berger, Karlhanns. *Die Funktionsbestimmung der Musik in der Sowjetideologie.* Berlin: Osteuropa-Institut, Freie Universität, 1963.
Blair, Katherine Hunter. *A Review of Soviet Literature.* London: Allen & Unwin, 1967.
Boelza, Igor. *Handbook of Soviet Composers.* Edited by Alan Bush. London: Pilot Press, 1943.
Bowers, Faubion. *Broadway, U.S.S.R.* Edinburgh and New York: Thomas Nelson, 1959.
Braun, Joachim. *Jews and Jewish Elements in Soviet Music.* Tel Aviv: Israeli Music Publications, 1978.
Brown, Edward J. *The Proletarian Phase in Russian Literature, 1928–1932.* London, 1953; (*Proletarian Episode in Russian Literature*) New York: Octagon, 1970.
Bukovsky, Vladimir. *To Build a Castle—My Life as a Dissenter.* Translated by Michael Scammell. New York: The Viking Press, 1979.
Byrnes, Robert F. *Soviet-American Academic Exchanges, 1958–1975.* Bloomington: Indiana University Press, 1976.
Calvocoressi, Michel D. *A Survey of Russian Music.* London: Penguin, 1944.
Chaliapin, Fedor. *Pages from My Life.* Translated by H. M. Buck, edited by K. Wright. New York and London: Harper, 1927.
———. *An Autobiography as Told to Maxim Gorky.* Translated and edited by N. Froud and J. Hanley. London: Macdonald, 1967.
Conquest, Robert, *Russia after Khrushchev.* London: Pall Mall Press and New York: Praeger, 1965.
Counts, George S., and Lodges, Nucia. *The Country of the Blind: The Soviet System of Mind Control.* Boston: Houghton Mifflin, 1949.

Crankshaw, Edward. *Khrushchev's Russia*. London and Baltimore: Pelican Special, 1959.

Ehrenburg, Ilya. *People and Life, 1891–1921*. Translated by A. Bostock and Y. Kapp. London: MacGibbon & Kee, 1961; New York: Knopf, 1962.

———. *Memoirs: 1921–1941*. Translated by T. Shebunina and Y. Kapp. London: MacGibbon & Kee, 1963; New York: World, 1964.

———. *Memoirs: The War, 1941–1945*. Translated by T. Shebunina and Y. Kapp. London: MacGibbon & Kee, 1964; New York: World, 1964.

———. *Memoirs: Post-War Years, 1945–1954*. Translated by T. Shebunina and Y. Kapp. London: MacGibbon & Kee, 1966; New York: World, 1967.

Fischer, Louis. *The Life of Lenin*. New York: Harper & Row, 1964; London: Weidenfeld & Nicholson, 1965.

Gojowy, Detlef. *Neue sowjetische Musik der 20er Jahre*. Laaber: Laaber-Verlag, 1980.

Grechaninov, Alexander. *My Life*. Translated by N. Slonimsky. New York: Coleman-Ross, 1952.

Hofmann, Michel-R. *La musique en Russie des origines à nos jours*. Paris, 1956.

Horecky, Paul, ed. *Basic Russian Publications: A Selected and Annotated Bibliography on Russia and the Soviet Union*. Chicago and London: University of Chicago Press, 1962.

———. *Russia and the Soviet Union: A Bibliographic Guide to Western-Language Publications*. Chicago: University of Chicago Press, 1965.

Ikonnikov, Alexei. *Myaskovsky, His Life and Work*. New York: Philosophical Library, 1946.

Jelagin, Juri. *Taming of the Arts*. Translated by N. Wreden. New York: Dutton, 1951.

Johnson, Priscilla, and Labedz, Leopold. *Khrushchev and the Arts*. Cambridge: M.I.T. Press, 1965.

Jusefovich, Viktor. *David Oistrakh: Conversations with Igor Oistrakh*. Translated by N. de Pfeiffer. London: Cassell & Company, 1979.

Kaiser, Robert G. *Russia: The People and the Power*. New York: Atheneum, 1976.

Kay, Norman. *Shostakovich*. London: Oxford University Press, 1971.

Krebs, Stanley D. *Soviet Composers and the Development of Soviet Music*. London: Allen & Unwin and New York: Norton, 1970.

Laux, Karl. *Die Musik in Russland und in der Sowjetunion*. Berlin, 1958.

Layton, Robert, "The Symphonies of Prokofiev" and "The Symphonies of Shostakovich" in *The Symphony*, edited by R. Simpson. Vol. 2. London and Baltimore: Penguin, 1967.

Lenin, Vladimir. *New Economic Policy*. New York, 1937.

Leonard, Richard A. *A History of Russian Music*. London: Jarrolds, 1956; New York: Funk & Wagnalls, 1968.

London, Kurt. *The Seven Soviet Arts*. London: Faber, 1937; New Haven: Yale University Press, 1938.

Lourié, Arthur. *Sergei Koussevitzky and His Epoch*. Translated by S. W. Pring. New York: Knopf, 1931.

Lualdi, Adriano. *Viaggio musicale nel U.R.S.S*. Milan, 1941.

MacDonald, Malcolm, comp. *Dmitri Shostakovich—A Complete Catalogue*. London: Boosey & Hawkes, 1977.

Malko, Nikolai. *A Certain Art*. New York: Morrow, 1966.

Meyer, Krzysztof. *Dmitri Schostakowitsch*. Translated by Ilona Reinhold. Leipzig: Verlag Philipp Reclam jun, 1980.

Moisenko, Rena. *Realist Music: Twenty-five Soviet Composers*. London: Meridian, 1949.

Mooser, R.-Aloys. *Regards sur la musique contemporaine*. Lausanne, 1946.

Nestyev, Israel. *Sergei Prokofiev, His Musical Life*. Translated by Rose Prokofieva. New York: Knopf, 1946.

———. *Prokofiev*. Translated by Florence Jonas. Stanford: Stanford University Press and London: Oxford University Press, 1960.

The New Grove: Dictionary of Music and Musicians. Edited by Stanley Sadie. 6th ed. London: Macmillan, 1980.

Norris, Christopher, ed. *Shostakovich: the Man and His Music*. London: Lawrence and Wishart and Boston: Marion Boyars, 1982.

Olkhovsky, Andrei. *Music under the Soviets: The Agony of an Art*. New York: Praeger and London: Routledge, 1955.

Polyakova, Lyudmila. *Soviet Music*. Translated by X. Danko. London: Central Books, 1961.

Prieberg, Fred. *Musik in der Sowjetunion*. Cologne: Verlag Wissenschaft und Politik, 1965.

Prokofiev, Sergei. *Autobiography, Articles, Reminiscences*. Translated by R. Prokofieva. London: Central Books, 1960.

———. *Prokofiev by Prokofiev: A Composer's Memoir*. Edited by David H. Appel, translated by Guy Daniels. New York: Doubleday, 1979.

Rabinovich, David. *Dmitri Shostakovich, Composer*. Translated by George Hanna. London: Lawrence & Wishart, 1960.

The Raised Curtain. Report of the Twentieth Century Fund Task Force on Soviet-American Scholarly and Cultural Exchanges. Background Paper by Herbert Kupferberg. New York: The Twentieth Century Fund, 1977.

Rauch, Georg von. *A History of Soviet Russia*. Translated by P. and A. Jacobsohn. 5th ed. London: Pall Mall Press and New York: Praeger, 1967.

Reed, John. *Ten Days that Shook the World*. New York, 1960; London: Penguin, 1970.

Sabaneyev, Leonid. *Modern Russian Composers*. Translated by J. A. Joffe. New York: International, 1927; New York: Da Capo Press, 1975.

Sadoul, Jacques. *The Socialist Soviet Republic of Russia*. London, 1920.

Salisbury, Harrison. *American in Russia*. New York: Harper, 1955.

———. *The 900 Days: The Siege of Leningrad*. New York: Harper & Row and London: Secker & Warburg, 1969.

————, ed. *The Soviet Union: The Fifty Years*. New York: Harcourt, Brace, 1967.

Seroff, Victor. *Dmitri Shostakovich*. New York: Knopf, 1943.

————. *Sergei Prokofiev: A Soviet Tragedy*. New York: Funk & Wagnalls, 1968; London: Frewin, 1969.

Shneerson, Grigory. *Musik im Dienste der Reaktion*. Halle: Mitteldeutscher Verlag, 1952.

————. *Aram Khachaturian*. Translated by X. Danko. Moscow, 1959.

Shostakovich, Dmitri. *Testimony: The Memoirs of Dmitri Shostakovich*, as related to and edited by Solomon Volkov. Translated by Antonina W. Bouis. New York: Harper & Row, 1979.

Slonimsky, Nicolas. *Music since 1900*. 4th ed. New York: Scribner, 1971.

Smith, Hedrick, *The Russians*. New York: Random House, 1976.

Smith, Moses. *Koussevitzky*. New York: Allen, Towne & Heath, 1947.

Sollertinsky, Dmitri and Ludmilla. *Pages from the Life of Dmitri Shostakovich*. Translated by Graham Hobbs and Charles Midgley. New York: Harcourt Brace Jovanovich, 1980.

Souvtchinsky, Pierre, ed. *Musique russe: études réunies*. 2 vols. Paris, 1953.

Stanislavsky, Constantin. *My Life in Art*. Translated by J. J. Robbins. London: Penguin, 1967.

Stravinsky, Igor. *Poetics of Music*. Translated by A. Knodel and I. Dahl. Cambridge, Mass., 1947; London: Hinrichsen, 1960.

Stravinsky, Igor, and Craft, Robert. *Dialogues and a Diary*. New York, 1963; London: Faber, 1968.

Struve, Gleb. *Geschichte der Sowjetliteratur* (expanded translation of *Soviet Russian Literature, 1917–1950* [Norman, Oklahoma, 1951]). Munich, 1957.

————. *Russian Literature under Lenin and Stalin*. Norman: University of Oklahoma Press, 1971.

Trotsky, Leon. *Literature and Revolution*. Ann Arbor: University of Michigan Press, 1960.

Ulam, Adam B. *The Bolsheviks*. New York: Macmillan, 1965; (*Lenin and the Bolsheviks*) London: Secker & Warburg, 1966.

Vodarsky-Shiraeff, A. *Russian Composers and Musicians*. . . . New York: H. W. Wilson, 1940; New York: Da Capo Press, 1969.

Wells, H. G. *Russia in the Shadows*. London, 1920.

Werth, Alexander. *Musical Uproar in Moscow*. London: Turnstile Press, 1949.

————. *The Khrushchev Phase*. London: Hale, 1961; (*Russia under Khrushchev*) New York: Hill & Wang, 1962.

————. *Russia at War*. London: Barrie & Rockliff and New York: Dutton, 1964.

Wolfe, Bertram D. *Khrushchev and Stalin's Ghost*. New York: Praeger, 1957.

Zetkin, Klara. *Reminiscences of Lenin*. London, 1929.

Zhdanov, Andrei. *Essays on Literature, Philosophy, and Music*. New York, 1950.

2. Books in Russian

(Books pertaining to a particular individual or place (Asafiev, Miaskovsky, Prokofiev, Shostakovich, etc.) are grouped under the name of the composer or the city. Publications written or edited by more than one author are listed by title. This list is highly selective; for complete information, consult the exhaustive Soviet bibliographies listed below.)

BIBLIOGRAPHIES, ANTHOLOGIES, ENCYCLOPEDIAS:
Startsev, I. *Sovetskaya Literatura o Muzyke, 1918–1947.* Moscow, 1963.
Uspenskaya, S. *Literatura o Muzyke, 1948–1953.* Moscow, 1955.
———. *Literatura o Muzyke, 1954–1956.* Moscow, 1958.
Uspenskaya, S., and Yagolim, B. *Sovetskaya Literatura o Muzyke za 1957 god.* Moscow, 1959.
Uspenskaya, S., and Koltypina, G. *Sovetskaya Literatura o Muzyke, 1958–1959.* Moscow, 1963.
Uspenskaya, Kolbanovskaya, Startsev, Yagolim. *Sovetskaya Literatura o Muzyke, 1960–62.* Moscow, 1967.
Antologia Sovetskoi Pesni, 1917–1957, 5 vols. Moscow, 1957–59.
Entsiklopedicheskii Muzykalnyi Slovar, 2d ed. Edited by B. Steinpress and I. Yampolsky. Moscow, 1966.
Kto pisal o muzyke, 4 vols. Edited by G. Bernandt and I. Yampolsky. Moscow, 1971–79.
Muzykalnaya Entsiklopedia, 5 vols. Edited by Yuri Keldysh. Moscow, 1973–81.
Slovar Oper, 1736–1959. Edited by G. Bernandt. Moscow, 1962.
Sovetskie Kompozitory: kratkii biograficheskii spravochnik. Edited by G. Bernandt and A. Dolzhansky. Moscow, 1957.
Sovetskie Kompozitory i muzykovedy, vol. 1. Edited by G. Bernandt and I. Yampolsky. Moscow, 1978. Vol. 2, 1981.

ASAFIEV:
Asafiev, Boris. *Izbrannye Trudy,* 5 vols. Moscow, 1952–57.
———. *Kniga o Stravinskom.* Leningrad, 1929.
Pamyati akademika Boris Vladimirovicha Asafieva. Moscow, 1951.
Orlova, Elena. *B. V. Asafiev. Put issledovatelya i publitsista.* Leningrad, 1964.

Danilevich, Lev. *Kniga o Sovetskoi Muzyke.* Moscow, 1962.
———. *Tvorchestvo D. B. Kabalevskovo.* Moscow, 1963.
De Musica (yearbook). Edited by B. Asafiev, et al. Leningrad, 1925, 1926, 1927. The 1928 issue was entitled *Muzykoznanie.*
Druskin, Mikhail. *Novaya Fortepiannaya Muzyka.* Leningrad, 1928.
———. *Russkaya Revolutsionnaya Pesnya.* Moscow, 1954.
———. *Igor Stravinsky.* Leningrad, 1979.
———. ed. *Voprosy Sovremennoi Muzyki.* Leningrad, 1963.
Glazunov, Alexander. *Issledovania, Materialy, Publikatsii, Pisma,* 2 vols. Moscow, 1959–60.

Gnessin, Mikhail. *Statii, Vospominanya, Materialy.* Moscow, 1961.
Gorky, Maxim. *O sotsialisticheskom realizme.* In *Collected Works,* vol. 27. Moscow, 1953.
Gozenpud, Abram. *Russkii Sovetskii Opernyi Teatr.* Leningrad, 1963.
Grosheva, Elena. *Bolshoi Teatr SSSR v proshlom i nastoyashchem.* Moscow, 1960.
Istoria Muzyki Narodov SSSR, 5 vols. Edited by Y. Keldysh. Moscow, 1966–74.
Istoria Russkoi Sovetskoi Muzyki, 5 vols. Moscow, 1956–63.
Iz proshlovo sovetskoi muzykalnoi kultury. Edited by Tamara Livanova. Moscow, 1975.
Kabalevsky, Dmitri. *Izbrannye Statii o Muzyke.* Moscow, 1963.
Keldysh, Yuri. *R.S.F.S.R., Russkaya Sovetkaya Muzyka.* Moscow, 1958.
————. *100 let Moskovskoi Konservatorii.* Moscow, 1966.
————. *Sergei Rachmaninov i evo vremya.* Moscow, 1973.
Khrennikov, Tikhon. *Noto-bibliograficheskii spravochnik.* Compiled by D. Person. Moscow, 1973.
————. *Statii o tvorchestva kompozitora.* Edited by I. Martynov. Moscow, 1974.
Khubov, Georgi. *Muzykalnaya Publitsistika raznykh let.* Moscow, 1976.
Korev, Semyon. *Muzyka i Sovremennost: sbornik statyei.* Moscow, 1928.
Kukharsky, Vassili. *Tikhon Khrennikov.* Moscow, 1957.
Lenin, Vladimir. *O Literature i Iskusstve.* Moscow, 1957.

LENINGRAD:
Muzykalnyi Leningrad. Edited by I. Golubovsky. Leningrad, 1958.
Muzykalnaya Zhizn Leningrada, sbornik statyei. Leningrad, 1961.
Muzykalnaya Kultura Leningrada za 50 let, muzykalno-istoricheskie ocherki. Leningrad, 1967.
Leningradskaya Konservatoria v vospominaniakh, 1862–1962. Leningrad, 1962.
100 let Leningradskoi Konservatorii: istoricheskii ocherk. Leningrad, 1962.
Leningradskaya Filarmonia: 10 let simfonicheskoi muzyki, 1917–27. Leningrad, 1928.

Lunacharsky, Anatol. *O Vladimire Ilyiche: sbornik statyei. . . .* Moscow, 1933.
————. *V Mire Muzyki.* Moscow, 1958.
Marxism i Ideologia, sbornik. Moscow, 1927.

MIASKOVSKY:
Miaskovsky, Nikolai. *Statii, Pisma, Vospominania,* 2 vols. Moscow, 1960.
Livanova, Tamara. *Nikolai Miaskovsky.* Moscow, 1953.
Vinogradov, Victor. *Spravochnik-Putevoditel po Simfoniam N. Miaskovskovo.* Moscow, 1954.

MOSCOW:
Morov, A. *Moskva muzykalnaya.* Moscow, 1964.
Moskovskaya Konservatoria, 1866–1966. Moscow, 1966.

Vospominania o Moskovskoi Konservatorii. Moscow, 1966.
Vydayushchiyesya deyateli teoretiko-kompozitorskovo fakulteta Moskovskoi Konservatorii. Moscow, 1966.
See also Grosheva, 1960; Keldysh, 1966.
Muzyka i Sovremennost, sbornik. (Irregular yearbooks.) Moscow, 1961–76, ten vols.
Muzyka XX veka, Part I: 1890–1917. Edited by D. Zhitomirsky. Moscow. 1977.
Nash Muzykalnyi Front. Edited by S. Korev. *Materialy vserossiiskoi muzykalnoi konferentsii* (1929). Moscow, 1930.
Novaya Muzyka, sborniki Leningradskoi ACM (Irregular yearbooks under various titles.) Leningrad, 1926ff.
Ocherki Sovetskovo Muzykalnovo Tvorchestva. Edited by Asafiev et al. (Essays.) Moscow and Leningrad, 1947.
Orlov, Genrikh. *Russkii Sovetskii Simfonism.* Moscow and Leningrad, 1966.
Pokrovsky, Boris. *Razmyshlenia ob opere.* Moscow, 1979.

PROKOFIEV:
Prokofiev, Sergei. *Materialy, Dokumenty, Vospominania.* Edited by S. Shlifstein. 2d. enlarged ed. Moscow, 1961.
———. *Statii i Materialy, 1953–1963.* Edited by I. Nestyev and G. Edelman. Moscow, 1962.
———. *Cherty Stilya S. Prokofieva.* Edited by L. Berger. Moscow, 1962.
———. Correspondence with V. Alpers; Correspondence with V. Meyerhold. *Muzykalnoye Nasledstvo,* vol. 1 (1962) and vol. 2 (1968).
———. *Avtobiografia.* Edited by M. Kozlova. Moscow, 1973.
———. *Correspondence with N. Miaskovsky.* Moscow, 1977.
Boganova, Tatiana. *Natsionalno-Russkie Traditsii v Muzyke S. Prokofieva.* Moscow, 1961.
Kremlev, Yuli. *Esteticheskie Vzglyady S. Prokofieva.* Moscow, 1966.
Nestyev, Israil. *Prokofiev.* Moscow, 1957.
———. *Zhizn' Sergeya Prokofieva.* 2d ed., enlarged and rev. Moscow, 1973.
Ordzhonikidze, Givi. *Fortepiannye Sonaty Prokofieva.* Moscow, 1962.
Slonimsky, Sergei. *Simfonii Prokofieva: opyt issledovania.* Moscow, 1964.
Tarakanov, Mikhail. *Stil simfonii Prokofieva.* Moscow, 1968.

Puti Razvitia Sovetskoi Muzyki: kratkii obzor. Edited by A. Shaverdyan. Moscow, 1948.
Raaben, Lev. *Sovetskaya kamerno-instrumentalnaya muzyka.* Leningrad, 1963.
———. *Mastera Sovetskovo kamerno-instrumentalnovo ansambla.* Leningrad, 1964.
———. *Sovetskii instrumentalnyi kontsert.* Leningrad, 1967.
———, ed. *Muzyka Sovetskovo baleta: sbornik statyei.* Moscow, 1962.
———, ed. *Krizis burzhuaznoi kultury i muzyka.* Moscow: vol. 1, 1972; vol. 2, 1973.

Sabaneyev, Leonid. *Muzyka posle oktyabrya.* Moscow, 1927.
Shebalin, Vissarion. *Statii, Vospominania, Materialy.* Moscow, 1970.
SHOSTAKOVICH:
Dmitri Shostakovich. Edited by L. Danilevich et al. (Collection of essays.)
    Moscow, 1967.
————. *Cherty stilya Shostakovicha.* Edited by L. Berger. Moscow, 1962.
————. *Notograficheskii i bibliograficheskii spravochnik.* Edited by E.
    Sadovnikov. 2d ed. Moscow, 1965.
Bobrovsky, Victor. *Kamernye instrumentalnye ansambli Shostakovicha.* Mos-
    cow, 1961.
Danilevich, Lev. *Nash Sovremennik: Tvorchestvo Shostakovicha.* Moscow,
    1965.
Dolzhansky, Alexander. *24 Preludii i fugi Shostakovicha.* Leningrad, 1963.
Orlov, Genrikh. *Simfonii Shostakovicha.* Moscow, 1961–62.
Sabinina, Marina. *Shostakovich—Simfonist.* Moscow, 1976.
Shneerson, Grigori. *D. Shostakovich, Statii i Materialy.* Moscow, 1976.
Shostakovich, D. *O Vremeni i o sebe, 1926–1975.* Edited by G. Pribegina.
    Moscow, 1980.

Sokhor, Arnold. *Russkaya Sovetskaya Pesnya.* Leningrad, 1959.
Sovetskaya Muzyka: statii i materialy, vol. 1. Moscow, 1956.
Sovetskaya Muzyka na podyome. Moscow, 1950.
Sovetskaya Simfonicheskaya Muzyka: sbornik statyei. Moscow, 1955.
55 Sovetskikh Simfonii. Leningrad, 1961.
Sovetskie Kompozitory. (Sketches about 36 composers, ill.) Leningrad,
    1938.

SVIRIDOV:
Sviridov, Georgi. *Noto-bibliograficheski spravochnik.* Compiled by D. Per-
    son. Moscow, 1974.
L. Polyakova. *Vokalyne cikly Sviridova.* Moscow, 1961.
V. Zhivov. *Pateticheskaya oratoria Sviridova.* Moscow, 1973.

Tarakanov, Mikhail. *Tvorchestvo Rodiona Shchedrina.* Moscow, 1980.
V Gody Velikoi Otechestvennoi Voiny. Edited by V. Bogdanov-Berezovsky
    and I. Gusina. Leningrad, 1959.
*V Pervye Gody Sovetskovo Muzykalnovo Stroitelstva, statii, vospominania,
    materialy.* Edited by V. Bogdanov-Berezovsky and I. Gusina. Lenin-
    grad, 1959.
Yarustovsky, Boris. *Simfonii o voine i mire.* Moscow, 1966.

3. Selected Articles in Non-Russian Publications
(See also Notes on Sources)

Anbruch, Musikblätter des. "Neue Russische Musik". June 1922.
————. "Musikschaffen in Russland". April-July 1923.
————. "Russland-Heft". March 1925.

―――. Various articles in 1926 and 1927.
―――. *U.S.S.R.*. November–December 1931.
Beiträge zur Musikwissenschaft. "Sowjetische Musikwissenschaft". Sonderhefte 1967: 3/4 and 1968: 1/2.
Belayev, Victor. "Russian Music since the Revolution". *Christian Science Monitor*, 7 February 1925.
―――. "The Moscow Musical Season". Ibid., 16 May 1925.
―――. "Russian Composers of Today". Ibid., 11 February 1928.
―――. "New Visions in the Russian Theatre". *Modern Music*, January–February 1926.
―――. "Russia's Newest Composers". Ibid., May–June 1926.
Boguslavsky, S. "La culture musicale en URSS". *Revue musicale* X (December 1929).
Brown, Malcolm H. "The Soviet Russian Concepts of 'Intonazia' and 'Musical Imagery'". *The Musical Quarterly*, 60:4 (October 1974), pp. 557–67.
―――. "Prokofiev's *War and Peace:* A Chronicle". *The Musical Quarterly*, July 1977, pp. 297–326.
Brown, Royal S. "An Interview with Shostakovich". *High Fidelity Magazine*, October 1973, pp. 86–89.
Cholopov, Jurij N. "Symmetrische Leitern in der Russischen Musik". Translated by Detlef Gojowy. *Die Musikforschung* 1975:4, pp. 379–407.
Craft, Robert. "Stravinsky's Return, a Russian Diary". *Encounter*, June 1963, pp. 33–48.
―――. Review of *Testimony, Prokofiev on Prokofiev*, et al. *The New York Review of Books*, 24 January 1980.
Fay, Laurel E. "Shostakovich versus Volkov: Whose *Testimony?*" *The Russian Review*, October 1980, pp. 484–93.
Fedorov, Vladimir. "Asafiev et la musicologie russe avant et après 1917". *Revue de Musicologie*, July 1958.
Gil-Marchex, Henri. "Back from a Trip to Russia". *The Chesterian*, January–February 1927.
Gojowy, Detlef. "Nikolai Roslawetz, ein früher 12-Ton Komponist". *Die Musikforschung* 1969:1.
―――. "Zwölftontechnik in Russland". *Melos* 1973:3, pp. 130–41.
―――. "Struktursegmente, Feen und Zwölftonkomplexe". *Die Musikforschung* 1975:4, pp. 435–37.
Graf, Herbert. "Oper im neuen Russland, Ergebnisse einer Studienfahrt". *Anbruch* XI:6 (1929).
Grosz, Georg. "Russlandreise 1922". *Der Monat* V:56 (May 1953).
Khrushchev on Culture. *Encounter* Pamphlet no. 9, London, 1963.
Krebs, Stanley. "Soviet Music Instruction: Service to the State". *Journal of Research in Music Education* IX (1961).
Lipman, Samuel. "The Russian Wave". *Commentary*, February 1980, pp. 68–73.
Lourié, Arthur. "The Russian School". *The Musical Quarterly*, XVIII (1932), pp. 519ff.

Melos (monthly journal): Important articles in IV:9 (April 1925) V:2 (December 1925); V:6 (March 1926); VI:1, 6, 8–9 (1927); VII (1928); VIII:8–9 (August-September 1929); IX (1930).

Meyer, Ernst H. "Musikfest in der Sowjetunion". *Melos* X:10 (October 1931.)

Miller, Arthur. "In Russia". *Harper's Magazine*, September 1969.

Musik, Die (monthly journal): Important articles in XVIII:4 (January 1926, see Schreker below); XIX:3 (December 1926); XIX:4 (January 1927); XXIII:11 (August 1931); also brief reviews by Soviet critic E. Braudo, April 1928, September 1929, and April 1930.

Musik und Zeit, vol. 6: *Probleme der sowjetischen Musik*. Edited by W. Sterz. (Translated articles from *Sovetskaya Muzyka* 1951.) Halle/S., 1953.

Neue Zeitschrift für Musik. "Musik in der Sowjetunion". 1981:2, pp. 105–54.

Prieberg, Fred. "The Sound of New Music". *Survey*, January and July 1963.

Rogal-Levitsky, D. "La Littérature orchestrale dans l'URSS". *Revue musicale* X (December 1929.)

Schloezer, Boris de. "Gegenwartsströmungen der russischen Musik". *Von Neuer Musik*, edited by H. Grues et al. Cologne, 1925.

Schreker, Franz. "Kunst und Volk im neuen Russland". *Die Musik*, January 1926.

Schwarz, Boris. "Musical Thought in Russia". *The Listener*, 7 July 1960.

———. "Stravinsky in Soviet Russian Criticism". *The Musical Quarterly* 48:3 (July 1962), pp. 340–61.

———. "Soviet Music since the Second World War". Ibid. 51:1 (January 1965), pp. 258–81.

———. "Arnold Schoenberg in Soviet Russia". *Perspectives of New Music*, Fall-Winter 1965, pp. 86–94.

———. "Shostakovich's Struggle for Creative Freedom". *Keynote*, September 1981, pp. 6–13.

———. "Shostakovich in Retrospect". *Festschrift in Honor of Paul Henry Lang*. New York: W.W. Norton, 1983.

Shostakovich, Dmitri. "My Opera Lady Macbeth of Mtsensk". *Modern Music* XII (1934).

Slonimsky, Nicolas. "D. D. Shostakovich". *The Musical Quarterly* 28:4 (October 1942).

———. "The Changing Style of Soviet Music". *Journal of the American Musicological Society*, Fall 1950.

Society for Cultural Relations with the USSR, London. Music Section Bulletins.

Souster, Tim. "Shostakovich's Fourth and Fifth Symphonies". *Tempo* 78 (Autumn 1966.)

Taruskin, Richard. "Molchanov's *The Dawns Are Quiet Here*". *The Musical Quarterly*, 62: 1 (January 1976), pp. 105–15.

Thomson, Virgil. "Socialism at the Metropolitan". *Modern Music*, April
  1935.
———. "From the U.S.S.R.". *Music, Right and Left*. New York: Henry
  Holt, 1951.
Union of Composers of the USSR. *Information Bulletin*, Moscow.
  (Monthly publications in Russian and English editions.)
Union musicologique, vol. 5, no. 1. The Hague, 1925.
VOKS Bulletins. Published in England as *Soviet Culture Bulletin*. Mos-
  cow, 1931ff.
Volkov, Solomon. "The 'New Folkloristic Wave' in Contemporary
  Soviet Music as a Sociological Phenomenon". *IMS Congress Berkeley
  1977*. Kassel: Bärenreiter, 1981, pp. 49–51.
Yarustovsky, Boris. "The Young [Soviet] Composers". *Atlantic Monthly*,
  June 1960.
———. "Soviet Musicology". *Acta Musicologica* 1974:1, pp. 50–57.

4. Selected Russian Music Periodicals from
1917 to the Present

(For detailed listings, see *Periodicheskaya Pechat SSSR, 1917–1949* (Moscow, 1955–), *Letopis Periodicheskikh Izdanii SSSR, 1950–4* (Moscow,
1955), and entries in Russian bibliographies. See also "Zhurnaly" in
Entsiklopedicheskii Muzykalnyi Slovar. For individual articles of special interest, see Notes.)

K Novym Beregam. Moscow, 1923 (3 issues). V. Belayev and V. Der-
  zhanovsky, eds.
Muzyka. Moscow, 1922 (4 issues).
Muzyka i Byt. Leningrad, 1927 (12 issues).
Muzyka i Oktyabr. Moscow, 1926 (5 issues).
Muzyka i Revolutsia. Moscow, 1926–29 (monthly).
Muzyka i Teatr. Leningrad, 1922–24.
Muzykalnaya Kultura. Moscow, 1924 (3 issues). Nikolai Roslavetz, ed.
Muzykalnaya Nov. Moscow, 1923–24 (12 issues).
Muzykalnaya Zhizn. Moscow, 1957 to present.
Muzykalnoye Obrazovanie. Moscow, 1926–30.
Persimfans. Moscow, 1926–29.
Proletarskii Muzykant. Moscow, 1929–32.
Sovietskaya Filamonia. Moscow, 1928–29 (bulletin).
Sovietskaya Muzyka, Moscow, 1933–41; 1943–45 (six "sborniki"); 1946 to
  present (monthly). Organ of Soviet Composers' Union.
Sovremennaya Muzyka. Moscow, 1924–29. V. Belayev, V. Der-
  zhanovsky, and L. Sabaneyev, eds. Published by Association for Con-
  temporary Music.
Za Proletarskuyu Muzyku. Moscow, 1930–32.
Zhizn Iskusstva. Leningrad, 1918–22 (daily); 1923–29 (weekly).

Index